HANDBOOK
ON THE
PROPHETS

HANDBOOK ON THE PROPHETS

Isaiah

Jeremiah

Lamentations

Ezekiel

Daniel

Minor Prophets

Robert B. Chisholm Jr.

Baker Academic
A Division of Baker Book House Co
Grand Rapids, Michigan 49516

Published by Baker Academic
a division of Baker Book House Company
P.O. Box 6287, Grand Rapids, MI 49516-6287

Printed in the United States of America

Library of Congress Cataloging-in-Publication Data

Chisholm, Robert B.
    Handbook on the prophets / Robert B. Chisholm, Jr.
        p. cm.
    Includes bibliographical references and index.
    ISBN 0-8010-2529-X (cloth)
    1. Prophets. 2. Bible. O.T. Prophets—Criticism, interpretation, etc. I. Title.

BS1505.2 .C53 2002
224'.06—dc21   2002071135

For information about Baker Academic, visit our web site:
http://www.bakeracademic.com

With love and admiration
to my wife Debra,
who rivals the prophets of old
in her devotion to God and his word

Contents

Preface

The prophetic literature of the Hebrew Bible presents great interpretive obstacles. Its poetry, though teeming with vivid imagery that engages the imagination and emotions, challenges the reader's understanding because of its economy of expression, rapid shifts in mood, and sometimes cryptic allusions. The reader of the prophetic literature quickly realizes that these books were written at particular points in time to specific groups of people with whom the modern reader seems to share little. Yet these books are more than just ancient documents written to a long-dead people. They contain the very word of the eternal God, the message of which transcends time and space. Like the ancient prophets, we too worship this God, and, through the mystery of inspiration, their words can provide us insight into God's character and challenge us to love him more and to serve him with greater devotion.

Because of its interpretive challenges and importance, the prophetic literature demands careful study. Scholars have produced large technical commentaries on each of the prophetic books in an effort to do these books justice and to provide enduring reference works for professional scholars. Such works address interpretive issues in great depth, attempting to leave no stone unturned. This book is not of this technical commentary genre. This volume gives an overview of the prophets' message through a running commentary that analyzes the structure, themes, and message of the prophets. Indeed, one must see the forest as well as the individual trees, for the individual parts will not make sense without a feel for the whole. However, out of necessity, I do at times address especially important interpretive issues in greater depth and attempt to synthesize and interact with the scholarly opinions expressed in the commentaries and technical literature. Much of this discussion appears in footnotes. For those wanting to delve deeper into scholarly work on the prophetic literature, bibliographies are provided at the end of each chapter. For the most part, these bibliographies are limited to works in English that have been completed since 1990.

This book's target audience is not the professional scholar or even advanced students, though hopefully they will find the book helpful. Rather it is aimed toward college students taking a survey course on the prophets, students taking introductory seminary courses on the prophets, pastors, and laypersons engaged in serious Bible study. My hope is that this book will provide some insight into this challenging, but exciting, portion of God's word.

ROBERT B. CHISHOLM JR.

Abbreviations

AB	Anchor Bible
AUSS	*Andrews University Seminary Studies*
BA	*Biblical Archaeologist*
BASOR	*Bulletin of the American Schools of Oriental Research*
BDB	Brown, F., S. R. Driver, and C. A. Briggs. *A Hebrew and English Lexicon of the Old Testament.* Oxford, 1907
Bib	*Biblica*
BRev	*Bible Review*
BSac	*Bibliotheca Sacra*
BT	*The Bible Translator*
BTB	*Biblical Theology Bulletin*
CBOTS	Coniectanea biblica: Old Testament Series
CBQ	*Catholic Biblical Quarterly*
CTA	*Corpus des tablettes en cunéiformes alphabétiques découvertes à Ras Shamra-Ugarit de 1929 à 1939.* Edited by A. Herdner. Mission de Ras Shamra 10. Paris, 1963
ETL	*Ephemerides theologicae lovanienses*
ExpT	*Expository Times*
FOTL	Forms of the Old Testament Literature
GKC	*Gesenius' Hebrew Grammar.* Edited by E. Kautzsch. Translated by A. E. Cowley. 2d ed. Oxford, 1910
HALOT	Koehler, L., W. Baumgartner, and J. J. Stamm, *The Hebrew and Aramaic Lexicon of the Old Testament.* Translated and edited under the supervision of M. E. J. Richardson. 4 vols. Leiden, 1994–99
HAR	*Hebrew Annual Review*
HSM	Harvard Semitic Monographs
HTR	*Harvard Theological Review*
HUCA	*Hebrew Union College Annual*
ICC	International Critical Commentary
Int	*Interpretation*
JANES	*Journal of the Ancient Near Eastern Society of Columbia University*
JAOS	*Journal of the American Oriental Society*

JBL	*Journal of Biblical Literature*
JETS	*Journal of the Evangelical Theological Society*
JJS	*Journal of Jewish Studies*
JNSL	*Journal of Northwest Semitic Languages*
JPSBC	The JPS Bible Commentary
JSNT	*Journal for the Study of the New Testament*
JSNTSup	Journal for the Study of the New Testament Supplements
JSOT	*Journal for the Study of the Old Testament*
JSOTSup	Journal for the Study of the Old Testament Supplements
JSS	*Journal of Semitic Studies*
JTS	*Journal of Theological Studies*
KJV	King James Version
NAC	New American Commentary
NASB	New American Standard Bible
NCB	New Century Bible
NET	New English Translation
NGTT	*Nederduitse gereformeerde teologiese tydskrif*
NICOT	New International Commentary on the Old Testament
NIV	New International Version
OTE	*Old Testament Essays*
OTL	Old Testament Library
OtSt	*Oudtestamentische Studiën*
RB	*Revue Biblique*
SBLDS	Society of Biblical Literature Dissertation Series
SBLMS	Society of Biblical Literature Monograph Series
SBLSP	*Society of Biblical Literature Seminar Papers*
SJT	*Scottish Journal of Theology*
SJOT	*Scandinavian Journal of the Old Testament*
TBT	*The Bible Today*
TDOT	*Theological Dictionary of the Old Testament.* Edited by G. J. Botterweck and H. Ringgren. Translated by J. T. Willis, G. W. Bromiley, and D. E. Green. 8 vols. Grand Rapids, 1974–
TJ	*Trinity Journal*
TOTC	Tyndale Old Testament Commentaries
TynB	*Tyndale Bulletin*
UF	*Ugarit-Forschungen*
VT	*Vetus Testamentum*
VTSup	Vetus Testamentum Supplements
WBC	Word Biblical Commentary
WTJ	*Westminster Theological Journal*
ZAW	*Zeitschrift für die alttestamentliche Wissenschaft*

Isaiah

Introduction

Isaiah's prophetic career spanned at least four decades. God commissioned him to be a prophet in 740 B.C., the year of King Uzziah's death (see Isa. 6:1). His ministry continued through the reigns of Jotham and Ahaz and lasted well into the reign of King Hezekiah, who led Judah from 715–686 B.C. (see Isa. 1:1).

These were eventful times. The mighty Assyrian Empire was expanding westward and swallowing up smaller kingdoms like Israel and Judah. By 722 B.C., the Assyrians had conquered Israel, taken its people into exile, and made its territory an Assyrian province. Judah also became an Assyrian subject. When Judah eventually rebelled, the Assyrians invaded the land (701 B.C.) and conquered the region surrounding Jerusalem. Only the Lord's miraculous intervention, in response to King Hezekiah's prayer, saved the city (see Isa. 36–37). Isaiah lived through all of this, prophesying these events and challenging God's people to repent.

The book containing Isaiah's prophecies has two major literary units. The first of these (chapters 1–39) reflects for the most part the concerns and sociopolitical realities of Isaiah's time. The book opens with a prophecy from 701 B.C., toward the end of Isaiah's career. In the aftermath of the Assyrian invasion, Isaiah urged Judah to repent, warning that persistence in sin would bring even more severe judgment. Chapter 39 tells of an episode from this same period in which Isaiah warned that the Babylonians would eventually take the people of Judah into exile. Chapters 1–39 may be subdivided into four sections: chapters 1–12, 13–27, 28–35, and 36–39.

The book's second major literary unit (chapters 40–66) anticipates the exile and addresses concerns of the future exiles in Babylon. It seeks to convince the exiles that their God is alive and well, despite appearances. He is willing and able to deliver them from exile and to usher in a bright new era

in the nation's history. The great Persian ruler Cyrus, who conquered Babylon in 539 B.C. and then decreed that the Judean exiles could return home,
is even mentioned by name (see Isa. 44:28–45:1). Chapters 40–66 may be
subdivided into two sections, chapters 40–55 and 56–66.

Because of the obvious exilic setting of chapters 40–66, most scholars
deny Isaianic authorship of these chapters and attribute them instead to an
unnamed individual (called "Second Isaiah" or "Deutero-Isaiah") who lived
during the exile. Some propose that a third individual (called "Third Isaiah"
or "Trito-Isaiah"), living in the postexilic period, wrote chapters 56–66.

While chapters 40–66 assume that the exile has already occurred and
that Jerusalem is in ruins, this does not preclude Isaianic authorship of the
section. One of the unit's major themes is that Israel's sovereign God controls history. He can decree and announce events long before they happen.
Having warned that the exile would come, this same God, speaking through
his prophet, addresses this future generation of exiles in advance and speaks
in very specific ways to their circumstances. Such a unique message, originating decades before the situation it addresses, was designed to challenge
the disheartened exiles to look to the future with hope and anticipation.

Isaiah's rhetorical approach in chapters 40–66 may be compared to an
aging grandfather who writes a letter to his baby granddaughter and seals it
with the words, "To be opened on your wedding day." The grandfather
knows he may not live to see his granddaughter's wedding, but he understands the challenges she will face as a wife and mother. He projects himself
into the future and speaks to his granddaughter as if he were actually present on her wedding day. One can imagine the profound rhetorical impact
such a letter would have on the granddaughter as she recognizes the foresight
and wisdom contained within it and realizes just how much her grandfather
cared for her. When God's exiled people, living more than 150 years after
Isaiah's time, heard his message to them, they should have realized that God
had foreseen their circumstances and that he cared enough about them to
encourage them with a message of renewed hope.

A Rainbow after the Storm (Isaiah 1–12)

Chapters 1–12 blend announcements of judgment with descriptions of a future era when justice and peace will fill the earth.[1] Though accusations
against God's rebellious people and images of impending judgment dominate the early chapters, the prophet foresees a better day beyond the smoke
of judgment (see 2:2–4; 4:2–6). This thin ray of hope then bursts into a

---

1. In the book's final canonical form, the heading in 1:1 appears to function as an introduction to the
entire Isaianic corpus, including chapters 40–66. From beginning to end the destiny of Judah and Jerusalem is the prophet's focus.

bright light (see 9:1–7) that dispels the darkness and dominates the concluding chapters (see chapters 11–12).

Obedience, Not Sacrifice (1:1–20)

In 701 B.C., the Assyrian army, led by Sennacherib, overran Judah, devoured its crops, and left its cities in ruins.[2] They besieged Jerusalem and threatened to reduce Judah to an Assyrian province, as they had done to the northern kingdom (Israel) twenty years before. In response to Hezekiah's prayer, the Lord miraculously delivered the city, forcing Sennacherib to scurry home with his tail between his legs (see Isa. 36–37).

In the aftermath of this invasion, the Lord confronted his people with their rebellion and issued an ultimatum. The message begins with a courtroom scene (1:2a). The Lord assumes the role of prosecutor, Judah (called Israel here) is the defendant, and the heavens and earth are summoned as witnesses. Long ago, in the days of Moses, the personified heavens and earth witnessed Israel's covenantal agreement with the Lord, whereby the nation agreed to keep God's law and to submit to God's disciplinary judgment if it violated his standards (see Deut. 4:26; 30:19; 31:28; 32:1). Now the Lord calls upon these witnesses to support his accusation by testifying that Israel has been unfaithful to its oath.

The Lord's accusation is direct and clear (vv. 2b–3). He accused Israel of rebellion and ingratitude. As Israel's father, the Lord did everything he could to meet his children's needs and to raise them properly. One would expect these children to have responded with gratitude, but instead they rebelled against God's authority. Even the most brutish animals (the ox and donkey) can recognize where their food comes from, but Israel refused to acknowledge the Lord as the source of its many blessings.

The Lord does not tolerate such rebellion. As Isaiah points out, he had already sent many of the judgments threatened in the Deuteronomic curse list, bringing Judah to the brink of extinction (vv. 4–9).[3] This next section of the speech begins with the sound of death. The interjection "ah" (the Hebrew word is sometimes translated "woe") was a cry of mourning heard at funerals (see 1 Kings 13:30; Jer. 22:18–19; Amos 5:16). When Isaiah's audience heard this word, images of death must have appeared in their minds. By prefacing his remarks with this word, the prophet suggested that the rebellious nation's funeral was imminent.

Isaiah reiterated the reason for this impending doom in strong language (v. 4). Israel was loaded down with the guilt of sin. It had rejected (note "forsaken," "spurned," "turned their backs on") the "Holy One of Israel." The

---

2. For Sennacherib's highly propagandized account of the invasion, see James Pritchard, *Ancient Near Eastern Texts Relating to the Old Testament* (Princeton: Princeton University Press, 1969), 287–88.

3. Compare the language used in these verses to Deut. 28:23, 33, 51–52, 62.

title "Holy One of Israel" is one of Isaiah's favorite ways to refer to God. It pictures the Lord as the sovereign king who rules over his covenant people and exercises moral authority over them (see Isa. 6). The basic sense of the word "holy" is "special, unique, set apart from that which is commonplace." The Lord's holiness is first and foremost his transcendent sovereignty as the ruler of the world. He is "set apart" from the world over which he rules.[4] At the same time, his holiness encompasses his moral authority, which derives from his royal position. As king he has the right to dictate to his subjects how they are to live; indeed, his own character sets the standard for proper behavior. He is "set apart" from his subjects in a moral sense as well. He sets the standard; they fall short of it.[5]

In its near-fatal condition, Israel resembled a severely battered human body that had been deprived of medical attention (vv. 5–9). A foreign army (the Assyrians) had invaded the land, burned its cities, and stripped its fields of produce. Only the preservation of Jerusalem (called here Daughter Zion) kept Israel from being annihilated like the ancient twin cities of Sodom and Gomorrah, prime examples of God's devastating judgment (see Isa. 13:19; Jer. 49:18; 50:40; Amos 4:11; Zeph. 2:9). The divine title "LORD Almighty" (traditionally "the LORD of Hosts") is especially appropriate here, for it often depicts the Lord as a mighty warrior-king who leads his armies into battle (see 1:9, 24; 2:12).

Having established Israel's guilt and its desperate need for restoration, the Lord was ready to point out the prerequisite for reconciliation between himself and his people. But before the Lord speaks, the prophet summons the citizens of Jerusalem into court, addressing them as "rulers of Sodom" and "people of Gomorrah" (v. 10). The sarcastic address reflects the Lord's perspective and emphasizes how sinful the nation was in his sight.

On the surface, such a comparison might seem unfair, for the people were quite religious. They observed the prescribed religious festivals, brought an abundance of sacrifices to the temple, and offered prayers to God (vv. 11–15). But the Lord was highly offended by all this religious ritual. He detested the people's sacrifices and incense and regarded their assemblies in the temple as burdensome. He refused to listen to their prayers, because the hands spread upward in prayer were covered with the spilled blood of their human victims.

This allusion to violent crime provides the transition to the climax of the Lord's speech. The citizens of Jerusalem needed to "wash" away their sins (vv. 16–17). How? By transforming their socioeconomic system. By this time, a huge, oppressive royal military bureaucracy had developed in Judah. As this

4. Note the emphasis on the elevated position of his throne in Isa. 6:1 and his designation as "the King" in 6:5.
5. In Isa. 6:5, the prophet laments that he is morally unworthy to be in the king's presence.

bureaucracy expanded, it acquired more and more land and gradually commandeered the economy and legal system. At various administrative levels it invited bribery and other dishonest practices (see Isa. 1:23). The common people outside the administrative centers, through confiscatory taxation, conscription, excessive interest rates, and other oppressive measures, were gradually disenfranchised and lost their landed property, and, with it, their means of survival and their rights as citizens.[6] The Lord demanded a radical change. The rich officials needed to dismantle their bureaucracy and to reinstate the poor to their land. Instead of accumulating wealth and exploiting the vulnerable farmers, the rich needed to promote fairness in the courts and marketplace.

The Lord concluded his speech with an ultimatum (vv. 18–20). He made it clear that forgiveness was still available to the sin-stained people. But the nation's future hinged on its response to the Lord's appeal for social justice. If the people obeyed, they would again experience divine blessing in the form of peace and agricultural prosperity. But if they continued to rebel, the final stroke of judgment would fall. Ironically, instead of eating the best the land could produce (v. 19), they would be "devoured" by the sword (v. 20).

Purifying Zion (1:21–31)

This speech gives a brief history of Zion. Once a "faithful city" and a center of justice, she became "a harlot," filled with murderers, rebels, thieves, dishonest officials, and idolaters. However, through God's purifying judgment she would become "the City of Righteousness, the Faithful City."

The prophet lamented Zion's moral and ethical condition. He compared the city to an unfaithful wife, impure silver, and diluted beer (vv. 21–22). In earlier days the leadership promoted justice (see 1 Kings 3:7–12, 16–28; 10:9; 2 Chron. 19:5–10), but now they were concerned only with financial gain and neglected the rights of society's most vulnerable members, such as the widow and orphan (v. 23). God, called here the "Lord Almighty" (literally, "the Lord of Armies," a title depicting the Lord as a mighty warrior leading his forces into battle), would defend the cause of the oppressed by seeking vengeance against Jerusalem's leaders, whom he regarded as "enemies" (v. 24).

The news was not all bad, however. This judgment had a positive goal. Developing further one of the metaphors utilized in verse 22, the Lord explained that his judgment would burn away Zion's impurities (v. 25). He would then restore just leadership to the city, which would again become a center for justice (vv. 26–27). Quickly returning to present realities, the Lord emphasized that the present sinful generation would be excluded from this future age (v. 28).

6. For a study of the socioeconomic background of the time, see J. A. Dearman, *Property Rights in the Eighth-Century Prophets* (Atlanta: Scholars Press, 1988).

At this point God addressed another major problem in Zion (vv. 29–31). Not only were the leaders and people guilty of social injustice, they were also worshiping pagan gods in orchards and gardens, apparently as part of some form of fertility cult. Appropriately, the Lord would make these sinners like a dying tree with fading leaves and like an unwatered garden. They would be deprived of the fertility they sought.

A Center of Justice (2:1–5)

In chapters 2–4, the prophet's focus remains on Judah and Jerusalem (see 2:1) as he develops more fully the major themes of the preceding speech. At the beginning and end of this section (2:2–5; 4:2–6), he envisions a day when purified Zion would be a center for justice and the Lord would restore his protective presence to the city (see 1:26–27). However, in between these poles, Isaiah confronted the people with their idolatry and injustice and described the impending judgment of Judah and its devastating effects (2:6–4:1).

Moving beyond the immediate situation and the coming judgment, Isaiah envisioned a time when the temple mount in Jerusalem would become the focal point of the world (vv. 2–4). The nations would stream to Jerusalem to learn the Lord's laws and to submit their disputes to his wise and fair judgment. Wars would cease as the nations devoted their energies to more peaceful and worthwhile endeavors.

This vision depicts nothing short of the transformation of human society. We tend to think of war as an aberration or abnormality. We fail to realize how fundamental it is to human civilization. Historian John Keegan states, "History lessons remind us that the states in which we live, their institutions, even their laws, have come to us through conflict, often of the most bloodthirsty sort."[7] Many professional, lifetime warriors testify to its horrors. Robert E. Lee said, "It is well that war is so terrible, or we should grow fond of it."[8] William T. Sherman observed, "War is at best barbarism. . . . It is only those who have neither fired a shot nor heard the shrieks and groans of the wounded who cry loud for blood, more vengeance, more desolation. War is hell."[9]

For Isaiah, living in the eighth century B.C. and facing the Assyrian menace, war meant bloody slaughter on the battlefield in hand-to-hand combat, as well as siege warfare, which often resulted in starvation and with it unthinkable atrocities, such as parents eating their own children. War meant the destruction of crops, the raping of helpless women, the slaughter of innocent children, slave trade, and the deportation of entire population groups

---

7. John Keegan, *A History of Warfare* (New York: Alfred A. Knopf, 1994), 4.
8. J. Kaplan, ed., *Bartlett's Familiar Quotations,* 16th ed. (Boston: Little, Brown, 1992), 440.
9. Ibid, 492.

to foreign lands. But all this will change when the Lord establishes his kingdom of peace and justice on the earth.

Though this kingdom was yet to come, Isaiah urged his countrymen to preview it by walking in "the light of the LORD" (v. 5), probably a reference to the Lord's commands and moral standards (see v. 3). Since it was inevitable that all nations would someday recognize the sovereign authority of Israel's God, it made sense that his people submit to that authority in the here and now.

Judgment Day Approaches (2:6–22)

Having envisioned the Lord's coming kingdom, Isaiah returned to his own time. He acknowledged that Judah was overrun by pagan influences. The people turned to diviners and omen readers in order to determine the future (v. 6). In the ancient Near Eastern world, divination was a means of discerning the intentions of the gods. Divination encompassed a variety of methods, including cataloging casual phenomena and accompanying events, examining the inner organs of animals, and observing astrological developments and patterns.[10] Though divination was popular among the nations surrounding Israel, the Lord prohibited it in Israel (Deut. 18:10–12). Instead, God revealed his will and intentions through prophets like Isaiah.

In violation of the Deuteronomic law, Judah's royal bureaucracy was also accumulating silver and gold, as well as horses and chariots (v. 7; see Deut. 17:16–17). In the ancient Near East, the most powerful nations utilized horse-drawn chariots in battle, but the Lord wanted his people to trust in his supernatural protective power, not a modernized army. He told the people not to fear chariots and promised them victory (Deut. 20:1–4). Time and time again the Lord demonstrated his ability to annihilate powerful chariot forces (see Exod. 14:23–28; Josh. 11:4–11; Judg. 4:15; 2 Sam. 8:4).

In blatant disregard of the first and second commandments of the Decalogue, the people of Judah also imported foreign gods and worshiped manmade idols (vv. 8–9a; see Exod. 20:3–5; Deut. 5:7–9). Some interpret verse 9a as a prediction of judgment (see vv. 11, 17), but it is better understood as a description of idolatrous worship and may be translated, "Men bow down to them in homage, they lie flat on the ground in worship" (NET). Isaiah emphasized that human beings actually bow down to and worship the lifeless products of their own hands. The moral absurdity of this prompted him to urge God not to spare these idolaters (v. 9b).

The prophet turned next to the sinful people and urged them to run and hide from the destructive judgment of the Lord, who would come with all the splendor of a terrifying warrior-king (v. 10). In this day of judgment,

---

10. See Robert R. Wilson, *Prophecy and Society in Ancient Israel* (Philadelphia: Fortress, 1980), 90–98. Wilson focuses on Mesopotamian divination theory and practice.

God would target proud men, whom he would humble as he triumphantly exalted himself (vv. 11, 17). Isaiah used several metaphors for these proud individuals (vv. 12–16). He compared them to the cedars of Lebanon and oaks of Bashan, which were well known for their size and make apt symbols for powerful men who think of themselves as prominent. These proud men considered themselves as secure as towering mountains, high hills, lofty towers, and fortified walls. They viewed themselves as the best of their class, like the large, impressive "trading" ships (literally, "ships of Tarshish") capable of traveling over the Mediterranean to distant western ports.

When the Lord appeared in judgment, Judah's panic-stricken idolaters would run into caves to escape the Lord's anger (vv. 18–21). They would carry their beloved idols with them, but then, ironically, throw them to the rodents living in the darkness, a telltale sign that these man-made "gods" were unable to protect them from the Lord's power.

Once more Isaiah drew a lesson for his audience (v. 22). If even the most powerful men were doomed, it made no sense to trust in them. Judah should not place its faith in its leadership or in foreign rulers, for all people are mortal, as the coming judgment would make crystal clear.

Chaos Is Coming (3:1–15)

Developing this theme further, Isaiah announced that the Lord was about to remove from power the corrupt leadership of Judah and Jerusalem, including warriors, judges, prophets, and divination experts (vv. 1–3). This would create a leadership void, which incompetent youths would seek to fill. Conflict would sweep through the land, neighbors would fight with each other, youths would rebel against their elders, and society's riffraff would challenge respected citizens (vv. 4–5). People would desperately beg men to lead them, but potential leaders would refuse to take up such a fool's errand (vv. 6–7).

The sin of the nation's leadership was the root problem that prompted divine judgment. The leaders had rebelled against God's authority with the same brazen attitude as ancient Sodom (vv. 8–9; see 1:10). Though the Lord would preserve a godly remnant and reward them for their deeds (v. 10), he would punish the sinful leaders who oppressed the poor (vv. 11–12). In his role as the nation's mighty warrior-king and judge, the Lord accused and passed sentence on the nation's leadership (vv. 13–15).

Beauty Disappears (3:16–4:1)

The wives and daughters of Zion's wealthy royal bureaucrats would not be insulated from the coming judgment. These women, who were the beneficiaries of their husbands' and fathers' oppressive measures against the poor, were proud of their beautiful jewelry and clothes (3:16), which Isaiah itemized ad nauseam in order to emphasize their materialism and excessive vanity (vv. 18–23). But the coming judgment would change all this. These women would be shaved bald, branded as slaves, deprived of their perfume, and hauled into exile (vv. 17, 24). Their husbands and fathers would be slaughtered (v. 25) and their city, personified as a mourning woman, would be abandoned (v. 26). Any women who remained would desperately beg the few male survivors to marry them (4:1).

The Aftermath of Judgment (4:2–6)

This coming judgment, though severe, would usher in a new era of divine blessing. The Lord would restore agricultural prosperity to the land (v. 2). Rather than taking pride in material possessions, the people would derive satisfaction from the Lord's provision ("finery" in 3:18 and "pride" in 4:2 translate the same Hebrew word).

Many interpreters see a messianic reference here and translate the first half of verse 2 as follows: "In that day the Branch of the LORD will be beautiful and glorious" (see NIV). Though the Hebrew word *tsemakh,* translated "Branch," is used by later prophets of a messianic figure (Jer. 23:5; 33:15; Zech. 3:8; 6:12), those passages contain clear contextual indicators that a human ruler is in view and that the word is being used, in a metaphorical way, of offspring. Jeremiah associated the "Branch" with David, and Zechariah identified him as the Lord's servant and as a man. In Isaiah 4:2, there are no such contextual indicators. On the contrary, in the parallel structure of the verse the phrase in question corresponds to "fruit of the land," which refers elsewhere exclusively to literal agricultural produce (see Num. 13:20, 26; Deut. 1:25).[11] In the majority of its uses, the word refers to literal crops or vegetation (see Gen. 19:25; Ps. 65:10 [where the Lord is the source of this vegetation]; Isa. 61:11; Ezek. 16:7; 17:9–10; Hos. 8:7). The picture of the Lord restoring crops makes excellent sense in this section of Isaiah (see 1:19). The prophets frequently included this theme in their visions of the future age (see, among others, Isa. 30:23–24; 32:20; Jer. 31:12; Ezek. 34:26–29; and Amos 9:13–14).

According to Isaiah, the coming judgment would also purify Jerusalem (vv. 3–4). The remnant surviving the judgment would be called "holy," for the Lord would wash away the "filth of the women of Zion," as well as "the bloodstains" left by the murderers of the poor (see 1:21). The language used to describe Zion's women is especially sarcastic and ironic. The word translated "filth" in verse 4 is used elsewhere in Isaiah of vomit and fecal material (28:8; 36:12). From the human perspective, Zion's women were beautifully

---

11. The proposal that "fruit of the land" is a reference to the Messiah's human origins should be rejected as allegorical. For a defense of this allegorical view, see J. Alec Motyer, *The Prophecy of Isaiah* (Downers Grove, Ill.: InterVarsity, 1993), 65.

adorned, but from God's perspective their clothes and jewelry were as detestable and defiling as excrement.

Isaiah's vision of purified Zion culminates with images of God as the protector of his people (vv. 5–6). As in the days of the exodus, God would supernaturally protect his people. Alluding to the exodus account, Isaiah used the symbolic metaphors of a cloud of smoke and fire to depict God's protective presence (see Exod. 13:21–22; 14:19, 24). As a huge canopy shelters those under it from heat and rain, so God would defend his people from harmful and dangerous forces.

An Off–Key Love Song (5:1–7)

Isaiah is at his rhetorical best in chapter 5. The chapter begins with what appears to be a love song offered by the covenant community (including both Israel and Judah) to the Lord (vv. 1–2a).[12] Using the metaphor of a vineyard to refer to herself (see Song of Sol. 8:12), the covenant community tells how the Lord made all of the usual preparations in anticipation of the vineyard producing tasty grapes.

But then the love song hits a sour note, as the Lord interrupts and transforms the song into an accusatory judgment speech. The Lord's vineyard yielded only sour grapes (v. 2b). Having done all he could to ensure a good crop (vv. 3–4), the Lord had no alternative but to abandon the vineyard (vv. 5–6).

Verse 7 explains the extended metaphor. The vineyard represents Israel and Judah. The anticipated crop of good grapes symbolizes justice and righteousness; the sour grapes represent bloodshed and cries of distress. Isaiah used wordplay to draw attention to the contrast between the Lord's expectations and reality. The Lord looked for "justice" (Heb. *mishpat*), but got only "bloodshed" (Heb. *mispakh*); he looked for "righteousness" (Heb. *tsedaqah*), but got only "cries of distress" (Heb. *tse'aqah*) from the oppressed.

The Sound of Death (5:8–30)

Isaiah employs a series of woe oracles to expand on the two major themes of the preceding "song"—the accusation of social injustice and the announcement of impending doom. Each of these oracles begins with the interjection "ah" or "woe," which was a cry of mourning heard at funerals (see 1 Kings 13:30; Jer. 22:18–19; Amos 5:16; see Isa. 1:4). By prefacing his accusations with this word, the prophet suggests that the rebellious nation's funeral was imminent because of its sins. The structure of verses 8–30 is as follows:

---

12. The identity of the speaker in vv. 1–2 is debated. According to some, the prophet, taking the role of best man, composes a love song for his friend on the occasion of his wedding. However, it is more likely that God's covenant community (including both Israel and Judah) is the speaker, at least through the middle of v. 2. The Hebrew word translated "loved one" in the second line of v. 1 is frequently used by the woman in the Song of Solomon to describe her lover.

Woe Oracle	Accusation	Announcement of Judgment
1	v. 8	vv. 9–10
2	vv. 11–12	vv. 13–17
3	vv. 18–19	—
4	v. 20	—
5	v. 21	—
6	vv. 22–23	vv. 24–30 (with a brief accusation in v. 24b)

The themes of the accusatory sections are presented in a chiastic manner (in which the second half of the unit mirrors the first):

> A Social injustice (v. 8)
>   B Carousing (vv. 11–12a)
>   C Spiritual insensitivity (v. 12b)
>   C′ Spiritual insensitivity (vv. 18–21)
>   B′ Carousing (v. 22)
> A′ Social injustice (v. 23)

In the first woe oracle, the prophet condemns the rich royal bureaucrats for building large houses and accumulating fields at the expense of the common people (v. 8). Their actions violated the covenantal principles that the Lord owned the land and that all Israelites were to possess their fair share of it (see Lev. 25:8–55). Ironically, the rich would not live to enjoy their fine houses, and their fields would not yield crops (vv. 9–10).

The second woe oracle focuses on the bureaucrats' excessive lifestyle, made possible by their dishonest and oppressive practices. The rich spent most of their waking moments at parties, where the booze flowed freely and the music played on (vv. 11–12a). They were insensitive to the Lord's "deeds" (v. 12b), probably referring here to the impending judgment approaching the land in the form of the imperialistic expansion of the mighty Assyrians (see v. 26). This lack of spiritual discernment would lead to exile, in which the leaders would die of hunger (v. 13). They would become the main course at Death's banquet, leaving only sheep to graze on the ruins of the large houses where the rich once held their parties (vv. 14, 17). In that day of judgment, proud men would be humiliated, and the Lord would demonstrate that he is the just and sovereign warrior-king who vindicates the oppressed (vv. 15–16; see 2:11, 17).

The next three woe oracles come in rapid succession and, like verse 12b, depict the spiritual insensitivity of the people. The rebellious people dragged their sin behind them and sarcastically challenged God to bring his plans to realization (vv. 18–19). They perverted God's ethical standards, calling "evil good and good evil" (v. 20). In the moral realm they could not tell the difference between light and darkness or what is sweet and what is bitter. Despite their obvious moral confusion, they thought they were wise (v. 21).

These three woe oracles are purely accusatory and contain no formal announcement of judgment. By focusing on the sin of the people, the oracles draw attention to the people's guilt. By delaying the announcement of judgment, the oracles create an ominous mood. As the evidence against the people accumulates, one expects the announcement of judgment, when it finally does come, to be particularly frightening.

The sixth and final oracle focuses on the people's social injustice and the excessive lifestyle to which injustice gave rise (vv. 22–23). The anticipated announcement of judgment finally appears with its visions of destructive fire consuming dry grass, decaying plants being blown away by the wind, an angry God striking the rebellious people who had rejected his law, and dead bodies lying in the streets (vv. 24–25a).

But these visions of divine judgment do not adequately depict the extent of God's rage (v. 25b). The announcement of judgment culminates with a frightening, detailed description of the invading Assyrian army. When God raises his rallying banner and summons them with a whistle, the Assyrians spring into action and march relentlessly and speedily toward their target (vv. 26–28). The arrogant people challenged the Lord to bring his "work" to pass quickly (see v. 19). Through the hard-charging Assyrian soldiers and chariots, the Lord would do just that. Like a growling lion, the enemy seizes its prey and drags its helpless victim to be devoured (v. 29). The roar of the attacking army is as loud as waves crashing against the seashore (v. 30a). The dark clouds of judgment descend on the land, signaling death for God's sinful people (v. 30b). Ironically, those who called light (symbolizing good) darkness (symbolizing evil) in the moral arena (see v. 20) would watch the darkness of God's destructive judgment swallow the light in which they lived.

Stepping into No–Man's–Land (6:1–13)

In the year of King Uzziah's death (740 B.C.), Isaiah saw a vision of the real King, the LORD Almighty (see Isa 6:5), enthroned in his heavenly court (Isa. 6:1) and attended by beings called "seraphs" (6:1–2).[13] These seraphs loudly proclaimed the Lord's holiness and declared that his royal splendor fills the entire earth (v. 3).

The threefold appearance of the word "holy" draws attention to the

13. The Hebrew word translated "seraph" means "burning one," perhaps suggesting that seraphs had a fiery appearance. Elsewhere in the Hebrew Bible the word "seraph" refers to poisonous snakes (Num. 21:6; Deut. 8:15; Isa. 14:29; 30:6). Perhaps they were called "burning ones" because of the effect of their venomous bite, which would cause the victim to burn with fever. It is possible that the seraphs seen by Isaiah were serpentine in appearance. Though it might seem strange for a snakelike creature to have wings, two of the passages using the term "seraph" of snakes describe them as "flying" (Isa. 14:29; 30:6), perhaps referring to their darting movements.

Lord's holiness. In Hebrew, a word is sometimes repeated for emphasis.[14] For example, in Isaiah 26:3 the word "peace" (Heb. *shalom*) is repeated to emphasize the degree of security God provides those who trust in him. The passage may be translated, "You will keep in perfect peace [literally, "peace, peace"] the one who is firm in purpose." Threefold repetition, though rare, is a particularly forceful way of emphasizing an idea. For example, in Ezekiel 21:27 the Lord announces that he will make Jerusalem "a ruin, a ruin, a ruin," meaning that he will reduce the city to a pile of rubble and debris. In Isaiah 6:3, the threefold repetition of "holy" emphasizes that the Lord is absolutely holy.[15] As noted earlier (see 1:4), God's holiness in this context refers first and foremost to his transcendent sovereignty over the world that he rules.[16] At the same time his holiness encompasses God's moral authority, which derives from his royal position.

As Isaiah listened to the seraphs and saw how their loud voices shook the very foundation of the heavenly temple, he realized he was in no-man's-land and expected to be destroyed (vv. 4–5).[17] Though praise was the order of the day, Isaiah was not qualified to praise the king. His lips (the instruments of praise) were "unclean" because he was contaminated by his sinful society, which had rejected the "Holy One of Israel" and his word (see Isa. 1:4; 5:24).[18] However, one of the seraphs placed a burning coal on Isaiah's lips to symbolize his spiritual cleansing, which was granted in response to his confession of his sinfulness (vv. 6–7).

Isaiah next heard the Lord ask for volunteers (v. 8). Speaking on behalf of the entire heavenly assembly, the Lord asked, "Whom shall I send? And who will go for us?"[19] Having been cleansed from his sin, Isaiah volunteers for spiritual service.

The Lord accepts Isaiah's offer and commissions him to preach a message to the covenant community, called here "this people," a designation that

14. See Bruce K. Waltke and M. O'Connor, *Biblical Hebrew Syntax* (Winona Lake, Ind.: Eisenbrauns, 1990), 233.

15. Some Christian theologians have seen an allusion to the Trinity in the seraphs' threefold declaration, "holy, holy, holy." This proposal has no linguistic or contextual basis and should be dismissed as fanciful.

16. Note the emphasis on the elevated position of his throne in v. 1 and his designation as "the King" in v. 5.

17. His declaration "I am ruined" employs a Hebrew perfect verbal form in a rhetorical manner. He used the perfect, which indicates completed action, at least from the standpoint of the speaker, to suggest that he was as good as ruined.

18. The principle of corporate solidarity undergirds Isaiah's thinking here. Though modern Westerners tend to emphasize individualism, ancient Israelites were very much aware that the actions of individuals profoundly affect others in their social context and that one's social context affects the individual adversely or positively. The principle is illustrated nicely in Joshua 7, in which God accuses Israel of having sinned (v. 11), even though an individual (Achan) was the actual culprit. For a discussion of the principle of corporate solidarity, see Joel S. Kaminsky, *Corporate Responsibility in the Hebrew Bible* (Sheffield: Sheffield Academic Press, 1995).

19. The first-person plural pronoun likely refers in this context to the Lord and the seraphs, though the entire heavenly assembly might be in view (see 1 Kings 22:19–22).

suggests a degree of alienation between God and his people. Verse 9, which ostensibly records the content of Isaiah's message to the people, is clearly ironic. As far as we know, Isaiah did not literally proclaim these exact words. The Hebrew imperatival forms are employed rhetorically and anticipate the response Isaiah would receive.[20] When all was said and done, Isaiah might as well have prefaced and concluded every message with these ironic words, which, though imperatival in form, might be paraphrased as follows: "You continually hear, but never understand; you continually see, but never perceive." Isaiah might as well have commanded them to be spiritually insensitive, because, as the preceding and following chapters make clear, the people were bent on that anyway.

Having given the content of the message, the Lord explained to Isaiah the nature of the commission: "Make the heart of this people calloused; make their ears dull and close their eyes. Otherwise they might see with their eyes, hear with their ears, understand with their hearts, and turn and be healed" (v. 10). Should we take this commission at face value? Did the Lord really want to prevent his people from understanding, repenting, and being healed? Verse 10b is clearly sarcastic. On the surface it seems to indicate that Isaiah's hardening ministry would prevent genuine repentance. But, as the surrounding chapters clearly reveal, the people were hardly ready or willing to repent. Therefore, Isaiah's preaching was not needed to prevent repentance. Verse 10b reflects the people's attitude and might be paraphrased accordingly: "Otherwise they might see with their eyes, hear with their ears, understand with their mind, repent, and be restored, and they certainly wouldn't want that, would they?!"

Within this sarcastic framework, verse 10a should also be seen as ironic. As in verse 9, the imperatival forms may be taken as rhetorical and as anticipating the people's response. One might paraphrase: "Your preaching will desensitize the minds of these people, make their hearing dull, and blind their eyes." From the outset, the Lord might as well have commanded Isaiah to harden the people, because his preaching would end up having that effect.

Despite the use of sarcasm and irony in verses 9–10, God's commissioning of Isaiah may be viewed as an act of divine hardening. After all, God did not have to send Isaiah. By sending him, God drove the sinful people farther from him, for Isaiah's preaching, which focused on the Lord's covenantal demands and impending judgment upon covenantal rebellion, forced the people to confront their sin and then continued to desensitize them as they responded negatively to the message. Ironically, Israel's rejection of Isaiah's preaching in turn expedited disciplinary punishment, and brought the battered people to a point where they might be ready for rec-

---

20. On the rhetorical use of the imperative, see Waltke and O'Connor, *Biblical Hebrew Syntax*, 571–72.

onciliation. The prophesied judgment (see 6:11–13) was fulfilled by 701 B.C., when the Assyrians devastated the land (a situation presupposed by Isa. 1:2–20; see especially vv. 4–9). At that time divine hardening had run its course, and Isaiah was able to issue an ultimatum (see 1:19–20), which Hezekiah apparently took to heart, resulting in the sparing of Jerusalem (see Isa. 36–39 and compare Jer. 26:18–19 with Mic. 3:12).

This interpretation, which holds in balance both Israel's moral responsibility and the Lord's sovereign work among his people, is consistent with other pertinent texts both within and outside the Book of Isaiah. Isaiah 3:9 declares that the people of Judah "have brought disaster upon themselves," but Isaiah 29:9–10 indicates that the Lord was involved to some degree in desensitizing the people. Zechariah 7:11–12 looks back to the preexilic era (see Zech. 7:7) and observes that earlier generations stubbornly hardened their hearts, but Psalm 81:11–12, recalling this same period, states that the Lord "gave them over to their stubborn hearts."[21]

Having received his commission, Isaiah asked the Lord how long the job would last (v. 11a). The Lord informed the prophet that he must preach until the land lay in ruins and the people had been taken into exile (vv. 11b–12). A concluding metaphor, which compares the demise of the people to the destruction of an idolatrous shrine, emphasizes the thorough nature of the coming judgment and at the same time hints at one of the major reasons why this divine judgment was necessary (v. 13).

Scholars have struggled to understand verse 13, the Hebrew text of which presents the interpreter with special challenges. As it stands, the text reads literally, "And still in it [is] a tenth, and it will again become firewood, like a terebinth and like an oak, which in the felling [have] a pillar [or "stump"] in them, offspring of holiness [is] its pillar [or "stump"]." Most agree that the first half of the verse means that even if the land were reduced to only a tenth of its population, that remnant would be further decimated.

The second half of the verse is more difficult to understand. Some see a ray of hope here. God's people would be like a tree that has been chopped down. But even chopped-down trees leave a stump that can produce new growth (see Job 14:7–9). Israel's "stump" was a holy remnant, which offered promise for the future.

However, this interpretation is problematic. Proponents of the view define the Hebrew noun *matsebet* as "stump," despite the fact that it refers to a pillar or monument in its only other use in the Hebrew Bible (see 2 Sam. 18:18). The term closely resembles the noun *matsebah*, which elsewhere refers to a sacred pillar. The Mosaic law commanded Israel to destroy the sacred pillars of the pagan Canaanites (Exod. 23:24; 34:13; Deut. 7:5; 12:3).

---

21. For a discussion of Isa. 6:9–10 in the larger context of the divine-hardening theme in the Hebrew Bible, see Robert B. Chisholm Jr., "Divine Hardening in the Old Testament," *BSac* 153 (1996): 410–34, especially 430–33.

Consequently, some prefer to understand the noun *matsebet* in Isaiah 6:13 as referring to one of these sacred pillars. By slightly emending the Hebrew text (changing *'asher,* "which," to *'asherah,* "Asherah," and *bam,* "in them," to *bamah,* "high place"),[22] one can paraphrase verse 13 as follows: "Even if a tenth remains in the land, it [either the land or the tenth] will again become firewood, like the terebinth or the oak tree of Asherah when a sacred pillar at the high place is thrown down. Its [the high place's] pillar is the holy offspring."

According to this view, the phrase "holy offspring" alludes to God's ideal for his covenant people, the offspring of the patriarchs. Ironically, that "holy" nation, which God had set apart for himself, was more like a pagan "pillar" (probably symbolizing the Canaanite god, Baal). It would be thrown down like a sacred pillar from a high place and its land ruined, just as the sacred trees located at shrines were reduced to firewood when pagan high places were destroyed. Understood in this way, the ironic statement is entirely negative in tone, just like the rest of the preceding announcement of judgment. It would also remind the people of their failure. They did not oppose pagan religion; instead, they embraced it. Now they would be destroyed in the same way they should have destroyed paganism (see Isa. 1:29–30).

A Challenge to Faith (7:1–9)

In 735 B.C., five years after his prophetic commission, Isaiah found himself thrust into the middle of an international political crisis. By this time, Ahaz, Uzziah's grandson, had joined his father Jotham as co-regent over Judah.[23] For almost a decade, the Assyrians, under Tiglath-pileser III, had been expanding their empire in the west. Syria and Israel formed an alliance in an effort to free themselves from Assyrian domination. When they sought to add Judah to their anti-Assyrian coalition, Ahaz refused to join, prompting the Syrians and Israelites to invade their southern neighbor (Isa. 7:1). They hoped to replace Jotham and Ahaz with a puppet king, called the "son of Tabeel" (see v. 6),[24] but the invasion was unsuccessful.

When the royal house of Judah first heard of the Syrian-Israelite coalition, they were struck with fear (v. 2). At this point the Lord instructed Isaiah to enter the scene and to assure the royal house of God's protection. The prophet was to take his son Shear-jashub and to confront Ahaz near the

22. Asherah symbols and high places are both associated with pagan pillars elsewhere. See Exod. 34:13; Deut. 7:5; 12:3; 16:21–22; 1 Kings 14:23; 2 Kings 17:9–10; 18:4; 23:13–14; Mic. 5:13–14. Asherah symbols appear to have been living trees or wooden poles. See J. C. de Moor, "אֲשֵׁרָה," *TDOT* 1:442–43.

23. For the chronology of this period, see Edwin R. Thiele, *The Mysterious Numbers of the Hebrew Kings,* 3d ed. (Grand Rapids: Zondervan, 1983), 131–34.

24. The Tabeel family was probably a Judahite family that had become prominent in Gilead. See Yohanan Aharoni, *The Land of the Bible: A Historical Geography,* translated and edited by A. F. Rainey, rev. ed. (Philadelphia: Westminster, 1979), 370.

aqueduct of the Upper Pool, where the king was inspecting the city's defenses and water supply (v. 3).

As Isaiah himself later explained, he and his sons had symbolic names (see Isa. 8:18). Isaiah's name, meaning "the LORD saves," was a reminder of the Lord's ability to deliver his people from crises. Shear-jashub's name, meaning "a remnant will return," probably had a positive connotation as well, perhaps suggesting that most of the enemy invaders would be defeated and only a remnant would return home.

Isaiah told Ahaz not to panic and assured him that the Lord intended to stop the invaders in their tracks (vv. 4–9). After all, Ahaz was a member of the house of David (see v. 2), which had been promised an eternal dynasty (2 Sam. 7:11b–16). By comparison, the invaders were insignificant, a fact Isaiah emphasized by calling King Pekah of Israel simply "the son of Remaliah" (vv. 4–5, 9).

While assuring Ahaz of deliverance from the Syrian-Israelite threat, Isaiah also challenged the royal house and the entire nation to trust in the Lord (v. 9).[25] Using wordplay, he warned that if they did not "stand firm," they would not "stand" at all. The exact meaning of this warning becomes apparent as the rest of the story unfolds.

Unbelief Forfeits a Blessing (7:10–25)

Perhaps realizing that twenty-year-old Ahaz (see 2 Kings 16:2) needed some extra encouragement, the Lord offered to give the king a confirming sign of his intention to protect Judah from the invaders (vv. 10–11). The Lord gave Ahaz a blank check; the king could ask for any sign he desired, including one beyond the bounds of ordinary human experience. But Ahaz, who had already decided to court the Assyrians rather than trust in God (see 2 Kings 16:7–8), balked, objecting that he did not want to "test" the Lord (v. 12). It is true that the Lord was angered by earlier generations of Israelites who "tested" him by questioning his goodness and ability to care for them (see Exod. 17:2–7; Num. 14:22; Deut. 6:16; Ps. 78:18, 41, 56; 95:9; 106:14). But the Lord was not above giving a confirming sign to those whose weak faith needed a boost (Judg. 6:17; 1 Sam. 10:7–9). The Lord's offer to Ahaz was a generous invitation designed to stimulate faith, not a trick designed to tempt Ahaz to sin. Ahaz's pious-sounding response was really a smoke screen sent up by one who preferred to walk by sight, not faith.

Isaiah was not about to let Ahaz sidestep the issue. Reminding the king of his spiritual heritage, the prophet addressed the entire "house of David,"

---

25. In v. 9b, the verbs "stand firm" and "stand" are plural forms in Hebrew, indicating that Ahaz is no longer the sole addressee (as in vv. 4–5, in which the second-person verbs and pronouns are singular in Hebrew). The plural in v. 9b probably encompasses Ahaz, the royal house (including Jotham), and the entire nation. See v. 2, which points out that Ahaz and "his people" responded in fear when they heard of the alliance.

warning them that they were trying not only Isaiah's patience, but the patience of God as well (v. 13).[26] In a subtle but sarcastic verbal shift, Isaiah called the Lord "my God," not "your God" (as in v. 11). The implication is clear; at this point, the prophet was not so sure the royal house regarded the Lord as their God.

Though Ahaz refused to ask for a sign, the Lord insisted on giving him one. This "sign" involved a series of events outlined in verses 14–25. A young woman known to the royal family would soon give birth to a boy whom the mother would name Immanuel (meaning "God is with us"). Eventually this child would eat sour milk (or "curds") and honey, an experience which would help him make wise moral decisions. Before this took place, however, the Syrians and Israelites would be defeated. The Lord would then usher in a period of time unlike any since the division of the nation into separate kingdoms almost two hundred years before.

Egypt and Assyria would both set their sights on Judah. Verse 18 compares the Egyptians to flies and the Assyrians to bees. Swarming flies are annoying; bees are irritating and especially dangerous because of the pain they inflict with their sting (see Deut. 1:44; Ps. 118:12). The metaphors are well chosen, for the Assyrians were much more powerful and dangerous than the Egyptians. Nevertheless, both would put pressure on Judah, for Egypt wanted Judah as a buffer state against Assyrian aggression, while Assyria wanted it as a base for operations against Egypt. Following the reference to sour milk and honey, the metaphors are especially appropriate, for flies are attracted to dairy products and bees can be found in the vicinity of honey. The Assyrians would overrun the land, destroy the crops, and force the people to subsist on goats' milk and honey. At that time, as the people saw Immanuel eating his sour milk and honey, they would be forced to acknowledge that God was indeed with them. God was present with them in the Syrian-Israelite crisis, fully capable of rescuing them; but he would also be present with them in judgment, disciplining them for their lack of trust.

Initially the prophecy appears to be a message of salvation. The name Immanuel seems to have a positive ring to it; curds and honey elsewhere symbolize prosperity and blessing (see Deut. 32:13–14); verse 16 announces the defeat of Judah's enemies; and verse 17 could be taken as predicting a return to the glorious days of David and Solomon. However, the message turns sour in verses 17b–25. God would be with his people in judgment, as well as in salvation. The curds and honey would be signs of deprivation, the relief announced in verse 16 would be short-lived, and the new era would be characterized by unprecedented humiliation, not a return to glory. Ahaz's refusal to

---

26. The second-person masculine verb forms and pronouns in vv. 13–14 are plural in Hebrew, indicating that the message is addressed to the entire royal house. In vv. 16–17, the prophet switches back to the singular, focusing again on Ahaz.

trust the Lord would transform potential blessing into judgment, just as Isaiah turned an apparent prophecy of salvation into a message of judgment.

We must look at verses 14–17 in more detail, for this passage has given rise to some spirited debates, primarily because of the use of verse 14 in Matthew 1:23. I present an annotated translation of verses 14–17 before discussing the identity of Immanuel and the New Testament's use of verse 14.[27]

An Annotated Translation of Isaiah 7:14–17

14 For this reason the sovereign master himself will give you a confirming sign.[28] Look, the young lady[29] over there[30] is about to conceive[31] and will give birth to a son. You, young lady, will name

27. The following translation is a revised version of a translation originally prepared by the author for the NET.

28. The Hebrew noun translated "sign," can refer to a miraculous event (v. 11 seems to anticipate this type of "sign"), but this is not the inherent meaning of the word. Elsewhere in Isaiah the word usually refers to a natural occurrence or an object/person vested with special significance (see 8:18; 19:20; 20:3; 37:30; 55:13; 66:19). Only in 38:7–8, 22 does it refer to a miraculous deed that involves suspending natural physical laws. The sign outlined in vv. 14–25 involves God's providential control over events and their timing, but not necessarily his miraculous intervention. Consequently, the use of the word "sign" does not demand that a miraculous birth be in view.

29. Traditionally, "virgin." Though the Hebrew noun *'almah* can refer to a woman who is a virgin (Gen. 24:43; see v. 16), it does not carry this meaning inherently. (It is important to distinguish referent and meaning. To illustrate the point, I offer the following scenario. Imagine a young lady is wearing a pin which broadcasts her virginity with the words, "Waiting for marriage." Now if I say to you, "Look at that gal! She's got a lot of moral courage," you would not assume that "gal" means "virgin." Even though I used a word ("gal") to refer to a young lady who is indeed a virgin, you understand that "gal" means "young lady," not "virgin." In a different context, "gal" might refer to a nonvirgin. In other words, the person to which a word refers may possess a certain quality without that quality having any bearing on the meaning of the word being used to refer to the person. The same appears to be true of Hebrew *'almah,* which approximates our term "gal." The word pertains to age, not sexual experience. In one context it may refer to a young woman who is a virgin, in another to a young lady who is a nonvirgin.) The word is the feminine form of the corresponding masculine noun *'elem,* meaning "young man" (1 Sam. 17:56; 20:22). A related abstract noun, *'alumim,* means "youth," not "virginity." Usage in cognate languages certainly does not suggest that the word has a specialized meaning, "virgin." The Aramaic cognate is used in the *Targum of Judges* 19:3–5 of the Levite's concubine, and the Ugaritic cognate refers to a goddess who has consummated her marriage and become pregnant (*CTA* 24). The very limited usage of the term in the Hebrew Bible is ambiguous (see Exod. 2:8; Ps. 68:25; Song of Sol. 1:3; 6:8), and the referent in Prov. 30:19 may even be a nonvirgin (depending on what type of romantic activity is envisioned there). The word seems to pertain to age, not sexual experience, and is best translated "young woman." At the same time, the term is flexible enough to accommodate the New Testament's application of the prophecy to the Virgin Mary, Jesus' mother.

30. The text reads simply "the young woman." The words "over there" are added in the translation to bring out the force of the article. It is very likely that Isaiah pointed to a woman who was present at the scene of the prophet's interview with Ahaz. Isaiah's address to the "house of David" and his use of second-person plural forms suggest other people were present, and his use of the second-feminine singular verb form ("you will name") later in the verse is best explained if addressed to a woman who is present.

31. Elsewhere the adjective *harah,* when used predicatively, refers to a past pregnancy (from the narrator's perspective, 1 Sam. 4:19), to a present condition (from the speaker's perspective, Gen. 16:11; 38:24; 2 Sam. 11:5), and to a conception that is about to occur (Judg. 13:5, 7). In Isa. 7:14, one could translate, "the young woman is pregnant." In this case, the woman may have been a member of the royal family. Another option, the one chosen in the translation above, takes the adjective in an imminent future sense, "the

him[32] Immanuel. **15** He will eat sour milk and honey, which will
help him know how[33] to reject evil and choose what is right.
16 Here's why this will be so.[34] Before the child knows how to reject
evil and choose what is right, the land whose two kings you fear will
become desolate. **17** The LORD will bring upon you, your people,
and your father's family, a time unlike any since Ephraim departed
from Judah—the king of Assyria will come![35]

The Identity of Immanuel

Who was the child Immanuel? Scholars have answered this question in a variety of ways. On the basis of Matthew 1:23, many propose an exclusively
messianic interpretation of Isaiah 7:14 and identify Immanuel solely with
Jesus. While the prophecy certainly does point ultimately to Jesus (see the
discussion below, "Immanuel as a Type"), an examination of verse 14 in its
immediate literary context precludes an exclusively messianic interpretation.
Verse 14 suggests that Immanuel's mother was present when Isaiah delivered
the prophecy, and verses 15–17 indicate that Immanuel functioned as a tangible sign of God's presence to the house of David and to the people of Judah
in the eighth century B.C. Like the entire nation, he eventually experienced
the devastation of the Assyrian invasion.

---

young woman is about to conceive." In this case, the woman could have been a member of the royal family,
or, more likely, the prophetess with whom Isaiah had sexual relations shortly after this (see 8:3).

32. The text literally reads, "and you will call his name." The words "young lady" are added in the
translation to clarify the identity of the addressee. The verb is normally taken as an archaic third-feminine-
singular form here and translated, "she will call." However, the form *qara't* is more naturally understood as
second-feminine-singular, in which case the words would be addressed to the young woman mentioned just
before this. In the three other occurrences of the third-feminine-singular perfect of *qara'* I, "to call," the
form used is *qare'ah* (see Gen. 29:35; 30:26; 1 Chron. 4:9). (A third-feminine-singular perfect, *qara't*, does
appear in Deut. 31:29 and Jer. 44:23, but the verb here is the homonym *qara'* II, "to meet, encounter.") The
form *qara'* I (from *qara'* I, "to call") appears in three other passages (Gen. 16:11; Isa. 60:18; Jer. 3:4 [Qere]),
and in each case is second-feminine-singular.

33. The text literally reads, "for his knowing." Traditionally the preposition has been translated in a
temporal sense, "when he knows." Though the preposition *le-* can sometimes have a temporal force, it never
carries such a nuance in any of the forty other passages where it is used with the infinitive construct of the
verb *yada'*, "to know." Most often the construction indicates purpose or consequence. This sense is preferable here. The following context indicates that sour milk and honey would epitomize the devastation that
God's judgment would bring upon the land. Cultivated crops would be gone, and the people would be
forced to live off the milk produced by their goats and the honey they found in the thickets. As Immanuel
was forced to eat a steady diet of this sour milk and honey, he would be reminded of the consequences of
sin and motivated to make correct moral decisions in order to avoid further outbreaks of divine discipline.

34. The text reads literally, "for, because." The particle introduces the entire following context (vv.
16–25), which explains why Immanuel was an appropriate name for the child, why he would eat sour milk
and honey, and why experiencing such a diet would contribute to his moral development.

35. The Hebrew text reads simply "the king of Assyria." Because these words are rather awkwardly
tacked on to the end of the sentence, some regard them as a later addition. (This implies, of course, that
later editors worked in a sloppy, ungrammatical fashion.) However, the very awkwardness of the construction may facilitate the prophet's rhetorical strategy here, as he suddenly turns what sounds like a positive
message into a judgment speech. Actually, "the king of Assyria" stands in apposition to the earlier object
"time" (literally, "days") and specifies who the main character of these coming "days" would be.

Who was this historical Immanuel? Some take Immanuel as a collective name for all children born from Judahite women who were pregnant at the time of the prophecy, but the singular forms used in verses 14–16 favor an individual referent. Immanuel may have been an otherwise unidentified child born to the house of David.[36] In this case, the young lady addressed by Isaiah may have been a queen or princess in the royal family (and possibly even a virgin at the time the prophecy was delivered).

A more likely option is that Immanuel and Maher-shalal-hash-baz (whose birth is recorded in chapter 8) were one and the same. The birth account in 8:3 could easily be interpreted as the fulfillment of the prophecy of 7:14. The presence of a formal record and witnesses (8:1–2) suggests a sign function for the child (see 7:14). As in 7:14–16, the removal of Judah's enemies would take place before the child reached a specified age (see 8:4). Both 7:17–25 and 8:7–8 speak of an Assyrian invasion of Judah following the defeat of the Syrian-Israelite alliance. The direct address to Immanuel at the end of 8:8 would make sense if his birth has been recorded in the previous verses.

The major objection to this view is the use of different names, but dual naming is attested elsewhere in the OT (see Gen. 35:18).[37] The name Immanuel (given by the mother; see 7:14) would emphasize the basic fact of God's presence, while the name Maher-shalal-hash-baz (given by Isaiah; see 8:3), meaning "one hastens to the plunder, one hurries to the loot," would explain exactly how God would be present (in judgment). Giving the child a different name at the time of his birth would also be highly ironic, for it highlights how God's presence, normally viewed as a positive reality, had been transformed into something dark and ominous by Ahaz's unbelief. Some argue that the phrase "your land" in 8:8 points to a royal referent (a child of Ahaz or the Messiah), but usage elsewhere shows that the phrase does not need to be so restricted. While the pronoun can refer to the king of a land (see Num. 20:17; 21:22; Deut. 2:27; Judg. 11:17, 19; 2 Sam. 24:13; 1 Kings 11:22; Isa. 14:20), it can also refer to one who is merely a native of a particular land (see Gen. 12:1; 32:9; Jon. 1:8). (See also the use of "his land" in Isa. 13:14, in which the pronoun refers to a native of a land, and in 37:7, in which it refers to a king.)

Immanuel as a Type

In addition to being a reminder of God's presence in the immediate crisis faced by Ahaz and Judah, Immanuel was a guarantee of the nation's future greatness in fulfillment of God's covenantal promises. Eventually God would

---

36. Some identify Immanuel with King Hezekiah, but Hezekiah was born five years earlier in 740 B.C. See E. H. Merrill, *Kingdom of Priests* (Grand Rapids: Baker, 1987), 404, 426 n. 102.

37. It is also interesting that Jesus was not actually named Immanuel, nor is there any evidence that he was ever called by this name.

deliver his people from the hostile nations (see 8:9–10) through another child, an ideal Davidic ruler who would embody God's presence in a special way (see 9:6–7).[38]

Jesus the Messiah is the fulfillment of the Davidic ideal prophesied by Isaiah, the one whom Immanuel foreshadowed. Through the miracle of the incarnation he is literally "God with us," not merely a tangible reminder of God's presence. Matthew realized this and applied Isaiah's ancient prophecy of Immanuel's birth to Jesus (Matt. 1:22–23). The first Immanuel was a reminder to the people of God's presence and a guarantee of a greater child to come who would manifest God's presence in an even greater way. The second Immanuel is "God with us" in a heightened and infinitely superior sense. He "fulfills" Isaiah's Immanuel prophecy by bringing the typology intended by God to realization and by filling out or completing the pattern designed by God. Of course, in the ultimate fulfillment of the type, the incarnate Immanuel's mother must be a virgin, so Matthew uses a Greek term (*parthenos*) that carries that technical meaning (unlike the Hebrew word *almah,* which has the more general meaning "young woman," but is flexible enough to include a virgin as its referent).

This is not the only passage in which Matthew draws an analogy between events surrounding the birth of Jesus and events from Israel's history referred to in the prophets. The linking of these passages by analogy is termed "fulfillment." In 2:15, God calls Jesus, his perfect Son, out of Egypt, just as he did his son Israel in the days of Moses, a historical event referred to in Hosea 11:1. In so doing Matthew makes it clear that Jesus is the ideal Israel prophesied by Isaiah (see Isa. 49:3), sent to restore wayward Israel (see Isa. 49:5 and Matt. 1:21). Matthew 2:18 views Herod's slaughter of the infants as another instance of the oppressive treatment of God's people by cruel tyrants. Herod's actions are analogous to those of the Assyrians, who deported the Israelites, causing the personified land to lament as inconsolably as a mother robbed of her little ones (Jer. 31:15). Neither of the prophetic texts refers in their original context to the events of Jesus' time, but from Matthew's perspective these episodes in Israel's history foreshadowed those of Jesus' time.

A Sign–Child Enters the Picture (8:1–10)

Having sent Isaiah to challenge and warn the king, the Lord next commanded the prophet to write the name Maher-shalal-hash-baz, meaning "one hastens to the plunder, one hurries to the loot," on a scroll (8:1). He even summoned two reliable witnesses to watch this symbolic act (v. 2). Isaiah then had sexual relations with one called "the prophetess" (presumably

---

38. Note how the reference to the king's birth in 9:6a links this passage with the texts describing the birth of Immanuel (7:14) and Maher-shalal-hash-baz (8:3).

his wife), who conceived and gave birth to a son (v. 3a). The Lord instructed Isaiah to give the child the symbolic name Maher-shalal-hash-baz (v. 3b), which provided a word-picture of the impending divine judgment on Damascus (the capital city of Syria) and Samaria (the capital city of Israel). Before the child reached the age at which he could address his parents as "father" and "mother," both of the nations represented by these cities would be plundered and looted (v. 4). God's instrument of judgment would be the Assyrians, who would sweep through the area like a powerful flood (vv. 5–7).[39]

But the judgment foreshadowed by the sign-child's name was not restricted to Judah's enemies. Because of Ahaz's refusal to trust in the Lord, the Assyrian flood would sweep into Judah as well (v. 8a). Switching metaphors, Isaiah depicts the Assyrians as a large bird spreading its wings over the entire land of Judah (v. 8b). This final announcement of judgment is addressed to Immanuel (Maher-shalal-hash-baz's other name, in my view). The text drips with irony at this point. One would think that God's presence with his people would ensure their safety, but in this case he would be with his people in judgment through the instrumentality of Assyria, the very nation to whom Ahaz turned for help.

The Lord's warning quickly became a reality. In 734 B.C., Tiglath-pileser III invaded the west, first conquering the coastal areas of Tyre and Philistia. In 733–732 B.C., he conquered Syria and Israel. He executed King Rezin of Damascus and made Syria into an Assyrian province (see 2 Kings 16:9). In Israel, Hoshea assassinated King Pekah and became an Assyrian puppet king (see 2 Kings 15:29–30). Israel's territory was greatly reduced, as the northern regions of the nation became Assyrian provinces.[40] All of this happened before little Immanuel, born in late 735 B.C. or early 734 B.C., could differentiate right from wrong (see Isa. 7:16) or address his parents as "daddy" or "mommy" (see Isa. 8:4).

While Ahaz's agreement with the Assyrians seemed to get Judah off the hook, the alliance actually proved to be the kiss of death. Judah was now bound to the Assyrians by a treaty that demanded regular tribute payments and drained the royal house and nation of their wealth (see 2 Chron. 28:20–21). When Judah, under Ahaz's son Hezekiah, eventually rebelled against oppressive Assyrian rule, the Assyrian king Sennacherib invaded the land. In

39. The precise meaning of v. 6 is uncertain. If the phrase "this people" refers to Samaria/Israel, then the verse depicts the northern kingdom's rejection of the Lord, symbolized by the "gently flowing waters of Shiloah" (probably a reference to a spring that supplied Jerusalem with water). However, the phrase "this people" could refer to the people of Judah. In this case, the word translated "rejoices" would have to be derived from a different Hebrew lexical form and assigned a meaning "melts in fear." Verse 6 would then describe how the people of Judah were so paralyzed by fear of the Syrian-Israelite alliance that they refused to trust in the Lord's promise of deliverance.

40. For more detailed accounts of the Assyrian invasion of the west in 734–732 B.C., see Wayne T. Pitard, *Ancient Damascus* (Winona Lake, Ind.: Eisenbrauns, 1987), 186–89, and B. Otzen, "Israel under the Assyrians," in *Power and Propaganda*, ed. M. T. Larsen (Copenhagen: Akademisk Forlag, 1979), 251–61.

701 B.C., the Assyrian army swept into Judah like a flood (see Isa. 8:7–8), devastated the countryside, and destroyed the crops (see Isa. 7:17–25, as well as 1:7 and 37:30–31). Sennacherib conquered several fortified cities and villages (see 2 Kings 18:13), and took a huge number of people and livestock into exile.[41] Immanuel, now a young man in his early thirties, experienced the aftermath of this invasion. As he was forced to subsist on a steady diet of sour milk and honey, he was undoubtedly reminded of the consequences of sin and motivated to make correct moral decisions (see Isa. 7:15). As people observed him eating his sour milk and honey, many must have recalled the words of Isaiah and lamented the day that Ahaz chose to walk by sight, rather than by faith.

But Sennacherib's invasion had a surprise ending. As Sennacherib's armies surrounded Jerusalem, Hezekiah begged the Lord to intervene (see Isa. 36–37). The Lord sent a killer angel who destroyed the Assyrians in one night, forcing Sennacherib to retreat with his tail between his legs (Isa. 37:36–37). Hezekiah's faith reversed the effects of Ahaz's unbelief, and Judah once more experienced the presence of God as its deliverer, rather than its judge.

Isaiah himself foresaw this in 735–734 B.C., when he delivered his judgment oracle in conjunction with his son's birth. Having described how the Assyrians would flood the land of Judah and cover it with the dark, ominous shadow of judgment (Isa. 8:7–8), Isaiah suddenly turns to the invaders and taunts them. In 8:9–10, he challenges the "nations" (a reference to the Assyrian army, which utilized soldiers from various conquered nations throughout the Assyrian Empire)[42] to prepare for battle, but confidently announces that their attack would fail.[43] Why? That question could be answered in one word—the name Immanuel (see "God is with us" at the end of v. 10). When all was said and done, Judah's savior-turned-judge would reprise his role of deliverer and demonstrate his sovereignty over the raging nations that he had used as instruments of judgment.

Persevering during Dark Times (8:11–22)

The Syrian-Israelite threat caused many in Judah to panic. As fear expelled reason, some even accused others of being part of a conspiracy to overthrow

41. For Sennacherib's highly propagandized account of the invasion, see Pritchard, *Ancient Near Eastern Texts,* 287–88.

42. J. H. Hayes and S. A. Irvine identify the "nations" here as Syria and Israel. See *Isaiah* (Nashville: Abingdon, 1987), 152. In this case, the prophet finishes his message as he started it by focusing on the more immediate future and the deliverance it would bring. But the reference to "distant lands" suggests that Assyria, which in vv. 7–8 takes center stage, is still in view (see 5:26 as well). This becomes even more likely when one considers 10:5–34, which develops in detail the brief but confident cry of 8:9–10.

43. The threefold imperative in vv. 9–10 ("be shattered") is rhetorical and equivalent to a prediction, "you will be shattered." It expresses Isaiah's firm conviction of the outcome of the nations' attack. The repetition of the imperative creates a taunting mood.

the government. The Lord warned Isaiah and his followers not to get caught up in the panic (vv. 11–12).[44] In the midst of all the fear and confusion, the faithful remnant was to stay focused on the Lord, its sovereign king (v. 13).

The people of Israel and Judah, including the residents of Jerusalem, had abandoned the Lord. That decision would prove to be their downfall. Rather than being their source of security, the Lord would bring about their demise. In the past, his intervention for his people had been commemorated by a "stone of help" (see 1 Sam. 7:12). He was Israel's "rock" of defense and security (see Deut. 32:4; 2 Sam. 22:32). Now, ironically, he would become a stone/rock over which both Israel and Judah would trip and fall, and a snare that would entrap the people of Jerusalem (vv. 14–15).

In light of these coming events, it was important that a written record of "the testimony" and "the law" be preserved among the faithful remnant (v. 16).[45] The "testimony" probably refers here to the prophetic messages God had given the prophet, the "law" to the prophet's commands and warnings. When the prophecies were fulfilled and the warnings had materialized, God's followers could then produce an official record to confirm the authenticity of Isaiah's ministry and to impress upon the people the reality of God's authority over them.

Isaiah affirmed that he would maintain his trust in the Lord through the coming time of judgment, when God's face would be hidden from God's people (v. 17). Isaiah and his children (Shear-jashub and Maher-shalal-hash-baz) would continue to stand firmly as reminders of the Lord's willingness to help his people (v. 18). Isaiah's name (which means "the LORD saves") was a reminder that the Lord was the nation's only source of protection; Shear-jashub's name ("a remnant will return") was meant, at least originally, to encourage Ahaz (see 7:3); and Maher-shalal-hash-baz's name ("one hastens to the plunder, one hurries to the loot") was a guarantee of Syria's and Israel's defeat (see 8:4). Sadly, the people, because of their lack of faith, had forfeited the divine security that the names suggested.

As the darkness of judgment settled over the land, the people were turning to pagan occult practices in an effort to discover and control the future (v. 19).[46] The "mediums and spiritists" referred to here utilized pits dug into

44. The second-person verbal and pronominal forms in vv. 12–13 are plural, indicating that these warnings are directed to Isaiah and other followers of the Lord who looked to the prophet for leadership (see v. 16).

45. If the Lord is speaking (as in vv. 12–15) to Isaiah here (the second-person verb forms are singular), then "my disciples" refers to the Lord's followers. If Isaiah is speaking (as in v. 17), the addressee is not specified and "my disciples" refers to the prophet's followers.

46. It is not clear if the prophet or the Lord is speaking in vv. 19–22. If Isaiah is the speaker, then he is probably addressing the Lord's followers (the second-person pronoun and verb in v. 19 are plural). If the Lord is speaking, then vv. 19–22 resume the speech recorded in vv. 12–15, in which he addressed Isaiah and the faithful remnant.

the ground in an effort to tap into the subterranean world of the dead.[47] The mediums whispered and muttered incantations designed to conjure up the spirits of the dead who would in turn give an oracle to the one making inquiry.[48] In the midst of such spiritual darkness, the faithful remnant must follow the compass of God's prophetic word, referred to once more as "the law" and "the testimony" (v. 20; see v. 16). Through Isaiah, the Lord had already told the people that their future was dark. In the aftermath of invasion, refugees would roam through the land looking for food as they angrily cursed both their king and their God (vv. 21–22).[49]

A Light Dispels the Darkness (9:1–7)

The darkness of judgment would not cover the land forever. Focusing on the northern regions of Israel, Isaiah described a time when God would reverse the humiliating judgment he had poured out on the ancient tribal regions of Zebulun and Naphtali (v. 1).[50] In 734–732 B.C., Tiglath-pileser III of Assyria annexed much of Israel's territory and reduced Samaria to a puppet state, governed by a ruler handpicked by the Assyrians. The Assyrians organized the annexed areas into the three provinces mentioned in verse 1: Megiddo (= "Galilee of the Gentiles"), Dor (= "the way of the sea"), and Gilead (= "[the region] along [better, beyond] the Jordan").[51] The light of God's deliverance would dispel the darkness that shrouded this region (v. 2). A conquering Davidic king (see v. 7 and 11:1, 10) would deliver Israel from their oppressive enemies, just as Gideon of old had shattered the cruel Midianites (vv. 4–5; see Judg. 7).

This great victory would prompt a joyous outburst from God's people (v. 3). Focusing on their king, the people recall his birth, affirm his willingness to shoulder the responsibility of leadership, and rehearse his royal titles, which emphasize his military ability (v. 6).[52] The king's military strength

47. King Saul consulted such a medium (see 1 Sam. 28). For more on these mediums and their rituals, see H. Hoffner, "אוֹב" *TDOT* 1:130–34.

48. Verse 19b is typically translated as the speaker's (Isaiah's or God's) response to the idolaters (see, for example, NIV). However, the Hebrew text reads literally, "Should a people not seek its God/gods, on behalf of the living the dead?" It is more likely that this is a continuation of the mediums' words, the citation of which begins in v. 19a. See John Day, *Yahweh and the Gods and Goddesses of Canaan* (Sheffield: Sheffield Academic Press, 2000), 218. Verses 19–20a may be paraphrased: "When they say to you, 'Consult the mediums and spiritists, who whisper and mutter! Should not a people consult its gods? [Should they not consult] the dead on behalf of the living?' then [go] to the law and the testimony!"

49. The traditional translation assumes that the Hebrew word *'elohim,* as usual, refers to the one true God, whom the people recognize as the source of their distress. Another option in this context is to understand the word as a true plural referring to the pagan gods whom the people hoped would deliver them. As they wander through the land, they curse these gods for their failure to protect them (see 2:20).

50. In vv. 1–5, Isaiah takes a rhetorical stance in the future age of restoration and describes future events as if they have already occurred.

51. See Aharoni, *Land of the Bible,* 374–75.

52. The Hebrew verb forms in v. 6 indicate completed action; they reflect the perspective of the future generation that would experience this great victory.

makes the nation secure, and his commitment to justice assures the continuation of the Davidic dynasty (v. 7a). The secret to his success is the Lord,
whose "zeal" for (that is, intense devotion to and love for) his people prompts
him to vindicate them and to fulfill his promises to David and the nation.

The king's royal titles deserve special attention for they characterize and
epitomize his reign. Unfortunately, the grammatical structure of verse 6b is
not entirely clear. In the Hebrew text the sentence begins "and he calls his
name," but no subject is indicated for the verb "he calls." Some suggest that
one or more of the titles that follow refer to God, not the king. For example,
the traditional Hebrew text, as punctuated by medieval Hebrew scribes, suggests the translation "and the Wonderful Counselor, the Mighty God, calls his
name, 'Everlasting Father, Prince of Peace.'" However, it is more likely that
the subject of the verb is indefinite, "one calls." In such cases it is possible to
translate the verb as passive, making the grammatical object the subject in the
translation, "and his name is called." This use of "he calls/called" with an indefinite subject followed by the object "name" occurs elsewhere in the Hebrew Bible (see Gen. 25:26; 35:8; 38:29–30; Num. 11:3; 21:3; Josh. 5:9).

Traditionally "Wonderful" and "Counselor" have been taken separately,
yielding a total of five titles (see KJV). However, the pattern of the second,
third, and fourth titles, each of which combines two elements, suggests the
first title is also a compound, "Wonderful Counselor" (see NIV). Some understand this first royal title as referring to the king's wisdom in a general
sense, but the immediate context suggests a more specific idea is in view. The
preceding verses focus on the king's military victory, and the very next title
("Mighty God") highlights his divinely bestowed strength. Therefore the
title "Wonderful Counselor" probably depicts this warrior-king as an extraordinary military strategist. A related noun, translated "counsel" or "strategy," is associated with military might in Isaiah 11:2 and 36:5.

The second title, "Mighty God," portrays the king as God's representative on the battlefield. God supernaturally empowers the king for battle.
When the king's enemies oppose him on the battlefield, they are, as it were,
fighting against God himself. Though we might in retrospect see this title as
indicating the coming king's deity, it is unlikely that Isaiah or his audience
would have understood the title in such a bold way. Psalm 45:6 addresses the
Davidic king as "God" because he ruled and fought as God's representative
on earth. Ancient Near Eastern art and literature depict gods training kings
for battle, bestowing special weapons, and intervening in battle. According
to Egyptian propaganda, the Hittites described Rameses II as follows: "No
man is he who is among us, It is Seth great-of-strength, Baal in person; Not
deeds of man are these his doings, They are of one who is unique."[53] The

---

53. Miriam Lichtheim, *Ancient Egyptian Literature,* 3 vols. (Berkeley: University of California Press,
1975–80), 2:67.

royal title in Isaiah 9:6 probably envisions a similar kind of response when friend and foe alike look at the Davidic king in full battle regalia.[54]

The third title, "Everlasting Father," pictures the king as the protector of his people (for a similar use of "father" see Isa. 22:21 and Job 29:16). This figurative, idiomatic use of "father" is not limited to the Bible. In a Phoenician inscription (dating to approximately 825 B.C.), the ruler Kilamuwa declares: "To some I was a father, to others I was a mother." In another inscription (dating to approximately 800 B.C.), the ruler Azitawadda boasts that the god Baal made him "a father and a mother" to his people.[55] Isaiah and his audience probably understood the term "everlasting" as royal hyperbole emphasizing the king's long reign or enduring dynasty (for examples of such hyperbolic language used of the Davidic king, see 1 Kings 1:31; Ps. 21:4–6; 61:6–7; 72:5, 17). The hyperbolic language (as in the case of the title "Mighty God") is literally realized in the ultimate fulfillment of the prophecy, for Jesus will rule eternally.

The fourth title, "Prince of Peace," pictures the king as one who establishes a safe sociopolitical environment for his people. It hardly depicts him as meek and mild, for he establishes peace through military strength. His people experience safety and prosperity because their invincible king has annihilated their enemies (see Ps. 29 for a similar example of God providing peace through power).

The Lord's Hand of Judgment Remains Upraised (9:8–10:4)

Having previewed the messianic era, the prophet returns to the harsh realities of his own time. In the next speech Isaiah depicts the Lord's unrelenting judgment upon the northern kingdom. This speech assumes that God had already sent devastating judgment (see v. 10),[56] but it emphasizes that God's anger had not subsided and that another round of divine judgment was coming (10:1–4). The speech was probably given just prior to the Assyrian conquest of the northern kingdom in 734–732 B.C. or sometime between that invasion and the downfall of Samaria in 722 B.C. The speech is divided into four parts, each of which ends with the refrain, "Yet for all this, his anger is not turned away, his hand is still upraised":

> Part I (9:8–12)
>   A   Description of past judgment (9:8)
>   B   Description of the people's attitude toward past judgment (9:9–10)
>   C   Description of past judgment (9:11–12a)
>   D   Refrain (9:12b)

---

54. See Hayes and Irvine, *Isaiah*, 181–82.

55. For these two inscriptions see Pritchard, *Ancient Near Eastern Texts*, 499–501.

56. The Hebrew verb forms in vv. 8–9, 14, 17–20 are best translated with the past tense (contrary to NIV, which uses the future or present tense).

Part II (9:13–17)
- A   Description of the people's attitude toward past judgment (9:13)
- B   Description of past judgment (9:14–17a)
- C   Refrain (9:17b)

Part III (9:18–21)
- A   Description of past judgment (9:18–21a)
- B   Refrain (9:21b)

Part IV (10:1–4)
- A   Woe oracle announcing future judgment (10:1–4a)
- B   Refrain (10:4b)

Israel experienced the devastating effects of divine judgment. This judgment, though announced by God, had no effect on the proud people, who optimistically boasted that they would rebuild their ruined cities and replace their destroyed sycamore trees with cedars (vv. 8–10). The Lord brought the Syrians and Philistines against the land, but the people refused to repent of their sins (vv. 11–13).[57] The Lord removed many of the nation's most prominent leaders, including the lying prophets who misled the people (vv. 14–16). From top to bottom, Israel was corrupt (v. 17). This widespread evil ignited the fires of divine judgment that scorched the land (vv. 18–19). Civil war tore the nation in two and spilled over into Judah, as the northern kingdom, under Pekah, tried to force the southern kingdom to join its anti-Assyrian alliance (vv. 20–21; see 2 Kings 15:10–16:6).

All of this was a mere prelude to an even more devastating judgment that was about to fall. The leaders of the northern kingdom were doomed (note "woe" in 10:1) because they had failed to promote justice. They instituted oppressive measures against the poor, denied the people justice, and even exploited the weak and helpless, epitomized by the widows and fatherless (10:1–2). In the day of divine reckoning these leaders would have no one to help them and nowhere to hide their money (v. 3). Those who escaped the invader's sword would be captured and taken away into exile (v. 4).

God Cuts the Assyrians Down to Size (10:5–34)

God's severe judgment of Israel would not quench his thirst for justice. Once more his upraised hand (see v. 4b) would strike his enemies, but this time the proud Assyrians would get a taste of what they had been dishing out.

The Lord used the Assyrians as his instrument of judgment against godless Israel (vv. 5–6), but the Assyrians did not recognize this. The imperialistic Assyrian kings boasted of their victories over Syria, Israel, and other western states. They thought of Judah as just another weak kingdom whose

---

57. Since the Syrians and Israelites were allies by 735 B.C. (see 7:1), v. 11 must refer to an earlier Syrian attack on the northern kingdom, probably during Menahem's reign over Israel (752–742 B.C.). See J. Bright, *A History of Israel,* 3d ed. (Philadelphia: Westminster, 1981), 271–72. Unlike Pekah, who allied with Syria against Assyria, Menahem followed a pro-Assyrian policy (see 2 Kings 15:19–20).

gods were incapable of stopping the Assyrian onslaught (vv. 7–11).[58] The Lord would use the Assyrians to discipline Judah, but once that task was accomplished he would teach the Assyrians a lesson (v. 12). The proud Assyrians attributed their success to their own strength and wisdom, and boasted that their conquests had been as easy as stealing eggs from an abandoned bird's nest (vv. 13–14). The Assyrians were a mere tool in the Lord's hand, but they were acting as if they were superior to him. This, of course, was absurd, comparable to a tool swinging a workman or a weapon brandishing a warrior (v. 15). Assyria's excessive pride demanded God's attention. Israel's divine warrior-king would demonstrate his majesty and power by destroying the Assyrians, just as a raging fire quickly consumes a forest (vv. 16–19).

The Lord's victory over Assyria would open the door to a new era for Israel. The remnant of the northern kingdom would renew their trust in and allegiance to the Lord, their true king (vv. 20–21). Appropriately, the Lord is called the "Holy One of Israel," a title indicating his sovereignty (see 1:4 and 6:3), and the "Mighty God," a reminder of the power he revealed when he "struck them down" (v. 20). Sadly, only a remnant would participate in the coming reconciliation with God, for Israel's population would be decimated by judgment (vv. 22–23).

The title "Mighty God" appears only here (v. 21) and in Isaiah 9:6, where it is one of the epithets of the coming ideal Davidic king. It is possible that Isaiah 10:20–21 pictures the Israelites returning to both the Lord ("the Holy One of Israel") and to the Davidic king ("the Mighty God"), as in Hosea 3:5. However, the Davidic king is not mentioned in the immediate context of verse 21 (see chapter 11, however). The preceding verse mentions Israel relying on the "LORD, the Holy One of Israel," so it is likely that the title "Mighty God" refers to the Lord as well. Two similar titles, both of which refer to God, appear in Deuteronomy 10:17 and Nehemiah 9:32 ("the great, mighty, and awesome God") and in Jeremiah 32:18 ("the great and powerful God").

Twice in verses 21–22 the statement "a remnant will return" appears. The statement echoes and plays off the symbolic name of Isaiah's son Shear-jashub, who accompanied the prophet on his initial meeting with King Ahaz (see Isa. 7:3). On that occasion Isaiah tried to encourage the king by assuring him that the Lord was capable of delivering him from the Syrian and Israelite invaders. Shear-jashub's name, meaning "a remnant will return," probably had a positive connotation at that time, perhaps suggesting that most of the enemy invaders would be defeated and only a remnant would return home. Isaiah 10:21–22 shows that the prophecy inherent in Shear-jashub's name was realized, as God's judgment reduced the once great nation

---

58. The Assyrians conquered the states mentioned in v. 9 between 740–717 b.c. Verse 11, which assumes that Samaria had already fallen, indicates this oracle against Assyria dates sometime after 722 b.c.

of Israel to a mere remnant. Yet there is good news here as well. Eventually a remnant would return to God and be reunited with Judah under the rule of the ideal Davidic king (see chapter 11).

Having stopped to describe the reconciliation of Israel to God, the prophet returned to his major theme—Assyria's demise (v. 24; see vv. 5–19). Addressing the people of Jerusalem on behalf of the Lord, he assured them that their mighty, divine warrior-king would protect them from the Assyrian threat. Though the Lord had used the Assyrians to punish his people (v. 24), his anger toward Judah would soon be transferred to Assyria (v. 25). He would strike down the Assyrians (v. 26) and deliver Judah from Assyria's oppressive and burdensome rule (v. 27).

He would defeat the Assyrians, just as he had annihilated the Midianites in the days of Gideon (v. 26a). The reference to "the rock of Oreb" recalls the incident recorded in Judges 7:25. In the aftermath of Gideon's victory over the Midianites, the Ephraimites captured and beheaded the Midianite general Oreb at a rock subsequently named for this executed foe.

This display of might would be reminiscent of the power God unleashed against Egypt in the days of Moses (v. 26b). The Hebrew text of verse 26b reads literally, "and his staff [will be] against [or "over"] the sea, and he will lift it in the way [or "manner"] of Egypt." If the text is retained as it stands, "the sea" symbolizes hostile Assyria. In this case the word-picture probably recalls how Moses lifted his staff/hand to cause the Red Sea to destroy the pursuing Egyptian army (see Exod. 14).[59]

In a highly dramatic manner, verses 28–32 describe an Assyrian invasion of Judah from the north.[60] The Assyrians march closer and closer to Jerusalem and defiantly shake their fist at the city. But then the Lord suddenly strikes. Comparing the Lord to a mighty woodsman and Assyria to a forest, the prophet pictures the Lord cutting the trees to the ground with his ax (vv. 33–34).

This prophecy was essentially fulfilled in 701 B.C. when Sennacherib invaded Judah.[61] Historical records and the biblical text (see Isa. 36:2) indicate Sennacherib approached Jerusalem from the southwest, not the north.[62] Consequently the account in verses 28–32 should probably be understood as rhetorical-prophetic. It was not necessarily intended to be a literal itiner-

---

59. However, some emend the phrase "against the sea" (Heb. 'al-hayyam) to "against them" (Heb. 'alehem). In this case the word-picture probably refers more generally to the way in which the Lord used Moses' staff to bring judgment down on Egypt.

60. On the geographical details of the account, see Aharoni, *Land of the Bible*, 393.

61. Hayes and Irvine (*Isaiah*, 209–10) suggest the text describes the Israelite-Syrian invasion of Judah (735 B.C.), but this proposal disregards the preceding context, which prophesies the destruction of Assyria. Some suggest that this invasion occurred in conjunction with Sargon's western campaign of 713–711 B.C., but there is no historical evidence of such an invasion at that time.

62. John N. Oswalt (*The Book of Isaiah, Chapters 1–39* [Grand Rapids: Eerdmans, 1986], 274–75) prefers to see the description as rhetorical and as not corresponding to any particular historical event, but Hayes and Irvine argue that the precise geographical details militate against such a proposal.

ary of the Assyrians' movements; rather, its primary purpose was to create a foreboding mood. The geographical references contribute to this purpose, though they merely reflect how one might expect an Assyrian invasion to proceed, not necessarily how the actual invasion progressed.[63]

An Ideal King Brings Peace (11:1–9)

Returning to the messianic theme introduced earlier (see 9:1–7), Isaiah envisions a day when an ideal Davidic king would rule, guaranteeing justice and peace. This king is pictured as a shoot or branch growing from the root or trunk of Jesse (v. 1). By associating the king with Jesse, rather than David, the prophet pictures this ruler as a new David, not just another disappointing Davidic descendant. Other prophets call this coming ideal king "David" or picture him as the second coming of David, as it were. (See Jer. 30:9; Ezek. 34:23–24; 37:24–25; Hos. 3:5; and Mic. 5:2.) Like David of old (see 1 Sam. 16:13), this king is energized by God's Spirit, who gives him extraordinary wisdom, enables him to execute God's plans, and instills within him absolute loyalty to the Lord (vv. 2–3a).

The phrase "of wisdom and of understanding" (v. 2) combines synonyms to emphasize the degree of discernment the king possesses. This supernatural wisdom makes the king capable of just decisions based on truth, rather than mere appearances (v. 3b).

The phrase "of counsel and of power" (v. 2), which combines related ideas, refers to his supernatural ability to execute the plans or strategies he devises. This ability enables him to defend the oppressed by implementing just policies and eliminating their oppressors (v. 4). Indeed, his commitment to justice is the foundation of his rule; it provides stability and support, like a belt worn around the waist (v. 5).

The phrase "of knowledge and of the fear of the LORD" (v. 2) depicts this king's absolute loyalty to the Lord. "Knowledge" is used here in its covenantal sense and refers to a recognition of God's authority and a willingness to submit to it. (See Jer. 22:16, where "knowing" the Lord is defined as a commitment to justice.) "Fear of the LORD" refers here to a healthy respect for God's authority that produces obedience. Taken together the two terms emphasize the single quality of loyalty to the Lord. This loyalty guarantees that he makes just legal decisions and implements just policies (vv. 3–5).

In Isaiah's vision the transformation of human society is accompanied by a radical transformation within the animal kingdom (vv. 6–9). The animal kingdom as we know it is characterized by the "rule of tooth and claw," where predators stalk and devour weaker animals. But during the ideal king's reign, this basic structure changes. Predators no longer attack and eat weaker

---

63. For further discussion of the problem, see R. E. Clements, *Isaiah 1–39* (Grand Rapids: Eerdmans, 1980), 117–19.

animals. Instead, the predators' fundamental nature is altered, and they become herbivores. This startling vision may be purely figurative, with the predators symbolizing human oppressors and the prey their helpless victims (see vv. 4–5), but it is possible that it describes a literal change that mirrors the transformation in human society, where the categories "oppressor" and "oppressed" are eliminated.

While this kingdom of peace is certainly worldwide (see 2:2–4 and 11:10), verse 9 focuses on the change that takes place in Jerusalem and in the land of Israel. Verse 9 states that "they [apparently referring to the predators just mentioned, which in turn symbolize the wicked mentioned in v. 4] will neither harm nor destroy on all my holy mountain, for the earth will be full of the knowledge of the LORD as the waters cover the sea." The Lord's "holy mountain" is Mount Zion/Jerusalem (see Ps. 2:6; 15:1; 43:3; 48:1; 99:9; Isa. 56:7; 57:13; 65:11, 25; 66:20; Dan. 9:16, 20; Joel 2:1; 3:17; Obad. 16). This suggests that the Hebrew term 'erets, translated "earth" by NIV, refers to the "land" of Israel here and in verse 4.

The Exiles Return Home (11:10–12:6)

This ideal king also reclaims God's exiled people (vv. 10–12). In 722 B.C., the Assyrians deported the people of Israel to Mesopotamia and regions beyond (see 2 Kings 17:6; 18:11). In 701 B.C., Sennacherib, though defeated outside the walls of Jerusalem, took a large number of Judahites into exile.[64] Isaiah also foretold the Babylonian exile of Judah, which took place in 605–586 B.C. (see Isa. 39:6–7). However, in Isaiah's vision of the ideal king's reign, the once hostile nations of the earth allow the exiles to return to their homeland from the four quarters of the earth.

Once they return to their land, God's people enjoy renewed national strength (vv. 13–14). The northern kingdom (represented here by Ephraim) no longer opposes Judah. Instead, they unite against the hostile nations around them, including the Philistines to the west and Edom, Moab, Ammon, and the desert tribes to the east. As in the glorious days of the united monarchy under David and Solomon, they subdue these nations and force them to pay tribute.

Isaiah pictures the mass return of God's people as a second exodus. The Lord dries up seas and rivers, allowing his people to return from exile in Egypt and Assyria (vv. 15–16). As in the days of Moses, the Lord's people praise his mighty deeds (12:1–6). They thank him for replacing his anger with salvation and, with words reminiscent of the Song of Moses (see Exod. 15:2), they praise him as their protector and savior, as they drink in his salvation as if it were fresh water drawn from a well. God's restored people then turn to the

---

64. See Pritchard, *Ancient Near Eastern Texts,* 287–88. Sennacherib claims to have taken 200,150 (certainly an inflated number) of Hezekiah's people captive. Isa. 6:11–13 anticipated this devastation, and Isa. 1:9 seems to presuppose it.

residents of Zion and urge them to proclaim the Lord's mighty deeds among the nations as they celebrate the sovereign God's presence among his people.

Will this prophecy of Israel's return to the land be fulfilled in a literal way? Some insist that the prophecy will be fulfilled just as it is described, but others point out that a literal fulfillment of all the details of the prophecy is impossible. After all, in the course of time the exiles of the northern kingdom disappeared as a distinct ethnic entity as they were assimilated into the surrounding culture of their new homes. Likewise, the Philistines, Edomites, Moabites, and Ammonites no longer exist. Some propose that the geopolitical structures and ethnic realities of Isaiah's time will somehow reappear in the future. Others associate the present occupants of these lands with their ancient predecessors and look for a fulfillment through these supposed modern counterparts. But such hyperliteralism fails to account for the way in which prophetic messages were contextualized for the sake of the original audience. It is more likely that the prophecy will be fulfilled in its essence, not in an exact manner. As the Apostle Paul makes clear (Rom. 11:25–32), there will be a future restoration of ethnic Israel, whom we know as the Jewish people (primarily descended from the tribes of Judah, Benjamin, and Levi).[65] However, many of the precise details of the prophecy, which is culturally conditioned and reflects the perspective of Isaiah's context, were included to make the prophecy understandable and relevant to Isaiah's audience and should be understood as archetypal.[66] Rather than describing literal geopolitical realities of this future age, Isaiah 11:13–14 affirms that the restored Israel of the future will be unified and secure.

In depicting the return from exile as a second exodus (11:15–16), Isaiah employed a "back to the future" technique that linked God's future act of deliverance with his mighty deeds in salvation history. In this way he emphasized that the God of Israel's early history was still active and capable of intervening in power to form his people's future. This use of earlier traditions must be viewed as a creative form of literary allusion, not necessarily a literal description of the future. This rhetorical technique makes it clear that Israel's future will be marked by the same miraculous divine intervention that highlighted Israel's deliverance from Egypt in the days of Moses.

Worldwide Judgment (Isaiah 13–27)

This second section of the book's first main unit presents a series of judgment oracles against various nations (chapters 13–23). This litany of judgment sets the stage for a vision of worldwide judgment that ushers in the Lord's kingdom on earth (chapters 24–27).

65. See Ezra 1:5; 4:1; 10:9; Neh. 11.
66. For a brief discussion of archetypal language in prophetic literature, see Robert B. Chisholm Jr., *From Exegesis to Exposition* (Grand Rapids: Baker, 1998), 173–74.

A Litany of Judgment (Isa. 13–23)

Though no date is attached to most of the oracles, it appears that they originate from different periods in Isaiah's career. For example, the oracle
against the Syrian-Israelite coalition (17:1–11) must have been given prior
to their defeat by Tiglath-pileser III in 733–732 B.C. The oracle against the
Philistines (14:28–32) was delivered in the year of King Ahaz's death (715
B.C.), while the prophecy against Egypt and Cush (20:1–6) dates to 712
B.C., the year in which King Sargon's Assyrian forces attacked the Philistine
city of Ashdod. The oracle against Tyre (23:1–18) speaks of the Assyrian
destruction of Babylon (which took place in 689 B.C.) as a past event
(v. 13).

The oracles in chapters 13–23 are arranged as follows:

Oracle concerning Babylon	13:1–14:27
Oracle concerning the Philistines	14:28–32
Oracle concerning Moab	15:1–16:14
Oracle concerning Damascus[67]	17:1–11
Woe oracle concerning the nations	17:12–14
Woe oracle concerning Cush	18:1–7
Oracle concerning Egypt	19:1–25
Prophecy concerning Egypt and Cush	20:1–6
Oracle concerning Babylon	21:1–10
Oracle concerning Dumah	21:11–12
Oracle concerning Arabia	21:13–17
Oracle concerning Jerusalem	22:1–25
Oracle concerning Tyre	23:1–18

It is likely Isaiah proclaimed these oracles to Judah, not the actual foreign nations addressed. The prophecies probably had a dual purpose. For
those leaders who insisted on getting embroiled in international politics,
these oracles were a reminder that Judah need not fear foreign nations or
seek international alliances for security reasons. For the loyal remnant within
the nation, the oracles were a reminder that their God was indeed the sovereign ruler of the earth, worthy of his people's trust.

An Oracle Concerning Babylon (13:1–14:27)

The first oracle, which pertains primarily to Babylon (see 13:1), includes an
introduction depicting worldwide judgment (13:2–16),[68] a lengthy description of God's judgment on Babylon (13:17–14:23), a brief judgment speech
against Assyria (14:24–25), and a concluding summary that returns to the
theme of worldwide judgment (14:26–27).

---

67. The oracle in chapter 17 is addressed to Damascus (the capital of Syria), but Syria was an ally of
Israel (see 7:1) and the oracle contains judgment pronouncements against Israel (see vv. 3, 10).

68. Note especially the reference to the "world" in v. 11. Verse 5 also refers to God's destruction of "all
the earth" (Heb. *kol-ha'arets*), though the NIV translates the phrase "the whole country" here.

The oracle displays the following structure:

> Heading (13:1)
> Worldwide setting of the judgment (13:2–16)
> Babylon falls (13:17–14:23)
>> Babylon reduced to rubble (13:17–22)
>> Salvation for Israel (14:1–2)
>> Israel taunts the king of Babylon (14:3–21)
>> Babylon reduced to rubble (14:22–23)
> Assyria defeated (14:24–25)
> Worldwide setting of the judgment (14:26–27)[69]

The oracle begins dramatically with the Lord rallying his warriors for battle (vv. 2–3). The prophet hears and sees a mighty army gathering among the nations with the "LORD Almighty" (lit., "LORD of Hosts/Armies," see 1:9) at its head (vv. 4–5). As the Lord's day of judgment approaches, it causes widespread mourning and terror, for it is a time when the "Almighty" destroys his enemies (vv. 6–8).

In the Hebrew Bible the title "Almighty" (Heb. "Shaddai") depicts God as the sovereign king and judge of the world who both gives and takes away life.[70] The patriarchs knew God primarily as El (meaning "God") Shaddai (Exod 6:3). In the patriarchal stories the name is used in contexts where God appears as the source of fertility and life (see Gen. 17:1–8; 28:3; 35:11; 48:3). When blessing Joseph, Jacob referred to Shaddai (we should probably read "El Shaddai" here, along with several ancient textual witnesses) as the one who bestows blessing, including children, alluded to here in the expression "blessings of the breast and womb" (49:25). Outside Genesis the name Shaddai (minus El, "God") depicts God as the sovereign king who protects or judges. The name is especially prominent in the Book of Job, where it occurs thirty-one times. Job and his "friends" regard Shaddai as the sovereign king of the world (11:7; 37:23a) who is the source of life (33:4b) and promotes justice (8:3; 34:10–12; 37:23b). He provides blessings, including children (22:17–18; 29:4–6), but he also disciplines, punishes, and destroys (5:17; 6:4; 21:20; 23:16). Naomi uses the name when accusing the Lord of mistreating her by taking the lives of her husband and sons (Ruth 1:20–21). Psalm 91:1 pictures Shaddai as his people's protector, while Psalm 68:14 and Joel 1:15, like Isaiah 13:6, depict him as making war against his enemies.

Isaiah characterizes the "day of the LORD" as a time when God pours out

<hr>

69. NIV's "the whole world" in 14:26 translates the Hebrew phrase kol-ha'arets, "all the earth" (see 13:5 and the previous note).

70. The derivation and meaning of the name are uncertain. The most likely proposal is that the name means "the one of the mountain" (an Akkadian cognate means "mountain," to which Heb. shad, "breast," is probably related). For a discussion of proposed derivations see T. N. D. Mettinger, In Search of God, trans. F. Cryer (Philadelphia: Fortress, 1988), 70–71. The name may originally depict God as the sovereign judge who, in Canaanite style, rules from a sacred mountain. Isa. 14:13 and Ezek. 28:14, 16 associate such a mountain with God, while Ps. 48:2 refers to Zion as "Zaphon," the Canaanite mountain of the gods.

his anger upon the wicked sinners of the world (vv. 9, 11). The heavenly luminaries grow dark and the entire world shakes violently (vv. 10, 13). The devastating judgment is thorough, relentless, and merciless (vv. 12, 14–15). Not even helpless infants and women are spared (v. 16).

The expression "day of the Lord" appears frequently in the Hebrew Bible.[71] In the most basic sense it is a day when the Lord intervenes in the world to judge his enemies. The phrase is applied to various events, including the Assyrian conquest of Israel in the eighth century B.C. (Amos 5:18–20), the Babylonian conquest of Judah in 586 B.C. (Ezek. 13:5; Zeph. 1:7, 14), the judgment on the postexilic community threatened by the prophet Joel (1:15; 2:1, 11), the worldwide judgment associated with the fall of various nations and with the deliverance of Jerusalem (Joel 2:31; 3:14; Obad. 15), and the Lord's purifying judgment of his covenant community (Mal. 4:5). Here in Isaiah 13 the "day of the Lord" refers to a time of worldwide divine judgment that begins with the downfall of the historical Babylonian Empire.

In verses 17–19 the focus of this terrifying prophecy sharpens, as we see the Medes ruthlessly attacking Babylon. Babylon's destruction is like that of Sodom and Gomorrah in its severity, for the city is left in ruins and overrun by wild animals (vv. 20–22).

The fall of Babylon would mean deliverance for God's exiled people (14:1–2). The Lord would extend his mercy to Israel and restore them to their land. Israel would now gain the upper hand over the nations that once oppressed them. The prophecy anticipates Israel's release from exile following Cyrus's conquest of Babylon, but the language also transcends that event and envisions a time when Israel will become the dominant nation on earth (see 11:14).

Freed from bondage and suffering, God's people taunt their defeated oppressor, the king of Babylon (14:3–21). This taunt song begins with a vision of the worldwide celebration that follows the king's fall. Though the king of Babylon once conquered the world (v. 6), he is no match for the Lord (vv. 4–5). His demise enables the nations to breathe a sigh of relief (v. 7), while the personified trees of Lebanon no longer have to worry about the king of Babylon cutting them down (v. 8). This alludes to the practice of Mesopotamian kings, including Nebuchadnezzar of Babylon, who transported timber from Lebanon for their building projects.[72]

The song next pictures the defeated king's arrival in the land of dead

---

71. For studies of the origin and usage of the phrase, see Gerhard von Rad, "The Origin of the Concept of the Day of the Lord," *JSS* 4 (1959): 97–108; A. J. Everson, "The Days of Yahweh," *JBL* 93 (1974): 329–37; and Douglas Stuart, "The Sovereign's Day of Conquest," *BASOR* 220/221 (December 1975–February 1976): 159–64.

72. For references to Nebuchadnezzar's utilization of Lebanon timber in his building projects, see Georges Roux, *Ancient Iraq* (Middlesex, England: Penguin Books, 1966), 345–46, 359–60.

spirits and the reception he receives there (vv. 9–15). The many kings of the nations who have preceded the king of Babylon to the underworld rise to greet him (vv. 9–10a). With a tone of sarcasm in their voice, they point out that he has become like them (v. 10b).[73] Despite all his former splendor, maggots and worms now devour his corpse (v. 11). Drawing on their own mythological traditions, these kings compare the once proud, but now humiliated king to "morning star, son of the dawn," a lesser deity in the West Semitic pantheon who, according to tradition, tried to usurp the place of the high god (vv. 12–13).[74] Despite his arrogance, this god was hurled down to the grave (vv. 14–15).

Because of the imagery used in verses 12–15, many interpreters have seen an allusion to the fall of Satan here, but this is contextually unwarranted.[75] Verses 4–21 are directed to the king of Babylon, who is depicted as a human ruler. He is called "the man" (v. 16) and possesses a physical body (vv. 11, 19–20). Nevertheless because of the language of verses 12–15 some see a dual referent in the taunt song or at least a comparison of the proud king of Babylon to Satan. However, these verses, which are spoken by pagan kings to another pagan king (see vv. 9–11), contain language known from West Semitic mythology. The birth of the deity Shachar (translated "dawn" by NIV), identified in verse 12 as the father of "morning star" (Heb. "Helel," a proper name or title meaning "shining one"), is described in an Ugaritic myth.[76] The phrase "stars of God" (v. 13, Heb. "El," the name of the West Semitic high god) refers to the assembly of gods that congregated on "the mount of assembly."[77] NIV's "sacred mountain" translates the Hebrew "Zaphon," the name of a mountain specifically associated with the god Baal in the Ugaritic myths.[78] These verses appear to allude to a myth about the minor god Helel's attempt to dethrone the high god El or the storm god

73. Verses 10b–15 are spoken by the kings to the king of Babylon. Their words constitute a taunt song embedded within the larger taunt song of vv. 4b–21.

74. The identity of "morning star, son of the dawn" has been debated, but the referent is probably Venus. See Day, *Yahweh and the Gods,* 167–70.

75. John Martin writes, "Though many hold that verses 12–14 refer to the entrance of sin into the cosmos by Satan's fall, that subject seems a bit forced in this chapter." See "Isaiah," in *The Bible Knowledge Commentary: Old Testament,* ed. J. F. Walvoord and R. B. Zuck (Wheaton: Victor Books, 1985), 1061. See also E. J. Young, *The Book of Isaiah,* 3 vols. (Grand Rapids: Eerdmans, 1965–72), 2:441. He affirms that the passage "cannot apply to Satan." John Calvin vehemently rejected the view that Isa. 14:12–15 refers to Satan, calling it "useless" and attributing it to "very gross ignorance" and inattention to context. See *Calvin's Commentaries,* trans. W. Pringle, 22 vols. (reprint, Grand Rapids: Baker, 1999), 7:442. For the history of interpretation of these verses, see Gerald Keown, "A History of the Interpretation of Isaiah 14:12–15," Ph.D. diss., Southern Baptist Theological Seminary, 1979.

76. See J. C. L. Gibson, *Canaanite Myths and Legends,* 2d ed. (Edinburgh: T. & T. Clark, 1978), 123–27.

77. The divine assembly is called the "congregation of the stars" in Ugaritic myth. For studies of the West Semitic divine assembly, see Lowell K. Handy, *Among the Host of Heaven: The Syro-Palestinian Pantheon as Bureaucracy* (Winona Lake, Ind.: Eisenbrauns, 1994), and E. Theodore Mullen, *The Divine Council in Canaanite and Early Hebrew Literature* (Chico, Calif.: Scholars Press, 1980).

78. See Day, *Yahweh and the Gods,* 107–8.

Baal. His attempted revolt failed, and he was thrown down into the under-world.[79] The king of Babylon is taunted for having similar delusions of grandeur. If Zaphon here symbolizes Mount Zion (see Ps. 48:2), it is possible that the reality underlying the mythological imagery is Nebuchadnezzar's assault upon Jerusalem and his desecration of the temple.[80]

Who was the historical king of Babylon referred to here? If the prophecy anticipates the fall of Babylon in 539 B.C. (as I argue below), then the king of Babylon taunted here may be Nabonidus (the official king of Babylon when it fell), Belshazzar (who was functioning as king at the time; see Dan. 5:1), or even Nebuchadnezzar, who ruled from 605–562 B.C. and made Babylon a world power.[81] However, it is unnecessary to put a specific name and face with the king described here. Perhaps the "king of Babylon" simply symbolizes Babylonian power as embodied in her successive kings, beginning with Nebuchadnezzar or his predecessor Nabopolassar.

Leaving mythological imagery behind, Israel's taunt song returns to reality and focuses on the humiliating death of the king of Babylon. As by-standers observe his corpse, they find it hard to believe that this humiliated king is the same individual who once terrorized and conquered the world (vv. 16–17). Other kings' corpses lie in stately tombs, but this king's dead body lies exposed and unburied among others who have fallen by the sword (vv. 18–20a). To make matters worse, the king's dynasty is terminated as his sons are executed for their forefathers' sins (vv. 20b–21).

As the taunt song ends, the Lord himself speaks again (vv. 22–23; see 13:3, 11–13, 17). Once more he declares that he will wipe out the people of Babylon (v. 22; see 13:18–19) and destroy the city, leaving it populated only by wild animals (v. 23; see 13:20–22).

Returning to the more immediate future, the Lord reminds his audience that he will also defeat the Assyrians, the major power of Isaiah's time (vv. 24–25; see 10:5–34). Though a reference to Assyria may seem awkward in an oracle against Babylon, its placement here makes sense if we remember that Assyria exercised political control of Babylon in Isaiah's time and that the famed warrior and hunter Nimrod founded both Babylon and Nineveh (a major Assyrian city), according to biblical tradition (see Gen. 10:8–10).

The oracle ends where it began, as the Lord makes it clear that the judgment just described is part of his larger plan for the whole world (v. 26). The

---

79. Though the general parallels cited indicate the imagery originates in West Semitic myth, scholars have yet to pin down the precise mythological background of the text. For studies of the issue, see, among others, P. C. Craigie, "Helel, Athtar, and Phaethon (Isa. 14:12–15)," *ZAW* 85 (1973): 223–25; Day, *Yahweh and the Gods*, 166–84; J. W. McKay, "Helel and the Dawn-Goddess: A Re-examination of the Myth in Isaiah XIV 12–15," *VT* 20 (1970): 451–64; Hugh R. Page, *The Myth of Cosmic Rebellion* (Leiden: Brill, 1996), 120–40; and W. S. Prinsloo, "Isaiah 14:12–15: Humiliation, Hubris, Humiliation," *ZAW* 93 (1981): 432–38.

80. See Day, *Yahweh and the Gods,* 183–84.

81. Day makes a strong case for the referent being Nebuchadnezzar. See ibid., 180–84.

Lord has raised his hand of judgment, and no one is able to prevent him from carrying out his purposes (v. 27).[82]

When and how was this prophecy of Babylon's fall fulfilled? Some argue that the prophecy was fulfilled in 689 B.C. when the Assyrians under Sennacherib sacked and desecrated the city, an event mentioned in 23:13.[83] However, the demise of Babylon in 689 B.C. did not lead to the restoration of Israel, as 14:1–3 suggests would happen. Furthermore, this view has a hard time explaining the reference to the Medes in 13:17, for they participated in Cyrus's conquest of Babylon in 539 B.C. (see Jer. 51:11, 28). Proponents of the view must argue that the Medes were mercenaries in the Assyrian army or that the reference is purely literary, symbolizing fearsome enemies.[84] The king of Babylon addressed in the taunt is depicted as a great world conqueror (see 14:4–7). Some see the addressee as an Assyrian king (Tiglath-pileser, Sargon, or Sennacherib), but this is contrived and unconvincing.[85] It is true that Assyrian rulers conquered Babylon; Tiglath-pileser even assumed a Babylonian name, Pul. But in the biblical reference to this in 2 Kings 15:29 he is still called "the king of Assyria," not "the king of Babylon." If we are to use Isaiah himself as a guide, then a Chaldean king must be in view, for in 39:1 the prophet refers to the Chaldean ruler "Merodach-baladan son of Baladan king of Babylon." In 39:7 he anticipates the Babylonian exile, when Hezekiah's offspring would become eunuchs in the palace of "the king of Babylon." However, neither of the Chaldean rulers of Babylon during Isaiah's time, Merodach-baladan and Mushezib-marduk (the Chaldean ruler of the city in 689 B.C.), could be classified as great conquerors.[86] Neither was able to maintain rule over Babylon for a significant period of time, let alone create a vast world empire.

For these reasons it is more likely that the oracle prophesies the fall of Babylon to the Persian army led by Cyrus in 539 B.C. This view accommodates nicely the reference to the Medes and the portrayal of the king of Babylon as a world conqueror. (Nebuchadnezzar was certainly that!)[87] Further-

---

82. The reference to the Lord's "stretched out" (or "upraised") hand (v. 27) echoes the refrain from an earlier judgment speech (see 9:12b, 17b, 21b; 10:4b).

83. See, among others, Seth Erlandsson, *The Burden of Babylon* (Lund: CWK Gleerup, 1970). For a refutation of Erlandsson's view, see Day, *Yahweh and the Gods*, 180–81. Erlandsson applies only 13:19–22 and 14:22b–23 to Babylon and sees the rest of the material as applying to Assyria. As Day observes, "this view . . . is forced."

84. 2 Kings 17:6 (see also 18:11) does indicate that the "towns of the Medes" were under Assyrian control at this time.

85. See Day, *Yahweh and the Gods*, 181–82, for a critique of such proposals.

86. See H. W. F. Saggs, *The Greatness That Was Babylon* (New York: New American Library, 1962), 129–30.

87. Edwin Yamauchi writes that following the absorption of the Median kingdom into the Persian empire, "the Medes were to play a subordinate though important role under the Persians in the Achaemenid period (550–330 B.C.)." See his *Persia and the Bible* (Grand Rapids: Baker, 1996), 57. Isaiah probably mentions the Medes, rather than the Persians, because in his day the Medes were the dominant element. (See

more, the fall of Babylon to Cyrus paved the way for Israel's return from exile and freed many nations from Babylon's oppressive rule.

However, this view is not without its problems. Cyrus did not destroy Babylon. In fact his takeover of the city, though preceded by a military campaign, was relatively peaceful and even welcomed by some Babylonian religious officials. How then does one explain the prophecy's description of the city's violent fall? It is possible that the fall of Babylon in 689 B.C. has contributed to the imagery of the oracle. However, it is more likely that the language is stylized and exaggerated. For dramatic effect, the prophets sometimes used such stereotypical language to describe the divine judgment of a city or nation.[88] In the case of Isaiah 13–14, the use of this style drives home the point that the Babylonian Empire would fall and disappear forever. Cyrus's conquest of the city, while not accompanied by the atrocities and destruction described in the oracle, did bring this empire to an end and essentially fulfilled Isaiah's prophecy.[89]

Though this prophecy of Babylon's fall was essentially fulfilled in 539 B.C., it does have an archetypal dimension that transcends that event. Babylon's fall is just one event in the widespread judgment described in chapters 13–23. This judgment of the nations in turn foreshadows the culminating worldwide judgment depicted in chapters 24–27. Because the fall of the Babylonian Empire is associated with this final judgment (see 13:1–16; 14:26), it takes on typological potential that is developed in the Book of Revelation, where John uses Babylon as an archetype of the hostile world powers that are destroyed by God (see Rev. 14:8; 16:19; 17:5; 18:2,10, 21).

An Oracle Concerning the Philistines (14:28–32)

In this brief oracle the prophet warns the Philistines of impending judgment. The Philistines were apparently rejoicing because a king who had oppressed them (called the "rod that struck you" and "that snake") had passed from the scene (v. 29a). However, they should have been in mourning, for a "viper" would spring forth from the "snake" (v. 29b) and invade Philistine territory

---

Yamauchi, p. 23, who notes that the Medes "dominated the Persians until the rise of Cyrus.") The first biblical reference to Persia does not appear until Ezekiel's time (see Ezek. 27:10; 38:5).

88. See Isa. 34:11–15; Jer. 50:39–40; 51:36–37; Zeph. 2:13–15. Both Jeremianic prophecies refer to the fall of Babylon in 539 B.C. See especially 50:28; 51:11, 24, 34–35, 59–63, all of which make it clear that the referent in this prophecy is the kingdom ruled by Nebuchadnezzar in the sixth century B.C. Ancient Near Eastern literature also employs such stylized language on occasion for dramatic effect. Homer Heater Jr. calls this imagery "destruction language." For a helpful study of the relevant biblical texts and motifs, as well as samples of "destruction language" from ancient Near Eastern sources, see his article, "Do the Prophets Teach That Babylonia Will Be Rebuilt in the *Eschaton?*" *JETS* 41 (1998): 31–36. (It should be noted that Heater argues for a fulfillment of Isa. 13–14 in 689 B.C. See pp. 25–31.)

89. If we see Isa. 13–14 as prophesying the events of 539 B.C., rather than the fall of Babylon in 689 B.C., this does not mean the chapters had to be written in the exilic or postexilic period, rather than by Isaiah. Isaiah anticipated the rise of Babylon and a Babylonian exile for Judah (Isa. 39), as well as God's deliverance of his people from Babylonian power through Cyrus (Isa. 40–55).

from the north, bringing famine and death in its wake (vv. 30b–31). The widespread destruction would leave the poor and homeless to inherit the lands of the wealthy rulers (v. 30a). While the Philistines would experience the terrors of an invasion, the Lord would protect the people of Jerusalem. For this reason, it was unnecessary to form an alliance with the Philistines when they sent their envoys to Jerusalem (v. 32).

The identity of the rulers referred to in verse 29 is uncertain. The image of a "viper" springing up from a "snake" seems to suggest that the "viper" is the next king in the dynastic line of the "snake." Since the oracle is dated to the year of Ahaz's death (715 B.C.), some suggest he is the "snake" of verse 29 and his son Hezekiah the "viper."[90] However, this seems unlikely since there is no record of Ahaz conquering the Philistines. On the contrary, the Philistines took territory from Judah during the early years of Ahaz's reign (2 Chron. 28:18). Hezekiah did conquer Philistine territory (1 Kings 18:8), but he would have invaded Philistia from the east, not the north.

It seems more likely that the "snake" and "viper" would be Assyrian rulers, for the Assyrians exercised authority over the Philistines during this period and one would expect them to invade Philistine territory from the north. However, if the oracle dates to 715 B.C., it is difficult to harmonize it with Assyrian chronology. Sargon replaced Shalmaneser V as Assyrian king in 722 B.C. and ruled until 705 B.C., when Sennacherib succeeded him. There was no change of king in 715 B.C. Perhaps the imagery does not point to a dynastic connection between the "snake" and "viper" after all.

The identification of the rulers behind the imagery must account for both of the events to which the oracle refers, namely, Ahaz's death in 715 B.C. (v. 28) and the invasion of Philistine territory from the north (v. 31, suggesting the Assyrians are in view). Perhaps the rod/snake of verse 29a is Ahaz. Though Ahaz himself did not conquer Philistine territory, surely his loyalty to Assyria was resented by anti-Assyrian elements in Philistia. In fact, some may have viewed Ahaz as responsible for the oppressive Assyrian presence in the west, for it was he who twenty years before had invited the Assyrian king Tiglath-pileser III to deliver him from his enemies, including the Philistines (2 Chron. 28:16–20). From that point on the Philistines were subject to the Assyrians. When viewed against this background, it is possible to understand how Ahaz could be viewed (admittedly, somewhat hyperbolically) as an oppressor of the Philistines. So when Ahaz died, the Philistines would have celebrated, perhaps thinking (correctly) that his death would bring Hezekiah of Judah over to the anti-Assyrian cause. This in turn might be the catalyst for a more powerful western alliance that would free the Philistines and others from Assyrian rule.

Isaiah was quick to correct such false hope. Any anticipated lessening of

90. On the date of Ahaz's death, see Merrill, *Kingdom of Priests,* 403–4.

Assyrian influence prompted by Ahaz's death would fail to materialize. The Assyrian presence in the west would continue and renewed resistance to Assyrian rule would prompt Assyrian reprisals. In 712 B.C., Sargon invaded Philistine territory in order to put down an uprising in Ashkelon (see Isa. 20). In 701 B.C., Sennacherib severely punished anti-Assyrian elements in Philistia when he invaded the west. The "viper" of verse 29b probably symbolizes Assyria's menacing presence in the west, embodied in both of these rulers.

An Oracle Concerning Moab (15:1–16:14)

The next oracle turns our attention eastward as it describes God's judgment upon the Moabites, descendants of Lot who lived east of the Dead Sea. The oracle depicts a devastating invasion of Moabite territory, though the invader is not specifically identified. An appendix to the oracle (see 16:13–14) indicates the prophecy had been given sometime in the past and announces that its fulfillment would occur within three years. Unfortunately we are not able to pinpoint the date of the original prophecy or the appended announcement, nor do extrabiblical texts corroborate the invasion of Moab portrayed in the oracle.

The opening verses of the prophet's lament picture the widespread mourning that follows the sudden destruction of the land (15:1–4). The men shave their heads and facial hair, put on sackcloth, and wail publicly over their loss. These were common expressions of sorrow in the ancient Near East. Playing the dramatic role of a mourner, the prophet joins the weeping Moabite refugees as they flee through their devastated land carrying their possessions (vv. 5–7). The sound of their weeping is so loud it echoes throughout Moabite territory and reaches the borders of the land (v. 8).

The shocking scene of Dibon's (the Hebrew text has "Dimon" here) blood-filled waters would seem to elicit nothing but pity and mercy, but the Lord chimes in at this point and announces that his judgment upon Moab is not over (v. 9). A "lion" would attack the helpless fugitives who had survived the disaster.[91] The metaphor probably symbolizes an invading army or the neighboring peoples who would rush into Moab in the aftermath of the invasion to collect the spoils.

The Moabites' only hope is to turn to Judah (16:1–5). Isaiah urges the defeated Moabites to declare their allegiance to the king of Judah, who rules in Jerusalem (called here "the mount of the Daughter of Zion," v. 1). Before elaborating on this theme, he again pictures the desperate condition of the Moabite fugitives. The excited women, whose panic is like that of mother birds forced from their nests (v. 2), beg their neighbors to offer them shelter

---

91. This interpretation follows the traditional reading of the Hebrew text. Some prefer to emend "lion" (*'aryeh*) to "I see, look upon" (*'er'eh*) (the two readings look quite similar in Hebrew). In this case, the prophet simply announces that his vision of the Moabite fugitives' plight is not yet exhausted; there is more to describe. See Hayes and Irvine, *Isaiah*, 241–42.

(vv. 3–4a). The prophet responds by assuring them that their cruel enemy will be defeated and that a just king, worthy of Moab's allegiance, will rule from David's throne (vv. 4b–5).

What king did the prophet have in mind? Verse 4b, which envisions the invading army's demise, may refer to Assyria's defeat outside Jerusalem in 701 B.C. In this case, verse 5 may anticipate Hezekiah's rise to prominence following this event. Of course, this event foreshadows the eventual ascendancy of the ideal Davidic ruler depicted in Isaiah 9:6–7 and 11:1–10. He would make restored Israel secure (see 11:13–14). At that time surrounding nations like Moab would be wise to submit to his just rule and find security in him (see Isa. 2:2–4).

The prophet returns to his role of mourner (vv. 9, 11; see 15:5) as he focuses on the destruction of Moab's agriculture (vv. 6–12). Moab was proud of its fields and vineyards, but the coming invasion would leave the land's crops and vines in ruins. The Moabites would offer up many prayers to their god(s), but to no avail.

An Oracle Concerning Damascus (17:1–11)

This next oracle, which anticipates the demise of the Syrian-Israelite coalition, must have been given prior to Tiglath-pileser's invasion in 733–732 B.C., when he defeated both Damascus and Samaria. The prophet announced the downfall of Damascus (the Syrian capital), the cities of Aroer,[92] and the fortified cities of Israel (called "Ephraim" here) (vv. 1–3, 9). With vivid word-pictures the oracle depicts Israel's splendor fading away. The once prominent nation would be like a malnourished man whose body is reduced to skin and bones (v. 4). The land's population would all but disappear, as when reapers strip a field of its grain (v. 5).

This judgment would fall because Israel had rejected the God who had delivered and protected them in the past (v. 10). They built altars and worship centers to pagan gods (v. 11a). Their attempt to grow imported vines symbolized their commitment to foreign gods (vv. 11b–12). But just as these vines would not yield a crop, so Israel's paganism would fail to bring prosperity.

Nevertheless, some survivors would remain, comparable to the few ears of grain left behind by reapers or the few olives left near the top of the tree following the olive harvest (v. 6). The devastating judgment would have a positive effect on the survivors. They would reject their pagan practices and turn back to their creator and sovereign king (vv. 7–8).

A Woe Oracle Concerning the Raging Nations (17:12–14)

Even though the immediate future looked bleak, there was a light at the end of the tunnel. God would use the mighty Assyrian army, which included sol-

---

92. Aroer probably refers here to a city located east of the Dead Sea near the Arnon River. This region was conquered by Israel and later taken by the Syrians. See Josh. 12:2; 13:9, 16; Judg. 11:26; 2 Kings 10:33.

diers from many nations, as his instrument of judgment. The invading army, whose roar sounded like surging waters, would threaten even Judah, but in the end they would be swept away like tumbleweed before the powerful wind of divine judgment. Once again the prophet anticipates the destruction of Sennacherib's army in 701 B.C.

A Woe Oracle Concerning Cush (18:1–7)

The next oracle concerns the distant land of Cush (modern Ethiopia), located south of Egypt. Cush is called "the land of whirring wings" (v. 1), an odd designation that has puzzled interpreters. It may depict Cush as a land filled with insects, or it possibly alludes to the swift movement of the Cushite ships (their sails being compared to wings). During Isaiah's time the Cushites gained political control of Egypt and eventually became the main rival of the Assyrians in the west. Perhaps verse 2a alludes to their attempts to solidify an anti-Assyrian alliance with Palestinian states, including Judah.

The meaning of verse 2b is obscure. The identity of both the messengers and the distant nation to whom they are sent is unclear. The messengers addressed in verse 2b may be the same as the envoys mentioned in the first half of the verse. If so, then the Cushite envoys to Judah are told to return to their distant home. However, it is more likely that the Lord, in response to Cushite efforts to form an alliance, dispatches his own messengers to Cush with a message (vv. 3–6) that is pertinent to all the nations.

The Lord was ready to assemble his troops for battle (v. 3; see 13:2–5). He was an ever-present observer, much like the shimmering summer heat and the misty clouds were characteristic features of harvest time in ancient Israel (v. 4).[93] At the appropriate time he would intervene. Picking up on the agricultural imagery introduced in verse 4, the prophet compares God's judgment to a farmer pruning his vines (v. 5). The Lord would "prune" the nations and leave the discarded branches on the hills for wild animals and birds to eat (v. 6). The imagery probably anticipates the Assyrians' defeat in 701 B.C. (see 14:25; 16:4; 17:12–14), but since this is a woe oracle against Cush (v. 1) it must also include God's judgment on the Cushites (see 20:3–6).

For Judah the message was loud and clear. God would judge all of the world's powerful nations, including Assyria and Cush. For this reason, Judah must avoid entangling foreign alliances and trust instead in God's protective power. After all, a day would come when the Cushites would send their tribute to Jerusalem, the place where the Lord Almighty (Lord of Armies) ruled (v. 7; see 24:23).

93. G. B. Gray, *The Book of Isaiah I–XXVII*, ICC (Edinburgh: T. & T. Clark, 1912), 314.

An Oracle Concerning Egypt (19:1–25)

This oracle was probably given sometime between 720–702 B.C., for it seems to reflect the political situation in Egypt during this period.[94] This was an eventful time, during which Cushite kings took control of Egypt. King Shabaka, who succeeded Piankhy around 716 B.C., solidified an unstable political situation in Egypt and united Egypt with Cush. He seems to have maintained peaceful relations with the Assyrians, but by 701 B.C. his successor, Shebitku, came into conflict with Sennacherib as Assyrian and Cushite interests began to collide.

The oracle begins with a vivid picture of the Lord riding toward Egypt on a swift moving cloud (v. 1). His approach caused the Egyptian idol-gods and their worshipers to shake with fear. The Lord announced he would bring conflict to Egypt in the domestic sphere (note "brother will fight against brother") and at the national level (note "kingdom against kingdom") (v. 2). The panic-stricken Egyptians would look to their gods for help, but the Lord would frustrate their attempts to know and control the future through divination (v. 3).

The Lord would hand Egypt over to a foreign conqueror (v. 4). Though there is no scholarly consensus on the identity of this prophesied king, the most likely candidate is the aforementioned Cushite ruler Shabaka, who conquered Egypt shortly after coming to power. At this time Egypt had divided into three factions as Osorkon IV, Shoshenk VI, and Bakenranef vied for power. Verse 2 alludes to this instability.

The vision of God's judgment on Egypt culminates in the drying up of the Nile, upon which Egypt was dependent for its very life (vv. 5–10).[95] As the river dries up, its dead fish rot and its plants wither. The surrounding fields, which depend on the waters of the Nile for irrigation, wither as well. Those dependent on the Nile for their livelihood, such as fishermen and linen workers, lament their fate.[96]

Egypt's royal advisers, upon whom the nation relied for guidance, are not able to help, for the Lord deceives them and causes them to give bad advice to the rulers (vv. 11–14a).[97] Egypt becomes as confused as a drunkard wallowing in his own vomit, and the nation's rulers and prophets (called the "head" and "tail," respectively; compare v. 15 with 9:14) are helpless to do anything about it (vv. 14–15). In the face of God's powerful judgment, the Egyptians tremble in fear and are forced to recognize the superiority of Judah and its God (vv. 16–17).

94. See John D. Currid, *Ancient Egypt and the Old Testament* (Grand Rapids: Baker, 1997), 232–40, for a discussion of the date and historical background of this oracle.

95. Ibid., 240–45.

96. Flax was used to make rope and linen yarn, but the drying up of the Nile meant that no flax would grow. See ibid., 242.

97. For a study of the theme of divine deception in the Hebrew Bible, see Robert B. Chisholm Jr., "Does God Deceive?" *BSac* 155 (1998): 11–28.

At this point the oracle takes on a more positive note as it anticipates a time when Egypt is assimilated into God's kingdom (vv. 18–22). The Egyptians speak the Hebrew language and declare their allegiance to the God of Israel.[98] Even "the city of the sun," a center of worship to Re, the Egyptian sun god, turns to the Lord.[99] A monument dedicated to the Lord stands at the Egyptian border, declaring where Egypt's loyalty lies. In the middle of the land the Egyptians build an altar to the Lord that serves as a constant reminder of his willingness to protect them from their enemies. In response to the Lord's self-revelation, the Egyptians worship him with their sacrifices. Curse turns to blessing as the Lord heals their land and answers their prayers.

As if this vision of Egypt's spiritual transformation is not enough, Isaiah next pictures a time of unparalleled peace when Egypt and Assyria, rivals in Isaiah's day, become allies (vv. 23–25). They march hand-in-hand with Israel to worship the Lord, who regards all three as his people.

Though the Assyrian king Sargon (722–705 B.C.) did promote peaceful relations with Egypt's Cushite rulers,[100] his policies hardly satisfy the language of this prophecy. Sargon's successor, Sennacherib, quickly came in conflict with Egypt, and neither the Assyrians nor Egyptians became worshipers of the Lord. The prophecy's fulfillment clearly awaits a future day.

How will the prophecy be fulfilled? After all, the Assyrian Empire has long since disappeared from the earth (see Zeph. 2:13–15), and modern Egypt can hardly be viewed as the geopolitical child of eighth-century-B.C. Egypt. As is often the case in prophecies in which the fulfillment transcends the era in which the prophecy was given, one must look for an essential, rather than literal, realization of the prophet's vision. Though Isaiah may not have realized it, God contextualized the prophecy for him and the people of Judah. Using realities familiar to the prophet and his contemporaries, the Lord gave Isaiah a vision in which the two major powers of Judah's world become allies and worshipers of the one true God. Though that reality did not materialize in Isaiah's time, the prophecy has not failed. Assyria and Egypt were archetypes of the powerful, warring kingdoms of the earth that would one day lay down their weapons and acknowledge the Lord as the one true God (see Isa. 2:2–4; 11:1–10).[101]

---

98. The reference to "five" cities of Egypt in v. 18a has puzzled interpreters, especially since it seems to suggest a relatively small number. For a discussion of interpretive options, see Oswalt, *Isaiah, Chapters 1–39*, 376–77, and Clements, *Isaiah 1–39*, 171.

99. The Hebrew text reads "the city of destruction" here, but such a negative idea does not fit the positive emphasis of vv. 18–22. A manuscript of Isaiah from Qumran and some medieval Hebrew manuscripts read instead "the city of the sun" (i.e., Heliopolis). The word used here (*heres*, "destruction") is almost identical to the term *kheres*, "sun," making it easy for a scribe to make a transcriptional error. Several other ancient textual witnesses also support the reading "city of the sun," including Symmachus's Greek version, the Aramaic Targum, and the Latin Vulgate.

100. See Currid, *Ancient Egypt and the Old Testament*, 239, and Hayes and Irvine, *Isaiah*, 265.

101. For a brief discussion of archetypal language in prophetic literature and in this text, see Chisholm, *From Exegesis to Exposition*, 173–74.

A Prophecy Concerning Egypt and Cush (20:1–6)

In 712 B.C., the Assyrian king Sargon sent troops to the Philistine town of Ashdod to put down a rebellion (v. 1). Iamani, the king of Ashdod, attempted to find asylum in Egypt, but the Cushite ruler Shabaka, apparently not wanting to tangle with the Assyrians, captured Iamani and sent him to the Assyrians.[102] The Lord decided to use the occasion to give his people an important object lesson. He instructed Isaiah to walk around barefoot and only lightly dressed (v. 2).[103] The prophet was to do this for three years as a sign of what would happen to the Egyptians and Cushites (v. 3). The Assyrians, whose most recent show of strength was fresh in the people's minds, would eventually conquer Egypt and lead the Egyptians and Cushites away into exile (v. 4). At that time those who trusted in Egypt would be terrified and embarrassed, for their faith would prove to be misplaced (vv. 5–6). Isaiah's actions and the prophecy itself were designed to discourage the people of Judah from placing their trust in an anti-Assyrian alliance with Egypt. Instead, they were to maintain their neutrality and rely on the Lord to protect them.

This prophecy of Egypt's defeat was partially fulfilled in 701 B.C., when Sennacherib defeated an Egyptian-led western coalition at Eltekeh.[104] The vision was more fully realized in the seventh century B.C., when the Assyrian kings Esarhaddon (680–669 B.C.) and Ashurbanipal (668–627 B.C.) defeated the Cushites and conquered Egypt.[105]

An Oracle Concerning Babylon (21:1–10)

This next oracle concerns Babylon (see v. 9), called "the Desert by the Sea" in the introduction to the prophecy. The significance of this name is not entirely clear. Southern Mesopotamia was known in ancient times as "the land of the sea." Perhaps Isaiah's title is a derogatory alteration of this name. By substituting "desert" for "land," he anticipated the coming judgment on the region, which would be reduced to a wasteland.[106]

The oracle pictures a military force from the east invading Babylon like a destructive whirlwind (v. 1). Through this instrument of judgment the Lord puts an end to the suffering experienced by Babylon's victims (v. 2). The invaders are identified as Elamites and Medes, who were in Isaiah's day the two most powerful ethnic groups living east of Babylon. As in 13:17, the

---

102. See Currid, *Ancient Egypt and the Old Testament*, 238–39.

103. The Hebrew word used here (translated "stripped" in NIV) sometimes means "naked," but here it probably means "lightly dressed," that is, stripped to one's undergarments.

104. For Sennacherib's account of the battle, see Pritchard, *Ancient Near Eastern Texts*, 287–88.

105. For a summary of the Assyrian conquest of Egypt during this period, see William W. Hallo and William K. Simpson, *The Ancient Near East: A History* (New York: Harcourt Brace Jovanovich, 1971), 291–92.

106. This same word, translated "desert" in NIV, is used in Isa. 14:17 to describe how the king of Babylon conquered the world and reduced it to a "desert."

oracle anticipates Cyrus's invasion of Babylon in 539 B.C.[107] The first part of the verse, which suggests betrayal is involved, probably reflects the fact that, as far back as Isaiah's time, the Elamites had been traditional allies of the Chaldeans against the Assyrians.[108] But now they turn on their former friends and contribute to their demise.

The prophet plays the role of a participant in the invasion as he describes the terror and panic caused by the invaders (vv. 3–4). The attack comes so suddenly it interrupts normal activity (v. 5). The drama continues as the Lord instructs the prophet to post a watchman on the walls of an unidentified town, which seems to be representative of Israel (vv. 6–7; see v. 10). A messenger finally arrives with the news that Babylon has fallen (vv. 8–9). The prophet assures God's downtrodden people that the message is indeed true (v. 10). The judgment announced here parallels the events described in chapters 13–14, where the news of Babylon's demise frees God's people from oppression and ignites a celebration (see 14:3).

An Oracle Concerning Dumah (21:11–12)

This oracle concerns Dumah, an oasis located in the Arabian desert.[109] The prophet hears someone calling to him from Seir, located in Edom in the direction of Dumah. This individual may represent the refugees from Dumah, or the Edomites, whose economic interests would be adversely affected by the fall of Dumah. This unidentified individual asks a watchman if the night (symbolizing judgment and hard times) is ready to pass (v. 11). The watchman responds that morning (symbolizing relief from suffering) is indeed coming, but then adds that night (symbolizing renewed hardship) will follow (v. 12).

The background of this oracle is uncertain. Some suggest that it reflects an Assyrian invasion of the Arabian desert, perhaps during the time of Sargon. If the defeat of Dumah occurred at the same time as Kedar's downfall, then the oracle must refer to an event during Isaiah's lifetime (see vv. 16–17). Another possibility is that the oracle anticipates political developments in the sixth century B.C., when Nabonidus conquered Arabia (this would correspond to the night mentioned in v. 11) before being defeated by the Persians (the morning mentioned in v. 12), who then extended their empire westward (the night mentioned in v. 12).

An Oracle Concerning Arabia (21:13–17)

This oracle mentions Dedan and Tema, two more oases in Arabia. The residents of both are instructed to bring water and food for refugees who have

---

107. It is possible that the reference to Elamite hostilities against Babylon anticipates the Elamite raid on southern Mesopotamia in 546 B.C. On this invasion, see Saggs, *The Greatness That Was Babylon,* 155.

108. Ibid., 121, 128–32.

109. Gen. 25:14 lists Dumah as one of the sons of Ishmael.

escaped the slaughter of the battlefield (vv. 13–15). This exhortation is linked to the announcement of judgment in verses 16–17 (the Hebrew text has an explanatory particle, "for, because," at the beginning of v. 16 which is left untranslated by NIV). The refugees are apparently the survivors of the Arabian region of Kedar, which would suffer a humiliating and devastating military defeat within a year of the time of the prophecy. The reference to "within one year" places the prophecy in Isaiah's time and probably anticipates one of the Assyrian campaigns into Arabia.

An Oracle Concerning Jerusalem (22:1–25)

This oracle pertains to "the Valley of Vision" (vv. 1, 5), which is associated here with the city of Jerusalem (vv. 8–11). The significance of this title is uncertain, though it apparently refers to one of the valleys in the Jerusalem vicinity. Perhaps it is called the "valley of vision" because the prophet received this oracle there or because this valley plays a central role in the prophetic vision (v. 5).

The prophet plays the role of a mourner who laments the calamity that is overtaking his people (v. 4). Convinced that death is right around the corner, the people are partying one last time (vv. 1b–2a, 13), though they should be mourning and repenting (v. 12). Some have died of starvation and leaders have tried to escape, only to be captured by the enemy (vv. 2b–3). The Lord's day of judgment has arrived as warriors from the distant lands of Elam and Kir invade Judah and surround Jerusalem (vv. 5–8a). The people of Jerusalem have strengthened the city's defenses and secured its water supply, but have not turned to God for help (vv. 8b–11). For this reason, the Lord announces that their sin of unbelief will not be forgiven (v. 14).

The background of this oracle is not certain. Both the content and style of the message suggest that the oracle reflects an event contemporary with the prophet. The actions described in verses 8b–11a seem to refer to the measures taken by Hezekiah to defend Jerusalem against Sennacherib (see 2 Chron. 32:1–5). The Hebrew verbs used in verses 5–12 appear to be narratival and seem to point to events that have already taken place. If so, the "day" mentioned in verse 5 was not future from the prophet's perspective, but had already arrived or taken place (see "in/on that day" in vv. 8 and 12). For this reason, some argue that the oracle reflects the Assyrian crisis of 701 B.C., when Sennacherib invaded the land and threatened Jerusalem. Though verses 5 and 14 indicate the city would fall, it is possible that the oracle preceded Hezekiah's prayer, which prompted the Lord to turn back the Assyrians and deliver the city (see Jer. 26:17–19).

However, the reference to Elam and Kir (v. 5) is problematic for this view because it is difficult to see how these lands represent Assyria. Though Elam is associated with Ashur (or Assyria) in Genesis 10:22 and Kir, the original home of the Arameans (Amos 9:7), may have been an Assyrian province (see 2 Kings 16:9; Amos 1:5), this would still be a rather cryptic way of referring to the Assyrian army. For this reason, some prefer to understand the oracle as referring to the Babylonian conquest of Jerusalem in 586 B.C. The reference to Elam makes more sense in this case for the Elamites were traditional allies of the Babylonians. In this case the prophet takes a visionary stance in the future and describes the invasion as if it were already underway. Perhaps events surrounding the Assyrian crisis in 701 B.C. influenced the prophet's language and served as a catalyst for this prophecy about a more distant event. Some contend that the original Isaianic prophecy, delivered in the midst of the crisis in 701 B.C., was reapplied in 586 B.C. In this case verse 6 may be viewed as a later addition to the prophecy to adapt it to this later situation.

The second part of the oracle (vv. 15–25) pertains to a high government official named Shebna, who epitomized the pride that characterized Judah's royal bureaucracy at this time. Shebna had built a fine tomb for himself, as if he deserved to be remembered as a prominent national leader (vv. 15–16). But the Lord would judge Shebna's pride by removing him from office and causing him to die in disgrace (vv. 17–19).

The Lord would replace him with Eliakim, who would receive Shebna's symbols of honor and become a fatherlike protector to the people (vv. 20–21). As the possessor of the "key to the house of David," Eliakim would have the authority to grant or exclude access to the king (v. 22). Initially, Eliakim's position would be secure, like a peg driven into a firm place (v. 23). His family would gain respect, and his descendants, compared to bowls and jars hanging from the peg, would gain positions of honor and receive special benefits (v. 24). But nepotism inevitably dilutes the quality of leadership, and the house of Eliakim would eventually fall. Utilizing the metaphor of verse 23, the prophet compares this to a peg giving way and breaking, causing everything hanging on it to crash to the floor (v. 25).

An Oracle Concerning Tyre (23:1–18)

This oracle pertains to Tyre, a seaport located north of Israel along the Mediterranean coast. The prophet must have received this oracle toward the end of his career, for verse 13 seems to assume that the Assyrian destruction of Babylon (which occurred in 689 B.C.) had already taken place.[110]

Isaiah dramatically calls upon the large trading ships (literally, "ships of Tarshish," see 2:16) to lament Tyre's destruction (vv. 1, 14). Because Tyre was a thriving commercial center, merchants all around the Mediterranean world mourned her downfall (vv. 2–7). Tyre epitomized human pride. For this reason, the Lord decreed that she would be humiliated (vv. 8–9). Tyre's fall left the merchants of Tarshish and Sidon without a port to buy and sell

---

110. For Sennacherib's account of this event, see Roux, *Ancient Iraq,* 291–92.

goods (vv. 10–12). Like the land of the Babylonians, which had been ravaged by Sennacherib's Assyrian armies, Tyre was ruined (v. 13).

In the second part of the oracle, Isaiah indicated that Tyre would be forgotten for seventy years, the average life span of a typical king (v. 15a). The
number seventy, being a multiple of the symbolic number seven, may be
used here in a stereotypical, nonliteral manner to indicate a long period of
time that satisfies completely the demands of divine judgment. It also suggests that the fulfillment of the prophecy would not be witnessed by most of
those hearing it. However, the Lord would eventually restore Tyre as a prominent commercial center. Comparing the city to a prostitute, Isaiah pictured
a time when she would again attract clients (vv. 15b–17). However, her profits would no longer be hoarded by merchants. Instead, they would be given
to the Lord, who would in turn distribute them to his people (v. 18).
Though the image of the Lord collecting prostitute Tyre's profits may be offensive to some modern readers, Isaiah's point is clear. Tyre would be incorporated into God's kingdom and offer tribute to Israel's God.

The background of this oracle is not entirely clear. Though many kings
attacked and besieged Tyre, the city was not actually destroyed until 332
B.C., when Alexander the Great conquered it. For this reason, some see the
oracle as containing a long-range prediction of this event. However, the oracle seems to assume that Tyre had already fallen. For this reason, it may be
preferable to associate Tyre's fall with events occurring in Isaiah's time. In
709 B.C., Sargon of Assyria instituted commercial policies in the west that
diminished Tyre's prominence well into the seventh century B.C. The Assyrian kings Sennacherib, Esarhaddon, and Ashurbanipal periodically threatened the city, making it risky to trade with Tyre. Using the stereotypical and
exaggerated language of destruction, the oracle refers to Tyre's fall from economic prominence.[111]

The prophecy of Tyre's assimilation into God's kingdom is more problematic, for there is no indication that Tyre was ever subservient to Judah.
For this reason, it is best to regard this Tyre of the future as archetypal. Tyre
represents the great commercial powers of the earth who will one day recognize the Lord's authority and honor him with their wealth (see Isa. 60:5–9;
Hag. 2:7).

The Lord Establishes His Kingdom (Isa. 24–27)

The litany of divine judgment on the nations of Isaiah's day (chapters 13–
23) forms a fitting prelude to chapters 24–27, which depict God's culminating worldwide judgment and the establishment of his earthly kingdom.
In many ways these chapters pick up the theme of worldwide judgment in-

---

111. In this regard see especially Hayes and Irvine, *Isaiah,* 288–90, and Motyer, *The Prophecy of
Isaiah,* 192. On the language of destruction, see my earlier comments on Isa. 13–14.

troduced in 13:1–16 and develop it further. Scholars sometimes label chapters 24–27 "The Little Apocalypse," for the literary style and thematic emphases of these chapters resemble the Book of Revelation, also known as "The Apocalypse."

A Curse Overtakes the Earth (24:1–20)

The "Little Apocalypse" begins with a description of God's devastating worldwide judgment. God plays no favorites; the judgment touches everyone, including the most prominent and the most lowly in society (vv. 1–3). A "curse" overtakes the earth, bringing with it infertility and famine (vv. 4, 6). Those who love to party and have a good time are especially disappointed, because the destruction of the vines and crops deprives them of wine and beer (vv. 7–9). Revelry and carousing turn into anguish and sorrow in the city streets (vv. 10–11). Destruction sweeps through the cities, leaving only a handful of survivors in its wake (vv. 12–13).

This "curse" falls on the earth because its inhabitants have broken "the everlasting covenant" and violated its "laws" and "statutes" (v. 5). The association of a curse with a covenant is common in the Bible and in the ancient Near East. Such curses typically threaten the loss of agricultural fertility. For example, the Mosaic covenant concludes with a list of judgments to be poured out on those who disobey God's commands. Drought, loss of crops, and famine highlight the list (Deut. 28:17–18, 22–23, 38–42). Likewise the Assyrian king Esarhaddon's treaty with his vassals concludes with a lengthy curse list that threatens subject nations with severe judgments if they dare disobey the stipulations of the agreement. One of these curses calls for drought to come upon the land of any subject who disobeys.[112]

To what "everlasting covenant" does verse 5 allude? Some scholars identify this as a worldwide covenant supposedly made between God and Adam at the time of creation, but the Bible does not clearly refer to any such covenant.[113] The references to "laws" and "statutes" in verse 5 causes some to identify the covenant as the Mosaic law, but this covenant is never called an "everlasting covenant"[114] and it is difficult to see how the nations of the earth could be judged on the basis of a covenant made between God and Israel. Still others identify this covenant as the one made by God with Noah and, by extension, with all his descendants. Isaiah 24 refers to a covenant which

---

112. See Pritchard, *Ancient Near Eastern Texts,* 534–41. See especially paragraph 64 of the treaties.

113. W. J. Dumbrell (*Covenant and Creation* [Nashville: Thomas Nelson, 1984], 20–39) argues that Gen. 6:18 presupposes the existence of such a covenant, but this statement, rather than referring back to an unmentioned covenant, seems to anticipate the ratification of the Noahic covenant (see 9:8–17). Some see a reference to a divine covenant with Adam in Hos. 6:7, but the meaning of this text is uncertain.

114. Judg. 2:1 and Ps. 111:5, 9 possibly refer to the Mosaic covenant, but it is more likely that God's promise to Abraham is in view. Exod. 31:16 calls the Sabbath an everlasting covenant (or, in this case, "sign" or "guarantee") of God's relationship with Israel, but it is not certain if this implies that the law, in which observance of the Sabbath is commanded and regulated, is viewed as everlasting as well.

humankind has broken by shedding blood unjustly, as the reference to the earth being "defiled" (v. 5) suggests and Isaiah 26:21 specifically states.[115] The Noahic mandate commands humankind to populate the earth and makes murder a capital offense (Gen. 9:1–7). Furthermore, God's promise to Noah (Gen. 9:8–17) is specifically called an "everlasting covenant" (v. 16). However, it appears that the covenant is restricted to the promise outlined in Genesis 9:8–17 and does not include the mandate to populate the earth in verses 1–7.

Perhaps Isaiah's language is intentionally ambiguous and designed to encompass both Israel and the foreign nations. If so, then the "everlasting covenant" is, from Israel's perspective, the Mosaic law, which includes specific legislation outlawing murder. At the same time, from the perspective of other nations, the "everlasting covenant" is the Noahic mandate, which makes it clear that humankind is to populate the earth, not destroy one another. In this case Isaiah, with a stroke of irony, links the divine promise made to Noah with the mandate to populate the earth. In so doing he stresses the grave importance of the mandate and perhaps, with a touch of hyperbole, suggests that humankind's failure to carry it out even jeopardizes the promise in some way. Isaiah 24:18 offers support for this, for it depicts the coming worldwide judgment as a reenactment of the Noahic flood (see Gen. 7:11, as well as Zeph. 1:2–3).[116]

Another debated interpretive issue concerns the identity of the "city" portrayed in Isaiah 24:10–12. Many understand the city to be typical or symbolic of proud human society in rebellion against God. The general, somewhat stereotypical language of verses 10–12 supports this view. However, others see behind the vague language an allusion to a specific city or nation. Some identify the city with a foreign power, such as Moab (see Isa. 25:10–12) or Babylon,[117] while others see Jerusalem (compare 24:8–9 with 5:11–14) or Samaria (compare 27:9–11 with 17:8) lurking behind the prophet's description. As in the case of the "everlasting covenant," Isaiah's language may be intentionally ambiguous here. The "ruined city" of 24:10–12 represents all the cities of the world that oppose God and experience his destructive judgment, but the language and imagery of chapters 24–27 also point to specific manifestations of such cities in Isaiah's day, including the kingdoms of Moab, Babylon, Jerusalem, and Samaria.

This outpouring of divine judgment prompts the surviving nations to praise God's majesty (vv. 14–16a). But their reaction is premature. The

---

115. See also Num. 35:33–34, where the shedding of blood "defiles" a land.

116. On the other hand, Isa. 54:9 views the Noahic promise as unconditional and everlasting.

117. The oracle against Babylon (Isa. 13:1–14:27) begins with a description of universal judgment that resembles Isa. 24. Isa. 24 also contains verbal echoes of the Tower of Babel story in Gen. 11. See Robert B. Chisholm Jr., "The 'Everlasting Covenant' and the 'City of Chaos': Intentional Ambiguity and Irony in Isaiah 24," *Criswell Theological Review* 6 (1993): 242–43.

prophet does not join them in praising God, but instead laments the sin that continues to weigh down the earth (see v. 20), for he knows that this "treachery" will prompt another outpouring of divine anger (v. 16b). This next round of judgment will bring inescapable destruction (v. 17) that will rival the Noahic flood in its intensity and devastating effects (vv. 18–19).

In verses 17–18 Isaiah pictures the agents of judgment as "terror and pit and snare." The three agents are depicted as allies who conspire to capture the victim. This is even more apparent in Hebrew, where these three words sound the same. (Phonetically the three words sound as follows: *pakhad, pakhat, pakh.*) If someone runs at the sound of terror, he will fall into a pit. If he is able to climb out of the pit, then he will be caught in a snare. The point is clear; judgment will be inescapable.

The Lord Becomes King (24:21–26:7)

God's day of judgment culminates in the defeat of the cosmic alliance arrayed against him. These forces are identified as "the powers in the heavens above and the kings on the earth below" (v. 21). The "powers in the heavens above" (literally, "the host of the height in the height") are viewed as members of God's heavenly assembly (see 1 Kings 22:19) and are associated in pre-scientific Israelite thinking with the stars and planets.[118]

The Lord captures these enemies and herds them into a prison to await their final punishment (v. 22). In the progress of biblical revelation, one discovers that the driving force behind this coalition is none other than Satan, whose defeat and imprisonment the Apostle John describes (see Rev. 20:2–3).[119] Isaiah's imagery may have its roots in Mesopotamian myth, which tells how the Babylonian god Marduk defeated Tiamat, a symbol of the destructive forces that threaten world order, and then imprisons her demonic allies.[120]

Having subdued his enemies, the Lord establishes his rule in Jerusalem on Mount Zion (see Isa. 2:2–4). To emphasize the Lord's royal splendor, Isaiah pictures both the moon and sun being darkened (literally, "ashamed") as

118. See Deut. 4:19; 17:3; 2 Kings 17:16; 21:3, 5; 23:4–5; 2 Chron. 33:3, 5, Isa. 34:4, where the "host of heaven" is identified as the heavenly luminaries. In Judg. 5:20 the stars fight on the Lord's behalf. According to Job 38:7, the "morning stars" (also called the "sons of God") celebrated God's creative work. The reference to the "stars of God" in Isa. 14:13 may refer to the Canaanite god El's divine assembly, which is referred to as the "congregation of the stars" in Ugaritic mythology.

119. Both Peter (see 2 Pet. 2:4) and Jude (see v. 6) tell of rebellious angels who were imprisoned by God. However, these texts are not speaking of the end-time rebellion envisioned by Isaiah. Both are referring to the angelic rebellion described in Gen. 6:2, which tells how the "sons of God" (members of God's heavenly assembly, see Job 1:6; 2:1; 38:7, as well as Ps. 89:5–8) cohabited with women and polluted the human race. For the intertestamental Jewish literary tradition that has apparently impacted Peter's and Jude's thinking, see 1 Enoch 6–10 and Jubilees 5. Translations of these texts are available in James H. Charlesworth, ed. *The Old Testament Pseudepigrapha,* 2 vols. (Garden City, N.Y.: Doubleday, 1983, 1985), 1:15–18 and 2:64–65, respectively.

120. See tablet IV of the Babylonian creation epic, known as Enuma Elish. A translation of pertinent sections of the epic is available in Pritchard, *Ancient Near Eastern Texts,* 60, 66–69, 514.

they surrender their rulership of the night and day, respectively (see Gen. 1:16–18), to the God who created them (see Isa. 60:19–20).[121]

This event prompts God's people to break out in praise (25:1–5). Representing this future generation and speaking from their perspective, the prophet declares his allegiance to God and his intention to praise him for his faithful, mighty deeds. God announced his plan for the world and then brought it to pass. He defeated the powerful nations of the earth and forced them to recognize his authority. They threatened to destroy his people, but God proved to be "a shelter from the storm and a shade from the heat."

Having assumed his rightful place as king of the earth, the Lord holds a banquet on Mount Zion (25:6–8). The people of the earth gather to celebrate the dawning of a new era in which death, the most terrifying of all humankind's enemies, is eliminated. Using vivid imagery, Isaiah pictures the Lord swallowing up Death and then wiping the tears from the faces of those who have experienced its terrors. The death of Death prompts this future generation of God's people to affirm their loyalty to him and celebrate the salvation he provides (25:9).

The word-picture of the Lord swallowing Death is especially appropriate in its ancient Near Eastern context. Death is portrayed in both the Hebrew Bible (Prov. 1:12; Isa. 5:14; Hab. 2:5) and Ugaritic myth as voraciously swallowing up its prey. In the myths we read of Death having "a lip to the earth, a lip to the heavens . . . and a tongue to the stars."[122] Deified Death describes his own appetite as follows: "But my appetite is the appetite of lions in the waste. . . . If it is in very truth my desire to consume 'clay' [a reference to his human victims], then in truth by the handfuls I must eat it, whether my seven portions [indicating fullness and completeness] are already in the bowl or whether Nahar [the god of the river responsible for ferrying victims from the land of the living to the land of the dead] has to mix the cup."[123] How appropriate that the Lord swallows up the great swallower of mankind, putting an end to his reign of terror.[124]

121. The language should not be interpreted in an overly literal manner. The point is that God's royal glory will exceed all else, even the light of the moon and sun. The language is clearly metaphorical, for Isa. 30:26 pictures a scenario that is just the opposite of the situation described in 24:23 and 60:19–20. According to 30:26, the moon and sun will grow seven times brighter in the era of salvation. In this case light symbolizes the Lord's saving presence, which will be apparent to everyone. It is obvious that the heavenly luminaries cannot be both darkened and brightened at the same time. Once one understands the metaphorical and hyperbolic nature of these texts, the apparent contradiction is resolved. For further discussion see Chisholm, *From Exegesis to Exposition,* 176.

122. Gibson, *Canaanite Myths and Legends,* 69.

123. Ibid., 68–69.

124. The Hebrew Bible stops short of deifying death, but we probably should not retreat to the opposite extreme and reduce the Hebrew Bible's depiction of death to mere personification. Perhaps a mediating position would be to say that the Hebrew Bible "demonizes" death. This is consistent with Heb. 2:14, which observes that the devil "holds the power of death."

Isaiah next contrasts the future security of Mount Zion with the fate of the proud nations that oppose God (25:10–12). Using Moab as an archetype of the hostile nations, Isaiah uses a vivid metaphor to depict their humiliating demise. God's enemies are trampled down like straw in a manure pile. They are utterly humiliated, like someone who falls flat on his face into a manure pile and then flails his arms like a swimmer in an effort to extricate himself from the disgusting mess. The walls of their fortified cities, symbolic of their power and pride, collapse.

The defeat of the nations once again prompts God's people to break forth in praise (26:1–7; see 25:1–5, 9). In contrast to the ruined cities of God's enemies, Jerusalem stands firm. God protects his faithful people and rewards their trust in him with national security. The one "whose mind is steadfast" (v. 3) is the righteous nation mentioned in verse 2. He gives them "perfect peace" (literally "peace, peace" in the Hebrew text— the repetition is for emphasis), which likely refers in this context to national security, rather than emotional composure. To his people God is like a high rocky cliff (NIV "Rock") where they can flee for safety. God brings the walls of his enemies' cities down to the dust and allows his once oppressed people to stomp on the ruins. He levels the path for his people, a word-picture that refers here to the vindication and security he provides.

Longing for the Vision to Become Reality (26:8–18)

At this point, God's suffering people address the Lord. Having heard Isaiah describe the nation's glorious future, they declare their allegiance to the Lord and anticipate the prophet's vision becoming a reality. They anxiously await the coming of God's judgment, because it alone will convince sinners of his justice and majesty (vv. 8–9). Sinners are calloused to God's mercy and justice; they need vivid, incontrovertible proof of his moral authority (vv. 10–11). As they continue their prayer, God's people recall how he delivered them from oppressive rulers and expanded their borders (vv. 12–15), yet they also remember their past pain and frustration (vv. 16–18). Israel's distress, compared here to the pains of childbirth, seemed to have no purpose. A woman in labor endures pain with the hope that a child will be born, but Israel's suffering yielded nothing but wind. Israel was like a woman who strains to bring forth a child but who cannot push the baby through to daylight.

The Vision Renewed (26:19–27:13)

The Lord responds to Israel's prayer with an encouraging word of hope. He announces that Israel's dead will rise from the grave (v. 19). It is unclear if this promise refers to a literal resurrection of Israelite dead (see Dan. 12:2) or speaks metaphorically of the deliverance of Israelites from the "grave" of exile in a foreign land (see Isa. 27:12–13; Ezek. 37:1–14).[125]

The Lord also warns his people to seek shelter until the full fury of his judgment has passed (v. 20). As previously announced by Isaiah, the Lord is ready to emerge from his dwelling place and punish the people of the earth for their violation of the Noahic mandate (v. 21; see 24:5). Rather than populating the earth, they have defiled it with the blood of their fellow human beings.

When the Lord comes in judgment he defeats those who oppose his rule, symbolized here by the sea monster Leviathan (27:1). In West Semitic mythology, Leviathan was a seven-headed serpentine sea creature which, as a symbol or ally of the sea god, threatened to destroy the established world order. Isaiah here applies this mythological imagery and language to the heavenly and earthly coalition that opposes the Lord in the culminating battle (see 24:21–22). Elsewhere in the Hebrew Bible similar imagery and language are used to describe the Lord's victories over hostile forces at creation and in history (cf. Ps. 74:13–14; 77:16–20; 89:9–10; Isa. 51:9–10). The Lord's superiority to the unruly waters demonstrates his sovereignty (see Ps. 29:3, 10; 93:3–4).[126]

Following the Lord's victory over his enemies, he abundantly blesses his people. They become a well-watered vineyard that produces tasty fruit under the Lord's protective care (vv. 2–6). The metaphor of a fruitful vineyard reverses the imagery of 5:1–7, where the Lord compares the sinful generation of Isaiah's day to a vineyard that fails to produce good grapes, despite all the attention and care it receives from its divine owner. This idolatrous generation would be subjected to merciless judgment that would leave the pagan worship centers and cities in ruins and culminate in the exile (vv. 7–11). However, the day would come when the Lord would gather his exiled people from foreign lands and reestablish them in their land, where they would worship him on Mount Zion in Jerusalem (vv. 12–13).

Death Gives Way to Deliverance (Isaiah 28–35)

This section of Isaiah begins with warnings of impending judgment on Samaria and Jerusalem, but ends with a picture of God's exiled people celebrating as they return to Zion. The section displays the following structure:

> Woe oracle against proud Samaria (28:1–4)
> The transformation of society announced (28:5–6)

---

125. For a summary of the debate and a defense of the metaphorical view, see Day, *Yahweh and the Gods*, 123–24. Day acknowledges that the language of Dan. 12:2 is dependent on Isa. 26:19, but he argues that Dan. 12:2 adapts the imagery and makes it refer to a literal resurrection.

126. For mythological descriptions of Leviathan, the wording of which is identical or synonymous to the language of Isa. 27:1, see Gibson, *Canaanite Myths and Legends*, 50, 68.

Chapters 28–32 focus on God's people and oscillate between the poles of judgment and deliverance. Messages of judgment predominate in 28:1–30:17 (fifty-six of the seventy verses focus on judgment), but salvation becomes the dominant theme in 30:18–32:20 (thirty-six of forty-five verses anticipate a time of deliverance and spiritual transformation). In chapter 33 the focus of judgment changes from God's people to Assyria. Chapter 34 expands the scope of God's judgment to all nations, though the Edomites receive special attention. The culminating vision (chapter 35) moves beyond the immediate future, which would be highlighted by God's deliverance of Jerusalem from the Assyrian threat, to a more distant time, when God would bring his exiled people back to Jerusalem.

Samaria's Beauty Fades (28:1–4)

This oracle anticipates Samaria's downfall, which came in 722 B.C. The prophet pictures the city as a splendid wreath and a beautiful flower in which the people of the northern kingdom take great pride. But the wreath would be thrown to the ground and trampled underfoot; the flower would fade and wither (vv. 1, 3–4a). The Lord's judgment, likened to a destructive thunderstorm, would devastate Samaria (v. 2) and swallow it up, much like one devours a ripe fig (v. 4b).

A Glimpse of a Better Day to Come (28:5–6)

Before developing this message of impending judgment in more detail, the prophet stops to interject a word of encouragement (vv. 5–6). The dark storm clouds of divine judgment have a silver lining. When the judgment passes, those who remain will take pride in the Lord, for he will reestablish national security by giving the nation just leaders and by protecting his people from invading armies.

The Gibberish of Judgment (28:7–13)

This glimpse of the future stands in stark contrast to the realities of Isaiah's day. In Isaiah's time, Israel's spiritual leaders were incompetent (vv. 7–8). The prophet depicted them as drunkards who stagger around in their own vomit as they attempt to render judicial decisions and to receive prophetic visions. This may be a literal, though somewhat exaggerated, description of the priests and prophets, but it is possible that Isaiah used drunkenness as a metaphor to emphasize their spiritual insensitivity and incompetence.

The prophet next asked, "Who is it he is trying to teach? To whom is he explaining his message?" (v. 9a). As verse 12 seems to indicate, the LORD is the subject of the verbs "trying to teach" and "explaining." The prophet quickly answered his own question (v. 9b). As far as he was concerned, the Lord was trying to communicate to people who were moral infants. They stubbornly rejected God's offer of peace and blessing (v. 12), as if they were babies incapable of understanding what he was saying to them.

The Lord's punishment would be appropriate. He would speak to them, as it were, through foreign invaders who would devastate the land (vv. 10–11). These verses are best translated: "Indeed, they will hear meaningless gibberish, senseless babbling, a syllable here, a syllable there. For with mocking lips and a foreign tongue he will speak to these people" (see NET). The meaning of verse 10 has been debated. The text reads literally, "indeed [or "for"] *tsav latsav, tsav latsav, qav laqav, qav laqav;* a little there, a little there." The repetitive syllables are gibberish that resembles baby-talk and mimics what the people would hear when foreign invaders conquered the land. In this case "a little" refers to the short syllabic structure of the babbling.[127] The prophet alluded to the coming Assyrian invasion, when the people would hear a foreign language that would sound like gibberish to them. The Lord once spoke in meaningful terms, but in the coming judgment he would speak to them, as it were, through the mouth of foreign oppressors. The gibberish would be an outward reminder that God had decreed and brought to pass their defeat.

In fact, this gibberish would actually begin prior to the foreign invasion (v. 13). The Lord's prophetic appeals to them, like the appeal quoted in verse 12, were crystal clear. However, these appeals had no impact on the people. They dismissed prophetic preaching as gibberish, but ironically, without this divine guidance, their downfall was inevitable.

127. Some take *tsav* as a derivative of the Hebrew verb *tsavah,* "to command," and translate the first part of the statement as "command after command, command after command." Proponents of this position also take *qav* as a noun meaning "measuring line" (see v. 17), understood here in the abstract sense of "standard" or "rule." In this case the people make fun of the prophet, suggesting he is always shouting out commands and reminding them of rules they must follow.

Jerusalem's Leaders Would Not Be Spared (28:14–29)

The prophet next turned to Jerusalem's smug leaders, who thought their alliance with Egypt (see Isa. 30:1–7; 31:1–3) would protect them from the Assyrians and insulate them from destruction. Isaiah sarcastically depicted them as boasting of their "covenant with death" (vv. 14–15).

Ironically, the Lord did intend to make Zion secure someday. Using the imagery of building construction, the Lord announced that he would establish in Zion "a precious cornerstone for a sure foundation" (v. 16). The imagery suggests that God intended to rebuild Zion and populate it with people who would experience the security that faith produces (see Isa. 4:3–6; 31:5; 33:20–24; 35:10). More specifically, the cornerstone may represent the ideal Davidic ruler through whom this security would be realized (see Isa. 32:1). By calling justice and fairness his measuring line and plumb line, respectively (v. 17a), the Lord emphasized that this new Zion would be established and characterized by these qualities (see Isa. 1:26–27).

However, before this new Zion could become a reality, the present leadership had to be removed. Judah's agreement with death would prove futile when God's judgment swept through the land like a powerful rainstorm (vv. 17b–19). Isaiah compared the people's false sense of security to a bed that is too short and a blanket that is too narrow (v. 20). They may promise rest and protection from the cold, but in the end they are useless. In the same way, Judah's supposed treaty with death would prove disappointing.

Pouring out severe judgment on his own people was certainly not God's ideal. In fact, he called it his "strange work" and his "alien task" (v. 21). He would attack his own people just as he had fought against the Philistines at Mount Perazim in the days of David (see 2 Sam. 5:20) and against the Canaanites at Gibeon in the days of Joshua (see Josh. 10:10–11).

Though Isaiah's complacent audience might have been inclined to mock his message, they needed to pay close attention to his words (vv. 22–23). The coming judgment was an important element in God's plan for his people and a testimony to his wisdom (vv. 24–29). Just as farmers utilize divinely imparted wisdom to grow and harvest crops, so God's dealings with his people exhibit wisdom and order. Judgment would be accomplished according to a divinely ordered timetable and, while severe enough, would not be excessive. Judgment was inevitable, just as planting inevitably follows plowing. God would, as it were, thresh his people, but he would not crush them to the point where they would be of no use to him.

Jerusalem Is Surrounded (29:1–4)

The drumbeat of judgment continues as the Lord pronounces a woe oracle against Jerusalem, addressed here as "Ariel" (29:1–4). Some understand "Ariel" as a compound name, meaning "lion of God." However, it seems more likely that the term here means "altar hearth," for this same Hebrew term is used as a common noun in verse 2, where the Lord compares Jerusalem to an altar hearth. Just as an altar hearth is heated for a sacrifice, so Jerusalem would experience the heat of God's judgment as an enemy army besieged the city. At that time, the humbled and frightened people of the city would barely be able to speak. Their voices would resemble the sound of a spirit speaking from a diviner's ritual pit or the chirping of a sorcerer as he mutters an incantation.[128]

A Miraculous Deliverance (29:5–8)

The tone of Isaiah's message suddenly changes. Jerusalem would be surrounded by foreign armies, but the Lord would come like a powerful storm and sweep away the invaders. Though Jerusalem's enemies anticipated victory, their expectations would not be realized. They would be like a hungry and thirsty man who thinks he is eating and drinking, only to wake up and realize that it was all just a dream. This prophecy anticipates the Lord's miraculous deliverance of Jerusalem in 701 B.C. (see Isa. 37:36–37).

Spiritual Insensitivity (29:9–16)

In typical fashion the prophet again shifts his tone as he denounces his spiritually insensitive contemporaries. Utilizing the metaphor of drunkenness once more (see 28:7–8), he depicts the people as blind, drunk, and asleep (vv. 9–10a). Prophetic revelation had ceased for the most part, and the people were incapable of responding to Isaiah's message (vv. 10b–12). For them, Isaiah's prophetic vision was like a scroll that is sealed and is incapable of being read. Of course the people possessed a semblance of religion. They claimed to be loyal to the Lord, but their worship was nothing but meaningless ritual, devoid of genuine devotion (v. 13).

For this reason, the Lord would shock his people out of their lethargy by doing amazing things (v. 14). The sinful people thought they could hide their evil plans from God, as if they were sovereign over him (vv. 15–16). Isaiah illustrated their perverted way of thinking with the absurd image of a piece of pottery denying that the potter has made it. The people would discover just how ridiculous this attitude was. Through his "strange work" (see 28:21) of purifying judgment (see 29:21–22), God would demonstrate his sovereignty over the nation (see 28:14–29). Then he would transform the nation's spiritual condition, demonstrating that true security can be found only in him (see 29:17–24).

Society Transformed (29:17–24)

This transformation would be as radical as if the great forest of Lebanon were reduced to a common orchard[129] or a common orchard were to grow

128. On the background of the imagery used here, see my comments on Isa. 8:19.
129. NIV translates the Hebrew word *karmel* as "fertile field," but the term more likely refers to an orchard (see *HALOT* 499).

into a forest (v. 17). It is possible that the Lebanon forest symbolizes the high and mighty (see 2:13; 10:34), who would be humbled by God (see vv. 20–21) and that the orchard represents the lowly and oppressed, who would be vindicated (see v. 19).

Utilizing a second metaphor, the prophet compared the coming transformation to a deaf man suddenly being able to hear and to a blind man receiving his sight (v. 18). Perhaps the imagery is symbolic, depicting the spiritual renewal of those who were once insensitive to God (see vv. 9–12, 24, as well as 6:9–10).

God's justice highlights the prophet's vision of this new era (vv. 19–21). The poor and needy rejoice in God's intervention, for his judgment rids society of ruthless evildoers, epitomized by those who lie in court in order to deny the innocent justice.

Decimated by divine judgment, God's people were embarrassed by their condition and their heritage, but their shame would disappear, for the Lord would multiply the nation's population (vv. 22b–23a). Just as he had delivered aging Abraham from shame by giving him a son (see v. 22a), so he would give children to humiliated Israel. This renewed fertility would prompt the people to honor God as their sovereign king and to treat him with the respect he deserves (v. 23b). The nation that had strayed from God and complained of his ways would gain spiritual insight and humbly submit to his authority and instruction (v. 24; see Jer. 31:27–34).

Egypt Cannot Help (30:1–17)

As Assyria became more menacing, Judah turned to Egypt for help (30:1–2). Prior to Sennacherib's invasion in 701 B.C., Hezekiah formed an alliance with Pharaoh in hopes that the Egyptians might provide some security, compared here to shade.[130] Judah sent officials to the Egyptian cities of Zoan, located in the Egyptian delta in the north, and Hanes (or Tahpanhes), located in the southern region of lower Egypt, south of Memphis (v. 4). To illustrate Judah's desperation, Isaiah described how envoys of Judah braved the dangers of the desert to transport their tribute to Pharaoh (v. 6).

Hezekiah formed this alliance without consulting the Lord's Spirit (see v. 1) through prophets like Isaiah and his contemporary Micah, who were energized by the divine spirit as they communicated God's will to his people (see Mic. 3:8). In fact, the rebellious people rejected the prophets' warnings and demanded instead that God's spokesmen paint pleasant pictures of the future (vv. 9–11).

But God refused to bow to these demands. He warned that Egypt, sarcastically called Rahab, "Proud One" (v. 7), would be helpless before Assyria's

---

130. The ruler mentioned in v. 3 was either Shabaka, who died in 702 or 701 B.C., or his successor Shebitku. Sennacherib alludes to this treaty in his letter to Hezekiah (see Isa. 36:6, 9).

might and a source of embarrassment to Judah (vv. 3–7). He instructed Isaiah to record this message on a scroll as an enduring witness (v. 8). This would enable the prophet to use it in the future as evidence that God had warned his people of impending judgment.

God's people needed to repent and to trust in the Lord as their protector (v. 15). Their refusal to do so made judgment inevitable. The nation was like a high wall that is unstable and ready to fall (vv. 12–13). In an instant it collapses and shatters. In the same way Judah's destruction would be sudden and complete. Isaiah compared the devastation to a piece of pottery that is shattered into such small pieces that the fragments cannot be used for any useful purpose (v. 14). When the Assyrians invaded the land, the people of Judah would flee in panic and only a remnant would survive the onslaught (vv. 16–17).

God's Merciful Intervention (30:18–33)

Despite the need for judgment, the Lord longed to show Jerusalem compassion, and anticipated a time when his relationship to his people would be restored. Though severe judgment and suffering would come (see v. 20a), the Lord envisioned a time when sorrow would pass (v. 19a). The people would discard their idols like a menstrual cloth (v. 22) and turn to the Lord (v. 19b). The Lord would respond to their prayers (v. 19b), give them moral guidance (vv. 20b–21), and restore his agricultural blessings (vv. 23–25). His blessings would, like exceedingly bright light, be obvious to everyone (v. 26). To emphasize the reality of God's saving and healing presence, Isaiah compared it to the moon becoming as bright as the sun and to the sun becoming seven times brighter. Light here symbolizes salvation and restored blessing, while the number "seven" is used symbolically to indicate intensity.[131]

To inaugurate this time of divine blessing, God would intervene in awesome power and destroy the Assyrian invaders who threatened the city (vv. 27–33; see 8:9–10; 10:5–34; 14:25; 17:12–14; 29:5–8). In the role of helper, the Lord would come in fire and a storm and shatter Assyria's power.[132] The enemy king would be killed, with his corpse being cremated in Topheth, a burial ground located near Jerusalem (see Jer. 7:32; 19:11). The residents of Jerusalem would celebrate their miraculous deliverance by

---

131. In Isa. 60:19–20 (see also 24:23 and the earlier note on that text), the prophet goes one step further in his use of hyperbole and symbolism; he describes the sun and moon as actually disappearing in the era of salvation and being replaced by God himself.

132. The "Name" of the Lord sometimes stands by metonymy for the Lord himself. (See Exod. 23:21; Lev. 24:11; Ps. 54:1; 124:8.) In Isa. 30:27, where the "Name of the Lord" is described as coming to the aid of his people, the point is that he reveals that aspect of his character that his name suggests. In other words, he comes as "the Lord," Hebrew "Yahweh," meaning "he is/will be [present]." He is the ever-present helper of his people. The name "Yahweh" originated in a context in which God assured Moses that he would be with him as he confronted Pharaoh and delivered Israel from slavery in Egypt (see Exod. 3).

singing praises to the "Rock of Israel," a divine title that pictures God as the protector of his people.

The imagery used here to depict the coming judgment is, of course, stereotypical and hyperbolic. God's destruction of the Assyrians in 701 B.C. essentially fulfilled the prophetic vision, though the Lord did not literally appear in fire or in a storm on that occasion, nor was the Assyrian king Sennacherib killed and buried nearby. The imagery of fire and storm emphasizes God's destructive power.[133] By depicting the Assyrian king as dying, the prophet emphasized that his power would be removed and that he would be humiliated.

Let Me Repeat—Egypt Cannot Help (31:1–3)

Once more the prophet denounced Judah's reliance on Egypt. Rather than trusting their sovereign king, the "Holy One of Israel" (see 1:4), Judah looked to Egypt and its military might for protection (v. 1). Judah's royal advisers thought this was the wise decision, but the Lord possessed wisdom as well and would thwart the advisers' plans by decreeing and executing judgment against Judah's sinful rebels and their Egyptian allies (v. 2). The Egyptians and their war horses were composed of flesh and bone. As such they were unable to resist the Lord's power, which is far superior to what is merely physical and material (v. 3).

But the Lord Can Help! (31:4–9)

In what appears to be a description of the judgment announced in the preceding verses, Isaiah depicted the Lord as a roaring, fearless lion ready to do battle on Mount Zion (v. 4). But he comes as protector, not as destroyer (v. 5). Once more the prophet chose to look past the approaching judgment and focus instead on the deliverance of Jerusalem to follow. The Lord would supernaturally strike the Assyrian invaders down and cause them to flee in panic (vv. 8–9; see 37:36–37). Such a mighty protector was worthy of his people's allegiance. The prophet urged the people to repent of their rebellious deeds and to turn to the Lord (v. 6). When the Lord miraculously delivered them, they would recognize their sin and throw away their manmade idols (v. 7). Isaiah reasoned that they might as well turn to the Lord immediately, rather than waiting.

There may be an echo of the exodus tradition in verse 5. The verb translated "pass over" occurs only here and in Exodus 12:13, 23, 27, where the Lord "passes over" (that is, "spares") the Israelite homes as he comes to judge their Egyptian oppressors.[134] By using this verb in verse 5, Isaiah may be al-

---

133. For a discussion of the use of stereotypical imagery in prophetic judgment speeches, see Chisholm, *From Exegesis to Exposition,* 174–75.

134. The noun "Passover" is derived from this verb.

luding to the exodus event. As in the days of Moses, the Lord would spare his people as he judged their enemies.

New Leaders Appear, Fools Disappear (32:1–8)

Isaiah envisioned a time when Judah would be led by a king and royal officials who would promote justice and protect the weak and vulnerable (32:1). He compared these leaders to a refuge from the wind and rain, to life-giving waters in a desert, and to shade in a sun-scorched region (v. 2). The prophet likened this radical transformation of the nation's spiritual condition to a blind man receiving his sight, a fool acquiring wisdom, and a person with a speech impediment becoming articulate (vv. 3–4). In contrast to Isaiah's day, fools would no longer be elevated to prominent positions and be treated with respect (v. 5). Showing fools such honor is totally inappropriate, for fools, in contrast to the godly, devise evil plans and oppress, rather than help, the poor and needy (vv. 6–8).

Genuine Security Replaces False Confidence (32:9–20)

Isaiah next addresses the complacent, self-assured women of Jerusalem (v. 9; see 3:16). Rather than feeling secure and smug, they should have trembled with fear and lamented, for within a year the land would be devastated. The harvest would fail and cities would be reduced to ruins (vv. 10–14).

However, Isaiah again looked beyond the judgment to a happier time. God would intervene and restore agricultural fertility to the land (v. 15). The NIV translates here "till the Spirit is poured upon us from on high," as if this were a reference to God's personal spirit, but it is more likely that the Hebrew term *ruakh*, which appears here without a definite article (the text does not say "*the* spirit"), a pronominal qualifier (such as "*my* spirit," see 44:3), or a modifying noun (such as "the spirit *of the* LORD"), carries an impersonal nuance here, referring to "vigor" or "life."

This renewal of the fields would be accompanied by a transformation of society. Justice would prevail (v. 16), and the land would experience peace, security, and prosperity, in contrast to the destruction that would arrive in the immediate future (vv. 17–20).

A Prayer for God's Help (33:1–9)

Isaiah once again pronounced doom (see 28:1; 29:1, 15; 30:1; 31:1), but this time he anticipated the judgment of God's enemies, called here the "destroyer" and "traitor" (33:1). In this case the enemies are identified as the hostile nations (see vv. 3–4), though the Assyrians, who utilized warriors from many nations, were certainly in the forefront of the prophet's mind (see 8:9–10; 17:12–14).

In dramatic style the prophet offered up a prayer on behalf of God's people, which includes a petition for God's intervention (v. 2), a confident affirmation of faith (vv. 3–6), and a lament over the destruction that had taken place in the land (vv. 7–9). Isaiah asked for God's merciful deliverance because society was in chaos and the land ravaged by invaders. The destructive effect of the invading army on the crops of the land had been as devastating as if Lebanon, Sharon, Bashan, and Carmel, all regions known for their rich vegetation, had withered. But the prophet was confident that God would drive the enemies away and deprive them of their plunder, just as locusts deprive farmers of their crops. Isaiah affirmed that the Lord is the sovereign king of the world who guarantees justice and gives a treasure of wisdom and security to his loyal followers, referred to here as those who "fear" the Lord.

A Refuge for the Godly (33:10–24)

In response to the prophet's petition and lament, the Lord announced that he would intervene and demonstrate his power (v. 10; see Ps. 12:5). He then taunted the nations, making it clear that their efforts to destroy his people would prove futile and self-destructive (v. 11). God's judgment, compared to a raging inferno, would destroy the hostile nations, prompting the Lord to demand that all witnesses of the event acknowledge his power (vv. 12–13).

The prospect of divine judgment being unleashed terrified the sinful inhabitants of Jerusalem, for they recognized that they too were objects of God's anger. These panic-stricken sinners asked rhetorically, "Who of us can dwell with the consuming fire? Who of us can dwell with everlasting burning?" (v. 14). One would think that the answer to their question would be "no one," but the prophet (or perhaps God himself?) affirmed that the godly were insulated from divine rage (v. 15). The godly could be recognized by their lifestyle and speech. Unlike the unjust leaders of Judah, the godly refused to oppress others by accepting bribes and committing violent crimes. Though God's judgment would destroy sinners, the godly would be secure and have their needs met (v. 16).

The prophet encouraged the godly with a message of hope (vv. 17–24). He promised them that a better day was coming, when stable leadership and national security would be restored. With their own eyes they would actually see the "king" (v. 17), the Lord himself (see v. 22). The Assyrian tax collectors would disappear (vv. 18–19), and the residents of Jerusalem would experience peace and safety under the protective rule of their divine king (vv. 20–22), who would bring prosperity to the city and forgive his people's sins (vv. 23–24).

The prophet uses two nautical metaphors to facilitate his message. In verse 21 he pictures Jerusalem as having broad rivers and streams, suggesting an abundance of life-giving water (see Ps. 46:4). At the same time no invading ships threaten the city, for the Lord makes it secure. In verse 23 Isaiah compares the Jerusalem of his day to a ship that is unprepared or unable to sail. Perhaps the image suggests the city's inability to extricate itself from danger and highlights its desperate need for divine intervention.

The Lord's Terrible, Swift Sword (34:1–17)

Isaiah next summoned all the nations, because the message to follow pertains specifically to them (v. 1). God was angry with the nations and intended to slaughter their armies, leaving their corpses to rot on the blood-soaked terrain (vv. 2–3). Divine judgment would not be confined to the earthly realm. God would also defeat the rebellious heavenly forces arrayed against him, referred to here as the "stars of the heavens" (lit., "host of heaven," v. 4; see 24:21–23). As elsewhere, the "host of heaven" is identified with the heavenly luminaries,[135] which are depicted as fading, rolling up like a scroll, and withering like leaves or figs.

Once God's mighty sword had defeated these heavenly forces, it would descend in vengeance on Edom (vv. 5, 8) because of its hostility toward Judah, a hostility that began as far back as the days of Moses (see Num. 20:14–21). Isaiah compared God's judgment of Edom to a grisly sacrificial scene, filled with the blood, suet, and internal organs of the sacrificial victims (vv. 6–7). Edom would be reduced to a burning wasteland (vv. 9–10), populated only by screeching wild birds and other scavengers to whom the Lord had allotted Edomite territory (vv. 11–17).

This description of Edom's judgment is stylized and exaggerated. The prophets used such "destruction language" for rhetorical effect to emphasize that the object of God's anger would experience severe punishment.[136] The prophecy was essentially fulfilled by the time of Malachi (see Mal. 1:3), though its cosmic dimension transcends historical developments and points to an end-time judgment of worldwide proportions. When viewed in this larger eschatological context, Edom serves as an archetype for all God's enemies, who will be crushed by his angry judgment (see also 63:1–6, as well as the Book of Obadiah).

Marching to Zion (35:1–10)

In this vision, which concludes this section of the prophecy, God reveals his royal splendor and transforms the circumstances of his suffering people. When the Lord vindicated and delivered his people, it would be as if a wasteland had suddenly become a forest or a rich valley (vv. 1–4). The transformation would be comparable to someone who is blind, deaf, lame, or mute being freed from his handicap (vv. 5–6a; see 29:18). Returning to his initial

---

135. See Deut. 4:19; 17:3; 2 Kings 17:16; 21:3, 5; 23:4–5; 2 Chron. 33:3, 5.
136. See Isa. 13:20–22; 14:23; Jer. 50:39–40; 51:36–37; Zeph. 2:13–15, as well as Heater, "Do the Prophets Teach That Babylonia Will Be Rebuilt in the *Eschaton?*" 31–36.

metaphor (see v. 1), the prophet pictures a desert gushing with streams and an arid wilderness being filled with pools and springs as plant life begins to sprout and grow (vv. 6b–7). The image of water suggests life and renewed divine blessing. Isaiah next describes a road called the "Way of Holiness," upon which the returning exiles travel back to Zion (vv. 8–9). Sinners and fools would not be allowed on this road, nor would dangerous predators, perhaps symbolizing hostile nations, lurk there. As the exiles entered Zion, they would joyfully sing (v. 10). The comparison of joy to a crown (see 2 Sam. 1:10) may involve an ironic twist on the idiom "earth on the head" (see 2 Sam. 1:2; 13:19; 15:32; Job 2:12), which refers to a mourning practice. God's people were once overwhelmed with sorrow and could do nothing but mourn their circumstances, but the returning exiles would be overcome with happiness as they celebrated their deliverance.

The Lord Saves a King and a City (Isaiah 36–39)

These final chapters of the first main unit of the Book of Isaiah are primarily narratival in form and correspond for the most part to 2 Kings 18:17–20:19.[137] Chapters 36–37 describe the Assyrian siege of Jerusalem in 701 B.C. and the Lord's miraculous deliverance of the city in that same year.[138] (Isa. 37:38 jumps ahead to 681 B.C. and describes the assassination of the Assyrian king Sennacherib.) Chapter 38 tells of Hezekiah's illness and miraculous recovery. Verse 6 suggests that this illness occurred just before or during the Assyrian siege of Jerusalem (cf. 37:35). Chapter 39 describes a visit by Babylonian envoys following Hezekiah's recovery (see v. 1). If Hezekiah's illness and recovery took place just before or during the siege, then this visit probably occurred shortly after the miraculous deliverance of Jerusalem, for it is difficult to envision Babylonian envoys visiting the city during the Assyrian crisis.

Some prefer to place both Hezekiah's illness and the envoys' visit earlier, prior to the Assyrian siege. They point out that Merodach-baladan, called "the king of Babylon" in verse 1, was in power in Babylon from 721–710 B.C. and again from 705–703 B.C., but not after 703 B.C. However, though he lost control of the city in 703 B.C., Merodach-baladan continued to organize a rebellion against the Assyrians for three more years.[139] So it is certainly possible that he could have contacted Hezekiah in 701 or 700 B.C. and

---

137. The prayer of Isa. 38:9–20 is unique to Isaiah.
138. Isa. 36:1 (= 2 Kings 18:13) refers to the fourteenth year of Hezekiah's sole reign over Judah, which began in 715 B.C. Prior to this, from 729–715 B.C., Hezekiah served as a co-regent with his father Ahaz. See 2 Kings 18:1, 9–10, which refer to the first, fourth, and sixth years of Hezekiah's co-regency. See Leslie F. McFall, "Did Thiele Overlook Hezekiah's Co-regency?" *BSac* 146 (1989): 393–404, who corrects E. Thiele on this point.
139. See Roux, *Ancient Iraq*, 290.

that he could still be called "the king of Babylon" by a narrator assuming an anti-Assyrian perspective.

Proponents of the earlier date also argue that one would expect Isaiah 39:1 to mention the deliverance of the city if it had just taken place. But this is an argument from silence. Furthermore, the demise of the Assyrian army while attacking Jerusalem would have made Hezekiah a more attractive ally and might explain in part why Merodach-baladan showed such interest in him.

Proponents of an earlier date for the envoys' visit also point out that Isaiah 39:2 indicates Hezekiah possessed great riches at the time of the visit. Since the Assyrians carted off much of Hezekiah's wealth (see 2 Kings 18:13–16), the incident described in verse 2, they argue, seems to predate the Assyrian invasion. However, if the envoys' visit preceded the incident recorded in 2 Kings 18:13–16, then how does one explain Isaiah 39:6, which predicts that the treasures mentioned in verse 2 would be taken captive by the Babylonians (not the Assyrians)? Furthermore, 2 Kings 24:10–17 tells how the Babylonians, in fulfillment of Isaiah's prophecy (compare v. 13 with 2 Kings 20:17 = Isa. 39:6), took away the riches of the temple and palace.

These chapters make an important thematic contribution to the Book of Isaiah. Chapters 36–37 record the fulfillment of Isaiah's earlier prophecies of Assyria's demise and Jerusalem's deliverance. In chapter 38, Hezekiah, like the city of Jerusalem, which he leads and represents, gets a new "lease on life." However, in chapter 39 the story turns a bit sour, as Hezekiah, filled with royal pride, begins to flirt again with potential foreign allies. The king now epitomizes the self-sufficient attitude that had troubled Judah in the past and would lead to its ultimate demise. Isaiah used the occasion to announce that Judah would someday be exiled to Babylon. With its prophecy of exile, this chapter paves the way for chapters 40–66, which address this future exilic generation.

An Intimidating Invader Arrives (36:1–20)

In 701 B.C., Hezekiah allied with the kings of Sidon and Ashkelon and the leaders of Ekron in an attempt to overthrow Assyrian rule.[140] Sennacherib came west to put down the rebellion. The king of Sidon fled to Cyprus, the king of Ashkelon was carried away into exile, and the rebel leaders in Ekron were impaled. Sennacherib then invaded Judah.[141] His army first advanced through central Judah and established a line of approach and supply through the northern Shephelah. They captured Azekah, Gath, and the cities of the

---

140. On Hezekiah's reforms and anti-Assyrian policies, see Oded Borowski, "Hezekiah's Reforms and the Revolt against Assyria," *BA* 58 (1995): 148–55.

141. See N. Na'aman, "Sennacherib's Campaign to Judah and the Date of the *lmlk* Stamps," *VT* 29 (1979): 61–86.

Shephelah, including Lachish, located about thirty miles southwest of Jerusalem.[142] A large force then moved from Lachish up to Jerusalem (Isa. 36:1–2a). In his annals Sennacherib boasted that he captured forty-six walled cities (see Isa. 36:1), took more than two hundred thousand captives, forced Hezekiah to pay a large amount of tribute (see 2 Kings 18:13–16), and trapped him in his royal city "like a caged bird."[143]

One of Sennacherib's chief officials met three of Hezekiah's officials at the aqueduct near the Upper Pool (vv. 2–3a), the same site where Isaiah and his son Shear-jashub had met King Ahaz several years before (see Isa. 7:3).[144] This Assyrian official delivered a message from Sennacherib in which the Assyrian king attempted to convince Hezekiah to surrender without a fight.

Sennacherib argued that Hezekiah's decision to rebel against Assyria was the product of misplaced confidence (vv. 4–5). If Hezekiah was trusting in his alliance with Egypt, he would be disappointed, for Egypt was like a "splintered reed" that wounds, rather than supports, the one who leans on it (v. 6). If the king was trusting in Judah's God to defend him, his faith would prove to be misplaced, because, Sennacherib reasoned, Hezekiah had angered the Lord by shutting down the idolatrous worship centers throughout the land and insisting that the people worship only in Jerusalem (v. 7). Sennacherib's argument reflects his pagan mentality and wrongly assumes that Hezekiah's centralization of worship was displeasing to God (see 2 Kings 18:3–4).

Before continuing Sennacherib's message, the chief official interjected some words of his own (vv. 8–9). He urged Hezekiah to capitulate and even promised in return that he would begin to rebuild Judah's decimated military forces. If Hezekiah agreed to Sennacherib's terms, the chief official would give Judah more horses than Hezekiah was capable of outfitting. If a royal official could supply that many horses, just think what the king him-

142. On the siege of Lachish, see D. Ussishkin, "The Destruction of Lachish by Sennacherib and the Dating of the Royal Judean Storage Jars," *Tel Aviv* 4 (1977): 28–60.

143. For Sennacherib's highly propagandized account of the invasion, see Pritchard, *Ancient Near Eastern Texts*, 287–88. Some argue that there were actually two invasions of Judah by Sennacherib, separated by fifteen years. According to this view, 2 Kings 18:14–16 tells of the first, 2 Kings 18:17–19:35 of the second. For presentations, discussion, and critiques of this view, see, among others, Bright, *History of Israel*, 284–88; J. B. Geyer, "2 Kings XVIII 14–16 and the Annals of Sennacherib," *VT* 21 (1971): 604–6; S. H. Horn, "Did Sennacherib Campaign Once or Twice against Hezekiah?" *AUSS* 4 (1966): 1–28; K. A. Kitchen, "Late-Egyptian Chronology and the Hebrew Monarchy," *JANES* 5 (1973): 225–33; Merrill, *Kingdom of Priests*, 414–15 n. 74; and W. H. Shea, "Sennacherib's Second Palestine Campaign," *JBL* 104 (1985): 401–18.

144. This official's title was "Rab-shakeh," meaning "chief butler." The "chief butler" was a court official who did not normally go on military campaigns. But on this occasion Sennacherib decided to personally lead his army to the west. As Cogan and Tadmor point out, "[I]t was only natural that he be accompanied by his personal attendants." They also suggest that this particular official may have been chosen to negotiate with Hezekiah because of his facility in Hebrew (see v. 11). See M. Cogan and H. Tadmor, *II Kings*, AB (New York: Doubleday, 1988), 230.

self could do for Judah. Certainly it made more sense to deal with Assyria than to trust in Egypt.

Having made this seemingly attractive offer, the official finished delivering Sennacherib's message (v. 10). According to Sennacherib, Hezekiah had alienated the Lord by destroying the land's worship centers (see v. 7). Now the Assyrian king takes the argument one step further by claiming that the Lord himself had commissioned Assyria as his instrument of discipline and judgment. Assyria's presence in the land was the Lord's doing. Sennacherib's claim was correct up to a point (see 10:5–6), but even so, this did not mean that Hezekiah needed to surrender or that the proud Assyrians were immune from divine judgment (see 10:5–34).

Concerned that the people listening on the city walls would hear Sennacherib's message, Hezekiah's officials asked the Assyrian envoy to speak in Aramaic, the diplomatic language of the western portion of the Assyrian Empire, rather than in the Hebrew dialect of Judah (v. 11). But the Assyrian official refused to do so, pointing out that a prolonged siege of Jerusalem would have horrible effects on all the people, not just the leaders. Everyone inside the city would suffer from starvation and would resort to eating their own excrement and drinking their own urine (v. 12). Since the entire population would be affected adversely by the siege, the Assyrian envoy insisted on addressing all the people lined up on the city wall (v. 13). Certainly he was also hoping that popular opinion would turn against Hezekiah and force him to surrender before his own people rebelled against him.

The Assyrian official next proclaimed Sennacherib's message to the people of Jerusalem. He warned the people not to place their trust in Hezekiah or in his pious-sounding promises of divine deliverance (vv. 14–15). If the people surrendered, he promised they would have plenty to eat and drink. Though the Assyrians would be forced to deport the people of Judah, he promised that their new home would be an agriculturally rich land where they could prosper (vv. 16–17). Having made this seemingly attractive offer, Sennacherib further developed his earlier point that Hezekiah's promise of divine deliverance (see v. 15) was hollow. The Lord was angry with Hezekiah and had actually commissioned the Assyrians to attack Judah (see vv. 7, 10). But, Sennacherib argued, even if the Lord were to try to deliver Jerusalem, he could not (vv. 18–20). All one had to do was look at the track record. None of the gods of the surrounding nations had been able to prevent the Assyrians from conquering their lands. To back up his claim, Sennacherib reminded them of how Hamath, Arpad, Sepharvaim, and Samaria had fallen before Assyrian might.[145] At this point, Sennacherib's rhetoric went too far; he was treading on thin ice, as we shall see shortly.

145. Tiglath-pileser III conquered Arpad in 741 b.c. (see Roux, *Ancient Iraq,* 279), Samaria fell in 722 b.c., and Sargon conquered Hamath in 720 b.c. (see ibid., 282). The precise location of Sepharvaim is not known.

Hezekiah Turns to Isaiah for Help (36:21–37:7)

The people, as ordered by Hezekiah, refused to respond to the message (v. 21), but Hezekiah's officials tore their clothes as a sign of mourning and reported the envoy's words to the king (v. 22). When Hezekiah heard the bad news, he tore his garments, put on mourning clothes, went to the temple to pray (37:1), and sent two of his officials, along with a contingent of priests, to the prophet Isaiah with a report of what had happened (v. 2). After lamenting the humiliating events of the day (v. 3), Hezekiah expressed his hope that the Lord would judge the Assyrians for their arrogance and asked Isaiah to intercede for the people of Jerusalem (v. 4).

Isaiah sent the officials back to Hezekiah with an assuring word from the Lord. Just as he had urged Ahaz not to fear the threats of the Aramean-Israelite coalition many years before (see Isa. 7:4), the Lord urged Hezekiah not to fear the blasphemous words of Sennacherib's underlings (vv. 5–6). The Lord would instigate and manipulate events so that Sennacherib would hear an alarming report that would cause him to abandon his campaign and return to Assyria (v. 7). The precise meaning of the statement "I am going to put a spirit in him" is not entirely clear. It may refer to a personal spirit sent by God to control the king's mind (see 1 Kings 22:19), or it could refer to a disposition of concern and fear. In either case the Lord's sovereignty over the king is apparent.

Sennacherib Taunts Hezekiah (37:8–13)

When Sennacherib's envoy to Jerusalem heard that the Assyrian king had attacked Libnah, located a few miles northwest of Lachish, he returned to the main army (v. 8). Since there is no mention of the army leaving with him, the large force sent to Jerusalem with this official (see 36:2) may have stayed there and kept the city under guard.

In the meantime, Sennacherib heard that Tirhakah, the Cushite commander of the Egyptian forces, was marching toward him (v. 9).[146] Initially one suspects that this is the report referred to by the Lord in his earlier response to Hezekiah (see v. 7), but, if so, Sennacherib gave no sign of retreating. Instead he sent another intimidating message to Hezekiah in which

146. According to the Assyrian annals, Sennacherib had already defeated an Egyptian force at Eltekeh. For this reason, some argue that the chronology of events in Isa. 36–37, which seems to place Sennacherib's battle with Egypt after his attack on Judah (see 36:1–2), is confused. However, Isa. 37:9 does not say a battle was actually fought with Tirhakah. Furthermore, it is possible that Sennacherib fought the Egyptians on two separate occasions and that the annals either omit reference to the second battle or telescope two battles into one. For examples of this technique in the annals, see A. Laato, "Assyrian Propaganda and the Falsification of History in the Royal Inscriptions of Sennacherib," *VT* 45 (1995): 198–226. Others point out that the reference to Tirhakah as "king of Egypt" (Isa. 37:9) is erroneous, because Tirhakah did not become king until 690 B.C. The reference is obviously anachronistic and reflects later developments. Such proleptic references are not uncommon in ancient or even modern literature. See K. A. Kitchen, *Ancient Orient and Old Testament* (Downers Grove, Ill.: InterVarsity, 1966), 82–83.

he again argued that Hezekiah's God was unable to deliver Jerusalem from the invincible Assyrian army (vv. 10–13; see 36:18–20). This time Sennacherib even suggested that the Lord was deceiving Hezekiah (see v. 10). The point seems clear—when Sennacherib was through with the Egyptians, he intended to finish his business with Hezekiah. The dramatic tension heightens as Sennacherib responds to the report of Tirhakah's approach with bravado, not fear. The Lord's plan, as announced in verse 7, appears to be thwarted.

Hezekiah Begs for Help from Above (37:14–20)

Faced with such a determined and powerful foe, Hezekiah, in contrast to his father Ahaz, turned to the Lord for help. He went to the temple and placed the scroll containing Sennacherib's message before the Lord, as if to say, "Here, read for yourself what this blasphemous enemy is saying about you!" (v. 15). Hezekiah then offered a brief but powerful prayer that exhibits penetrating theological insight. He began by acknowledging, contrary to Sennacherib's boastful claim, that the Lord God of Israel is the most powerful of all warriors (note the title "Lord Almighty," literally, "Lord of Armies"; see Isa. 1:9) and the sovereign creator and king of the world (v. 16). He then asked the Lord to consider Sennacherib's insulting taunts (v. 17). Yes, one could not deny the Assyrians' past military successes (v. 18), but these victories were overrated, for in actuality the Assyrians had only defeated worshipers of man-made pagan "gods," who were really nothing but wood and stone (v. 19). Hezekiah concluded by asking the Lord to deliver his people and, in so doing, to demonstrate to the surrounding nations that the Lord is the only true God (v. 20).

The Lord Does Taunting of His Own (37:21–29)

The Lord responded to Hezekiah's prayer via Isaiah, who sent a divine message to the king (v. 21).[147] The Lord began by taunting Sennacherib with an image of personified Jerusalem defiantly mocking the Assyrian king (v. 22). He then accused Sennacherib of insulting and blaspheming him with his arrogant boasting (vv. 23–25). Sennacherib was proud of his military accomplishments in the west,[148] but he did not realize that his success was merely an outworking of the Lord's sovereign plan and decree (vv. 26–27). However, once the Lord had used Sennacherib as his instrument of judgment on

147. Isa. 37:21 gives the impression that Hezekiah's prayer was the catalyst for God's intervention (note "because you have prayed to me"), but the text may be corrupt at this point. The parallel account in 2 Kings 19:20 reads, "I have heard your prayer concerning Sennacherib king of Assyria." The verb "I have heard" does not appear in Isa 37:21.

148. In vv. 24b–25, the Lord quotes Sennacherib. It is not certain if these exact words were spoken by the Assyrian king, but they accurately reflect his arrogant attitude and his tendency to exaggerate his successes. The final statement in v. 25 ("I have dried up all the streams of Egypt") is obviously exaggerated, for Sennacherib did not conquer Egypt.

the western states, he would turn on the Assyrian ruler and punish him for his pride (v. 28). The Lord would put his "hook" in Sennacherib's nose and his "bit" in his mouth, and make him return to his homeland (v. 29). The image of the hook in the nose depicts a captive being led away by a conqueror (see 2 Chron. 33:11),[149] while the accompanying image of a bit in the mouth likens Sennacherib to a stubborn horse or donkey (see Ps. 32:9; Prov. 26:3).

Good News for Hezekiah (37:30–35)

Having made it clear that he would get rid of the Assyrian king, the Lord assured Hezekiah that better days were ahead. Normal agricultural activity had been interrupted by the Assyrian invasion, preventing the planting of crops for the following year and forcing the people to eat crops that had grown without cultivation from the seed planted in past years. However, by the time the next planting season came around, agricultural activity would resume according to its usual cycle (v. 30).[150] This announcement is called a "sign." Sometimes a sign is a guarantee of a future development (see Isa. 8:18; 20:3; 38:7–8), but here it appears to be a future reminder of God's intervention designated before the actual intervention takes place (see Exod. 3:12 and Isa. 7:14–25).

The crops would not be the only thing growing in the days ahead. The "remnant of the house of Judah," those who had survived the Assyrian invasion, would also "take root" and "bear fruit" (v. 31). The invasion had decimated the population (see Isa. 1:9). Many had died or been carried away into exile. But the survivors left in Jerusalem would move out into the land and, with the Lord's enablement, repopulate it (v. 32).

Returning to the present crisis, the Lord affirmed that Sennacherib would not invade the city. In fact, he would not even attack it or besiege it (vv. 33–34), for the Lord would defend it for the sake of his own honor, which Sennacherib had insulted, and because of his promise to David (v. 35). The Lord had promised David an enduring dynasty (see 2 Sam. 7:12–16). Though this promise did not insulate the Davidic kings from di-

---

149. The image may liken Sennacherib to a captured lion that is forced into a cage by means of hooks (see Ezek. 19:4, 9).

150. The reference to three years is problematic. If the Assyrians were to be eliminated soon, why would it take so long for normal agricultural activity to resume? If the defeat of the Assyrians occurred close to or during the fall, it would be too late to recover from the devastation of the invasion, repopulate the land, and plant crops for the following year. (Cereal crops were usually planted in November–December. See Oded Borowski's *Agriculture in Ancient Israel* [Winona Lake, Ind.: Eisenbrauns, 1987], 34.) The next planting would not occur until the following fall, but that crop would not be harvested until the following spring. So "this year" refers to the present agricultural year, which may have been almost over. Obviously, there was no harvest available because the Assyrians had consumed or destroyed the crops (see Isa. 1:7). "The second year" refers to the next agricultural year, for which there would be no harvest because fall planting would be impossible. "The third year" would begin with the following fall's planting, only thirteen or fourteen months away. See Oswalt, *Isaiah, Chapters 1–39*, 664–65.

vine discipline, it did guarantee the preservation of the dynasty and the protection of godly kings like Hezekiah, who followed the moral example of David (see 2 Kings 18:3).

A Killer Angel and Two Assassins (37:36–38)

The Lord does not make idle threats and promises. His angel (literally, "messenger") killed 185,000 Assyrian soldiers in one night (v. 36).[151] One cannot escape the irony here. Sennacherib sent messengers to intimidate Hezekiah (see 36:2 and 37:9); the Lord sent a messenger to destroy Sennacherib's mighty army. With his army decimated, Sennacherib was forced to break camp and return home, just as the Lord had promised (v. 37).

Many of the details surrounding this event are not entirely clear. It is not certain if the angel attacked Sennacherib's main army, which does not appear to have been at Jerusalem (see v. 9), or a force left at Jerusalem (assuming that the army accompanying the Assyrian official to Jerusalem remained there when the official went to Libnah; see my comments on 37:8). Verse 36 reads literally, "They woke up early in the morning and look, all of them

---

151. An angel designated "the angel of God" and "the angel of the LORD" (the two titles appear to be interchangeable in Judg. 6:20–22 and 13:3, 9, 13) has an especially prominent role in the Hebrew Bible. It is not clear if the title refers to just one angel. The phrase is definite because of the genitival proper name, but it may simply refer to a definite angel in any given context without implying the same angel is always the referent. (See the use of the phrase "the servant of the LORD," which refers to a servant who is definite in a given context, but the phrase does not refer to the same servant in every passage.) Those who assume a particular angel is in view in every passage debate this angel's precise identity. Some have argued that he is God himself (or perhaps the second person of the Trinity in a preincarnate form), while others contend that the angel, though distinct from God, comes with divine authority and can therefore speak and be treated as God himself.

Several texts equate this angel with God/Yahweh. The angel seems to speak as God at times (Gen. 31:11–13; Exod. 3:2, 4; Judg. 2:1–3), while humans who encounter the angel sometimes react as if they have seen God himself (Gen. 16:13; Judg. 6:22; 13:22; see also Gen. 32:28–30 in light of Hos. 12:3–4). On the other hand, the angel sometimes speaks as if he is distinct from God (Gen. 21:17; 22:11–12, 15–17; Zech. 1:12). In certain texts a close reading reveals that the angel and God are distinct entities (see Exod. 3:2–4; Judg. 6:11–23). The angel who accompanied Israel out of Egypt (called the "angel of God" in Exod. 14:19) is distinct from God (see Num. 20:16), yet he is called the "angel of his [God's] presence" (Isa. 63:9) and possesses God's "name" or full authority (Exod. 23:21).

It is more likely that the angel should be equated with God in a representative, not an essential or personal sense. (The passages that distinguish the angel from God in essence must be determinative.) The angel comes with full divine authority and can therefore speak in God's behalf (sometimes in the first person). Those who encounter the angel realize his authoritative representative status and therefore act appropriately. As James Ross states, "It would seem that the question of the messenger's authority could be answered simply: it is that of the one who sends him. Thus a messenger is to be treated as if he were his master." See "The Prophet as Yahweh's Messenger," in *Prophecy in Ancient Israel,* ed. David L. Petersen (Philadelphia: Fortress, 1987), 114.

Supporting evidence for this proposal can be found in the Ugaritic Baal myth. In an early scene in the myth Yam's messengers, in the appearance of fire, enter the divine assembly and report Yam's words to El: "The message of Yam your lord, of your sire judge Nahar is this: 'Give up, gods, him whom you protect, him whom you protect, o multitude, give up Baal and his lackeys, the son of Dagon, that I may possess his gold.' El answers as if Yam is personally present: "Baal is your slave, O Yam, Baal is your slave, O Nahar, the son of Dagon is your prisoner. Even he must bring you tribute like the gods, even he must bring you gifts like the sons of the Holy one." See Gibson, *Canaanite Myths and Legends,* 42.

[were] dead bodies." The identity of the subject of the verb "woke up" is not entirely clear. It could refer to the remainder of the Assyrian army (whether it be with Sennacherib or at Jerusalem), or to the people of Jerusalem (assuming a force remained there).

Some find the figure given for the number of Assyrian dead (185,000) to be unlikely or even impossible. A full treatment of the use of large numbers in the Hebrew Bible is beyond the scope of the present discussion, but it is essential to at least outline some of the options available to the interpreter. Some take the number at face value, while others consider it to be proof that the account is fanciful. However, these extreme positions are not the only ones available. It is possible that the Hebrew term 'elep, normally understood as "a thousand," refers in military contexts to a military contingent comprised of a much smaller number of soldiers. Another option is that numbers were sometimes purposely exaggerated to emphasize the relative magnitude of an event. In either case, the actual number of Assyrian dead would have been much less than 185,000, but still a remarkable figure.[152]

Some doubt the historicity of this account because Sennacherib does not mention it in his records of the campaign. However, the omission of any reference to his defeat should come as no surprise, given Sennacherib's well-attested tendency to falsify history in his royal annals.[153] One should also note that Sennacherib does not claim to have taken Jerusalem or to have deposed Hezekiah. In this case his silence speaks volumes.

A later historical tradition preserved by Herodotus tells how Sennacherib's army, while fighting in the Delta of Egypt, was forced to retreat when mice ate their quivers, bowstrings, and shield grips. Some conjecture that the reference to mice may be a clue to what really happened. Perhaps bubonic plague broke out among the Assyrian army, forcing them to retreat. If so, it is possible that this plague was the instrument used by the Lord's killer angel. However, when the legend is examined carefully, it appears to have nothing to do with the biblical account.[154]

Another problem concerns the relationship of this event to the promise made by the Lord in verse 7. Was the Lord's word of assurance, in which he promised to make Sennacherib retreat through a mere report, fulfilled as prophesied? If one understands the report of Tirhakah's approach (see v. 9) as the referent, then it appears that the prophecy was not exactly fulfilled. Following this line of thinking, one might reason that Sennacherib's pride and persistent blasphemy (see vv. 10–13) prompted God to alter his initial plan and to judge him more severely. However, it is possible that the report referred to in verse 9 is not the one foreseen by the Lord, but is mentioned

152. For a study of the use of large numbers in the Hebrew Bible see D. M. Fouts, "The Use of Large Numbers in the Old Testament," Ph.D. diss., Dallas Theological Seminary, 1992.

153. See Laato, "Assyrian Propaganda," 198–226.

154. See Cogan and Tadmor, II Kings, 250–51.

by the author merely to heighten the story's dramatic tension. No other report is specifically mentioned in the chapter, but if an army was left at Jerusalem, as suggested earlier, one might imagine that Sennacherib, while fighting against Tirhakah (see v. 9), received the bad news from Jerusalem and decided to retreat. In this case a report, as prophesied, would have been the catalyst for his retreat.[155] Another option is that Sennacherib received an alarming report from home which, in conjunction with the disaster recorded in verse 36, prompted him to leave Judah.

No matter how one resolves this problem, one thing is clear—the second half of the prophecy made in verse 7, in which the Lord announced he would engineer the assassination of Sennacherib in his homeland, was fulfilled as stated. According to verse 38, Sennacherib was killed by two of his sons while he was worshiping in the temple of his god Nisroch. Ironically, Sennacherib's god could not save his devotee, even in his own temple. By way of contrast, when Hezekiah entered the temple of the Lord, he received an assuring promise of protection which was fulfilled. The assassins escaped to Ararat (that is, Urartu), located north of Assyria, and Esarhaddon succeeded his father on the Assyrian throne.

Secular history corroborates and clarifies some of the details of this account. Several ancient sources, including the Babylonian Chronicle, inform us that Sennacherib was indeed assassinated.[156] The secular traditions mention only one son as the culprit, but it is certainly reasonable that a second son (mentioned in the biblical text) might have served as an accomplice in the crime. The secular records identify the assassin as Arda-milissu (i.e., Arad-ninlil), who was upset that his father chose a younger son, Esarhaddon, as his successor.[157] According to Assyrian chronology, this incident occurred in 681 B.C., twenty years after Sennacherib's invasion of Judah.[158] Esarhaddon's reign, which lasted until 669 B.C., is well attested in Assyrian records.

Hezekiah Gets a New Lease on Life (38:1–8, 21–22)

Sometime shortly before or during Sennacherib's invasion of the land, Hezekiah became very ill. Isaiah, speaking for the Lord, notified the king that the illness was terminal and told him to get his house in order (v. 1). How-

---

155. Of course, if the army sent to Jerusalem returned with the Assyrian official, then v. 36 refers to the destruction of Sennacherib's main force, a disaster which the king would have witnessed firsthand.

156. For a concise discussion of the evidence, see Cogan and Tadmor, *II Kings*, 239–40. For a more thorough study of the incident, see S. Parpola, "The Murder of Sennacherib," in *Death in Mesopotamia*, ed. B. Alster (Copenhagen: Akademisk Forlag, 1980), 171–82.

157. The biblical form of the name, Adrammelech, is slightly different and may be the result of scribal errors during the transmission of the text.

158. Several details of the story receive no secular corroboration. As noted above, there is no record of Sennacherib having a son named Sharezer, and there is no evidence of a Mesopotamian god by the name of Nisroch.

ever, the king did not accept the news stoically. He wept bitterly and reminded the Lord that he had been a faithful and obedient servant (vv. 2–3).
The Lord was moved by Hezekiah's prayer and sorrow and decided to grant
him fifteen more years of life. Isaiah arrived on the scene, reported the good
news to the king, and gave Hezekiah's attendants medical instructions on
how to treat the king's illness (vv. 4–5, 21).[159]

Isaiah also brought an additional word from the Lord. Not only would
Hezekiah recover, but the Lord also promised that he would deliver both
Hezekiah and the city of Jerusalem from Sennacherib (v. 6). The close association of Hezekiah's recovery with the city's deliverance suggests that the
king epitomizes the city. Both Hezekiah and Jerusalem came to the threshold of death, but both were given a new lease on life because of the king's
faithful deeds.

Apparently overwhelmed by the news, Hezekiah asked for a sign that he
would truly recover and be able to worship at the temple once more (v. 22).
As a guarantee of his promise, the Lord refracted the sun's rays so that the
shadow they cast was reversed (vv. 7–8). Ironically this "sign" took place at
the "stairway of Ahaz," a structure named for the king who, in contrast to
Hezekiah, had rejected a confirming sign of divine deliverance (see Isa.
7:10–17).

Hezekiah Gives Thanks (38:9–20)

Following his recovery, Hezekiah offered up a prayer, in which he recalls his
lament and cry for help (vv. 10–16) and expresses his gratitude to God for
healing him (vv. 17–20). When initially told that he would not recover, Hezekiah lamented that he would die in the prime of life (he was only thirty-
eight or thirty-nine at this time)[160] and no longer be able to worship the Lord
(vv. 10–11). He compared his death to a shepherd folding up his tent, to a
weaver cutting fabric from a loom, and to the darkness of night replacing
daylight (v. 12). He felt like God had attacked him like a lion. In his intense
pain he suffered through the night and looked longingly toward the sky for
some relief (vv. 13–14). Though he felt victimized by God's sovereign will
(v. 15), he recognized that some divine decisions can be reversed and asked
that the Lord heal him and extend his life (v. 16).

Then the good news came and the king recovered. In retrospect he recognized that his suffering brought some benefit, perhaps because it drew him
closer to God and gave him renewed appreciation for the Lord's forgiveness
(v. 17). The reference to forgiveness of sins may suggest that Hezekiah considered his illness to be a form of divine punishment inflicted on him be-

159. Verses 21–22 were somehow misplaced in the transmission of the text and belong between vv.
6–7. See 2 Kings 20:6–9.

160. Second Kings 18:2 says Hezekiah was twenty-five when he succeeded Ahaz in 715 B.C. See Merrill, *Kingdom of Priests,* 410.

cause of his sinful human condition. As illustrated in the Book of Job, it was quite common in biblical times to interpret serious illness as a punishment for sin. Hezekiah did not want to go to the grave, for, in the worldview of the Hebrew Bible, the land of the dead was not a place where God was praised (v. 18). Only the living praise God's faithfulness (v. 19), and Hezekiah, confident of God's continuing protection, anticipated doing just that in the Lord's temple (v. 20).

Babylonian Envoys Pay Hezekiah a Visit (39:1–8)

Following Hezekiah's recovery, Merodach-baladan, who was attempting to regain control of Babylon from the Assyrians, decided to court Hezekiah's friendship (v. 1). As noted earlier, this incident probably followed God's deliverance of Jerusalem, an event that would have made Hezekiah an especially attractive ally to the anti-Assyrian crowd in the Near East.

Hezekiah greeted the envoys and showed them his wealth (v. 2), as if to say, "Yes, I would make a powerful ally, wouldn't I?" Hezekiah's actions were evidence of his pride and a self-sufficient attitude. Isaiah used this occasion to announce that Judah would someday be exiled to Babylon (vv. 3–5). The Babylonians would carry away the riches they had seen in Hezekiah's storehouses and palace (v. 6). The Davidic dynasty would even be jeopardized, as Hezekiah's descendants would be taken captive and forced to be eunuchs in the Babylonian king's palace (v. 7). These prophecies were fulfilled during the years 605–586 B.C., when Nebuchadnezzar carried off members of the royal family and the riches of the royal treasuries (see 2 Kings 24–25; Dan. 1).

In contrast to the way he had reacted to the announcement of his death (see 38:1–3), Hezekiah's response to this prophecy was quite stoical (v. 8). He acknowledged the Lord's decision was appropriate and seemed content that he would experience peace and security during his lifetime. How should one interpret the king's reply to God's word? On the one hand, his response seems rather self-centered, but, on the other hand, he may have been admitting his own guilt and recognizing God's mercy in delaying punishment.

Restoration and Renewal (Isaiah 40–55)

In these chapters Isaiah assumes the perspective of the future exiles. Having announced the exile, he projects himself into the future and speaks to the exiles as if actually present with them in captivity. As noted earlier, most assume that this part of the book originated with an anonymous exilic prophet (designated "Second Isaiah" or "Deutero-Isaiah") who sought to carry on the tradition of Isaiah of Jerusalem. But chapters 40–55 emphasize that the sovereign creator can announce how the future of Israel will ultimately turn out because he decrees what will transpire and then works in history to assure that his decree becomes reality. God transcends history and controls the rise and fall of nations. What better way to drive home this point than to speak to a future generation as if present?

The unit opens with a prologue in which the Lord promises to restore downtrodden Jerusalem (40:1–11). He attempts to convince the discouraged exiles that he is able to accomplish what he has promised (40:12–31). While emphasizing divine sovereignty, the Lord makes it apparent that the exiles are responsible for their future as well. They are in exile because of sin, and they must repent and accept God's offer of forgiveness and of covenantal renewal before God's promise can be fully realized. This offer, which holds divine sovereignty and human responsibility in careful balance, culminates with a call to covenantal renewal in chapter 55.

In between these poles the Lord stresses his superiority to the idol-gods of the Babylonians and makes it clear that these so-called deities will be unable to thwart his purposes for his people. The Lord will use as his instrument a pagan ruler, Cyrus, to deliver his people from exile. The Lord also introduces another key figure in Israel's future, a special servant who plays both royal and prophetic roles and is depicted as a new Moses who leads a new exodus out of captivity (see 42:1–7).

In chapters 49–55, Cyrus fades into the background, and this special servant takes center stage. At the beginning of this subunit, his roles and purpose are reiterated (see 49:1–13). He will experience opposition (see 50:4–9) and will suffer rejection (see 52:13–53:12), but, ironically, his suffering actually brings redemption for Israel and makes the offer of a new covenant possible. Interspersed between these passages dealing with the Lord's servant are portraits of Zion's restoration, a theme introduced in the prologue (see 49:14–26; 50:10–52:12; 54:1–17).

Comfort for Downtrodden Jerusalem (40:1–11)

Isaiah begins his message to the future exiles with a comforting announcement of Jerusalem's restoration. God instructs unidentified messengers[161] to comfort his people by announcing to Jerusalem that she has paid for her sins in full and that her time of hardship is over (vv. 1–2). The personified city represents its exiled people, whose rebellion against God resulted in the devastation of Jerusalem by the Babylonians. In the aftermath of this tragic event, Jerusalem lay uninhabited and in ruins for several years. The exiles probably wondered if God really cared about them and if they still had a fu-

---

161. The Hebrew verb forms translated "comfort," "speak," and "proclaim" in vv. 1–2 are all plural, as is the pronoun translated "your." The heralds in vv. 1–11 probably have no real identity, but are utilized for dramatic effect.

ture as a nation (see Isa. 40:27). This announcement makes it clear that God has not abandoned them and opens the door to a bright future.

A herald (called simply "a voice of one calling") shouts instructions to prepare the way for the Lord's return to Jerusalem (vv. 3–5). This voice is later associated with John the Baptist (see Matt. 3:3; Mark 1:3; Luke 3:4–6; John 1:23), but there is nothing in this context to suggest a prophet is in view.[162] The New Testament makes the addressees John's Jewish audience, but it is unlikely that God's people are addressed in Isaiah 40, for just after this they are pictured as lambs returning from exile (see v. 11). In Isaiah 40 the addressees probably have no real identity, but, like the unidentified heralds in verses 1–2, are utilized strictly for dramatic effect.[163]

The herald tells his audience to construct a processional highway for the Lord, who is ready to return victoriously to Jerusalem (v. 3; see v. 10). This road is to be built through the desert lying to the east, for the Lord will come from Babylon with his exiled people (see v. 11, as well as Isa. 35:1, 6–10). The herald envisions all obstacles being removed (v. 4). Utilizing hyperbole, he pictures the valleys being elevated and the mountains leveled. The king will then appear in his glory, which will be visible to everyone (v. 5). In this context God's "glory" is his outward royal splendor, which radiates like a light (see Isa. 24:23; 35:2; 60:1). The herald concludes with an assuring affirmation that this promise of the Lord's return comes from the Lord himself. As elsewhere in Isaiah, the words "for the mouth of the LORD has spoken" lend emphasis to a divine pronouncement concerning the future (see Isa. 1:2; 58:14).

This vision of the king's return continues in verse 9, but first there is a parenthesis (vv. 6–8). An unidentified herald says, "Cry out," to which another responds, "What shall I cry?"[164] The first herald then tells the second what he is to say. The message contrasts the frailty of human beings and their unreliable promises with the sovereign power of God and the trustworthiness of his word. Like grass, which withers before the hot wind (called here the "breath of the LORD"), human beings are here today and gone tomorrow.

---

162. The identification with John the Baptist is facilitated in the New Testament by connecting the phrase "in the desert" with the preceding "a voice of one calling." In the Hebrew text, "in the desert" goes with the following "prepare," and corresponds in the synonymous parallelism to "in the wilderness" in the next line. The New Testament rendition of the verse follows the Septuagint, which is apparently based on a Hebrew original where the phrase "in the wilderness" was accidentally omitted.

163. In the larger context of Isa. 40–55, it becomes apparent that the full restoration of Zion is contingent on the people's repentance. For this reason, the language of vv. 4–5 may be interpreted, when read in its larger context, as referring to moral preparation. Realizing that he was the prophet predicted by Malachi (see Mal. 4:5) and that Jesus the king would soon appear in Jerusalem in fulfillment of the promise of Isa. 40:3–5, John the Baptist identified himself as the voice of Isa. 40:3 and appropriated the message of Isa. 40:4 as his own.

164. Once again the heralds appear to be utilized strictly for dramatic purposes. However, the Septuagint reads, "and I said" in the second line of v. 6. In this case the prophet is speaking and is the addressee in the preceding line.

Their promises are short-lived and unreliable as well. In verse 6b many translations, like NIV, read, "All men are like grass, and all their glory is like the flowers of the field." However, the Hebrew word rendered "glory" (following the Septuagint) is the well-attested noun *khesed*, which means "faithfulness, devotion, loyalty, commitment." This nuance fits very well in this context. Human beings and their faithfulness (verbal expressions of faithfulness are specifically in view in this context, which focuses on the Lord's promise) are short-lived and unreliable, in stark contrast to the decrees and promises of the eternal God. In this context, "the word of our God" (v. 8) refers specifically to the promise of the king's return (see vv. 5, 10–11). Verses 1–5 announce, "Jerusalem's trouble is over! The king is returning! God promises!" Verses 6–8 then affirm, "You can bank on it! God's promises are reliable!"

Having been informed that relief is in sight, personified Jerusalem is now instructed to climb up on a high mountain and to proclaim the good news of the Lord's return to the other towns of Judah (v. 9). Many translations, like the NIV, read, "You who bring good tidings *to* Zion . . . You who bring good tidings *to* Jerusalem." However, in the Hebrew text there is no preposition "to" before "Zion" or "Jerusalem." The participle translated "you who bring good tidings" is feminine singular in form,[165] as are the verbs translated "go up" and "lift up." The grammatical evidence suggests that the instructions in verse 9 are addressed to personified Zion/Jerusalem.[166] The statement is better translated: "Go up on a high mountain, O herald Zion! Shout out loudly, O herald Jerusalem!" (NET).

As Jerusalem announces to the towns of Judah, "Here is your God," the Lord appears as a mighty warrior-king returning from battle with the spoils of victory, called here his "reward" and "recompense" (v. 10). The metaphor shifts in verse 11, which pictures the Lord as a shepherd leading his flock and holding the lambs in his arms. The sheep are his exiled people, whom he has taken as his reward.[167]

The metaphor of the "arm of the LORD" is used in an ironic manner in verses 10–11. In verse 10 it suggests military strength, which is its usual connotation (see Isa. 48:14; 51:9; 59:16; 63:5, 12). But in verse 11 the Lord's arm holds his lambs close to his heart. Here the image suggests tenderness, not violence. The twofold use of the image reminds us that one's view of God's awesome power is a matter of perspective. To his enemies his powerful arm is terrifying for it is the instrument of their defeat. But to his people this same arm should be a reassuring symbol for it reminds us of his ability to protect his own.

165. Isa. 41:27 and 52:7 speak of a herald sent *to* Zion, but there a *masculine* singular form is used to refer to the messenger.

166. "Zion" and "Jerusalem" are in grammatical apposition to "you who bring good tidings."

167. See Isa. 62:10–12, in which v. 12 indicates that the returning exiles (the Lord's "redeemed") are the "reward" which accompanies the Lord as he travels the highway back to Jerusalem.

The Lord Can Do What He Promises (40:12–31)

Having announced his intention to deliver his people, the Lord reminds them that he is fully capable of doing so. The exiles may have thought their God was restricted by time or space or limited in wisdom and power. Perhaps he was inferior to the Babylonian gods and his people were doomed to a life in exile. This section of the prologue corrects such thinking by affirming that the Lord is the eternal creator and king of the world whose authority, power, and wisdom have no limits.

The case for the Lord's sovereignty begins with a series of rhetorical questions (v. 12) that expect the answer, "No one but the LORD!" The Lord alone created the world, establishing its components (including the water, the heavens, and the mountains) in precise proportions, much as a merchant weighs out items in his scales.

Another set of questions follows (vv. 13–14), each of which anticipates the answer, "No one!" According to Babylonian myth, the god Marduk received advice from Ea, the god of wisdom, when he created the world. The Lord, the real creator of the world, consulted no one. He needed no advice or blueprint; his wisdom and skill were sufficient.[168]

In the presence of the sovereign creator and king, the nations are insignificant, like a mere drop in a bucket or dust on a scale (v. 15). The Lord's greatness transcends anything that humankind can imagine. Even if all the trees of the Lebanon forest were cut down for fuel and all its animals were killed for burnt offerings, the resulting sacrifice would not be an adequate testimony to the Lord's greatness (v. 16). When compared to the king, the nations lack real substance (v. 17), for it is the Lord, not the nations, who determines the outcome of history. The Lord is the incomparable God who is infinitely superior to the man-made metal and wooden idols of the pagans (vv. 18–20). He sits enthroned over the earth, whose puny inhabitants appear like little grasshoppers before him (vv. 21–22a). He stretches out the sky like a tent (v. 22b) and assigns the stars their places (vv. 25–26). He has the power to eliminate the earth's rulers; with a mere breath he blows them away like chaff in a windstorm (vv. 23–24). It is obvious that no nation, king, or god can thwart the Lord's purposes or prevent him from keeping his promises.

For this reason, the exiles need not feel abandoned by God or discouraged about the future. Exiled Israel's complaint (v. 27) suggests that the Lord might be limited in some way. Perhaps he, like so many of the pagan gods, has died, or maybe his jurisdiction is limited to Judah and does not include Babylon. Perhaps he is unable to devise an adequate plan to save his people or lacks the strength or energy to execute it. But such thinking is wrong. The prophet affirms that the God of Israel is the eternal God who transcends his-

---

168. See R. Whybray, *The Heavenly Counsellor in Isaiah xl 13–14: A Study of the Sources of the Theology of Deutero-Isaiah* (Cambridge: Cambridge University Press, 1971), 64–77.

tory and the creator of the world who rules over all nations (v. 28a). He never grows fatigued, nor is he ever lacking in wisdom (v. 28b). On the contrary, he grants supernatural power to those who maintain their faith in him (vv. 29–31). Even if robust young men wilt and stumble, the Lord's supernatural strength enables the faithful to endure hardship and "soar on wings like eagles." For this reason, the exiles should look to the future with anticipation and renewed hope.

The Nations Are Helpless (41:1–7)

The sovereign God turns to the nations and challenges them to a public debate (v. 1). The nations have rejected the one true God in favor of idols, but the Lord refuses to accept this offense to his reputation. He presents his control over human history as evidence of his incomparability and sovereignty. Speaking from the perspective of the future exiles, he points to Cyrus the Persian, called here "one from the east," as exhibit A. As he decreed through Isaiah, the Lord raised up Cyrus as his servant and allowed him to conquer kingdoms (vv. 2–3; see 44:28–45:4). The Lord's ability to announce events before they happen and then to bring them to pass proves that he rules the world (v. 4). Before God's conquering servant Cyrus, the helpless nations panic and frantically try to thwart God's power by making more idol-gods (vv. 5–7). But the immobility of these "gods" (see v. 7b) stands in stark contrast to the active power of the one true God who controls human history.

Encouraging News for the Exiles (41:8–20)

The Lord speaks next to his exiled people and assures them of his saving presence. He reminds them that they are his chosen servant. They have a privileged position as the descendants of Abraham, whom God calls his "friend" (v. 8; see 2 Chron. 20:7). This term probably reflects Abraham's covenantal relationship with God whereby the patriarch became God's partner in a special arrangement.[169] The Lord announces that he is ready to bring the exiles back from the distant land of Babylon (v. 9).[170] In contrast to the panic-stricken nations (see v. 5), the exiles need not fear, for the Lord promises to be with them and to strengthen them (vv. 10, 13). He is their "Redeemer" (v. 14), a title that recalls the exodus traditions (see Exod. 6:6; 15:13; Ps. 74:2; 77:16). In the sphere of Israelite family life, a "redeemer" was one who protected the interests of his extended family in a variety of ways. By applying the title to himself, the Lord reminds Israel that they are

169. See 1 Kings 5:1, in which Hiram of Tyre and David are described as "friends," that is, partners in a treaty arrangement.

170. Many translate the verbs in v. 9 with the past tense (see NIV "I took," "I called," "I said"), as if the Lord refers here to some past event. But in this context they are better taken as present perfect or simple present (with a factual, descriptive nuance). The Lord has taken hold of his people with the intention of bringing them back from exile, he summons them to return from that distant place, and he declares that they are his servant.

his family and that he intends to protect the family interests by delivering them from their bondage in exile.

Israel is viewed as an insignificant little worm (v. 14) by its adversaries, but that is about to change. Their enemies will dissolve before them (vv. 11–12), for the Lord will energize his people for battle and enable them to annihilate their foes (vv. 15–16). The destruction of these enemies is compared to the threshing process. Farmers used a threshing sledge to separate the grain from the chaff and then winnowed the grain by tossing it in the air. This allowed the wind to blow away the chaff.[171] In the extended metaphor Israel is the threshing sledge, equipped with sharp teeth that tear and rip. The powerful and proud enemies are compared to mountains and hills that are reduced to chaff. The Lord himself provides the wind that blows away the chaff (see 40:24).

In their afflicted and oppressed condition the exiles are like an extremely dehydrated man who cannot find the water he so desperately needs (v. 17a). But the Lord promises to intervene and create for his people a garden land filled with water (vv. 17b–18) and capable of sustaining lush growth (v. 19). The imagery symbolizes the restoration of life and divine blessing (see also 35:1, 6–7).

God's ultimate purpose in delivering his people is self-glorification (v. 20). When observers see God radically transform the circumstances of the exiles, they will recognize the awesome creative power of the sovereign king ("the Holy One of Israel"). Recognizing God as creator and as the sovereign authority in the universe is a prerequisite to genuine worship.

A Challenge to the Gods (41:21–29)

The Lord next turns to the pagan gods, who, for the sake of argument, are addressed as if they really do exist. He speaks as "Jacob's King," a title that affirms his right to rule his covenant people. For the nations to resist his salvific work on Israel's behalf, their gods must prove to be superior to the Lord. So he challenges them to present evidence of their divine character and power (v. 21). More specifically, he demands that they demonstrate their ability to predict events and then bring them to pass (vv. 22–23). If they really are sovereign over the affairs of history, they should be able to point to past predictions they made and brought to pass and they should not hesitate to offer new predictions about the future. However, the pagan gods are silent, for they lack real substance and do nothing (vv. 24, 29). By way of contrast, the Lord is active in history. He has raised up Cyrus the Persian as a world conqueror (v. 25), an event that he alone announced beforehand, through Isaiah the prophet (vv. 26–28).

Cyrus is here called "one from the north," whereas in verse 2 he is re-

171. On threshing and winnowing in ancient Israel, see Borowski, *Agriculture in Ancient Israel*, 62–69.

ferred to as "one from the east." C. R. North explains: "Cyrus' empire, now incorporating Media and Lydia, stretched in an arc from east of Babylonia round to the Aegean. He could thus be said to come from both the north and east."[172] The Persian ruler is also described as one who "calls on" the Lord's "name." This would seem to conflict with 45:4–5 and the extrabiblical Cyrus Cylinder, in which Cyrus attributes his success to various Mesopotamian deities, including Marduk.[173] However, the statement in 41:25 need not imply exclusive worship of Israel's God, and historiographical texts do indicate that Cyrus recognized the Lord's involvement in his success (see 2 Chron. 36:22–23; Ezra 1:1–4). Furthermore, his positive attitude toward the Babylonian gods, as expressed in the Cylinder, was, according to Yamauchi, "primarily . . . a propagandistic effort to manipulate public opinion and to legitimate Cyrus's authority over Babylon."[174]

A Champion of Justice (42:1–12)

As further evidence of his sovereignty, the Lord makes a new prediction. He announces that his "servant," energized by the divine Spirit, will bring justice to the earth (vv. 1–4). The Lord then addresses the servant and commissions him to be a covenant mediator and deliverer (vv. 5–7).

The identity of this servant has been hotly debated. Since Cyrus's success as God's instrument is depicted just before this, it would be natural to see 42:1–7 as also describing his work. However, Cyrus is portrayed as a violent conqueror (41:2–3, 25), while this servant is meek (42:2–3). Both Cyrus and the servant play important and interrelated roles in the outworking of God's plan for his people and the nations, but those roles appear to be distinct, suggesting that distinct individuals are in view.

The Septuagint (the ancient Greek version of the Old Testament) identifies the servant as "Jacob/Israel." This interpretation seems sound, for several times in chapters 40–48 Israel is designated as the Lord's servant (see 41:8–9; 42:19; 43:10; 44:1–2, 21; 45:4; 48:20). Furthermore, there are several verbal connections between 41:8–13 and 42:1–6. In both passages the Lord chooses (41:8–9; 42:1), upholds (41:10; 42:1), calls (41:9; 42:6), and grasps the hand of the servant (41:13; 42:6). However, there appear to be some differences between the servant depicted in 42:1–7 and the exiled nation Israel. While Israel is pictured as a blind servant (42:19) in need of forgiveness and deliverance, this servant opens blinded eyes and fulfills the role of deliverer (42:7). There is a close connection between Israel and the servant, but there is also a distinction.

That distinction comes into sharper focus later in this section. In 49:1–13, a passage that closely parallels 42:1–7 in many ways, the servant is

172. *The Second Isaiah* (Oxford: Clarendon, 1964), 105.
173. See Pritchard, *Ancient Near Eastern Texts,* 315–16.
174. Yamauchi, *Persia and the Bible,* 88.

specifically called "Israel" (v. 3), yet he is commissioned, as if he were a new Moses, to deliver exiled Israel (vv. 5–6), to mediate a new covenant for the nation (v. 8), and to lead God's people back to their land (vv. 9–13). It seems apparent that the servant, though "Israel" in some sense, is also distinct from exiled Israel. Later references to this servant support this conclusion, for the servant suffers on behalf of Israel (see the commentary below on 52:13–53:12, especially my observations concerning 53:8). Like many of the prophets, he faces opposition and oppression, but ironically his suffering plays a vital part in God's redemption of his sinful, exiled people. When viewed in this larger context, the servant is apparently an "ideal" Israel who is closely linked to, but nevertheless distinct from, the sinful nation.[175] The four passages that depict his ministry are appropriately labeled the "servant songs" (42:1–7; 49:1–13; 50:4–9; 52:13–53:12). Further discussion of this servant's identity and ministry must await our study of these texts.

The Lord singles out his servant for special attention because he has chosen and empowered him for the special task of establishing justice on the earth (vv. 1, 4). The servant will not be self-promoting (v. 2), nor will he exploit or oppress the weak and poor, compared here to a "bruised reed" and a "smoldering wick" (v. 3).

The image of a Spirit-empowered individual championing the cause of justice reminds one of the portrayal of the messianic king in Isaiah 11:1–9. In the ancient Near East, promoting justice in society was a royal responsibility.[176] Both the parallel to Isaiah 11 and the cultural context strongly suggest that the servant is a king. Though none of the servant songs connect this king to the Davidic dynasty, one must conclude that the servant and the ideal Davidic ruler of Isaiah 11 are one and the same.[177]

Having announced the servant's role, the Lord now gives the servant his formal commission. The Lord introduces himself as the one true God[178] who has created the world and gives life to the people who live on the earth (v. 5). This introduction is appropriate, for this servant song is part of the polemic against the pagan gods that begins in 41:21. The Lord promises to sustain and protect the servant as he carries out his task (v. 6a). This task is twofold: the servant is to mediate a covenant "for the people" and bring "light" to the Gentiles (v. 6b).

The Hebrew text actually says that God will make the servant "a covenant of people." Since a person cannot literally be a covenant, the term "co-

175. For further development of this point, see the commentary on 49:1–13 below.

176. See Moshe Weinfeld, *Social Justice in Ancient Israel and in the Ancient Near East* (Jerusalem: Magnes, 1995), 45–56.

177. See Richard Schultz, "The King in the Book of Isaiah," in *The Lord's Anointed*, ed. P. E. Satterthwaite, R. S. Hess, and G. J. Wenham (Grand Rapids: Baker, 1995), 154–59. Schultz suggests that Isaiah does not identify the servant with the Davidic line because, if he did so, it would detract from the distinct thematic emphases of this section of the prophecy.

178. The Hebrew text of v. 5a reads, "This is what *the* God, the LORD says." The definite article on "God" indicates that he is unique and superior to all other so-called gods.

venant" must be used here of one who inaugurates or mediates a covenant. The precise identity of "people" is uncertain. In verse 5 the term refers to humankind, and the reference to the "Gentiles" in the next line of verse 6 also suggests that all people are in view. In this case the servant is commissioned to be a covenant mediator between God and humankind. However, in Isaiah 49:8, in which the Lord also commissions the servant to be "a covenant of people," Israel seems to be in view (see vv. 9–13). Furthermore, other texts in Isaiah 40–66 anticipate God making a covenant with Israel (see 55:3; 59:21; 61:8), but no other texts in these chapters speak of a covenant between God and the nations. So it is possible that Isaiah 42:6b describes the servant's ministry to Israel as covenant mediator and his broader mission to the Gentiles as God's "light" bearer.

In this context, "light" symbolizes deliverance from bondage and oppression (see 49:6b and 51:4–6). One of the ways the servant will establish justice on the earth (see 42:1, 4) is by freeing prisoners from dark dungeons (v. 7). This probably does not refer to hardened, dangerous criminals, but to political prisoners or victims of social injustice. As they sit for prolonged periods in their dark cells, their eyes go blind, but the servant will release them and "open their eyes," as it were, by leading them out into the sunlight (see Ps. 146:7–8 for similar imagery).

The Lord concludes his argument by insisting that he will not share his sovereign glory with the gods of the nations (v. 8). In contrast to the idol-gods (see 41:22–23), the Lord has brought former predictions (in this case concerning Cyrus) to pass, and he has announced new things (related to the ministry of the servant) that will take place (v. 9). His sovereignty over history should be apparent to all. In response to the Lord's declaration of his sovereignty, the prophet calls upon all the earth's inhabitants, even those living on the distant horizons, to sing praises to the Lord and acknowledge his greatness (vv. 10–12).

The Incomparable Savior (42:13–44:23)

This section reiterates and develops the major themes of 40:1–42:12. Israel need not fear, for the Lord is superior to the gods of the nations and is both willing and able to deliver his people from exile. These chapters also raise the issue of Israel's sin, which is, of course, the reason why the nation is exiled and the sole obstacle to its restoration. The Lord is indeed ready and willing to deliver his people and to fulfill his promises to them, but before that can happen, they must come to grips with their sin.

This section displays a paneled structure in which the second half mirrors the thematic sequence of the first half:

Part One (42:13–43:13)
  A The Lord announces Israel's coming deliverance (42:13–17)

    B   The Lord confronts Israel over the issue of sin (42:18–25)
    C   The Lord encourages Israel not to fear (43:1–7)
    D   The Lord affirms his superiority to the idol-gods (43:8–13)

Part Two (43:14–44:20)
    A′ The Lord announces Israel's coming deliverance (43:14–21)
    B′ The Lord confronts Israel over the issue of sin (43:22–28)
    C′ The Lord encourages Israel not to fear (44:1–5)
    D′ The Lord affirms his superiority to the idol-gods (44:6–20)

Epilogue (44:21–23)

The Divine Warrior Strikes (42:13–17)

The prophet pictures the Lord as a mighty warrior marching into battle. He raises his battle cry and reveals his power (v. 13). We hear the Lord speaking. He acknowledges that he has "kept silent" as his people have suffered the humiliation of defeat and exile. But he can no longer restrain himself. Like a woman overcome with labor pains, he pants and gasps in his eagerness to launch an attack against his enemies (v. 14). The Lord will annihilate all opposition. He compares the destructive effects of his attack to a widespread drought that causes the trees on the mountains to wither and the rivers and pools to dry up (v. 15). Having released the blind prisoners (see v. 7), he will guide them back home, lighting up the path before them and removing the obstacles from their way (v. 16). The hostile nations, who trust in idols, will be humiliated (v. 17; see 41:5–7).

The Blinding Effects of Sin (42:18–25)

The Lord now takes the metaphor of blindness and gives it an ironic twist. In the preceding context (vv. 7, 16) blindness was associated with the exiles' imprisonment and depicted their afflicted condition. But here the Lord addresses the exiles as blind and deaf as he confronts them with their spiritual dullness (vv. 18–20). He chose Israel as his servant and messenger. He gave his people the Mosaic law and expected them to obey it. The law was intended to regulate Israelite society in such a way that the surrounding nations would be impressed by Israel's wisdom (v. 21; see Deut. 4:5–8). By showcasing God's law and attracting others to the one true God, Israel would be a "messenger" to the nations. But Israel was spiritually deaf and blind (see Isa. 6:9–10). Though her citizens witnessed God's self-revelation through his mighty deeds and through the law, they rebelled against the Lord (vv. 23–24), forcing him to unleash his inescapable, destructive judgment upon them (vv. 22, 25). Even then, they failed to respond properly to God's discipline (v. 25b). Instead of realizing that their sin was the primary reason why they were in exile, they complained that God had forgotten them (see 40:27), as if he was responsible for their condition.

Israel's Redeemer and Protector (43:1–7)

Despite their past failures, the Lord urges his people not to fear and assures them that he will ransom them from exile. Speaking as Israel's creator and sovereign king (vv. 1, 3), the Lord promises that he will protect them from all the forces that threaten to destroy them (v. 2). Using two metaphors, he promises to be with them when they pass through dangerous streams and when they walk through flaming fire. The first of these metaphors recalls the exodus tradition, while the second ironically reverses the imagery of the preceding oracle. In 42:25 flaming fire symbolized God's judgment on Israel, but now he promises that such fire will not hurt them.

The Lord affirms his special love for Israel (v. 4). He created Israel for his glory (v. 7), and he will not abandon his purpose. He will restore them from the distant lands where they have been scattered (vv. 5–6), even if it means that other nations must suffer (v. 3). Again utilizing metaphorical language, the Lord explains that he will offer Egypt, Cush, and Seba (all regions in Africa populated by descendants of Ham; see Gen. 10:6–7), as a ransom payment for Israel's release. The sovereign Lord, of course, does not need to "pay off" anyone in order to save his people, but the metaphor of a ransom price stresses the importance of Israel in God's eyes. The reality behind the imagery is the Persian conquest of Egypt. By raising up Cyrus as a conqueror and allowing the Persians to establish an empire, God doomed these foreign peoples to be subjects of the Persians. But he also made it possible for his own people to return from exile by decree of Cyrus.

Blind and Deaf Witnesses (43:8–13)

While the Lord promises to deliver exiled Israel, he also gives the nation an important task to accomplish. Before the gathered nations, he expects them to testify of his greatness and his superiority to the gods of the nations (vv. 8, 10). No one among the nations predicted the rise of Cyrus or announced Israel's coming deliverance (v. 9). Only the Lord proclaimed these things because he alone is worthy of the title "God" and is sovereign over history. For this reason, he alone can save his people (vv. 11–12). When he decides to act, no one is able to prevent him from accomplishing what he has decreed (v. 13).

Deliverance from Babylon (43:14–21)

Speaking as Israel's creator, king, and savior, the Lord affirms that he will defeat Babylon and release his people from bondage (vv. 14–15). The exodus was the defining moment in Israel's history. God miraculously divided the sea and allowed them to escape the pursuing Egyptians (v. 16). When the Egyptians chased them into the sea, the Lord annihilated the Egyptian soldiers and chariots (v. 17). However, the coming deliverance of the exiles, called here a "new thing" (v. 19), will overshadow anything God did in the past (v. 18). The Lord will lead his people back home, protecting them from dangerous animals and providing for their needs along the way (vv. 19–21).

Facing Up to an Ugly Past (43:22–28)

Before developing this vision of future deliverance (see 44:1–5), the Lord again raises the issue of Israel's sinful past (see 42:18–25). Though the Lord created Israel to worship him (see 43:21), they rejected him (v. 22). At this point the exiles probably would have objected, pointing out that Israel had always offered plenty of sacrifices to the Lord. However, from the Lord's perspective such ritual was unacceptable, because the ones offering the sacrifices were so sinful. To make this point, the Lord actually denies that Israel has brought him offerings (vv. 23–24). On the surface these verses appear to be condemning Israel for failing to bring the proper sacrifices, but such an accusation is problematic and seemingly unfair. The Lord cannot be referring to the nation's behavior while in exile, for sacrificial rituals were impossible under such conditions and could hardly have been expected by the Lord. If these verses refer to the nation's conduct before the exile, they seem to contradict other passages that depict preexilic Israel as bringing excessive sacrifices (see, for example, Isa. 1:11–14; Jer. 6:20; Amos 4:4–5, 5:21–23). Rather than being a condemnation of Israel's failure to bring sacrifices, these verses are better taken as a highly rhetorical comment on the worthlessness of Israel's religious ritual. As noted above, Israel may have brought sacrifices, but not to the Lord, for he did not accept them or even want them.[179]

The Lord was ready to forgive Israel's sin (v. 25), but Israel must first own up to her sinful past and stop claiming to be innocent (v. 26). The father of the nation, Jacob, was a sinner and a whole series of national leaders since that time had rebelled against the Lord (v. 27).[180] This rebellion forced the Lord to take drastic measures and to bring severe judgment down upon the nation.[181]

---

179. For fuller discussion, see North, *Second Isaiah,* 127, and R. Whybray, *Isaiah 40–66,* NCB (Grand Rapids: Eerdmans, 1975), 91.

180. The identity of the nation's "first father" has been debated. The phrase could refer to Abraham (see 51:2), but Isaiah does not refer to him in a negative way elsewhere (see 29:22; 41:8; 63:16). A more likely candidate is Jacob, also referred to as the nation's "father" elsewhere in the book (see 58:14; 63:16). Jacob was the father of the twelve tribes that comprised Israel, and his struggle with God foreshadowed the rebellion of his descendants (see Hos. 12:2–4).

181. NIV translates v. 28 with the future tense, but in this context judgment has already taken place. The prefixed verbal forms with the prefixed, non-consecutive form of the conjunction, are normally taken as imperfect and cohortative, respectively. However, the forms are better understood as preterites and better translated with the past tense. Some want to emend the prefixed conjunctions on both forms to the consecutive form, but this is unnecessary. In poetry the preterite can appear with *waw*-conjunctive or even without a *waw.*

A Thirsty Land Drinks (44:1–5)

The Lord again assures his chosen people of his help (vv. 1–2). Comparing the exiled nation to parched ground, the Lord promises that he will send his blessings like rain and renew Israel (v. 3). The descendants of the exilic community will flourish like trees growing beside a stream (v. 4) and will unashamedly declare their allegiance to the Lord (v. 5).

In verse 2 the Lord addresses Israel as "Jeshurun," which means "upright one." This title appears only here and in Deuteronomy 32–33. In Deuteronomy 32:15, Jeshurun (= Israel) becomes prosperous through the Lord's blessings (see vv. 13–14), but then rebels against its Lord by turning to other gods (vv. 16–18). In Deuteronomy 33, the Lord, as Jeshurun's king (v. 5), superintends the blessings of the tribes, which conclude with the affirmation that "there is no one like the God of Jeshurun" (v. 26) who, as Israel's helper, blesses the nation in both military and agricultural endeavors (vv. 27–29). The appearance of the title Jeshurun in Isaiah 44:3 is appropriate because the context deals with the same themes associated with the title in Deuteronomy 32–33, namely the Lord's helping presence (see Isa. 44:2b and Deut. 33:26), the futility of idolatry (see Isa. 44:6–20 and Deut. 32:15–21), and the Lord's blessings (see Isa. 44:3–5 and Deut. 32:13–15; 33:26–29).

Lampooning the Gods (44:6–20)

Once more the Lord affirms that he is the one true God and challenges anyone to present evidence to the contrary (vv. 6–7). He urges Israel to testify to his incomparability and declares that he is the nation's only reliable protector (v. 8).

The titles "God" and "Rock" in the poetic parallelism of verse 8b, like Jeshurun in verse 3, echo Deuteronomy 32, where they are used of the Lord as the God who gave Israel birth (vv. 15, 18) and rules as the nation's faithful king (vv. 4, 15). Deuteronomy depicts rebellious Israel turning to false gods (vv. 15, 17–18), prompting an outburst of God's wrath (v. 30). However, the Lord promises to avenge his people by destroying their enemies, whose gods are incapable of defending them (vv. 31, 37). The Lord proves to be the only capable God and reliable protector ("Rock"). In the chronological scheme of Deuteronomy 32 the generation addressed by the Lord in Isaiah 44 stands between judgment and deliverance. They have already experienced the judgment threatened in Deuteronomy 32. However, by addressing them as Jeshurun and identifying himself as the "Rock" in a context of reassurance and promise, the Lord invites exiled Israel to turn their attention to the promises of Deuteronomy 32:34–43.

With biting sarcasm the Lord lampoons the pagan gods and their worshipers. Those who trust in idols are certain to be disappointed and humiliated, for these so-called gods are the products of human hands (vv. 9–11).

Two verbal links between verses 9–11 and verses 1–8 highlight the contrast between the Lord and the pagan gods. First, the Lord "formed" (Heb. *yatsar*) his people Israel (v. 2); those "who make" (*yatsar* again) idols (v. 9) and one "who shapes" (*yatsar*) a god produce the pagan gods. The point is clear—the Lord is the creator, but the pagan gods are created. Second, Israel need not "be afraid" (v. 8, Heb. *pakhad*), but the worshipers of idols are terrified before their enemies (see "terror" in v. 11, which translates Heb. *pakhad*). The point is clear—the Lord makes his people secure, but the pagan gods are incapable of helping their devotees.

The Lord drives home these points by focusing on the man-made character of the idols. Blacksmiths and carpenters work hard to create an idol-god, which is made in the image of man and is confined to a shrine where it sits and does nothing (vv. 12–13). The exertion robs the workers of their strength, but apparently they never stop to connect the dots. If the creators are so susceptible to weakness and fatigue, how inadequate and weak must the power of the idol-god be. By way of contrast, the Lord empowers his weary people with supernatural strength (see 40:29–31). The idols sit in little shrines, but the Lord sits on the earth's horizon and rules over the affairs of men (see 40:22–23).

The lampooning of the man-made idol-gods continues in verses 14–20. The idol is made of wood taken from a tree planted by a man (v. 14). A man uses half of the wood to build a fire so he can warm himself and cook his food. He then forms the other half of the wood into an image to which he offers worship and appeals for aid (vv. 15–17). Idol worshipers are blind to the absurdity of all this (v. 18). Their eyes are plastered over, as it were, and they never stop to think that the idol-god they worship is made of the same substance as the wood burning in the fire (vv. 19–20).

An Invitation and Response (44:21–23)

The Lord concludes the lengthy argument of this section with an invitation to his people. He urges them to consider carefully all that he has said to them and assures them that forgiveness is available (vv. 21–22a). In fact, the Lord declares that he has already forgiven them and removed their sins, which he compares to a cloud in the sky that is visible one minute and then quickly vanishes (see Job 7:9; 30:15; Hos. 6:4; 13:3). All Israel must do is appropriate this offer by repenting (v. 22b). Since the call to covenant renewal in Isaiah 55:7 views forgiveness as being the consequence of repentance, it is likely that the Lord uses hyperbole here in 44:22. By speaking of their sins as being forgiven prior to repentance, he emphasizes his willingness to restore Israel. From his standpoint, repentance is the lone remaining condition to reconciliation. In response to the Lord's invitation, the prophet calls upon the heavens and earth, as well as the personified mountains and forests, to praise the Lord and acknowledge his kindness to Israel (v. 23).

Cyrus, the Lord's Anointed One (44:24–45:8)

Having described the victories of a mighty conqueror from the east/north (see 41:2–3, 25), the Lord now identifies this king by name and assures him of success. As the sovereign creator of the world (v. 24), the Lord controls history. He decrees through his prophetic messengers, one of whom was Isaiah, that Jerusalem and the towns of Judah will be rebuilt (v. 26). His instrument in accomplishing this will be Cyrus, called here God's "shepherd," for his conquests and decrees will benefit God's people (v. 28). Of course, there will be opposition, but just as he dried up the Red Sea in the days of Moses, so the Lord will remove all obstacles that stand in the way (v. 27).

The Babylonian prophets and omen readers (see NIV "diviners") will try to thwart the Lord's purposes (v. 25). Omen reading was indispensable to Mesopotamian religion and society. By observing casual phenomena, examining animals' inner organs, and making astrological observations, the Babylonian omen readers believed they could discern the will of the gods and control the future. They catalogued omens and concocted counteromens to ward off disaster.[182] As Cyrus marches toward Babylon, the prophets and omen readers will try to stave off defeat, but to no avail, for the Lord has chosen the Persian king for this special task and will empower him (45:1). He even refers to Cyrus as his "anointed" one, a title normally reserved for an Israelite priest or king,[183] and he announces that he will take hold of Cyrus's right hand, guaranteeing the Persian's success.

Speaking directly to Cyrus, the Lord promises that he will go before the king and remove all obstacles (v. 2). As a reward for his service, the Lord will give Cyrus the riches of his defeated foes (v. 3a). Though the pagan king Cyrus does not presently realize the Lord is the one true God, he will come to recognize the sovereign power of Israel's God (vv. 3b–6).[184] The Lord's ultimate purpose in this is to deliver his people and to reveal his greatness to Cyrus and the nations. Through his control of historical events, the Lord will demonstrate that he is sovereign over his world. In accordance with his de-

---

182. For a helpful study of Mesopotamian divination, see Wilson, *Prophecy and Society in Ancient Israel*, 90–110, as well as A. Leo Oppenheim, *Ancient Mesopotamia*, rev. ed. (Chicago: University of Chicago Press, 1977), 206–27.

183. The title is most often used of David or one of his royal descendants.

184. Though the evidence suggests that Cyrus did remain a polytheist (see the Cyrus Cylinder, where he gives praise to Marduk and the Babylonian gods), the Bible does indicate that he recognized the role of Israel's God in his success (see 2 Chron. 36:22–23; Ezra 1:2–4). For fuller discussion see my earlier comments on Isa. 41:25.

creed will, he creates both "light," here symbolizing life and prosperity, and "darkness," here symbolizing disaster and death (v. 7). He can cause wars to cease and peace to predominate (as he was about to do for his exiled people through Cyrus), or he can bring calamity and judgment on nations (as he was about to do to Babylon through Cyrus).[185]

To emphasize his commitment to his people's restoration, the Lord once more utilizes the metaphor of water (v. 8). In dramatic style he commands the clouds in the sky to send their showers and cause crops to spring up from the earth. The rain symbolizes deliverance, and the growth of vegetation pictures the renewed vitality of God's restored people.

For many, the naming of Cyrus in these verses is a telltale sign that this section of the prophecy originates in the sixth century b.c., during the reign of the Persian king. Some reject the idea of predictive prophecy out of hand. To such skeptics we point out that the sovereign Creator who speaks so eloquently of his greatness in this passage is certainly capable of foretelling and determining the future. Indeed, his ability to do so is one of the key themes of this section of Isaiah. Others, though agreeing that the Bible contains predictive prophecy, point out that such prophecy does not include the names of future individuals. For these critics, the question is not "Could God predict an individual's name decades before he was born?" but "Does God, in predicting future events, actually give such specific details?" Defenders of Isaianic authorship often point out that King Josiah's name was prophesied more than three hundred years before he was born (1 Kings 13:2). Nevertheless, this kind of specificity is limited to these two texts. For this reason, some, while understanding both prophecies as genuine predictions that were fulfilled, prefer to take the proper names in both prophecies as later scribal additions designed to link the historical fulfillment with the prophecy.[186]

A Warning to Skeptics (45:9–19)

The Babylonian omen readers were not the only ones opposing the Lord. Apparently, some of the exiles were doubting his wisdom (vv. 9–11) and complaining that he was a hidden God (v. 15). Comparing these critics to an insignificant piece of pottery lying on the ground, the Lord argued that

---

185. Verse 7 should not be understood as teaching divine pancausality. As Fredrik Lindström observes, "[H]ere the positive phrases have to do with YHWH's salvific intervention on behalf of his people, while the negative phrases refer to the destruction of Babylonian power. Thus the activity ascribed to YHWH in this passage has exclusively to do with the imminent liberation of Israel from her Babylonian captivity." See his *God and the Origin of Evil* (Lund: CWK Gleerup, 1983), 236.

186. R. K. Harrison, for example, prefers "to regard the references to Cyrus in Isaiah 44:28 and 45:1 as constituting explanatory glosses imposed upon the original text by a post-exilic copyist." He adds that "it seems most probable that they comprise scribal additions inserted in order to explain what was thought to be the real significance of the prophecy." See his *Introduction to the Old Testament* (Grand Rapids: Eerdmans, 1969), 794. Oddly, however, Harrison understands the inclusion of Josiah's name in 1 Kings 13:2 as genuine prediction. (See pp. 754, 757.)

it is absurd and arrogant for that which is created to question the work of the creator. This is especially true when the creator is the sovereign God who made the world with a distinct design in mind (vv. 12, 18). The Lord knows what he is doing. He will raise up Cyrus, who will deliver his people from exile and restore them to their city (v. 13). Foreigners will become Israel's subjects and be forced to acknowledge the incomparability of the Lord as they pay their tribute (v. 14). The worshipers of idols will be humiliated, but Israel will be vindicated and never again subjected to shame (vv. 16–17). Contrary to the opinion of some, the Lord is not a hidden God, but rather a God who reveals his purposes and proves worthy of his people's allegiance (v. 19).

An Appeal to the Nations (45:20–25)

Once more the Lord confronts the idolatrous, pagan nations. He points out the futility of worshiping false gods (v. 20) and challenges the nations to consider the facts. It is the Lord alone who controls history (v. 21). He then appeals to the nations to turn to him in faith and accept the salvation he offers (v. 22). It makes sense to respond positively to this offer, for a day is coming when everyone will be forced to bow the knee and acknowledge the Lord's sovereignty (v. 23). On that day the enemies of God will be humiliated, while Israel will be vindicated (vv. 24–25).

Babylon's Demise Is Israel's Opportunity (46:1–48:22)

These three chapters display the following structure:

> A   Taunt against the Babylonian gods (46:1–2)
> B   Appeal to Israel (46:3–13)
> A´ Taunt against Babylon (47:1–15)
> B´ Appeal to Israel (48:1–22)

Helpless Gods (46:1–2)

The Lord begins by lampooning the Babylonian gods Bel and Nebo. "Bel," meaning "lord," was a title for Marduk, the patron deity of Babylon. Nebo (or Nabu) was Marduk's son and the patron deity of Borsippa. He was closely associated with the scribal arts and viewed as a god of wisdom.[187] The images of these gods will be carted away into exile in the aftermath of Babylon's fall. The idols are so heavy they weigh down and exhaust the poor animals assigned to carry them. The point is clear: these so-called gods cannot rescue their worshipers or even prevent their own capture. Consequently, they should not be feared and are certainly not worthy of worship.

---

187. See Helmer Ringgren, *Religions of the Ancient Near East*, trans. J. Sturdy (Philadelphia: Westminster, 1973), 67.

Israel's Incomparable God (46:3–13)

In contrast to the inactive, man-made pagan gods, who are carted around by animals (vv. 1–2) or carried on the shoulders of their worshipers (vv. 6–7), Israel's God has carried his people from the very beginning of their history and promises to sustain them in the future (vv. 3–5). He challenges his rebellious exiled people to consider the facts carefully (v. 8). He has demonstrated his incomparability in the past and will once again reveal his greatness in the days ahead. He will bring his purposes to pass through Cyrus, who is called here "a bird of prey" from the east (vv. 9–11). Though Israel is stubborn and disobedient, the Lord will open the door to a new and exciting future (vv. 12–13).

The Humiliation of Queen Babylon (47:1–15)

The Lord once again taunts Babylon. He pictures the city as a proud, wicked queen who is confident that she is secure from any danger (vv. 7–8, 10). However, disaster will strike suddenly. All of her attempts to ward off destruction through omen reading, counteromens, and incantations will fail (vv. 9, 11–13). The diviners and astrologers will be helpless before the Lord's fiery judgment (vv. 14–15), and Babylon will be humiliated. The Lord uses a vivid metaphor to depict Babylon's demise (vv. 1–5). The delicate and pampered queen will be forced to descend from her throne and sit mourning in the dirt. She will be reduced to excruciating slave labor and taken into exile. As she crosses streams on foot, she will be forced to remove her skirt and expose her private parts for all to see. The punishment, though harsh, is appropriate, for the Lord must repay Babylon for her mistreatment of his people (note "I will take vengeance," v. 3). The Lord used the Babylonians as his instrument of discipline, but they were merciless and even made the elderly perform hard labor (v. 6).

Israel Must Pay Attention (48:1–22)

The Lord again addresses his exiled people and urges them to pay attention to what he has to say (vv. 1–2). He begins with a history lesson (vv. 3–6a). In Israel's past the Lord announced events before they happened and then brought them to pass. The Lord did this because he knew how stubborn idolatrous Israel is. He had to make it clear that he, not the pagan gods, controls his people's destiny.

For the same reason he now announces "new things" before they transpire (vv. 6b–7). Because of Israel's rebellion (v. 8), the Lord was forced to discipline them severely (v. 10). However, he could not totally destroy them, for that would cause some to call into question his reputation as a faithful God (v. 9). For the sake of his own honor, the Lord must intervene (v. 11). Speaking as the sovereign lord of history and as the creator of the world (vv.

12–13), he asserts that he, not one of the idol-gods, has announced the appearance of Cyrus, who will carry out the Lord's purpose by attacking Babylon (vv. 14–16a). Cyrus himself is even depicted as agreeing with this, as he declares that the Lord has commissioned him and supernaturally energized him (v. 16b). The identity of the speaker in verse 16b is not given. Some identify the speaker as the prophet or as the Lord's special servant (note the reference to the Lord's Spirit and compare this to 42:1 and 61:1). However, verse 14 suggests that the speaker here is Cyrus, called the "Lord's chosen ally" and depicted as the conqueror of Babylon.

The tone now becomes more positive, as the Lord, speaking as Israel's redeemer and sovereign king, identifies himself as his people's teacher and moral guide (v. 17). The Lord has always wanted to bless Israel with security and numerous descendants, but Israel's sinful rebellion prevented that from happening (vv. 18–19). The time has come for God's ideal to be realized. The Lord urges the exiles to leave Babylon (v. 20) and to celebrate God's deliverance and provision (v. 21), which is described with imagery that echoes the exodus tradition (see Exod. 17:6; Num. 20:11). This speech ends with a sobering reminder that the wicked will not experience the peace promised by God (v. 22).

A Vindicated Servant and a Restored City (49:1–54:17)

In chapters 49–54, the focus oscillates between the Lord's special servant (49:1–13; 50:4–9; 52:13–53:12) and Zion's restoration and renewal (49:14–50:3; 50:10–52:12; 54:1–17). Despite opposition and suffering, the servant persists in his mission to lead sinful Israel back to God. This paves the way for the restoration of Jerusalem and the renewal of God's covenant relationship with his people (see chapter 55).

The Servant Guides Israel Home (49:1–13)

Cyrus now fades from the picture, and the Lord's special servant, introduced in the first of the so-called servant songs (see 42:1–9), takes center stage. This second servant song begins with the servant addressing the distant nations (v. 1a). This is appropriate because the servant's task is to extend God's salvific work to the ends of the earth (see v. 6 and 42:6).

The servant describes his special relationship to God. Even before the servant's birth, the Lord chose and equipped him for a special task (vv. 1b–2). The servant's mouth (which stands for the words he speaks) is compared to a sharp sword. This could suggest that his words will have the power to destroy, but in the context of the servant songs, which do not portray the servant as a conquering hero, the imagery probably means simply that the servant will be an effective spokesman for God (see 50:4). God keeps his hand on this "sword" so he can draw it for use at the appropriate time. The servant himself is compared to a sharpened arrow placed in a quiver, reserved for an opportune time. Again the image of an arrow might suggest a violent mission, but it is more likely that the servant's effectiveness in accomplishing God's purposes is the main point here.

The servant next recalls his commission from God (v. 3). The Lord addresses his servant as "Israel" (v. 3), suggesting that the nation Israel is in view. Yet the matter is not this simple. This servant "Israel" is commissioned to deliver exiled Israel (vv. 5–6), to mediate a new covenant for the nation (v. 8), and to lead God's people back to their land (vv. 9–13). As noted earlier, it seems clear that the servant, though "Israel" in some sense, is also distinct from exiled Israel. The servant is apparently an "ideal" Israel who is closely linked to, but nevertheless distinct from the sinful nation. He can be addressed as "Israel" because he embodies God's ideal for his people. He will restore the wayward, exiled nation to God and fulfill the role of God's messenger to the nations. God had always intended that Israel be a beacon to the nations by obeying his law and demonstrating to the watching world what a just society looks like (see Deut. 4:5–8; Isa. 42:21). In this way God would be glorified. Israel failed in its mission, but the servant will succeed (see v. 6).

Yet the pathway to success is not smooth. The servant confesses some discouragement because he feared that his hard work was in vain (v. 4a). This theme is developed more fully in the third and especially fourth servant songs, where we discover that opposition and suffering are the catalyst for this concern. However, despite the apparent lack of positive results, the servant remains confident that the Lord will eventually reward him for his efforts (v. 4b).

The servant next informs his audience of his renewed and expanded commission from the Lord (vv. 5–6). The servant's initial task was to restore Israel to a proper relationship with God, but his mission will include far more than that. He will also be "a light for the Gentiles." As noted earlier, "light" here symbolizes deliverance from bondage and oppression (see 42:6–7 and 51:4–6). When this task is accomplished, the servant, though once despised and subservient to rulers, will be vindicated by God (v. 7; see 52:13–15).

The servant's ministry to Israel now receives special attention. Energized by God, the servant will mediate a new covenant between God and Israel and lead God's people back to their land (v. 8). After releasing them from prison, he will guide them back home (v. 9). Along the way, God will provide food and water, and remove all obstacles (vv. 10–11). God's exiled people will return from all directions, prompting all observers to celebrate God's mercy toward his people (vv. 12–13). As one reads this portrayal of the servant, one cannot help but think of Moses. Like Moses of old, the servant is God's instrument in delivering his people from bondage, mediating a covenant with them (see Exod. 34:27 in this regard), and guiding them to their home.[188]

Zion's Children Return (49:14–50:3)

The scene now shifts from the returning exiles to the desolate city of Jerusalem. Pictured as a woman who has been abandoned by her husband, Zion laments that the Lord has forsaken her (v. 14). In response the Lord argues that Zion's complaint is unfounded. His attachment to Zion is as strong as a mother's love for her child. There is a natural bond that unites a mother and child, causing the mother to treat her baby with compassion (v. 15a). But even if mothers began to disregard that bond and neglect their babies, the Lord's devotion to Zion would remain (v. 15b), for she is always in the forefront of his thoughts (v. 16).

The scene shifts back to the returning exiles. As they arrive in the land and begin to repopulate it, the hostile invaders who destroyed the city and devastated the land disappear (v. 17). The returning exiles will become a source of pride to Zion, like a bride's jewelry (v. 18). These "children born during" Zion's "bereavement" will be so numerous that the land will not be able to hold them all (vv. 19–20). All of this will overwhelm bewildered Zion, who will confess that she does not even remember giving birth to these children (v. 21). Even the once hostile nations will get in on the act and transport Zion's children back home (v. 22). Kings and queens will become the caretakers of Zion's children and submit to Zion's authority (v. 23a). Zion will recognize that her Lord really is true to his name "Yahweh," which means "he will be (with you)" (see Exod. 3:12–15), and does not disappoint those who place their trust in him (v. 23b).[189]

The exiles might find this announcement of Zion's restoration difficult to believe. After all, the Babylonian conquerors were powerful and would

---

188. For a detailed study of the servant as a second Moses, see G. P. Hugenberger, "The Servant of the Lord in the 'Servant Songs' of Isaiah: A Second Moses Figure," in Satterthwaite, Hess, and Wenham, *The Lord's Anointed*, 105–40.

189. The name Yahweh is derived from an original root *hwh* or *hwy* (= Hebrew *hyh*), "to be." It is not certain if the form is basic (Qal/G stem) or causative (Hiphil/H stem). The basic form would highlight God's existence or presence, "he is/will be," while the causative form would focus on his creative power, "he causes (something) to be, he creates." Exod. 3:12–16 suggests the former is correct. When Moses asks God his name, the Lord responds by identifying himself as "I am/will be" (basic form, first person; v. 14), which he then converts to "Yahweh" (third person; vv. 15–16) to facilitate reference. (It is far less confusing to refer to God as "he is/will be" than to call him "I am/will be." On the other hand it is much more natural for God to refer to himself as "I am/will be" than to call himself "he is/will be.") The context suggests that the name points to God's enabling and saving presence with his people, not to his mere existence (vv. 12, 15–17). I would paraphrase God's words to Moses in vv. 14–15 as follows: "Call me I AM/WILL BE THE EVER PRESENT HELPER because I am/will be indeed the ever present helper. This is what you should say to the Israelites: 'I AM/WILL BE THE EVER PRESENT HELPER has sent me to you'. . . . Say to the Israelites, 'HE (WHO) IS/WILL BE THE EVER PRESENT HELPER, the God of your fathers, the God of Abraham, the God of Isaac, and the God of Jacob has sent me to you.' This will be my name forever, by which I will be remembered from generation to generation."

not relinquish their captives without a fight. Even though one cannot normally take plunder away from a victorious warrior (v. 24), the Lord is capable of doing just that. He will steal mighty Babylon's plunder (his exiled people) away from the captors (v. 25) and annihilate the oppressors (v. 26a). Those who witness the bloodbath will recognize that the Lord is indeed Israel's deliverer, protector, and mighty king (v. 26b).

Babylonian military power was not the real issue anyway. The Israelites were in exile because of their sins, not because of Babylonian military superiority (50:1). The same God who sent them into exile because of their sins was certainly capable of delivering them from captivity. He controls the forces of nature and with a mere word can dry up the sea (vv. 2–3).

Some find the logic of the argument in verse 1 a bit difficult to follow. On the surface the rhetorical questions in the first half of the verse might seem to imply that the Lord did not divorce his "wife" (Zion) or sell his children (the Israelites) into slavery. Yet the second half of the verse indicates that he did just that. He admits that he did sell the Israelites into slavery, but it was because of their sins, not because of some debt he owed. He also admits he divorced Zion, but that too was the result of the nation's sins. So the first rhetorical question, rather than implying no divorce occurred, asks for the certificate to be produced so the accuser can see the reason for the divorce in black and white. The second question, rather than implying no sale occurred, simply makes the point that the Lord did not sell them into slavery to pay off a debt, but to punish them for their sins.

The Servant Expresses His Trust (50:4–9)

Like the second servant song (see 49:1–4), this third servant song contains the servant's confession of trust in the Lord. This song, unlike the others, does not specifically identify the servant as such, but several clues suggest he is the speaker. His role as the Lord's spokesman (v. 4; see 49:2), his willingness to suffer (v. 6; see 52:13–53:12), his persistence in the face of opposition (v. 7; see 42:4), and his confidence that the Lord will vindicate him (vv. 8–9; see 49:4; 52:13–15; 53:10–12) are themes that appear in the other songs. Furthermore, in verse 10 the Lord, as if responding to the servant's confession, asks Israel, "Who among you fears the LORD and obeys the word of his servant?"

The servant begins this confession of trust by affirming that the sovereign Lord has given him the capacity to encourage those who are beaten

---

For a more detailed defense of this interpretation see Mettinger, *In Search of God,* 33–36. In addition to highlighting God's active presence with his people, the name Yahweh also points to his faithfulness to his promises. In the role of El Shaddai, God had promised the fathers that he would bless their descendants; now he comes as Yahweh to be with their descendants and fulfill those promises. In other words, Yahweh's presence must be understood within a covenantal framework, where his enablement is an outward expression of his faithfulness to his promise.

down (v. 4a). He follows the Lord's daily instructions and does not withdraw when opposition arises (vv. 4b–5). He willingly submits to physical violence and insults (v. 6) because he is confident the Lord will vindicate him (vv. 7–8a). He challenges his opponents to confront him with their accusations (v. 8b) because he knows the Lord is his helper and that his accusers will be destroyed in due time, just like a garment eaten by moths (v. 9).

The Lord Returns to Zion (50:10–52:12)

As if to affirm that the servant's confidence is well-placed, the Lord now speaks.[190] He first addresses his loyal followers, who are identified as those who fear him and obey the servant's instructions (v. 10a). Though these godly individuals are living in the darkness of exile, they, like the servant, must maintain their trust in the Lord (v. 10b), for vindication will come (see 51:1–8). The Lord also addresses the evildoers who attack his servant so violently. He warns them that their violence will be self-destructive and that they will be special objects of divine wrath (v. 11).

Resuming his address to the godly, the Lord urges them to recall their heritage (51:1–2). Their ancestors Abraham and Sarah were childless, but then the Lord intervened, endued them with the potency to reproduce, and gave them numerous descendants. In the same way he will miraculously restore barren and devastated Zion, transforming her ruins into an Eden-like garden and filling her streets and homes with joy and singing (v. 3). The Lord will extend his just rule to the remote regions of the earth and vindicate his people, while the enemies of God will disappear (vv. 4–8).

The prophet, speaking for the exiled people, responds with a prayer that the Lord's promise might quickly become reality.[191] Addressing the "arm of the LORD," which symbolizes divine strength, he asks the Lord to reveal the power he demonstrated when he delivered his people from Egypt (vv. 9–10). On that occasion the Lord dried up the waters of the sea, allowing his people to cross over to safety and freedom. This mighty deed is depicted as a victory over a sea monster, called here Rahab, meaning "Proud One." This sea monster, also known in the Bible and in Ugaritic myth as Leviathan (see Isa. 27:1), elsewhere symbolizes the forces of chaos that seek to destroy the created order (see Job 26:12; Ps. 89:10). Here the title refers more specifically to the waters of the Red Sea, but the underlying reality is the Egyptian army that opposed Israel at the Red Sea (note also Isa. 30:7 and Ps. 87:4, where

---

190. Because the Lord is mentioned in the third person in v. 10, one might conclude that the servant continues to speak here. However, the servant is also mentioned in the third person in v. 10, and v. 11b is most naturally seen as a statement by God (see especially, "this is what you shall receive from my hand"). Furthermore, the immediately following verses (51:1–8) are clearly statements by God.

191. The speaker in vv. 9–11 is not clearly identified, but since vv. 1–8 and vv. 12–15 are spoken to God's exiled people, it is natural to see them responding to God in vv. 9–11. Since the exiles are mentioned in the third person in v. 11, it is possible that the prophet speaks here as the representative of the righteous remnant within the exilic community.

the title is used of Egypt). Anticipating the Lord's positive response, the prayer suddenly describes how the exiles will enter Jerusalem with joyful singing (v. 11; see 35:10). They are called the "ransomed of the LORD" because they will experience the Lord's saving work in a second exodus from Babylon in the same way that the "redeemed" (see v. 10b) Israelites did in the first exodus from Egypt.

The Lord now addresses the exiled nation. Speaking as the one who encourages his people (see 40:1; 49:13; 51:3), he rebukes them for their fear (v. 12).[192] They have no reason to fear mortal men, for their God is the creator of the world (v. 13) and is fully capable of delivering them from bondage (v. 14).[193]

The Lord continues to speak in verses 15–16, but the identity of the addressee is not entirely clear.[194] The exiles are addressed in the immediately preceding verses (note especially the critical tone of vv. 12–13), but there seems to be a shift here, where the Lord announces that he has made the addressee his spokesman and his effective instrument. The language is reminiscent of the servant's words in 49:2 and 50:4. Perhaps the Lord, having spoken to the exiles in the immediately preceding verses (see 50:10–51:8 as well), now responds to the servant, who spoke just prior to this (see 50:4–9).

The correct translation of verse 16 is debated. The NIV takes the second half of the verse as referring to God, but the original text does not support this. The Hebrew text reads: "I have put my words in your mouth and covered you with the shadow of my hand in order to set the heavens in place (lit., "in order to plant the heavens")[195] and to establish the earth and to say to Zion, 'You are my people.'" The three infinitives in the second half of the verse are most naturally understood as indicating the purpose of the divine actions described in the first half of the verse. The meaning of the third infinitive is clear enough—the Lord has commissioned the servant to remind Zion of God's commitment to the city. But how do the first two infinitives relate to the servant's ministry? They seem to indicate that the Lord has commissioned the servant to create the universe. Perhaps creation imagery is employed metaphorically here to refer to the transformation that Jerusalem will experience. In Isaiah 65:17–18 the renewal of Jerusalem is viewed as the creation of "new heavens and a new earth."

---

192. The second half of v. 12 appears to be addressed to personified Zion, for the second-person pronoun and verb are feminine singular in the Hebrew text. God's people and personified Zion are closely connected (see v. 16b, in which Zion is addressed as God's people).

193. In v. 13, the second-person verb forms are masculine singular, apparently indicating that the exiled nation is addressed as a collective whole.

194. Verses 15–16 must be taken as a unit, for there is a grammatical break between vv. 14–15 (NIV "for" at the beginning of v. 15 is interpretive and misleading) and v. 16 is connected grammatically to v. 15.

195. Some prefer to emend the text to "stretch out" (see v. 13, as well as 40:22; 42:5; 44:24; 45:12).

The next message is directed to personified Jerusalem.[196] The down-trodden city is compared to an intoxicated woman who drinks from the cup of the Lord's anger. She now staggers through the streets and falls to the ground in a drunken stupor (vv. 17–19). Her enemies taunt her and stomp on her back (v. 23b), but her children can offer no help, for they, like their mother, have been incapacitated by God's judgment (v. 20). But the tables are about to turn. Jerusalem's divine protector will remove the cup from her hand and force her enemies to drink from it (vv. 21–23a).

The time has come for Zion to throw aside her chains, to lift herself from the dust, and to put on beautiful clothes, for foreign invaders will never again defile the holy city (52:1–2). God's people have been oppressed and humiliated, first in Egypt in the days of Moses, then by the Assyrians in the time of Isaiah, and finally by the Babylonians (vv. 3–4). God's reputation has even been slandered (v. 5), but the Lord is about to change that (v. 6). The Lord will reveal his power to all the nations as he delivers his people from exile and establishes his sovereign rule in Zion (vv. 7–10). The time has come for the exiles to leave ritually unclean Babylon and head for home (v. 11). However, in contrast to the first exodus, when Israel hurried out of Egypt (see Exod. 12:11; Deut. 16:3), there is no need for undue haste or concern, for the Lord will be both his people's vanguard and rear guard, insulating them from all danger (v. 12).

From Rags to Riches: The Servant's Vindication (52:13–53:12)

This fourth and most famous of the servant songs describes the servant's rejection and suffering, but it also anticipates his eventual vindication. The song begins (52:13–15) and ends (53:11b–12) with the Lord announcing the servant's exaltation. In between, once-wayward Israel acknowledges its former unbelief and articulates its newfound insight into the significance of the servant's suffering (53:1–11a).

As noted above, the servant's identity has been a hotly debated issue. Many interpreters, both Christian and Jewish, identify the servant as the personified nation Israel. Though he is addressed as Israel in the second servant song (see 49:3), that same song pictures the servant, like a second Moses, delivering the exiled nation and mediating a new covenant between God and his people (see 49:5–8). For this reason, it is best to identify the servant as an ideal Israel who, though closely related to the nation, is nevertheless distinct from it.

---

196. Since the servant's task is to encourage the city (v. 16b), it is possible that he is the speaker at this point. Having been commissioned as God's spokesman (see 49:4; 50:4), he begins to fulfill his task by communicating a message of hope to the downtrodden city. In this case, 51:17–22a; 52:1–3, 7–12 are spoken by the servant, who also reports to Jerusalem the word of God (see 51:22–23; 52:3–6). Further support for this view comes in 52:13–53:12, in which the Lord commends the servant for successfully completing his mission.

The fourth servant song also distinguishes the servant from the nation. The group speaking in 53:1–6 (note the use of the pronouns "we," "our," and "us" in these verses) is identified as God's people in verse 8 (if we retain the reading "my people" there).[197] Israel is the benefactor of the servant's ministry, not the servant. Furthermore, if Israel were the servant, how could the sinful, exiled nation be viewed as suffering innocently on behalf of the Gentiles (who, in this case, would have to be the group speaking in verses 1–6)? This section of Isaiah consistently affirms that Israel suffered in exile because of its own sins (see 40:2; 42:24–25; 43:24–25; 44:21–22; 48:1–8, 18; 50:1).[198]

Some scholars identify the servant as the so-called Second Isaiah, the supposed anonymous author of this section of the book who, according to the modern scholarly consensus, ministered among the exiles just prior to Cyrus's invasion of Babylon and the release of the exiles. In this highly speculative scenario, which has no supporting evidence from within or outside the Bible, this prophet risked his life and even endured persecution and imprisonment in order to proclaim his message of redemption to the exiles. While the theory certainly attests to the creativity of its proponents, it is nothing more than scholarly fiction. No prophet prior to Jesus fits this portrait of a servant who, as the covenant mediator depicted in the second servant song, reconciles Israel to God through his suffering and is eventually exalted above the kings of the earth. In the aftermath of Jesus' crucifixion and resurrection, the servant's identity came into sharper focus. When the Ethiopian eunuch, while reading Isaiah 53:7–8, asked if the prophet spoke of himself or someone else, Philip, "began with that very passage of Scripture and told him the good news about Jesus" (Acts 8:35).

As the song begins, the Lord draws attention to his servant and announces that he will eventually succeed and be elevated to a position of great honor (52:13).[199] During the time of his suffering, this servant was once so disfigured and marred that he no longer looked even human (v. 14).[200] He was repulsive to observers, and kings had certainly not been very impressed with him. But now this servant will be elevated to a lofty royal position, and kings will stand before him in shocked silence (v. 15).[201]

197. One of the Qumran manuscripts has "his people," that is, the servant's people, who are equated with the group speaking in vv. 1–6 (compare v. 8 with v. 5).

198. On this point see Harry M. Orlinsky, *The So-Called "Suffering Servant" in Isaiah 53* (Cincinnati: Hebrew Union College Press, 1964), 8–10. Orlinsky observes that Isa. 53:9b "alone at once excludes the people Israel from further consideration" as the servant (8).

199. The first line of v. 13 reads literally, "See, my servant will act wisely." The verb "act wisely" here has the connotation "will succeed." In biblical thought, wisdom characteristically results in success and prosperity. The heaping up of synonymous verbs in the second half of v. 13 emphasizes the certainty and degree of the servant's exaltation.

200. The text probably alludes here to the terrible beating Jesus endured just prior to his crucifixion.

201. Traditionally, the Hebrew verb has been understood as a causative of a verb meaning "spurt, spatter," and has been translated "sprinkle." In this case, the passage pictures the servant as a priest who

The prophet Isaiah hears this announcement and speaks on behalf of the nation Israel in 53:1–11a. Assuming a dramatic role, the prophet positions himself at a point in time after the servant's suffering (he speaks of that as already accomplished), but before the servant's full vindication and exaltation (he speaks of that as still future).

In this speech the people of Israel finally come to their senses. They suddenly realize that the one whom they rejected and wrote off as an object of divine anger is really their savior and destined to be king. Israel has not yet as a nation come to the realization that Jesus Christ, the servant foreseen by Isaiah, is their savior and king, but according to the Scriptures this will happen someday (see Rom. 11:26–27). Perhaps we can think of this as their confession of faith on that future day when they finally acknowledge their savior.

Verse 1a is traditionally translated, "Who has believed our report?" or "Who has believed our message?" as if the group speaking is lamenting that no one believes what it has to say. But that does not seem to be the point in this context. Here the group speaking does not cast itself in the role of a preacher or evangelist. They are repentant sinners, who finally see the light. The phrase "our report" can mean "the report which we proclaim," or "the report which was proclaimed to us." The latter fits better here, where the report is most naturally taken as the announcement that has just been made. A better translation would be, "Who would have believed what we just heard?" The rhetorical question expresses their shock at hearing the news of the servant's coming exaltation.

Stunned Israel also asks an accompanying question, "To whom has the arm of the LORD been revealed?" (v. 1b). Through this rhetorical question they confess that they did not see the arm of the LORD at work in the servant. In the Hebrew Bible the "arm of the LORD" is a metaphor of military power; it pictures the LORD as a warrior who bares his arm, takes up his weapon, and crushes his enemies (see Isa. 51:9–10; 63:5–6). Israel had not seen any such display of divine power in the servant's ministry.

On the contrary, the servant was seemingly insignificant, like a little twig growing out of a tree or a little root that pops up out of dry ground only to be withered by the sun (v. 2a). This servant had no majestic, royal aura about him (v. 2b). In fact, he was rejected by others and experienced intense

---

"sprinkles" (or spiritually cleanses) the nations. This interpretation, however, is problematic. In all other instances where the object or person sprinkled is indicated, the verb is combined with a preposition. This is not the case in Isa. 52:15, unless one takes the following phrase, "on him," with the preceding line. But then one would have to emend the verb to a plural, make the nations the subject of the verb "sprinkle," and take the servant as the object. However, the resulting picture of the nations "sprinkling" the servant fails to fit the preceding context. Others propose a homonymic verbal root meaning "spring, leap," which in the causative stem could mean "cause to leap, startle" and would fit the parallelism of the verse nicely. The servant's exaltation startles the nations and leaves their rulers speechless.

suffering; he was like a terminally ill person who is shunned by others because of his disease (v. 3).

Reflection replaces shock, as Israel suddenly realizes that appearances can be deceiving. They thought he was being punished by God for some horrible thing he had done (v. 4b), but they were only partially correct. He was indeed being punished by God, but not for his own sin. He was being punished for Israel's sins. The servant picked up the heavy burden of their sin, put it on his shoulders, and carried it (v. 4a). The servant was wounded and crushed, not because of something he had done, but because of what they had done (v. 5a). As sinners, they were like sheep who had wandered from the moral path of God's law (v. 6a). They were vulnerable to attack; the guilt of their sin was ready to attack and destroy them. But then the servant stepped in and took the full force of the attack (v. 6b).[202] They were spiritually ill and diseased, but because the servant accepted God's punishment for them, they were now healed and well (v. 5b).

Israel had missed its calling, compromised its special position before God, and experienced humiliation. But God's special servant, the ideal "Israel" who, in contrast to the exiled nation, remained faithful to God, suffered on the nation's behalf, making reconciliation with God possible. Israel here begins to realize that the work of this suffering servant opened the way for a new relationship between them and their God.

Israel continues to reflect on the servant's suffering. The nation remembers how he silently endured the harsh treatment. He did not even speak up in his own defense (v. 7a); he was like an unsuspecting sheep being led to the slaughtering block or to the shearing grounds (v. 7b).[203]

The servant's trial was a real kangaroo court if there ever was one. He was unjustly accused and condemned, but no one really gave it much thought (v. 8a).[204] They took him away and killed him, and he just allowed it to happen without protest because he was taking the punishment for Israel's rebellion against God (v. 8b).

202. The verb form in v. 6b is best translated "caused to attack." Elsewhere the form means "to intercede verbally" (Jer. 15:11; 36:25) or "to intervene militarily" (Isa. 59:16), but neither meaning fits this context. The form is the causative of the verb's basic meaning, "encounter, meet, touch," which sometimes refers to a hostile encounter or attack. The Lord caused Israel's sin to attack him, as it were. He experienced the punishment that these guilty sinners deserved.

203. The metaphor emphasizes the servant's silent submission; it does not necessarily suggest a sacrificial background. Sheep were slaughtered for food as well as for sacrifice, and the term translated "slaughter" need not refer to ritual sacrifice. See the use of the term in Gen. 43:16; Prov. 7:22; 9:2; Jer. 50:27; as well as the use of the related verb in Exod. 21:37; Deut. 28:31; 1 Sam. 25:11.

204. The text reads literally, "and his generation, who considers?" Since "his generation" is preceded by the accusative sign, some understand the phrase as the object of the verb "considers" and interpret it as referring to the servant's descendants. In this case the rhetorical question makes the point that he has no descendants. However, in this context it seems more likely that the so-called accusative sign highlights a new subject ("as for his generation"). In this case "his generation" probably refers to the servant's own generation and the question makes the point that none of his contemporaries paid much attention to the unjust treatment of the servant.

However, even in his death there was a hint of his coming vindication and exaltation. His executors intended to bury him with common criminals, but he ended up in a rich man's tomb (v. 9a).[205] That was more fitting than a criminal's burial, because he had done nothing wrong (v. 9b). He was simply submitting to the sovereign will of God, who had determined to crush this servant in Israel's place (v. 10a).

But this apparent alienation was not final. Having obediently accomplished God's will, the servant will be reconciled to God (v. 10b). The second poetic line of verse 10b is notoriously difficult to understand. It reads literally, "if you (or "she") makes a reparation offering, his life." The verb form is either second masculine singular or third feminine singular. If the former, it must be addressed to the servant or to God. However, the servant is only addressed once in this song (see 52:14a), and God either speaks or is spoken about in this song; he is never directly addressed. Furthermore, the idea of God himself making a guilt offering makes no sense. If the verb is taken as third feminine singular, then the grammatically feminine noun "life" at the end of the line is the likely subject. In this case one may take "his life" as equivalent to a pronoun and understand it as the subject of the verb, "if he (lit., "his life") makes a guilt offering." But does the image of the servant presenting such an offering make any sense? The servant's suffering might constitute such an offering, but the preceding context views his suffering as past, while the verb form here is imperfect, suggesting the offering is something the servant presents after his suffering has been completed. Perhaps the background of the image can be found in the Mosaic law, where a healed leper would offer a guilt offering as part of the ritual designed to restore him to ceremonial cleanliness (see Lev. 14). Earlier in the song the servant is pictured as being severely ill (v. 4a). This illness (a metaphor for the guilt of the people's sin) separated him from God. However, here we discover the separation is not final; God is willing to receive an offering from him, as it were.

Once reparation is made, so to speak, he will again experience the Lord's blessing and accomplish God's purposes (v. 10c).[206] In the end the servant will look back on his work and find great satisfaction in what he has accomplished (v. 11a).

205. The poetic parallelism of v. 9a is problematic. The text reads literally, "and he assigned with criminals his grave, and with the rich in his death." The parallelism appears to be synonymous (note the corresponding terms "his grave" and "in his death"), but "criminals" and "the rich" hardly make a compatible pair in this context, for these two groups would not be buried in the same kind of tomb. Some emend the term translated "the rich" to "doers of evil," while others relate it to an alleged Arabic word meaning "mob." However, it is possible that the statements are contrastive, not synonymous. In this case, the servant's burial in a rich man's tomb, in contrast to a criminal's burial, is highly ironic, but appropriate, for he had done nothing wrong.

206. The description of the servant having descendants and reaching a ripe old age need not be taken literally or allegorically. The stereotypical language emphasizes the servant's restoration to divine favor. Having numerous descendants and living a long life were considered outward signs of divine favor. See Job 42:13–16.

At this point God speaks once more and again announces that the servant will be exalted and greatly rewarded for his obedience (vv. 11b–12). Because the sinless servant identified with the rebels, took their sin on his shoulders, and gave his life for them, he will emerge victorious and will be richly rewarded by God for what he has done.

God's servant will justify (or better, "acquit") many; he will declare them innocent (see v. 11b). The precise meaning of the verb translated "justify" is debated. Elsewhere the form is used at least six times in the sense of "make righteous" in a legal sense, that is, "pronounce innocent, acquit" (see Exod. 23:7; Deut. 25:1; 1 Kings 8:32 = 2 Chron. 6:23; Prov. 17:15; Isa. 5:23). It can also mean "render justice" (as a royal function, see 2 Sam. 15:4; Ps. 82:3), "concede" (Job 27:5), "vindicate" (Isa. 50:8), and "lead to righteousness" (by teaching and example, Dan. 12:3). In this context the legal sense of the term makes excellent sense. Because the servant is willing to carry the people's sins, he is able to "acquit" them.

Some have objected to this legal interpretation of the language, arguing that it would be unjust for the righteous to suffer for the wicked and for the wicked to be declared innocent.[207] However, such a surprising development is consistent with the ironic nature of this song. It does seem unfair for the innocent to die for the guilty, but what is God to do when all have sinned and wandered off like stray sheep (see v. 6)? Covenantal law demands punishment, but punishment in this case would mean annihilation of what God has created. God's justice, as demanded by the law, must be satisfied. To satisfy his justice, he does something seemingly unjust. He punishes his sinless servant, the only one who has not strayed off. In the progress of biblical revelation, we discover that the sinless servant is really God in the flesh, who offers himself because he is committed to the world he has created. If his justice can only be satisfied if he himself endures the punishment, then so be it. What appears to be an act of injustice is really love satisfying the demands of justice.

The servant's suffering satisfied God's holiness and justice and made it possible for God to forgive sin. The suffering servant's death inaugurated a new covenant. At the Last Supper, Jesus held up the cup of wine, symbolic of the blood he would shed on the cross, and declared, "This cup is the new covenant in my blood, which is poured out for you" (Luke 22:20). Why is this new covenant important? Because it fulfills the demands of the old covenant and replaces it. The old covenant said "obey or else;" the new covenant gives the capacity to obey through the gift of the Holy Spirit (see Jer. 31:33 and Ezek. 36:25–27). The New Testament tells us this new covenant is not just for Israel, but is broader in scope. It includes all the nations of the earth, as Isaiah had already hinted (see 49:6).

207. See, for example, Orlinsky, *The So-Called "Suffering Servant,"* 22.

Zion's Marriage Restored (54:1–17)

Having focused on the servant's ministry, the prophet again turns to personified Zion, for she will be one of the primary beneficiaries of the servant's work. Zion was once barren and, for this reason, abandoned by her husband (vv. 1a, 4, 6–7a).[208] Left alone, she was overcome by shame and depression (v. 6a). But all that is about to change. Zion's husband, the sovereign Lord (v. 5), readily acknowledges that he divorced her in a fit of anger, but he is now ready to take her back (vv. 7–8). Furthermore, once-barren Zion will have numerous children (v. 1b), who will repopulate the desolate towns throughout the land and even conquer surrounding nations (vv. 2–3). Of course, the reality behind the imagery is the exile of God's people, which left Jerusalem uninhabited and in ruins. This happened because of Judah's sin, but the theme of rebellion is not the thrust of this passage. In this text the prophet portrays Zion in a very sympathetic light. Her suffering is highlighted, and she even appears to be an innocent victim of her husband's anger. The rhetorical tone draws attention to her great need and to the Lord's tender compassion.

To emphasize his renewed commitment to Zion, the Lord compares his promise to the covenant he made with Noah (v. 9). Following the flood, God promised never again to destroy the earth in such a way (Gen. 9:9–11, 15). In the same way he now promises Zion that she will never again experience his angry judgment. Even if the mountains, symbols of stability, were to disintegrate, the Lord's "covenant of peace" with Zion will remain firm (v. 10). The phrase "covenant of peace" also appears in Numbers 25:12, where it refers to the Lord's promise to Phinehas (see also Mal. 2:5), and in Ezekiel 34:25 and 37:26, where it is used of God's new covenant with restored Israel. The phrase describes a covenant that inaugurates peaceful relations between the parties involved.

Zion's restoration will usher in an era of glory and peace. Though the city had suffered terribly in the past, the Lord would rebuild it with precious gems (vv. 11–12). The imagery, which depicts the city as a lady covered with jewels from head to toe, points to the prosperity Zion will experience. Zion's children will become disciples of the Lord (v. 13), and the city will never again be threatened by enemy armies (v. 14). If anyone does have the audacity to launch an attack against Zion, they will be defeated (v. 15), for the Lord, who is sovereign over the weapon makers of the earth (v. 16), will personally protect and vindicate his people (v. 17).

---

208. Verse 4b in the NIV refers to the "reproach of her widowhood," but the surrounding context pictures her husband, the Lord, divorcing her, not dying. The prophet possibly uses a bold mixed metaphor, but it is more likely that the word translated "widowhood" actually refers to divorce here. See S. L. Stassen, "Marriage (and Related) Metaphors in Isaiah 54:1–17," *Journal for Semitics* 6 (1994): 65.

The Promise of a Permanent Covenant (55:1–13)

This section of the book culminates with a call to covenantal renewal that is patterned after an invitation to a feast. The Lord has announced his intention to restore Zion through the work of Cyrus and his special servant. He has confronted the exiles with their sin and urged them to come to grips with it. Now he makes an impassioned appeal to his people to return to him.

The exiles are pictured as thirsty, hungry, and penniless. Using an oxymoron for rhetorical effect, the Lord invites them to "buy" for no cost the delicious food and beverage that he offers (v. 1). It makes no sense for them to spend the little money they have worked so hard to earn on something that will not satisfy (v. 2). The material blessings of a renewed covenantal relationship are the reality underlying the imagery of food and drink, as the next verse makes clear. If the people return to the Lord, they will experience life (v. 3a), which refers here to material prosperity and national security (see Deut. 30:6, 15, 19–20). This life will be the product of a renewed covenantal relationship.

In contrast to the Mosaic covenant, this new covenant will be a permanent one, patterned after God's promissory covenant with David (vv. 3b–5).[209] The Lord chose David to rule over his people and, in response to David's faithful service, made an unconditional covenant with him (see 2 Sam. 7; Ps. 89). God promised David an eternal dynasty, adopted the Davidic king as his "son," and guaranteed the dynasty an inheritance, which included worldwide rule (see Ps. 2:7–9; 72:8–11; 89:25). The Davidic king was to testify of the Lord's greatness to the nations of the earth (see Ps. 18:50; 22:28). The Lord promised him that even distant nations, previously unknown to him, would submit to his rule.[210] The implication seems to be that the restored nation would experience the same kind of prominence.

Following this promise, the appeal to covenantal renewal continues (vv. 6–7). God's people should seek reconciliation with him while the time is opportune and he is predisposed to mercy. Sinners should forsake their evil plans and ways, for the Lord is willing to forgive their sins. The terminology of this appeal echoes the words of Moses (see Deut. 4:25–31; 30:1–10) and

209. The last line of v. 3 reads literally, "the reliable expressions of loyalty of David." Some understand "David" as a subjective genitive and understand this as the basis for the preceding promise. One might paraphrase, "Then I will make an unconditional covenantal promise to you, because of David's faithful acts of covenantal loyalty." But "David" is best understood as an objective genitive; he is the recipient of covenantal promises (see 2 Chron. 6:42). The syntactical relationship of "expressions of loyalty," to the preceding line is unclear. If the term is appositional to "covenant," then the Lord democratizes the promises of the Davidic covenant by transferring them to the entire nation. Another option is to take "expressions of loyalty" as an adverbial accusative and to translate, "according to the reliable covenantal promises." In this case the new covenant is an extension or fulfillment of the Davidic promises. A third option is to take the last line as comparative. In this case the new covenant is patterned after the Davidic covenant.

210. On the surface one might understand v. 5 as addressed to the exiles. However, the second-person verbs and pronouns in v. 5 are singular in the Hebrew text, suggesting that this verse is a quotation of what the Lord promised David when he promised him dominion over the nations. Plural forms are used in vv. 1–3, 6, 8–9, 12 when the exiles are addressed.

the prayer of Solomon (see 1 Kings 8:46–53). Both looked forward to a time when the exiled nation would seek the Lord and repent of their rebellion, prompting the Lord to compassionately forgive them.

Verses 6–7 bring the earlier promises of divine deliverance (see especially 40:1–11) into sharper focus. Though earlier promises emphasized God's determination to restore his people and may have had an unconditional ring to them, there is a conditional side as well. The people must return to the Lord and embrace his mercy.

Having confronted the people with their responsibility, the Lord affirms the reliability of his promises (vv. 8–11). If Israel repents, she can be certain that her sins will be forgiven and that God will renew his covenantal relationship.

Verses 8–9 are frequently interpreted to mean that God's ways are incomprehensible to mankind. However, this is not the point of the passage when it is viewed in its immediate context. Verses 10–11 emphasize that the Lord's ways and plans are accomplished. By way of contrast, Israel's ways and plans (see v. 7), if not abandoned, will lead only to death (v. 3 implies this). Elsewhere sinful mankind's plans (or "thoughts") are called a mere breath, for they are destined to amount to nothing (Ps. 94:11) apart from divine approval (Prov. 19:21). Human deeds (or "ways") are typically evil and lead to destruction (Prov. 1:15–19; 3:31–33; 4:19). In contrast to empty human plans and ways, God's plans are realized and his ways accomplish something positive. For this reason, his promises can be trusted.

In verses 10–11, his promise of forgiveness (see v. 7) is compared to the rain and snow. Once it begins to fall toward the ground, it does not suddenly reverse its course. Instead, it waters the ground and contributes to agricultural growth. In the same way the Lord's promise of forgiveness will not return to him without being fulfilled.

The Lord expands the promise of restoration in verses 12–13. If Israel responds positively to God's appeal, his promised forgiveness will bring the joy of deliverance. All nature will celebrate Israel's release from exile. Pine trees and myrtles will replace the thornbushes and briers. The picture of luxuriant renewed growth is a logical development of verses 10–11, which compare the Lord's word of promise to rain. The transformation of the arid wilderness, symbolizing an accursed condition resulting from God's judgment, into a forest, symbolizing restored blessings, will serve, like the rainbow of the Noahic covenant (see Isa. 54:9), as an external, permanent reminder (or "sign") of the Lord's promise to never again judge his people.

Beyond Exile (Isaiah 56–66)

Picking up where the preceding chapters left off, this concluding section of the book assumes that Jerusalem lies in ruins (see 63:18; 64:10–11) and anticipates the return of the exiles (see 56:8; 57:14), the rebuilding of Judah's towns (see 58:12; 60:10; 61:4), and the Lord's return to Zion (see 59:20; 62:10–12). Continuing the hortatory tone of chapter 55, the Lord makes it clear that the returning exiles must maintain the moral and ethical standards prescribed in the law. Restoration to the land is no guarantee of restored blessing. The Lord distinguishes between the godly and the ungodly, and warns that he will once again purify the covenant community through judgment in conjunction with a new creation.

An Invitation to Outsiders (56:1–8)

The Lord exhorts his people to promote justice and godly living, for the promised deliverance is right around the corner (v. 1). Those who commit themselves to keeping the law of God will experience joy (v. 2). The reference to keeping the Sabbath and keeping one's hand from doing evil is probably a shorthand way of referring to the Ten Commandments (also known as the Decalogue). Keeping the Sabbath refers to the first half of the Decalogue, which is more Godward in orientation and stresses the need to recognize divine authority. Keeping one's hand from evil refers to the second half of the Decalogue, which is more manward in orientation and stresses the need to respect the lives and property of one's fellow human beings.

After emphasizing the need to recommit themselves to the law of God and its principles of social justice, the Lord announces that he is ready to expand the ranks of the covenant community (vv. 3–8). He opens the doors of his temple to foreigners and eunuchs, both of whom were previously excluded from the worshiping community (see Deut. 23:1–8). From this time forward one's ethnicity or physical defects will no longer exclude a person from worship. All that will count is loyalty to the Lord as expressed through observance of the Sabbath and obedience to his commands. All who love the Lord and are loyal to him will join the returning exiles in offering sacrifices to the Lord. The rebuilt temple will be known as "a house of prayer for all nations" (v. 7). This vision of an expanded worshiping community depicts the realization of Solomon's wish for the temple to become a worship center for all nations (see 1 Kings 8:41–43).

In its original context the vision anticipates developments in the postexilic period. However, in the progress of revelation and history, it finds its ultimate fulfillment in the new covenant community, in which Gentiles find access to God through Jesus Christ (see Eph. 2:11–22, as well as Gal. 3:28). This new covenant community is no longer bound by the Decalogue and its Sabbath rules (Eph. 2:15; Col. 2:16), for Christ has fulfilled the law (Matt. 5:17). In fulfillment of the new covenant prophecies of Jeremiah and Ezekiel (see Jer. 31:33; Ezek 36:27), Christ creates a new covenant people who, through the gift of the divine Spirit, keep the essence of the law (Matt. 22:37–40), while being freed from its outer shell (Eph. 2:15) and its enslaving commands. Rather than bringing sacrifices to a temple, the new covenant community becomes the very temple of God (Eph. 2:21–22) and celebrates the ultimate, final sacrifice that makes its precursors obsolete (Heb. 7:27; 9:28). Rather than observing the Sabbath, this new community of worshipers enters through faith into a permanent "Sabbath-rest" (see Heb. 4:3, 9) that frees them from their own efforts to please God (Heb. 4:10) and motivates them to remain firm in their faith.

Greed and Idolatry Denounced (56:9–57:13a)

The Lord's tone shifts abruptly as he denounces the sinners within the community. At this point the speech sounds almost preexilic in its condemnation of greed and idolatry, but the surrounding context indicates that the early postexilic community is addressed. The Lord anticipates that some of the returning exiles would repeat the sins of their fathers. Projecting himself into the future, he addresses these future sinners with the same intensity as he did the preexilic generations.[211]

The Lord sarcastically invites the wild animals of the fields and forests to come and devour the objects of his anger (v. 9). He denounces Israel's "watchmen," probably a reference to Israel's leaders, comparing them to lazy dogs with big appetites, to mercenary shepherds who care nothing about the sheep placed under their care, and to self-assured drunkards who live to carouse (vv. 10–12). Godly individuals are disappearing, but no one really notices (57:1–2), for the rebellious people are too caught up in idolatry to care (vv. 3–4). Their pagan practices include fertility rites and child sacrifice (v. 5). The Lord has no alternative but to judge these idolaters, whose obsession with paganism is vividly depicted as erotic lust (vv. 6–8) and as an irrational attachment to that which is ultimately destructive (vv. 9–10). Though the Lord has been relatively silent in the past, he is ready to intervene in judgment and punish those who have forgotten him (vv. 11–13a).

Vindication for the Godly (57:13b–21)

Though the godly are disappearing from the land (see vv. 1–2), they will be vindicated in the end. The Lord promises that his loyal followers will inherit the Promised Land and enjoy access to God's presence on the temple mount (vv. 13b–14). Though the sovereign God sits exalted as the eternal king, he is not inaccessible. He condescends to live among the downtrodden in order to encourage them (v. 15). The Lord angrily punishes sin, but he realizes humankind's inherently fragile nature and is willing to heal those whom he has

---

211. Some of those scholars who assign these chapters to so-called Third Isaiah recognize the preexilic flavor of these verses. For example, Claus Westermann argues that "prophetic oracles of doom of the preexilic period were revised and directed against" the "transgressors" within the postexilic community. See his *Isaiah 40–66*, OTL (Philadelphia: Westminster, 1969), 302, 320.

wounded and console those who mourn over their sin (vv. 16–18). He offers peace to those he has punished, but he also warns the wicked that persistence in sin makes reconciliation to God impossible (vv. 19–21).

The Lord Demands Sincerity, Not Ritual (58:1–14)

Continuing to anticipate future developments, the Lord confronts the postexilic community, which, like earlier generations, is susceptible to religious hypocrisy. The Lord denounces such hypocrisy, making it clear that he values obedience and social justice, not empty formalism. Rituals of lamentation and fasting, even when accompanied by an apparent desire to know God better, are meaningless if one continues to pursue an evil lifestyle. The people addressed here seem pious enough on the surface (v. 2), but their violent treatment of others exposes them as hypocrites (vv. 1, 3–4). The Lord wants them to cease their oppressive ways (vv. 5–6) and to reach out to the homeless and starving within their community (vv. 7, 9b, 10a). Only then will they experience God's favor, protection, and renewed blessings, symbolized here by light (vv. 8–9a, 10b–11). Only then will God enable them to rebuild the ruined towns of the land (v. 12).

In addition to promoting social justice, the Lord demands something more fundamental from his people—observance of the Sabbath (v. 13). Having just denounced religious ritualism earlier in this speech, the Lord is not advocating mere formalism. He is exposing the people's underlying sin. The group addressed here is selfish; their failure to observe the Sabbath is a symptom of a deeper problem—lack of respect for God and his authority. This underlying selfishness is the root of their oppressive practices and mistreatment of others. The Lord makes it clear that this problem must be rectified. Only then will God's people find their relationship with him satisfying (v. 14a) and enjoy the blessings of the Promised Land (v. 14b).

Sin Exposed and Confessed (59:1–15a)

The prophet confronts the people, pointing out that their sins have alienated them from God (v. 2). The Lord is able and willing to deliver them (v. 1), but not while their hands are covered with the blood of their innocent victims and they use their lips to deceive and exploit others (v. 4). They are as crafty as spiders, which trap their victims in their web, and as deadly as poisonous snakes, which kill with their venomous bite (v. 5). They devise evil plans against others, which they then carry out with speed and violence (vv. 6–8).

Speaking as a representative of this sinful society, the prophet confesses the people's sin before the Lord. Because of their sin, the people have experienced the darkness of judgment, rather than the bright light of divine deliverance (v. 9). Separated from God and his blessings, they grope like blind men for something stable to hold, but God's salvation does not arrive (vv. 10–11). The prophet readily admits that the people's blatant rebellion against God (vv. 12–13) has destroyed society, leaving it devoid of justice and truth (vv. 14–15a).

Divine Intervention (59:15b–21)

The Lord cannot tolerate such injustice (v. 15b). Much to his dismay, no one intervenes on behalf of the oppressed (v. 16a), so the Lord decides to take matters into his own hands (v. 16b). The prophet pictures him as a warrior preparing for battle. His commitment to justice is compared to a breastplate, his determination to rescue the helpless is like a helmet, and his strong desire to avenge the oppressed is depicted as his battle robes (v. 17). He will unleash his anger against his enemies near and far, prompting people everywhere to recognize his royal splendor (vv. 18–19). True to his promise, he will return to Zion, where only those who repent of their sinful rebellion will be left to celebrate his arrival (v. 20). A new era will be inaugurated as the Lord makes a new covenant with his people, who, energized by the divine Spirit, will become his spokesmen for endless generations (v. 21).

Zion's Glory (60:1–22)

Having announced he will return to Zion (see 59:20), the Lord now addresses personified Zion and describes her future glory in vivid detail. Zion will shine like a beacon in a dark world (vv. 1–2), and the nations and kings of the earth will be drawn to her (v. 3). Zion's exiled people, pictured as her sons and daughters, will return (v. 4), prompting their delighted mother to smile with pride (v. 5a). The nations will bring their riches as tribute to the Lord (vv. 5b–9, 16–17) and will rebuild Zion's walls (v. 10). The flow of tribute will be so steady that the city's gates will remain open at all times to receive it (v. 11). Those who formerly oppressed and despised her will grovel at her feet (vv. 14–15), and any nation that attempts to free itself from the dominion of Zion's God will perish (v. 12). Like Solomon of old (see 1 Kings 5:6), the Lord will import lumber from the mighty Lebanon forest to beautify his temple (v. 13). Zion will never again experience the horrors of war and invasion (v. 18), for the Lord's presence, compared to a blinding light that replaces the sun and moon, will ensure her safety and prosperity (vv. 19–20).[212] Zion's citizens, who will all be loyal followers of the Lord, will spread out and occupy the Promised Land forever (v. 21a). The Lord will plant them, as it were, in the soil of the land, and they will multiply like a rich crop, bringing glory to the Lord (vv. 21b–22). This vision of a great nation forever occupying the Promised Land alludes to God's unconditional

---

212. On the use of the imagery of light here, see my earlier comments on 24:23 and 30:26.

promise to Abraham which, despite Israel's sin and exile, is certain of fulfillment (see Gen. 12:2; 13:15–16; 15:5; 17:2, 4–6, 8; 18:18; 22:17).[213]

This promise will be realized "in its time" (v. 22b), that is, "when the
right time comes" (NET). When will that be? According to Genesis 18:18–
19, the fulfillment of God's promise to Abraham will occur once Abraham's
offspring follow his example of faithful obedience. How will this happen?
According to the prophets, Israel will wholeheartedly follow the Lord once
the new covenant is implemented. This covenant, with its gift of the divine
Spirit, will transform Israel so that they all become loyal, obedient subjects
(see Isa. 59:21; Jer. 31:31–34; Ezek. 36:27; 37:26).

Good News for the Oppressed (61:1–11)

In this passage several voices can be heard. One anointed with the Lord's
Spirit announces his divine commission in verses 1–3, the Lord himself
speaks assuring words in verses 7–9, and personified Zion responds in verses
10–11. At some point between verses 3 and 7, the anointed one stops speaking and gives way to the Lord, but it is not entirely clear where this change
occurs. The third-person verb forms in verses 3b–5 appear to be linked with
verses 1–3a, so it may be that "and you" at the beginning of verse 6 marks
the transition.

The precise identity of the speaker in verses 1–3 has been debated, but
a close examination of the evidence points to the servant of the Lord depicted in the earlier servant songs. Like the servant in the songs, the speaker
is empowered by the divine Spirit to free those who are imprisoned (compare v. 1 with 42:1, 7; 49:9). Using language that recalls the Year of Jubilee
(see Lev. 25:10), he announces that the prisoners will be freed (v. 1b) and
that the Lord will vindicate his suffering people, turning their sorrow into
joy (vv. 2–3a).

This mission of deliverance and justice is a distinctly royal task that links
the speaker with the royal figure of the first two servant songs and with the
ideal just king portrayed in Isaiah 11. In the progress of revelation and history,
Jesus emerges as the fulfillment of these prophecies. It is no wonder that Jesus
boldly identifies himself with the speaker of Isaiah 61:1–2 (see Luke 4:18–21).

Released from their prison in exile and restored to their land, the people
will rebuild the cities that had been in ruins for so long (v. 4). Foreigners,
who once robbed God's people of their harvest (see Isa. 62:8), will take care
of their sheep, fields, and vineyards (v. 5). In fulfillment of the ancient
covenantal ideal (see Exod. 19:6), the restored community will serve as the
Lord's priests and collect tribute from the nations (v. 6). Divine blessing and
joy will replace disgrace and shame (v. 7), for the Lord is committed to jus-

213. On the unconditional nature of the Abrahamic covenant and the intertwined promises of numerous offspring and eternal possession of the land, see Robert B. Chisholm Jr., "Evidence from Genesis,"
in *A Case for Premillennialism,* ed. D. K. Campbell and J. L. Townsend (Chicago: Moody, 1992), 35–54.

tice and is determined to vindicate his people (v. 8a; see vv. 1–3). The Lord's devotion to them will culminate in a renewed covenant relationship that will be permanent (v. 8b; see 55:3; 59:21). The nations of the earth will take notice of this new covenant community and acknowledge that they are indeed an object of divine blessing (v. 9).

This glowing portrait of the future prompts a response from the recipient of God's blessings, personified Zion (vv. 10–11; see v. 3 and 62:1). Anticipating her deliverance, Zion bursts out in joy and pictures herself clothed in beautiful garments (see vv. 3, 7), like those of a bridegroom and bride. She celebrates God's vindication of his people and the praise it will elicit from the nations, comparing it to a plant springing up from the soil (see vv. 3, 9).

Waiting and Praying for Zion's Restoration (62:1–11)

A new voice now chimes in, declaring his resolve to pray for Zion until the day of her deliverance arrives (v. 1). The identity of the speaker is unclear, but the most likely candidates are the Lord's servant (see 61:1–3) or the prophet. The speaker, whoever he may be, looks forward to a time when Zion will be vindicated and exalted in the sight of the nations (v. 2a). She will receive from the Lord a new name, epitomizing her new status and glory (v. 2b), and will be like a beautiful royal crown in his hand (v. 3). Actually Zion receives four new names in the following context (see vv. 4, 12). Two of these are given in verse 4. Once called "Deserted" and "Desolate," Zion will now be called "Hephzibah," meaning "my delight is in her," and "Beulah," meaning "married" (v. 4). The Lord had, as it were, divorced Zion (see 54:5–7), but now he will remarry her (v. 5).[214]

The speaker, playing to the hilt the role of intercessor, now announces that he has posted watchmen on Zion's walls. As they scan the horizon looking for the new era to dawn, they pray without ceasing, asking the Lord to intervene on behalf of the city (vv. 6–7). How can they be so bold and persistent? Because the Lord has promised on oath that he will restore Zion's fortunes; his sovereign power, symbolized by his "right hand" and "mighty arm," guarantees that his word will be realized (vv. 8–9). A day will come when Zion's residents will enjoy the fruit of their labors and will never again worry about foreign invaders stealing their crops and wine.

Overcome with emotion, the speaker urges an unidentified group, cast in the role of workmen, to prepare the way for the return of God's exiled people (v. 10a). They are to construct a highway and then send a signal to the distant nations that the stage is set for this grand event. The Lord himself has announced that he will return to Zion, bringing the exiles with him as the spoils of his victory over Babylon (v. 11; see 40:10). Those saved from

214. The Hebrew text reads in v. 5, "your sons will marry you," but the metaphor is at best bizarre. Better parallelism is achieved (see the following, "so will your God rejoice over you") if "your sons" is emended to "your builder" (see Ps. 147:2, which calls the Lord the builder of Jerusalem).

exile will be set apart to God and called "the Holy People, the Redeemed of the LORD." Zion, their destination and new home, will be given two more new names, "Sought After" and "the City No Longer Deserted" (v. 12).

The Grapes of Wrath (63:1–6)

The stage is set for the victorious king's return to Zion. Suddenly the prophet (or perhaps the watchmen on Zion's walls; see 62:6) sees a royal figure marching confidently from Edom and asks him to identify himself (v. 1a). The Lord simply responds, "It is I," and then boasts that he is able to accomplish what he announces (v. 1b; see NET's translation, "It is I, the one who announces vindication, and who is able to deliver!"). The prophet (or watchmen?) then asks the Lord why his garments are red, as if he had been stomping grapes in a winepress (v. 2). The Lord explains that he has returned from stomping on the nations; it is their blood that is spattered over his robes (vv. 3, 6). When the time came for the Lord to avenge the atrocities committed against his people, no one volunteered to come to his aid (vv. 4–5a; see 59:16). Though outnumbered, the Lord's rage spurred him on and he single-handedly defeated his enemies (v. 5b). As in chapter 34, Edom serves as an archetype for all God's enemies, who will be crushed by his angry judgment (see also the Book of Obadiah).

Confessing Sin and Seeking Mercy (63:7–64:12)

The prophet, speaking as the representative for God's sinful people, now offers a lengthy prayer on their behalf. The prayer begins with an historical review of God's faithfulness to his people (v. 7). The Lord chose Israel with the hope they would prove faithful (v. 8a). He delivered them from bondage, demonstrating his love and mercy (vv. 8b–9). He led them safely through the sea and was present with them in a very intimate and personal way (vv. 11–14). Despite God's kindness to his people, they rebelled, prompting God to turn on them and become their enemy (v. 10).

Verse 9, as translated in NIV and many other English versions, indicates that God identified with the people in their suffering and then sent a special angel, called here "the angel of his presence" (literally, "the angel of his face") to protect and guide his people. This reading follows a marginal reading that accompanies the traditional Hebrew text. If this reading is original, the "angel" may be the one mentioned in Exodus 14:19. However, a different reading, which follows in part the traditional Hebrew text in its consonantal form and is reflected in the Septuagint, understands vv. 8b–9a as follows: "He became their savior in all their distress. Not an ambassador or a messenger, but he himself [lit., "his face"] saved them."[215] In this case, the text

---

215. For discussion of the two readings, see Whybray, *Isaiah 40–66*, 257. The Septuagint reading reflects the Kethib (Heb. *lo*), "not," rather than "to him" (the reading of the Qere). It also takes the beginning of v. 9 with the end of v. 8 and understands the Hebrew *tsir*, "ambassador," instead of *tsar*, "distress."

emphasizes that the Lord personally intervened in Israel's experience, rather than sending a mere envoy. There is apparently an allusion to Exodus 33:14–15, which speaks of the Lord's presence (lit., "face") accompanying the Israelites on their journey (see also Deut. 4:37).

Verses 10–11 mention God's "Holy Spirit." Though "the Spirit of God" is mentioned frequently in the Hebrew Bible, the expression "Holy Spirit" occurs only in this passage and in Psalm 51:11, where the psalmist begs that God not remove his "Holy Spirit." Here in Isaiah this "Holy Spirit" is viewed as personal (he can be "grieved") and is closely associated with the Lord's very presence (see v. 9 and Ps. 139:7) and with "the Spirit of the LORD" (see v. 14).

Having acknowledged God's goodness to his people and having confessed Israel's sinfulness, the prophet asks the Lord to take notice of his needy children, for he longs to see the Lord's power and compassion (vv. 15–16). Ironically the prophet attributes Israel's sinful, rebellious condition to divine hardening (v. 17a).[216] It is possible that the Lord directly hardened his people's hearts as an act of judgment, just as he did to Pharaoh at the time of the exodus and to the Amorite and Canaanite kings during the time of the Israelite conquest of the Promised Land. However, it seems more likely that this hardening was indirect. The Lord temporarily turned his back on the exiled people (see 64:7), causing them to become discouraged and bitter. Perhaps as a rhetorical technique, the language of lamentation often ignores intermediate causes and takes a deterministic view that attributes hardship and suffering directly to God (see, for example, Ruth 1:20–21 and Ps. 88).[217] Whether this hardening is viewed as direct or indirect, it was an aspect of divine judgment on Israel's sin.

The prophet asks the Lord to intervene on behalf of his people (vv. 17b–19). He stresses that they are indeed the Lord's people (note "your servants," "your inheritance," "your people," "we are yours"). In this way he implies that God's reputation is at stake. In fact, it is the Lord's sanctuary that has been violated. The situation could be remedied by a new display of God's awesome power (64:1). The prophet prays that the Lord would split the sky and descend to the earth in a great display of power, as he did in earlier times. The Hebrew verb translated "tremble" is used only here and in Judges 5:5, which describes in poetic terms the Lord's intervention on behalf of Israel. In both texts the mountains are the subject of the verb, and their re-

216. Some understand the Hiphil verb forms in v. 17a as tolerative, rather than causative. In this case one might translate: "Why do you allow us to wander from your ways and allow our hearts to be stubborn so that we do not revere you?" The verb used in the first line is rare, occurring only here and in Job 39:16, where it appears to mean "treat harshly." The verb used in the second line does have a tolerative sense in Jer. 50:6, but it is causative in the other passages where it occurs (see Isa. 3:12; 9:16; 30:28; as well as Gen. 20:13; 2 Kings 21:9; Job 12:24–25; Prov. 12:26; Jer. 23:13, 32; Hos. 4:12; Amos 2:4; and Mic. 3:5).

217. For a discussion of Isa. 63:17 in the larger context of the divine-hardening theme in the Hebrew Bible, see Chisholm, "Divine Hardening in the Old Testament," 410–34, especially 433.

sponse is prompted by the Lord's appearance as a warrior. It is likely that the prophet here employs a verbal allusion to this ancient poem. He is asking for a new display of the great power God revealed in days gone by. Such a display would exonerate God's reputation (or "name") and put the hostile nations in their place (v. 2).

Recalling God's past intervention for his people, the prophet affirms the uniqueness of Israel's God. No other god, he argues, has demonstrated such power and willingness to save his people (vv. 3–4). But there is a catch. As sinful Israel found out, God intervenes on behalf of those who remain faithful to him (v. 5a). When Israel rebelled against him, they forfeited his protective care and became objects of his disciplinary anger (v. 5b).

Speaking as the representative of God's exiled people, the prophet confesses that the entire nation stands guilty in the sight of God (v. 6), like one who has become ritually contaminated. What they consider righteous deeds, the Lord views as worthless rags (literally, menstrual cloths). The sinful nation lacks vitality and stability; they are like a dried up leaf or chaff that is blown about by the wind. The people forget about God, perhaps sensing that he has rejected and punished them (v. 7).

Despite the rift in God's relationship to his people, the prophet longs for reconciliation. He reminds the Lord that he is the nation's father and creator (v. 8). He begs the Lord to relent from his anger and not hold their sins against them (v. 9). To motivate a positive divine response, the prophet describes the lamentable condition of the Promised Land (vv. 10–11). The Lord's cities, including Jerusalem, lie in ruins. The temple, once a center for praise and worship, is charred rubble. The situation would seem to demand a response from the Lord (v. 12).

The Righteous and the Wicked: A Study in Contrasts (65:1–66:24)

The Lord responds to the prophet's prayer. He makes it clear that he has revealed himself to his people, even though they have not looked for him or invoked his name in prayer (v. 1). The Lord has gone out of his way to seek reconciliation with his obstinate people (v. 2), but they have persisted in their sinful ways, pagan practices, and religious pride (vv. 3–5).[218] For this reason, the Lord will persist in his judgment (vv. 6–7). The judgment poured out on the fathers will continue to fall on the sons. As noted earlier (see my introductory comments to 56:9–57:13a), the Lord anticipates that many of the returning exiles will repeat the sins of their fathers. Projecting himself

218. Some take the Hebrew perfect verbal forms in vv. 1–2 as referring to past actions, but the following context makes it clear that the early postexilic generation is primarily in view. For this reason, the perfects are best understood in a gnomic or descriptive present sense (see Westermann, *Isaiah 40–66*, 398–99) or as present perfects. In this way the generation in view here is linked with their ancestors (see v. 7).

into the future, he describes these future sinners and links them with the pre-exilic generation that ignored him.

As always, the Lord's judgment on sinners is discriminating and does not sweep away the righteous with the wicked. Even though a cluster of grapes may have many bad grapes in it, the pickers will take the time to save the good grapes in the cluster before discarding it. In the same way the Lord will preserve the righteous remnant among his sinful people (v. 8). This remnant, whom the Lord calls "my servants," will inherit the Promised Land (v. 9), where they will graze their livestock in peace (v. 10).[219]

However, idolaters will have no place in this coming era. Because they have rejected the Lord for pagan gods (v. 11), they will be cut down by the sword (v. 12). The Lord's servants will enjoy God's blessings, but the wicked will starve and be put to shame (vv. 13–14). The Lord's servants will receive a new name, symbolizing the dawning of this new era, but the names of the wicked will be remembered only as they are used in curse formulas (v. 15). In the era to come the Lord's people will be loyal to him and take their oaths in his name (v. 16a).

Using the language of creation, the Lord announces that he will "create new heavens and a new earth" (v. 17a). Past troubles will be forgotten (vv. 16b, 17b) as the Lord's people focus their attention on the transformation of Zion and its restoration to divine favor (vv. 18–19).[220] Death's power will all but disappear (v. 20), and the people will enjoy peace and prosperity (vv. 22–23).[221] Before they even voice their requests to God, he will answer (v. 24). Violence and hostility, epitomized by the "rule of tooth and claw" that permeates the animal kingdom, will disappear (v. 25). The image of predator and prey lying down together in peace has already appeared in Isaiah 11:6–9, where the predators symbolize human oppressors and the prey their helpless victims. The language may be strictly metaphorical, but it may describe a literal change that will mirror the transformation in human society, where justice and peace will prevail.

Some take the reference to "dust" being "the serpent's food" as an allusion to Genesis 3:14 and understand the statement as a prophecy of God's continuing judgment on Satan. However, this allegorical interpretation finds

219. Sharon, located along the Mediterranean coast to the west, and the Valley of Achor, located near Jericho to the east, here represent the entire breadth of the land from west to east.

220. In the context of Isaiah's prophecy, this passage, like so many others in chapters 40–66, anticipates the Lord's return to downtrodden Jerusalem, the rebuilding of the city, and the prosperity of the restored covenantal community. By hyperbolically comparing these events to a new creation of the cosmos, the prophet emphasizes the transformation that will take place. In Rev. 21–22, the Apostle John also combines new-creation imagery with the motif of a new Jerusalem as he describes the glorious future in store for those whom the Lamb of God has redeemed, including both Israel and the church (see Rev. 21:12–14).

221. The description in v. 20 does not go quite as far as the earlier portrayal of the death of Death. In 25:6–8, Isaiah pictures the utter demise of death, which is swallowed up once and for all by the Lord himself in conjunction with the establishment of his universal reign from Zion. Here in 65:20 longevity, not immortality, is envisioned. Death continues to exist, though its power over humankind is greatly weakened.

no support from the context. The point of the statement is that the snake, like other dangerous animals, will no longer pose a danger to those it once terrorized (note the parallelism within verse 25, as well as Isa. 11:8).

Perhaps some might consider this glowing vision of the future too good to be true. The Lord reminds any would-be skeptics that he is the sovereign creator and ruler of the world (66:1–2a). His sanctuary lies in ruins (see 63:18), but that does not mean he has become limited in some way, for he does not really reside in a house built by human hands.

Continuing to contrast the righteous and wicked, the Lord affirms that he shows special favor to those who are humble and repentant (v. 2b). On the other hand, he will severely punish idolaters who persist in evil and ignore his attempts at reconciliation (vv. 3–4). Verse 3 gives a detailed description of these hypocritical evildoers.[222] They offer sacrifices and incense, but at the same time they are guilty of violent crimes, infractions of rituals prescribed by the Mosaic law, and idolatry.[223] These evildoers persecute the godly, but the Lord assures his loyal followers he will repay these enemies for their sins (vv. 5–6).

The Lord now returns to the theme of Zion's restoration, comparing her to a pregnant woman who gives birth without having to endure labor pains (v. 7). In the same way Zion's exiled children will suddenly be restored to her (v. 8), as the Lord delivers what he has promised (v. 9). This announcement should bring great joy to those who love Zion and mourn over her past demise (v. 10), for they will be the beneficiaries of her restoration. Zion's citizens will collect the wealth of the nations with all the eagerness of a thirsty infant drinking from its mother's milk-filled breasts (vv. 11–12a). Zion's residents will feel as secure as a child in its mother's arms (vv. 12b–13).

The Lord's servants will rejoice as they see his power bring about Zion's restoration (v. 14a), but the Lord's enemies will be the objects of his angry judgment (vv. 14b–16). He will come as a mighty warrior and punish all men, many of whom will fall by his sword. The special target of divine wrath will be those within the covenant community who engage in pagan religious practices and ritually defile themselves by eating prohibited, unclean food (v. 17; see vv. 3–5). This group will be completely destroyed.

This revelation of God's power and glory will have a worldwide impact (v. 18). When the dust of divine judgment settles, there will be a few sur-

222. The NIV translation assumes that there is a series of comparisons here, but this is interpretive; there are no indicators in the Hebrew text that comparisons are in view. It is preferable to see here a list of the evildoers' practices, which combine traditional cultic rites with pagan behavior.
223. The significance of breaking a dog's neck is unclear. Perhaps some type of cultic infraction is in view. According to Deut. 21:1–9, if a man was found murdered in a field, the closest town was to make atonement for the deed by breaking a heifer's neck. Since the preceding line in Isa. 66:3 refers to a violent crime, it is possible that such a scenario is in the background. Perhaps the sinners described in v. 3 were carrying out the prescribed ritual with dogs rather than heifers. The same Hebrew verb is used of breaking the neck in Deut. 21:4 and Isa. 66:3.

vivors among the enemies of God (see v. 16, which says that "many," but not all, of God's enemies will die). Having personally witnessed God's power, they will be sent among the distant nations to testify of his majesty and to retrieve the rest of God's exiled people (vv. 19–20). Some of those who return from exile will be designated as priests and Levites (v. 21).[224]

The prophecy ends with a vision of the future. The Lord makes a promise to his loyal followers (v. 22). Just as the new heavens and new earth (see 65:17) will be permanently established, so the reputation and descendants of the godly will endure. As for the Gentile nations, they will worship the Lord on a regular (monthly and weekly) basis (v. 23). Perhaps as an incentive to remain loyal to the Lord, they will gaze on the corpses of the rebels who were destroyed by God's judgment (v. 24; see vv. 15–17). The rebels' burial site is depicted as a maggot-infested mass grave from which the smoke of burning corpses ascends continually.

Toward the beginning of Isaiah's prophecy, there is a denunciation of "rebels" who engage in pagan practices in "gardens." They are destroyed by the unquenchable fire of divine judgment that purifies Zion and makes it the center of worldwide worship (see 1:27–2:4). The prophecy now comes full circle as it ends with an assuring word to the godly remnant, a vision of worldwide worship, and a vivid portrait of the demise of God's rebellious enemies.

Bibliography

Commentaries

Blenkinsopp, J. *Isaiah 1–39*. AB. New York: Doubleday, 2000.

Childs, B. S. *Isaiah*. OTL. Louisville: Westminster John Knox, 2001.

Clements, R. E. *Isaiah 1–39*. NCB. Grand Rapids: Eerdmans, 1980.

Gray, G. B. *A Critical and Exegetical Commentary on the Book of Isaiah I–XXVII*. ICC. Edinburgh: T & T Clark, 1912.

Hayes, J. and S. Irvine. *Isaiah the Eighth-Century Prophet: His Times and His Preaching*. Nashville: Abingdon, 1987.

Kaiser, O. *Isaiah 1–12*. OTL. 2d. ed. Philadelphia: Westminster, 1972.

———. *Isaiah 13–39*. OTL. 2d ed. Philadelphia: Westminster, 1974.

Motyer, J. A. *The Prophecy of Isaiah*. Downers Grove, Ill.: InterVarsity, 1993.

North, C. R. *The Second Isaiah*. Oxford: Clarendon, 1964.

Oswalt, J. N. *The Book of Isaiah: Chapters 1–39*. NICOT. Grand Rapids: Eerdmans, 1986.

———. *The Book of Isaiah: Chapters 40–66*. NICOT. Grand Rapids: Eerdmans, 1998.

Seitz, C. R. *Isaiah 1–39*. Interpretation. Louisville: John Knox, 1993.

Watts, J. D. W. *Isaiah 1–33*. WBC. Waco, Tex.: Word, 1985.

———. *Isaiah 34–66*. WBC. Waco, Tex.: Word, 1987.

---

224. I understand "some of them" in v. 21 to refer to the returning exiles, called "your brothers" in v. 20, in which the addressees are the Lord's faithful followers who love Zion (see vv. 5, 10). Some understand the Gentile messengers to be in view in v. 21, in which case this is a startling prediction that Gentiles will be incorporated into the covenant community in a priestly role.

Westermann, C. *Isaiah 40–66*. OTL. Translated by D. M. G. Stalker. Philadelphia: Westminster, 1969.

Whybray, R. N. *Isaiah 40–66*. NCB. Grand Rapids: Eerdmans, 1981.

Wildberger, H. *Isaiah 1–12*. Translated by T. H. Trapp. Minneapolis: Fortress, 1991.

———. *Isaiah 13–27*. Translated by T. H. Trapp. Minneapolis: Fortress, 1997.

Young, E. J. *The Book of Isaiah*. 3 vols. Grand Rapids: Eerdmans, 1965–72.

Recent Studies

General

Aitken, K. T. "Hearing and Seeing: Metamorphoses of a Motif in Isaiah 1–39." In *Among the Prophets: Language, Image and Structure in the Prophetic Writings,* edited by P. R. Davies and D. J. A. Clines, 12–41. Sheffield: JSOT, 1993.

Barton, J. "Ethics in the Book of Isaiah." In *Writing and Reading the Scroll of Isaiah: Studies of an Interpretative Tradition,* edited by C. C. Broyles and C. A. Evans, VTSup 70, 67–77. Leiden: Brill, 1997.

———. *Isaiah 1–39*. Old Testament Guides. Sheffield: Sheffield Academic Press, 1995.

Broyles, C. C., and C. A. Evans, eds. *Writing and Reading the Scroll of Isaiah: Studies of an Interpretative Tradition*. 2 vols. Leiden: Brill, 1997.

Brueggemann, W. "Planned People/Planned Book?" In *Writing and Reading the Scroll of Isaiah: Studies of an Interpretative Tradition,* edited by C. C. Broyles and C. A. Evans, VTSup 70, 19–37. Leiden: Brill, 1997.

Carr, D. M. "Reaching for Unity in Isaiah," *JSOT* 57 (1993): 361–80.

———. "Reading Isaiah from Beginning (Isaiah 1) to End (Isaiah 65- 66): Multiple Modern Possibilities." In *New Visions of Isaiah,* edited by R. F. Melugin and M. A. Sweeney, JSOTSup 214, 188–218. Sheffield: Sheffield Academic Press, 1996.

Carroll, R. P. "Blindsight and the Vision Thing: Blindness and Insight in the Book of Isaiah." In *Writing and Reading the Scroll of Isaiah: Studies of an Interpretative Tradition,* edited by C. C. Broyles and C. A. Evans, VTSup 70, 79–93. Leiden: Brill, 1997.

Clements, R. E. "A Light to the Nations: A Central Theme of the Book of Isaiah." In *Forming Prophetic Literature: Essays on Isaiah and the Twelve in Honor of John D. W. Watts,* edited by J. W. Watts and P. R. House, 57–69. Sheffield: JSOT, 1996.

———. "Zion as Symbol and Political Reality: A Central Isaianic Quest." In *Studies in the Book of Isaiah: Festschrift Willem A. M. Beuken,* edited by J. van Ruiten and M. Vervenne, 3–17. Louvain: Peeters, 1997.

Clifford, R. J. "The Unity of the Book of Isaiah and Its Cosmogonic Language." *CBQ* 55 (1993): 1–17.

Coggins, R. J. "New Ways with Old Texts: How Does One Write a Commentary on Isaiah?" *ExpT* 107 (1995–96): 362–67.

Conrad, E. W. "Prophet, Redactor, and Audience: Reforming the Notion of Isaiah's Formation." In *New Visions of Isaiah,* edited by R. F. Melugin and M. A. Sweeney, JSOTSup 214, 306–26. Sheffield: Sheffield Academic Press, 1996.

———. *Reading Isaiah*. Minneapolis: Fortress, 1991.

———. "Reading Isaiah and the Twelve as Prophetic Books." In *Writing and Reading the Scroll of Isaiah: Studies of an Interpretative Tradition,* edited by C. C. Broyles and C. A. Evans, VTSup 70, 3–17. Leiden: Brill, 1997.

Darr, K. P. *Isaiah's Vision and Family of God*. Literary Currents in Biblical Interpretation. Louisville: Westminster John Knox, 1994.

Davies, A. *Double Standards in Isaiah: Re-evaluating Prophetic Ethics and Divine Justice*. Leiden: Brill, 2000.

de Waard, J. *A Handbook on Isaiah*. Winona Lake, Ind.: Eisenbrauns, 1997.

Doorly, W. J. *Isaiah of Jerusalem: An Introduction.* New York: Paulist, 1992.

Gitay, Y. "Back to the Historical Isaiah: Reflections on the Act of Reading." In *Studies in the Book of Isaiah: Festschrift Willem A. M. Beuken,* edited by J. van Ruiten and M. Vervenne, 63–72. Louvain: Peeters, 1997.

———. "Why Metaphors? A Study of the Texture of Isaiah." In *Writing and Reading the Scroll of Isaiah: Studies of an Interpretative Tradition,* edited by C. C. Broyles and C. A. Evans, VTSup 70, 57–65. Leiden: Brill, 1997.

Hill, L. H. "Reading Isaiah as a Theological Unity Based on an Exegetical Investigation of the Exodus Motif." Ph.D. diss., Southwestern Baptist Theological Seminary, 1993.

Holladay, W. L. *Isaiah: Scroll of a Prophetic Heritage.* Grand Rapids: Eerdmans, 1978.

Laato, A. *"About Zion I Will Not Be Silent": The Book of Isaiah as an Ideological Unity.* Stockholm: Almqvist & Wiksell, 1998.

Love, N. P. "The Mountain of the Lord in the Book of Isaiah: Prominent Themes in Contexts Mentioning the Mountain of the Lord and Related Terminology." Ph.D. diss., Trinity Evangelical Divinity School, 1996.

Ma, W. "The Spirit (רוּחַ) of God in the Book of Isaiah and Its Eschatological Significance." Ph.D. diss., Fuller Theological Seminary, 1996.

Melugin, R. F. "The Book of Isaiah and the Construction of Meaning." In *Writing and Reading the Scroll of Isaiah: Studies of an Interpretative Tradition,* edited by C. C. Broyles and C. A. Evans, VTSup 70, 39–55. Leiden: Brill, 1997.

Miscall, P. D. *Isaiah.* Readings: A New Biblical Commentary. Sheffield: JSOT, 1993.

———. "Isaiah: The Labyrinth of Images." *Semeia* 54 (1991): 103–21.

Mosley, H. R. "The Concept of Faith in Isaiah 1–39." Ph.D. diss., New Orleans Baptist Theological Seminary, 1992.

O'Connell, R. H. *Concentricity and Continuity: The Literary Structure of Isaiah.* JSOTSup 188. Sheffield: Sheffield Academic Press, 1994.

O'Kane, M. "Isaiah: A Prophet in the Footsteps of Moses." *JSOT* 69 (1996): 29–51.

———. "Wisdom Influence in First Isaiah." *Proceedings of the Irish Biblical Association* 14 (1991): 64–78.

Oswalt, J. N. "Judgment and Hope: The Full-Orbed Gospel." *Trinity Journal* 17 (1996): 191–202.

———. "The Kerygmatic Structure of the Book of Isaiah." In *"Go to the Land I Will Show You": Studies in Honor of Dwight W. Young,* edited by J. E. Coleson and V. H. Matthews, 143–57. Winona Lake, Ind.: Eisenbrauns, 1996.

Rendtorff, R. "The Book of Isaiah: A Complex Unity. Synchronic and Diachronic Reading." In *New Visions of Isaiah,* edited by R. F. Melugin and M. A. Sweeney, JSOTSup 214, 32–49. Sheffield: Sheffield Academic Press, 1996.

Roberts, J. J. M. "Double Entendre in First Isaiah." *CBQ* 54 (1992): 39–48.

Rooker, M. F. "Dating Isaiah 40–66: What Does the Evidence Say?" *WTJ* 58 (1996): 303–12.

Seitz, C. R. "How Is the Prophet Isaiah Present in the Latter Half of the Book? The Logic of Chapters 40–66 within the Book of Isaiah." *JBL* 115 (1996): 219–40.

———. *Zion's Final Destiny: The Development of the Book of Isaiah.* Minneapolis: Fortress, 1991.

Sheppard, G. T. "The 'Scope' of Isaiah as a Book of Jewish and Christian Scriptures." In *New Visions of Isaiah,* edited by R. F. Melugin and M. A. Sweeney, JSOTSup 214, 257–81. Sheffield: Sheffield Academic Press, 1996.

———. "Two Turbulent Decades of Research on Isaiah." *Toronto Journal of Theology* 9 (1993): 107–10.

Sommer, B. D. "Allusions and Illusions: The Unity of the Book of Isaiah in Light of Deutero-Isaiah's Use of Prophetic Tradition." In *New Visions of Isaiah,* edited by R. F. Melugin and M. A. Sweeney, JSOTSup 214, 156–86. Sheffield: Sheffield Academic Press, 1996.

Sweeney, M. A. "The Book of Isaiah as Prophetic Torah." In *New Visions of Isaiah,* edited by R. F. Melugin and M. A. Sweeney, JSOTSup 214, 50–67. Sheffield: Sheffield Academic Press, 1996.

———. "The Book of Isaiah in Recent Research." *Currents in Research: Biblical Studies* 1 (1993): 141–62.

———. *Isaiah 1–39 with an Introduction to the Prophetic Literature.* FOTL. Grand Rapids: Eerdmans, 1996.

Tate, M. E. "The Book of Isaiah in Recent Research." In *Forming Prophetic Literature: Essays on Isaiah and the Twelve in Honor of John D. W. Watts,* edited by J. W. Watts and P. R. House, 22–56. Sheffield: JSOT, 1996.

Webb, B. G. *The Message of Isaiah: On Eagles' Wings.* The Bible Speaks Today. Leicester, England, and Downers Grove, Ill.: InterVarsity, 1996.

Williamson, H. G. M. *The Book Called Isaiah: Deutero-Isaiah's Role in Composition and Redaction.* Oxford: Clarendon, 1994.

———. "First and Last in Isaiah." In *Of Prophets' Visions and the Wisdom of the Sages: Essays in Honour of R. Norman Whybray on His Seventieth Birthday,* edited by H. A. McKay and D. J. A. Clines, JSOTSup 162, 95–108. Sheffield: JSOT, 1993.

———. "Isaiah and the Wise." In *Wisdom in Ancient Israel: Essays in Honour of J. A. Emerton,* edited by J. Day, 133–41. Cambridge: Cambridge University Press, 1995.

———. "Synchronic and Diachronic in Isaiah Perspective." In *Synchronic or Diachronic? A Debate in Old Testament Exegesis,* edited by J. C. de Moor, 211–26. Leiden: Brill, 1995.

Willis, J. T. "Exclusivistic and Inclusivistic Aspects of the Concept of 'The People of God' in the Book of Isaiah." *Restoration Quarterly* 40 (1998): 3–12.

Wong, G. C. I. "The Nature of Faith in Isaiah of Jerusalem." Ph.D. diss., Cambridge University, 1995.

Wong, Y. C. "A Text-Centered Approach to Old Testament Exegesis and Theology and Its Application to the Book of Isaiah." Ph.D. diss., Trinity Evangelical Divinity School, 1994.

Isaiah 1–12

Bartelt, A. H. *The Book around Immanuel: Style and Structure in Isaiah 2–12.* Winona Lake, Ind.: Eisenbrauns, 1996.

———. "Isaiah 5 and 9: In- or Interdependence." In *Fortunate the Eyes That See: Essays in Honor of David Noel Freedman in Celebration of His Seventieth Birthday,* edited by A. B. Beck et al., 157–74. Grand Rapids: Eerdmans, 1995.

Beale, G. K. "Isaiah vi 9–13: A Retributive Taunt against Idolatry." *VT* 41 (1991): 257–78.

Ben Zvi, E. "Isaiah 1,4–9, Isaiah, and the Events of 701 BCE in Judah: A Question of Premise and Evidence." *SJOT* 1 (1991): 95–111.

Brenneman, J. E. "Canon(s) in Conflict: Negotiating Texts in True and False Prophecy: Isaiah 2:2–4 / Micah 4:1–4 vs. Joel 4:9–12 (Eng. 3:9–12)." Ph.D. diss., Claremont Graduate School, 1994.

Brown, W. P. "The So-Called Refrain in Isaiah 5:25–30 and 9:7–10:4." *CBQ* 52 (1990): 432–43.

Clements, R. E. "The Immanuel Prophecy of Isa. 7:10–17 and Its Messianic Interpretation." In *Die hebräische Bibel und ihre zweifache Nachgeschichte: Fst. R. Rendtorff,* edited by E. Blum et al. 225–40. Neukirchen-Vluyn: Neukirchener Verlag, 1990.

Dearman, J. A. "The Son of Tabeel (Isaiah 7.6)." In *Prophets and Paradigms: Essays in Honor of Gene M. Tucker,* edited by S. B. Reid, 33–47. Sheffield: JSOT, 1996.

Dennison, C. G. "Isaiah's Christmas Children: Shear-jashub." *Kerux* 14, no. 3 (1999): 36–42.

Emerton, J. A. "The Translation of Isaiah 5,1." In *The Scriptures and the Scrolls: Studies in Honour of A. S. van der Woude on the Occasion of His Sixty-fifth Birthday,* edited by F. G. Martínez et al., VTSup 49, 18–30. Leiden: Brill, 1992.

Eshel, H. "Isaiah viii 23: An Historical-Geographical Analogy." *VT* 40 (1990): 104–9.

Eslinger, L. "The Infinite in a Finite Organical Perception (Isaiah vi 1–5)." *VT* 45 (1995): 145–73.

Finley, T. J., and G. A. Payton. "A Discourse Analysis of Isaiah 7–12." *Journal of Translation and Textlinguistics* 6 (1993): 317–35.

Friesen, I. D. "Composition and Continuity in Isaiah 1–12." Ph.D. diss., St. Michael (Toronto), 1990.

Gitay, J. *Isaiah and His Audience: The Structure and Meaning of Isaiah 1–12.* Assen-Maastricht: Van Gorcum, 1991.

Goldingay, J. "The Compound Name in Isaiah 9:5(6)." *CBQ* 61 (1999): 239–44.

———. "Isaiah i 1 and ii 1." *VT* 48 (1998): 326–32.

Gosse, B. "Isaiah 8.23b and the Three Great Parts of the Book of Isaiah." *JSOT* 70 (1996): 57–62.

House, P. R. "Isaiah's Call and Its Context in Isaiah 1–6." *Criswell Theological Review* 6 (1993): 207–22.

Irsigler, H. "Speech Acts and Intention in the 'Song of the Vineyard' Isaiah 5:1–7." *OTE* 10 (1997): 39–68.

Irvine, S. A. *Isaiah, Ahaz, and the Syro-Ephraimitic Crisis.* SBLDS 123. Atlanta: Scholars Press, 1990.

———. "Isaiah's She'ar-Yashub and the Davidic House." *Biblische Zeitschrift* 37 (1993): 78–99.

———. "Problems of Text and Translation in Isaiah 10,13b." In *History and Interpretation: Essays in Honour of John H. Hayes,* edited by M. P. Graham et al., 133–44. Sheffield: JSOT, 1993.

———. "The Isaianic *Denkschrift:* Reconsidering an Old Hypothesis." *ZAW* 104 (1992): 216–31.

Jones, B. C. "Isaiah 8.11 and Isaiah's Vision of Yahweh." In *History and Interpretation: Essays in Honour of John H. Hayes,* edited by M. P. Graham et al., 145–59. Sheffield: JSOT, 1993.

Kamesar, A. "The Virgin of Isaiah 7:14: The Philological Argument from the Second to the Fifth Century." *JTS* 41 (1990): 51–75.

Korpel, M. C. A. "Structural Analysis as a Tool for Redactional Criticism: The Example of Isaiah 5 and 10.1–6." *JSOT* 69 (1996): 53–71.

Landy, F. "Strategies of Concentration and Diffusion in Isaiah 6." *Biblical Interpretation* 7 (1999): 58–86.

Lind, M. "Political Implications of Isaiah 6." In *Writing and Reading the Scroll of Isaiah: Studies of an Interpretative Tradition,* edited by C. C. Broyles and C. A. Evans, VTSup 70, 317–38. Leiden: Brill, 1997.

McLaughlin, J. L. "Their Hearts *Were* Hardened: The Use of Isaiah 6, 9–10 in the Book of Isaiah." *Bib* 75 (1994): 1–25.

Melugin, R. F. "Figurative Speech and the Reading of Isaiah 1 as Scripture." In *New Visions of Isaiah,* edited by R. F. Melugin and M. A. Sweeney, JSOTSup 214, 282–305. Sheffield: Sheffield Academic Press, 1996.

Menzies, G. W. "To What Does Faith Lead? The Two-Stranded Textual Tradition of Isaiah 7.9b." *JSOT* 80 (1998): 111–28.

Ogden, G. "Translating Isaiah 5.1: What Does the Poet Sing?" *BT* 49 (1998): 245–46.

Olivier, H. "God as Friendly Patron: Reflections on Isaiah 5:1–7." In *"Feet on Level Ground": A South African Tribute of Old Testament Essays in Honor of Gerhard Hasel,* edited by K. Van Wyk, 301–28. Berrien Center, Mich.: Hester, 1996.

Olivier, J. P. J. "Rendering ידיד as Benevolent Patron in Isaiah 5:1." *JNSL* 22 (1996): 59–65.

Oswalt, J. N. "The Significance of the '*Almah* Prophecy in the Context of Isaiah 7–12." *Criswell Theological Review* 6 (1993): 223–35.

Prinsloo, W. S. "Isaiah 12: One, Two, or Three Songs?" In *Goldene Äpfel in silbernen Schalen,* edited by K.-D. Schunck and M. Augustin, 25–33. Frankfurt am Main: Peter Lang, 1992.

Roberts, J. J. M. "Whose Child Is This? Reflections on the Speaking Voice in Isaiah 9:5." *HTR* 90 (1997): 115–29.

Robinson, G. D. "The Motif of Deafness and Blindness in Isaiah 6:9–10: A Contextual, Literary, and Theological Analysis." *Bulletin of Biblical Research* 8 (1998): 167–86.

Sailhamer, J. H. "Evidence from Isaiah 2." In *A Case for Premillennialism,* edited by D. Campbell and J. Townsend, 79–102. Chicago: Moody, 1992.

Schibler, D. "Messianism and Messianic Prophecy in Isaiah 1–12 and 28–33." In *The Lord's Anointed,* edited by P. E. Satterthwaite, R. S. Hess, and G. J. Wenham, 87–104. Grand Rapids: Baker, 1995.

Schultz, R. "The King in the Book of Isaiah." In *The Lord's Anointed,* edited by P. E. Satterthwaite, R. S. Hess, and G. J. Wenham, 141–65. Grand Rapids: Baker, 1995.

Schwartz, B. J. "Torah from Zion: Isaiah's Temple Vision (Isaiah 2:1–4)." In *Sanctity of Time and Space in Tradition and Modernity,* edited by A. Houtman et al., 11–26. Leiden: Brill, 1998.

Sweeney, M. A. "A Philological and Form-Critical Reevaluation of Isaiah 8:16–9:6." *HAR* 14 (1994): 215–31.

———. "Jesse's New Shoot in Isaiah 11: A Josianic Reading of the Prophet Isaiah." In *A Gift of God in Due Season: Essays on Scripture and Community in Honor of James A. Sanders,* edited by R. D. Weis and D. M. Carr, 103–18. Sheffield: Sheffield Academic Press, 1996.

———. "Sargon's Threat against Jerusalem in Isaiah 10,27–32." *Bib* 75 (1994): 457–70.

Tomasino, A. J. "Isaiah 1,1–2,4 and 63–66, and the Composition of the Isaianic Corpus." *JSOT* 57 (1993): 81–98.

van Wieringen, A. L. H. M. *The Implied Reader in Isaiah 6–12.* Leiden: Brill, 1998.

———. "Isaiah 12,1–6: A Domain and Communication Analysis." In *Studies in the Book of Isaiah: Festschrift Willem A. M. Beuken,* edited by J. van Ruiten and M. Vervenne, 149–72. Louvain: Peeters, 1997.

Wegner, P. D. "A Re-examination of Isaiah ix 1–6." *VT* 42 (1992): 103–12.

———. *An Examination of Kingship and Messianic Expectation in Isaiah 1–35.* Lewiston, N.Y.: Mellen Biblical Press, 1992.

———. "Another Look at Isaiah viii 23b." *VT* 41 (1991): 481–84.

Williamson, H. G. M. "Isaiah 6,13 and 1,29–31." In *Studies in the Book of Isaiah: Festschrift Willem A. M. Beuken,* edited by J. van Ruiten and M. Vervenne, 119–28. Louvain: Peeters, 1997.

———. "Isaiah XI 11–16 and the Redaction of Isaiah I–XII." In *Congress Volume: Paris, 1992,* edited by J. A. Emerton, VTSup 61. Leiden: Brill, 1995.

———. "The Messianic Texts in Isaiah 1–39." In *King and Messiah in Israel and the Ancient Near East,* edited by J. Day, JSOTSup 270, 238–70. Sheffield: Sheffield Academic Press, 1998.

———. "Relocating Isaiah 1:2–9." In *Writing and Reading the Scroll of Isaiah: Studies of an*

Interpretative Tradition, edited by C. C. Broyles and C. A. Evans, VTSup 70, 263–77. Leiden: Brill, 1997.

Willis, J. T. "Isaiah 2:2–5 and the Psalms of Zion." In *Writing and Reading the Scroll of Isaiah: Studies of an Interpretative Tradition,* edited by C. C. Broyles and C. A. Evans, VTSup 70, 295–316. Leiden: Brill, 1997.

Wong, G. C. I. "A Cuckoo in the Textual Nest at Isaiah 7:9b?" *JTS* 47 (1996): 123–24.

———. "Is 'God with Us' in Isaiah viii 8?" *VT* 49 (1999): 426–32.

Isaiah 13–27

Anderson, B. W. "The Slaying of the Fleeing, Twisting Serpent: Isaiah 27:1 in Context." In *Uncovering Ancient Stones: Essays in Memory of H. Neil Richardson,* edited by L. M. Hopfe, 3–15. Winona Lake, Ind.: Eisenbrauns, 1994.

Auret, A. "A Different Background for Isaiah 22:15–25 Presents an Alternative Paradigm: Disposing of Political and Religious Opposition?" *OTE* 6 (1993): 46–56.

Biddle, M. E. "The City of Chaos and the New Jerusalem: Isaiah 24–27 in Context." *Perspectives in Religious Studies* 22 (1995): 5–12.

Boshoff, F. J. "A Survey into the Theological Function of the Oracles against the Nations in the Old Testament with Special Reference to Isaiah 13–23." Ph.D. diss., University of Pretoria, 1992.

Chisholm, R. B., Jr. "The 'Everlasting Covenant' and the 'City of Chaos': Intentional Ambiguity and Irony in Isaiah 24." *Criswell Theological Review* 6 (1993): 237–53.

Day, J. "The Dependence of Isaiah 26:13–17 on Hosea 13:4–14:10 and Its Relevance to Some Theories of the Redaction of the 'Isaiah Apocalypse'." In *Writing and Reading the Scroll of Isaiah: Studies of an Interpretative Tradition,* edited by C. C. Broyles and C. A. Evans, VTSup 70, 357–68. Leiden: Brill, 1997.

Day, J. N. "God and Leviathan in Isaiah 27:1." *BSac* 155 (1998): 423–36.

Doyle, B. "A Literary Analysis of Isaiah 25,10a." In *Studies in the Book of Isaiah: Festschrift Willem A. M. Beuken,* edited by J. van Ruiten and M. Vervenne, 173–93. Louvain: Peeters, 1997.

Ellington, J. "A Swimming Lesson (Isaiah 25.11)." *BT* 47 (1996): 246–47.

Fouts, D. M. "A Suggestion for Isaiah xxvi 16." *VT* 41 (1991): 472–75.

Franke, C. A. "The Function of the Oracles against Babylon in Isaiah 14 and 17." *SBLSP* (1993): 250–59.

———. "Reversals of Fortune in the Ancient Near East: A Study of the Babylon Oracles in the Book of Isaiah." In *New Visions of Isaiah,* JSOTSup 214, edited by R. F. Melugin and M. A. Sweeney, 104–23. Sheffield: Sheffield Academic Press, 1996.

Fry, M. J. "The 'Oracles Concerning Babylon': An Exegetical Study of Isaiah 13:1–14:27." Ph.D. diss., Union Theological Seminary, 1992.

Gallagher, W. R. "On the Identity of Hêlēl Ben Šaḥar of Is. 14:12–15*." *UF* 26 (1994): 131–46.

Geyer, J. B. "The Night of Dumah (Isaiah xxi 11–12)." *VT* 42 (1992): 317–39.

Heater, H. "Do the Prophets Teach that Babylonia Will Be Rebuilt in the *Eschaton?*" *JETS* 41 (1998): 23–43.

Hendrik, J. B., and H. van Grol, eds. *Studies in Isaiah 24–27: The Isaiah Workshop.* Leiden: Brill, 2000.

Holladay, W. L. "Text, Structure, and Irony in the Poem on the Fall of the Tyrant, Isaiah 14." *CBQ* 61 (1999): 633–45.

Irwin, W. H. "The City of Chaos in Isa 24,10 and the Genitive of Result." *Bib* 75 (1994): 401–3.

Israelit-Groll, S. "The Egyptian Background to Isaiah 19.18." In *Boundaries of the Ancient*

Near Eastern World: A Tribute to Cyrus H. Gordon, edited by M. Lubetski et al., JSOTSup 273, 300–303. Sheffield: Sheffield Academic Press, 1998.

Itoh, R. "Literary and Linguistic Approach to Isaiah 24–27." Ph.D. diss., Trinity Evangelical Divinity School, 1995.

Jensen, J. "Helel Ben Shahar (Isaiah 14:12–15) in Bible and Tradition." In *Writing and Reading the Scroll of Isaiah: Studies of an Interpretative Tradition,* edited by C. C. Broyles and C. A. Evans, VTSup 70, 339–56. Leiden: Brill, 1997.

Jones, B. C. *Howling over Moab: Irony and Rhetoric in Isaiah 15–16.* SBLDS 157. Atlanta: Scholars Press, 1996.

Lubetski, M., and M. Gottlieb. "Isaiah 18: The Egyptian Nexus." In *Boundaries of the Ancient Near Eastern World: A Tribute to Cyrus H. Gordon,* edited by M. Lubetski et al., JSOTSup 273, 364–84. Sheffield: Sheffield Academic Press, 1998.

Nakamura, C. L. "Monarch, Mountain, and Meal: The Eschatological Banquet of Isaiah 24:21–23; 25:6–10a." Ph.D. diss., Princeton Theological Seminary, 1992.

Niccacci, A. "Isaiah xviii–xx from an Egyptological Perspective." *VT* 48 (1998): 214–38.

Pagán, S. "Apocalyptic Poetry: Isaiah 24–27." *BT* 43 (1992): 314–25.

Poirier, J. C. "An Illuminating Parallel to Isaiah xiv 12." *VT* 49 (1999): 371–89.

Polaski, D. C. "Destruction, Construction, Argumentation: A Rhetorical Reading of Isaiah 24–27." In *Vision and Persuasion: Rhetorical Dimensions of Apocalyptic Discourse,* edited by G. Carey and L. G. Bloomquist, 19–39. St Louis: Chalice, 1999.

———. "The Politics of Prayer: A New Historicist Reading of Isaiah 26." *Perspectives in Religious Studies* 25 (1998): 357–71.

———. "Reflections on a Mosaic Covenant: The Eternal Covenant (Isaiah 24.5) and Intertextuality." *JSOT* 77 (1998): 55–73.

Sawyer, J. F. A. "'My Secret Is with Me' (Isaiah 24.16: Some Semantic Links between Isaiah 24–27 and Daniel)." In *Essays in Honour of George Wishart Anderson,* edited by G. Auld, 307–17. Sheffield: JSOT, 1993.

Schoubye, H. "Isaiah's Damascus Oracle: Responding to International Threats." Ph.D. diss., Concordia Seminary, 1996.

Skjoldal, N. O. "The Function of Isaiah 24–27." *JETS* 36 (1993): 163–72.

Smothers, T. G. "Isaiah 15–16." In *Forming Prophetic Literature: Essays on Isaiah and the Twelve in Honor of John D. W. Watts,* edited by J. W. Watts and P. R. House, 70–84. Sheffield: JSOT, 1996.

Uffenheimer, B. "The 'Desert of the Sea' Pronouncement (Isaiah 21:1–10)." In *Pomegranates and Golden Bells: Studies in Biblical, Jewish, and Near Eastern Ritual, Law, and Literature in Honor of Jacob Milgrom,* edited by D. P. Wright et al., 677–88. Winona Lake, Ind.: Eisenbrauns, 1995.

van Grol, H. W. M. "Isaiah 27,10–11: God and His Own People." In *Studies in the Book of Isaiah: Festschrift Willem A. M. Beuken,* edited by J. van Ruiten and M. Vervenne, 195–209. Louvain: Peeters, 1997.

Williamson, H. G. M. "Sound, Sense, and Language in Isaiah 24–27." *JJS* 46 (1995): 1–9.

Willis, J. T. "An Interpretation of Isaiah 22.15–25 and Its Function in the New Testament." In *Early Christian Interpretation of the Scriptures of Israel: Investigations and Proposals,* edited by C. A. Evans and J. A. Sanders, JSNTSup 148, 334–51. Sheffield: Sheffield Academic Press, 1997.

———. "Historical Issues in Isaiah 22,15–25." *Bib* 74 (1993): 60–70.

———. "Textual and Linguistic Issues in Isaiah 22,15–25." *ZAW* 105 (1993): 377–99.

Willis, T. M. "Yahweh's Elders (Isa 24,23): Senior Officials of the Divine Court." *ZAW* 103 (1991): 375–85.

Wodecki, B. "The Religious Universalism of the Pericope Is 25:6–9." In *Goldene Äpfel in sil-*

bernen Schalen, edited by K.-D. Schunck and M. Augustin, 35–47. Frankfurt am Main: Peter Lang, 1992.

Youngblood, R. "The Fall of Lucifer (in More Ways Than One)." *Biblical Research* 14 (1998): 22–31, 47.

Isaiah 28–35

Asen, B. A. "The Garlands of Ephraim: Isaiah 28.1–6 and the *Marzēaḥ.*" *JSOT* 71 (1996): 73–87.

Barré, M. L. "Of Lions and Birds: A Note on Isaiah 31.4–5." In *Among the Prophets: Language, Image, and Structure in the Prophetic Writings,* edited by P. R. Davies and D. J. A. Clines, 55–59. Sheffield: JSOT, 1993.

Beuken, W. A. M. "Isa 29,15–24: Perversion Reverted." In *The Scriptures and the Scrolls: Studies in Honour of A. S. van der Woude on the Occasion of His Sixty-fifth Birthday,* edited by F. G. Martínez et al., VTSup 49, 43–64. Leiden: Brill, 1992.

———. "Isaiah 28: Is It Only Schismatics That Drink Heavily? Beyond the Synchronic versus Diachronic Controversy." In *Synchronic or Diachronic? A Debate in Old Testament Exegesis,* edited by J. C. de Moor, 15–38. Leiden: Brill, 1995.

———. "Isaiah 30: A Prophetic Oracle Transmitted in Two Successive Paradigms." In *Writing and Reading the Scroll of Isaiah: Studies of an Interpretative Tradition,* edited by C. C. Broyles and C. A. Evans, VTSup 70, 369–97. Leiden: Brill, 1997.

———. "Isaiah 34: Lament in Isaianic Context." *OTE* 5 (1992): 78–102.

———. "What Does the Vision Hold: Teachers or One Teacher? Punning Repetition in Isaiah 30:20." *Heythrop Journal* 36 (1995): 451–66.

———. "Women and the Spirit, the Ox and the Ass: The First Binders of the Booklet Isaiah 28–32." *ETL* 74 (1998): 5–26.

Dicou, B. "Literary Function and Literary History of Isaiah 34." *Biblische Notizen* 58 (1991): 30–45.

Eidevall, G. "Lions and Birds as Literature: Some Notes on Isaiah 31 and Hosea 11." *SJOT* 7 (1993): 78–87.

Harrelson, W. "Isaiah 35 in Recent Research and Translation." In *Language, Theology, and the Bible: Essays in Honour of James Barr,* edited by S. E. Balentine and J. Barton, 247–60. Oxford: Clarendon, 1994.

Holmyard, H. R., III. "Does Isaiah 33:23 Address Israel or Israel's Enemy?" *BSac* 152 (1995): 273–78.

———. "Mosaic Eschatology in Isaiah, Especially Chapters 1, 28–33." Ph.D. diss., Dallas Theological Seminary, 1992.

Landy, F. "Tracing the Voice of the Other: Isaiah 28 and the Covenant with Death." In *The New Literary Criticism and the Hebrew Bible,* edited by J. C. Exum and D. J. A. Clines, 140–62. Sheffield: JSOT, 1993.

Mathews, C. R. *Defending Zion: Edom's Desolation and Jacob's Restoration (Isaiah 34–35) in Context.* Berlin and New York: de Gruyter, 1995.

Miscall, P. D. *Isaiah 34–35: A Nightmare/A Dream.* JSOTSup 281. Sheffield: Sheffield Academic Press, 1998.

Routledge, R. L. "The Siege and Deliverance of the City of David in Isaiah 29:1–8." *TynB* 43 (1992): 183–90.

Stansell, G. "Isaiah 28–33: Blest Be the Tie that Binds (Isaiah Together)." In *New Visions of Isaiah,* edited by R. F. Melugin and M. A. Sweeney, JSOTSup 214, 68–103. Sheffield: JSOT, 1996.

Weis, R. D. "Angels, Altars, and Angles of Vision: The Case of אֶרְאֶלָּם in Isaiah 33:7." In *Tradition of the Text: Studies Offered to Dominique Barthélemy in Celebration of His Seven-*

tieth Birthday, edited by G. J. Norton and S. Pisano, 285–92. Freiburg: Universitätsverlag, 1991.

Wong, G. C. I. "Faith and Works in Isaiah xxx 15." *VT* 47 (1997): 236–46.

———. "Isaiah's Opposition to Egypt in Isaiah xxxi 1–3." *VT* 46 (1996): 392–401.

———. "On 'Visits' and 'Visions' in Isaiah xxix 6–7." *VT* 45 (1995): 370–76.

Isaiah 36–39

Barré, M. "Restoring the 'Lost' Prayer in the Psalm of Hezekiah (Isaiah 38:16–17b)." *JBL* 114 (1995): 385–99.

Darr, K. P. "No Strength to Deliver: A Contextual Analysis of Hezekiah's Proverb in Isaiah 37.3b." In *New Visions of Isaiah,* edited by R. F. Melugin and M. A. Sweeney, JSOTSup 214, 219–56. Sheffield: Sheffield Academic Press, 1996.

Hoffer, V. "An Exegesis of Isaiah 38:21." *JSOT* 56 (1992): 69–84.

Konkel, A. H. "The Sources of the Story of Hezekiah in the Book of Isaiah." *VT* 43 (1993): 462–82.

Kruger, H. A. J. "Gods', for Argument's Sake: A Few Remarks on the Literature and Theological Intention of Isaiah 36–37." *OTE* 9 (1996): 52–67, 383–99.

Seitz, C. *Zion's Final Destiny: The Development of the Book of Isaiah. A Reassessment of Isaiah 36–39.* Minneapolis: Fortress, 1991.

Isaiah 40–55

Abma, R. "Traveling from Babylon to Zion: Location and Its Function in Isaiah 49–55." *JSOT* 74 (1997): 3–28.

Bailey, D. P. "Concepts of *Stellvertretung* in the Interpretation of Isaiah 53." In *Jesus and the Suffering Servant,* edited by W. H. Bellinger Jr., and W. R. Farmer, 223–50. Harrisburg, Pa.: Trinity Press International, 1998.

———. "The Suffering Servant: Recent Tübingen Scholarship on Isaiah 53." In *Jesus and the Suffering Servant,* edited by W. H. Bellinger Jr., and W. R. Farmer, 251–59. Harrisburg, Pa.: Trinity Press International, 1998.

Balentine, S. E. "Isaiah 45: God's 'I Am,' Israel's 'You Are.'" *Horizons in Biblical Theology* 16 (1994): 103–20.

Baltzer, K. R. "The Polemic against the Gods and Its Relevance for Second Isaiah's Conception of the New Jerusalem." In *Second Temple Studies,* vol. 2: *Temple Community in the Persian Period,* edited by T. Eskenazi and K. H. Richards, JSOTSup 175, 54–59. Sheffield: JSOT, 1994.

Barré, M. "Textual and Rhetorical-Critical Observations on the Last Servant Song (Isaiah 52:13–53:12)." *CBQ* 62 (2000): 1–27.

Barstad, H. M. "Akkadian 'Loanwords' in Isaiah 40–55—And the Question of Babylonian Origin of Deutero-Isaiah." In *Text and Theology: Studies in Honour of Professor Dr. Theol. Magne Saebø Presented on the Occasion of His Sixty-fifth Birthday,* edited by A. Tångberg, 26–48. Oslo: Verbum, 1994.

———. *The Babylonian Captivity of the Book of Isaiah: 'Exilic' Judah and the Provenance of Isaiah 40–55.* Oslo: Novus forlag, 1997.

———. "The Future of the 'Servant Songs': Some Reflections on the Relationship of Biblical Scholarship to Its Own Tradition." In *Language, Theology, and the Bible: Essays in Honour of James Barr,* edited by S. E. Balentine and J. Barton, 261–70. Oxford: Clarendon, 1994.

Bergey, R. "The Rhetorical Role of Reiteration in the Suffering Servant Poem (Isa 52:13–53:12)," *JETS* 40 (1997): 177–88.

Biddle, M. E. "Lady Sion's Alter Egos: Isaiah 47.1–15 and 57.6–13 as Structural Counterparts." In *New Visions of Isaiah,* edited by R. F. Melugin and M. A. Sweeney, JSOTSup 214, 124–39. Sheffield: Sheffield Academic Press, 1996.

Birch, B. C. *Singing the Lord's Song: A Study of Isaiah 40–55.* Nashville: Abingdon, 1990.

Boer, R. "Deutero-Isaiah: Historical Materialism and Biblical Theology," *Biblical Interpretation* 6 (1998): 181–204.

Boyce, R. N. "Isaiah 55:6–13." *Int* 44 (1990): 56–60.

Brassey, P. D. "Metaphor and the Incomparable God in Isaiah 40–55." Ph.D. diss., Harvard University, 1997.

Brooks, R. "A Christological Suffering Servant? The Jewish Retreat into Historical Criticism." In *Hebrew Bible or Old Testament? Studying the Bible in Judaism and Christianity,* edited by R. Brooks and J. J. Collins, 207–10. Notre Dame, Ind.: University of Notre Dame Press, 1990.

Broyles, C. C. "The Citations of Yahweh in Isaiah 44:26–28." In *Writing and Reading the Scroll of Isaiah: Studies of an Interpretative Tradition,* VTSup 70, edited by C. C. Broyles and C. A. Evans, 399–421. Leiden: Brill, 1997.

Cajot, R. M. "Second Isaiah's Servant of Yahweh Revisited." *Philippinana Sacra* 34 (1999): 201–18.

Car, D. McL. "Isaiah 40:1–11 in the Context of the Macrostructure of Second Isaiah." In *Discourse Analysis of Biblical Literature: What It Is and What It Offers,* edited by W. R. Bodine, 51–74. Atlanta: Scholars Press, 1995.

Carroll, R. P. "Biblical Idolatry: Ideologiekritik, Biblical Studies, and the Problematics of Ideology." *JNSL* 24 (1998): 101–14.

Ceresko, A. R. "The Rhetorical Strategy of the Fourth Servant Song (Isaiah 52:13–53:12): Poetry and Exodus–New Exodus." *CBQ* 56 (1994): 42–55.

Clements, R. E. "Isaiah 53 and the Restoration of Israel." In *Jesus and the Suffering Servant,* edited by W. H. Bellinger Jr. and W. R. Farmer, 39–54. Harrisburg, Pa.: Trinity Press International, 1998.

———. "'Who Is Blind but My Servant?' (Isaiah 42:19): How Then Shall We Read Isaiah?" In *God in the Fray: A Tribute to Walter Brueggemann,* edited by T. Linafelt and T. K. Beal, 143–56. Minneapolis: Fortress, 1998.

Coggins, R. J. "Do We Still Need Deutero-Isaiah?" *JSOT* 81 (1998): 77–92.

Collins, A. Y. "The Suffering Servant: Isaiah Chapter 53 as a Christian Text." In *Hebrew Bible or Old Testament? Studying the Bible in Judaism and Christianity,* edited by R. Brooks and J. J. Collins, 201–6. Notre Dame, Ind.: University of Notre Dame Press, 1990.

Davidson, R. "The Imagery of Isaiah 40:6–8 in Tradition and Interpretation." In *The Quest for Context and Meaning: Studies in Biblical Intertextuality in Honor of James A. Sanders,* edited by C. A. Evans and S. Talmon, 37–55. Leiden: Brill, 1997.

Davies, P. R. "God of Cyrus, God of Israel: Some Religio-Historical Reflections on Isaiah 40–55." In *Words Remembered, Texts Renewed: Essays in Honour of John F. A. Sawyer,* edited by J. Davies et al., JSOTSup 195, 207–25. Sheffield: Sheffield Academic Press, 1995.

Davis, E. F. "A Strategy of Delayed Comprehension: Isaiah liv 15." *VT* 40 (1990): 217–21.

de Moor, J. C. *The Structure of Classical Hebrew Poetry: Isaiah 40–55.* Leiden: Brill, 1998.

Dempsey, D. A. "A Note on Isaiah xliii 9." *VT* 41 (1991): 212–15.

DeRoche, M. "Isaiah xlv 7 and the Creation of Chaos?" *VT* 42 (1992): 11–21.

Dijkstra, M. "Lawsuit, Debate, and Wisdom Discourse in Second Isaiah." In *Studies in the Book of Isaiah: Festschrift Willem A. M. Beuken,* edited by J. van Ruiten and M. Vervenne, 251–71. Louvain: Peeters, 1997.

———. "YHWH as Israel's *gōʾēl:* Second Isaiah's Perspective on Reconciliation and Restitution." *Zeitschrift für die Althebraistik* 5 (1999): 236–57.

Dion, P. E. "The Structure of Isaiah 42.10–17 as Approached through Versification and Distribution of Poetic Devices." *JSOT* 49 (1991): 113–24.

Echigoya, A. "Deutero-Isaiah's Polemics as Communicative Discourse: The Intended Audiences of the Trial and Disputation Speeches." Ph.D. diss., Vanderbilt University, 1994.

Ekblad, E. R., Jr. *Isaiah's Servant Poems According to the Septuagint: An Exegetical and Theological Study.* Louvain: Peeters, 1999.

Ferrie, J. J. "Meteorological Imagery in Isaiah 40–55." Ph.D. diss., Catholic University of America, 1993.

Fokkelman, J. P. "The Cyrus Oracle (Isaiah 44,24–45,7) from the Perspective of Syntax, Versification, and Structure." In *Studies in the Book of Isaiah: Festschrift Willem A. M. Beuken,* edited by J. van Ruiten and M. Vervenne, 303–23. Louvain: Peeters, 1997.

Franke, C. A. "The Function of the Satiric Lament over Babylon in Second Isaiah (xlvii)," *VT* 41 (1991): 408–18.

———. "Is DI 'PC'? Does Israel Have Most-Favored Nation Status? Another Look at 'The Nations' in Deutero-Isaiah." *SBLSP* (1999): 272–91.

———. *Isaiah 46, 47, and 48: A New Literary-Critical Reading.* Winona Lake, Ind.: Eisenbrauns, 1994.

Franzmann, M. "The City as Woman: The Case of Babylon in Isaiah 47." *Australian Biblical Review* 43 (1995): 1–19.

Gaiser, F. J. " 'Remember the Former Things of Old': A New Look at Isaiah 46:3–13." In *All Things New: Essays in Honor of Roy A. Harrisville,* edited by A. J. Hultgren et al., 53–63. St. Paul: Word & World, 1993.

Gelston, A. " 'Behold the Speaker': A Note on Isaiah xli 27." *VT* 43 (1993): 405–8.

———. "Isaiah 52:13–53:12: An Eclectic Text and a Supplementary Note on the Hebrew Manuscript Kennicott 96." *JSS* 35 (1990): 187–211.

———. "Knowledge, Humiliation, or Suffering: A Lexical, Textual, and Exegetical Problem in Isaiah 53." In *Of Prophets' Visions and the Wisdom of the Sages: Essays in Honour of R. Norman Whybray on His Seventieth Birthday,* edited by H. A. McKay and D. J. A. Clines, JSOTSup 162, 126–41. Sheffield: JSOT, 1993.

———. "Universalism in Second Isaiah." *JTS* 43 (1992): 377–98.

Goldingay, J. "Isaiah 40–55 in the 1990s: Among Other Things, Deconstructing, Mystifying, Intertextual, Socio-critical, and Hearer-Involving." *Biblical Interpretation* 5 (1997): 225–46.

———. "Isaiah 42.18–25." *JSOT* 67 (1995): 43–65.

———. "Isaiah 43,22–28." *ZAW* 110 (1998): 173–91.

———. "What Happens to Ms Babylon in Isaiah 47, Why, and Who Says So?" *TynB* 47 (1996): 215–43.

Grisanti, M. A. "The Relationship of Israel and the Nations in Isaiah 40–55." Ph.D. diss., Dallas Theological Seminary, 1993.

Hamlin, E. J. "Deutero-Isaiah's Picture of Cyrus as a Key to His Understanding of History." *Proceedings Eastern Great Lakes and Midwest Biblical Societies* 14 (1994): 105–11.

———. "Deutero-Isaiah's Reinterpretation of the Exodus in the Babylonian Twilight." *Proceedings Eastern Great Lakes and Midwest Biblical Societies* 11 (1991): 75–80.

———. "Isaiah 47: The End of Empire." *Proceedings Eastern Great Lakes and Midwest Biblical Societies* 16 (1996): 127–39.

Hanson, P. D. "Second Isaiah's Eschatological Understanding of World Events." *Princeton Seminary Bulletin Supplementary Issue* 3 (1994): 17–25.

———. "The World of the Servant of the Lord in Isaiah 40–55." In *Jesus and the Suffering Servant,* edited by W. H. Bellinger Jr., and W. R. Farmer, 9–22. Harrisburg, Pa.: Trinity Press International, 1998.

Helberg, J. L. "The Revelation of the Power of God according to Isaiah 40–55." *OTE* 8 (1995): 262–79.

Heyns, D. "God and History in Deutero-Isaiah: Considering Theology and Time." *OTE* 8 (1995): 340–55.

Holter, K. "A Note on שביה/שבי in Isa 52.2." *ZAW* 104 (1992): 106–7.

———. *Second Isaiah's Idol-Fabrication Passages.* Frankfurt am Main: Lang, 1995.

———. "The Wordplay on אל('God') in Isaiah 45,20–21." *SJOT* 7 (1993): 88–98.

Hudson, M. H. "Creation Theology in Isaiah 40–66: An Expression of Confidence in the Sovereignty of God." Ph.D. diss., Southwestern Baptist Theological Seminary, 1996.

Hugenberger, H. P. "The Servant of the Lord in the 'Servant Songs' of Isaiah: A Second Moses Figure." In *The Lord's Anointed,* edited by P. E. Satterthwaite, R. S. Hess, and G. J. Wenham, 105–40. Grand Rapids: Baker, 1995.

Jacobson, H. "A Note on Isaiah 51:6." *JBL* 114 (1995): 291.

Jeppesen, K. "From 'You, My Servant' to 'The Hand of the Lord Is with My Servants': A Discussion of Is 40–66." *SJOT* 1 (1990): 113–29.

———. "Mother Zion, Father Servant: A Reading of Isaiah 49–55." In *Of Prophets' Visions and the Wisdom of the Sages: Essays in Honour of R. Norman Whybray on His Seventieth Birthday,* edited by H. A. McKay and D. J. A. Clines, JSOTSup 162, 109–25. Sheffield: JSOT, 1993.

Jonston, A. "A Prophetic Vision of an Alternative Community: A Reading of Isaiah 40–55." In *Uncovering Ancient Stones: Essays in Memory of H. Neil Richardson,* edited by L. M. Hopfe, 31–40. Winona Lake, Ind.: Eisenbrauns, 1994.

Kim, H. C. P. "An Intertextual Reading of 'A Crushed Reed' and 'A Dim Wick' in Isaiah 42.3." *JSOT* 83 (1999): 113–24.

Kohn, R. L., and W. H. C. Propp. "The Name of 'Second Isaiah': The Forgotten Theory of Nehemiah Rabban." In *Fortunate the Eyes That See: Essays in Honor of David Noel Freedman in Celebration of His Seventieth Birthday,* edited by A. B. Beck et al., 223–35. Grand Rapids: Eerdmans, 1995.

Koole, J. L. *Isaiah,* pt. 3, vol. 2: *Isaiah 49–55.* Translated by A. P. Runia. Louvain: Peeters, 1998.

Korpel, M. C. A. "The Female Servant of the Lord in Isaiah 54." In *On Reading Prophetic Texts,* edited by B. Becking and M. Dijkstra, 153–67. Leiden: Brill, 1996.

———. "Metaphors in Isaiah lv." *VT* 46 (1996): 43–55.

———. "Soldering in Isaiah 40:19–20 and 1 Kings 6:21." *UF* 23 (1991): 219–22.

Kruger, P. A. "The Slave Status of the Virgin Daughter Babylon in Isaiah 47:2: A Perspective from Anthropology." *JNSL* 23 (1997): 143–52.

Kuntz, J. K. "The Form, Location, and Function of Rhetorical Questions in Deutero-Isaiah." In *Writing and Reading the Scroll of Isaiah: Studies of an Interpretative Tradition,* edited by C. C. Broyles and C. A. Evans, VTSup 70, 121–41. Leiden: Brill, 1997.

Laato, A. "The Composition of Isaiah 40–55." *JBL* 109 (1990): 207–28.

———. *The Servant of YHWH and Cyrus: A Reinterpretation of the Exilic Messianic Programme in Isaiah 40–55.* Stockholm: Almqvist & Wiksell, 1992.

Labahn, A. "The Delay of Salvation within Deutero-Isaiah." *JSOT* 85 (1999): 71–84.

Landy, F. "The Construction of the Subject and the Symbolic Order: A Reading of the Last Three Suffering Servant Songs." In *Among the Prophets: Language, Image, and Structure in the Prophetic Writings,* edited by P. R. Davies and D. J. A. Clines, 60–71. Sheffield: JSOT, 1993.

Leene, H. "History and Eschatology in Deutero-Isaiah." In *Studies in the Book of Isaiah: Festschrift Willem A. M. Beuken,* edited by J. van Ruiten and M. Vervenne, 223–49. Louvain: Peeters, 1997.

Lindblad, U. "A Note on the Nameless Servant in Isaiah xlii 1–4." *VT* 43 (1993): 115–19.

Melugin, R. F. "Israel and the Nations in Isaiah 40–55." In *Problems in Biblical Theology: Essays in Honor of Rolf Knierim,* edited by H. T. C. Sun, 249–64. Grand Rapids: Eerdmans, 1997.

Mettinger, T. N. D. "In Search of the Hidden Structure: YHWH as King in Isaiah 40–55."

In *Writing and Reading the Scroll of Isaiah: Studies of an Interpretative Tradition,* edited by C. C. Broyles and C. A. Evans, VTSup 70, 143–54. Leiden: Brill, 1997.

Olley, J. W. "'No Peace' in a Book of Consolation: A Framework for the Book of Isaiah." *VT* 49 (1999): 351–70.

Pilkington, C. "The Hidden God in Isaiah 45:15—A Reflection from Holocaust Theology." *SJT* 48 (1993): 285–300.

Prinsloo, W. S. "Isaiah 42.10–12: 'Sing to the Lord a New Song . . .'" In *Studies in the Book of Isaiah: Festschrift Willem A. M. Beuken,* edited by J. van Ruiten and M. Vervenne, 289–301. Louvain: Peeters, 1997.

Reichenbach, B. R. "'By His Stripes We Are Healed,'" *JETS* 41 (1998): 551–60.

Reventlow, H. G. "Basic Issues in the Interpretation of Isaiah 53." In *Jesus and the Suffering Servant,* edited by W. H. Bellinger Jr., and W. R. Farmer, 23–38. Harrisburg, Pa.: Trinity Press International, 1998.

Rosenbaum, M. *Word-Order Variation in Isaiah 40–55.* Assen: van Gorcum, 1997.

Sapp, D. A. "The LXX, 1QIsa, and MT Versions of Isaiah 53 and the Christian Doctrine of Atonement." In *Jesus and the Suffering Servant,* edited by W. H. Bellinger Jr., and W. R. Farmer, 170–92. Harrisburg, Pa.: Trinity Press International, 1998.

Skjoldal, N. O. "The Election of the People of God: A Rhetorical Analysis of Isaiah 41:1–44:23." Ph.D. diss., Trinity Evangelical Divinity School, 1995.

Sommer, B. D. *A Prophet Reads Scripture: Allusion in Isaiah 40–66.* Stanford, Calif.: Stanford University Press, 1998.

Stassen, S. L. "Marriage (and Related) Metaphors in Isaiah 54:1–17." *Journal for Semitics* 6 (1994): 57–73.

Stern, P. "The 'Blind Servant' Imagery of Deutero-Isaiah and Its Implications." *Bib* 75 (1994): 224–32.

Stone, B. W. "Second Isaiah: Prophet to Patriarchy." *JSOT* 56 (1992): 85–99.

Terlan, A. "The Hunting Imagery in Isaiah li 20a." *VT* 41 (1991): 462–71.

Trudinger, P. "On Not Seeing the 'Tree' Because of the 'Wood': A Note on Isaiah 40:18–20." *Downside Review* 115 (1997): 23–28.

Turner, E. A. "The Foreign Idols of Deutero-Isaiah." *OTE* 9 (1996): 111–28.

van der Kooij, A. "'The Servant of the Lord': A Particular Group of Jews in Egypt according to the Old Greek of Isaiah. Some Comments on LXX Isa 49,1–6 and Related Passages." In *Studies in the Book of Isaiah: Festschrift Willem A. M. Beuken,* edited by J. van Ruiten and M. Vervenne, 383–96. Louvain: Peeters, 1997.

Van Winkle, D. W. "Proselytes in Isaiah XL–LV: A Study of Isaiah XLIV 1–5." *VT* 47 (1997): 341–59.

Walsh, J. T. "Summons to Judgment: A Close Reading of Isaiah xli 1–20." *VT* 43 (1993): 351–71.

Watts, R. E. "Consolation or Confrontation? Isaiah 40–55 and the Delay of the New Exodus." *TynB* 41 (1990): 31–59.

Willey, P. T. *Remember the Former Things: The Recollection of Previous Texts in Second Isaiah.* SBLDS 161. Atlanta: Scholars Press, 1997.

Zvi Brettler, M. "Incompatible Metaphors for YHWH in Isaiah 40–60." *JSOT* 78 (1998): 97–120.

Isaiah 56–66

Beuken, W. A. M. "Isaiah Chapters lxv–lxvi: Trito-Isaiah and the Closure of the Book of Isaiah." In *Congress Volume Leuven 1989,* edited by J. A. Emerton, VTSup 63, 204–21. Leiden: Brill, 1991.

———. "The Main Theme of Trito-Isaiah: 'The Servants of YHWH.'" *JSNT* 47 (1990): 67–87.

Burghardt, W. J. "Isaiah 60:1–7." *Int* 44 (1990): 396–400.

Clements, R. E. "'Arise, Shine, for Your Light Has Come': A Basic Theme of the Isaianic Tradition." In *Writing and Reading the Scroll of Isaiah: Studies of an Interpretative Tradition,* edited by C. C. Broyles and C. A. Evans, VTSup 70, 441–54. Leiden: Brill, 1997.

Collins, J. J. "A Herald of Good Tidings: Isaiah 61:1–3 and Its Actualization in the Dead Sea Scrolls." In *A Gift of God in Due Season: Essays on Scripture and Community in Honor of James A. Sanders,* edited by R. D. Weis and D. M. Carr, 225–40. Sheffield: Sheffield Academic Press, 1996.

Dafni, N. "Isaiah 56–66: Prophecy or Apocalypse? The Nature of the Eschatological Beliefs of Isaiah 56–66 and the Investigation of the Problem of Its Unity within the Rest of the Isaianic Corpus." Ph.D. diss., King's College (London), 1997.

de Gruchy, J. W. "A New Heaven and a New Earth: An Exposition of Isaiah 65:17–25." *Journal of Theology for Southern Africa* 105 (1999): 65–74.

de Moor, J. C. "Structure and Redaction: Isaiah 60,1–63,6." In *Studies in the Book of Isaiah: Festschrift Willem A. M. Beuken,* edited by J. van Ruiten and M. Vervenne, 325–46. Louvain: Peeters, 1997.

Emmerson, G. I. *Isaiah 56–66.* Sheffield: JSOT, 1992.

Halpern, B. "The New Names of Isaiah 62:4: Jeremiah's Reception in the Restoration and the Politics of 'Third Isaiah.'" *JBL* 117 (1998): 623–43.

Harrelson, W. "Why, O Lord, Do You Harden Our Heart? A Plea for Help from a Hiding God." In *Shall Not the Lord of All the Earth Do What Is Right? Studies on the Nature of God in Tribute to James L. Crenshaw,* edited by D. Penchansky and P. L. Redditt, 163–74. Winona Lake, Ind.: Eisenbrauns, 2000.

Holladay, W. L. "Was Trito-Isaiah Deutero-Isaiah after All?" In *Writing and Reading the Scroll of Isaiah: Studies of an Interpretative Tradition,* edited by C. C. Broyles and C. A. Evans, VTSup 70, 193–217. Leiden: Brill, 1997.

Hurowitz, V. A. "A Forgotten Meaning of *Nepeš* in Isaiah LVIII 10." *VT* 47 (1997): 43–52.

Japhet, S. "שם יד (Isa 56:5)—A Different Proposal." *Maarav* 8 (1992): 69–80.

Koole, J. L. *Isaiah III.* Kampen: Kok Pharos, 1997.

Kruger, H. A. J. "Who Comes, Yahweh or Nahar: A Few Remarks on the Translation of Isaiah 59:19c–d and the Theological Meaning of the Passage." *OTE* 10 (1997): 84–91, 268–78.

Oswalt, J. N. "Righteousness in Isaiah: A Study of the Function of Chapters 55–66 in the Present Structure of the Book." In *Writing and Reading the Scroll of Isaiah: Studies of an Interpretative Tradition,* edited by C. C. Broyles and C. A. Evans, VTSup 70, 177–91. Leiden: Brill, 1997.

Polan, G. J. "Still More Signs of Unity in the Book of Isaiah: The Significance of Third Isaiah." *SBLSP* (1997): 224–33.

Sawyer, J. F. A. "Radical Images of Yahweh in Isaiah 63." In *Among the Prophets: Language, Image, and Structure in the Prophetic Writings,* edited by P. R. Davies and D. J. A. Clines, 72–82. Sheffield: JSOT, 1993.

Schramm, B. *The Opponents of Third Isaiah: Reconstructing the Cultic History of the Restoration.* JSOTSup 193. Sheffield: Sheffield Academic Press, 1995.

Smith, P. A. *Rhetoric and Redaction in Trito-Isaiah: The Structure, Growth, and Authorship of Isaiah 56–66.* VTSup 62. Leiden: Brill, 1995.

Song, T. B. H. "The Loftiness of God, the Humility of Man, and Restoration in Isaiah 57:14–21: A Text Linguistic Analysis of their Convergence." Ph.D. diss., Trinity Evangelical Divinity School, 1997.

Sweeney, M. A. "Prophetic Exegesis in Isaiah 65–66." In *Writing and Reading the Scroll of Isaiah: Studies of an Interpretative Tradition,* edited by C. C. Broyles and C. A. Evans, VTSup 70, 455–74. Leiden: Brill, 1997.

van Ruiten, J. "The Intertextual Relationship between Isaiah 65,25 and Isaiah 11,6–9." In *The Scriptures and the Scrolls: Studies in Honour of A. S. van der Woude on the Occasion of His Sixty-fifth Birthday,* edited by F. G. Martínez et al., VTSup 49, 31–42. Leiden: Brill, 1992.

Van Winkle, D. W. "An Inclusive Authoritative Text in Exclusive Communities." In *Writing and Reading the Scroll of Isaiah: Studies of an Interpretative Tradition,* edited by C. C. Broyles and C. A. Evans, VTSup 70, 423–40. Leiden: Brill, 1997.

———. "Isaiah LVI 1–8." *SBLSP* (1997): 234–52.

———. "The Meaning of *yād wāšēm* in Isaiah LVI 5." *VT* 47 (1997): 378–85.

Webster, E. C. "The Rhetoric of Isaiah 63–65." *JSNT* 47 (1990): 89–102.

Wells, R. D., Jr. "'Isaiah' as an Exponent of Torah: Isaiah 56:1–8." In *New Visions of Isaiah,* edited by R. F. Melugin and M. A. Sweeney, JSOTSup 214, 140–55. Sheffield: Sheffield Academic Press, 1996.

Williamson, H. G. M. "Isaiah 63,7–64,11: Exilic Lament or Post-exilic Protest?" *ZAW* 102 (1990): 48–58.

Jeremiah and Lamentations

The Weeping Prophet (Jeremiah)

Introduction

Jeremiah's prophetic career began in 627 B.C. (the thirteenth year of Josiah's reign) and ended shortly after the fall of Jerusalem in 586 B.C. (see Jer. 1:1–3).[1] He persevered despite intense opposition from the royal authorities. By and large, his warnings of coming disaster went unheeded. In the end his message and ministry were vindicated when Jerusalem fell, just as he had announced would happen.

The book contains a variety of literary genres, including prophetic oracles in poetic form, Jeremiah's so-called confessions, biographical highlights from the prophet's ministry, and prophetic sermons in a more prosaic style.[2] This variety in style has given rise to several complex theories of how the book evolved into its present form. A comparison of the traditional Hebrew (Masoretic) text with the ancient Greek version (Septuagint) suggests that the book existed in at least two canonical forms in ancient times. The Greek version is approximately one-eighth shorter than the Hebrew version. Furthermore, the oracles against the nations, which appear in chapters 46–51 in the Hebrew text, follow 25:13 in the Greek version and display a different internal arrangement.[3]

In the Hebrew version, which is used as the basis for the commentary that follows, the book displays the following structure. In 1:1–25:13, the focus is on Judah's sin and impending doom. Prophetic messages dominate the section. The second major section of the book consists of chapters 26–

---

1. For a chart showing the dated material in Jeremiah, see Raymond B. Dillard and Tremper Longman III, *An Introduction to the Old Testament* (Grand Rapids: Zondervan, 1994), 302.

2. For a discussion of the different genres in Jeremiah, see C. Hassell Bullock, *An Introduction to the Old Testament Prophetic Books* (Chicago: Moody, 1986), 204–6.

3. See Longman and Dillard, *Introduction*, 291–94, and Bullock, *Introduction*, 206–7.

45, which are primarily biographical and trace the downfall of Judah, culminating in the Babylonian conquest of Jerusalem in 586 B.C. Oracles announcing judgment upon the nations frame this lengthy section. In 25:14–38, the theme of worldwide judgment is introduced, while the actual oracles appear in chapters 46–51. The "words of Jeremiah" end with chapter 51 (see v. 64b), but the book contains an epilogue (chapter 52) that parallels the account of Jerusalem's fall in 2 Kings 24–25. The epilogue was probably included to demonstrate that Jeremiah's ministry and message were fully vindicated by history.[4]

On the Brink of Disaster (Jeremiah 1–25)

This first major section of the book focuses on Judah's sin and impending doom. Following the book's heading (1:1–3) and an introductory call narrative recounting Jeremiah's commissioning as a prophet (1:4–19), the section includes several extended speech units, each of which is introduced by a reference to Jeremiah receiving the word of the LORD:

> Chapters 2–6 (note "The word of the LORD came to me" in 2:1)[5]
> Chapters 7–10 (note "This is the word that came to Jeremiah from the LORD" in 7:1)
> Chapters 11–12 (note "This is the word that came to Jeremiah from the LORD" in 11:1)
> Chapters 13–17 (note "This is what the LORD said to me" in 13:1 and 17:19)[6]
> 18:1–19:13 (note "This is the word that came to Jeremiah from the LORD" in 18:1)[7]

At this point a narrative (referring to Jeremiah in the third person) appears (19:14–20:6), to which is appended one of the prophet's so-called confessions (20:7–18). Another lengthy speech unit follows, introduced by the formula "The word came to Jeremiah from the LORD" (21:1).[8] In 24:1–25:14 one finds two messages dated to specific time periods, both of which deal with the theme of Judah's exile. A judgment speech against the nations (introduced by "this is what the LORD, the God of Israel, said to me," see 25:15) concludes the section.[9]

4. See J. A. Thompson, *Jeremiah*, NICOT (Grand Rapids: Eerdmans, 1980), 773–74.

5. In its later uses in chapters 1–25 (see 13:3, 8; 16:1; 18:5; 24:4), this formula does not introduce a major speech unit. The word choice is probably influenced in 2:1 by the appearance of the formula in the preceding commissioning account (see 1:4, 11, 13). The appearance of this formula at the beginning of the book's first major speech unit links it with the commissioning account.

6. The two units introduced in this way form a bracket around this section. The statement "This is what the LORD said" (Heb. *koh 'amar adonai*) appears frequently in chapters 1–25, but only in these two texts and in 25:15 is "to me" (referring to the prophet) added.

7. The introductory formula is the same as the one used in 7:1 and 11:1.

8. Though the NIV translates it differently here, the formula in the Hebrew text is identical to the one used in 7:1; 11:1; and 18:1.

9. The formula is almost identical to the one appearing in 13:1 and 17:19. In 25:15, the phrase "God of Israel" is added, perhaps to emphasize that it is Israel's God who is sovereign over the nations.

Jeremiah's Commission (1:4–19)

There was never any doubt that Jeremiah would be a prophet. Before he was even born, the Lord chose Jeremiah to be his prophetic spokesman to the nations (vv. 4–5). Aware of his youth and inexperience, Jeremiah objected that he was not articulate (v. 6), but the Lord would not accept any excuses. He commissioned Jeremiah to proclaim his word and assured him of his protective presence (vv. 7–8). As God's spokesman, Jeremiah would possess divine authority. When the prophet announced a nation's downfall or rise to prominence, God's power would make his message a reality (vv. 9–10).

To convince Jeremiah of the power of the prophetic word, the Lord gave him two symbolic visions. In the first vision Jeremiah saw the branch of an "almond tree" (Heb. *shaqed*). The Lord then explained that he was "watching" (Heb. *shoqed*) events carefully to assure that his word was fulfilled (vv. 11–12). The significance of the vision derives from the similarity in sound between the key terms. Every time the prophet saw an almond tree, he must have been reminded that the Lord guaranteed the fulfillment of the prophetic word.

In the second vision the prophet saw a boiling pot tipped toward Judah from the north (v. 13). The boiling contents of the pot symbolized the disaster that would come upon Judah in the form of invading armies from the northern regions (vv. 14–15). This disaster would take place because of Judah's idolatry (v. 16). This foe from the north eventually proved to be the Babylonians and their northern allies (see Jer. 25:9, 26, as well as 46:20, 24).[10]

Having promised Jeremiah that he would personally see to it that his judgment pronouncements came to pass, the Lord urged the prophet to proclaim fearlessly the divine word (v. 17). Opposition would inevitably come from those in high places and from the population in general, but the Lord assured Jeremiah that he would be insulated from their attacks. Jeremiah would stand firm like "a fortified city, an iron pillar, and a bronze wall," for the Lord would be with his servant and rescue him (vv. 18–19).

The Lord Must Punish Unfaithful Judah (2:1–6:30)

This extended speech contains two major sections (2:1–3:5; 3:6–6:30), which are distinguished by the chronological heading in 3:6. Within the second of these, the focus of 3:6–4:2 is on exiled Israel, while 4:3–6:30 is addressed to the people of Judah and Jerusalem.

---

10. In the past some scholars identified these northern invaders with the Scythians, but it is more likely, in light of subsequent historical developments, that the Chaldeans (i.e., Babylonians) are in view. (See Thompson, *Jeremiah*, 86–87.) Though Babylon lies to the east of Judah, the Babylonians, like the Assyrians before them (see Isa. 14:31), invaded Palestine from the north (see Ezek. 26:7), and Babylon was viewed as a northern land (see Zech. 2:6; 6:8). Edwin M. Yamauchi suggests that Scythian mercenaries may have served in the Babylonian army. See his *Foes from the Northern Frontier* (Grand Rapids: Baker, 1982), 87–99.

An unfaithful nation chases her lovers (2:1–3:5). Utilizing the metaphor of marriage and speaking as if he were Israel's husband, the Lord recalled the loving devotion his bride exhibited toward him in the early years of their relationship (2:1–3). Israel followed the Lord through the wilderness and occupied a special, unique position. The Lord valued her, like one does the firstfruits of the harvest, which were reserved for the Lord. He sent disaster upon any who dared try to devour her.

This exaggerated portrayal of Israel's early history is so obviously idealized that it seems laughable. A quick survey of the Pentateuch and the historical books shows that Israel frequently rebelled against the Lord and was unfaithful to her covenantal commitment almost from the very beginning of her history. (See, among many other texts, Exod. 32; Num. 14 and 25; Judg. 2. Note also the summary in Ezek. 20:10–21.) However, with the passing of time there was undoubtedly a tendency to look back with nostalgia at the early days as a time when, at least relatively speaking, Israel's relationship with God seemed to have been more intimate and vital than it eventually came to be. The Lord here exploits this nostalgic viewpoint for rhetorical purposes. (This same strategy is apparent in Hos. 2:14; 13:5.)[11]

In time, Israel abandoned the Lord and turned to idolatry (vv. 4–5). The people forgot how the Lord delivered their ancestors from Egypt and led them through the dangerous wilderness to the fertile Promised Land (vv. 6–7). Priests ignored the Lord, and the prophets served other gods (v. 8). Their rejection of their God was unprecedented among the nations and completely irrational (vv. 9–12). It made no sense to exchange their glorious divine king for worthless idols. The Lord was like a spring that provides fresh water (symbolizing his rich, life-giving blessings), but the people preferred idols, compared here to cracked cisterns that cannot hold water (v. 13).[12]

Israel occupied a special position before the Lord; the nation was no mere slave. But despite their special status, the people had been carried off, like the prey of a ferocious lion, and the land left in ruins (vv. 14–15). The Lord may allude here to the Assyrian invasions of the prior century, especially those of Tiglath-pileser III in 733 B.C., Shalmaneser V in 722, and Sennacherib in 701. Danger had also arrived from the south. The Egyptians (represented here by the towns of Memphis and Tahpanhes, see 44:1; 46:14) had also inflicted a defeat on God's people (v. 16).[13] The text may allude to

11. Jer. 7:25–26 makes clear that the Lord was no romantic idealist wallowing in syrupy nostalgia. He was well aware of the "dark side" of Israel's early history.

12. Cisterns were man-made receptacles designed to catch and hold runoff water. They were typically lined with lime plaster to make them waterproof. In the Judean hill country the impermeable limestone bedrock served as a natural waterproofing, making it unnecessary to seal them. The cisterns envisioned in v. 13 were hewn out of porous rock and had not been properly sealed. See Philip J. King, *Jeremiah: An Archaeological Commentary* (Louisville: Westminster John Knox, 1993), 154–57.

13. In v. 16, the traditional Hebrew text reads literally, "they grazed [on] you, a forehead." The verb "graze" (Heb. *ra'ah*) is often taken in a metaphorical sense here to mean "strip" or "shave." However, it is

the Egyptian victory over Josiah at Megiddo in 609 B.C., a battle that cost Judah's king his life (see 2 Kings 23:29–30; 2 Chron. 35:20–24).

God's people could blame no one but themselves for the disasters that had overtaken them (vv. 17–19). They had forsaken the Lord and were paying the consequences for their rebellion. The nation's leadership had traditionally tried to find security in foreign alliances, but this strategy, which demonstrated an underlying lack of faith in the Lord's protective power, was futile.

The people had long ago rejected the Lord's authority over them and prostituted themselves to other gods, especially the Canaanite fertility deity Baal (v. 20). They were like a grapevine that yielded wild, bitter fruit, even though it came from high-quality, domesticated stock (v. 21).[14] Their guilt was obvious, like a stain on a garment that even soap cannot remove (v. 22). In her wild pursuit of Baal, the nation had acted like the typical young female camel that exhibits total lack of discipline (v. 23) or the typical female donkey in heat that frantically seeks a mate (v. 24).[15] Searching for her false gods, the idol-obsessed nation ran, as it were, until her sandals were worn out and her throat was dry (v. 25). Israel's idolatry ultimately proved futile and humiliating, especially to the leaders of the community (v. 26).

The sins of the past had continued into the present. Jeremiah's contemporaries in Judah (note "O Judah" in v. 28 and "this generation" in v. 31), like the house of Israel, worshiped false gods and rejected their true Creator. Yet when trouble arrived they turned to the Lord, as if they intuitively knew he was the only God who was really capable of helping them (v. 27). But the Lord would not be manipulated by such expedient "worship." He sarcastically urged them to seek help from their idols (v. 28). Despite their denial, the nation's rebellion was obvious (v. 29). The Lord had tried to get their attention, but they had violently struck down his prophets (v. 30), as if they viewed the Lord as being like a danger-filled "desert" or dark land (v. 31). The nation's reaction to the Lord made no sense whatsoever. A young woman is typically preoccupied with her appearance and makes sure to beautify herself with jewelry. A bride never forgets to put on her bridal attire prior to her wedding. In the same way, the Lord's people should have been preoccupied with him, but instead they chased other gods with such passion that they became prime examples of how to do evil (vv. 32–33).

The nation had compounded its guilt by adding the sin of social injustice to that of idolatry (v. 34). Their idolatry demonstrated their refusal to

---

better to emend the text and read a form of either the verb *ra'a'*, "break" ("they shattered you on the forehead") or the verb *'arah*, "lay bare" ("they laid you bare on the forehead").

14. For a discussion of viticulture in ancient Israel, see Oded Borowski, *Agriculture in Iron Age Israel* (Winona Lake, Ind.: Eisenbrauns, 1987), 102–14.

15. For a description of the behavior of these two animals, see William L. Holladay, *Jeremiah 1* (Philadelphia: Fortress, 1986), 100.

love the Lord their God, while their oppression of the poor revealed their failure to love their neighbor. As Jesus once explained, love for both God and one's neighbor is the essence of the Law and the Prophets (see Matt. 22:37–40), but God's people had rejected his standards. Remarkably, the people had the audacity to claim innocence, but judgment would fall, and the nation's foreign alliances, which demonstrated her lack of faith, would prove worthless (vv. 35–37).

Though sensing the Lord's anger, the nation apparently thought reconciliation would be easy (see 3:4–5a). However, the Lord reminded them of a legal principle found in the law (v. 1a). According to the law, if a divorced woman remarried, she could not later return to her first husband (see Deut. 24:1–4). If this principle applied to a woman who remarried, how much more would it apply to the idolatrous nation, for she had turned to prostitution and given herself to many lovers (vv. 1b–2). Appropriately, the Lord withheld the rain that Israel's pursuit of Baal was designed to elicit, yet the nation brazenly refused to admit her guilt and even appealed to the Lord for help (vv. 3–5a). She addressed him as both father and husband, suggesting they had enjoyed a long-standing relationship of intimacy. Her questions about the duration of God's anger implied that his treatment of her was perhaps unfeeling and unjustified.[16] Yet her persistence in sin exposed her words as empty and devoid of truth (v. 5b).

Calling wayward Israel home (3:6–4:2). Comparing Israel and Judah to two sisters, the Lord accused both of adultery (vv. 6–11). Israel, the northern kingdom, had worshiped fertility gods (see v. 6, as well as 2:20). The Lord expected Israel to repent and return to him, but she refused to do so and persisted in her sin (v. 7a).[17] The Lord was forced to "divorce" Israel and send her into exile as punishment for her unfaithfulness (v. 8a). This "divorce" occurred in 722 B.C., when the Assyrians took the Israelites into exile and made Israel's territory into an Assyrian province.

Judah, Israel's "sister" to the south, was watching all this transpire

16. The Hebrew phrase translated "my friend from my youth" (lit., "companion of my youth") is used in Prov. 2:17 (cf. "partner of her youth," lit. "companion of her youth") of the husband of an adulteress (see v. 16).

17. Most interpreters understand Hebrew *wa'omar,* "and I said," in the sense of "and I thought" (i.e., "said to myself") and take the imperfect that follows as indicative ("she will return"), yielding a translation, "I thought: 'After she has done all these things, she will return to me.' But she did not return." In the same way vv. 19b–20 are typically translated, "I thought: 'You will call me "My father," and will not turn back from following me.' But like a woman unfaithful to her husband so you have been unfaithful to me, O house of Israel." Another, less likely, option is to translate v. 7 as follows: "I said . . . 'She must return to me.' But she did not return." In this interpretation the imperfect ("she must return") is understood as obligatory. In this case the Lord's command is disregarded, rather than his expectations being unrealized. In the same way vv. 19b–20 may be translated: "I said, 'You must call me "My father," and you must not turn back from following me.' But like a woman unfaithful to her husband so you have been unfaithful to me, O house of Israel." For this interpretation of vv. 19b–20, see Thompson, *Jeremiah,* 204, 206–7. (However, Thompson does not treat v. 7 in this manner. See p. 193, where he translates, "I thought she would come back to me. But she did not come back.")

(v. 7b). She should have taken the episode to heart and remained faithful to the Lord, but instead she too committed spiritual adultery by worshiping idols (vv. 8b–9).[18] Though she made a pretense of repentance (Josiah's reforms may be in view), her actions were hollow and did not reflect genuine, heartfelt change (v. 10). As far as the Lord was concerned, Judah was more culpable than Israel, because Judah had the advantage of witnessing Israel's punishment, yet still persisted in her adultery (v. 11).

This reference to Israel's relative innocence prompted the Lord to issue a call to repentance to faithless, exiled Israel (v. 12a). He encouraged her by reminding her that he is merciful and by promising that he would not stay angry forever (v. 12b). All the Lord required was a confession of guilt (v. 13). As Israel's husband, he was more than ready to deliver the exiles and bring a remnant to his home in Zion (v. 14). He would give the nation new leaders who would be loyal to him. The nation would experience a population explosion (vv. 15–16a). The ancient ark of the covenant, a symbol of the Lord's presence, would not even be missed, for the Lord's presence in Jerusalem would be obvious to all, including the once rebellious nations of the earth (vv. 16b–17). Israel and Judah, divided since the days of Rehoboam and Jeroboam, would be reunited in the Promised Land (v. 18).

The Lord wanted only the best for Israel (v. 19a). He expected Israel to acknowledge him as her fatherly protector and to remain faithful to him, but she disappointed him (vv. 19b–20). The mixing of metaphors (God is both father and husband) heightens the pathos of the speech and helps one empathize with God in his disappointment and emotional pain.[19] Israel's cries of pain and prayers for deliverance could be heard on the hilltops, giving evidence that the people were paying the consequences for their sins (v. 21). In response the Lord summoned his wayward people to return and promised to cure them of their propensity to wander off (v. 22a).

At this point the people, in highly dramatic fashion, answer the Lord's call to repentance by announcing their intention to return to him (v. 22b), repudiating their idolatry (vv. 23–24), and confessing their past sins (v. 25). Of course, these words were not actually spoken by exiled Israel. This is a model prayer in which the prophet, speaking on behalf of the exiles, demonstrates what an appropriate response to God's call would look like, in hopes that it might be recited by a future repentant generation.[20] (Hosea uses a similar technique in Hos. 6:1–3 and 14:2–4.)

18. Within the framework of the marriage metaphor being employed here, the Lord is pictured as having two wives, the sisters Israel and Judah (see also Ezek. 23). Though the law prohibited a man marrying sisters (Lev. 18:18), the practice is not unknown in the Bible (cf. Jacob). The Lord here uses a contextually conditioned metaphor for illustrative purposes. The use of such an illustration does not mean that the Lord condoned bigamy.

19. In this regard, see the insightful comments of Terence Fretheim, *The Suffering of God* (Philadelphia: Fortress, 1984), 116.

20. See Thompson, *Jeremiah*, 209.

The Lord responds to this model prayer by urging Israel to follow its good impulses (4:1a). He assures the nation that if they do indeed put away their idols and renew their allegiance to the Lord, the impact of such a change will be worldwide in its scope (vv. 1b–2). As the nations see obedient Israel experience the Lord's renewed blessing, they will flock to Jerusalem (see 3:16–17) and become worshipers of the one true God (4:2b). The nations will pronounce blessings by the Lord's name and make Israel's God the object of their pride.[21]

An invader sweeps through Judah (4:3–6:30). The Lord, who desired the ultimate reunification of Israel and Judah (see 3:18), next turned to the men of Judah and Jerusalem and urged them to repent of their sins. Using agricultural imagery, he exhorted them to plow their fields in preparation for planting (see Hos. 10:12) and warned against simply scattering seed on thorny, unplowed ground (v. 3). The point seems to be this: They must make the effort to cultivate a new spiritual relationship with the Lord by truly repenting of their sins (see 3:10). Only in this way would a crop of restored divine blessings appear.

Utilizing the imagery of circumcision, the Lord also urged them to "circumcise" their "hearts" (v. 4a; see Deut. 10:16; 30:6, as well as Lev. 26:41). Circumcision of the foreskin was the outward sign that a man was a member of the Lord's covenant community, but the Lord wanted something more profound. He wanted his people to have hearts and minds that were committed to him. In this way their obedient lifestyle would mark them out as the Lord's special people. Failure to respond to the Lord's appeal would bring the fiery anger of God down upon the evil nation (v. 4b).

In dramatic fashion the Lord urged the people of Judah and Jerusalem to prepare for an invasion from the north (vv. 5–6; see 1:13–15). He compared the invader (the Babylonian army) to a lion that has come out in search of prey (v. 7). The time had come to lament over the impending judgment, which would leave Judah's leaders paralyzed with fear (vv. 8–9).

The prophet responded to this announcement of judgment (v. 10). He attributed Jerusalem's complacency in the face of impending doom to the Lord himself, who, Jeremiah asserted, had thoroughly deceived the people.[22] Jeremiah affirmed that the Lord had used a misleading message of hope

21. NIV translates the first line in Jer. 4:2b "then the nations will be blessed by him," but the Hithpael verbal form of the verb "to bless" is better taken in a reflexive-reciprocal sense, "then the nations will bless one another by him." In this way they will copy Israel, who will make formal pronouncements using the formula, "As surely as the LORD lives" (see v. 2a).

22. The construction in the Hebrew (infinitive absolute + finite verb) is emphatic. The verb translated "deceived" here is used elsewhere of the snake deceiving Eve through half-truths and outright lies (Gen. 3:13), of a king or god misleading people into false confidence (2 Kings 18:29 = 2 Chron. 32:15 = Isa. 36:14; 2 Kings 19:10 = Isa. 37:10), of an ally deceiving a treaty partner (Obad. 7), of false prophets instilling their audience with false hope (Jer. 29:8), and of pride producing self-deception (Jer. 37:9; 49:16; Obad. 3).

("You will have peace") to deceive the people and expedite their downfall. This prediction of peace was the hallmark of the false prophets (see 6:13–14; 8:10–11; 14:13; 23:17). Elsewhere in the book the Lord, in contrast to Jeremiah's claim, seems to disavow any connection with this false message (see 14:14–15; 23:16, 18, 32). For this reason, some contend that Jeremiah was simply wrong in attributing deceit to God (in this regard, see 20:7).[23] However, it is possible that the prophets who opposed Jeremiah and preached this false message were unwitting agents of divine deceit, just like Ahab's prophets were when they promised the king victory on the battlefield and opposed Micaiah (see 1 Kings 22). Like the prophets of Ahab, the false prophets of Jeremiah's time had not stood in the Lord's council or received a commission from him. The Lord had not spoken to them directly; their message of peace originated in their own minds. But at the same time the Lord may in some way have energized their activity and, as a form of judgment, caused the sinful people to believe their message.[24]

The days ahead would hardly be peaceful. Judgment would sweep through like a destructive windstorm (vv. 11–12). The chariots of the invading army were moving swiftly toward Jerusalem (v. 13), making repentance a necessity (v. 14). The residents of Dan, located in the far north of the land, and those living in the Ephraimite hill country just north of Judah sent out a warning cry to Judah in the south, announcing the approach of this foreign army (vv. 15–17a). Judah had no one to blame but herself, for her behavior had prompted this disaster (vv. 17b–18).

Jeremiah was overwhelmed with terror as he anticipated the sights and sounds of warfare (vv. 19–21). He lamented the moral folly of his sinful contemporaries (v. 22) and described the devastation of judgment as a reversal of creation (vv. 23–26). The land appeared to be "formless and empty," as if it had returned to the primordial chaos described in Genesis 1:2. The light of the heavens disappeared, the mountains shook, people and birds were gone, and the once fruitful land had been reduced to a desert. This impending destruction was inevitable, for the Lord had decreed that judgment would fall, and he would not revoke his word (vv. 27–28).[25]

The presence of this unalterable decree suggests this speech (or at least this portion of it) dates from a time relatively late in Jeremiah's career, because

23. See, for example, Walter C. Kaiser Jr., *Toward Old Testament Ethics* (Grand Rapids: Zondervan, 1983), 257–58.

24. For a fuller discussion of this issue, see Robert B. Chisholm Jr., "Does God Deceive?" *BSac* 155 (1998): 18–19, as well as Robert P. Carroll, *Jeremiah*, OTL (Philadelphia: Westminster, 1986), 161–62.

25. Many passages in the Hebrew Bible depict God relenting after he has announced judgment. In fact, Joel 2:13–14 and Jon. 4:2 indicate that his capacity to relent is a fundamental divine attribute that grows out of his compassion and mercy. However, there are occasions when God declares his refusal to relent (see, for example, Num. 23:19 and 1 Sam. 15:29). In such cases the declaration marks the statement as an unalterable divine decree. For fuller discussion see Robert B. Chisholm Jr., "Does God 'Change His Mind'?" *BSac* 152 (1995): 387–99.

during the prophet's early ministry the Lord made it clear that he would relent from sending judgment if Judah repented (see 18:1–12; 26:3, 13, 19, as well as 15:6, where God declares that he is weary of relenting). The decree may seem to contradict the calls to repentance in 4:14 and 5:1, but the latter are directed to Jerusalem, not Judah as a whole. Apparently at the point when this decree was given, Judah's fate was sealed, but not Jerusalem's.[26]

This portrait of judgment continues as Jeremiah pictures the people of every town fleeing into the countryside to escape the onslaught of the invaders (v. 29). He then turns to Jerusalem and asks why she continues to persist in her idolatry, compared here to a prostitute vainly pursuing her lovers (v. 30). Jerusalem would suffer greatly, like a woman experiencing labor pains for the first time (v. 31).

Though Judah's doom was certain (see 4:28), there appeared to be a glimmer of hope for Jerusalem (5:1; see 4:14). With a touch of hyperbole, the Lord promised that if one honest person could be found in Jerusalem, he would spare the city. But the language actually seems more sarcastic than hopeful. The implication seems to be that everyone in Jerusalem was corrupt. Indeed the people broke oaths taken in the Lord's name and refused to repent, even when the Lord disciplined them (vv. 2–3). This rebellious attitude characterized the leadership as well as the common people (vv. 4–5). For this reason, the invaders would be turned loose in Judah, like a vicious predator that attacks and mauls its victims (v. 6). As long as the people persisted in their idolatry and pagan fertility rites, the Lord had no alternative but to withhold forgiveness and punish them severely (vv. 7–9). The Lord had to prune the branches of his vineyard, as it were, for Judah had followed in the adulterous footsteps of the northern kingdom (vv. 10–11).

Yet the people were convinced there would be no judgment and ignored the warnings of prophets like Jeremiah, whom they dismissed as windbags (vv. 12–13). To preserve the honor and integrity of the prophetic word, the Lord had to act decisively. Jeremiah's message of judgment would materialize in the form of a distant nation speaking an unknown tongue (vv. 14–15).[27] The invaders would sweep through the land, destroying virtually everyone and everything in their path (vv. 16–17). However, the Lord would preserve a remnant (v. 18). When this remnant asked why the Lord had brought such disaster upon the land, Jeremiah was to tell them that this was God's way of punishing their sin (vv. 18–19). Appropriately and ironically,

---

26. The call to repentance in 4:3–4, which is directed to both Judah and Jerusalem, must come from an earlier period in the prophet's career.

27. In v. 15, the addressee is the "house of Israel." In v. 11, this expression refers to the northern kingdom of Israel, as distinct from the southern kingdom of Judah (see also 3:18, 20; 11:10, 17; 13:11). This is problematic in v. 15 because Israel had long since been invaded and carried away into exile. Perhaps Jeremiah here uses an ancient prophecy against Israel, applying it to his Judahite audience. Having made the point that Judah shared in Israel's sin (v. 11; see also 3:7–10), he then addressed Judah as if it were Israel in order to drive home the point and make it clear that Judah would share the fate of Israel.

those who had served "foreign gods" would now serve "foreigners" on foreign soil. In this way the punishment mirrored the crime.

The people of Judah were spiritually blind and deaf (vv. 20–21). They should have feared the Lord, the sovereign creator who set a boundary for the raging sea so that it could not inundate the earth (v. 22). In biblical and ancient Near Eastern thought, the sea was viewed as a dangerous entity that threatened to destroy the world order. In the Bible it often symbolizes the hostile nations that threaten to destroy God's people. The affirmation in verse 22 serves as a reminder of the Lord's ability to protect his people from these hostile forces. In verse 24b, he reminds them that he is the sovereign lord over nature, who provides the rains in their season so that the people might have an abundant harvest. The implication is clear: God insulates his people from danger and provides them with food.

Judah should have feared their protector and provider, but instead they rebelled against him by ignoring the fundamental principles of his law (vv. 23–24a). Wicked men violated God's principles of social justice and became wealthy by exploiting the weak and vulnerable (vv. 26–28). Prophets and priests operated outside God's authority, with the approval of the people (v. 30). For these reasons God decided to withhold his blessings (v. 25) and, as the avenger of the downtrodden, was compelled to bring judgment on the nation (v. 29).

The time had come to flee for safety, for the invader was already looming on the northern horizon and would soon surround Jerusalem (6:1–3). In dramatic fashion Jeremiah lets us hear the enemy's call to attack (vv. 4–5), as well as the Lord's instructions to the invaders (vv. 6–7). The Lord commands them to besiege the city, explaining that it must be punished for the wickedness that it continually produces. However, the Lord's mercy and patience still shine through as he once more urges Jerusalem to repent so that disaster may be averted (v. 8; see 4:14; 5:1).

Utilizing the imagery of the vineyard once again (see 5:10), the Lord authorizes the invaders to "glean the remnant of Israel" (probably a reference to Judah as all that is left of the original covenant community comprised of the twelve tribes) as thoroughly as the harvesters do the grapevine (v. 9). Jeremiah chimes in, complaining that the people refuse to listen to the word of God (v. 10). When the prophet observes that he is "full of the wrath of the LORD" and "cannot hold it in" (v. 11a), the Lord gives him permission to "pour it out" on the people (vv. 11b–12). The point of this dialogue seems to be this: As Jeremiah encountered stubborn, sinful Judah, he became more and more convinced of the necessity of divine judgment and was overwhelmed by a desire to proclaim judgment against the nation. God concurred and urged him to make his pronouncements, which would activate divine judgment.

The judgment, though severe, would be well-deserved. The entire society was corrupted by greed (v. 13a). Both prophets and priests misled the people by overlooking the magnitude of the people's sins and promising them peace (vv. 13b–15). They misrepresented the Lord by giving people the impression that adherence to God's ethical standards does not really matter.

The Lord had tried to get their attention, urging them to walk in the moral path he had prescribed for them in his law. This path would lead to blessing and security, but the people refused to follow it (v. 16). The Lord's prophets, compared here to watchmen on a city wall, warned of impending judgment, but the people refused to listen to them (v. 17). Of course, the people maintained a semblance of religion. They offered aromatic incense and sacrifices to God, apparently thinking that such devotion to ritual insulated them from judgment (v. 20). But such sacrifices are not God's priority; he desires obedience. Only then do sacrifices have any real meaning (see as well 1 Sam. 15:22; Isa. 1:11–17; Hos. 6:6; Amos 5:21–24; Mic. 6:6–8).

The Lord announced to the watching nations that he would punish his stubborn, misguided people (vv. 18–19) by putting "obstacles" before them, over which they would stumble (v. 21). The image of stumbling over obstacles picks up on the metaphor of the "way" mentioned in verse 16. The people refused to travel on the "good way" leading to blessing. Instead, they took a different path (see 18:15; 23:12), which would be filled with dangers and lead to their demise.

The reality behind the imagery was the Babylonian army, which would invade the land from the north (v. 22; see 1:13–15; 4:6). Its fully armed, merciless regiments would march against Jerusalem (v. 23). The people would be paralyzed with fear and unable to escape (vv. 24–25). Realizing their doom was certain, they would lament their fate with the same intensity as a parent who has just lost an only son (v. 26).

Jeremiah was like a "tester of metals" whose job is to refine the ore until the impurities are burned away by the intense fire of the furnace (v. 27). As such he observed the people's moral condition and proclaimed God's word to them, including the announcements of doom that activated God's purifying judgment. But the people were hardened in their sin, epitomized by the way they slandered others (v. 28a). They were like inferior metals, such as bronze and iron, which were considered dross in comparison to silver (v. 28b; see Ezek. 22:18). The refining fire burned intensely, but the impurities (the wicked) remained (v. 29), forcing the Lord to conclude that his people were incapable of being purified (v. 30).

False Confidence Dashed to Pieces (7:1–10:25)

The Lord instructed Jeremiah to stand at the gate of the temple and urge the people of Judah to repent so they might be spared (7:1–3). Since the Lord attaches a promise to the warning, this message must have been delivered by Jeremiah earlier in his career, before God decreed Judah's demise (see 4:28).

Jeremiah's generation thought it was insulated from judgment because the Lord's temple, symbolizing the Lord's presence with his people, stood in its midst. However, the presence of the temple was no guarantee of peace and prosperity (v. 4). They would survive only if they abandoned their evil deeds, including the oppression of the poor and idolatry (vv. 5–8). The temple would provide no asylum for a society that violated God's law by stealing, murdering, committing adultery, breaking oaths, and worshiping other gods (vv. 9–11). A brief history lesson would prove this (vv. 12–15). Shiloh was once a religious center where God made his presence known in conjunction with the ark of the covenant (see 1 Sam. 1–3). But when Eli's family sinned, the ark was captured by the Philistines and the Lord abandoned Shiloh (1 Sam. 4; see also Ps. 78:60). In the same way, the Lord would abandon the temple in Jerusalem and drive his people from his presence, just as he had done to the northern kingdom (represented by Ephraim; see v. 15) many years before.

In the past, God had sometimes spared his people when a godly leader interceded on their behalf (see, for example, Exod. 32:7–14; Amos 7:1–6). But it was too late for intercession to be effective. The Lord told Jeremiah not to pray for the people (v. 16). They could be saved only if they repented en masse by changing their evil ways (see v. 3). Entire families were engaging in the shameful worship of pagan gods, with the "Queen of Heaven" being the major attraction (vv. 17–19).[28] Such blatant idolatry necessitated drastic measures (v. 20).

Despite their idolatry, the people continued to offer sacrifices to the Lord, apparently in an effort to "cover all their bases," as it were (v. 21). Somehow they had failed to realize that obedience, not religious ritual, is God's major concern (see 6:20). Once more the Lord offered a history lesson to drive home his point (vv. 22–26; see vv. 12–15). From the very beginning of the nation's history, the Lord's first priority was obedience, not sacrifice.[29] Yet the people disregarded God's commands and refused to listen

---

28. For a detailed discussion of the cult to the Queen of Heaven, see King, *Jeremiah*, 102–7. The precise identity of the "Queen of Heaven" is uncertain. Proposals include Astarte (= Mesopotamian Ishtar), Anat, and Asherah. For a discussion of the various views, see John Day, *Yahweh and the Gods and Goddesses of Canaan* (Sheffield: Sheffield Academic Press, 2000), 144–50. Day concludes (p. 150) that the "Queen of Heaven" was probably the West Semitic goddess Astarte, though he admits "it is possible . . . that what we have is not simply Astarte, but Astarte in syncretism with her Mesopotamian equivalent Ishtar."

29. In the Hebrew text, v. 22 reads literally, "I did not speak with your fathers and I did not command them . . . concerning matters related to a burnt offering and a sacrifice." This raises a problem since the Pentateuch clearly depicts Israel sacrificing to God during this period. It is possible that Jeremiah alludes to an alternative tradition, but the statement may be exaggerated for effect. Though Moses gave Israel numerous laws about sacrifices and offerings, the sacrificial system per se could not be fully implemented until the people settled in the land. Though important, sacrifices were never the essence of God's relationship with

when the Lord sent his prophets to confront them with their sin. The Lord warned Jeremiah that he would be treated no differently than the other prophets (v. 27). Therefore Jeremiah was to rebuke them for their sin (v. 28) and tell them to prepare for judgment (v. 29).

To support his accusation against the people, the Lord again focused on their idolatry (v. 30; see vv. 6, 18). The people had the audacity to set up idols in the Lord's temple. This practice began in the days of King Manasseh (see 2 Kings 21:3–7). Though Josiah purged the temple (2 Kings 23:4–6), idols reappeared there following his death (see Ezek. 8:3–16). In violation of God's law (see Lev. 18:21; 20:2–5; Deut. 12:31; 18:10), the people also offered their children as sacrifices in the Valley of Hinnom, just outside Jerusalem to the southwest (v. 31; see also 19:5; 32:35).[30] The Lord certainly did not command them to do this; in fact, the thought of demanding such sacrifices never even entered his mind.[31]

The Lord would severely punish those who engaged in this horrible sin. In the aftermath of the coming invasion, the Valley of Hinnom would be renamed "the Valley of Slaughter," for it would be turned into a mass burial ground for the victims of divine judgment (v. 32). When there was no room left to bury the dead, the corpses would be stacked up on the surface of the ground and devoured by birds and wild animals (v. 33). Against the backdrop of a desolate land (v. 34), tombs would be desecrated (8:1) and the bones would lie exposed beneath the heavenly lights that the deceased once worshiped before their deaths (v. 2).[32] Meanwhile, those who survived would long for death to put them out of the misery of life in exile (v. 3).

Judah's persistence in sin was irrational and obsessive (vv. 4–5). The Lord patiently waited for the people to repent and return to him, but they stubbornly refused to acknowledge any wrongdoing and insisted on following their own desires (v. 6). Migratory birds instinctively know when it is time to move on in accordance with the natural order established by God,

---

his people. Loyalty, expressed through obedience, was always the highest priority. Sacrifices had significance only when offered by one who was committed to God and obedient to his moral will. One could rephrase the statement, "I did not speak with your fathers and I did not command them . . . *only* concerning matters related to a burnt offering and a sacrifice." Amos 5:25 appears to make a similar point. See my comments on that text, as well as the sources cited there. In a similar way Hos. 6:6a declares: "For I desire mercy, not sacrifice," which really means, "I desire mercy more than sacrifice," as v. 6b indicates.

30. On the practice of child sacrifice in Judah, see King, *Jeremiah*, 136–39, and Jack R. Lundbom, *Jeremiah 1–20*, AB (New York: Doubleday, 1999), 496–97. The site where these child sacrifices were offered was also known as Topheth (see 2 Kings 23:10; Isa. 30:33; Jer. 19:6, 11–14).

31. Modern readers of the text might be tempted to condemn in a self-righteous manner the primitive practice described in v. 31. But, as Lundbom points out, "the Western world in the 1990s has been scarcely better" (see ibid., 503). In condemning modern crimes against children, Lundbom denounces the "unrepentant attitude of many regarding the callous, irreverent, and immoral injustices to the not-yet born." He then asks this haunting question: "Do modern parents care any more for the children they conceive and bring into the world than their ancient counterparts?"

32. On tomb desecration in the ancient Near Eastern world, see my remarks on Amos 2:1–3.

but God's own people ignored the moral order he had established through his law (v. 7).[33] Of course, the people boasted about possessing the law, which they claimed made them wise (v. 8a). But what good did the law do them when the greedy priests and prophets (v. 10b) responsible for instructing the people mishandled it (v. 8b) and overlooked the sin of their society (v. 11a)? These teachers, who thought they were so wise, would be humiliated like fools, for they shamelessly rejected the Lord's moral standards and told the people what they wanted to hear (vv. 9, 11b–12). Their property, including their wives, would be taken from them (vv. 10a, 13).

We next hear the voice of the people as they anticipate the invasion announced by God. Their false confidence has been shattered as they suddenly realize that judgment is on the horizon (vv. 14–15). The invaders are moving southward and will soon sweep through the land with the deadly power of poisonous snakes (vv. 16–17). Jeremiah expresses his grief as he hears the people asking if their divine protector still resides in Jerusalem (vv. 18–19a). The Lord then asks a question of his own, inquiring as to why the people have angered him with their idolatry (v. 19b). The point seems clear: Rather than playing the role of Jerusalem's protector, the Lord stands as her judge. The people, albeit unwittingly, give witness to this as they complain that their deliverance is overdue (v. 20). The delay speaks louder than words.

Jeremiah lamented over the prospects of his countrymen being crushed by God's judgment (v. 21). He asked hopefully, "Is there no balm in Gilead? Is there no physician there?" (v. 22). Gilead, located on the east side of the Jordan River, was known for its balm, which could be used for medicinal purposes (see Gen. 37:25; Jer. 46:11).[34] Of course, the language is metaphorical here. Judah's "illness" was spiritual in nature (see v. 19, as well as 9:2b). Jeremiah's grief over his people's impending doom was uncontrollable. He wished that he had an unending supply of tears to shed (9:1). But his grief did not blur his spiritual insight. He realized that judgment was deserved. In fact, he longed to run away to the desert to get away from the sinful society in which he lived (v. 2).

Just in case anyone had doubts about the propriety of divine judgment, the Lord provided more evidence for why this sinful society needed to be punished. The people slandered and deceived one another (vv. 3, 8). Brothers and friends could not even be trusted (vv. 4–5). Because of their refusal to acknowledge the Lord's authority (v. 6; see also v. 3b), the Lord had no alternative but to purify the land through judgment (vv. 7, 9). Though judgment was deserved, this fact did not make it any easier for Jeremiah, who would have to watch the disaster unfold. Once more he expressed his sorrow as he anticipated the desolation that would result from judgment (v. 10).

33. For an excellent discussion of the migratory patterns and habits of the various birds mentioned here, see ibid., 510–13.
34. See King, *Jeremiah*, 153–54.

As if answering the questions he asked earlier (see vv. 7, 9), the Lord formally announced his intention to devastate the land (v. 11). In response to Jeremiah's question as to why this was necessary (v. 12), the Lord accused the people of breaking his law and worshiping other gods (vv. 13–14). For this reason, disaster and exile would come (vv. 15–16), prompting widespread wailing (vv. 17–19). The mourners would lament death's intrusion into their homes (vv. 20–21), while the fields would be littered with the corpses of Judah's men (v. 22).

Human wisdom, strength, and riches would not be able to insulate anyone from the devastation of the coming judgment. For this reason, the wise, strong, and rich should not boast in their endowments (v. 23). The only ones who could legitimately boast were those who understood and knew the Lord, the faithful God and righteous judge of the earth, for it was this group alone that was the object of divine favor (v. 24). In this context, "understanding" and "knowing" the Lord do not refer to mere intellectual knowledge. The verb translated "knows" (Heb. *yada'*) is used here in its covenantal sense of "acknowledge (or "recognize") as Lord." Such recognition of lordship required faithfulness demonstrated concretely through obedience to the Lord's commands (cf. v. 13, see as well Hos. 2:20 and Jer. 22:16).

Neither would the nation's special status as God's covenant community, tangibly symbolized by the circumcised foreskins of its males, insulate it from judgment (vv. 25–26). Other nations also engaged in the rite of circumcision, but God's judgment would still fall upon them.[35] Though circumcision had special significance for God's people, in the Lord's eyes they were no different morally and ethically than the pagans around them. All of these nations, Judah included, were really "uncircumcised in heart" for their attitudes and thoughts were opposed to God and his moral standards (see as well Jer. 4:4).

As noted earlier in this speech, one of Judah's major problems was its idolatry (see 7:18; 8:19; 9:14). The Lord now addresses this issue at length. He warns his people not to follow the practices of the pagan nations, who place great stock in omens and worship lifeless, man-made idols forged out of wood and metal (10:1–5).[36] Jeremiah responds by affirming that the Lord is unique and incomparable (v. 6). He alone is worthy of worship, for he alone is the sovereign king over the nations (v. 7). Unfortunately the self-pro-

35. The extrabiblical and biblical evidence for the practice of circumcision among the peoples mentioned in v. 26 is discussed by Lundbom, *Jeremiah 1–20*, 573–74.

36. In 10:1, the Lord addresses the "house of Israel." In Jeremiah this phrase usually refers to the exiled northern kingdom of Israel, as distinct from Judah (see, for example, 3:18, 20; 5:11; 11:10, 17; 13:11). In 10:1–5, the Lord possibly addresses the exiled northerners. If so, the message also applies to Judah, which would soon follow the northern kingdom into exile (see 9:16). A similar technique is apparently employed in 5:15 (see the earlier note on this verse). However, it is possible that "Israel"/"house of Israel" is used in this particular speech (chapters 7–10) of the entire covenant community with Judah being the primary focus (see 7:12; 9:26; 10:16).

claimed wise men among the nations fail to recognize this and look to wooden idols for guidance (v. 8). The pagan idols look quite impressive, for they are made of precious metal and clothed in beautiful garments, but the Lord is the "true God" who lives forever and has the authority and power to judge the nations (vv. 9–10). The pagan gods, who do not have the capacity to create, will perish from the earth (v. 11). By way of contrast, the Lord created the world and controls the powerful forces of nature, which he can utilize as instruments of judgment (vv. 12–13). Those who make and worship idols will someday be put to shame, for their so-called gods will prove worthless in the day of judgment (vv. 14–15). Israel's God, as the creator of all things, stands alone as sovereign king (v. 16).

Returning to the theme of Judah's impending doom, the prophet urges his countrymen to prepare for exile, for the Lord has announced that he will "hurl" the people out of the land (vv. 17–18). Speaking for the people, the prophet anticipates the "incurable" wound that is ready to beset the nation, mourns the loss of its children, bemoans the failures of its leaders, and announces the approach of the invaders from the north who will devastate the land (vv. 19–22). Still assuming his role as the nation's representative, he acknowledges the Lord's sovereign right to judge, but begs that his anger might not be excessive. Otherwise the nation would be annihilated (vv. 23–24). He then asks God to pour his angry judgment out on the invaders once they have accomplished their divinely assigned task because, though they are instruments of God, they do not acknowledge him as their sovereign king (v. 25; see vv. 2–5).

Plots against God and His Prophet (11:1–12:17)

The Lord commissioned Jeremiah to confront the people with their covenantal obligations (11:1–2). When the Lord delivered their forefathers from Egyptian slavery, he made a covenant with them. If they obeyed his commandments, he would be their God and would give them the land he promised to their ancestors (vv. 4–5; see Gen. 15:18–21; 26:3; 28:13; 35:12). However, disobedience would activate the covenant curses, or threatened judgments (v. 3). After the people settled in the land, they rejected his commandments, despite his continual warnings and calls to repentance. For this reason, he brought the threatened judgments upon them (vv. 6–8). But Jeremiah's contemporaries had not learned from the past. They persisted in their sins and turned to other gods, following in the footsteps of the northern kingdom (vv. 9–10). Disaster would soon overtake Judah. The many foreign gods worshiped by the people would be unable to save their devotees from judgment (vv. 11–13). Furthermore, Jeremiah should not bother interceding for the people (v. 14a). Intercession was one of a prophet's typical roles, but in this case only wholesale repentance could avert the impending disaster (see 7:3, 16). It would soon be too late for the people to repent, and

the Lord would not pay attention to their cries for help once judgment fell
upon them (v. 14b; see v. 11). The Lord once viewed his people as his
"beloved" and as a fruit-bearing olive tree, but their sin negated their attempts at worship, and their idolatry provoked the Lord's anger (vv. 15–17).

Because he was the Lord's spokesman and the nation's moral conscience,
Jeremiah had become the target of evildoers. The prophet was as naive as a
lamb being led to the slaughtering block, but the Lord revealed to him that
the men in his hometown of Anathoth were planning to kill him (vv. 18–19,
21). Jeremiah asked the Lord, the just king of the world, to intervene and
vindicate his cause, which he had committed to the Lord (v. 20). The Lord
answered his request and assured him that he would punish these evil men
by completely destroying the young men and children of the town (vv. 22–
23). The judgment may seem harsh, but this is just one of many instances in
the Hebrew Bible where children experience the consequences of their fathers' sins. The principle of corporate solidarity was integral to Israelite
thinking. Ancient Israelites realized that the actions of individuals profoundly affect others in their social context and that one's social context affects the individual adversely or positively.[37]

Jeremiah was not entirely satisfied with the Lord's response to his prayer.
He acknowledged that the Lord had been fair to him in the past (12:1a), but
he was still troubled by the apparent prosperity of the wicked (v. 1b). The
Lord seemingly blessed them, even though their claims of allegiance were
not genuine (v. 2). Arguing that his own motives were pure, Jeremiah called
upon the Lord to destroy these evildoers so the land might be freed from the
consequences of their sin and their wrong ideas about God might be corrected (vv. 3–4). The Lord responded with a mild rebuke. If Jeremiah was
discouraged over what happened in Anathoth, how would he manage when
opposition to his ministry intensified (v. 5)? In fact, his very own brothers
had joined the plot against him and he must be on his guard against their
flattering deception (v. 6).

Jeremiah was not the only one alienated from his family.[38] The Lord was
also treated as an enemy. His hostile people are compared to a lion that snarls
at an enemy and to a bird of prey that circles over its victim (vv. 8a, 9a). This
prompted the Lord to abandon them (vv. 7, 8b).[39] Ironically, he would call

---

37. For a discussion of the theological principle of corporate solidarity, see Joel S. Kaminsky, *Corporate Responsibility in the Hebrew Bible* (Sheffield: Sheffield Academic Press, 1995).

38. The connection between Jeremiah's experience and the Lord's situation is made through the repetition of the word "house." Jeremiah's "own family" (literally, "the house of your father") had plotted
against the prophet (v. 6). The Lord would forsake his people, called here his "house," because they had rejected him (v. 7).

39. The Lord's statement in v. 8b ("therefore I hate her") is startling, but it does express the intense
emotion he felt as his people roared at him like a lion (v. 8a). Some prefer to downplay the emotional element here and understand the term as carrying the force of "reject." (See Gen. 29:31, 33, in which the term
is used of Leah, who was treated as "second fiddle" to Rachel. See v. 30. NIV's "not loved" softens the lan-

in "birds of prey" and "wild beasts" (metaphors for the Babylonian army) to attack and devour his people (v. 9b). Foreign rulers (ironically called "shepherds" here, see 6:3 as well) would devastate the vineyards and fields (v. 10), leaving the land a desolate waste (vv. 11–13). Apparently the image is that of shepherds (the Babylonian officers) turning their flocks (the Babylonian soldiers) loose and letting them devour everything in their path.

The surrounding nations would exploit the weakness of the Lord's people and seize their territory. But the Lord would not let this hostility go unpunished. He would "uproot" the nations from their lands, in the process delivering the people of Judah from exile (v. 14). However, in an act of compassion the Lord would eventually restore the nations to their lands and give them the opportunity to become his worshipers (vv. 15–16). Those nations that refuse to do so will be eliminated from the face of the earth (v. 17).

The Cessation of Intercession (13:1–17:27)

The Lord instructed Jeremiah to purchase and then to wear a linen belt (13:1–2). After the prophet complied, the Lord told him to bury the belt and then, after many days, to dig it up (vv. 3–6). When Jeremiah retrieved the belt, it was ruined by such prolonged exposure to the elements (v. 7). What was the point of this object lesson? The belt symbolized God's people. Just as one binds a belt to one's waist, so the Lord had bound himself by covenant to his people. He hoped that they would bring honor to his name, just as an attractive belt draws attention to its owner (v. 11). But his defiant people had turned to idols (v. 10a). For this reason, the Lord would "ruin" their pride (vv. 8–9) and discard them as useless, just as Jeremiah's belt had been rendered useless by the elements (v. 10b).

The Lord also instructed Jeremiah to deliver a parable to the people. He was to say to the people, "Every wineskin should be filled with wine" (v. 12a). When they rebuked him for stating the obvious (v. 12b), he was to announce that the Lord was ready to fill the land with "drunkenness," a metaphor for the violent, merciless judgment that would sweep through the land and leave the people reeling like a drunkard (vv. 13–14).

The urgency of the situation demanded a prompt, decisive response from the people. Jeremiah urged them to abandon their pride and take heed to the Lord's warning (v. 15). They must show the Lord the respect he deserved before it was too late and the darkness of judgment settled over the land, leaving the prophet to weep over the proud nation's demise (vv. 16–17).[40] The king and the queen mother should take the lead in demon-

---

guage of the text, which literally reads "hated" in both instances.) In this case, the term points to the fact that God would oppose his people and bring about their demise.

40. The phrase rendered "give glory" by NIV (v. 16) does not refer here to praise or worship per se. Rather here it has the nuance of showing respect through humility, repentance, and obedience (see Mal. 2:2).

strating humility, for otherwise they would lose their royal positions of prominence (v. 18).[41] The invader from the north would sweep through Judah to its southernmost borders (note the reference to "the cities in the Negev") and carry its people into exile as if they were helpless sheep (vv. 19–20).[42]

As the speech unfolds, the addressee, who appears to be the queen mother (see v. 18), changes to personified Jerusalem (see v. 27). In the aftermath of the invasion, Jerusalem would experience terror and humiliation because of her many sins (vv. 21–22). The people had become ingrained in their sinful behavior, which was as unchangeable as the appearance of a leopard or Ethiopian (v. 23).[43] The Lord would scatter them to the wind (v. 24) because of Jerusalem's idolatry (v. 25). Since the city had committed spiritual adultery, it would be subjected to the same humiliating punishment that an adulteress receives (vv. 26–27; see Ezek. 16:37; Hos. 2:3).

Just as the Lord had threatened in the covenantal curses (see Deut. 28:22–24), drought had overtaken the land of Judah, prompting widespread lamentation (14:1–2). The cisterns were empty and the ground cracked because no rain had fallen (vv. 3–4). Even the wild animals were starving because the vegetation had withered (vv. 5–6).

Speaking for the people, Jeremiah confessed the nation's sins, lamented the Lord's apparent absence, and asked for his intervention (vv. 7–9). But the Lord rejected Jeremiah's plea and told him not to intercede for the people (vv. 10–11; see 7:16; 11:14). He would not accept their religious rituals, for he was intent upon destroying them (v. 12).

Jeremiah, however, was not ready to give up. He pointed out that the

41. The command to "come down" is an example of double entendre. On the surface it is a call to repent in humility (see v. 16), but the rejection of the call transforms it into an ironic statement announcing in highly rhetorical fashion the demise of the king and queen mother. Perhaps one could paraphrase the statement as follows: "One way or another you must come down from your thrones. You should do so in humility before God, for otherwise you will be humbled before your enemies and your royal status will be taken from you." The identities of the king and queen mother are unclear. Some propose that Jehoiakim and his mother Zebidah (2 Kings 23:36) are in view, while others identify the referents as Jehoiachin and his mother Nehushta (2 Kings 24:8).

42. The identity of the addressee in v. 20 is uncertain. In the Hebrew consonantal text the verbs "lift up" and "see" are feminine singular, while the traditional marginal reading understands them as masculine plural. The second-person pronoun attached to "eyes" is masculine plural, while the second-person pronouns in v. 20b are feminine singular. Because of the feminine forms, some see personified Jerusalem as the addressee (see vv. 21–27, especially v. 27). However, the reference to the addressee being entrusted with a flock suggests the royal leaders addressed in v. 18 may still be in view. In this case, the feminine singular forms would be addressed to the queen mother, while the plural forms would encompass both the king and queen mother. Despite the inconsistency in style, the variation is what one might expect in an impassioned speech directed to the king and queen mother. In such speech one can shift focus from one to both and vice versa.

43. In v. 23, the second-person forms switch from feminine singular (see vv. 21–22) to masculine plural, indicating that the addressee changes briefly from personified Jerusalem to the people who live within the city. In vv. 25–27 feminine singular forms are used again as the address to the personified city resumes. (In v. 24, the Hebrew text reads literally, "I will scatter them," referring to the people, rather than "I will scatter you" [see NIV].)

false prophets were misleading the people by promising peace (v. 13). The Lord denounced these prophets, pointing out that that they had not received their message from him (v. 14). Because these lying prophets told the people that sword and famine would not touch the land, they and their families would perish by the sword and famine (vv. 15–16). But the guilt of the prophets hardly exonerated the people, who should have been able to discern truth from error. The time for intercession had passed. Rather than praying for the people, Jeremiah was to lament their tragic demise (vv. 17–18).

But Jeremiah persisted in his intercessory role. Once more he appealed to the Lord, confessing the nation's sins and expressing his trust in the faithfulness of God to his covenantal promises (vv. 19–22). Once more the Lord refused to accept the prophet's prayer. He explained that not even Moses or Samuel could persuade him to show compassion (15:1). The statement is startling, for both of these ancient prophets were famous for their success in interceding with the Lord. Following the golden-calf incident, Moses talked God out of destroying the Israelites by appealing to God's reputation and promise (see Exod. 32:7–14). Samuel's intercession for Israel was instrumental in the nation's liberation from the Philistines (see 1 Sam. 7:1–14). After God reprimanded the Israelites for demanding a king, Samuel promised to intercede for them (see 1 Sam. 12:23).

If the people in desperation asked for Jeremiah's advice on what to do, he was to tell them with biting sarcasm that destruction was inevitable and escape impossible (v. 2). The sword-wielding invaders would be followed by wild dogs, birds, and wild animals that would devour the carcasses of the dead (v. 3). This disaster would come because the people had persisted in the sins inaugurated by wicked King Manasseh several years before (v. 4).

On the surface, verse 4 gives the impression that the coming judgment was solely a divine response to the sins of Manasseh, who ruled over Judah from 696–642 B.C. This king's reign was marred by widespread idolatry and social injustice (see 2 Kings 21:1–16; 23:26; 24:3–4). But Jeremiah's prophecies make it clear that the prophet's contemporaries were punished for their own sins (see 14:20, for example). How then is one to understand verse 4 and integrate it into Jeremiah's argument? Manasseh planted the seed that had developed into a fully grown poisonous plant by Jeremiah's time. Jeremiah's contemporaries had perpetuated his sins. By judging this Manasseh-like generation, the Lord would continue to punish this wicked king for his sins. This passage thus provides further evidence for the concept of transgenerational guilt and punishment in ancient Israelite thought.

The Lord's punishment of Jerusalem would be extremely harsh (v. 5). Though the Lord had time and time again relented from sending disaster, the people continued to reject him.[44] Judgment could no longer be post-

---

44. In the Hebrew text the last statement in v. 6 reads literally, "I am weary of relenting."

poned (v. 6). Like the farmer who removes the chaff from his grain through the winnowing process, so the Lord would purge his stubborn people through warfare (v. 7). Wives would lose their husbands, and children would be deprived of their mothers (vv. 8–9a). Refugees would be cut down by the sword (v. 9b).

The Lord's reference to mothers dying prompts Jeremiah to lament that his own mother has given him birth (v. 10). As God's prophet of doom, he faced intense hostility from the people (v. 10). Unfortunately, the Lord's response to the prophet seems garbled and is unclear. In verses 13–14, the Lord is clearly speaking to the sinful people of Judah, but the addressee in verse 11 is uncertain, as is the point of the statement, which reads literally, "Surely I will . . . you for good.[45] Surely I will cause to confront you in the time of calamity and in the time of distress the enemy."[46] Because the meaning of verse 11 is so uncertain, the point of the proverbial-like saying in verse 12 is also unclear. Understandably, interpreters are divided as to how these verses function in the text. Some see the Lord trying to encourage Jeremiah before resuming his announcement of judgment against the people. Others argue that these verses are spoken to the people, not the prophet, in which case the Lord ignores Jeremiah's complaint and continues the announcement of judgment.

In verses 15–18, Jeremiah pursues the complaint he began in verse 10. He prays for the Lord's protection and for divine vengeance against his enemies (v. 15a). He reminds the Lord of how he has suffered because of his commitment to preach faithfully God's word (vv. 15b–16). He deprived himself of the ordinary joys of life as he devoted himself to God's cause (v. 17). Yet despite his faithfulness, he suffers unrelenting pain (v. 18a). Almost at his breaking point, he suggests the Lord is unreliable (v. 18b). The Lord mildly rebukes Jeremiah, indicating that he needs to repent and no longer express such insulting words (v. 19). If he repents, he can continue as the Lord's spokesman, but he must not fall into the sinful nation's way of thinking. As if to energize Jeremiah, the Lord assures him of protection from his violent enemies (vv. 20–21).

Despite the Lord's assuring words, Jeremiah's life did not get any easier. More object lessons were in order. The Lord prohibited Jeremiah from marrying and having children (16:1–2). After all, the Lord explained, starting a family would be pointless in light of the coming judgment, which would annihilate the families of the land (vv. 3–4). Furthermore, Jeremiah was prohibited from attending any funerals and from mourning for the dead (v. 5). Again this was to foreshadow the coming judgment, which would bring such

---

45. The meaning of the verb is uncertain, hence the ellipsis in the translation. See *HALOT* 1652–53, 1658, for a list and discussion of options.

46. For another example of the grammatical construction used here (Hiphil of *paga'* with preposition *be-* and accusative introduced by *'et*), see Isa. 53:6. See as well Holladay, *Jeremiah 1*, 453.

widespread destruction and death that people would not have the opportunity to bury the dead, let alone mourn their demise or console those left behind (vv. 6–7). The Lord also told the prophet to stay away from feasts because all celebrations, including wedding festivities, would soon come to an end (vv. 8–9).

When the people demanded to know why the Lord intended to judge them, Jeremiah was to point out that they had surpassed the sins of their idolatrous fathers and were stubbornly disobeying his commands (vv. 10–12). For this reason, the Lord would send them into exile, where they could worship foreign gods to their heart's content (v. 13). In so doing their actions would ironically mirror those of their ancestors (see v. 11). Before continuing this announcement of judgment (see vv. 16–18), the Lord looks beyond the day of judgment to a time when he would deliver his people from Babylonian exile and restore them to their land (vv. 14–15). But in the meantime the invaders would sweep through the land. As a fisherman gathers fish in a net, so the enemy would gather its victims en masse. Like hunters, the invaders would relentlessly pursue their victims (v. 16). The Lord's idolatrous people would be repaid double (the language is hyperbolic, indicating full payment) for their sins (vv. 17–18). In contrast to the scene described in verse 18, Jeremiah anticipated a time when foreigners would come to the Lord and confess their sin of idolatry (vv. 19–20). In that day the Lord would instruct the nations (v. 21). They would come to know his powerful, protective presence, just as the prophet did (see v. 19a).

Once again a brief flight into the distant future is followed by a return to the present (see 16:14–16), which was marred by sinful Judah's obsession with idols (17:1–2). This idolatrous worship was designed to ensure the nation's prosperity, but the Lord would hand their wealth over to the invaders (vv. 3–4).

In the face of the coming judgment, what chance did anyone have of escaping destruction and death? That question must have tormented the faithful few who remained in Judah and heard Jeremiah's prophecies of doom. Here the Lord encourages the remnant by reminding them that those who trust in the Lord can never be shaken. Those who trust in human strength and ignore the Lord are doomed (vv. 5–6), but the Lord's loyal followers are like a well-watered tree that always yields its fruit (vv. 7–8; see Ps. 1). While encouraging, these words were also a challenge to Jeremiah to maintain his faith in the Lord and avoid following the example of the masses (see 15:19b), whose moral nature was contaminated (v. 9). These sinners could not escape the penetrating gaze of the Lord, who knows people's hearts and deeds and judges them accordingly (v. 10). Many in Judah had accumulated wealth through oppressive means, but the Lord's just judgment would cause their riches to disappear (v. 11; note how this verse correlates thematically with v. 3).

In response, Jeremiah praised the Lord as the only hope of his people and acknowledged that those who rejected the Lord were indeed doomed (vv. 12–13). Utilizing the metaphor of physical healing, he begged the Lord to deliver him from the threats of his enemies, who taunted him and questioned his prophetic authority (vv. 14–15). Jeremiah had faithfully carried out his commission (v. 16). He needed to be vindicated, so he prayed that the Lord would indeed bring the prophesied judgment to pass (vv. 17–18).

The Lord instructed Jeremiah to move from gate to gate in Jerusalem, beginning at the royal gate (v. 19). As the people came and went, Jeremiah was to warn them not to violate the ancient Sabbath laws, as their fathers had done (vv. 20–23). If the people responded positively to Jeremiah's challenge and observed the Sabbath, the Lord would make the city secure and accept the worship of those who brought offerings to his temple (vv. 24–26). But if they persisted in violating the Sabbath, fire would destroy the city (v. 27).

This emphasis on Sabbath worship may seem to overlook the more fundamental issues facing sinful Judah, namely, idolatry and social injustice. Sabbath breaking was certainly a serious sin (see Exod. 20:8; Num. 15:32–36), but it would seem that people could easily observe the Sabbath in an outward manner without changing their hearts. But this apparently simple challenge to the people is actually profound. Their failure to keep the Sabbath was a symptom of their deep-rooted greed and lack of respect for the Lord (see Amos 8:4–6).[47] As a symptom it would not disappear until its underlying causes were eliminated. The Lord knew this generation could never keep such a seemingly arbitrary commandment like the Sabbath law unless their hearts were right and their commitment to him renewed. So keeping the Sabbath becomes a metonymy for a wholesale change of heart.

Lessons from the Potter (18:1–19:13)

The Lord sent Jeremiah down to the potter's house for an object lesson (18:1–2). As the potter shaped his pot according to a specific design, the clay proved to be unpliable, so the potter reshaped it into a different type of pot (vv. 3–4). In the same way that the potter improvised his design for the unpliable clay, so the Lord would change his plans for Israel if necessary (vv. 5–6). If the Lord intends to destroy a nation, but that kingdom then repents when warned of its impending doom, the Lord will relent from sending the threatened judgment (vv. 7–8). On the other hand, if the Lord intends to make a nation secure, but that kingdom then disobeys him, the Lord will change his mind and not bless that rebellious nation (vv. 9–10). In other words, God's announcements of judgment and blessing are not necessarily

---

47. In this regard, note the observation of Lundbom (*Jeremiah 1–20*, 810): "It [Sabbath-breaking] is an evil rooted in greed, which according to Amos 8:4–6, is the handmaiden of social injustice and what leads to the breakdown of community well-being."

set in stone, as if he has decreed unconditionally what will take place.[48] God makes plans and announces his intentions, but how nations respond to his warnings and moral standards can and often does determine what actually transpires. Despite the imagery of the potter and clay, there is no room for fatalistic determinism here, for the "clay" is depicted as exercising its own will, prompting an appropriate response from the divine "potter."

In the case of Jeremiah's generation, the Lord was planning to send judgment (v. 11a). The proper response was repentance (v. 11b), but the Lord was skeptical about that happening and expected the people to persist in their sins (v. 12).[49] Judah's decision to reject the Lord in favor of idols (v. 15a) was unprecedented among the nations, who typically remained loyal to their gods (v. 13; see 2:10–12). Judah's idolatry was totally irrational and as unbelievable as if the snows of Lebanon were to dry up (v. 14). The people had wandered away from the Lord and would suffer the severe consequences of their actions (vv. 15–17).

As if to affirm the Lord's evaluation of the people, Jeremiah described how they plotted against him and refused to listen to his message (v. 18). He had been willing to intercede for the people, but they repaid his good with evil (v. 20). Appealing to God as the just judge (v. 19), he called a curse down upon his enemies and asked that the Lord repay their evil appropriately (vv. 21–23). This curse may seem harsh and vindictive, but it should be understood as a genuine appeal for justice and deliverance from one who is outnumbered and helpless apart from divine intervention. Such appeals for divine justice, though prohibited in the present era (see, for example, Luke 6:28; Rom. 12:14), were in Old Testament times perfectly legitimate, for God's positive response to such prayers would have a powerful impact on observers (see Ps. 58:10–11).[50]

Another object lesson was in order. The Lord instructed Jeremiah to buy a clay jar from a potter and then take some civil leaders and priests to the Potsherd Gate in the Valley of Ben Hinnom, located on the southwest side of the city (19:1–2). The prophet was to announce that the Lord was about to bring disaster on the city because of the people's idolatrous behavior, which included sacrificing their children to the god Baal in Topheth (vv. 3–5; see 7:31). In the aftermath of the coming invasion, Topheth/the Valley

48. For a helpful study of contingency in prophecy see R. L. Pratt Jr., "Historical Contingencies and Biblical Predictions," in *The Way of Wisdom: Essays in Honor of Bruce K. Waltke,* ed. J. I. Packer and S. K. Soderlund (Grand Rapids: Zondervan, 2000), 180–203.

49. The Lord's willingness to repent, which seems to contrast with what he says in 15:1–5, suggests that the episode recorded in 18:1–10 occurred earlier in the prophet's ministry, before the Lord decreed the fall of Jerusalem (see chapter 26, which dates from early in Jehoiakim's reign). See my earlier comments on 4:28.

50. For a more detailed discussion of imprecations (or "curses"), see Robert B. Chisholm Jr., "A Theology of the Psalms," in *A Biblical Theology of the Old Testament,* ed. R. B. Zuck (Chicago: Moody, 1991), 282–83.

of Hinnom would be renamed "the Valley of Slaughter," for it would be
turned into a mass burial ground for the victims of divine judgment (vv.
6–8; see 7:32). During the siege that preceded the city's downfall, starving
parents would actually eat their own children and cannibalism would become rampant (v. 9; see Deut. 28:53–57; Lam. 2:20; 4:10). After proclaiming this message, Jeremiah was to break the clay jar, symbolizing the way the
Lord would "smash" the nation to bits because of its idolatry (vv. 10–13).

Conflict and Complaint (19:14–20:18)

After discharging his duties at Topheth, Jeremiah proceeded to the court of
the temple, where he repeated his announcement of impending disaster (vv.
14–15). When the priest Pashhur, the chief of temple security, heard him,
he arrested Jeremiah and had him beaten and placed in stocks (20:1–2).
When Pashhur released Jeremiah the next day, the prophet lashed out at the
priest, sarcastically calling him Magor-Missabib, which means "terror all
around" (v. 3). This was an appropriate name, for horrifying terror would
soon overtake Pashhur and his associates (vv. 4–6). He would watch in horror as his associates were cut down by the sword and the Babylonians hauled
away Judah's people and riches. Pashhur would die in exile in Babylon.

Jeremiah's humiliating experience shook him to the core and prompted
him to cry out to the Lord. His prayer (vv. 7–20) is an odd mixture of complaint and praise, of despair and confidence. It is difficult to understand how
all of these elements could be present in one short prayer, but the apparent
inconsistency is testimony to Jeremiah's disturbed emotional state at this
time. Part of him wanted to strike out and complain to God, while the other
part of him wanted to affirm that God was his protector.[51]

Jeremiah began by accusing the Lord of deceiving and bullying him
(v. 7a). He faithfully preached God's word, but all it brought him was
ridicule and shame (vv. 7b–8). He thought about resigning his commission,
but God's word was like a fire inside him that demanded to burst forth (v. 9).
What is one to make of Jeremiah's charge that God had deceived him? Perhaps he believed that God had made the commission sound more attractive
than it proved to be or that God had failed to warn him adequately about
the opposition he would face. However, the charge may be more serious than
this. Because of the opposition he faced, Jeremiah may have come to the
point where he feared that he was a false prophet, like the divinely deceived
prophets described in 1 Kings 22. His enemies certainly suspected as much
and were eagerly waiting for his messages to fail so they could get rid of him
(see v. 10). Of course, Jeremiah's charge was unfounded, not because God

---

51. The quick changes in mood and thematic discontinuities in vv. 7–20 cause many to conclude that
this is not a continuous prayer uttered on one occasion, but separate prayers that have been gathered together. See, for example, William McKane, *Jeremiah*, 2 vols., ICC (Edinburgh: T. & T. Clark, 1986, 1996),
1:468, and Holladay, *Jeremiah 1*, 548.

would never deceive a prophet (see 1 Kings 22 as well as Jer. 4:10), but because Jeremiah's message was true to the covenant. Jeremiah's denunciation of sin was in line with the moral and ethical commandments of God's law, and his warnings of impending doom were consistent with the covenantal principle that sin will be punished.[52]

Though pressured by his enemies, Jeremiah experienced a sudden burst of confidence. He believed the Lord was his protector and avenger (vv. 11–12). His enemies would stumble and fall, because the Lord, whose penetrating gaze can reach into the hearts and minds of men, would act justly and vindicate his faithful prophet. Overcome with joy, the prophet calls upon others to praise the Lord because he delivers his beleaguered people from their wicked enemies (v. 13).

But Jeremiah descends the mountain as quickly as he ascended it. The emotional roller coaster takes a swift dive as Jeremiah curses the day of his birth and levels a violent imprecation against the one who announced to his father that a son had been born (vv. 14–16). The prophet wishes that this messenger had killed him in his mother's womb so that he could have escaped the trouble and sorrow that have characterized his life (vv. 17–18).

Confronting Kings and Prophets (21:1–23:40)

In 588 B.C., as the Babylonian army attacked Jerusalem, King Zedekiah sent two envoys to Jeremiah asking him to inquire of the Lord (21:1–2a). The king hoped the Lord would miraculously deliver Jerusalem as he had in the past (v. 2b). He undoubtedly had in mind the incident in 701 B.C., when the Lord rescued the city from Sennacherib, king of Assyria (see Isa. 37:36–37).

But the time for deliverance had come and gone. The Lord announced that he would personally lead the Babylonian charge against the city and strike down every living thing within its walls, including even the animals (vv. 3–6). The Lord would hand Zedekiah and his officials over to Nebuchadnezzar, who would ruthlessly cut them down (v. 7). When Jerusalem fell two years later, Nebuchadnezzar actually spared Zedekiah's life, but he executed Zedekiah's sons before blinding the king and carrying him into exile (see Jer. 52:10–11). However, the Lord did offer some consolation to the people of Jerusalem (v. 8). Anyone who remained in the city would die from starvation or disease, or be cut down by the sword, but anyone willing to surrender to the Babylonians would escape the destruction that would soon overtake the city (vv. 9–10).

At first it appears that verses 11–14 continue the speech begun in verse 3, but it quickly becomes apparent that this is not the case. The call to establish social justice (v. 11a) comes from an earlier period in Jeremiah's ca-

---

52. See Chisholm, "Does God Deceive?" 17–18.

reer, and the second half of verse 11 makes judgment on the royal house conditional, while in the preceding verses destruction is inevitable. Despite the
traditional chapter division, it is much more likely that verses 11–14 form an
introduction to what follows.[53] This general appeal to the royal house, which
continues in 22:1–9, serves as an appropriate prelude to the following series
of messages, which pertain to the kings Jehoahaz (Shallum) (22:10–12), Jehoiakim (Eliakim) (22:13–19), and Jehoiachin (Coniah) (22:24–30), respectively. A judgment speech against Jerusalem is tucked between the second and third of these (see 22:20–23). A postlude (23:1–8) addresses the
kings of Judah in general (utilizing the metaphor of "shepherds") and anticipates the coming of an ideal Davidic ruler who will establish justice.[54]

The prelude summarizes Jeremiah's message to the royal house of Judah.
Through his prophet the Lord challenged the king and his officials to establish social justice in the land and defend the cause of the oppressed (vv. 11–
12a). Otherwise God's fiery judgment would come upon them for their oppressive policies (v. 12b). Though the people of Jerusalem felt secure, the
Lord had determined to attack the city and punish its people for their sinful
deeds (vv. 13–14).

The Lord sent Jeremiah to the royal palace to confront the king and his
officials with their responsibilities (22:1–2). He commanded these leaders to
promote social justice in the land by aggressively defending the rights of the
weak and vulnerable in society (v. 3). Their willingness to obey this command
would determine their destiny. Obedience would make the Davidic throne
secure, but disobedience would bring ruin (vv. 4–5). The royal palace was an
impressive structure, built in part with timber from the forests of Gilead and
Lebanon (v. 6a). But its splendor did not make it secure. If the king who lived
within it did not carry out his duties as God's delegated authority, the palace
would go up in smoke (vv. 6b–7). When observers inquired as to why the
Lord would destroy his own city, the answer would be clear and simple—the
people had broken his covenant and worshiped other gods (vv. 8–9).

The series of specific messages begins with a call to lament the fate of
King Jehoahaz (also known as Shallum; see vv. 10–12). In 609 B.C., the people were still lamenting the tragic death of King Josiah (see 2 Kings 23:29–
30). But Jeremiah urged them to mourn instead the fate of Josiah's son and
successor, Jehoahaz, who had ruled for only three months before being taken
captive by Pharaoh Necho of Egypt (2 Kings 23:31–34). This unfortunate
king would die in exile and never again see his homeland.

Next comes a judgment oracle against Jehoiakim (also known as Eliakim, see 2 Kings 23:34), the half-brother and successor of Jehoahaz (see

---

53. See Thompson, *Jeremiah*, 466, 470, 473.

54. There is no specific message to Judah's last king, Zedekiah, but, as Thompson observes, the
prophecy of the ideal king in 23:5–6 plays on Zedekiah's name and thus sets up an implied contrast between the ideal king and Zedekiah. See ibid., 486, 490–91.

2 Kings 23:36) who ruled from 608–598 B.C. When building his extravagant royal palace, Jehoiakim forced some of his countrymen to work as slaves (vv. 13–14, 17). He had failed to follow the example of his father, Josiah. Having a beautiful palace is not the essence of kingship (v. 15a). The primary duty of kings was (and still is) to promote social justice by defending the cause of the weak and vulnerable (v. 16). Josiah did this and was blessed by God (v. 15b). His obedience demonstrated that he truly "knew" the Lord. The term "know" does not mean here "be aware of," but is used in the sense of "recognize the authority of."[55] "Knowing" God does not involve just intellectual awareness or even a declaration of allegiance. Knowing God, in the sense in which the term is used here, means recognizing his authority and demonstrating such recognition by obedience. Josiah was a prime example of this. He understood that he was subject to God and that his role as king was to carry out God's wishes concerning social justice. He proved he recognized God's authority by taking up the cause of the poor and needy.

Because Jehoiakim, in contrast to his father, oppressed his countrymen (v. 17), he would be punished severely (vv. 18–19). People would not mourn his passing, and his corpse would not receive a proper burial (see also Jer. 36:30). Indeed, he would be dragged outside the city gates like a dead donkey. There is no evidence that Jehoiakim actually died such a humiliating death. Second Kings 24:6 states simply that he "rested with his fathers," while 2 Chronicles 36:6 tells how Nebuchadnezzar bound him in shackles with the intent of taking him to Babylon. While the evidence does not corroborate the fulfillment of the prophecy, neither does it preclude it.[56] However, it seems likely that the language of the diatribe in verses 18–19 is hyperbolic or that other factors subsequently prompted God to cancel the prophecy or alter the details of its fulfillment.[57]

Before denouncing the next king, the Lord speaks to personified Jerusalem about the tragedy that is about to overtake her.[58] While the appearance

55. The term also carries this nuance in 1 Sam. 2:12, Isa. 11:2, and Hos. 4:1, 6. The idiom also appears in 1 John 2:3–4; 4:8.

56. For an attempt to harmonize Jer. 22:19 with 2 Kings 24:6 in such a way that Jer. 22:19 is literally fulfilled, see Charles L. Feinberg, "Jeremiah," in *The Expositor's Bible Commentary*, vol. 6, ed. F. E. Gaebelein (Grand Rapids: Zondervan, 1986), 514–15. He points outs that after Ahab's violent and humiliating death (see 1 Kings 22:34–38), it is stated that he "rested with his fathers" (v. 40), just as 2 Kings 24:6 states with respect to Jehoiakim. However, 1 Kings 22:37 says that Ahab was buried, in contrast to Jer. 22:19, which indicates Jehoiakim would not be buried. For a critique of harmonizing efforts like those of Feinberg, see Carroll, *Jeremiah*, 432–34.

57. On the use of stereotypical, hyperbolic language in prophetic judgment oracles, see my discussion of Isa. 13–14. For an attempt to explain Jer. 22:19 in this way, see Carroll, *Jeremiah*, 432. On contingency in implicitly conditional prophecies, see my discussion of Jer. 26:17–19 (in conjunction with Mic. 3:12), as well as my observations on Joel 2:18–27, Jon. 3:9–10, and Hag. 2:6–9, 20–23. In this regard it is also instructive to compare 1 Kings 21:19 with 22:37–38 (Naboth was executed in Jezreel, not Samaria), and 2 Kings 22:20 with 23:29–30 (does death on a battlefield constitute being buried "in peace"?).

58. The identity of the addressee as Jerusalem is especially apparent in the Hebrew text, where second feminine singular pronouns and verb forms are employed in vv. 20–23. Jerusalem is frequently personified as a woman in prophetic literature.

of this speech may seem to interrupt the sequence of messages pertaining to the kings, its placement here is appropriate, for the fall of Jerusalem and the demise of the Davidic dynasty were two sides of the same coin. The reference to "shepherds" (i.e., leaders, especially the royal house) being swept away also links the speech to its context thematically.

The Lord urged Jerusalem to ascend a high place and wail, for her allies were defeated (v. 20). The Lord had warned Jerusalem that judgment would come, but the confident city refused to listen and persisted in sin (v. 21). Like a mighty wind, the coming judgment would sweep away the city's leaders (compared here to "shepherds") and allies, leaving the city humiliated (v. 22). Utilizing Lebanon as a symbol for proud Jerusalem, the Lord then compares the city's day of judgment to the painful experience of childbirth (v. 23).

The Lord next turns to Jehoiachin (also known as Coniah), the son and successor of Jehoiakim who ruled for only three months before being taken into exile by Nebuchadnezzar in 597 B.C. (2 Kings 24:8–16). In a scathing diatribe the Lord formally disowns Jehoiachin and announces that both he and his mother would be taken into exile (vv. 24–26). Jehoiachin would die there without ever again seeing his native land (v. 27). Furthermore, his dynasty would come to an end (vv. 28–30). For all intents and purposes, he would be childless. Though he actually had seven sons (see 1 Chron. 3:17–18), none of his descendants would occupy his throne.[59] Jehoiachin is compared to a signet ring that the Lord removes from his hand, symbolizing that he no longer functions as God's representative. This oracle, seemingly finalized by oath (see v. 24), places the future of the Davidic dynasty in jeopardy, but the announcement to Jehoiachin's grandson Zerubbabel (see Hag. 2:20–23) reverses the curse. The Lord promises Zerubbabel that he will make him his signet ring, restoring the divine authority of the Davidic dynasty.

Having denounced specific kings, the Lord pronounced a "woe" against the "shepherds" (a symbol for Judah's kings) who had destroyed God's sheep (a symbol for the people) by not caring for them properly (23:1–2). However, the Lord, the true shepherd of his people, would someday restore the remnant of his flock from exile, just as he had earlier delivered Israel from bondage in Egypt (vv. 3, 7–8). He would place over his people competent shepherds who would protect them (v. 4; see Mic. 5:5). At the head of this contingent of shepherds would be a Davidic descendant, called here "a righteous Branch" (v. 5a). The imagery pictures this king as a branch that shoots from the Davidic family tree. The qualifying adjective, translated "righteous," may depict the king as just and fair (see v. 5b), though usage of a cognate term in Phoenician and Ugaritic suggests it may designate this king as

---

59. Zedekiah, Jehoiachin's successor, was Josiah's son and Jehoiachin's uncle. See 2 Kings 24:17.

"worthy, legitimate."[60] This wise ruler would promote justice (v. 5b; see Isa. 11:1–5) and bring security to the land (v. 6a). The people would call him "The LORD [is] Our Righteousness," for he would be the Lord's instrument of justice.[61]

Verses 5–6 contain a wordplay on the name of Zedekiah, the last king of Judah. The adjective "righteous" (Heb. *tsaddiq*) comes from the same root as Zedekiah's name (Heb. *tsidqiyahu*, meaning "My righteousness is the LORD"). The name given the king in verse 6 (Heb. *'adonai tsidqenu*, meaning "the LORD is our righteousness") is clearly a deliberate play on Zedekiah's name. In light of his character, Zedekiah's name was a sham (see 34:8–22), for he was unworthy to sit on the throne and was rejected by the Lord. But the ideal Davidic king would be a worthy ruler through whom the Lord would establish justice among his people.

Judah's civil leaders were not the only culprits. Her religious leaders, especially the majority of the prophets, were also corrupt. Jeremiah was deeply disturbed by the priests' and prophets' sinful behavior, which had prompted divine judgment in the form of drought and famine (vv. 9–11). These false prophets were headed for disaster (v. 12). In God's eyes they were just as repulsive as the Israelite prophets of earlier days who encouraged the people to worship Baal (vv. 13–14). When God looked on Jerusalem and its leaders, he saw another Sodom and Gomorrah (see Isa. 1:10), prompting him to announce that severe judgment would come upon the land (v. 15).

The Lord warned the people not to listen to the false prophets, who assured the people they were insulated from disaster (vv. 16–17). However, these prophets had not stood in God's council and, in contrast to Jeremiah, had not received a divine commission (vv. 18, 21). Contrary to their assuring messages, the Lord was ready to explode upon the people in angry judgment (vv. 19–20). If they were really the Lord's spokesmen, they would have confronted the sin of the people, for it was obvious that the Lord's covenant had been violated (v. 22). The people acted as if they believed the Lord was restricted to one place. The reference to "a God nearby" probably alludes to his residing in the Jerusalem temple. In their thinking he was a myopic deity who was unaware of what was going on outside his own little corner of the world (v. 23). Such a notion is, of course, absurd. The Lord is the ruler of the world who sees all that happens. The people could not hide anything, including their sinful deeds (see v. 22), from him (v. 24; see Ps. 11:4–5).

On the surface the false prophets seemed to possess divine authority.

---

60. For the evidence from the cognate languages, see Holladay, *Jeremiah 1*, 618; McKane, *Jeremiah*, 1:561; and J. Hoftijzer and K. Jongeling, *Dictionary of the North-West Semitic Inscriptions*, 2 vols. (Leiden: Brill, 1995), 2:962.

61. Another option is to translate the name without the connecting verb, "The LORD Our Righteousness." The name highlights the fact that through this king the Lord would establish justice and peace in the land (see especially v. 5b).

They prophesied in the Lord's name and claimed to receive prophetic visions (v. 25). But these prophecies actually originated in the prophets' own deluded minds and misrepresented the Lord (vv. 26–27). The false prophets' dreams of peace and security would be exposed as empty lies when set alongside genuine prophecy, just as straw is easily recognized when compared to grain (v. 28). The messages of true prophets of the Lord, like Jeremiah, were characterized by power in that they denounced sin and announced judgment (v. 29). As such, they were like destructive fire or a powerful hammer blow. Three times the Lord solemnly declares his opposition to the false prophets, whose deceptive lies mislead the people (vv. 30–32).

If the people, including the priests or prophets, were to ask Jeremiah, "What is the oracle of the LORD?" he was to respond sarcastically, "You are the burden! (v. 33 NET)."[62] A wordplay is involved in the Hebrew text; the terms translated "oracle" and "burden" are homonyms (Heb. *massa'*). When the people inquired about the latest *massa'* (i.e., oracle) from the Lord, Jeremiah was to inform them that they were the *massa'* (i.e., burden), as far as the Lord was concerned. Their sinful behavior was like a heavy burden that he was anxious to discard (v. 34; see v. 39). The Lord would punish all who had the audacity to speak in his name when they had not received a message from him (vv. 35–38). He would drive them away from his presence into exile and bring lasting shame upon them (vv. 39–40).

An Object Lesson Using Figs (24:1–10)

Sometime after 597 B.C., when Nebuchadnezzar deported King Jehoiachin and other prominent citizens of Judah to Babylon (see 2 Kings 24:10–17), the Lord used two baskets of figs to teach Jeremiah a lesson (24:1). One basket contained tasty figs from the season's first crop, which ripens in June.[63] The other contained rotten, inedible figs (vv. 2–3). The good figs symbolized those who had recently been taken into exile (vv. 4–5). Just as one takes delight in tasty figs, so the Lord would show favor to these exiles by eventually transforming them into a repentant community of worshipers and restoring them to the land (vv. 6–7). The prophecy can hardly apply literally to Jehoiachin (see 22:24–30) and those exiled with him, but must instead refer to their descendants. In this regard Jeremiah's letter to these exiles, recorded in 29:1–23, makes it clear that the prophecy would not be realized until seventy years had passed (see 29:10, as well as 25:11–12). The rotten figs symbolized King Zedekiah and the others who were left in Judah. Just as one throws away rotten figs, so the Lord would reject those remaining in

---

62. The traditional Hebrew text has suffered from misdivision. Following the lead of the Septuagint, one can reconstruct the text to read, "You [are] the burden!" See McKane, *Jeremiah*, 1:599, and Holladay, *Jeremiah 1*, 647.

63. See Borowski, *Agriculture in Iron Age Israel*, 115.

the land (v. 8). He would devastate the land, making Judah abhorrent in the eyes of neighboring nations (vv. 9–10).

A Lifetime Spent in Exile (25:1–14)

In Jehoiakim's fourth year (605 B.C.) the Lord formally announced the coming Babylonian exile (25:1). For the past twenty-three years Jeremiah had confronted the people with their sin, but they had rejected his message (vv. 2–3). Jeremiah and other prophets like him had called the people to repentance and warned about the consequences of idolatry, but to no avail (vv. 4–7). For this reason, the Lord was ready to summon Nebuchadnezzar, the newly crowned king of Babylon, as his instrument of judgment (vv. 8–9a). The Babylonian armies would devastate the land and eliminate the sounds of joy and everyday activity (vv. 9b–10).[64] With Judah left a wasteland, the exiled people would be forced to serve the Babylonians for a period of seventy years (v. 11).

The figure "seventy" should probably not be taken too precisely. Though Nebuchadnezzar invaded Judah in 605 and again in 597 (see 2 Kings 24:1–2, 10–16; 2 Chron. 36:6–7, 10; Dan. 1:1–2), the text closely associates Judah's period of servitude with the devastation of the land (cf. 25:9–11 with 24:8–10), which is most naturally understood as beginning with the fall of Jerusalem in 586 B.C.[65] In this case, the period of servitude was forty-seven to forty-eight years, not seventy years. In chapter 29, a seventy-year period is mentioned again (see v. 10), this time in a letter to the exiles written sometime after the deportation of Jehoiachin in 597 (see v. 2). If the "seventy years" referred to here begins in 597, then the period of servitude is actually 58–59 years in length, not seventy. Either way the period in question did not last seventy years.[66] For this reason, it seems preferable to take the number as an idiomatic expression which is used in a stereotypical, non-literal manner to indicate a long period of time that satisfies completely the demands of divine judgment. Being a multiple of the symbolic number seven, it indicates

---

64. The phrase "everlasting ruin" in v. 9b is obviously hyperbolic, for the Lord promised to restore the land someday.

65. Second Chronicles 36 favors this as well, for the seventy-year period of desolation mentioned in 2 Chron. 36:21 most naturally begins with the events of 586 mentioned just before this in vv. 17–20. The Chronicles passage, furthermore, specifically relates the events it records to Jeremiah's prophecy of a seventy-year exile.

66. Some start the period of exile in 605, in which case it lasted 66–67 years. However, this view must distinguish between the time of Judah's desolation referred to in 25:11 (which began in 586) and the period of its servitude to Babylon (which began in 605). Proponents of this view understand the seventy years of 29:10 as the time period of Babylon's dominance (note the statement, "when seventy years are completed for Babylon"), taken as beginning in 605. In this view the figure of "seventy" years is fairly literal, though still approximate. Some find support for this interpretation in Dan. 9:2, reasoning that Daniel understood the period of seventy years to have begun in 605, when he was taken into exile. As the termination of the period drew closer, Daniel was compelled to pray for divine intervention. However, there is nothing in Daniel's prayer that demands this more literal interpretation of the number.

completeness. Since it also designates an average life span (see Ps. 90:10; Isa. 23:15), it suggests that the exile would extend beyond the lifetime of most of those who were taken captive to Babylon.[67]

Though the Babylonians would dominate God's people for many years, the Lord would eventually turn the tables on them (vv. 12–14). In fulfillment of Jeremiah's prophecies (see chapters 50–51), the Lord would repay the Babylonians for their pride and cruel excesses. This prophecy was fulfilled in 539 B.C. when the Persian ruler Cyrus conquered Babylon and brought the Neo-Babylonian Empire to an end.

God's Judgment on the Nations (25:15–38)

The announcement of Babylon's eventual demise (vv. 12–14) provides a nice transition into the next speech, in which the Lord declares that he will unleash his judgment on all nations. Comparing judgment to a cup of intoxicating wine, the Lord announces he will force the nations to gulp it down (v. 15). Under the influence of God's wrath, they will stagger as if intoxicated (v. 16). The scope of this judgment will be virtually worldwide, as the lengthy list of nations indicates (see vv. 17–26, especially v. 26). It will encompass Egypt to the south, Uz to the east, the Philistines to the west, the trans-Jordanian kingdoms to the east, Tyre and Sidon to the north, the Arabian tribes, and the kings of distant Elam and Media (located east of Babylon), as well as all the kings of the north. The judgment will culminate with the king of "Sheshach," a cryptic reference to Babylon.[68] None of the nations will be exempt (vv. 27–28). After all, if even Jerusalem, God's special city, must experience disaster, then how much more should the pagan nations suffer(v. 29)?

The judgment will be terrifying. The sovereign Lord, enthroned in heaven, will roar like a lion and shout like those who celebrate the grape harvest as they stomp on the grapes in the winepress (v. 30). Since God's judgment is sometimes compared to treading grapes (see Isa. 63:3; Joel 3:13), the metaphor is ominous. As the Lord executes judgment upon humankind with his mighty sword, destruction will spread from nation to nation (vv. 31–32), leaving piles of unburied corpses in its wake (v. 33). Comparing the leaders of the nations to shepherds, the Lord announces their demise (vv. 34–35).

67. See Holladay, *Jeremiah 1*, 669, and, for a balanced discussion of competing views, Carroll, *Jeremiah*, 493–96. Support for the idiomatic interpretation can be found in an inscription from the Assyrian king Esarhaddon that speaks of Marduk decreeing seventy years of desolation for Babylon. See H. W. F. Saggs, *The Greatness That Was Babylon* (New York: New American Library, 1962), 133, and Georges Roux, *Ancient Iraq* (Middlesex, England: Penguin Books, 1966), 294.

68. The technique used is called "atbash," in which the letters of a name are replaced by the corresponding letters when the alphabet is read in reverse order. In Hebrew the name "Babel" consists of the consonants *beth-beth-lamed*. *Beth* is the second letter in the Hebrew alphabet, *lamed* the twelfth. The cryptic name "Sheshach" consists of the consonants *shin-shin-kaph; shin* is the twenty-first letter of the alphabet, while *kaph* is the eleventh. If one reads the alphabet in reverse, *shin* is the second letter, *kaph* the twelfth.

He will lay waste the pasturelands and then attack the sheep (symbolizing humankind) like a raging lion (vv. 36–38).

A Prophet in the Storm (Jeremiah 26–45)

This next major section of the book can be divided into two literary units, both of which are framed with material dating to the reign of King Jehoiakim.[69] The first of these units begins in chapter 26 with an account of how the nation rejected the prophetic message at the Jerusalem temple. This unit concludes in chapter 35 with an encouraging message to the loyal Rechabites, who are contrasted with the unfaithful nation. In a similar way the second unit begins in chapter 36 with another account (which, like chapter 26, dates to the reign of Jehoiakim) of how the nation rejected the prophetic message at the Jerusalem temple. This unit ends in chapter 45 (which, like chapter 35, dates to the reign of Jehoiakim) with an encouraging message to loyal Baruch.

Within the framework of the first literary unit (chapters 26–35), chapters 27–29, which date to the reign of King Zedekiah, focus on Jeremiah's conflict with the authorities. Chapters 30–33 look ahead to the ultimate restoration of the exiled people, while chapter 34, which dates to the reign of Zedekiah, highlights the nation's unfaithfulness. Within the framework of the second literary unit (chapters 36–45), chapters 37–39, which date to Zedekiah's reign, focus on Jeremiah's conflict with the authorities. Chapters 40–44 describe the aftermath of judgment and make it clear that disobedience persisted within the covenant community. For this reason, the restoration anticipated in chapters 30–33 would not take place in the immediate future.

Jeremiah's Life Is Threatened (26:1–24)

Early in the reign of Jehoiakim, who ruled from 608–598 B.C., the Lord instructed Jeremiah to confront the people who came to worship in the Jerusalem temple (26:1–2). If the people persisted in their sin and refused to listen to the Lord's prophets, Jerusalem would be invaded and the Lord would abandon his temple, just as he had abandoned the sanctuary at Shiloh (vv. 4–6; see 7:14). The Lord hoped this warning would bring the people to their senses and prompt them to repent. If they did so, he promised to relent from sending the prophesied disaster (v. 3; see 18:7–8).[70]

Jeremiah's message did not have the desired effect on those who heard it. In fact, the prophets, priests, and "all the people" attacked him. As far as they

69. For an analysis of the structure of chapters 26–45, see Gary E. Yates, "'The People Have Not Obeyed': A Literary and Rhetorical Study of Jeremiah 26–45" (Ph.D. diss., Dallas Theological Seminary, 1998).

70. For a discussion of God's use of "perhaps" in prophetic literature, see Fretheim, *The Suffering of God*, 45–47.

were concerned, the prophet deserved to die because he prophesied that the temple and city would be destroyed (vv. 7–9). Their peculiar brand of Zion theology taught that Jerusalem was immune to judgment because it was the Lord's dwelling place (see 7:4).

When the news reached the officials of the royal court, they went to the temple to investigate the matter (v. 10). The priests and prophets lodged a formal accusation against Jeremiah and demanded that he be executed (v. 11). In stating his own defense Jeremiah pointed out that the Lord sent him to warn the nation about impending judgment (v. 12). Once again he urged the people to repent and promised that if they did so, the Lord would relent from sending judgment (v. 13; see v. 3). He also warned the officials that if they put him to death, God would hold them responsible for shedding innocent blood (vv. 14–15).

Jeremiah's defense convinced the officials and the fickle crowd that he spoke the Lord's word and that he should not be executed (v. 16). Some of the elders then stepped forward and addressed the people (v. 17). They reminded the crowd of something that had happened about a century before this, in the days of Hezekiah. Micah the prophet had announced, in seemingly unconditional terms, that Jerusalem would be destroyed (v. 18; see Mic. 3:12). Hezekiah and the people did not put him to death but instead repented, prompting the Lord to relent from sending the prophesied judgment (v. 19a). Micah's prophecy thus proved to be implicitly conditional. In the same way, the people must respond appropriately to Jeremiah's explicitly conditional prophecy of judgment (see vv. 3–6, 13). If they harmed him, they would bring a "terrible disaster" upon the nation (v. 19b).

Hezekiah's reaction to Micah's message stood in stark contrast to Jehoiakim's treatment of one of Jeremiah's prophetic contemporaries, Uriah son of Shemaiah. Like Jeremiah, he had warned that judgment was ready to fall on Judah and Jerusalem (v. 20). King Jehoiakim and his officials wanted to kill Uriah, but he ran away to Egypt (v. 21). Not to be denied, Jehoiakim sent some of his men to Egypt, where they managed to get Uriah extradited (v. 22). Upon his return to Judah, Uriah was executed by order of the king and then placed in a common burial plot (v. 23). The words of the elders, coupled with the insertion of this brief account of Uriah's tragic death, heighten the tension of the narrative. Despite the officials' declaration of Jeremiah's innocence (v. 16), one wonders if they might change their mind, or if the king himself might overrule their decision.

The tension is resolved in verse 24, which informs us that Ahikam son of Shaphan intervened and kept Jeremiah from being executed. We know very little about Ahikam, though it is apparent that he and his family were among Jeremiah's supporters. Ahikam's father, Shaphan, had served as King Josiah's secretary, and Ahikam himself was part of the royal court at that time (see 2 Kings 22:3–14). His brother Gemariah advised Jehoiakim not to destroy Jeremiah's prophetic scroll (see Jer. 36:25), and his son Gedaliah took protective custody of Jeremiah after the Babylonians released the prophet from prison (see Jer. 39:14).

A Babylonian Victory Is Inevitable (27:1–22)

In the fourth year of Zedekiah's reign (594 or 593 B.C., see 28:1) the Lord gave Jeremiah a message for the surrounding nations (27:1).[71] Jeremiah was to place a wooden yoke on his neck as a symbol of how these nations would be subjugated by and forced to serve the king of Babylon (v. 2). Then the prophet was to send a message to the kings of Edom, Moab, Ammon, Tyre, and Sidon (v. 3), informing them that the Lord God of Israel, who created the earth and all that is in it, had decided to hand their kingdoms over to Nebuchadnezzar of Babylon, whom the Lord calls his "servant" (vv. 4–6). These nations would serve Nebuchadnezzar and his dynasty for a predetermined period of time, but then the Babylonian empire would be conquered by other nations (v. 7). The first part of this prophecy was fulfilled shortly afterward as Nebuchadnezzar conquered these western states. The second part of the prophecy came to pass in 539 B.C. when the Medo-Persian armies of Cyrus conquered Babylon and brought the Neo-Babylonian Empire to an end.[72]

If any nation resisted Nebuchadnezzar, it would suffer the horrors of military invasion (v. 8). The kings of the surrounding nations must not listen to those who prophesied that they would escape the king of Babylon (v. 9). Any such messages of hope were false and would only lead to serious repercussions (v. 10). Those who voluntarily submitted to Babylon would maintain their national identity and be allowed to remain in their native lands (v. 11).

This same message applied to Zedekiah and the people of Judah. Judah must willingly submit to Babylon in order to escape the devastation of war (vv. 12–13). Zedekiah and the people must not listen to the reassuring words

71. The Hebrew text erroneously dates this message to the reign of Jehoiakim (608–598 B.C.), but a few medieval Hebrew manuscripts, as well as the Syriac and Arabic versions, correctly read "Zedekiah" here. Verses 3 and 12 make it clear that Zedekiah was king at the time the message was given, while v. 20 refers to the captivity of Jehoiachin, Jehoiakim's successor, as having already taken place.

72. Verse 7 gives the impression that these nations would serve Nebuchadnezzar, his son, and his grandson until the kingdom of Babylon fell. This is not quite the way the history of the Babylonian Empire unfolded. Nebuchadnezzar reigned for forty-three years (605–562 B.C.) and was succeeded by his son Evil-merodach, who ruled briefly (561–560). Evil-merodach was succeeded by Nebuchadnezzar's son-in-law Neriglissar (559–556) and then the latter's son, Labashi-marduk (556), who was a grandson of Nebuchadnezzar. At that point Nabonidus, who was not a member of the royal family, joined with other conspirators to assassinate Labashi-marduk and seized the throne, ruling from 555–539. At the time the kingdom fell, Nabonidus and his son Belshazzar ruled the kingdom. (For a brief survey of the period, see Bill T. Arnold, "Babylonians," in *Peoples of the Old Testament World*, ed. A. J. Hoerth, G. L. Mattingly, and E. M. Yamauchi [Grand Rapids: Baker, 1994], 64–66.) It is likely that the reference in v. 7 to Nebuchadnezzar, his son, and his grandson is simply a stereotypical way of referring to the empire he established. See Carroll, *Jeremiah*, 527–28, and Thompson, *Jeremiah*, 533.

of the false prophets, who promised that Judah would not serve Babylon and that the items taken from the temple in 597 would soon be returned (vv. 14–16). The proper course of action was to submit to Babylon, for only in this way would the city avoid disaster and ruin (v. 17). The false prophets, who were so concerned about the temple articles that had already been taken away (see v. 16), should pray to the Lord that the articles which still remained in the temple and the royal palace might not be carried off to Babylon (v. 18). Though the Lord had already announced that these remaining items would be taken to Babylon, at least for a time (vv. 19–22), he might be persuaded to alter his plans if the nation submitted to Babylon and the false prophets accepted the nation's destiny and begged for divine mercy.

Dueling Prophets (28:1–17)

Later that same year the court prophet Hananiah publicly confronted Jeremiah in the temple (28:1). Claiming to be the Lord's spokesman, Hananiah prophesied that the Lord would deliver Judah from Babylonian rule and soon restore the articles that had been taken from the temple in 597 (vv. 2–3). According to Hananiah, the Lord would also bring back King Jehoiachin from exile, as well as the others who had been taken into Babylonian captivity (v. 4).

Jeremiah sarcastically prayed that Hananiah's words might be fulfilled (vv. 5–6). After all, it would be wonderful if the Lord did restore the temple articles and the exiled people. However, Hananiah's prophecy could not be taken at face value. Traditionally the prophets were God's messengers to a sinful people who warned of impending judgment (vv. 7–8). Any prophet who, like Hananiah, proclaimed a message of peace should be recognized as the Lord's spokesman only if his words were fulfilled (v. 9).

In response to this challenge, Hananiah removed from Jeremiah's neck the symbolic yoke the prophet had been wearing (see 27:2). He then broke it and announced that within two years the Lord would break the harness that Nebuchadnezzar had placed upon the necks of all the nations, including Judah (vv. 10–11a). Content to wait for a prophetic word from the Lord, Jeremiah simply walked away (v. 11b).

Shortly after this episode, the Lord gave Jeremiah a message for Hananiah (v. 12). To symbolize Judah's deliverance from Babylonian power, Hananiah had broken the symbolic wooden yoke worn by Jeremiah. But Judah would not be delivered. Instead, the Lord would place an iron yoke, as it were, around the necks of the nations. Nebuchadnezzar's grip on the western nations, Judah included, would be even stronger than previously announced. Even the wild animals would be subservient to him (vv. 13–14).

Jeremiah denounced Hananiah as a false prophet who, though not commissioned by the Lord, had misled the people with his prophecies (v. 15). The Lord regarded Hananiah as a traitor and announced that he would punish this lying prophet by taking his life (v. 16). The appropriate nature of the punishment is emphasized in the Hebrew text by a wordplay involving the verb "to send." In verse 15 Jeremiah states that the Lord did not "send" Hananiah. In verse 16 the Lord announces that he will "send away" this false prophet by taking his life from him. Approximately two months later, the word of the Lord was fulfilled (v. 17; see v. 1).

Letters to the Exiles (29:1–32)

Sometime after the exile of Jehoiachin in 597, Jeremiah sent a letter to the people who had been taken captive to Babylon (29:1–3). Speaking as the Lord's prophetic spokesman, Jeremiah urged the exiles to settle down in Babylon, to have children, and to pray for the well-being of their new home (vv. 4–7). They were not to listen to the prophets and diviners who promised them a swift release from captivity (vv. 8–9). In accordance with the Lord's plan, they would remain in Babylon for the remainder of their lives (v. 10a).[73] When the appointed time was over, the Lord would, in fulfillment of his promise, bring the exiles back to Judah (v. 10b). The Babylonian exile was a mere delay in God's plan for his people. He had a bright future in store for them (v. 11). A time would come when the people would sincerely seek the Lord's favor (vv. 12–13) and the Lord would respond to their prayers by bringing them back to their homeland (v. 14). But that time had not yet arrived.

Two individuals in particular, Zedekiah son of Maaseiah (not to be confused with King Zedekiah) and Ahab son of Kolaiah, were giving the exiles false hope (see v. 21). Though some regarded them as prophets (v. 15), their messages, like their actions, lacked integrity (vv. 21, 23). Jerusalem would not be delivered and the exiles would not return to their homeland anytime soon. On the contrary, the Lord would destroy those who remained in Judah and make them an object of ridicule among the nations (vv. 16–18), because they had rejected the genuine messages of his true prophets (v. 19a). The exiles must not repeat this mistake by rejecting Jeremiah's words in favor of the false prophets' lies (v. 19b). Zedekiah and Ahab would soon be executed by Nebuchadnezzar, most likely because their activities would be judged by the Babylonian authorities as promoting insurrection (vv. 20–21). The execution of these two false prophets would remain so vivid in the exiles' minds that they would use their names in formulating curses (vv. 22–23).

When Jeremiah's letter to the exiles arrived, Shemaiah the Nehelamite, another of the false prophets in Babylon, objected to its contents (v. 28, cf. vv. 5–10). He wrote to the priests in Jerusalem and told Zephaniah, the overseer of the temple, that he should arrest Jeremiah, whom Shemaiah regarded as a "madman" and false prophet (vv. 24–27). When Zephaniah informed

---

73. On the idiomatic use of "seventy years," see my discussion of Jer. 25:11.

Jeremiah of Shemaiah's accusation, the Lord gave Jeremiah a personalized message for Shemaiah (vv. 29–31a). Jeremiah informed the exiles that the Lord would punish Shemaiah for his lies (v. 31b). His offspring would be cut off and would not live to see the day when the exiles returned to Judah (v. 32).

Better Days Ahead (30:1–31:40)

In Jeremiah's letter to the exiles, the Lord made it clear that he would at the appointed time deliver his people from captivity and bring "good things" their way (see 29:10–15, 32). In chapters 30–31 the Lord develops this theme of restoration in greater detail.

The approaching judgment would be a terrifying event that would paralyze even strong men (30:4–7a), but it would not completely destroy God's covenant community (v. 7b). In due time the Lord would free his people from bondage to their foreign oppressors (v. 8), restore them to their land (vv. 1–3), and reestablish the Davidic dynasty (v. 9).[74] The exiles should not fear or despair, because the Lord would rescue them (v. 10a) and once again make them secure in their own land (v. 10b). Though the Lord had been forced to discipline his people, he was still watching over them and would eventually punish their oppressors (v. 11).

The Lord next turns to personified Zion (that is, Jerusalem) and encourages her (see v. 17b).[75] Zion was wounded, as it were, and abandoned by those who were once her allies (vv. 12–14a). The Lord had severely punished the city for its sins (vv. 14b–15). But the tables would someday be turned. Those who had invaded and ransacked Zion would themselves be defeated (v. 16), while Zion would experience restoration (v. 17). Because of his mercy, God would cause the city to be rebuilt, including the royal palace, a symbol of the nation's independence (v. 18). People would celebrate the city's rejuvenation, and the population of the land would greatly increase, bringing the community renewed respect among the nations (vv. 19–20a). Foreign rulers would no longer oppress them (v. 20b). Instead, one of their own, a Davidic descendant (see v. 9, as well as 23:5–6; 33:15–16), would lead them and enjoy an intimate relationship with the Lord (v. 21). The Lord would reestablish his relationship with his people, fulfilling the ancient covenant ideal (v. 22; see also 24:7, as well as Exod. 6:7 and Lev. 26:12). Judgment would indeed come, but it would purify the community by removing the wicked people who had contaminated it (vv. 23–24). This purifying judgment would open the door to a bright future in which God would be reconciled to his people (31:1).

74. Verse 9 speaks of the people serving "David their king," a reference to the ideal Davidic king of the future who will rule in the spirit and power of his illustrious ancestor. See my comments on Hos. 3:5.

75. Throughout the Hebrew text of vv. 12–17, the second-person pronouns are feminine singular, indicating that personified Zion, viewed as a woman, is being addressed.

Judah and Jerusalem would not be the only recipients of the Lord's salvation. As an expression of his everlasting love and faithfulness, the Lord would also restore the exiles of the northern kingdom to their land, prompting the people to celebrate (vv. 2–4). The people would again grow crops and enjoy the fruits of their labor (v. 5). As in the distant days of the Davidic empire, they would look toward Jerusalem as their worship center (v. 6). In anticipation of this glorious day, those who heard the prophecy were to praise the Lord and pray that the prophetic vision might soon be realized (v. 7).

Israel's return from exile would be a sight to behold. The people would stream back en masse from their place of exile in the north (v. 8a). Their ranks would include even those normally unfit for travel, such as the blind, the lame, and pregnant women (v. 8b). Shedding tears of joy, they would experience the Lord's fatherly provision and protection (v. 9). The message should be proclaimed among the nations loudly and clearly—the same God who sent his people into exile would deliver them from their powerful captors and, like a shepherd, lead them back to their homeland (vv. 10–11). To celebrate the restoration of the Lord's agricultural blessings, they would make a pilgrimage to Zion, where even their old men would sing and dance with joy (vv. 12–14).

This outburst of joy would stand in marked contrast to Israel's past suffering. The exile of the northern kingdom was accompanied by inconsolable sorrow. Verse 15 uses a vivid metaphor to depict this. From the town of Ramah, located in Benjaminite territory about five miles north of Jerusalem, one hears intense weeping. It is Rachel, weeping for her children, who are being taken from her and carried into exile. Rachel, the mother of Benjamin and Joseph, is utilized here as a metaphor for the land of Israel, for she was the grandmother of two of Israel's most prominent tribes, Ephraim and Manasseh. Ramah may be mentioned because Rachel was buried in Benjaminite territory (1 Sam. 10:2).[76] Another option is that the reference to

76. Later tradition erroneously located Rachel's tomb near Bethlehem, perhaps due to a misreading of Gen. 35:19–20 and 48:7. Both texts indicate that Rachel was buried along the road leading from Benjamin to Ephrath, which is glossed as Bethlehem. Some argue that the Ephrath mentioned here must have been in Benjaminite territory. See P. Kyle McCarter Jr., *1 Samuel*, AB (New York: Doubleday, 1980), 181. The tradition that Rachel was buried near Bethlehem may have influenced Matthew to utilize Jer. 31:15 in conjunction with his account of Herod's slaughter of Bethlehem's infant males (see Matt. 2:16–18). According to Matthew, Jeremiah's words were "fulfilled" when Herod committed this atrocity. In its literary and historical context Jeremiah's statement obviously does not refer to Herod's deed. Rather than being a prophecy, it looks back to an event that occurred approximately a century before. Furthermore, Jer. 31:16–17 picture Rachel's children returning to her. Matthew is not suggesting that a prediction made by Jeremiah literally came to pass in Herod's time. Rather, in retrospect he is drawing an analogy between the exile of Israel in the eighth century B.C. and Herod's slaughter of the innocents shortly after Jesus' birth. Like the Assyrians' treatment of Israelite exiles, Herod's atrocity was a cruel act that brought great suffering to God's covenant people. In this respect it "filled out" the pattern of oppression and cruelty established by the ancient Assyrians. It was as if history repeated itself through Herod's actions, and Jeremiah's description

Ramah reflects the fact that in Jeremiah's time the site was a staging area where the Babylonians took captives prior to sending them away into exile (see Jer. 40:1). The mere name "Ramah" would connote exile to Jeremiah's contemporaries.

However, this story would not end in tears and sorrow. "Rachel's" strenuous lamentation would pay off, and her children would return from exile (vv. 16–17). The psalmists utilized lamentation to move God to deliver them from their suffering. Their songs of thanksgiving attest to the fact that such prayers were often the catalyst for divine intervention. Such is the case here, as the return of Rachel's children is depicted as the reward or "payoff" for her mourning, called here her "work." In captivity the exiles (called here "Ephraim") recognize that they have been disciplined for their rebellion, and repent of their sins (vv. 18–19). The Lord, who loved Ephraim like a son, responds with compassion (v. 20) and invites the exiles to return to their homeland without delay (vv. 21–22a).

In conjunction with Israel's return to the land, the Lord states, "I will create a new thing on earth" (v. 22b). Unfortunately, we are not in a position to identify this "new thing" because of the cryptic way in which it is described ("a woman will surround a man"). Interpreters have tried to make sense of this riddle, but it remains unintelligible. Some understand the woman in the metaphor as the virgin Israel (see v. 21, as well as v. 4) and the man as the Lord (note the love imagery of v. 3). In this case she is pictured as passionately embracing him and renewing an intimate relationship. Perhaps the reality behind the image is the people's renewed worship of the Lord in Zion (see vv. 6, 12). Others understand the verb in the statement in the sense of "protect." In this case the statement depicts the unusual image of a woman shielding a man from harm. The Lord's restoration of his people would be as new and different as a woman protecting a man from danger.[77]

In verse 23, the focus shifts back to Judah. When Judah's exiles returned from Babylon, they would pronounce a blessing upon Zion, the "sacred mountain." The people would settle down in the land and resume the normal activities of life (v. 24). Refreshed by God's blessing, they would enjoy rest and security (vv. 25–26).[78]

Both Israel and Judah would return to the land (v. 27). In the past the Lord had carefully superintended their downfall, but he would restore them

---

of Israelite suffering was once more realized in space and time. One might call Matthew's use of Jeremiah's statement "retrospective typology."

77. One of the more bizarre and humorous interpretations of this passage is Jerome's allegorical view that it pictures Jesus encased within the womb of the Virgin Mary.

78. NIV translates v. 26 as if Jeremiah is speaking. Understood in this way, the prophet awakes from a trance or dream in which he received the preceding prophetic vision. However, it seems more likely that one of the returning exiles speaks here about how secure he feels in the environment described in the preceding verses.

(v. 28). Using a proverb, the exiles complained that they had unfairly suffered for their fathers' sins (v. 29; see also Lam. 5:7; Ezek. 18:2). While it is true that children suffer the consequences of their fathers' sins (see comments on Jer. 11:22–23), the exiles' view of their situation was faulty. Those who went into exile were punished for their own sins, which exceeded those of their fathers (see Jer. 3:25; 16:10–13; 32:18–19). Once the people realized this, repented (see Jer. 31:18–19), and experienced God's renewed favor, they would no longer recite this proverb. Instead they would acknowledge that God fairly judges each individual (v. 30).[79]

There are two primary ways in which verse 30 may be understood in relation to verse 29. One view understands verse 30 as articulating an actual change in divine policy. In the past God did indeed judge the children for the fathers' sins (as v. 29 implies), but in the future he would punish strictly on an individualized basis. A second view, the one favored here, is that the text is elliptical at the beginning of verse 30 and should be paraphrased, "Instead [they will say] . . ." In this case, there is a change in the people's *perception* of God's activity. In the past they erroneously accused him of being unfair, but in the future they would recognize that divine justice is fairly administered on an individualized basis.

The new era to come would be highlighted by the inauguration of a new covenant with Israel and Judah (v. 31). It would differ from the old covenant, the Mosaic code, not in its demands, but in its effectiveness. The Mosaic law demanded allegiance to the Lord, demonstrated through obedience to its regulations. But it had no power, in and of itself, to make the people obey. Despite the Lord's love and care, the people violated the covenant (v. 32). The new covenant would operate differently. It would make the same essential demands on the people, but this time God's law, rather than being recorded on stone tablets, would be inscribed on the hearts and minds of God's people (v. 33). The point of the metaphor is that the people would have an inherent capacity and desire to obey God's demands. There would be no more need for exhortations to "know the LORD," for the people would automatically "know" him as they experienced the forgiveness of sin (v. 34). "Know" is here used in its covenantal sense of "recognize and obey" (see my comments on Jer. 22:16). The prophet Ezekiel associates this inner renewal with the gift of the divine Spirit who purifies the people from sin and supernaturally prompts them to obey the Lord (see Ezek. 36:24–27).

The Lord concludes this promise of a new covenant with an assuring word. He affirms that his commitment to Israel's descendants (both Israel and Judah are probably in view here; see v. 31) is as constant as the cycles of nature he has set in place (vv. 35–36). To emphasize the point, he states that

---

79. For a defense of this view, see Kaminsky, *Corporate Responsibility in the Hebrew Bible,* 141–54, especially 147–48.

it is as impossible for him to reject his people as it is for a mere human being to measure the extent of the heavens or the subterranean regions (v. 37). Restoration would indeed come, highlighted by the rebuilding of Jerusalem, which in its entirety would be set apart as a sacred city (vv. 38–40).

In what way(s) is this promise of the new covenant realized? While Jeremiah seems to indicate that this promise is strictly for Israel and Judah, the New Testament makes it clear that the new covenant has already been implemented with the church (see Luke 22:20; 1 Cor. 11:25; 2 Cor 3:6; Heb. 8:13; 9:15; 12:24). Through his sacrificial atonement Jesus inaugurated this new covenant community, which fulfills the law by obeying it (see Matt. 5:17–20), not in the contextualized time-bound particulars of the Mosaic code, but in its essence as articulated by Jesus (see Matt. 22:36–40). How does one reconcile the apparent conflict between the Hebrew prophets, who foresaw God making the new covenant with Israel, and the New Testament, which associates this covenant with the church? Some have tried to circumvent the problem by proposing that there are two new covenants—one for Israel and one for the church—but the New Testament clearly sees the present covenant with the church as a fulfillment of the Old Testament promise (see Heb. 8). Others reinterpret the language of the Old Testament so that the church becomes the new Israel and inherits its promises, but Romans 11, which makes a clear distinction between ethnic Israel and the church in God's future program, undermines this position. There is a better explanation that does justice to all of the evidence. As foreseen by the prophets, the new covenant will be fulfilled in conjunction with the future salvation of ethnic Israel. Indeed, Romans 11:26–27 anticipates this event. However, the prophets' focus was limited in its scope. In the progress of history and revelation, we discover that this new covenant has a broader application. Prior to the restoration of ethnic Israel, God has implemented this new covenant with the followers of Christ, who are being transformed through the gift of the divine Spirit.

Perhaps an illustration will help us better understand this dual fulfillment of the new-covenant prophecy. Standing with Jeremiah and Ezekiel at their vantage point in history, we are in a dark tunnel. As we look with them toward the light at the end of the tunnel, we see God making a new covenant with ethnic Israel. We then move through the tunnel and emerge into the light. There ahead of us we see the same scene we saw from afar—God implementing his covenant with ethnic Israel. But now that we have stepped out of the tunnel into the light, our peripheral vision is expanded. To the side of us, incapable of being seen from back in the tunnel, is another scene—God implementing this same covenant with the church of the present era, comprised of both Jews and Gentiles. The prophets were not wrong—they simply had "tunnel vision" because their focus was on ethnic Israel.

However, there is another significant problem related to the fulfillment of the prophecy through ethnic Israel. Unlike the exiles from Judah (including Judahites, Benjaminites, and Levites), some of whom returned from Babylonian captivity in the sixth century B.C., the Israelite exiles never did return to the land. They disappeared as a distinct national entity and were assimilated into the nations. This means that the prophecy of a future reunion of Israel and Judah and the implementation of a new covenant with both cannot be literally fulfilled. This does not mean that God's promise has failed, however. There will be an essential fulfillment of the prophecy when the Lord establishes his covenant with the Jewish people (see Rom. 11:25–32, as well as my discussion of Isa. 11:13–14).

Jeremiah Buys Some Real Estate (32:1–33:26)

In 587 B.C., as the Babylonian army besieged Jerusalem, Jeremiah was placed under arrest and confined to the royal guard's courtyard in the king's palace because his prophecies of impending judgment on the city had angered King Zedekiah (32:1–5). However, as chapters 30–31 demonstrate, Jeremiah's message was not entirely one of doom and gloom. He also prophesied that the Lord would someday restore the exiles to the land and make a new covenant with them. To emphasize this positive side to Jeremiah's message, the Lord instructed him to buy some land from his cousin Hanamel, who offered the prophet a field near their hometown of Anathoth (vv. 6–7). Jeremiah obediently closed the transaction before legal witnesses and instructed his friend Baruch to place the deed of purchase in a clay jar where it could be preserved for a long period of time (vv. 8–14). Jeremiah's purchase of the field appeared to make little sense in light of his prophecy that the people would soon be exiled to Babylon. But the action had symbolic value, for it anticipated a time when the people would return to the land and again buy and sell property (v. 15).

At first this was difficult for the prophet himself to fathom. After giving the deed to Baruch, he prayed to the Lord (v. 16) and expressed his bewilderment. The prayer begins as a hymn of praise in which the prophet declares that the Lord is the omnipotent creator and just ruler of the world (vv. 17–19). He rehearses the Lord's mighty deeds in Israel's early history, but acknowledges that God's people have sinned, prompting the Lord to bring judgment upon the nation (vv. 20–23). As the Lord had announced, the Babylonians had surrounded the city and would soon conquer it (v. 24). Why then would the Lord tell the prophet to buy land, as if life would go on as usual (v. 25)?

In his response to Jeremiah, the Lord reminds the prophet of what he had already affirmed in his prayer—the Lord is the sovereign ruler over mankind and is capable of doing whatever he desires (vv. 26–27; see v. 17). His instructions to Jeremiah did not mark a sudden change in plans. The

Babylonians would indeed destroy Jerusalem (v. 28). The city's rebellious residents would die by the sword, famine, and plague because they had aroused God's anger with their idols and pagan practices (vv. 29–36). But death and destruction would not be the end of the story. The Lord would bring the exiles back to their homeland and reestablish his relationship with them (vv. 37–38). He would transform them into an obedient people (v. 39), make an everlasting covenant with them (v. 40), and restore his blessings (v. 41). Prosperity would replace calamity (v. 42). At that time people would once more own and exchange land (vv. 43–44). Jeremiah's symbolic act foreshadowed this reversal in the people's fortunes.

While still confined in the royal guard's courtyard, Jeremiah received a second message from the Lord (33:1). Speaking as the creator of the world, the Lord invited Jeremiah to pray to him (vv. 2–3a). He promised that he would give him additional information about what the future held (v. 3b). Using the Babylonians as his instrument of punishment, the Lord would fill Jerusalem with corpses (vv. 4–5). But the story would have a happy ending. The Lord would someday make the city secure, bring back the exiles of both Judah and Israel to the land, and forgive his people (vv. 6–8). All the nations would hear of Jerusalem's restoration and praise God (v. 9). The empty, desolate streets of Jerusalem and Judah would be filled with the sounds of celebration and joy, as people praised the Lord for his faithful love (vv. 10–11). Flocks of sheep would once more graze throughout the land of Judah under the watchful care of their shepherds (vv. 12–13).

The Lord would also provide a shepherd for his people. He would raise up a king from the line of David who would promote justice in the land and protect it from hostile forces (vv. 14–16a; see 23:5–6). Jerusalem would receive a new name, epitomizing its newfound security (v. 16b).[80] The Lord promised that the Davidic throne would be established and that the Levites would again minister in his presence (vv. 17–18). The Lord had made unconditional promises to David (see 2 Sam. 7:16) and the Levites, and his commitment to them was as secure as the natural cycle of day and night (vv. 19–22). As the Babylonian shadow grew darker over the land, many of the people lamented that the Lord had rejected his ancient covenant people (vv. 23–24). Though divine discipline was necessary, it did not negate God's covenants with the patriarchs and David. His promises were as secure as the natural laws he set in place at creation. One of David's sons would indeed rule over the descendants of Abraham, Isaac, and Jacob (vv. 25–26).

The background for the Levitical covenant mentioned in verses 21–22 is not certain. The covenant seems to ensure that Levi will minister before the Lord and have numerous descendants. No such covenant is recorded in

---

80. According to 23:6, this name ("The Lord our Righteousness") would be given to the ideal king. Here Jerusalem receives the same name.

the Pentateuch; this may refer to the Lord's choice of the Levites, especially Aaron, to serve him in a priestly role (see Num. 3:12). A formal covenant with the Levites, also referred to in Malachi 2:4–5 and Nehemiah 13:29, was apparently made on this occasion.[81] However, the covenant in view in Malachi 2:4–5 is a bilateral agreement in which blessing was contingent upon loyalty, while the Levitical covenant described in Jeremiah 33:21–22 appears to be an unconditional promise. The Lord made an unconditional covenant with Phinehas and his descendants (see Num. 25:12–13). It is possible that this promise was later expanded to include the entire family of Levi, but this seems unlikely.

Zedekiah's Options (34:1–7)

During the Babylonian invasion of Judah in 588, Jeremiah confronted King Zedekiah with his options (vv. 1–2a). The Babylonians had already conquered most of Judah; only Jerusalem, Lachish, and Azekah were still holding out (vv. 6–7). If the king tried to hold out against the Babylonians, Jerusalem would fall into Nebuchadnezzar's hands and Zedekiah would have to face the wrath of the Babylonian king (vv. 2b–3). However, there was an alternative. If Zedekiah surrendered to Nebuchadnezzar, his life would be spared. In fact, he would remain in Jerusalem and enjoy the honor and respect of his countrymen (vv. 4–5).

On the surface, verses 2–5 seem to contain contradictory prophecies about Zedekiah's fate. According to verses 2–3, Jerusalem would fall and Zedekiah would be exiled, but verses 4–5, without laying down any conditions, assume the king would be spared and remain in his homeland.[82] The best way to resolve this tension is to understand the text as a juxtaposition of two implicitly conditional prophecies representing the alternatives facing Zedekiah.[83] The account of Jeremiah's encounter with Zedekiah in 38:17–18 supports this interpretation. There the prophet promises Zedekiah that he, the royal family, and the city would be spared if the king surrendered.[84]

Zedekiah's Injustice (34:8–22)

As the Babylonians threatened Jerusalem, Zedekiah, his royal officials, and the city's upper class had by royal decree released their slaves (vv. 8–10). The Mosaic law demanded that Hebrew slaves be freed after six years of service (see Deut. 15:12), but the men of Jerusalem had ignored this command (vv. 12–14). Apparently, under the pressure of the Babylonian threat, they felt compelled to repent and decided that showing kindness to their slaves would

---

81. Num. 18:19 mentions a "covenant of salt" between the Lord and the Levites, but this pertains to the priests' assigned portion of a sacrifice, not priestly service in general.

82. See Carroll, *Jeremiah*, 642.

83. In this regard see William L. Holladay, *Jeremiah 2,* Hermeneia (Minneapolis: Fortress, 1989), 233.

84. See Carroll, *Jeremiah*, 642.

be a good way of demonstrating to God that they had changed (see v. 15). They had even solemnized the proceedings by making a covenant before the Lord in which they cut up a calf, arranged its carcass in two rows, and walked between its pieces as a self-imprecation (vv. 18–19). In doing this they were giving God permission to judge them severely (that is, make them like the cut-up calf) if they went back on their promise to their slaves. Unfortunately, their repentance was short-lived. They broke their covenant and took back their slaves (vv. 11, 16). For this reason, the Lord would punish them severely. They had failed to grant freedom to their slaves, so the Lord would grant freedom to the sword, plague, and famine to destroy the slaveholders (v. 17). Like the pieces of the calf used in their covenant ritual, their corpses would lie exposed and be eaten by birds and wild animals (vv. 19–20). Though the Babylonians had withdrawn from the city (perhaps prompting the people to think the threat was over and to return to their old sinful ways?), they would return in full force and conquer the city (vv. 21–22).

A Model of Loyalty (35:1–19)

During the reign of Jehoiakim, the Lord instructed Jeremiah to visit the nomadic Rechabite family (vv. 1–2). He was to invite them to the temple and offer them some wine. The prophet did as instructed, but when he set the wine before the Rechabites, they refused to drink it, explaining that their forefather Jonadab had commanded them to abstain from drinking wine (vv. 3–6). Jonadab had also instructed them to live a nomadic lifestyle (v. 7). The Rechabites had obeyed Jonadab's instructions for more than two hundred years.[85] None of them had ever drunk wine, and they had maintained a nomadic lifestyle until the Babylonian invasion forced them to seek protection within the walls of Jerusalem (vv. 8–11). The Rechabites' devotion to their traditions was both an object lesson and an indictment of the people of Judah and Jerusalem (vv. 12–13). In contrast to the Rechabites, who faithfully obeyed Jonadab's commands, God's people had disobeyed his commands and ignored the warnings of his prophets (vv. 14–16). For this reason, the Lord would bring disaster upon his people (v. 17). But the Rechabites, because of their integrity and faithful character, would become servants of the Lord (vv. 18–19). It is unclear what type of service is envisioned here or how the prophecy was fulfilled.

Prophecy Goes Up in Flames (36:1–32)

In 605 B.C. (the fourth year of King Jehoiakim's reign), the Lord instructed Jeremiah to write down all of the prophecies he had received (36:1–2). The Lord hoped that the cumulative effect of the judgment speeches, when read

---

85. Jonadab lived during the ninth century B.C. Second Kings 10:15–23 indicates that he was a contemporary of Jehu, who ruled Israel from 841–814 B.C.

to the people (see v. 6), would prompt them to repent, enabling him to for-give their sins (v. 3; see 26:3 as well). Jeremiah summoned Baruch, who wrote down the prophecies as Jeremiah dictated them (v. 4). Jeremiah had been banned from the temple, so he instructed Baruch to go there and read the prophetic scroll to the people in hopes that they might repent (vv. 5–7). Baruch did as he was told, reading the scroll to the people while they were gathered at the temple to fast before the Lord (vv. 8–10). Baruch was sum-moned before the royal officials and told to read the scroll (vv. 11–15). When the officials heard the prophecies, they told Baruch that its contents must be reported to the king (v. 16). However, rather than arresting Baruch they advised him and Jeremiah to go into hiding (vv. 17–19). When the king heard the report of what had happened, he demanded that the scroll be read in his presence (vv. 20–21). An official named Jehudi brought it to the king, who was sitting in his royal apartment in front of a fire (it was wintertime). As the scroll was being read, the king cut off three or four columns at a time and threw them into the fire (vv. 22–23). The king showed no fear or re-morse (v. 24). Some of the officials urged him not to destroy the prophecy, but he rejected their advice and even commanded his servants to arrest Baruch and Jeremiah, who by this time had gone into hiding (vv. 25–26).[86]

The scroll was gone, but the king's arrogant action could not silence the word of God. The Lord instructed Jeremiah to produce another copy of the prophecy (vv. 27–28), a command that the prophet obeyed with the assis-tance of Baruch (v. 32). The Lord also gave the prophet a message for the king. Jehoiakim had destroyed the first scroll because he objected to the mes-sage of judgment it contained (v. 29). Yet judgment would come, and it would strike Jehoiakim in an especially severe way. Jehoiakim's dynasty would end (v. 30a). The king himself would be killed, and his corpse would not receive a proper burial (v. 30b).[87] His family and royal court would be punished, and God would bring disaster upon Jerusalem and Judah (v. 31).

Jeremiah in Jail (37:1–38:28)

In 588 b.c., during Zedekiah's reign, the king sent a messenger and a priest to Jeremiah, requesting that the prophet pray for the king and the nation (37:1–3). This was a desperate move on the king's part, for prior to this he had ignored Jeremiah's prophecies. At the time of the king's request, Jere-miah had not yet been imprisoned, and the Babylonians had withdrawn from Jerusalem in order to confront an Egyptian army that had advanced

---

86. The Hebrew text of v. 26 states that "the LORD hid them," but the Septuagint has simply "they were hidden" with no reference to the Lord. The divine name may have been accidentally omitted in the textual tradition underlying the Septuagint, but it seems more likely that the name was added in the Hebrew tradition. For a fuller discussion of the textual issues involved, see McKane, *Jeremiah*, 2:909.

87. A similar prophecy appears in 22:18–19. For a discussion of the prophecy's fulfillment, see my comments on that passage.

against them (vv. 4–5). However, the Babylonian withdrawal was only temporary. The Lord answered the king's request for prayer with a judgment speech (vv. 6–10). The Egyptians would retreat before the Babylonians, who would return to the city and capture it. Zedekiah and his royal court should not get their hopes up, for a Babylonian victory was inevitable.

Jeremiah's response to the king's request must have angered the royal officials, for shortly after this he got into trouble with the authorities. During the time of the Babylonian withdrawal, Jeremiah decided to make a trip to Benjaminite territory to transact some business. As he was leaving the city, the captain of the guard accused him of treason and arrested him (vv. 11–13). Despite Jeremiah's plea of innocence, the prophet was beaten and imprisoned in a dungeon, where he remained for a lengthy period of time (vv. 14–16).

When Zedekiah finally summoned him, the king asked Jeremiah if he had received any divine revelation (v. 17a). Answering in the affirmative, Jeremiah informed the king that he would be handed over to the Babylonians (v. 17b). The prophet also protested his mistreatment and requested that he not be sent back to the dungeon (vv. 18–20). The king permitted him to stay in the courtyard of the royal guard, where the prophet was fed daily (v. 21; see 32:2).

The precise chronological relationship of chapter 38 to chapter 37 is uncertain. Some see the accounts as referring to the same events, but there are apparent differences, suggesting that two different episodes are involved.[88] At the beginning of chapter 38, Jeremiah appears to be out among the people preaching (cf. 37:4). However, if chapter 38 follows chapter 37 chronologically, it is more likely that Jeremiah preached to the people indirectly (perhaps through Baruch) while confined in the courtyard of the royal guard (see chapter 32 in this regard).[89]

Jeremiah's unpopular message about Jerusalem's impending doom angered several important royal officials (38:1–3), who reported his words to Zedekiah. They advised the king to execute the prophet as a traitor (v. 4). Zedekiah gave them permission to deal with Jeremiah as they saw fit (v. 5). They lowered the prophet into a muddy cistern with the apparent intention of starving him to death (v. 6; see v. 9). At this point an unlikely hero steps to the forefront. Ebed-melech, a Cushite (i.e., Ethiopian) serving in the royal palace, interceded for the prophet. Accusing Jeremiah's enemies of wrongdoing, he asked the king to deliver Jeremiah from the cistern (vv. 7–9). This

---

88. For a summary of the differences between the accounts, see Carroll, *Jeremiah*, 679.

89. McKane (*Jeremiah*, 2:962–63) criticizes this approach. He writes: "If Jeremiah, while he was held in the palace-yard, had the liberty to broadcast his prophetic message by addressing 'all the people', his confinement served no purpose and he might as well have been free from any constraint whatever. Further, it is arguable that if he addressed 'all the people', this implies that he was not suffering any kind of restriction and is incompatible with his being kept in custody in the palace-yard."

official, whose name means "servant of the king," must have had some leverage with Zedekiah, for the vacillating king ordered that Jeremiah be released (v. 10). Ebed-melech, with the help of thirty men, then pulled Jeremiah up from his muddy prison (vv. 11–13). The text does not at this point tell us why Ebed-melech interceded for Jeremiah, but we discover in 39:18 that his faith in the Lord motivated his actions.

Zedekiah summoned Jeremiah for a private audience (v. 14; see v. 27b). Jeremiah was hesitant to tell Zedekiah the truth, for he feared the king would kill him (v. 15). However, the king swore an oath that he would not kill Jeremiah or hand him over to those who sought his life (v. 16). Satisfied that Zedekiah was sincere, Jeremiah gave the king two options. If he surrendered immediately to the Babylonians, he and his family would be spared and the city would not be destroyed (v. 17). But if he held out, the city would be burned and Zedekiah would be captured (v. 18). Zedekiah was afraid that, if he surrendered, the Babylonians would hand him over to the pro-Babylonian Jews who had already surrendered (v. 19). Jeremiah assured the king that the Babylonians would not do this (v. 20a). He urged Zedekiah to obey the Lord and surrender, for this was the only way he could spare his life (v. 20b). If he rejected the Lord's command, both he and the city would experience disaster (vv. 21–23).

Before sending Jeremiah back to the courtyard, Zedekiah warned him not to tell the royal officials about their conversation (v. 24). If the officials got wind of the meeting and demanded that Jeremiah tell them what had transpired, then Jeremiah should lie to them and tell them that he was begging the king not to send him back to prison (vv. 25–26; see 37:15–20). As the king suspected, the officials did indeed find out about the meeting, but when they interrogated the prophet, he lied to them, just as the king had ordered (v. 27). Jeremiah remained confined in the courtyard of the palace guard until the day the city fell to the Babylonians (v. 28).

Prophecy Fulfilled (39:1–10)

Jeremiah's prophetic warning was soon fulfilled. In January, 588 B.C., Nebuchadnezzar had set up a siege around Jerusalem; the Babylonian armies broke through the city's defenses in July 586 (39:1–2).[90] As Babylonian officials took control of the city (v. 3), Zedekiah and his soldiers tried to escape by night (v. 4), but they were captured by the Babylonian army and taken to Nebuchadnezzar's headquarters (v. 5). Just as Jeremiah had warned, the Babylonian king was merciless in his treatment of the rebels. He killed Zedekiah's sons before the king's very eyes, executed Judah's nobles, and put out

---

90. On the dating of the events, see Edwin R. Thiele, *The Mysterious Numbers of the Hebrew Kings*, rev. ed. (Grand Rapids: Zondervan, 1983), 190. The city was not actually burned until August 586 (see Jer. 52:12–13).

Zedekiah's eyes before binding the king in bronze shackles and taking him to Babylon (vv. 6–7). In the meantime the Babylonians burned Jerusalem to the ground (v. 8) and took most of its residents into exile (v. 9). They did leave behind the very poorest of Judah's people, to whom they gave the fields and vineyards (v. 10).

Jeremiah and Ebed-Melech Are Vindicated (39:11–40:6)

In the aftermath of the Babylonian invasion, Jeremiah was vindicated. Because Jeremiah, at the Lord's command, had advised capitulation to the Babylonians, Nebuchadnezzar ordered the prophet released from the courtyard of the palace. Nebuzaradan, commander of Nebuchadnezzar's royal guard, placed Jeremiah under the care of Gedaliah and allowed him to stay in the land (vv. 11–14).

Prior to his release the prophet had received a message from the Lord pertaining to Ebed-melech, the Ethiopian servant who had rescued Jeremiah from certain death in Malkiah's cistern (vv. 15–18; see 38:7–13). The Lord promised Ebed-melech that his faithfulness would be rewarded. When the Babylonians took the city, they would spare his life.

Chapter 40 begins with an account of how Jeremiah was rescued from being sent into exile. It is not certain how this account is to be harmonized with the episode recorded in 39:11–14.[91] The latter tells how Nebuzaradan and other Babylonian officials ordered Jeremiah's release from the courtyard of the royal palace and placed him in the custody of Gedaliah. But, according to 40:1–6, Jeremiah had been taken to Ramah with the other captives and was ready to be shipped off to Babylon (v. 1). Nebuzaradan approached Jeremiah and, after making an insightful theological observation about the underlying reason for Judah's demise (vv. 2–3), unchained the prophet. Nebuzaradan told Jeremiah he was welcome to come to Babylon, but he also gave the prophet the option of staying in the land (v. 4). Sensing that Jeremiah wanted to stay among his own people, Nebuzaradan gave the prophet provisions and advised him to live with Gedaliah, the newly appointed governor of Judah (vv. 5–6).

The Assassination of Gedaliah (40:7–41:18)

The Babylonians appointed Gedaliah as governor of Judah and put him in charge of the poor people who were allowed to remain in the land (v. 7). Some of the officers and soldiers in Judah's army had escaped capture. When they heard about Gedaliah's appointment, they approached him at Mizpah (v. 8). Gedaliah promised on oath that he would not take action against

---

91. For an attempted harmonization, see Holladay, *Jeremiah 2*, 293. He suggests that Jeremiah, after being released from the courtyard and assigned to Gedaliah's care, was rearrested by accident and taken to Ramah, where Nebuzaradan rescued him and sent him back to Gedaliah.

them and encouraged them to accept Babylonian authority (v. 9). He gave them permission to settle in the towns and become farmers (v. 10). Jewish refugees who had fled to Transjordan returned to the land and resumed agricultural activities (vv. 11–12).

Despite the restoration of peace to the land, trouble was brewing. Johanan son of Kareah, one of the military men with whom Gedaliah had made an agreement, informed him that one of their number, Ishmael son of Nethaniah (see v. 8), had been hired by Baalis, the Ammonite king, to assassinate Gedaliah (vv. 13–14).[92] Apparently the Ammonite king was anti-Babylonian in his sentiments and feared the presence of a pro-Babylonian governor on his borders. He found a willing accomplice in the fanatical Ishmael, who must have viewed Gedaliah as a traitor. Unfortunately, Gedaliah refused to believe the report and rejected Johanan's offer to kill Ishmael (vv. 15–16).

Shortly thereafter, in October, Ishmael carried out his assassination plot with the help of ten henchmen. They came to Gedaliah on peaceful pretenses, but as Gedaliah entertained them, they drew their swords and murdered him, other Jews who were present, and the Babylonian guards stationed there (41:1–3). Bloodthirsty Ishmael was not finished. Eighty unsuspecting mourners arrived from the north, on their way to Jerusalem to lament the destruction of the temple, which had been burned to the ground two months before (see Jer. 52:12–13), and to offer sacrifices at the temple site (vv. 4–5).[93] Pretending that he shared their sorrow, Ishmael invited them into Mizpah on the pretense of meeting Gedaliah (v. 6). Once they were inside, he and his men murdered seventy of the northerners in cold blood and threw them into a cistern (vv. 7, 9). However, ten of the mourners successfully bargained for their lives by promising to give Ishmael some provisions they had hidden in a field (v. 8). Ishmael's motive for killing these worshipers is not clear. Various proposals have been suggested, but the most likely explanation is that he was simply an angry, cruel man whose appetite for violence was not easily satisfied.[94]

Ishmael took captive the people of Mizpah, including Zedekiah's daughters, and set out for Ammon (v. 10).[95] However, when Johanan son of Kareah and his men heard what Ishmael had done, they chased him and over-

---

92. An Ammonite seal impression dating from around 600 B.C. mentions this king. See Randall W. Younker, "Ammonites," in *Peoples of the Old Testament World*, ed. A. J. Hoerth, G. L. Mattingly, and E. M. Yamauchi (Grand Rapids: Baker, 1994), 313–14.

93. Shaving one's beard, tearing one's clothes, and cutting one's body (see v. 4) were gestures of lamentation. See Jer. 16:6; 47:5; 48:37.

94. For a discussion of Ishmael's possible motives, see Holladay, *Jeremiah 2*, 297, and McKane, *Jeremiah*, 2:1027–28. Carroll (see *Jeremiah*, 711) aptly calls Ishmael a "psychotic bandit."

95. According to the prophecy recorded in Jer. 38:22–23, the women of Zedekiah's palace would be taken captive to Babylon. However, the reference to the "king's daughters" in 41:10 makes it clear that some escaped that fate.

took him in Gibeon (vv. 11–12). Realizing he was outnumbered, Ishmael released his captives and escaped to Ammon (vv. 13–15). Afraid that the Babylonians might blame them for allowing Gedaliah's assassination to occur,
Johanan and his men, along with those they had rescued, headed south toward Egypt (vv. 16–18).

Rejecting God's Word (42:1–43:7)

At this point Jeremiah reemerges in the story. Apparently he was among
those whom Ishmael had kidnapped from Mizpah (see 40:6). Johanan, accompanied by his fellow soldiers and all the people who had been rescued,
approached Jeremiah and asked him to pray for a word of guidance from the
Lord (42:1–3). Jeremiah assured them that he would do so, and the people
promised on oath that they would obey the Lord's instructions (vv. 4–6).
Ten days later Jeremiah received an answer to his prayer and summoned the
people to hear the Lord's word (vv. 7–8). The Lord urged them to stay in the
land and promised to bless and protect them (vv. 9–12). He also warned
them that if they refused to obey his command, he would punish them. If
they insisted on going to Egypt, they would experience the Lord's angry
judgment, just as Jerusalem had in recent days (vv. 13–18). Jeremiah suspected that this divine command would come as a shock to the people.
Though they had asked for the Lord's guidance, they had their hearts set on
going to Egypt and were merely looking for divine confirmation of their
plans. For this reason, the prophet once more warned them of the consequences of disobedience (vv. 19–22).

As Jeremiah suspected, the people did not approve of the Lord's message.
Several of the men, including Johanan, called Jeremiah a liar and accused
him of plotting with Baruch to hand them over to the Babylonians (43:1–3).
Led by Johanan, the people blatantly disobeyed the Lord's command. Forcing Jeremiah to go with them, they went to Egypt, where they settled in Tahpanhes, located in the eastern region of the Nile delta (vv. 4–7).

Denouncing the Egyptian Exiles (43:8–44:30)

After Jeremiah arrived in Egypt, the Lord instructed him to carry out another of the symbolic acts that had been such an important part of his
prophetic ministry. The prophet was to take some large stones and bury
them in clay at the entrance of the royal palace where the Pharaoh stayed
when visiting Tahpanhes (vv. 8–9). Jeremiah was then to announce that
Nebuchadnezzar, referred to here as God's "servant" because he would be an
instrument of divine judgment, would invade Egypt and spread his royal
canopy over these very stones (v. 10). Nebuchadnezzar and his armies would
strike down everyone in their path and burn the temples of Egypt's gods, including the temple of Re, the sun god (vv. 11–13). The point of the
prophecy seems clear: By fleeing to Egypt, the Jewish refugees hoped to es-

cape the wrath of Nebuchadnezzar. But Egypt would not prove to be a place of asylum, for the Babylonians would invade its borders, bringing death and destruction with them. The prophecy was fulfilled, at least to some degree, when Nebuchadnezzar invaded Egypt in 568–567 B.C.[96]

Trouble would follow the exiles to Egypt. Judgment had fallen on Judah because the people persisted in idolatry and rejected the warnings of the Lord's prophets (44:1–6). The exiles in Egypt would be cut off from God's covenant community because they were following in the footsteps of their fathers by worshiping foreign gods (vv. 7–10). The sword and famine would virtually wipe out the exilic community in Egypt, making them a byword among the nations (vv. 11–14). Only a few refugees would ever return to Judah.

The Egyptian exiles rejected Jeremiah's warning (vv. 15–16). They wanted to worship the "Queen of Heaven" (vv. 17–19; see 7:18).[97] They pointed out that prior to Jerusalem's fall they had worshiped this goddess and prospered. It was only when they stopped worshiping her that disaster fell. Their sin-blinded eyes could not see that judgment came because they had abandoned the Lord and disobeyed his commandments (vv. 20–23). Instead, they attributed their misfortune to a pagan fertility goddess, whom they believed they had offended. So they insisted on making renewed vows to worship this deity (vv. 24–25). However, their obsession with the Queen of Heaven would be their demise. The Lord's destructive judgment would fall upon them, forcing them to acknowledge, albeit too late, that the Lord's word is certain to be fulfilled (vv. 26–28). As a guarantee that this announcement of judgment would be fulfilled, the Lord gave the exiles a sign of their impending doom (v. 29). Hophra, king of Egypt, would be handed over to his enemies, just as Zedekiah, Judah's last king, had been handed over to Nebuchadnezzar (v. 30). This sign was fulfilled in 570 B.C. when Amasis, a military general, usurped Hophra's authority.

A Promise for Baruch (45:1–5)

The second major subunit (chapters 36–45) of the book's second major section (chapters 26–45) ends where it began, with an episode dating to the fourth year of King Jehoiakim's reign (v. 1; see 36:1). Baruch served as Jeremiah's faithful assistant and shared in the prophet's suffering (vv. 2–3). In response to Baruch's lament, the Lord urged Baruch to come to grips with the reality of impending judgment and the disaster that would overtake the land (vv. 4–5a). However, the Lord also assured Baruch that his life would be spared (v. 5b). In contrast to the idolatrous Egyptian exiles, who would experience the continuing judgment of God (chapter 44), Baruch, who repre-

---

96. For a fragmentary report of this event, see James Pritchard, *Ancient Near Eastern Texts Relating to the Old Testament* (Princeton: Princeton University Press, 1969), 308.

97. On the identity of the "Queen of Heaven," see my earlier comments on Jer. 7:18.

sents a genuine remnant of the Lord's faithful followers, would be preserved through judgment.

The Lord Judges the Nations (Jeremiah 46–51)

These chapters contain a series of nine judgment oracles against various nations (46:1). The speeches are arranged as follows in the Hebrew text:[98]

>Judgment of Egypt (46:2–28)
>Judgment of the Philistines (47:1–7)
>Judgment of Moab (48:1–47)
>Judgment of Ammon (49:1–6)
>Judgment of Edom (49:7–22)
>Judgment of Damascus (49:23–27)
>Judgment of Kedar and Hazor (49:28–33)
>Judgment of Elam (49:34–39)
>Judgment of Babylon (50:1–51:64)

The arrangement reflects a general movement from the southwest to the distant east. We move from Egypt in the southwest to Philistia in the west, before crossing the Dead Sea to Moab. We then journey northward to Ammon, back south to Edom, and then on to Damascus in the northeast and to Kedar and Hazor in the Syrian desert. From there we head to distant Elam, located east of Babylon, before terminating our journey in Babylon.

Judgment on Egypt (46:2–28)

In 605 B.C., Pharaoh Necho led his army northward to fight the Babylonians. Nebuchadnezzar defeated the Egyptians at Carchemish, located on the Euphrates River in what is today northern Syria. Just before or after this battle, the Lord delivered a taunt against the Egyptians (v. 2). The Egyptians appeared to be primed for battle, but they retreated in fear and were humiliated (vv. 3–6). Egypt proudly boasted that she would conquer the earth, but the Lord opposed her and brought her down (vv. 7–11). The day of the Egyptians' defeat is called the Lord's "day of vengeance." The language may be stylized and stereotypical (see Isa. 34:8; 61:3; 63:4), but perhaps it suggests that the Lord was repaying the Egyptians for killing King Josiah four years before (see 2 Kings 23:29–30). Though the Egyptians might try to recover from this embarrassing defeat, their shame would be broadcast among the nations (vv. 11–12).

To make matters worse, Nebuchadnezzar would eventually press his advantage and invade Egypt (vv. 13–14; see 43:11–13).[99] Egypt's gods would be unable to defend their land (v. 15). Following the traditional text of verse 15a, NIV translates, "Why will your warriors be laid low? They cannot stand."

---

98. As noted earlier, the arrangement differs in the ancient Greek version. See Bullock, *Introduction*, 207.

99. The invasion of Egypt did not take place until 568–567 B.C.

However, it is better to follow the lead of the Septuagint and read, "Why has Apis fled? Your bull did not stand his ground."[100] Apis, a bull-god worshiped at Memphis, was viewed as the incarnation of the deity Ptah.[101] The troops assigned to defend the land would lose confidence in Pharaoh and run back to their homes (vv. 16–17). Taunting the Egyptians, the Lord announces that one like Mount Tabor or Mount Carmel will invade the land, and he urges the residents of Egypt to prepare for exile (vv. 18–19). The mountain imagery suggests prominence and symbolizes Nebuchadnezzar.

The Lord uses a series of additional images to depict Egypt's destiny. The Babylonians would be like a buzzing, stinging fly that torments a heifer (v. 20). Helpless before the onslaught, Egypt's mercenary troops would panic and run, but they would be slaughtered like fattened calves (v. 21). Egypt would flee before the invaders like a snake, unable to do anything more than hiss its disapproval as the Babylonian invaders swept through the land like locusts and ravaged it like lumberjacks in a forest (vv. 22–23). The Lord would hand the Egyptians, including even their god Amon and their rulers, over to the Babylonians (vv. 24–26a). However, Egypt's defeat would be temporary. Eventually she would be inhabited as in the past (v. 26b).

This oracle against Egypt culminates with an encouraging word for God's people. He urged his exiled people not to fear, for he was with them and would someday rescue Israel from bondage and make them secure in their own land (vv. 27–28a). The Lord must discipline his people, but he would never annihilate them (v. 28b).

Judgment on the Philistines (47:1–7)

Sometime before an Egyptian attack on the Philistine town of Gaza, the Lord announced the downfall of the Philistines (47:1). The precise date of this attack is not known, though it is reasonable to conclude that it occurred sometime between 610–601 B.C.[102] Oddly enough, however, the oracle seems to refer to a Babylonian, rather than an Egyptian, attack upon Philistia. The imagery of "waters rising in the north" most naturally points to Babylon, not Egypt. Apparently the Egyptian attack on Gaza was simply a harbinger of a worse disaster to follow and provided an ideal occasion to prophesy Philistia's ultimate demise. On the other hand, the statement "before Pharaoh attacked Gaza" does not appear in the ancient Greek version and may represent a later misinterpretation of the historical occasion of the prophecy.

As the invaders' chariots approached, the Philistines would panic. Fathers would not even stop to help their own children (v. 3). The Lord would

---

100. See Thompson, *Jeremiah,* 690–92.

101. George Steindorff and Keith C. Seele, *When Egypt Ruled the East,* rev. ed. (Chicago: University of Chicago Press, 1957), 140–41.

102. For a discussion of specific options, see Holladay, *Jeremiah 2,* 336–37.

devastate Philistia, leaving the Phoenicians, who also lived along the coast to the north, without allies (v. 4). The personified cities of Gaza and Ashkelon are pictured mourning their demise (v. 5). For dramatic effect the sword of the Lord is told to return to its scabbard (v. 6). But the reply comes back that it cannot do so, for it is carrying out the Lord's command to attack and destroy (v. 7, see also Hab. 3:9).

Judgment on Moab (48:1–47)

The next oracle announces the fall of Moab. The Lord pronounces a "woe" over Nebo and Kiriathaim, signaling their impending doom (vv. 1–2).[103] In dramatic fashion he depicts the widespread suffering and lamentation that would characterize the aftermath of Moab's defeat (vv. 3–4). Moabite refugees would be forced to flee for their lives (vv. 5–6), while the leaders of the land, along with the Moabite god Chemosh, would be hauled away into exile (v. 7). The language probably depicts the idols of Chemosh being removed from their shrines. The invader would sweep through the land, destroying every single town (vv. 8–9).[104] An observer chimes in, pronouncing a curse on any soldier who is lax in doing the Lord's work of shedding Moabite blood (v. 10).

From the time she became a nation, Moab had been relatively secure and had grown complacent (v. 11), but all this would change. Moab would be shattered like empty wine jars (v. 12). When Chemosh proved incapable of delivering his people, the Moabites would be ashamed of him, just as the Israelites had been ashamed of Bethel, where Jeroboam I had placed an idolatrous calf-idol (v. 13; see 1 Kings 12:28–31). The Assyrians carried this idol away when they conquered the northern kingdom in the eighth century B.C. (see Hos. 10:5–6). The Lord taunts the Moabite warriors, who would soon be cut down (vv. 14–16). Bystanders are told to mourn Moab's demise, as are the inhabitants of Dibon, another prominent Moabite town (vv. 17–18). Refugees are pictured running for their lives, as judgment sweeps over Moab town by town (vv. 19–25).

Moab's judgment was well-deserved, for the Moabites had defied the Lord by taunting his people in the day of their calamity (vv. 26–28). The proud Moabites would be put to shame and become a pathetic object of pity, for their once rich orchards and fields would be empty (vv. 29–33). The Moabites' cry of despair would resonate over the countryside, as the people

103. Both towns once belonged to the tribe of Reuben (see Num. 32:3, 38; Josh. 13:19), but, according to the Moabite Stone, Mesha king of Moab seized them during the ninth century B.C. See Pritchard, *Ancient Near Eastern Texts*, 320–21.

104. The NIV translation in v. 9a ("Put salt on Moab") assumes that the Hebrew term *tsits,* which normally means "blossom, flower," is related to a Ugaritic word supposedly meaning "salt." In this case, the enemy is pictured sowing the Moabites' fields with salt (cf. Judg. 9:45). A better option might be to follow the lead of the Septuagint and to emend the Hebrew text to *tsiyun,* meaning "signpost, monument." In this context it would refer metaphorically to a gravestone (cf. 2 Kings 23:17).

shaved their hair and slashed their skin as part of their lamentation rites (vv. 34–38). They once taunted God's people, but now they would be taunted and ridiculed by the surrounding nations (v. 39). The invader would swoop down on the land like a powerful eagle, causing Moab's warriors to be panic-stricken (vv. 40–41). Because Moab had "defied" the Lord, it would be over-whelmed by God's inescapable judgment, compared here to terror, a pit, and a snare (vv. 42–44; see Isa. 24:17–18). The blazing fire of divine judgment would bring death, destruction, and exile to Moab (vv. 45–46), but a day would eventually come when the Lord would restore Moab's fortunes (v. 47).[105] This prophecy of Moab's defeat and destruction may have been fulfilled in 582 B.C. According to Josephus, Nebuchadnezzar and his Baby-lonian army conquered Moab in that year.[106]

Judgment on Ammon (49:1–6)

Ammon, Moab's neighbor to the north, would also experience divine judg-ment. The Ammonites had taken away territory from the Israelite tribe of Gad (v. 1), but the Lord would personally lead an attack against the Am-monite town of Rabbah and reduce it to ruins (v. 2a). Heshbon too would fall, and Milkom, the Ammonites' national god, would be taken into exile, along with the leaders of the land (v. 3).[107] The complacent, self-assured Ammonites would be stricken with panic and forced to flee for their lives (vv. 4–5), while God's people would reclaim the territory the Ammonites had taken from them (v. 2b). However, as in the case of Moab, the Lord would someday restore Ammon's fortunes (v. 6; see 48:47). This prophecy of Ammon's defeat may have been fulfilled in 582 B.C.[108]

Judgment on Edom (49:7–22)

Divine judgment would also overtake Edom. The Edomites' vaunted wis-dom would forsake them, as disaster swept through their land (vv. 7–8). The invaders sent by the Lord would ransack Edom and rob it of all its wealth, including its hidden treasures (vv. 9–10a; see Obad. 5–6). Thieves typically take what they desire, leaving unwanted items behind. Even grape pickers normally miss or drop a few grapes. But Edom's invaders would miss noth-ing and leave nothing behind. Edom's population would perish (v. 10b), though the Lord does mercifully offer asylum to the few orphans and wid-ows who might survive the disaster (v. 11).

That Edom should be the object of divine anger should come as no sur-

---

105. The reference to a fire coming from Sihon is an allusion to the ancient poem recorded in Num. 21:27–30, which recalls how the Amorite king Sihon had conquered Moab. Ancient history would repeat itself.

106. See Gerald L. Mattingly, "Moabites," in *Peoples of the Old Testament World,* ed. A. J. Hoerth, G. L. Mattingly, and E. M. Yamauchi (Grand Rapids: Baker, 1994), 328.

107. In the Hebrew text, the name Milkom is vocalized "their king."

108. See Younker, "Ammonites," in *Peoples of the Old Testament World,* 314.

prise. After all, if God's judgment extended to nations who were less culpable than Edom, then certainly Edom would be punished for its sins (v. 12; see Obad. 10–14). The Lord vowed that he would reduce Edom's towns to ruins and make it an object of scorn among the nations (v. 13). The Lord was summoning an army to attack proud Edom, who thought of itself as insulated from disaster (vv. 14–16; see Obad. 1–4). But Edom would be humiliated and suffer the same fate as the ancient cities of Sodom and Gomorrah (vv. 17–18). Comparing himself to a raging, hungry lion and the Edomites to a helpless flock of sheep, the Lord boasted that no shepherd would be able to fight him off (v. 19). He would, as it were, drag off the sheep and destroy the pasture (v. 20). Edom's death cries would be heard as far off as the Red Sea (v. 21). The Lord would swoop down like an eagle on Edom, causing the Edomite warriors to melt in fear (v. 22; see 48:40).

By Malachi's time (approximately 450 b.c.), Edom had suffered a devastating defeat (see Mal. 1:1–4), though not of the magnitude envisioned by Jeremiah.[109] The prophet's description of Edom's judgment is probably to some degree stylized and exaggerated.

Judgment on Damascus (49:23–27)

The next oracle pertains to Damascus, which had already been reduced to an Assyrian province in 732 b.c., long before Jeremiah's time. To what extent Assyria's fall freed Damascus from foreign rule is not certain, but Jeremiah makes it clear that the Arameans would not escape the coming judgment. The city would be gripped with terror (vv. 23–24) as her soldiers fell in battle (vv. 25–26) and her defenses went up in smoke (v. 27; see Amos 1:4).

Judgment on Kedar and Hazor (49:28–33)

God's judgment would also overtake the Arab tribes of the Syrian desert, represented here by Kedar and Hazor. Nebuchadnezzar, God's instrument of judgment, would attack them and carry off their wealth (vv. 28–29, 32a). The Arab tribes would flee for their lives and scatter in every direction, abandoning the regions they once called home (vv. 30–31, 32b–33). The background for this prophecy may be Nebuchadnezzar's raid on the Arabs in 599–598 b.c.[110]

Judgment on Elam (49:34–39)

Even the most distant lands were under the Lord's dominion. Early in the reign of Zedekiah (which began in 597 b.c.), the Lord announced that he would bring disaster on Elam, located east of Babylon (vv. 34–38). However, though the Elamites would be scattered, the Lord promised to someday re-

---

109. See Kenneth G. Hoglund, "Edomites," in *Peoples of the Old Testament World,* ed. A. J. Hoerth, G. L. Mattingly, and E. M. Yamauchi (Grand Rapids: Baker, 1994), 342–43.

110. See Thompson, *Jeremiah,* 726.

store their fortunes (v. 39; see 48:47; 49:6). In addition to illustrating the Lord's sovereignty, this oracle may have been included to emphasize the extent of Babylon's power.[111] Surely Judah would not be able to resist such a powerful, divinely energized nation.

Judgment on Babylon (50:1—51:64)

Mighty Babylon would serve as the Lord's instrument of judgment upon various nations, but eventually the Lord would turn on the proud Babylonians and repay them for their sins. In this final and longest oracle against the nations, the prophet describes Babylon's demise in vivid detail. During Zedekiah's fourth year (594–593 b.c.), Jeremiah gave a copy of the oracle to Seraiah, one of Zedekiah's staff officers who was to accompany the king on a visit to Babylon. The prophet instructed Seraiah to read the oracle publicly when he arrived in Babylon. Then he was to tie it to a stone and throw it into the Euphrates River as an object lesson. In the same way that the stone sank to the bottom of the river, so Babylon would fall, never to rise again (51:59–64).

The oracle begins with a public announcement to the nations (vv. 1–2a). An invader from the north would devastate and capture Babylon (vv. 2b–3). Babylon's idol-gods, including her patron deity Bel (i.e., Marduk), would be unable to defend the city. The prophecy anticipates the fall of Babylon to the Persian army led by Cyrus in 539 b.c. Though Persia was located to the east of Babylon, it could be called "a nation from the north" because Cyrus's conquests included regions north of Babylon and his invasion route came from the north (see Isa. 41:25).

Contrary to what the prophecy may suggest, Cyrus did not actually destroy Babylon. In fact, his takeover of the city, though preceded by a military campaign, was relatively peaceful and even welcomed by some Babylonian religious officials. How then does one explain the prophecy's description of the city's violent fall (see especially 50:39–40 and 51:37)? The language is undoubtedly stylized and exaggerated. For dramatic effect the prophets sometimes used such stereotypical language to describe the divine judgment of a city or nation.[112] In Jeremiah's prophecy (see Isa. 13–14 as well), the use of this style drives home that the Babylonian Empire would fall and disappear forever. Cyrus's conquest of the city, while not accompanied by the atrocities and destruction described in the oracle, did bring this empire to an end and essentially fulfilled Jeremiah's prophecy.

---

111. Ibid., 728.

112. See Isa. 13:17–22; 14:22–23; 34:11–15; Zeph. 2:13–15. Ancient Near Eastern literature also employs such stylized language on occasion for dramatic effect. Homer Heater Jr. calls this imagery "destruction language." For a helpful study of the relevant biblical texts and motifs, as well as samples of "destruction language" from ancient Near Eastern sources, see his article, "Do the Prophets Teach That Babylonia Will Be Rebuilt in the *Eschaton?*" *JETS* 41 (1998): 31–36.

Like lost sheep without a shepherd, the exiles were helpless before their foreign oppressors (vv. 6–7a). The Babylonians justified their cruel treatment of the exiles by pointing out that God's people had sinned against the Lord (v. 7b). However, the Lord was offended by the Babylonians' sinful attitude (see vv. 11a, 14b) and would avenge his people (see v. 15b). He would use a powerful northern alliance to inflict a crushing, humiliating defeat upon Babylon (vv. 9–15, 17–18). Babylon's fall would signal the release of the exiles (vv. 8, 16). Like a shepherd, the Lord would gather his scattered flock (see v. 17a) and bring them back to their pasture, where they would enjoy his rich provision (v. 19) and once again worship him in Zion (vv. 4–5a). He would forgive their sins (v. 20), enabling them to renew their ancient covenantal relationship with him (v. 5b).

The Lord's diatribe against Babylon continues. He urges the invader to attack Babylon and kill its inhabitants (vv. 21–23).[113] He commands Babylon's conquerors to carry out his judgment by looting the city's granaries and ruthlessly slaughtering her people (vv. 24–30). The Lord viewed Babylon's arrogant attitude as open defiance (see vv. 24b, 29b) that must be punished (vv. 31–32). Furthermore, her cruel treatment of God's exiled people must be avenged (see v. 28). Though the oppressive Babylonians held the exiles firmly within their strong grasp (v. 33), the Lord of Armies (see NIV "Lord Almighty"), the Redeemer of his people, would "defend their cause" and vindicate them (v. 34).[114] Using both the sword of the invader as well as natural disasters, the Lord would overcome Babylon's institutionalized power and reduce the kingdom to uninhabited ruins (vv. 35–40). As the Lord's mighty northern army approached, the king of Babylon would be paralyzed with fear (vv. 41–43). The Lord would execute his plan against Babylon, and no one would be able to resist his power (vv. 44–45). All the world would tremble at the sound of Babylon's fall (v. 46).

The description of Babylon's demise continues in chapter 51, as if to emphasize the degree of the Lord's wrath and the extent of Babylon's impending doom. He is so angry at the Babylonians that his desire for vengeance will not easily be satisfied. The repetitious style and the sheer length of the prophecy reflect this.

Foreign invaders, functioning as God's instruments of vengeance, would ruthlessly cut down Babylon's young men (51:1–5). Speaking to a future generation of exiles, the prophet urged them to flee the doomed city, for it would be repaid by the Lord for its sins (v. 6). The Lord had used Babylon as his instrument of judgment, but her turn to experience divine wrath

113. Merathaim and Pekod (see v. 21) were regions located within Babylonian territory. See Thompson, *Jeremiah*, 741.

114. The divine title "Lord Almighty" (traditionally "the Lord of Hosts") is especially appropriate here, for it often depicts the Lord as a mighty warrior-king who leads his armies into battle (see Isa. 1:9, 24; 2:12).

would come in due time (vv. 7–8). The exiles should abandon any feelings they might have for doomed Babylon, return to Zion, and celebrate God's work on their behalf (vv. 9–10).

The Lord would use the Medes to take vengeance on the Babylonians for what they did to his temple (vv. 11–12; see Isa. 13:17). The invaders would rob Babylon of her great wealth (vv. 13–14). Before the incomparable sovereign creator of the universe, Babylon's lifeless idol-gods would be helpless (vv. 15–19). Babylon had been the Lord's hammer of judgment throughout the world, but he would repay the Babylonians for the way they treated Jerusalem (vv. 20–24). Babylon once towered over the nations like a great mountain, but it would be turned into a desolate mound, consumed by the smoke of judgment (vv. 25–26). Terrifying hordes from the north would answer the Lord's summons and overrun Babylon (vv. 27–33). The Babylonians would experience violence, just as Nebuchadnezzar had dished out violence to the people of Jerusalem (vv. 34–35). The vengeance of the Lord would reduce Babylon to a heap of ruins, overrun by wild animals (vv. 36–37).[115] The Babylonians had once fearlessly roared like lions, but now they would be overcome by judgment and slaughtered like sacrificial lambs (vv. 38–40). The raging sea, symbolizing the northern hordes, would overwhelm Babylon (v. 42). The nations, which once streamed to Babylon to do business, would look with horror on the ruins of the abandoned city (vv. 41, 43–44).[116]

Projecting himself into the future and speaking again to a future generation of exiles (cf. v. 6), the prophet emphasized that there was little time to spare (v. 45). Because of what the Babylonians had done to God's people, Babylon's fall was inevitable (vv. 46–49). The exiles should leave the city before judgment fell and turn their eyes toward home (v. 50). Babylon desecrated the Lord's temple and humiliated his covenant people (v. 51), but a time of retribution was coming. Mighty Babylon's fortifications would tumble, and her people would be silenced (vv. 52–58).

Epilogue (Jeremiah 52)

Jeremiah's prophecies end with the oracles against the nations (see 51:64b), but the Book of Jeremiah concludes with an epilogue (chapter 52) that parallels the account of Jerusalem's fall in 2 Kings 24–25. This epilogue was probably included to demonstrate that Jeremiah's ministry and message were fully vindicated by history.

This chapter begins with a negative assessment of Zedekiah's reign and observes that this king rebelled against Babylon (52:1–3). This defiant act prompted a Babylonian siege of Jerusalem in January 588 B.C. (vv. 4–5). The

---

115. On the use of stereotypical, hyperbolic destruction language here, see my discussion of Isa. 13–14, in which the fall of Babylon is depicted in similar terms.

116. Sheshach (v. 41) is a code name for Babylon (see 25:26).

siege continued until July 586, when the Babylonians finally breached Jerusalem's defenses and invaded the city (vv. 6–7a). They captured the fleeing Zedekiah, killed his sons and officials, put out his eyes, and took him away to Babylon (vv. 7b–11). In August 586 the Babylonians burned the temple and other buildings, tore down the city's walls, and took the upper classes away into exile, leaving only the poorest of the people in the land (vv. 12–16). According to verse 29, 832 people were deported at this time.[117] Before destroying the temple, the soldiers removed its bronze, gold, and silver items, which were taken to Babylon (vv. 17–23). The commander of the Babylonian army took Seraiah the chief priest, as well as other religious and civil leaders, to Nebuchadnezzar, who ordered them all to be executed (vv. 24–27). The book ends on a more positive note, as it tells how Evil-merodach, Nebuchadnezzar's successor, in 562–561 B.C. released the exiled King Jehoiachin from prison and treated him kindly (vv. 31–34).

Weeping for Zion (Lamentations)

Introduction

The Book of Lamentations was written in the aftermath of Jerusalem's fall to the Babylonians in 586 B.C. The author (whom we will call the "poet") depicts the intense suffering experienced by the city's inhabitants and laments the severity of God's judgment. But all is not lost. Rising above the horror of the tragedy, the poet affirms the Lord's abiding faithfulness, asks that God would avenge his people, and prays for the restoration of the covenant community.

The book's author is not identified, but tradition attributes it to Jeremiah. This tradition is reflected in the ancient Greek version (Septuagint), which includes a heading identifying Jeremiah as the book's author. In the Septuagint, Lamentations follows Jeremiah and the apocryphal Baruch. This tradition of Jeremianic authorship is also reflected in English translations, where Lamentations follows Jeremiah. It is certainly understandable that some would associate Jeremiah with the book. He experienced Jerusalem's demise firsthand and expressed his desire to weep for his people (see Jer. 9:1). Second Chronicles 35:25 informs us that the prophet composed laments (in this case for King Josiah). The Hebrew Bible, however, does not lend support to the notion of Jeremianic authorship. In the traditional Hebrew

---

117. Verses 28–30 mention two other deportations, in addition to the one in 586 B.C. In Nebuchadnezzar's seventh year (598–597 B.C.), he deported 3,023 people, while in his twenty-third year (582–581), he deported another 745. The three deportations totaled 4,600 people. In 2 Kings 24:14, 16, much larger figures are given for the first deportation. According to Cogan and Tadmor, 2 Kings 24 may give the number of deportees from Jerusalem, while Jeremiah 52 refers to the number of people from the countryside. See M. Cogan and H. Tadmor, *II Kings*, AB (New York: Doubleday, 1988), 312.

canonical arrangement, Lamentations appears in the third section of the canon, called the "Writings," where it is grouped with Ruth, Song of Songs, Ecclesiastes, and Esther under the heading of the "Scrolls."

The book is comprised of five poems, the first four of which are written in an acrostic form where successive stanzas begin with the successive letters of the Hebrew alphabet. The first two poems each contain twenty-two stanzas/verses, each of which has three poetic lines. In the second poem, the *ayin* and *pe* stanzas are reversed. The third poem contains sixty-six verses, comprised of twenty-two stanzas. Each stanza has three verses/poetic lines, each of which begins with the same letter of the alphabet. For example, the first three verses each begin with the letter *aleph,* verses 4–6 with *beth,* and so on. As in the second poem, the *ayin* and *pe* stanzas are reversed. The fourth poem has twenty-two stanzas/verses, each of which has two poetic lines. As in the second and third poems, the *ayin* and *pe* stanzas are reversed. The fifth poem is not an acrostic, but for the sake of symmetry with earlier poems it contains twenty-two verses, each of which has one poetic line. The book's acrostic/symmetrical structure gives the anthology an aura of completeness and also facilitates memorization and recitation.

An Abandoned City (Lamentations 1)

The poet mourns over Jerusalem, comparing the deserted city to a lonely widow and to a once prominent princess who has been reduced to the status of a common worker (v. 1). Jerusalem is like a woman who spends her nights weeping because she has been abandoned by her lovers and betrayed by her friends (v. 2). The reference to "lovers" and "friends" recalls Judah's foreign alliances, which were viewed by the Lord as spiritual adultery.[118] Judah had experienced difficult times, culminating in the Babylonian exile (v. 3). Utilizing the literary device of personification, the poet pictures the roads leading to Jerusalem as mourning due to the fact that no one travels on them to commemorate the religious feasts (v. 4a). The city's gates, which once bustled with the arrival of religious pilgrims, lie desolate, while the priests and young women, who once played a prominent role in the festivities, grieve (v. 4b).[119] Because of her rebellion, the Lord gave the city over to her enemies and sent her children into exile (v. 5). Her princes, once the pride of the city, are forced to run for their lives as their pursuers chase them down like deer (v. 6). In contrast to her past glory, Zion must now endure the taunts of her enemies (v. 7). As the consequence of her sins, she suffers humiliation, like a promiscuous woman whose nakedness is publicly ex-

---

118. Note the reference to "nations" in the preceding verse, as well as Jer. 3:1, in which NIV "lovers" translates the same Hebrew term rendered "friends" in Lam. 1:2.

119. Young women apparently danced at such festivities. See Judg. 21:19–21 and Jer. 31:13, as well as Delbert R. Hillers, *Lamentations,* AB (Garden City, N.Y.: Doubleday, 1972), 20.

posed as a penalty for her misdeeds (vv. 8–9).[120] Her treasure has been looted and her temple defiled by invaders, while her starving survivors must trade what material goods they have left for a little bit of food (vv. 10–11).

Beginning in verse 12, personified Zion speaks for herself. She urges passersby to consider the depth of her misery (v. 12a). She attributes her suffering to God's angry judgment (v. 12b), which she compares to fire that penetrates into her bones and to a net that has entrapped her (v. 13). Recognizing that her sinful rebellion has prompted God's anger (v. 14a), she laments her humiliating defeat (v. 14b), which she compares to being trampled in a winepress (v. 15b). She also mourns her abandonment (v. 16a) and the loss of her young men (vv. 15a, 16b). She extends her hands for help, but no one offers any comfort, for the Lord has decreed that she should be judged for her sins (v. 17). Zion acknowledges that the Lord is justified in punishing her rebellion (v. 18a; see also v. 20b). Once more she draws attention to her plight (v. 18b) and laments the starvation and death she sees all around her (vv. 19–20). No one helps her, while her enemies rejoice over the way God has treated her (v. 21a). In her pain and suffering, she appeals to God for vengeance on her enemies. She asks him to bring judgment on her enemies, as he announced he would eventually do (v. 21b). She prays that God will punish her enemies for their sins, just as he judged her rebellion (v. 22).

The Lord Is My Enemy (Lamentations 2)

The poet once more laments what has become of Zion. The city was once the Lord's "footstool," for he lived within its temple (v. 1; see Isa. 60:13 and Ps. 132:7, as well as Ps. 99:5 [cf. v. 2] and 1 Chron. 28:2). But the Lord's angry, fiery judgment has destroyed the city and humiliated the nation's leaders (vv. 2–3). The poet pictures the Lord cutting off "every horn of Israel." The image of an animal's horn is used here to symbolize the nation's strength, perhaps as embodied in its warriors and leaders. The Lord did not raise his right hand, a symbol of his military power, against the invaders (v. 3a).[121] Instead, he attacked his own people and used his right hand to shoot arrows at them (v. 4). Rather than being Israel's defender, the Lord became their enemy, swallowing up the nation and its strongholds (v. 5a, cf.

---

120. It is possible that the metaphorical language also depicts her as menstruous (and therefore ritually unclean). The Hebrew term translated "unclean" in v. 8 (*nidah*) occurs only here in the Hebrew Bible. It is understood by some to mean literally "a shaking of the head," that is, an object of scorn and ridicule (see *HALOT* 696). But others prefer to emend the term to *niddah*, which refers to the menstrual bleeding of a woman and, by extension, to ritual impurity (see *HALOT* 673). The NIV translation reflects the latter interpretation.

121. Hillers (*Lamentations*, 36) argues that Israel is the subject of the statement "he has withdrawn his right hand," but elsewhere in this context the Lord is the subject of the third-person masculine singular verb forms, while Israel/Judah/Zion are portrayed as feminine. Furthermore, if one understands "his right hand" in v. 3 as a reference to the Lord's power, we then have a nice contrast with the use of "his right hand" in v. 4, where the referent is clearly the Lord.

also v. 2) and leaving widespread mourning and lamentation in his wake (v. 5b). He even destroyed his own sanctuary, allowing the enemy to desecrate it (vv. 6–7). Jerusalem is in ruins, while her leaders are either exiled or reduced to silence (vv. 8–9). Everyone, from the elders to the young women, laments the city's demise (v. 10).

The poet is overcome emotionally by the scene that unfolds before his tear-filled eyes. Starving children die in their mothers' arms as they beg for something to eat and drink (vv. 11–12; see v. 19). Jerusalem's misery is unsurpassed (v. 13). The false prophets had promised deliverance but had failed to expose the nation's sin (v. 14). Their visions and oracles proved to be misleading, as the Lord mercilessly brought to pass the warnings of judgment that he had issued through his prophets decade after decade since at least the time of Isaiah (v. 17). The enemy overran the city and then boasted of their victory as they hurled their taunts and insults (vv. 15–16). The poet urges the personified "wall" of Daughter Zion to pour out her heart before the Lord in lamentation for the horrors taking place in the city's streets (vv. 18–19).

Personified Zion responds. She protests that the Lord has never treated anyone so harshly (v. 20a). Mothers, driven to insanity by their hunger, eat their own children (v. 20b). Priests and prophets lie dead in the Lord's temple (v. 20b). The streets are littered with the corpses of both the young and old, cut down by the sword (v. 21a). The Lord himself, overcome with anger, slaughtered Zion's people (v. 21b), replacing the animal sacrifices of her religious festivals with an overwhelming and inescapable human bloodbath (v. 22).

Reflecting on the Horror (Lamentations 3)

In this lengthy chapter, the poet bitterly laments what he has experienced (vv. 1–20), confesses his abiding faith in the Lord's covenantal love (vv. 21–26), acknowledges the propriety of divine disciplinary judgment (vv. 27–39), exhorts his contemporaries to confess their sins (vv. 40–47), and renews his lament (vv. 48–54) as a prelude to seeking God's vengeance upon his enemies (vv. 55–66). Speaking on behalf of his people and their ruined city, the poet represents the survivors within the covenant community who have experienced God's anger. At the same time he models for this remnant the proper response to what has transpired. Though there are plenty of reasons to despair and give up hope, the poet is able to see a faithful God through the smoking ruins. He points to repentance as a doorway to the future, which will include vindication for God's people and vengeance against their arrogant enemies.

The poet begins with a vivid description of how God ruthlessly attacked him, driving him from the light into darkness (vv. 1–3). Metaphors follow in rapid succession, each one further magnifying the horrors of divine judgment. The Lord shriveled up his skin and shattered his bones, surrounded him with hardship, put him in a dark dungeon where he was weighed down with chains, and refused to hear his shouts for help (vv. 4–8). The Lord put obstacles in his path, mangled him like a fierce lion or bear, shot arrows into his heart (vv. 9–13), and made him the laughingstock of everyone (v. 14). If this were not enough, the Lord made him eat bitter herbs, smashed his face into the gravel, and trampled him underfoot (vv. 15–16). Deprived of peace and prosperity, he reflected upon his suffering (vv. 17–20).

Weighed down by his discouragement and suffering, the poet nevertheless rises above his circumstances and gains new hope (v. 21). Though the covenant community had suffered terribly, it was not annihilated. The Lord spared a remnant, demonstrating that he was still committed to his people and capable of showing them compassion when they deserved none (v. 22). Despite the horror all around him, the poet affirms God's abiding faithfulness, declares his allegiance to the Lord, and anticipates God's saving intervention (vv. 23–25). He acknowledges that there is something therapeutic about submitting to divine discipline and suffering in humble silence (vv. 26–30). Though God disciplines his people, he does not permanently abandon them (v. 31). His love prompts him to extend his compassion (v. 32). He does not derive sadistic delight from seeing humans suffer. On the contrary, he sends his disciplinary judgment only as a last resort (v. 33). When humans suffer for their sins, it is not because God is unjust (vv. 34–36). On the contrary, God is a just king who fairly dispenses blessing and judgment so that everyone receives what he or she deserves (vv. 37–39). When calamity befalls sinners, it is because the Lord himself has decreed it as an appropriate punishment for sinful deeds.

Having made it clear that human sin, not divine injustice, was the underlying reason for the calamity that had overtaken the nation, the poet urges the survivors to cry out to God (vv. 40–41). They should confess their sins as a prelude to lamenting their rejection by God and the humiliation they were experiencing at the hand of their enemies (vv. 42–47). Having provided his contemporaries with a model prayer to offer up to God, the poet voices his own lament. As he considers the demise of his countrymen, tears flow from his eyes (vv. 48, 51). Only the Lord's saving intervention can bring him relief (vv. 49–50). His enemies seek his life and threaten to overwhelm him (vv. 52–54), but he has turned to the Lord for deliverance and vindication (v. 55). The Lord has responded to his cry for help with the assuring words, "Do not fear," guaranteeing that relief would indeed come (vv. 56–58). Convinced that the Lord was aware of his enemies' ruthless intentions (vv. 59–64), he appeals to the Lord for justice, asking him to destroy his foes (vv. 64–66).

On the surface the chronology of verses 52–66 appears to be confusing. On the one hand, the poet speaks of the attacks of his enemies and prays for divine intervention (vv. 59–66). On the other hand, he speaks as if God has already rescued him (vv. 55–58). However, the conflict is only apparent. The poet continues to face the threats of his enemies, who have not yet been subdued. However, he has prayed to the Lord and received an oracle of salvation, which allows the poet to speak of God's redemption as already accomplished while at the same time praying for its realization. These verses reflect the typical sequence of prayer and divine response seen in the psalms. When the psalmist faces a life-threatening crisis, he appeals to God for help (see, e.g., Ps. 12:1–4). Through an assuring oracle, God promises to intervene (v. 5). This in turn elicits a response of confidence from the psalmist (vv. 6–8) as he awaits and even prays for the realization of the divine promise.[122]

An Outpouring of Divine Anger (Lamentations 4)

The poet resumes his lament over Jerusalem's downfall. Using metaphorical language, he bemoans the fact that the gold has lost its luster and the jewels have been scattered in the streets (v. 1). In verse 2, he explains that Jerusalem's young men are the underlying reality behind the symbolism. They were once valued and respected, but now they are treated as common and ordinary. Famine has overtaken the city and, with it, slow, agonizing death by starvation. Desperate parents, driven to the edge of insanity by their hunger, eat what little food is available and let their children starve (v. 3). They are compared to the ostrich, which was viewed as cruel because it buried its eggs in the sand where they could be easily crushed underfoot (see Job 39:13–18). Infants are dehydrated and children beg for food, but no one responds (v. 4). People who once lived in the lap of luxury are destitute and homeless (v. 5), while once robust princes die from malnutrition (vv. 7–8). In the poet's opinion, Jerusalem's fate is worse than Sodom's, for that ancient city was destroyed in an instant and its people did not have to endure a slow, painful death (v. 6). He reasons that those who fell by the sword are better off than those who starve to death (v. 9). The victims of the sword die swiftly, but the starving survivors resort to hideous, cannibalistic practices (v. 10).

The Lord poured out his anger upon Jerusalem in full measure (v. 11). Though foreigners considered the city to be impregnable, her sin caused her downfall (vv. 12–13).[123] Religious leaders became corrupt and condoned the social injustice that stained the city with the blood of the oppressed. But now

---

122. This same sequence can be seen in Ps. 3, in which the lament proper (v. 1) is followed by an affirmation of confidence in God's ability to protect (vv. 2–3, 5–6) based on an oracle of salvation that the psalmist received (v. 4). A prayer for divine intervention (i.e., for the fulfillment of God's promise) then follows, accompanied by another expression of confidence (vv. 7–8). In Ps. 6 the lament proper (vv. 1–7) is followed by a statement of confidence based on an oracle of salvation (vv. 8–9) and a concluding prayer of imprecation (v. 10). For a discussion of salvation oracles in the Psalms, see Raymond J. Tournay, *Seeing and Hearing God with the Psalms*, trans. J. E. Crowley (Sheffield: JSOT, 1991), 160–98.

123. Following Sennacherib's defeat outside Jerusalem in 701 b.c., foreigners who heard about the incident must have viewed the city as invincible.

these same leaders are covered with blood and shunned by those who see them (v. 14). Is the blood that covers their clothes that of their victims? Or is it the blood of those who died by the sword when the Babylonians invaded the city? Perhaps some of both. At any rate, defiled by their bloodstained garments, they are forced to wander among the nations as outcasts (v. 15). Ultimately, it was the Lord himself who had scattered them and withdrawn his protective care from them (v. 16). Much to the shock of the people, no help came as the Babylonian army approached (vv. 17–18). The invaders proved to be powerful and effective predators, like eagles that swoop down upon their prey (v. 19). Even the king of Judah (Zedekiah is probably in view), to whom the people looked for protection, was captured (v. 20).

The poet suddenly turns on Edom, Judah's neighbor to the southeast. The Edomites relished Judah's downfall and exploited her weakness to their own benefit. The poet mockingly encourages them to celebrate all they want, but he warns them that they too must soon drink the cup of divine judgment (v. 21). Zion will find relief and her exiled people will return, but Edom will continue to suffer for its sins (v. 22).

Pleading for Restoration (Lamentations 5)

In his final prayer, the poet, speaking on behalf of his fellow survivors, begs the Lord to take a close look at their humiliating situation (v. 1). Foreigners have taken over their land, making them as vulnerable as orphans and widows (vv. 2–3). They are dependent on others for even the most basic essentials of life—water to drink and wood to build a fire (v. 4). They are beaten down and weary, but unable to find relief (v. 5).

In verses 6–7, the poet looks backward to find an explanation for the present situation. For economic reasons, Judah once made treaties with foreign powers, such as Egypt and Assyria (v. 6). These alliances were forbidden by the Lord, who expected his people to trust him alone for the essentials of life. God's judgment fell upon the nation and the poet's generation was experiencing the consequences of their ancestors' sins (v. 7). This statement should not be taken to mean that they felt as if they were being unfairly punished. Later in the poem they confess that they too have sinned (see v. 16). While the statements may seem contradictory, it is likely that both are true. As Kaminsky suggests, "the guilt of earlier generations was visited upon those who were themselves guilty."[124]

In verse 8, the poet resumes his description of the suffering endured by the community. They are subject to those who are "slaves" to other men (lower-level Babylonian officials are probably in view). They must risk their very lives just to get food, and they suffer from illnesses and diseases as a result of being malnourished (vv. 9–10). To make matters worse, images of horrify-

---

124. See Kaminsky, *Corporate Responsibility in the Hebrew Bible*, 44–45 n. 35.

ing scenes were fresh in their minds. Their women, including young virgins, had been brutally raped (v. 11). Their young men had been publicly humiliated and forced to do menial labor normally reserved for women or prisoners (vv. 12–13; see Judg. 16:21; Isa. 47:2). The community leaders who normally congregated at the city gates had disappeared, along with the sounds of festive celebration (vv. 14–15). Their sins had deprived them of the glory and respect they once enjoyed, compared here to a crown (v. 16). The sight of desolate Zion, overrun by wild scavengers, brought discouragement (vv. 17–18).

But hope was not gone. The destruction of the temple did not mean that God's throne had been toppled. Despite Zion's demise, the Lord still reigned as the everlasting king (v. 19). The poet asks why God continues to abandon his people (v. 20). He prays that the Lord might restore his people, for he realizes that God must take the initiative if genuine reconciliation is to occur (v. 21). Though the poet longs for covenantal renewal, the reconciliation which he desires stands in stark contrast to the present circumstances, which are the result of God's angry rejection of his people (v. 22).[125]

Bibliography (Jeremiah)

Commentaries

Brueggemann, W. *A Commentary on Jeremiah: Exile and Homecoming.* Grand Rapids: Eerdmans, 1998.

Carroll, R. P. *The Book of Jeremiah.* OTL. Philadelphia: Westminster, 1986.

Clements, R. E. *Jeremiah.* Interpretation. Atlanta: John Knox, 1988.

Craigie, P. C., P. H. Kelley, and J. F. Drinkard Jr. *Jeremiah 1–25.* WBC. Dallas: Word, 1991.

Holladay, W. L. *Jeremiah.* Hermeneia. 2 vols. Minneapolis: Fortress, 1986, 1989.

Huey, F. B., Jr. *Jeremiah, Lamentations.* NAC. Nashville: Broadman & Holman, 1993.

Jones, D. R. *Jeremiah.* NCB. Grand Rapids: Eerdmans, 1992.

Keown, G. L., P. J. Scalise, and T. G. Smothers. *Jeremiah 26–52.* WBC. Dallas: Word, 1995.

Lundbom, J. R. *Jeremiah 1–20.* AB. New York: Doubleday, 1999.

McKane, W. *A Critical and Exegetical Commentary on Jeremiah.* ICC. 2 vols. Edinburgh: T. & T. Clark, 1986, 1996.

Thompson, J. A. *The Book of Jeremiah.* NICOT. Grand Rapids: Eerdmans, 1979.

Recent Studies

General

Anderson, J. S. "The Metonymical Curse as Propaganda in the Book of Jeremiah." *Bulletin of Biblical Research* 8 (1998): 1–13.

Applegate, J. "The Fate of Zedekiah: Redactional Debate in the Book of Jeremiah." *VT* 48 (1998): 137–60, 301–8.

---

125. For a detailed analysis of the syntax of v. 22, see Hillers, *Lamentations,* 100–101. Hillers understands the Hebrew construction *ki 'im* at the beginning of the verse as expressing contrast. He translates it "But instead" (96). Another option is to take the construction as exceptive, "unless" (see NIV). In this case, the poet is tempering his prayer with a dose of realism by acknowledging that it may be too late for reconciliation. For a critique of this and other interpretive alternatives, see Hillers.

————. "'Peace, Peace, When There Is No Peace': Redactional Integration of Prophecy of Peace into the Judgement of Jeremiah." In *The Book of Jeremiah and Its Reception,* edited by A. H. W. Curtis and T. Römer, 51–90. Louvain: Peeters, 1997.

Bauer, A. *Gender in the Book of Jeremiah: A Feminist-Literary Reading.* New York: Lang, 1999.

Carroll, R. P. "Inscribing the Covenant: Writing and the Written in Jeremiah." In *Understanding Poets and Prophets: Essays in Honour of George Wishart Anderson,* edited by A. G. Auld, JSOTSup 152, 61–74. Sheffield: JSOT 1993.

————. "Intertextuality and the Book of Jeremiah: Animadversions on Text and Theory." In *The New Literary Criticism and the Hebrew Bible,* edited by J. C. Exum and D. J. A. Clines, JSOTSup 143, 55–78. Sheffield: JSOT, 1993.

————. "Jeremiah, Intertextuality, and Ideologiekritik." *JNSL* 22 (1996): 15–34.

————. "Surplus Meaning and the Conflict of Interpretations: A Dodecade of Jeremiah Studies (1984–95)." *Currents in Research: Biblical Studies* 4 (1996): 115–59.

————. "Synchronic Deconstructions of Jeremiah: Diachrony to the Rescue? Reflections on Some Reading Strategies for Understanding Certain Problems in the Book of Jeremiah." In *Synchronic or Diachronic? A Debate in Old Testament Exegesis,* edited by J. C. de Moor, 39–51. Leiden: Brill, 1995.

Curtis, A. H. W. and T. Römer, eds. *The Book of Jeremiah and Its Reception.* Louvain: Peeters, 1997.

Delamarter, S. "Thus Far the Words of Jeremiah." *BRev* 15, no. 5 (1999): 34–55.

Diamond, A. R. P. "Portraying Prophecy: Of Doublets, Variants, and Analogies in the Narrative Representation of Jeremiah's Oracles—Reconstructing the Hermeneutics of Prophecy." *JSOT* 57 (1993): 99–119.

Domeris, W. R. "Jeremiah and the Religion of Canaan." *OTE* 7 (1994): 7–20.

Gosse, B. "The Masoretic Redaction of Jeremiah: An Explanation." *JSOT* 77 (1998): 75–80.

Hoffman, Y. "Eschatology in the Book of Jeremiah." In *Eschatology in the Bible and in Jewish and Christian Tradition,* edited by H. G. Reventlow, JSOTSup 243, 75–97. Sheffield: Sheffield Academic Press, 1997.

House, P. R. "Plot, Prophecy, and Jeremiah." *JETS* 36 (1993): 297–306.

Jeremias, J. "The Hosea Tradition and the Book of Jeremiah." *OTE* 7 (1994): 21–39.

King, P. J. *Jeremiah: An Archaeological Companion.* Louisville: Westminster John Knox, 1993.

le Roux, J. H. "In Search of Carroll's Jeremiah (Or: Good Old Jerry, Did He Really Live? Question Irrelevant)." *OTE* 7 (1994): 60–90.

Lundbom, J. R. *The Early Career of the Prophet Jeremiah.* Lewiston, N.Y.: Mellen, 1993.

McConville, J. G. "Jeremiah: Prophet and Book." *TynB* 42 (1991): 80–95.

————. *Judgment and Promise: An Interpretation of the Book of Jeremiah.* Winona Lake, Ind.: Eisenbrauns, 1993.

McKane, W. "Jeremiah and the Wise." In *Wisdom in Ancient Israel: Essays in Honour of J. A. Emerton,* edited by J. Day, 142–51. Cambridge: Cambridge University Press, 1995.

Mulzac, K. D. "The Remnant and the New Covenant in the Book of Jeremiah." *AUSS* 35 (1997): 239–48.

————. "The Remnant Motif in the Context of Judgement and Salvation in the Book of Jeremiah." Ph.D. diss., Andrews University, 1995.

Parunak, H. van Dyke. "Some Discourse Functions of Prophetic Quotation Formulas in Jeremiah." In *Biblical Hebrew and Discourse Linguistics,* edited by R. D. Bergen, 489–519. Winona Lake, Ind.: Eisenbrauns, 1994.

Roberts, J. J. M. "The Motif of the Weeping God in Jeremiah and Its Background in the Lament Tradition of the Ancient Near East." *OTE* 5 (1992): 361–74.

Römer, T. C. "How Did Jeremiah Become a Convert to Deuteronomistic Ideology?" In *Those Elusive Deuteronomists: The Phenomenon of Pan-Deuteronomism,* edited by L. S. Schearing and S. L. McKenzie, JSOTSup 268, 189–99. Sheffield: Sheffield Academic Press, 1999.

Roshwalb, E. H. "Build-Up and Climax in Jeremiah's Vision and Laments." In *Boundaries of the Ancient Near Eastern World: A Tribute to Cyrus H. Gordon,* edited by M. Lubetski et al., JSOTSup 173, 111–35. Sheffield: Sheffield Academic Press, 1998.

Sommer, B. D. "New Light on the Composition of Jeremiah." *CBQ* 61 (1999): 646–66.

Steiner, R. C. "The Two Sons of Neriah and the Two Editions of Jeremiah in the Light of Two *Atbash* Code-Words for Babylon." *VT* 46 (1996): 74–84.

Stipp, H.-J. "Linguistic Peculiarities of the Masoretic Edition of the Book of Jeremiah: An Updated Index," *JNSL* 23 (1997):181–202.

———. "The Prophetic Messenger Formulas in Jeremiah According to the Masoretic and Alexandrian Texts." *Textus* 18 (1995): 63–85.

———. "Zedekiah in the Book of Jeremiah: On the Formation of a Biblical Character." *CBQ* 58 (1996): 627–48.

Stulman, L. "Insiders and Outsiders in the Book of Jeremiah: Shifts in Symbolic Arrangements." *JSOT* 66 (1995): 65–85.

———. *Order amid Chaos: Jeremiah as Symbolic Tapestry.* Sheffield: Sheffield Academic Press, 1998.

Thompson, H. O. *The Book of Jeremiah: An Annotated Bibliography.* London: Scarecrow, 1996.

Tov, E. "The Book of Jeremiah: A Work in Progress." *BRev* 16, no. 3 (2000): 32–38, 45.

White, R. E. *The Indomitable Prophet: A Biographical Commentary on Jeremiah. The Man, the Time, the Book, the Tasks.* Grand Rapids: Eerdmans, 1992.

Wilcox, B. K. "Rejection of the Word of Yahweh and Judgment in the Book of Jeremiah." Ph.D. diss., New Orleans Baptist Theological Seminary, 1990.

Williams, M. J. "An Investigation of the Legitimacy of Source Distinctions for the Prose Material in Jeremiah." *JBL* 112 (1993): 193–210.

Wilson, R. R. "Historicizing the Prophets: History and Literature in the Book of Jeremiah." In *On the Way to Nineveh: Studies in Honor of George M. Landes,* edited by S. L. Cook and S. C. Winter, 136–54. Atlanta: Scholars Press, 1999.

Youngblood, R. "The Character of Jeremiah." *Criswell Theological Review* 5 (1990–91): 171–82.

Zipor, M. A. " 'Scenes from a Marriage'—According to Jeremiah." *JSOT* 65 (1995): 83–91.

Jeremiah 1–25

Applegate, J. "Jeremiah and the Seventy Years in the Hebrew Bible: Inner-Biblical Reflections on the Prophet and His Prophecy." In *The Book of Jeremiah and Its Reception,* edited by A. H. W. Curtis and T. Römer, 91–110. Louvain: Peeters, 1997.

Becking, B. "Does Jeremiah x 3 Refer to a Canaanite Deity Called Hubal?" *VT* 43 (1993): 555–57.

Biddle, M. E. *Polyphony and Symphony in Prophetic Literature: Rereading Jeremiah 7–20.* Macon, Ga.: Mercer, 1996.

———. *A Redaction History of Jeremiah 2:1–4:2.* Zürich: Theologischer Verlag, 1990.

Bozak, B. A. "Heeding the Received Text: Jer 2,20a, a Case in Point." *Bib* 77 (1996): 524–37.

Christensen, D. L. "In Quest of the Autograph of the Book of Jeremiah: A Study of Jeremiah 25 in Relation to Jeremiah 46–51." *JETS* 33 (1990): 145–53.

Clements, R. E. "Jeremiah 1–25 and the Deuteronomistic History." In *Understanding Poets and Prophets: Essays in Honour of George Wishart Anderson,* edited by A. G. Auld, JSOTSup 152, 93–113. Sheffield: JSOT 1993.

Curtis, A. H. W. "Terror on Every Side!" In *The Book of Jeremiah and Its Reception,* edited by A. H. W. Curtis and T. Römer, 111–18. Louvain: Peeters, 1997.

Diamond, A. R. P., and K. M. O'Connor. "Unfaithful Passions: Coding Women, Coding Men in Jeremiah 2–3 (4:2)." *Biblical Interpretation* 4 (1996): 288–310.

Dubbink, J. "Jeremiah: Hero of Faith or Defeatist? Concerning the Place and Function of Jeremiah 20.14–18." *JSOT* 86 (1999): 67–84.

———. "Listen before You Speak: The Prophet as Spokesman and First Recipient of the Word of YHWH." In *The Rediscovery of the Hebrew Bible*, edited by J. W. Dyk, 69–83. Maastricht, the Netherlands: Shaker, 1999.

Gitay, Y. "The Projection of the Prophet: A Rhetorical Presentation of the Prophet Jeremiah (according to Jer 1:1–19)." In *Prophecy and the Prophets: The Diversity of Contemporary Issues in Scholarship,* edited by Y. Gitay, 41–55. Atlanta: Scholars Press, 1997.

Gladson, J. A. "Jeremiah 17:19–27: A Rewriting of the Sinaitic Code?" *CBQ* 62 (2000): 33–40.

Hayes, K. M. "Jeremiah iv 23: *tōhû* without *bōhû*." *VT* 47 (1997): 247–49.

Hess, R. S. "Hiphil Forms of *qwr* in Jeremiah vi 7." *VT* 41 (1991): 347–50.

Hoffman, Y. " 'Isn't the Bride too Beautiful?': The Case of Jeremiah 6.16–21." *JSOT* 64 (1994): 103–20.

Kessler, M. "Jeremiah 25,1–29, Text and Context: A Synchronic Study." *ZAW* 109 (1997): 44–70.

Kruger, H. A. J. "Ideology and Natural Disaster: A Context for Jeremiah 10:1–16." *OTE* 6 (1993): 367–83.

Kruger, P. A. "The Psychology of Shame in Jeremiah 2:36–37." *JNSL* 22 (1996): 79–88.

Lenchak, T. A. "Puzzling Passages: Jeremiah 20:14." *TBT* 37 (1999): 317.

Lundbom, J. R. "Jeremiah 15,15–21 and the Call of Jeremiah." *SJOT* 9 (1995): 143–55.

———. "Rhetorical Structures in Jeremiah 1." *ZAW* 103 (1991): 193–210.

Noegel, S. B. "*Atbash* in Jeremiah and Its Literary Significance." *The Jewish Bible Quarterly* 24 (1996): 160–66, 247–50.

O'Connor, K. M. "The Tears of God and Divine Character in Jeremiah 2–9." In *God in the Fray: A Tribute to Walter Brueggemann,* edited by T. Linafelt and T. K. Beal, 172–85. Minneapolis: Fortress, 1998.

Olson, D. C. "Jeremiah 4:5–31 and Apocalyptic Myth." *JSOT* 73 (1997): 81–107.

Olyan, S. M. " 'To Uproot and to Pull Down, to Build and to Plant': Jer 1:10 and Its Earliest Interpreters." In *Hesed ve-emet: Studies in Honor of Ernest S. Frerichs,* edited by J. Magness and S. Gitan, 63–72. Atlanta: Scholars Press, 1998.

Rudman, D. "Creation and Fall in Jeremiah x 12–16." *VT* 48 (1998): 63–73.

Scheffler, E. "The Holistic Historical Background against Which Jeremiah 7:1–5 Makes Sense." *OTE* 7 (1994): 381–95.

Shields, M. E. "Circumcision of the Prostitute: Gender, Sexuality, and the Call to Repentance in Jeremiah 3:1–4:4." *Biblical Interpretation* 3 (1995): 61–74.

———. "Circumscribing the Prostitute: The Rhetorics of Intertextuality, Metaphor, and Gender in Jeremiah 3:1–4:4." Ph.D. diss., Emory University, 1996.

Smit, J. H. "War-Related Terminology and Imagery in Jeremiah 15:10–21." *OTE* 11 (1998): 105–14.

Smith, M. S. *The Laments of Jeremiah and Their Contexts: A Literary and Redactional Study of Jeremiah 11–20.* Atlanta: Scholars Press, 1990.

Snyman, S. D. "Divine and Human Violence and Destruction in Jeremiah 20:7–13." *Acta Theologica* 19 (1999): 99–112.

———. "A Note on *pth* and *ykl* in Jeremiah XX 7–13." *VT* 48 (1998): 559–63.

———. "The Portrayal of Yahweh in Jeremiah 20:7–13." *Hervormd Teologiese Studies* 55 (1999): 176–82.

Steiner, R. C. "A Colloquialism in Jer. 5:13: From the Ancestor of Mishnaic Hebrew." *JSS* 37 (1992): 11–26.

———. "Incomplete Circumcision in Egypt and Edom: Jeremiah (9:24–25) in Light of Josephus and Jonckheere." *JBL* 119 (1999): 497–505.

Swart, I. "'Because Every Time I Speak, I Must Shout It Out, I Cry—"Violence and Oppression!"': The Polyvalent Meaning of חמס ושד in Jeremiah 20:8," *OTE* 7 (1994): 193–204.

Thelle, R. "דרש את־יהוה: The Prophetic Act of Consulting YHWH in Jeremiah 21,2 and 37,7." *SJOT* 12 (1998): 249–56.

van der Wal, A. J. O. "Jeremiah ii 31: A Proposal." *VT* 41 (1991): 360–63.

Wessels, W. J. "The Fallibility and Future of Leadership according to Jeremiah 23:1–4." *OTE* 6 (1993): 330–8.

Youngblood, R. "The Call of Jeremiah." *Criswell Theological Review* 5 (1990–91): 99–108.

Jeremiah 26–45

Becking, B. "Baalis, the King of the Ammonites: An Epigraphical Note on Jeremiah 40:14." *JSS* 38 (1993): 15–24.

———. "Jeremiah's Book of Consolation: A Textual Comparison. Notes on the Masoretic Text and the Old Greek Version of Jeremiah xxx–xxxi." *VT* 44 (1994): 145–69.

———. "Text-Internal and Text-External Chronology in Jeremiah 31:31–34." *Svensk Exegetisk Årsbok* 61 (1996): 33–51.

———. "The Times They Are A-Changing: An Interpretation of Jeremiah 30,12–17." *SJOT* 12 (1998): 3–25.

Berlyn, P. J. "Baruch Ben-Neriah: The Man Who Was Not a Prophet." *The Jewish Bible Quarterly* 25 (1997): 150–61.

Boyle, B. "Narrative as Ideology: Synchronic (Narrative Critical) and Diachronic Readings of Jeremiah 37–38." *Pacifica* 12 (1999): 293–312.

Bozak, B. A. *Life "Anew": A Literary-Theological Study of Jer. 30–31.* Rome: Pontifical Institute, 1991.

Brueggemann, W. "A 'Characteristic' Reflection on What Comes Next (Jeremiah 32.16–44)." In *Prophets and Paradigms: Essays in Honor of Gene M. Tucker,* edited by S. B. Reid, JSOTSup 229, 16–32. Sheffield: Sheffield Academic Press, 1996.

———. "The 'Baruch Connection': Reflections on Jer 43:1–7." *JBL* 113 (1994): 405–20.

Chavel, S. "'Let My People Go!': Emancipation, Revelation, and Scribal Activity in Jeremiah 34,8–14." *JSOT* 76 (1997): 71–95.

Cox, D. E. "The Book of Jeremiah: Jeremiah 30:5–31:22 and the Jeremiah Tradition." Ph.D. diss., St. Andrews University, 1993.

Dearman, J. A. "My Servants the Scribes: Composition and Context in Jeremiah 36." *JBL* 109 (1990): 403–21.

Heyns, D. "History and Narrative in Jeremiah 32." *OTE* 7 (1994): 261–76.

Hoffman, Y. "Aetiology, Redaction, and Historicity in Jeremiah xxxvi." *VT* 46 (1996): 179–89.

Huffmon, H. B. "The Impossible: God's Words of Assurance in Jer. 31:35–37." In *On the Way to Nineveh: Studies in Honor of George M. Landes,* edited by S. L. Cook and S. C. Winter, 172–86. Atlanta: Scholars Press, 1999.

Kessler, M. "The Judgment-Promise Dialectic in Jeremiah 26–36." *Amsterdamse Cahiers* 16 (1997): 60–72.

Knights, C. H. "Jeremiah 35 in the Book of Jeremiah." *ExpT* 109 (1997–98): 207–8.

———. "The Rechabites of Jeremiah 35: Forerunners of the Essenes?" *Journal for the Study of the Pseudepigrapha* 10 (1992): 81–87.

———. "'Standing Before Me for Ever': Jeremiah 35:19." *ExpT* 108 (1996–97): 40–42.

———. "The Structure of Jeremiah 35." *ExpT* 106 (1994–95): 142–44.

Leene, H. "Jeremiah 31,23–26 and the Redaction of the Book of Comfort." *ZAW* 104 (1992): 348–64.

Lust, J. "The Diverse Text Forms of Jeremiah and History Writing with Jer. 33 as a Test Case." *JNSL* 20 (1994): 31–48.

McKane, W. "Jeremiah 30,1–3, Especially 'Israel.'" In *The Scriptures and the Scrolls: Studies in Honour of A. S. van der Woude on the Occasion of His Sixty-fifth Birthday,* edited by F. G. Martínez and C. J. Labuschagne, VTSup 49, 65–73. Leiden: Brill, 1992.

Pettigrew, L. D. "The New Covenant." *The Master's Seminary Journal* 10 (1999): 251–70.

Renkema, J. "A Note on Jeremiah xxviii 5." *VT* 47 (1997): 253–55.

Sawyer, D. F. "Gender-Play and Sacred Text: A Scene from Jeremiah." *JSOT* 83 (1999): 99–111.

Schart, A. "Combining Prophetic Oracles in Mari Letters and Jeremiah 36." *JANES* 23 (1995): 75–93.

Sharp, C. J. "'Take Another Scroll and Write': A study of the LXX and the MT of Jeremiah's Oracles against Egypt and Babylon." *VT* 47 (1997): 487–516.

Shead, A. G. "Jeremiah 32 in Its Hebrew and Greek Recensions." *TynB* 50 (1999): 318–20.

Smelik, K. A. "Letters to the Exiles: Jeremiah in Context." *SJOT* 10 (1996): 282–95.

Sweeney, M. A. "Jeremiah 30–31 and King Josiah's Program of National Restoration and Religious Reform." *ZAW* 108 (1996): 569–83.

van der Kooij, A. "Jeremiah 27:5–15: How Do MT and LXX Relate to Each Other?" *JNSL* 20 (1994): 59–78.

van der Wal, A. J. O. "Themes from Exodus in Jeremiah 30–31." In *Studies in the Book of Exodus,* edited by M. Vervenne, 559–66. Louvain: Peeters, 1996.

van Heerden, W. "Preliminary Thoughts on Creativity and Biblical Interpretation with Reference to Jeremiah 30:12–17." *OTE* 6 (1993): 339–50.

Weaver, J. D. "Making Yahweh's Rule Visible." In *Peace and Justice Shall Embrace—Power and Theopolitics in the Bible: Essays in Honor of Millard Lind,* edited by T. Grimsrud and L. L. Johns, 34–48. Telford, Pa.: Pandora, 1999.

Yates, G. E. "'The People Have Not Obeyed': A Literary and Rhetorical Study of Jeremiah 26–45." Ph.D. diss., Dallas Theological Seminary, 1998.

Jeremiah 46–52

Bellis, A. O. *The Structure and Composition of Jeremiah 50:2–51:58.* Lewiston, N.Y.: Mellen, 1995.

Gershenson, D. E. "A Greek Myth in Jeremiah." *ZAW* 108 (1996): 192–200.

Jackson, J. J. "Jeremiah 46: Two Oracles on Egypt." *Horizons in Biblical Theology* 15 (1993): 136–44.

McKane, W. "Jeremiah's Instructions to Seraiah (Jeremiah 51:59–64)." In *Pomegranates and Golden Bells: Studies in Biblical, Jewish, and Near Eastern Ritual, Law, and Literature in Honor of Jacob Milgrom,* edited by D. P. Wright et al., 697–706. Winona Lake, Ind.: Eisenbrauns, 1995.

Reimer, D. J. *The Oracles against Babylon in Jeremiah 50–51: A Horror among the Nations.* San Francisco: Mellen Research University Press, 1993.

Watts, J. W. "Text and Redaction in Jeremiah's Oracles against the Nations." *CBQ* 54 (1992): 432–47.

Bibliography (Lamentations)

Commentaries

Hillers, D. R. *Lamentations.* AB. Garden City, N.Y.: Doubleday, 1972.

Huey, F. B., Jr. *Jeremiah, Lamentations.* NAC. Nashville: Broadman Holman, 1993.

Provan, I. *Lamentations*. NCB. Grand Rapids: Eerdmans, 1991.

Renkema, J. *Lamentations*. Translated by B. Doyle. Louvain: Peeters, 1998.

Recent Studies

Dobbs-Allsopp, F. W. "Tragedy, Tradition, and Theology in the Book of Lamentations." *JSOT* 74 (1997): 29–60.

Fretz, M. J. H. "Lamentations and Literary Ethics: A New Perspective on Biblical Interpretation." Ph.D. diss., University of Michigan, 1993.

Gous, I. G. P. "Exiles and the Dynamics of Experiences of Loss: The Reaction of Lamentations 2 on the Loss of Land." *OTE* 6 (1993): 351–63.

———. "Mind over Matter: Lamentations 4 in the Light of the Cognitive Sciences." *SJOT* 19 (1996): 69–87.

Guest, D. "Hiding behind the Naked Women in Lamentations: A Recriminative Response." *Biblical Interpretation* 7 (1999): 413–48.

Heater, H., Jr. "Structure and Meaning in Lamentations." *BSac* 149 (1992): 304–15.

Helberg, J. L. "Land in the Book of Lamentations." *ZAW* 102 (1990): 372–85.

Hunter, J. *Faces of a Lamenting City: The Development and Coherence of the Book of Lamentations*. Frankfurt am Main: Lang, 1996.

Joyce, P. "Lamentations and the Grief Process: A Psychological Reading." *Biblical Interpretation* 1 (1993): 304–20.

Krašovec, J. "The Source of Hope in the Book of Lamentations." *VT* 42 (1992): 223–33.

Miller, C. W. "Poetry and Personae: The Use and Functions of the Changing Speaking Voices in the Book of Lamentations." Ph.D. diss., Iliff School of Theology, 1996.

Neusner, J. *Israel after Calamity: The Book of Lamentations*. Valley Forge, Pa.: Trinity Press International, 1995.

Provan, I. "Feasts, Booths, and Gardens (Thr 2,6a)." *ZAW* 102 (1990): 254–55.

———. "Past, Present, and Future in Lamentations iii 52–66: The Case for a Precative Perfect Re-examined." *VT* 41 (1991): 164–75.

———. "Reading Texts against an Historical Background: The Case of Lamentations 1." *SJOT* 1 (1990): 130–43.

Renkema, J. "The Meaning of the Parallel Acrostics in Lamentations." *VT* 45 (1995): 379–83.

Reyburn, A. D. *A Handbook on Lamentations*. New York: United Bible Societies, 1992.

Saebø, M. "Who Is 'the Man' in Lamentations 3? A Fresh Approach to the Interpretation of the Book of Lamentations." In *Understanding Poets and Prophets: Essays in Honour of George Wishart Anderson,* edited by A. G. Auld, JSOTSup 152, 294–306. Sheffield: JSOT, 1993.

Salters, R. B. "Searching for Pattern in Lamentations." *OTE* 11 (1998): 93–104.

———. "Using Rashi, Ibn Ezra, and Joseph Kara on Lamentations." *JNSL* 25 (1999): 201–13.

Westermann, C. *Lamentations: Issues and Interpretation*. Translated by C. Muenchow. Minneapolis: Fortress, 1994.

Ezekiel

Introduction

Ezekiel received his prophetic call in July 593 B.C., approximately four years after the deportation of King Jehoiachin of Judah in 597 (see 1:2).[1] His prophetic ministry continued until at least 571 B.C. (see 29:17). If the phrase "the thirtieth year" in 1:1 refers to Ezekiel's age, he was born in 623.[2] Ezekiel was apparently taken to Mesopotamia in 597 (note the expression "our exile" in 40:1), where he lived in a community of fellow exiles near the city of Nippur.[3] Ezekiel was from a priestly family (1:3), though it is not clear if he actually served in the Jerusalem temple prior to his exile. His priestly background probably explains his interest in the temple and the sacrificial system.

The Book of Ezekiel may be divided into three major sections. Chapters 1–24 focus on the impending destruction of Jerusalem, while chapters 25–32 contain judgment oracles against several of the surrounding nations. The tone of the prophecy shifts in chapters 33–48, which anticipate reconciliation between God and Israel, as well as the return of the exiles.

Sin and Judgment (Ezekiel 1–24)

God Commissions Ezekiel (1:1–3:27)

The first three chapters of the book record Ezekiel's prophetic call. He first sees a magnificent vision of the Lord's royal splendor (chapter 1) as a prelude to his formal commissioning (chapters 2–3).

---

1. See Moshe Greenberg, *Ezekiel 1–20,* AB (Garden City, N.Y.: Doubleday, 1983), 8–10.
2. However, the significance of this chronological note is unclear. See Leslie C. Allen, *Ezekiel 1–19,* WBC (Dallas, Word, 1994), 20–21.
3. Greenberg, *Ezekiel 1–20,* 40.

Ezekiel Sees God's Glory (1:1–28)

Ezekiel's inaugural vision occurred in July 593 B.C., near the Kebar Canal (vv. 1–3). This elaborate vision began with a windstorm coming from the north, accompanied by a large cloud and a blazing fire, from which emanated a brilliant glow (v. 4). The imagery, which is rooted in the theophanies of the Hebrew Bible, signals the arrival of God.[4] Emerging from the fire were four "living creatures," each of which possessed a human form, four faces (that of a man, a lion, an ox, and an eagle), four wings, calflike feet, and human hands beneath their wings (vv. 5–8, 10). Each had two wings spread upward, while the other two covered the body (v. 11). The creatures proceeded straight ahead in unison, without having to wheel around (vv. 9, 12).[5] They glowed like fire and moved back and forth with the speed of lightning (vv. 13–14).

Though the description of these creatures may seem bizarre to the modern reader, their appearance would have been familiar to Ezekiel and his contemporaries. Ancient Near Eastern sculpture contains very similar images of part-human, part-animal creatures that serve as throne bearers and sky bearers.[6] Ezekiel's vision is a classic example of contextualization; God accommodates his divine self-revelation to the cultural situation in which his people find themselves.

As Ezekiel looked closer, he noticed a wheel beside each of the creatures (v. 15). Each of the four wheels sparkled and had high rims (vv. 16, 18). The reference in verse 16b to "a wheel intersecting a wheel" has puzzled interpreters. Some envision concentric rims, while others propose "a globe-like structure in which two wheels stand at right angles."[7] The wheels' capacity to change directions without turning (v. 17) favors the latter proposal. The wheels moved along with the creatures, which in turn followed the lead of "the spirit" that energized them (vv. 19–21; see as well v. 12).

Further attention to detail reveals that the creatures and their wheels function as the chariot of God. With half their wings the creatures held up a sparkling, transparent platform (v. 22). They used the remaining wings to propel themselves (v. 23). The sound of their wings was deafening, like the roar of waves, the tumult of an army, or the voice of God (v. 24). The prophet heard a voice coming from above the platform (v. 25). When he looked up, he saw a sapphire throne, on which was seated a human figure (v. 26). From the waist up he looked like glowing metal; from the waist

4. See Jeffrey J. Niehaus, *God at Sinai: Covenant and Theophany in the Bible and Ancient Near East* (Grand Rapids: Zondervan, 1995), 255–56. On the possible meteorological background of the windstorm from the north, see Greenberg, *Ezekiel 1–20*, 42–43.

5. Greenberg, *Ezekiel 1–20*, 45.

6. Allen, *Ezekiel 1–19*, 26–31. For a discussion of extrabiblical parallels in general, see D. N. Freedman and M. O'Connor, "כְּרוּב," *TDOT* 7:314–18.

7. Allen, *Ezekiel 1–19*, 33–34.

down his appearance was like fire (v. 27a). Around him was a bright light that was as impressive in appearance as a rainbow against the background of storm clouds (vv. 27b–28a). Recognizing that he was witnessing the glory of God, the prophet fell on his face (v. 28b).

God Calls Ezekiel to Be a Prophet (2:1–3:27)

The Lord addressed Ezekiel with the words "son of man," an idiom that simply means "human one." This designation distinguished him from the supernatural creatures that were present. When the Lord commanded him to stand, Ezekiel may have been inclined to remain on his face, but a "spirit" empowered him and raised him up (2:1–2).[8] Some see this "spirit" as an impersonal "spirit" of vigor or courage.[9] Others identify it with the spirit that energized the living creatures.[10] However, the spirit that energized the creatures is specifically called "the spirit" (*haruakh;* see 1:12, 20a) or "the spirit of the living creatures" (1:20b–21; see also 10:17). It is possible that the Lord's personal Spirit is the referent, but the absence of the article makes this unlikely. Elsewhere in Ezekiel the Lord's Spirit is referred to as "the Spirit of the Lord" (11:5; 37:1), "the Spirit of God" (11:24) or "my (i.e., the Lord's) Spirit" (36:27; 37:14; 39:29). It is more likely that the term refers in 2:2 to a wind sent from God closely associated with the invigorating life's breath that originates with him. The Hebrew word often refers to a wind in the Book of Ezekiel (see 1:4; 5:10, 12; 12:4; 13:11, 13; 17:10, 21; 19:12; 27:26; 37:9). In Ezekiel 37:5–10 a "breath" (Heb. *ruakh*) originates in the "four winds" (Heb. *rukhot*) and is associated with the Lord's Spirit, or life-giving breath (v. 14). This breath or wind enters into the dry bones and renews their life (v. 5). In the same way this wind/life-giving breath enters into the all-but-paralyzed Ezekiel (2:2; 3:24) and enables him to move. Furthermore, this is not the only place where a "spirit" is associated with the prophet's physical movement. In several texts it transports him from one place to another (3:12, 14; 8:3; 11:1, 24; 43:5).

At this point the Lord gave Ezekiel his formal commission as a prophet. The Lord could not guarantee that the rebellious and stubborn people would listen to Ezekiel, but whether they responded positively or not, they would know that a prophet had been among them (vv. 3–5). Though the opposition would be fierce, Ezekiel was to proclaim the word of the Lord fearlessly (vv. 6–8a).

As a vivid reminder of his commission, the Lord commanded his new prophet to eat a scroll containing messages of doom and destruction (2:8b–3:2). Surprisingly, when the prophet ate the scroll, it tasted sweet in his mouth, despite its contents (3:3). The point of the vision seems to be

---

8. NIV has "the Spirit," but the Hebrew text has simply *ruakh,* "[a] spirit," with no article prefixed to the word.

9. See, for example, Greenberg, *Ezekiel 1–20,* 62.

10. See, for example, Allen, *Ezekiel 1–19,* 38.

twofold: God's word would sustain the prophet in his dangerous mission, and his mission, though one of proclaiming judgment, would ironically bring him satisfaction, for he would serve as God's spokesman, a task that brings delight (see Jer. 15:16).

The Lord made it clear to Ezekiel that his mission would be difficult. One might think the task would be simple, for the Lord was sending Ezekiel to his own people, not foreigners who spoke another language (vv. 4–6a). However, in contrast to the pagans, who would have responded positively to God's word, Israel was obstinate (vv. 6b–7). To stand up to them one needed an extra measure of fortitude and resolve. The Lord would give Ezekiel the courage and determination he needed to confront such hostile people (vv. 8–9). Whether they listened or not, Ezekiel must carry out his mission (vv. 10–11).

At this point Ezekiel felt a mighty wind lifting him up and heard the Lord's living chariot moving (vv. 12–13).[11] Energized by God, the prophet found himself among the exiles at Tel Abib near the Kebar Canal (vv. 14–15a).[12] Emotionally overwhelmed by all he had seen and heard, he sat silently among them for one week (v. 15b).

After a week of sitting in numbed silence, Ezekiel received a message from the Lord (vv. 16–17). The Lord explained that Ezekiel's job was to warn sinners of the consequences of disobedience. If the Lord announced that a wicked man would be punished, Ezekiel must warn the sinner and try to convince him to repent. If the prophet failed to to do so, the Lord would hold him accountable for the sinner's death (v. 18). On the other hand, if Ezekiel did warn the man, he would not be held accountable for the unrepentant sinner's death (v. 19). In the same way, if a righteous man turned to evil, Ezekiel must warn him about the consequences. If he failed to do so, he would be held accountable for the man's death (v. 20). On the other hand, if the man turned back to God, Ezekiel would have saved both the sinner and himself (v. 21).

The Lord then instructed Ezekiel to go out to the Euphrates plain for further instructions (v. 22). When he arrived there, he once more saw the

---

11. NIV translates Hebrew *ruakh* as "the Spirit" in vv. 12, 14, but it is more likely that a powerful God-sent wind is in view. See my earlier comments on 2:2, as well as Greenberg, *Ezekiel 1–20*, 70, and Paul Joyce, *Divine Initiative and Human Response in Ezekiel* (Sheffield: JSOT, 1989), 110, 161 n. 11.

12. Verse 14 is traditionally understood to mean that Ezekiel felt "bitterness" and "anger." If this interpretation is sustained, then these feelings probably reflect God's attitude toward sinful Israel or the prophet's own feelings about the prospects of carrying out such a difficult task. See Greenberg, *Ezekiel 1–20*, 71, and Daniel I. Block, *The Book of Ezekiel Chapters 1–24*, NICOT (Grand Rapids: Eerdmans, 1997), 136–37. For a different understanding of the text, see Allen, *Ezekiel 1–19*, 13, who suggests that *mar*, "bitterness," may be a misplaced marginal note, and that *khemah*, usually understood as "anger," refers here to passion or fervor. Perhaps the term *mar* should be understood in the sense of "strengthened" or "empowered." The root *mrr* in Semitic languages can carry the sense "strong." See Cyrus Gordon, *Ugaritic Textbook* (Rome: Pontifical Biblical Institute, 1965), 438–39. Gibson, in his treatment of the Ugaritic *mr*, "be strengthened, fortified, blessed," suggests this nuance for Hebrew *mar* in Ezek. 3:14. See J. C. L. Gibson, *Canaanite Myths and Legends*, 2d ed. (Edinburgh: T. & T. Clark, 1978), 152.

Lord's glory and fell to the ground (v. 23). Again a powerful force (perhaps a wind or an invigorating breath; see 2:2) raised him to his feet (v. 24a). The Lord instructed him to go inside his house (v. 24b), where he would be tied up and prevented from going out among the people (v. 25). The Lord would paralyze Ezekiel's tongue so that he could not rebuke the sinful people (v. 26). However, at appropriate times of God's own choosing, he would loosen the prophet's tongue and speak through him (v. 27). It is uncertain who would tie Ezekiel up. Some suggest his enemies did this, but this is unlikely, for prior to this Ezekiel hardly had time to preach and alienate the people to the point where they would put him under house arrest. It is more likely that these verses describe a period of divinely imposed silence bringing the period of his commissioning to a conclusion. In this case the binding of the prophet was a symbolic act that he himself would have instructed others to perform.[13]

Object Lessons (4:1–5:17)

Ezekiel's ministry began with two object lessons that the prophet was to act out. The first depicts the siege of Jerusalem (chapter 4), while the second envisions the destruction and exile of God's people (chapter 5).

The Siege of Jerusalem (4:1–17)

The Lord instructed Ezekiel to draw a map or picture of Jerusalem on a brick (v. 1). The prophet was then to construct miniature siege works and to place them around the brick (v. 2). Next he was to take an iron pan, to set it up as a wall between himself and the brick, and to gaze toward the brick (v. 3). These items and actions were a "sign" to Israel. The pan symbolized the barrier that existed between God and his people, while the prophet's steady gaze depicted the Lord's determination to judge the city (see v. 7).

The object lesson was not finished. Ezekiel was to lie on his left side. Just as his left side bore the full weight of his body, so the people of Israel were weighed down by their sin (v. 4). Ezekiel was to go through this ritual for 390 successive days, representing the 390 years during which the people had been weighed down by sin (v. 5). If one counts backward 390 years from 593 B.C., the apparent date of the prophecy (see 1:2), one arrives at the year 983 B.C., which was during the reign of David. It is not clear how that date would mark the beginning of a period of sin. Obviously perplexed by the figure, the Septuagint reads "190" instead of "390." It apparently understands the period as extending from the time of Israel's exile in 722 B.C. until the return from exile in 538 B.C., a period of 184 (roughly 190) years. In this case the Hebrew term 'awon, translated "sin" in NIV, must be taken in its well-attested sense of "punishment."

13. See John B. Taylor, *Ezekiel*, TOTC (Downers Grove, Ill.: InterVarsity, 1969), 72–73.

Next the prophet was to turn on his right side and in so doing symbol-ically to "bear the sin of the house of Judah" (v. 6). He was to perform this ritual for forty days, representing forty years. Presumably these forty years corresponded to the time period in which Judah had sinned. Once again it is difficult to pinpoint the exact period that is envisioned. If one counts backward from 593 B.C., one arrives at 633 B.C., but it not clear how that date would mark the beginning of a period of sin, for Judah had often re-belled against the Lord prior to this. For this reason some prefer to see the forty years as looking ahead and as representing a period of punishment cor-responding to Judah's exile. If one begins the period in 586, when Jerusalem fell, moving ahead forty years places one in 546, just eight years before the return from exile. Since the exile actually lasted forty-eight years (586–538), one might have expected the number fifty, but forty may have been em-ployed because of its association with the wilderness wandering (see Amos 2:10) and because it was used idiomatically to indicate a generation (see Ezek. 29:11–12).

While lying on his side, Ezekiel was to face his model of the siege of Je-rusalem, to lay bare his arm, and to prophesy against the city (v. 7). The bared arm symbolizes the Lord's intention to come as a warrior and to judge the city. To facilitate Ezekiel's sign act, the Lord himself would tie the prophet up so that he would not be able to roll over to his other side (v. 8). One should not assume that the prophet remained on his side throughout each of the 430 days. He apparently carried out the prescribed ritual for an unspecified period of time each day.

During the 390-day period in which Ezekiel was to lie on his left side, he was to make bread according to a divinely prescribed recipe. He was to eat eight ounces of this bread and drink two-thirds of a quart of water each day at a specified time (vv. 9–11). This meager diet pictured the siege con-ditions which Jerusalem would endure, when food and water would be scarce (vv. 16–17). The Lord instructed Ezekiel to bake the bread over a fire fueled by human excrement (v. 12). Since this would make one ritually un-clean (see Deut. 23:13–14), this object lesson symbolized how the people would be forced to eat ritually defiled food in exile (v. 13).

Up to this point Ezekiel had offered no objections to the Lord's difficult instructions, but the command to eat defiled food seemed unreasonable and unfair. He balked at the Lord's command, explaining that he had rigidly ob-served a ritually clean diet since his youth (v. 14). The Lord revised his in-structions and gave him permission to bake the bread over cow manure (v. 15), which was apparently ritually less offensive.

Destruction and Exile (5:1–17)

Ezekiel's next sign act required him to shave his head and beard and to divide it into three piles of equal weight (5:1). After Ezekiel completed the first sign act (see chapter 4), he was to burn one pile of his hair in the city, to strike the second pile with a sword, and to scatter the third pile to the wind (v. 2). These actions foreshadowed what would happen to the people of Jerusalem. A third would be destroyed by plague and famine within the city, another third would fall by the sword outside the city walls, and still another third would go into exile, where they would continue to suffer (v. 12). Fire (v. 2) was used to symbolize famine and plague (v. 12) because starvation and disease would be accompanied by fever (see Lam. 5:10). The judgment would be thorough; only a very few would escape. To illustrate this, Ezekiel took a few strands of hair from the third pile and put them in the folds of his garment, as if to symbolize that a few would escape (v. 3). But then he was to take some of these and throw them into the fire, symbolizing that even the exilic remnant that survived the judgment would not be entirely secure (v. 4).

Why would the judgment be so severe? From the Lord's perspective, Jerusalem was central among the nations and occupied a privileged position (v. 5). But her people rebelled against his covenantal demands and descended to a level of morality lower than that of the pagan nations around them (vv. 6–7). These sins are outlined in detail in chapter 22; here the Lord focuses on their idolatry (vv. 9a, 11). Because Jerusalem's sins exceeded those of the nations, the Lord would publicly humiliate her in the sight of the nations (v. 8). The Lord would inflict unprecedented punishment upon her (v. 9b), prompting the nations to taunt her (vv. 14–15). He would send famine upon her, causing her starving residents to resort to cannibalistic practices (vv. 10, 16). Wild beasts, unable to find food in their natural habitat, would invade the city and prey on children (v. 17). The judgments outlined in this chapter recall the covenant curses threatened in Leviticus 26 (cf. v. 10 with Lev. 26:29; v. 12 with Lev. 26:33; v. 14 with Lev. 26:31; and v. 17 with Lev. 26:22).[14] Once the curses were implemented, the anger of the covenant Lord would subside (v. 13).

Prophecies of Judgment (6:1–7:27)

Chapters 6–7 contain two prophecies of judgment that reiterate the message conveyed by the object lessons of chapters 4–5. Each is introduced with the formulaic statement, "the word of the LORD came to me." The focus of the first speech (chapter 6) is God's judgment upon the land's idolatrous worship centers. The second speech (chapter 7) describes the devastation that would accompany the day of the Lord.

Smashing the High Places (6:1–14)

The people of Judah set up worship centers for their foreign gods throughout the land. Here the Lord announced that he would destroy these "high

14. For a chart showing the verbal and thematic parallels between Leviticus 26 and Ezekiel 4–6, see Allen, *Ezekiel 1–19,* 94.

places," which were elevated platforms containing sacrificial altars (6:1–3). He would smash the altars to pieces, litter the site with the corpses of the worshipers, and scatter their remains on the altars (vv. 4–6, 13). The people would be forced to recognize that he is Yahweh (NIV, "the LORD") (v. 7; see also vv. 10, 13–14). Though the judgment would be devastating (vv. 11–14), the Lord would spare a remnant (v. 8). Scattered among the nations, they would come to their senses, remember the Lord, and deeply regret their former sins (v. 9). They would also be forced to acknowledge Yahweh, who does not make idle threats when confronting his people's rebellion (v. 10).

The expression "you/they will know that I am Yahweh" occurs frequently in Ezekiel, indicating that it is a particularly important theme in the prophet's message.[15] What is the significance of Yahweh being recognized? The name Yahweh (meaning "he is" or "he will be") originally highlighted the fact that he would be with his people as their deliverer and protector (see Exod. 3:12–15). In Exodus the expression "you will know that I am Yahweh" is used in contexts that highlight Yahweh's commitment to his people (6:7; 29:46) and his sovereign power, which enables him to deliver and protect them (7:17; 10:2; 16:12). Subsequent usage (outside of Ezekiel) highlights these same themes (see Deut. 29:6; 1 Kings 20:13, 28; Isa. 49:23; Joel 3:17). In the time of Ezekiel, the people had forgotten who Yahweh is and had turned their backs on him. Despite the fact that Yahweh had rescued them from bondage and established a covenant with them, they had turned to other gods, presumably because of the benefits they believed these other gods could bestow upon them. They had to be reminded that it was Yahweh alone who deserved their exclusive worship, for it was Yahweh alone who possessed the sovereign power to meet their needs. Through judgment and eventually deliverance, God's people would be reminded that Yahweh was their covenantal Lord, the one who held their destiny in his hands.[16] They would be forced to acknowledge that the God of Moses was still alive, promising blessing in exchange for obedience, but also implementing the covenant curses against those who rejected his authority.

The Devastating Day of the Lord (7:1–27)

The Lord announced to the personified land of Israel that the "end" had come and judgment was imminent (7:1–3a, 5–7). He would exact punishment in fair measure, leaving no room for mercy (vv. 3b–4a, 8–9a). In the aftermath of judgment, the people would be forced to recognize the Lord's

---

15. In addition to the occurrences in chapter 6, see 7:4, 27; 11:10, 12; 12:15–16, 20; 13:14, 21, 23; 14:8; 15:7; 16:62; 20:38, 42, 44; 22:16; 24:27; 25:5, 7, 11, 17; 26:6; 28:22–23, 26; 29:9, 21; 30:8, 19, 25–26; 32:15; 33:29; 34:27; 35:4, 9, 15; 36:11, 38; 37:6, 13; 38:23; 39:6, 28.

16. Though it is usually judgment that prompts such recognition, the Lord's deliverance of his people also results in God's people recognizing that he is Yahweh. See 16:62; 20:38, 42, 44; 28:26; 29:21; 34:27; 36:11, 38; 37:6, 13; 39:28.

authority and power (vv. 4b, 9b; see 6:7–14).[17] Using the metaphor of a plant, the Lord explained that the people's injustice and pride were ready to bloom into the calamity of judgment (vv. 10–11).[18] The ordinary activities of life, such as buying and selling land, would be permanently disrupted (vv. 12–13). Though the watchman would sound the trumpet, signaling an impending battle, no defense would be offered (v. 14). Those outside the city would be cut down by the sword, while famine and plague would kill those inside its walls (v. 15). Any survivors would flee to the hills, moaning like doves over their destiny (v. 16). Fear would paralyze the people, who would be able to do nothing but put on sackcloth and mourn their demise (vv. 17–18).

In the "day of the LORD's wrath," their silver and gold jewelry, which they used to make idols, would be of no use (vv. 19–20). They would regard the riches they once valued as if they were a putrid, bloody menstrual rag (the more precise referent of the term *nidah*, translated by NIV as "unclean thing"). The Lord would hand their riches over to the foreign invaders, who would even desecrate the Lord's temple (vv. 21–22). The people had polluted the land with bloodshed; now the Lord would hand them over to foreigners so that they might experience the same kind of unbridled violence they had dished out to the poor and needy (vv. 23–24). As judgment drew closer, they would desperately try to dodge the inevitable (v. 25). But the prophets would have no encouraging visions, the priests would offer no moral direction, and the civil leaders would have no strategies (v. 26). A sense of fatalism would overtake everyone, from the king down to the common people (v. 27a). The Lord would give them what they deserved, demonstrating once again his sovereign authority and power as their covenant lord (v. 27b).

The Lord Leaves Town (8:1–11:25)

Ezekiel received a vision from the Lord in September 592 B.C. as he sat in his house in the presence of "the elders of Judah," probably a reference to those who had assumed a leadership role among the exiles.[19] Transported in his vision to Jerusalem, he saw the idolatry being practiced in the temple (chapter 8) and then witnessed the departure of God's glory from the temple and the city (chapters 9–11).

17. In vv. 3–4a, 6b, 8–9a, which are addressed to the "land of Israel" (see v. 2), the second-person pronouns are feminine singular (*'adamah*, "land," is a feminine noun in Hebrew), but in vv. 4b and 9b ("you will know") a second masculine plural form is used, indicating that the people are addressed.

18. In v. 10, the traditional Hebrew text reads "the rod has budded," but this is nonsensical. If the text is retained, then the term *matteh* should be understood as referring to the stem or branch of a plant (see its use in Ezek. 19:11–14). However, many prefer to revocalize Hebrew *matteh*, "the rod," to *mutteh*, "bending, perversion (of the law), injustice," a term that appears in 9:9. The emended form fits the poetic parallelism (note "arrogance" in the following line, and "violence" in v. 11a). The reading "rod" in v. 10 may have arisen under the influence of v. 11, in which the word "rod" appears as a metaphor of judgment.

19. The "sixth year" in 8:1 refers to the sixth year of Jehoiachin's exile. See 1:2.

Idolatry in the Temple (8:1–18)

Ezekiel again saw the fiery figure he encountered in his inaugural vision (8:1–2; see 1:26–27). According to 1:28, this figure was a manifestation of the glory of the Lord (see also 8:4). He grabbed Ezekiel by the hair, and a wind (see 2:2; 3:12, 14) swept the prophet away to Jerusalem (v. 3a). There, at the north gate of the temple's inner court, he saw an image, called "the idol that provokes to jealousy" (vv. 3b, 5). The term translated "idol" (Heb. *semel*) also appears in 2 Chronicles 33:7, 15, where it refers to an idol that Manasseh set up in the temple, probably the carved Asherah pole mentioned in 2 Kings 21:7. According to 2 Chronicles 33:15, Josiah removed this image from the temple and threw it outside the city, but by 592 B.C. it may have resurfaced in the temple area.

The Lord invited Ezekiel to look at the "detestable things" going on there and also gave notice that this idolatrous activity would force him to leave his own sanctuary (v. 6). The Lord then led Ezekiel closer to the entrance, where they spotted a hole in the wall (v. 7). In accordance with the Lord's instructions, Ezekiel dug into the wall, found a doorway, and went into the inner court (vv. 8–9). He saw inscribed on the walls the images of "all kinds of crawling things and detestable animals and all the idols of the house of Israel" (v. 10). The seventy elders of Israel offered incense to the false gods represented by the images (v. 11). These leaders were convinced the Lord did not see their actions, because they believed he had already abandoned the land (v. 12).

But Ezekiel had not yet seen the worst (vv. 13, 15). The Lord brought him out to the north gate of the temple's court, where he saw women mourning for Tammuz, a Mesopotamian god whose banishment to the underworld was lamented by his devotees (v. 14).[20] Moving back into the inner court, Ezekiel saw twenty-five men facing the east and bowing down to the sun (v. 16; cf. 2 Kings 23:5). Worship of the sun was widespread in the ancient Near East and was deeply rooted in Canaan.[21] In Israelite thought the sun was a member of the "host of heaven," which was viewed as the Lord's heavenly assembly (compare Deut. 4:19; 17:3; 2 Kings 23:5 with 1 Kings 22:19). This may explain why these men could worship the sun in the Lord's temple. Day explains: "The sun would thus have been considered part of the host of heaven, subordinate to Yahweh. As such one might argue that the worship of the sun in Yahweh's temple would have been seen by those who participated in it as, so to speak, all 'part of the package', just as Catholics

20. See Helmer Ringgren, *Religions of the Ancient Near East*, trans. J. Sturdy (Philadelphia: Westminster, 1973), 64–66; Greenberg, *Ezekiel 1–20*, 171; and Block, *Ezekiel Chapters 1–24*, 294–96.
21. See Ringgren, *Religions of the Ancient Near East*, 57–59, and John Day, *Yahweh and the Gods and Goddesses of Canaan* (Sheffield: Sheffield Academic Press, 2000), 152–54. Some argue that Yahweh was actually equated with the sun in the pagan thinking of this time. For a summary and refutation of this view, see Day, 156–61.

would regard veneration (not worship) of Mary as not being incompatible with worship of Christ."[22]

Idolatry was not Judah's only offense. Violence and social injustice also filled the land (v. 17). By worshiping idols the people had broken the first and second commandments of the Decalogue (Exod. 20:3–5) and violated the spirit of the command in Deuteronomy 6:5 to love the Lord. By oppressing the poor they had violated the commandment given in Leviticus 19:18 to love one's neighbor as oneself. According to Jesus, the essence of the law of Moses could be summarized in these two commandments (Matt. 22:36–40). Judah had thus broken the covenant at its most fundamental level. For this reason judgment was inevitable (v. 18).

The reference to the people "putting the branch to their nose" (v. 17b) has puzzled interpreters. Based on sculptural evidence from Mesopotamia, some suggest the gesture was a ritual associated with the worship of pagan gods, but the significance of the action remains uncertain.[23]

God's Glory Departs (9:1–11:25)

The Lord summoned "the guards of the city," each of whom had a weapon in his hand (9:1). In verse 2 they are simply called "six men" and are accompanied by another man dressed in linen and carrying a writing kit. His linen garments might suggest a priestly role (see Lev. 6:10; 16:4), but linen is also worn by angelic messengers in visionary literature (see Dan. 10:5; 12:6–7). At any rate, his primary task seems to be scribal. As for the "guards of the city," they are most likely angelic military personnel responsible for overseeing God's judgment of Jerusalem. The term used to describe them in verse 1 is used elsewhere of those given responsibility to oversee an assigned task (see Num. 3:2; 2 Chron. 24:11; Isa. 60:17; Ezek. 44:11).

As they stood before the bronze altar (v. 2b; see 1 Kings 8:64; 2 Kings 16:14), the glory of the Lord moved upward from his throne to the threshold of the temple (v. 3a). According to some interpreters, verse 3 describes the Lord's glory leaving the most holy place of the temple. In this case the cherubim are the ornamental ones within the temple, and the Lord's action shows he is ready to abandon his temple, just as he had indicated he would do (see 8:6). However, there is a problem with this view. Verse 3a reads literally, "And the glory of the God of Israel went up [or perhaps, "had gone up"] from the cherub." The singular form "cherub" is problematic since there were two cherubim ("cherubim" is the Hebrew plural form of the singular noun "cherub") in the most holy place.[24]

---

22. Day, *Yahweh and the Gods and Goddesses*, 158.

23. For a discussion of the evidence, see Allen, *Ezekiel 1–19*, 145–46; Block, *Ezekiel Chapters 1–24*, 299; and Greenberg, *Ezekiel 1–20*, 173. Greenberg doubts that the gesture should be associated with pagan worship in v. 17, for the first half of the verse deals with social injustice, not idolatry.

24. Allen (*Ezekiel 1–19*, 122, 147–48) translates the singular form "cherubim-structure," and sees it as referring to "a single, comprehensive entity," namely the "temple cherubim" which "formed a single structure."

It is more likely that the chariot throne described in chapter 1 is in view. In chapter 10 the living creatures who hold up and transport the throne are called cherubim (see especially 10:15, 20, which equate the living creatures with the cherubim). In 10:4 we are told, as in 9:3, that the glory of the Lord rose up from "the cherub" and moved to the temple threshold. Of course, it is problematic to identify the cherub of 9:3 with the living creatures/cherubim of chapter 10 since there were four of the latter. However, a close reading of 10:2, 7 appears to resolve this problem. In 10:2 the Lord instructs the scribe in linen to go beneath "the cherub" (singular, not plural as NIV translates) and fetch burning coals from among the cherubim (plural). In verse 7 "the cherub" (not "one of the cherubim" as NIV translates) reaches out its hand, takes the fire that is among the cherubim (plural), and gives it to the scribe. Both of these texts seem to indicate that there was another cherub in a central position beneath the throne, in addition to the four cherubim near the wheels (see 10:9). Perhaps Psalm 18:10 (see also 2 Sam. 22:11) has influenced the description, for it depicts the Lord riding a "cherub" (singular, contrary to NIV, which translates "cherubim" in both texts), which is viewed as birdlike and equated with the wind (note "wings of the wind" in the parallel line).[25] To summarize, the glory of the Lord was transported by four living creatures/cherubim who occupied positions near the four wheels of the chariot. Directly beneath the chariot was another cherub (called "the cherub" in 9:3 and 10:2, 4, 7). In 9:3, the Lord's glory, which was situated on a throne above the cherubim (cf. 1:26–27; 10:1), moved from his position directly above the central cherub to the temple threshold. Apparently having returned to his throne, the glory of the Lord made this same move in 10:4.

From his position at the temple threshold, the Lord instructed the scribe to go throughout the city and put a special mark on the foreheads of those who lamented over the idolatrous practices taking place in the city (vv. 3b–4). The word translated "mark" is Hebrew *tahv*, the name of the final letter of the Hebrew alphabet that, in Ezekiel's time, had the shape of an "X," or a cross. The Lord told the other six to follow the scribe through the city and mercilessly kill everyone, regardless of age or gender, who did not have the mark on his or her forehead (vv. 5–6a). As commanded by the Lord, they began by killing the elders who were in front of the temple and those who were worshiping within it (vv. 6b–7a). By littering the temple with corpses, they defiled it, making it unfit for worship. From there they moved out into the city and continued executing its residents (v. 7b).

The sight of such bloodshed was too much for Ezekiel to bear. He fell down before the Lord and asked if he intended to wipe out the entire population (v. 8). The Lord defended his actions by reminding his prophet that

---

25. As in Ezek. 10:2, burning coals are associated with the divine theophany in Ps. 18:8/2 Sam. 22:9.

the people themselves had filled the land with the shed blood of the innocent, so this judgment was only fitting (vv. 9–10). As the Lord finished
speaking, the scribe returned and announced that he had carried out the
Lord's command (v. 11). This apparent interruption of Ezekiel's dialogue
with the Lord should have reminded the prophet of the Lord's earlier command to the scribe. He was to mark all the righteous people, so that they
might be spared. The judgment, while merciless and severe, was at the same
time discriminating. A remnant would be spared.

At this point Ezekiel saw the sapphire throne that he had witnessed in
his inaugural vision (10:1; cf. 1:26). As before, it sat on a transparent platform supported by the living creatures (cf. 1:22), now referred to as cherubim (see vv. 15, 20, which specifically equate the "living creatures" of chapter 1 with these cherubim). According to Freedman and O'Connor, the term
"cherub" (plural "cherubim") "is a technical term for a class of hybrid beings" that "resemble birds, bipeds, and quadrupeds."[26]

The Lord instructed the man in linen (the scribe mentioned in chapter 9) to go to a spot beneath "the cherub" (see my earlier comments on 9:3)
between the wheels. Here he would find burning coals, which he was to scatter over the city, symbolizing its destruction (v. 2; see Gen. 19:24; Ps. 11:6;
140:10).

As the cherubim stood on the south side of the temple, a cloud symbolizing the Lord's glorious presence filled the temple's inner court, just as it had
done when Solomon dedicated the structure (v. 3; see 1 Kings 8:10–11). As
Niehaus observes, the scene is "sadly ironic." In Solomon's day, the Lord
came to bless his people with his presence, but now he would withdraw his
presence and abandon them to the curse of judgment.[27]

Once more the Lord's glory rose from his chariot throne directly above
"the cherub" and moved to the temple threshold (v. 4a; see 9:3). The radiance of his glory filled the sanctuary (v. 4b; see 1:27–28). At the same time
the cherubim flapped their wings, making a sound as loud as God's powerful voice (v. 5; see 1:24). Obeying the Lord's command (see v. 2), the man
in linen went under the chariot and stood by a wheel (v. 6). "The cherub"
(see 9:3; 10:2, 4) directly beneath the chariot gave him some of the fiery
coals (vv. 7–8).

Ezekiel again describes the appearance and movement of the wheels (vv.
9–11, 13; see 1:16–18) and tells us what the cherubim looked like (vv. 12,
14, 21–22; see 1:5–14). This description of the cherubim is not as detailed
as the earlier one, but it does provide one new bit of information. We now
discover that the cherubim, like the wheels, are filled with eyes. The description in verse 14 also differs from the earlier vision in one respect. Ac-

26. Freedman and O'Connor, "כְּרוּב," *TDOT* 7:318.
27. Niehaus, *God at Sinai*, 275.

cording to 1:10, the cherubim had the faces of a man, lion, ox, and eagle, but in 10:14 they have the faces of a cherub, man, lion, and eagle.[28] Some commentators suggest that a scribal error has occurred or that a cherub typically had the face of an ox. However, it is difficult to see how the Hebrew terms for "ox" (*shor*) and "cherub" (*kerub*) could be confused, and there is no evidence that the face of a cherub was typically that of an ox. On the contrary, the biblical evidence suggests a cherub's face was hybrid.

Suddenly the cherubim rose upward. As they did, the wheels of the chariot moved with them (vv. 16–17). The glory of the Lord left the temple threshold and assumed a position above the cherubim (v. 18). Apparently they came back to the ground near the east gate of the temple, for verse 19 describes them as once more rising from the ground.

The wind lifted Ezekiel up again and transported him to the east gate of the temple (11:1a; see 3:12, 14; 8:3). There he saw the twenty-five sun worshipers he had seen earlier in the inner court (v. 1b, cf. 8:16). The Lord accused them of making evil plans (v. 2). To prove his point, the Lord quotes their very words in verse 3, but unfortunately the precise meaning of their statement is not entirely clear. Some translate the first part of the statement as a rhetorical question, suggesting that they feel safe within the city and expect relief from the enemy threat. However, there is nothing in the Hebrew text that requires this to be a question. It is better taken as a descriptive statement, "It is not the time to build houses," perhaps suggesting that the proper policy was to strengthen the city's defenses. Another option is that the statement implies there is no need to build houses because they had already taken over the homes of those who had been exiled and because they had robbed others of their homes (see v. 6).[29]

The metaphorical statement in verse 3b probably expresses their high opinion of themselves. They thought they were the meat in the pot, while the scrap pieces had already gone into exile (cf. v. 15). They talked as if they were special, but the Lord knew their evil thoughts (vv. 4–5) and was aware of their murderous deeds (v. 6). As far as the Lord was concerned, the corpses of their victims were the meat in the pot (Jerusalem), and he would drive the murderers out of the city, where they would be cut down by the enemy's sword (vv. 7–10). God did not regard them as special. To use their own terms, they would not be the "meat" (special group) in the "pot" (Jerusalem) (v. 11a). They had violated the Lord's law, and they would pay dearly (vv. 11b–12).

As Ezekiel remained in a prophetic trance, Pelatiah son of Benaiah, one

---

28. Verse 14, which is omitted in the Septuagint, presents difficult textual problems. For a thorough discussion of the issues involved, see Allen, *Ezekiel 1–19*, 125–26, who suggests that the problem is as much redactional as textual. The problem is complicated by the fact that 10:22 says the faces of the cherubim had the same appearance as those of the living creatures described in chapter 1.

29. See Greenberg, *Ezekiel 1–20*, 187; Allen, *Ezekiel 1–19*, 160.

of the twenty-five men described earlier and a leader of the people (v. 1), died (v. 13a).[30] Though Pelatiah was an idolater, his death had a negative impact on the prophet, who once more asked if the Lord intended to wipe out "the remnant of Israel" (v. 13b; see 9:8). Because Pelatiah's name means "the Lord rescues," perhaps Ezekiel saw his death as an ironic and bad omen.[31]

The Lord responded to Ezekiel's lament with encouraging words. He pointed to the exilic community as the future hope of the nation. Those back in Jerusalem demeaned the exiles, thinking that they, not the exiles, were the heirs to the Promised Land (vv. 14–15). They apparently thought they had an edge on the exiles because of their access to the temple. The Lord had indeed scattered the exiles among the nations, but he had not abandoned them (v. 16a). He would be a "sanctuary" to them, even in the foreign countries where they lived (v. 16b). The metaphor indicates that one need not be in Jerusalem to have access to God's presence. God was not confined to his temple and could reveal his presence to whomever he desired, no matter where they happened to be living.

Furthermore, the Lord would someday restore the exiles to the Promised Land (v. 17). They would remove all the idols from the land, and the Lord would transform their hearts and spirits, enabling them to give him their undivided loyalty (vv. 18–19). The "heart" is viewed here as the seat of the will. At the present time they had a "heart of stone," that is, a dead heart (cf. 1 Sam. 25:37), an image suggesting they were stubborn and unresponsive. But the Lord would give them a "heart of flesh," that is a living, beating heart, an image suggesting responsiveness and life. With their inner nature transformed, the Lord's people would obey his commandments and would experience the ancient covenantal ideal, expressed in the statement, "They will be my people, and I will be their God" (v. 20, cf. Exod. 6:7). By way of contrast, the idolaters living in the land would experience the judgment they deserved (v. 21).

The Lord had announced that he would leave his sanctuary (8:6) and become a sanctuary for the exiles (11:16). The glory of the Lord had already moved from the temple threshold to the temple's east gate (10:18–19). Now that same glory leaves Jerusalem and hovers above the Mount of Olives, east of the city (vv. 22–23). The text does not describe the Lord leaving the area, though one might assume as much, in light of the statement in verse 16 and Isaiah's portrait of the Lord returning to Jerusalem with his exiled people

---

30. Presumably Ezekiel saw this in his vision. The statement "as I was prophesying" in v. 13 need not mean that Ezekiel was now relating his vision to the exiles in a formal manner. He does not do this until the vision ends (see vv. 24–25). "Prophesy" here refers to being in a prophetic trance (see 1 Sam. 10:11; 19:20). *HALOT,* 2:659, points out that the Hebrew term "does not just mean speaking," because several passages in Ezekiel have the expression "prophesy and say," which distinguishes prophesying from formal speech (see 21:9, 28; 30:2; 34:2; 36:1, 3, 6; 37:4, 9, 12; 38:14; 39:1).

31. See Allen, *Ezekiel 1–19,* 163.

(Isa. 40:1–11). At this point Ezekiel's vision ended, and the wind swept him
back to Babylon, where he told the exiles all he had seen (vv. 24–25).

Acting Out the Fall of Jerusalem (12:1–20)

The Lord reminded Ezekiel that his fellow exiles were rebellious people who
refused to see and hear the truth (vv. 1–2; see 2:5–8; 3:4–9). They needed
vivid object lessons to drive home the point of the prophetic message. They
thought Jerusalem would be delivered and that they would soon go home.
This faulty notion had to be corrected. The Lord told Ezekiel to pack his
bags like an exile might do and to bring them outside his house. Then in the
evening he was to pick up his belongings and walk away as if going into exile
(vv. 3–4). As the people watched him, he was to dig a hole through the town
wall (probably a clay wall is in view) and slip through with his bags in hand.
As he did so, he was to cover his face so that he could not see the land (vv.
5–6). Ezekiel did as instructed (v. 7).

Knowing that the people would ask Ezekiel about the meaning of his actions, the Lord explained to the prophet their significance (vv. 8–9). Ezekiel's
actions were a "sign," or object lesson, of what would transpire in Jerusalem
(vv. 10–11a; see v. 6b). The people would be taken into exile and scattered
among the the nations (vv. 11b, 15). Only a remnant would be spared
(v. 16). The prince of Jerusalem (probably a reference to King Zedekiah)
would try to sneak out of the city during the Babylonian siege (see 2 Kings
25:4). As he did so, he would cover his face, perhaps to disguise himself or
to express his grief and shame (cf. 2 Sam. 19:4) (v. 12). But the Lord would
trap him and send him into Babylonian exile (v. 13a; see 2 Kings 25:5a, 7).
The prince would lose his sight (see 2 Kings 25:7) and die in exile, while his
staff and troops would be hunted down (vv. 13b–14; see 2 Kings 25:5b).

Another object lesson was in order. Ezekiel was to tremble and shake
while he ate, as if he were afraid of something (vv. 17–18). In the same way,
the people living back in Jerusalem would eat in fear, realizing that their land
had been stripped clean and turned into a desolate ruin (vv. 19–20).

Messages about Prophecy and Prophets (12:21–14:11)

Back in Israel there was a popular saying which reflected the cynicism of the
people: "The days go by and every vision [a reference to prophetic visions
and messages] comes to nothing" (vv. 21–22). This may refer to prophecy in
general, including both the hopeful messages of the false prophets and the
messages of judgment by prophets like Jeremiah and Ezekiel, but the following context suggests that only the latter are in view.[32] The people accepted the messages of the false prophets as true (see chapter 13) but opposed God's true prophets. The Lord would put a stop to this. Soon the true

32. See Greenberg, *Ezekiel 1–20*, 230.

prophecies, warning of judgment, would come to pass, and the false prophets would be exposed (vv. 23–24). Many of the people thought the prophecies of doom applied to a far-off time (vv. 26–27), but the Lord would announce his intentions and then bring them to pass without delay (vv. 25, 28).

The Lord gave Ezekiel a message for the false prophets who were dreaming up prophecies (13:1–2). Their doom was certain (note "woe"), for these foolish prophets had the audacity to speak on the Lord's behalf when he had not revealed his word to them (vv. 3, 6–7). The interjection "ah" (sometimes translated "woe") was a cry of mourning heard at funerals (see 1 Kings 13:30; Jer. 22:18–19; Amos 5:16). By using it here the Lord suggested that the false prophets' funeral was imminent. They were like scavengers prowling around the ruins of the city, exploiting the situation for their own benefit (v. 4). They offered no genuine solution for the city's woes (v. 5), because they whitewashed the situation by promising peace (v. 10a) and failing to confront the people with their sin. It was as if they had erected a flimsy wall and covered it with whitewash (v. 10b). The Lord opposed these prophets and would exclude them from the covenant community (vv. 8–9). The rain of God's judgment would wash away their whitewash and the powerful wind of his anger would blow down their wall. The wall would collapse and destroy those who built it (vv. 11–16).

There were also women among the people who prophesied for a living (v. 19). They put homemade magic charms on their wrists and veils on their heads to look the part (v. 18). They too promised peace and by so doing discouraged those who had repented and encouraged sinners to persist in their evil ways (v. 22). The Lord opposed these prophets and announced their doom was certain (vv. 17–18; note "woe" in v. 18). The Lord would free his people from the magic spells of these fortune tellers (vv. 20–21, 23).

Some prophets cooperated with idolaters, but Ezekiel was to have nothing to do with such rebels. In 14:1, the prophet tells how some "elders of Israel" among the exilic community came to visit him. They were apparently seeking divine guidance or assurance about some plan or endeavor. However, the Lord revealed to Ezekiel that these men were not pure worshipers of God. They were actually syncretists, who attempted to worship the Lord while at the same time worshiping idol-gods (vv. 2–3). The Lord refused to tolerate such compromise. He told Ezekiel to warn them of the consequences of idolatry and call them to repentance (vv. 4–6).[33] Such idolaters would not receive the oracle they requested, but rather an "answer" from the Lord in the form of severe judgment (vv. 7–8).

---

33. Greenberg (*Ezekiel 1–20*, 250) argues that untimely death is the punishment in view. Perhaps the "answer" would consist of a prophetic announcement of judgment followed by the fulfillment of the divine word.

Verse 9 appears to describe a situation in which the Lord incites a prophet to cooperate with such idolaters and then judges him for his disobedience. But why would God incite someone to sin and then hold that individual accountable for his wrongdoing? What is one to make of this? The verb form (*piteti*) in verse 9 is usually translated as a present perfect, "I have enticed [or "deceived"]." In this case the Lord seems to be saying that he really is behind the deception mentioned in the first half of the verse. If we allow other texts describing divine deception to instruct us, it is possible this prophet's deception is a form of divine judgment on an underlying sin. Like the idolaters who come to him, he has a compromising spirit. Rather than denouncing their idolatry, as the Lord instructed Ezekiel to do (vv. 4–6), he is willing, for whatever reason, to give them an oracle. (This assumes that the prophet recognizes the idolaters as such.) In this case the Lord will deceive the prophet by giving him an oracle and then judge him for delivering it. If this scenario is correct, then the divine deception envisioned here, as in other texts, is an aspect of God's judgment on an underlying sin. When a prophet has a compromising spirit and wants to peek over the cliff of syncretism, the Lord will entice him to lean too far and then push him over with the rest of the crowd that is so enamored with idolatry.[34]

However, this is not the only option for understanding this verb. On the basis of the grammatical parallels in verses 4b and 7b–8, Allen argues for a future tense translation, "I will show him [that prophet] to be misled."[35] In this case the Lord is not deceiving the prophet. Rather he is showing through judgment that the prophet was self-deceived. Perhaps it would be even better to translate, "I will deceive that prophet." In this case the deception in verse 9a is distinct from the divine deception in the second half of the verse. When a prophet is enticed into compromising with idolaters, the Lord will then deceive him as part of his judgment upon him. The repetition of the verb "deceive" (translated "enticed" in NIV) highlights the appropriate nature of the punishment. When such idolaters and cooperating prophets are punished by God, the people will take notice, reject their sin, and return to the Lord (vv. 10–11).

Jerusalem's Doom Is Sure (14:12–23)

The Lord's next message emphasizes the inevitability of the coming judgment. Once the Lord determines to punish an unfaithful country for its sins, no one can deter him from carrying out his plan (vv. 12–20). Even if godly men were present in the land, the Lord would not spare the sinful nation for

34. Greenberg (*Ezekiel 1–20*, 254) appears to interpret the passage in this way. He writes, "Our passage ascribes the error of a prophet in responding to inquiry to divine misguidance. The obtuseness of the Israelites, including prophets, is culpable, and God punishes it by corrupting the spring of inspiration, leading inquirer and respondent alike to destruction."
35. See Allen, *Ezekiel 1–19*, 187, 193, 207–8.

their sake. He would spare the lives of the godly individuals, but everyone else would die, including the children of the godly.

To make his point more vivid, the Lord used three men as examples— Noah, Daniel, and Job (vv. 14, 20). Since Noah and Job were non-Israelite figures from the distant past, some find the reference to Daniel to be problematic. After all, Daniel was taken into exile in 605 B.C. and was still a young man at the time of Ezekiel's prophecy. By the end of his life he had become a paradigm of godliness, but one wonders if he had established such a reputation this soon. It is possible that the reference to Daniel is a later scribal addition dating to the postexilic period. In the apocryphal story of Susanna, Daniel appears as a wise judge whose insight saves the falsely accused heroine from death.

Another proposal is that the Daniel referred to here is not the Daniel of the Jewish exile, but the Daniel of Canaanite legend.[36] The latter (whose name is sometimes spelled Dan'el) is a major character in the Ugaritic legend of Aqhat, which depicts him as a just ruler who cares for the needs of widows and orphans.[37] This same individual may be referred to in Ezekiel 28:3, which seems to assume that the ruler of Tyre knew of him.[38] This view has the advantage of making all three of the individuals mentioned in Ezekiel 14:14, 20, non-Israelites. However, unlike Noah and Job, this Daniel is not mentioned elsewhere in the Bible, though a Daniel is mentioned in the intertestamental *Book of Jubilees* (4:20) as Enoch's uncle and father-in-law.[39] It is not clear what relationship, if any, the Daniel of *Jubilees* has to the Daniel of Canaanite legend. The major objection to identifying the Daniel of Ezekiel 14:14, 20 with the Canaanite Daniel is that the latter is portrayed in the Legend of Aqhat as a polytheistic worshiper of Baal.[40]

The principle outlined in verses 12–20 applied, of course, to Jerusalem (v. 21). The Lord had unleashed four instruments of judgment against it— sword (cf. v. 17), famine (cf. v. 13), wild beasts (cf. v. 15), and plague (cf. v. 19). Contrary to what one might have expected, some of the city's sons and daughters would be spared (v. 22a; contrast vv. 16, 18, 20). However, this is not as positive as it might initially seem. As these survivors arrived in the exilic community and the exiles saw their sinful behavior, they would be

36. See Walther Zimmerli, *Ezekiel 1,* trans. R. E. Clements, Hermeneia (Philadelphia: Fortress, 1979), 314–15.

37. See Gibson, *Canaanite Myths and Legends,* 103–22.

38. One should note that the name appearing in Ezek. 14:14, 20; 28:3 is spelled slightly differently in the Hebrew text than the name of the historical Daniel of the exile.

39. See James Charlesworth, ed., *The Old Testament Pseudepigrapha,* 2 vols. (Garden City, N.Y.: Doubleday, 1983–85), 2:62.

40. It is possible, as Taylor (*Ezekiel,* 129) suggests, "that ancient Hebrew traditions which have not survived incorporated material centered around a character of the same name and similar character to the Ugaritic Dan'el." For objections to the identification of Ezekiel's Daniel with the Ugaritic Daniel and a defense of the traditional view, see Block, *Ezekiel Chapters 1–24,* 448–49.

convinced that God's judgment of the city had been just, and would be con-soled to some degree (vv. 22b–23).

Parables about the Future: Useless Branches (15:1–8)

To drive home the point of the preceding message (Jerusalem's fall is in-evitable), the Lord gave the prophet a parable. He made the point that a grapevine is inferior to the trees of the forest (15:1–2). The wood of the larger trees can be put to a useful purpose, but the branches of a grapevine cannot (v. 3). The latter are only useful as kindling for a fire. Furthermore, once they are burned and charred by the fire, they are even more useless than before (vv. 4–5). In God's eyes the unfaithful people of Jerusalem had be-come as useless as the branches of a grapevine, so he had discarded them and burned them in the fire of judgment (v. 6). Some had survived the first wave of judgment, but the Lord would throw them back into the flames and make their land desolate (vv. 7–8).

An Unfaithful Wife (16:1–63)

The next parable confronts Jerusalem with her sin in a striking way (16:1–2). Jerusalem's history is rehearsed, beginning with her ignominious birth. The personified city was born in the land of the Canaanites from an Amorite father and a Hittite mother (v. 3). The parable reflects the fact that Jerusalem, prior to its conquest by David, was under the control of the na-tive Canaanite population (see Josh. 10:5; 15:63; Judg. 1:21; 2 Sam. 5:6). The city's later penchant for idols (see vv. 15–22) is rooted in her pagan ori-gins. In the very beginning Jerusalem had been a relatively unimportant city. The Lord compared her to an unwanted baby who is immediately tossed into a field and abandoned by her parents (vv. 4–5). But then the Lord came along and took pity on her as she squirmed in her blood. He sustained her life until she grew into a beautiful young woman, but she was naked and needed clothes (vv. 6–7). This part of the parable apparently refers to the city's growth in prominence in the pre-Israelite period. Once Jerusalem had grown up, the Lord passed by again. He noticed that she was ready for mar-riage, so he took her as a wife and made a marriage covenant with her (v. 8). He cleaned her up, gave her beautiful clothes and jewelry, and provided her with fine food (vv. 9–13). Her fame spread throughout the nations (v. 14). This portion of the allegory refers to the Davidic-Solomonic period, when Jerusalem became the capital of the united kingdom and the location of the Lord's temple.

But here the story takes a tragic turn. Jerusalem began flirting with every man who passed by and became a prostitute (v. 15). She built special struc-tures for her illicit activity (v. 16). She used her God-given jewelry to make idols and her God-given food to offer incense to them (vv. 17–19). To top it all off, she took the children she had borne to the Lord and sacrificed them to her idols (vv. 20–21). While doing all these things she forgot how the Lord had saved her life (v. 22). If this were not enough, she turned to the surrounding nations and offered them her sexual favors (vv. 23–26). The Lord disciplined her by giving some of her territory to the Philistines (v. 27), but this did not dissuade her, for she shared her favors with the Assyrians and Babylonians (vv. 28–29). She was even worse than a prostitute, for she gave herself to her lovers for free (vv. 30–31). In fact, she spurned her husband and paid her clients to have sex with her (vv. 32–34). This portion of the parable traces the history of Jerusalem from the Solomonic era to Ezekiel's time. It focuses on the city's idolatry and the foreign alliances that her kings made with various nations. While often designed to protect Judah's interests, these alliances were a symptom of the nation's lack of faith in the Lord's ability to protect and sustain her. They inevitably weakened the nation by draining her wealth and making her more dependent on foreign powers that cared only for their own interests.

Jerusalem's time of reckoning had arrived. Though the Lord had disciplined her in the past (v. 27), more drastic measures were now needed. The Lord would humiliate her in the sight of her lovers (vv. 35–37). She would be stripped naked in public, the appropriate penalty for an adulteress. Because she had shed the blood of her own children (see vv. 20–21), she would be executed as a murderer (v. 38). Ironically, the Lord would appoint her lovers to be her executioners. They would tear down her shrines, strip off her clothes and jewelry, stone her, and hack her to pieces with swords (vv. 39–40). Her prostitution would come to an end and the Lord's jealous anger would be appeased (vv. 41–42). The punishment, though harsh, was fair (v. 43a).

Those reflecting on adulterous Jerusalem's demise would quote the proverb, "Like mother, like daughter" (vv. 43b–44). Though her life was saved by the Lord, she returned to the pagan and idolatrous practices of her Hittite mother (v. 45; see v. 3).[41] The paganized Jerusalem of Ezekiel's time more closely resembled the pre-Israelite Canaanite city than it did the Jerusalem of David's day.

The Lord also depicts Jerusalem as having two sisters, Samaria and Sodom, who shared her immoral character (vv. 45–46). Jerusalem copied her sisters' immoral behavior and soon outdid them (vv. 47–48). Sodom and her daughters had been proud, self-assured, and unconcerned about the poor (v. 49).[42] Her abominable behavior prompted the Lord to destroy her (v. 50). The word translated "detestable things" in verse 50 most likely refers to her

41. Verse 45 says that Jerusalem's Hittite mother despised her husband (identified as an Amorite in vv. 3 and 45) and children. The reality behind this is unclear. The statement may be made simply for dramatic purposes.
42. Sodom's "daughters" (v. 49) were the nearby cities of Gomorrah, Admah, Zeboiim, and the other cities of the plain. Compare Gen. 19:24–25 with Gen. 14:8 and Hos. 11:8.

sexual perversity. The term is used in Leviticus 18:26–27, 29 at the end of a chapter listing all kinds of perverse sexual acts. Specifically the sin of homosexual behavior is probably in view (note the use of the term in Lev. 18:22 and 20:13). Samaria, Jerusalem's sister to the north, "did not commit half the sins" Jerusalem did (v. 51a). In fact Jerusalem was so sinful she made Sodom and Samaria "seem righteous" by comparison (vv. 51b–52). If God were to restore the fortunes of Jerusalem, it was only fair that he also restore Sodom and Samaria along with her (v. 53). When Jerusalem saw her sisters restored and understood the principle of justice that necessitated it, she would realize how sinful she had been and feel shame and disgrace over her past sins (vv. 54–55). Jerusalem had considered herself morally superior to Sodom, so much so that she would not even speak Sodom's name (v. 56). But now the Edomites and Philistines, neither of whom was a paradigm of moral behavior, looked down on Jerusalem in the same haughty way (vv. 57–58).

The conclusion to the prophecy takes a turn for the better. The Lord was forced to punish Jerusalem as she deserved, because she had broken her covenant with him (v. 59; see v. 8). However, the Lord would remember the promise he made to her when she was young, and would establish a new, lasting covenant with her (v. 60). Though his earlier promise did not include sovereignty over Samaria and Sodom, the Lord would give these cities to her as subjects ("daughters") (v. 61). When the Lord renewed his covenant with her, she would recognize him as Yahweh, the one who is present with his people to deliver, protect, and bless them (v. 62; see my earlier comments on chapter 6). The Lord would absolve her of her sins, but she would be so ashamed of her past deeds that she would remain speechless (v. 63).

How is one to interpret the references to the restoration of Samaria and Sodom in this chapter? When Jerusalem was restored after the Babylonian exile, this prophecy was not fulfilled. Furthermore, the disappearance of the exiles of the northern kingdom and the utter annihilation of Sodom preclude a hyper-literal interpretation that would see both of these cities actually being restored in the eschaton to their former condition (as v. 55 depicts). One is better off looking for an essential fulfillment. The main point seems to be that God's willingness to restore Jerusalem, despite the magnitude of her sin, offers hope for other sinful nations, even those who violate his moral standards in blatant ways.

Eagles and a Vine (17:1–24)

Ezekiel next saw a great eagle swoop down upon Lebanon and break off the highest branch of a cedar tree (vv. 1–3). He carried it away to "a land of merchants" and planted it in "a city of traders" (v. 4). This eagle-turned-horticulturist then took some seed from the land of Israel and planted it in fertile soil in a well-watered spot, where it grew into a healthy vine that branched out and sprouted leaves. The branches grew toward the eagle (vv. 5–6). But then another eagle appeared, and the vine's branches turned in his direction (vv. 7–8). The Lord asked a series of rhetorical questions that made it clear that the vine would be uprooted and its fruit destroyed. Even if it were transplanted, it would be withered by the hot east wind (vv. 9–10).

Verses 11–21 explain the meaning of the parable. The first eagle is Nebuchadnezzar, the king of Babylon, who swept down on "Lebanon" (= Jerusalem here) and took Jehoiachin and the nobility (= the cedar branch) into exile (the land/city of the traders) (vv. 11–12; cf. vv. 3–4). Nebuchadnezzar made a treaty with Zedekiah, who ruled over a weakened kingdom (= the vine) (vv. 13–14; cf. vv. 5–6). But then Zedekiah turned toward Egypt for help and shifted his allegiance to the pharaoh (Hophra by name) (v. 15a; cf. vv. 7–8), a policy that would prove disastrous for Zedekiah and Jerusalem (vv. 15b–21; cf. vv. 9–10). When Zedekiah made his oath of allegiance to Nebuchadnezzar, the Lord's name was invoked as a guarantor of the treaty (see 2 Chron 36:13). Consequently when Zedekiah broke his oath to Nebuchadnezzar, he in effect broke a treaty with God. The Lord would punish him severely for his unfaithfulness (vv. 19–20).[43]

The parable seems to end on a somber note, but another parable gives the prophecy a happy ending. Picking up on the imagery of verses 3–4, the Lord announced that he would take the top branch of a cedar and plant it, not in a land of traders, but on a high mountain, which here symbolizes the land of Israel (vv. 22–23a). It would grow into a tall cedar and provide shelter for the birds (v. 23b). At that time all the trees of the forest would recognize that the Lord brings down the tall tree and makes the short tree grow tall. He dries up the green tree and makes the dry tree flourish (v. 24).

No explanation is given for this parable, but the meaning seems clear. The Lord, not Nebuchadnezzar, was ultimately sovereign over his people. In contrast to Jehoiachin, the cedar branch taken into exile (see vv. 3–4, 12), the Lord would raise up an ideal Davidic ruler. His kingdom would extend over many nations (symbolized by the birds), whose people would find protection as his subjects. The kings of the nations (symbolized by the trees of the field that are dwarfed by God's mighty cedar) would recognize the Lord's sovereignty over the world and his ability to raise up and tear down kingdoms.

Each Individual Is Accountable (18:1–32)

The exiles liked to quote a popular proverb that suggested that they were unfairly suffering the consequences of their fathers' sins (18:1–2; see Jer. 31:29).[44] The Lord objected, pointing out that he holds each individual ac-

---

43. For this explanation of the oath and covenant of v. 19, see Allen (*Ezekiel 1–19,* 259), who argues convincingly that the oath and covenant of v. 19 must be equated with the oath and treaty/covenant of vv. 16 and 18. See as well Zimmerli, *Ezekiel 1,* 365, and Block, *Ezekiel Chapters 1–24,* 547.

44. The group quoting the proverb was the exilic community. See Joyce, *Divine Initiative and Human Response in Ezekiel,* 43, 55–56.

countable for his or her own sin (vv. 3–4). The Lord illustrated the point
with a series of case studies dealing with hypothetical situations. Suppose
there is a righteous man who obeys the Lord's law (v. 5). He does not worship idols, commit sexual sins, cheat, or steal. Instead he pays back his debts,
is generous to the poor, and tries to be fair in all he does (vv. 6–8). Such a
man will live (v. 9). But suppose he has a son who murders, worships idols,
commits adultery, oppresses the poor, and robs (vv. 10–13a). This man will
die because of his sins (v. 13b). Now suppose this sinner has a son who repudiates his father's sinful lifestyle and follows his godly grandfather's example (vv. 14–17a). The grandson will not be punished for his father's sins, but
will live because he is obedient to the Lord (v. 17b). The illustrations show
that the Lord deals with people on an individual basis based on their own
moral character, not that of their father or son (vv. 18–20).

However, this does not mean that the wicked have no hope. If a wicked
man repudiates his sin and turns to the Lord, the Lord will spare his life (vv.
21–22).[45] The Lord finds no pleasure in the death of the wicked. He is
pleased when they repent, and he can forgive them (v. 23). On the other
hand, a righteous man must sustain his righteous lifestyle. If he turns from
God and becomes wicked, he will die (v. 24).

Where do the exiles fit into the picture? Though they accused the Lord
of being unjust, they were the ones who were guilty of injustice (vv. 25, 29).
As the preceding illustrations make clear, the Lord operated according to a
clear-cut principle: The righteous live and the wicked die (vv. 26–28). The
Israelites correspond to the wicked son who needed to repent (v. 30). They
were not mere victims of God's judgment on their fathers. They too were
sinners and needed to take personal responsibility for their actions. God in
his grace did not sweep them away along with their fathers. He had given
them opportunity to repent of their evil and to do what is right. They
needed to turn from their sin and exhibit a changed attitude (v. 31). The
Lord did not want them to die; he wanted them to repent and live (v. 32).

How does one reconcile this passage, which emphasizes individual accountability, with the many texts that illustrate the principle of corporate responsibility? The Lord warned his enemies that their sin would have negative consequences for their family throughout their lifetime (Exod. 20:5;
34:7; Num. 14:18). Dathan's, Abiram's, and Achan's innocent children died
along with their sinful parents (Num. 16:27, 32; Josh. 7:24), and David,
with the Lord's approval, allowed the Gibeonites to execute Saul's seven sons
because of their father's crimes against that city (2 Sam. 21:1–9, 14). The
Lord also took the lives of four of David's sons because of his sin against

45. In this regard, Zimmerli (*Ezekiel 1*, 387) observes, "Any fatalism which sees the scales to be hope-
lessly weighed down by the burden of past sins is broken by the call to enter the open door to life. Any
ponderous 'doctrine of righteous retribution' is broken through by this unheard of freedom of God to
promise life, which itself penetrates into every guilty and rebellious person's experience."

Uriah (2 Sam. 12:5–6, 10; cf. 12:14–15; 13:28–29; 18:15; 1 Kings 2:25). Some suggest that there were two competing views in ancient Israel (individual accountability and corporate responsibility), while others propose that Ezekiel 18 rejects the earlier corporate concept and replaces it with a new divine policy. A better solution is to hold both principles in balance. Both are true, and neither should be elevated to universal status so that the other is canceled out. Children do experience the effects of a parent's sin. God even punishes children for a parent's sin on occasions where he deems such a punishment fitting. However, this is not always the case. Often, as in the case of the exilic generation in Ezekiel's day, the children are given the opportunity to obey or disobey the Lord. In such cases they can be assured that God will evaluate them on the basis of their own deeds, not those of their parent. In this regard Kaminsky concludes: "Although Ezekiel 18 is challenging certain ideas of individualized retribution, this passage is not signaling an evolution from older corporate concerns to newer individualistic concerns. Because the theology of divine retribution found in Ezekiel 18 is not a systematic doctrinal statement about how God always operates, one should not read it as an utter rejection of the older, more corporate model of divine retribution. Rather, one should see it as providing a new vision that attempts to challenge and qualify the older corporate ideas. Ultimately, the two conceptions function in a complementary, rather than in a contradictory fashion."[46]

A Lament for Israel's Princes (19:1–14)

The Lord gave Ezekiel a lament to recite for the princes (i.e., kings) of Israel (19:1). The lament contains two parables. In the first parable a great lioness is depicted as the "mother" of the addressee, presumably one of the princes mentioned in the heading of the lament (v. 2).[47] The most likely candidate is Zedekiah, the king of Judah at the time when Ezekiel prophesied.[48] The identity of the lioness is uncertain, but the imagery used in verses 10–14 suggests that it represents the Davidic dynasty (see the discussion below).[49]

The great lioness had cubs, one of which grew into a strong lion and gained a reputation among the nations before he was trapped and taken to Egypt (vv. 3–4). The lion represents King Jehoahaz, who succeeded Josiah. He ruled for only three months before Pharaoh Necho captured him and took him into exile (2 Kings 23:31–33).

The lioness was disappointed, so she took another of her cubs and made

---

46. Joel Kaminsky, *Corporate Responsibility in the Hebrew Bible* (Sheffield: Sheffield Academic Press, 1995), 177–78. See as well Joyce, *Divine Initiative and Human Response in Ezekiel*, 79–87.

47. The second-person pronoun modifying "mother" (see vv. 2, 10) is masculine singular in Hebrew, indicating that an individual, not the princes as a group, is being addressed.

48. Zedekiah is referred to as a "prince" (Heb. *nasi'*) in 12:10, 12 and 21:25.

49. See Zimmerli, *Ezekiel 1*, 393–94.

him strong (v. 5). He was a vicious lion who terrified people (vv. 6–7). But the nations attacked him, trapped him with a net, and took him to the king of Babylon, who put him into prison and silenced his terrifying roar (vv. 8–9). The identity of this lion is debated. An obvious candidate is Jehoiakim, the successor of Jehoahaz.[50] His reign (608–598 B.C.) was characterized by social injustice and oppressive policies (see Jer. 22:13–17). These deeds may be the reality underlying the imagery of the roaring, vicious lion of Ezekiel 19:6–7. Though Jeremiah threatened him with an ignominious death and burial (see Jer. 22:18–19; 36:30), 2 Kings 24:6 says he "slept with his fathers" and 2 Chronicles 36:6 tells how Nebuchadnezzar bound him in shackles with the intent of taking him to Babylon (see Ezek. 19:9). Some suggest that Jehoiachin, who ruled for just three months before being taken into Babylonian exile (2 Kings 24:8–15), is the lion in view here, but his brief reign does not satisfy the imagery of verses 6–7 as well as Jehoiakim's cruel exploits. Others identify the second lion as Zedekiah, though the text appears to describe an event (such as the demise of Jehoiakim or Jehoiachin) that had already occurred. If this lament, like the passages around it, dates to 592–591 B.C., then Zedekiah's exile to Babylon was still future (see 8:1; 20:1).[51] However, as Allen points out, in the lament genre events still future can be depicted as past.[52] Like Jehoiakim, Zedekiah was guilty of social injustice (see Jer. 34:8–16).

In the second parable the addressee's mother is compared to a well-watered, fruitful vine (v. 10). Its branches were so strong they were fit to be used for a ruler's scepter (v. 11a). The imagery here suggests that the vine is a source of royalty and points to the Davidic dynasty as the underlying reality. The vine grew tall and had many branches (v. 11b). This probably alludes to the prominence of the Davidic dynasty and the size of the royal house. But suddenly it was uprooted and withered by an east wind, a symbol for the Babylonians (v. 12; see 17:10). It was transplanted in a hot desert (v. 13, a symbol of Babylon, where Jehoiachin was already held prisoner), but a fire destroyed its fruit and the strong branches (v. 14). The language aptly describes the downfall of the Davidic dynasty and anticipates Zedekiah's demise.

Past, Present, and Future (20:1–44)

In August 591 B.C., some of the leaders of the exilic community came to Ezekiel to inquire of the Lord, perhaps to see if they would soon return to

---

50. See Block, *Ezekiel Chapters 1–24*, 604–7.

51. Those who take the lioness of v. 2 as Hamutal, the wife of Josiah and mother of Jehoahaz (the lion of vv. 3–4), prefer to see Zedekiah as the referent because he was the full brother of Jehoahaz (see 2 Kings 23:31; 24:18), whereas Jehoiakim was only a half-brother (2 Kings 23:36). Jehoiachin was Jehoiakim's son (2 Kings 24:6).

52. Allen, *Ezekiel 1–19*, 288.

their homeland (v. 1).[53] However, the Lord refused to cooperate with them (vv. 2–3). Instead, he told Ezekiel to confront them with their sinful history and heritage (v. 4). When the Lord chose Israel to be his covenantal people, he promised to deliver them from bondage in Egypt and to give them a fruitful land as their home (vv. 5–6). He also demanded their loyalty and commanded them to discard the idols of Egypt (v. 7), but they refused to do so (v. 8a). (The Pentateuch contains no reference to the people's idolatry in Egypt, but Josh. 24:14 appears to allude to such practices.) The Lord was angry and wanted to judge them, but he decided to deliver them for the sake of his reputation (vv. 8b–9).

The Lord led them into the desert, where he gave them his law (vv. 10–11). This included the Sabbath regulation, which was to serve as a reminder (or "sign") that he had chosen them to be his special, covenantal people (v. 12; see Exod. 31:13). But while they were still in the desert, the people violated his law and desecrated the Sabbath (v. 13a). Once more the Lord was tempted to destroy them, but for the sake of his reputation he tempered his judgment with mercy (vv. 13b–14). The adults were denied entry into the Promised Land, but the Lord did not annihilate the community (vv. 15–17). He gave the new generation an opportunity to live up to his ideal. He urged them to repudiate their parents' idols, to obey his law, and to observe the Sabbath (vv. 18–20). However, the children rebelled in the desert, prompting God's anger (v. 21). Once more the Lord withheld judgment for the sake of his reputation (v. 22), but he swore an oath in the desert that he would scatter them among the nations (vv. 23–24).

The Pentateuch seems to know nothing of this episode, but the tradition reflected in verses 23–24 may underlie Psalm 106:26–27. Perhaps the best way to harmonize verses 23–24 with the Pentateuchal material is to understand the oath referred to as conditional and to associate the threatened judgment of exile with the covenantal curses of Leviticus 26:33 and Deuteronomy 28:36–37.[54] However, verse 24 seems to indicate that the threat in verse 23 is based on past actions in the desert (see vv. 18–21), not future failure.

In addition to announcing the future exile of this disobedient generation, the Lord also gave them bad laws and defiled them through child sacrifice (vv. 25–26). The NIV translation softens the blow of these verses by rendering the main verbs, "I gave them over to" and "I let them become defiled." The Hebrew text reads simply, "I gave them" and "I defiled them," respectively. The text seems to say that God himself was responsible for Israel's moral failure, including the abominable practice of child sacrifice.

What exactly is the passage saying and implying? In answering this ques-

53. See Leslie C. Allen, *Ezekiel 20–48*, WBC (Dallas: Word, 1990), 9.
54. For examples of a conditional oath, see Deut. 28:9 and Jer. 22:5.

tion, some distinguish between God's perfect moral will and his permissive will. His moral will, as clearly stated in his law, was that Israel worship him alone, keep his commandments, and repudiate the practices of the pagan world, including child sacrifice. However, when his people disobeyed him, he gave them over to their own sinful desires and permitted them to follow pagan customs and rituals (cf. Rom. 1 for this same theme). According to this view, verses 25–26 refer to God's permissive will, which is ultimately designed to bring his people to their senses (see v. 26b). In this case the text uses deterministic language to emphasize God's sovereign control over the process and his purpose in letting Israel follow their own sinful inclinations. Indeed, sometimes the idiom of the Hebrew Bible attributes directly to God actions that were simply permitted by him or mediated through agents (see, for example, 2 Sam. 12:8). The NIV translation seems to reflect this interpretation of the text.

However, there is another interpretive option. One might take the language of the text in a straightforward manner and understand it as describing the direct judgment of God, rather than the simple permissive will of God as outlined in the preceding paragraph. The Hebrew Bible sometimes pictures God as punishing sin by causing the sinner to sin even more. For example, his sovereign hardening of Pharaoh's heart caused the stubborn king to disobey the divine command to release Israel from bondage.[55] When sinful Israel aroused him to anger, the Lord punished the nation by inciting David to sin (2 Sam. 24:1, 10).[56] Thus it is possible that Israel's paganism, as outlined in Ezekiel 20:25–26, was sent by God as punishment for their previous sins.

Despite their sin, the Lord allowed the people to enter the Promised Land, where they promptly began to engage in pagan rituals (vv. 27–29). The contemporary generation had persisted in these sins and had forfeited their right to inquire of the Lord (vv. 30–31). At this point we discover the reason for the Lord's initial response to the elders (see vv. 1–3).

However, the Lord did not leave them in the dark concerning the future. Israel wanted to worship idols as the other nations did (v. 32a). Being in exile might actually facilitate such idolatry, but the Lord would not let this happen (v. 32b). Using imagery from the exodus, the Lord announced that he would gather his exiled people and lead them into the desert, where he would subject them to purifying judgment (vv. 33–38). Like a shepherd who counts his sheep as they pass beneath his staff (see Lev. 27:32), so the Lord would count those destined to return to the land, while at the same time sifting out the rebels who would be denied entry to it.

55. For a discussion of this issue, see Robert B. Chisholm Jr., "Divine Hardening in the Old Testament," *BSac* 153 (1996): 410–34.
56. For a fuller discussion of this passage, see Robert B. Chisholm Jr., "Does God Deceive?" *BSac* 155 (1998): 21–22. For other instances in which the Lord causes individuals to act unwisely and even sinfully as punishment for prior sins, see 1 Sam. 2:25; 2 Sam. 17:14; 1 Kings 12:15; 2 Chron. 25:20.

Israel persisted in idolatry, but the Lord was determined to purify the nation so that they no longer profaned his holy name (v. 39). Someday the people would bring holy sacrifices to the Lord on his holy mountain (v. 40). He would gather them from the nations and reveal his holiness to them (v. 41). At that time they would deeply regret their past sins and acknowledge that Yahweh is the faithful God who forgives his people (vv. 42–44).

Fire and Sword (20:45–21:32)

Once more using a parable, the Lord told Ezekiel to "preach against the south and prophesy against the forest of the southland" (vv. 45–46). The Lord was about to send a fire through the forest that would consume both its green and dry trees and scorch every onlooker (vv. 47–48). When Ezekiel complained that the people were dismissing his messages as mere parables (v. 49), the Lord explained to him the meaning of the parable. The southern forest symbolized the land of Israel (i.e., Judah), specifically Jerusalem and its temple (21:1–2). It is not certain why the Lord speaks as if he and Ezekiel were north of Judah (Babylon was east of Judah), but later in the chapter the king of Babylon is pictured as invading Palestine from the north (vv. 20–22). Perhaps the Lord assumes the king's perspective here as he anticipates the announcement of the invasion.[57] The fire in the vision symbolized the sword of the Lord, which would cut off everyone, including the righteous (the green trees in the parable) and the wicked (the dry trees), from north to south (vv. 3–5).[58] Since Ezekiel elsewhere pictures God's judgment as discriminating (see 9:4–6; 18:1–20; see as well Ps. 1:6; 11:5) and promises the preservation of a remnant (3:21; 6:8; 12:16), this announcement is startling. Perhaps the Lord utilizes hyperbole here, overstating the case to squash any false optimism in Jerusalem.[59]

Ezekiel was to groan before the people (v. 6). When they asked him the reason for this, he was to explain that he was lamenting the impending slaughter depicted in the preceding prophecy (v. 7). The sword of the Lord was polished and sharpened in preparation for its deadly work (vv. 8–11). It would cut down the people and the princes of Israel (vv. 12–17).

One now discovers that the sword wielded by the Lord (see vv. 3–5, 9–17) is that of Nebuchadnezzar, the king of Babylon (vv. 18–19a). As he approached the land from the north, he would have two options before him (v. 19b). He could veer to the left and invade Ammon, located on the eastern side of the Jordan River, or he could turn to the right and attack Judah and its capital Jerusalem (v. 20). He would seek an omen before making a

---

57. See Zimmerli, *Ezekiel 1*, 423–24.

58. Elsewhere in Ezekiel, the expression "cut off from," when describing an action accomplished with a sword, refers to slaughtering people and animals (see 14:17, 21; 25:13; 29:8; 35:7–8).

59. See Allen, *Ezekiel 20–48*, 25–26; Block, *Ezekiel Chapters 1–24*, 669–70; and Zimmerli, *Ezekiel 1*, 424–25.

decision, for he believed that it was through such means that one could determine the will of the gods and know the future (v. 21a).[60] He might try a
variety of methods, including pulling marked arrows from a quiver, seeking
an oracle from his personal idols, and reading the liver of a sacrificial animal
(v. 21b).[61] The signs would point toward Jerusalem, against which Nebuchadnezzar would set a siege (v. 22). When the people of Judah heard the
news, they would object that the omen was false because they had sworn allegiance to the Babylonian king (v. 23a, cf. 17:13). But he would counter
that they had broken their treaty with him and must be taken into exile
(v. 23b, cf. 17:18). Of course, at a deeper level they had broken their
covenant with God, necessitating their punishment (v. 24). Their wicked
"prince" (Zedekiah is in view) had led them down an evil path, but he would
now be humiliated and dethroned, symbolized by the removal of his tur-
ban/crown (vv. 25–26).

Verse 27 is typically understood to mean that the city would be completely devastated until an individual chosen by God arrived to restore it.
However, this interpretation is problematic. The first statement of verse 27
reads literally, "A ruin, a ruin, a ruin I will make it." The pronoun following
the verb "make" is feminine singular in the Hebrew text. The closest antecedent is the turban/crown of verse 26.[62] Thus the statement likely depicts
the turban/crown being ruined as it is stomped underfoot (see v. 26b). The
second half of verse 27 is particularly difficult to decipher. It reads literally,
"Also this, it was[63] not, until the coming of one to whom is the judgment [or
"legal claim"], and I will place/give it."[64] The difficult and unique syntax
makes it virtually impossible to arrive at a definitive interpretation. Perhaps
the latter part of the statement refers to Nebuchadnezzar (cf. 23:24, which
reads literally, "they will come against you . . . and I will place/give before
them judgment, and they will judge you with their judgments").[65]

---

60. For a helpful discussion of Mesopotamian divination, including a study of the theory and practice
of omen reading, see Robert R. Wilson, *Prophecy and Society in Ancient Israel* (Philadelphia: Fortress, 1980),
90–110. See also A. Leo Oppenheim, *Ancient Mesopotamia*, rev. ed. (Chicago: University of Chicago Press,
1977), 206–27.

61. The term translated "idol" refers to household idols (see Gen. 31:19; 1 Sam. 19:13, 16) that were
used for divination. Their use was forbidden by the Lord (see 1 Sam. 15:23; 2 Kings 23:24; Hos. 3:4).

62. Both terms are feminine singular in Hebrew.

63. The verb is masculine singular and does not agree with the preceding "this," which is a feminine
singular form.

64. The pronoun after the verb "place/give" is masculine singular, apparently referring to the preceding noun "judgment, legal claim."

65. Many see in Ezek. 21:27b an allusion to Gen. 49:10b, which is traditionally translated, "until he
comes to whom it (the scepter mentioned in v. 10a) belongs" and understood as an early, albeit cryptic,
messianic prophecy. However, the verbal connections between the two texts are loose at best. Ezekiel
21:27b (v. 32b in the Hebrew text) reads *'ad-bo' 'asher-lo hammishpat*, "until the coming of one to whom is
the judgment," while Gen. 49:10b reads *'ad ki-bo' shiloh*, which has been translated in a variety of ways, depending on how one interprets the cryptic *shiloh*. The only terms the readings share in common are the
preposition *'ad*, "until," and the verb *bo'*, which appears in an infinitival form in Ezek. 21:27 and in an im-

When the Lord led Nebuchadnezzar to Jerusalem, rather than to Ammon (vv. 20–22), and allowed the Babylonians to sack the city, the Ammonites would rejoice over Jerusalem's fall and insult God's people (see 25:3, 6). However, their insults would be answered by the Lord's sword. The same sword that flashed against Jerusalem would strike down the Ammonites, despite Ammonite prophecies and omens to the contrary (vv. 28–29).

But suddenly a command is given to return the sword to its scabbard (v. 30a). The Lord then unleashes a judgment speech against it.[66] In the land of the sword's origin, the Lord would judge it (v. 30b). He would unleash his anger against it and turn it over to brutal destroyers (vv. 31–32). The sword addressed here must be that of the Babylonian king (vv. 19–20). While wielded by the Lord as he judged Judah and Ammon, it now becomes the enemy of the Lord.[67]

Since this would be the only place where Ezekiel prophesies Babylon's fall and since the heading to the oracle says that it pertains to Ammon (v. 28a), some interpret the sword in verses 28b–32 as that of the Ammonites.[68] In this case, verses 28–29 describe the Ammonites' hostile intentions toward Judah. But then God commands them to abandon their plan (v. 30a) and announces their punishment (vv. 30b–32). However, the close linguistic connections between verses 9–10 and 28 suggest that the same sword is the referent in both texts. Verse 20 identifies this sword as that of the king of Babylon, while verses 3–5 indicate that it is wielded by the Lord.

Bloodstained Jerusalem (22:1–31)

Ezekiel's next message denounces Jerusalem for its idolatry and bloodshed and announces the city's judgment and approaching humiliation (22:1–5). The princes (kings; see chapter 19) shed innocent blood, oppressed the weak and vulnerable, and desecrated what God considered holy, including the Sabbath (vv. 6–8). Rather than championing justice and morality, they tolerated injustice, idolatry, all kinds of sexual crimes, bribery, and oppressive economic practices (vv. 9–12a). Though they ignored the Lord, he would

---

perfect form in Gen. 49:10. Some emend *shiloh* to *shello,* "one to whom (it belongs)," a form that combines the relative pronoun *she-* with *lo* (consisting of the preposition *le-* and a third masculine singular pronominal suffix). In this case, the form would approximate the construction *'asher lo* in Ezek. 21:27, where the more common form of the relative pronoun is followed by *lo.* However, in light of the parallelistic structure, a more likely reading in Gen. 49:10 would be *shay loh,* "(until) tribute (comes) to him." In this case, the construction combines the noun *shay,* "gift, present," with *lo.* See Gordon Wenham, *Genesis 16–50,* WBC (Dallas: Word, 1994), 478. Due to the grammatical and lexical problems involved in both Ezek. 21:27 and Gen. 49:10, the attempt to link the texts is pure speculation.

66. The second-person verb forms and pronouns in vv. 30b–32 (see also v. 29a) are feminine singular in the Hebrew text, indicating that the personified sword (a feminine noun in Hebrew) is addressed.

67. See Allen, *Ezekiel 20–48,* 28; Block, *Ezekiel Chapters 1–24,* 695–96; and Zimmerli, *Ezekiel 1,* 448–49.

68. See, for example, Taylor, *Ezekiel,* 165.

not ignore their sin (vv. 12b–14). He would terminate their ungodly practices by scattering them among the nations (vv. 15–16).

To illustrate the moral condition of the people, the Lord used a metallurgical metaphor. He compared them to the dross, or scum, that is left in the furnace after the silver has been refined (vv. 17–18). Because of their blatant sin, they were worthless in his sight. The metaphor changes in verses 19–22, as the Lord pictures the coming judgment. The Lord compared them to the crude metal that is put into the furnace so the dross can be separated from the pure metal. The image of God melting them as he blows on them with the intense heat of his anger is an apt illustration of the severe judgment that would fall on the city.

More metaphors follow. Because it was contaminated by its sinful people, the land was morally unproductive and worthless, like a land that has dried up due to a drought (vv. 23–24). Like lions that devour their prey, Judah's princes (kings) robbed the weak and vulnerable (v. 25).[69] The priests did not distinguish between what is ritually clean (holy) and unclean, nor did they keep the Sabbath (v. 26). Civil officials, compared to hungry wolves, resorted to violence and injustice to line their pockets (v. 27). The prophets whitewashed these evil deeds and gave the perpetrators false hope through visions and omens that did not originate with the Lord (v. 28). The leaders were not the only offenders. The ordinary people of the land were dishonest and exploited the weak and vulnerable (v. 29). The community was like a broken-down wall in desperate need of repair. The image is foreboding, since it anticipates what would soon happen to Jerusalem's walls. The Lord looked for someone to step into the gap and rebuild it by championing justice and holiness, but no one stepped forward (v. 30). Consequently he was forced to punish them. When he poured his anger out on them, they would receive exactly what they deserved (v. 31).

A Parable of Two Sisters (23:1–49)

The Lord used another lengthy parable to illustrate how his people had abandoned him. This is the story of two sisters named Oholah and Oholibah (vv. 2, 4). Both names are derivatives of the Hebrew word *'ohel*, "tent," but the meaning of the names does not appear to be important or symbolic.[70] In the parable Oholah symbolizes Samaria, which represents the northern kingdom of Israel. Oholibah symbolizes Jerusalem, which represents the southern kingdom of Judah.

69. The Hebrew text reads "her prophets" in v. 25, but the Septuagint has "her princes." The latter seems to be preferable since the prophets are mentioned later (v. 28). Four groups are mentioned in vv. 26–29: priests, officials, prophets, people of the land. A dual reference to prophets would be odd, since none of the other groups are mentioned twice. A reference to the princes/kings in v. 25 would fit nicely in light of the focus of the earlier speech (see v. 6).

70. Oholah may mean "her tent"; Oholibah may mean "my tent is in her." The latter may allude to the fact that the Lord's "tent" (i.e., temple) was in Jerusalem.

Within the framework of the marriage metaphor being employed here, the Lord is pictured as having two wives, the sisters Israel and Judah (see also Jer. 3:6–11). Though the text does not specifically mention their being married to the Lord, the passage seems to assume this. The expression "while she was still mine" in verse 5 reads literally "[while she was] under me." In Numbers 5:19–20, 29 the expression "under her husband" is used of a wife being subject to her husband's authority. In verse 25 it is the Lord's jealousy that is aroused by Oholibah's sin, indicating that he is depicted as her husband. Though the law prohibited a man from marrying sisters (Lev. 18:18), such marriages are not unknown in the Bible (cf. Jacob). The Lord here uses a contextually conditioned metaphor for illustrative purposes. The use of such an illustration does not mean that the Lord condoned bigamy.

When the sisters were just young girls in the land of Egypt, they became prostitutes and freely offered their breasts to their lovers (v. 3). The reality behind the imagery is Israel's worship of idols while in Egypt (see 20:7–9; Josh. 24:14). Oholah continued her prostitution, giving herself to the Assyrian soldiers (vv. 5–8). The underlying reality is Israel's willingness to form alliances with Assyria. The Lord eventually handed Oholah over to her lovers, the Assyrians, who publicly humiliated her, stole her children, and then executed her (vv. 9–10). The text refers here to the fall of Samaria and the exile of the northern kingdom in 722 B.C.

Oholibah saw all of this happen, but she was even more of a nymphomaniac than her sister (v. 11). She gave herself to the Assyrians and then the Babylonians (i.e., Chaldeans) (vv. 12–17a). She turned in disgust from the Babylonians but persisted in her prostitution with the same vigor and lust she had displayed in her youth (vv. 17b, 19–21). The underlying reality behind the parable is the series of alliances that Judah made with Assyria, Babylon, and finally Egypt. The Lord turned from Oholibah in disgust (v. 18) and announced that he would turn her over to the Babylonians, whom she had jilted (v. 22). They now hated her and would subject her to their own twisted version of justice (vv. 23–24, 28–30). As agents of God's jealous anger, they would mutilate her, steal her children, and publicly humiliate her, bringing her adulterous ways to an abrupt end (vv. 25–27).[71] Comparing the desolation of judgment to an intoxicating beverage, the Lord announced that Oholibah would have to drink from the same cup as Oholah did, because she, like her sister, had rejected her husband for a life of prostitution (vv. 31–35).

The Lord then invited Ezekiel to testify on his behalf (v. 36). Once more he stated his case. The focus initially shifts from foreign alliances, the primary sin denounced in verses 1–35, to idolatry and its attendant horror,

---

71. The punishment of cutting off the nose and ears is attested among the Egyptians and Hittites. See Zimmerli, *Ezekiel 1,* 489.

child sacrifice. Both sisters worshiped idols, to which they sacrificed their own children (v. 37). On the very day they offered these human sacrifices, they had the audacity to enter the Lord's temple and defile it (vv. 38–39). The theme of foreign alliances again rears its ugly head. The sisters summoned men from far away (v. 40a). Suddenly, Oholibah becomes the focal point as the Lord describes the way she prepared a seductive scene for her lovers' arrival (vv. 40b–41).[72] Men flocked to the sisters and slept with them (vv. 42–44). However, righteous men like Ezekiel would recognize their sin and sentence them to a just punishment (v. 45). As the offended husband, the Lord summons a mob to execute them, kill their children, and burn down their houses (vv. 46–47). Only in this drastic way could he bring their prostitution to an end (vv. 48–49).

Put On the Cooking Pot (24:1–14)

On January 15, 588 B.C., the Lord told Ezekiel to mark the date carefully, because on that very day the Babylonian siege of Jerusalem had begun (24:1–2). The Lord then gave Ezekiel another parable to deliver to the people (v. 3a). He told the prophet to put a cooking pot over the fire, to pour water into it, and to fill it with choice pieces of meat still on the bone (vv. 3b–4). Then he was to build a strong fire beneath the pot, to bring the water to a boil, and to cook the meat (v. 5). This culinary episode was an object lesson of what the Lord would do to bloodstained Jerusalem, which had become like a cooking pot encrusted with hard-to-remove deposits (v. 6a). The meat within the pot would eventually be removed piece by piece (v. 6b). This apparently pictures the exile of Jerusalem's residents. The oppressive leaders within the city had openly shed innocent blood, and the Lord had not allowed the evidence of their guilt to be covered up (vv. 7–8). Because of its murderous deeds the city was doomed (v. 9a). The Lord would, as it were, build a hot fire beneath the cooking pot. As Ezekiel kindled the fire under his cooking pot and thoroughly cooked the meat until the bones were charred, he was previewing what would happen to Jerusalem (vv. 9b–10). The action envisioned here seems to precede the one described in verse 6b. Before the meat (the city's populace) was removed (v. 6b, picturing the exile), it would be subjected to the heat (vv. 9–10, depicting the suffering of the city's residents during the siege). Once the meat was emptied, Ezekiel was to place the pot directly on the coals and melt away its deposits, which up to this point had stubbornly remained despite attempts to remove them (vv. 11–12). This symbolic action previewed the final phase of God's merciless judgment against the city (vv. 13–14).

72. Beginning with "you bathed yourself" in v. 40b, the text uses singular verbal and pronominal forms, suggesting that Oholibah is being addressed. See also "her" in v. 42a. In v. 42b the use of the plural signals that Oholah has reentered the scene. Note "their heads." (NIV "the arms of the woman and her sister" reads literally in the Hebrew text, "their arms.")

Don't Cry for a Dead Wife (24:15–27)

The next object lesson would be the most difficult of all for Ezekiel to carry out. The Lord announced that he would suddenly take the life of Ezekiel's wife (vv. 15–16a). Yet the prophet was not allowed to lament her death in the normal manner or even shed tears for her (v. 16b). He was permitted to moan under his breath, but he could not follow the normal customs of mourners (v. 17). By evening Ezekiel's wife was dead, and the next morning, when the people saw his strange, seemingly dispassionate response, they correctly assumed this had something to do with them (vv. 18–19). The prophet explained the significance of his actions. Just as Ezekiel's wife had been the "delight" of the prophet's "eyes" (v. 16), so the Jerusalem temple was the "delight" of God's people and the object of their affection. But just as the Lord had taken the life of Ezekiel's wife, so he would desecrate his own temple through judgment and take the lives of the children of Jerusalem, some of whom belonged to the exiles (vv. 20–21). Just as Ezekiel did not lament his wife's death in the normal way, so the exiles would be so shocked by the news of Jerusalem's fall that they would sit in stunned silence, unable to perform the usual mourning customs (vv. 22–27).

Disaster for Judah's Neighbors (Ezekiel 25–32)

The next major section of the book contains judgment oracles against the neighboring nations. Seven nations are singled out, beginning in the east (Ammon, Moab, Edom) and then moving to the west (Philistia), the north (Tyre and Sidon), and finally the south (Egypt). Three oracles are delivered against Tyre; seven are directed against Egypt. Each of the seven oracles against Egypt begins with the formula, "the word of the LORD came to me." The sevenfold structures suggest completeness and finality. The section may be outlined as follows:

1. The judgment of Ammon (25:1–7)
2. The judgment of Moab (25:8–11)
3. The judgment of Edom (25:12–14)
4. The judgment of Philistia (25:15–17)
5. The judgment of Tyre (26:1–28:19)
   a. Tyre's downfall (26:1–21)
   b. Lamenting for Tyre (27:1–36)
   c. Taunting Tyre's king (28:1–19)
6. The judgment of Sidon (28:20–26)
7. The judgment of Egypt (29:1–32:32)
   a. The Lord opposes Pharaoh (29:1–16)
   b. Nebuchadnezzar's plunder (29:17–21)
   c. Lamenting for Egypt (30:1–19)
   d. Breaking Pharaoh's arm (30:20–26)
   e. A cedar falls (31:1–18)

   f. Lamenting for Pharaoh (32:1–16)
   g. The demise of Egypt's army (32:17–32)

The oracles against the first six nations make it clear that their judgment is due to the way they have mistreated God's people and/or gloated over their demise. Thus the primary role of the oracles seems to be to assure the exiles, or at least a godly remnant, that they would be avenged and restored to their land. The oracles against Egypt seem to have a different purpose. Since Judah was relying on Egypt for help against the Babylonians (see 17:15; 29:16), the news of Egypt's fall (see Jer. 37:5–7) confirmed Ezekiel's message: There was no hope for Jerusalem in the immediate future.[73]

Several of the oracles are dated to 587–585 B.C., while one (see 29:1–17) comes from the year 571. At least one of the undated oracles postdates the fall of Jerusalem (see 25:3).

Judgment East and West (25:1–17)

The Ammonites gloated over the fall of Jerusalem and the exile of her people (25:1–3). The Lord announced he would punish their arrogance by sending the "people of the East," probably a reference to desert tribes, against them (v. 4a).[74] These nomadic invaders would take away the Ammonites' fruit and flocks and turn the Ammonite capital, Rabbah, into a pastureland (vv. 4b–5). Because the Ammonites clapped their hands with delight when Judah fell, the Lord would stretch out his hand of judgment against them (vv. 6–7).

The Moabites also gloated over Judah's demise, so the Lord would bring the desert tribes across their borders as well (vv. 8–11). The Edomites treated Judah in a particularly hostile manner (see Obad. 1–14), so the Lord would annihilate Edom (vv. 12–13). In this case he would use his own people, Israel, as his instrument of vengeance (v. 14; see Obad. 15–21). Because the Philistines had also been hostile to Judah, the Lord would "carry out great vengeance" on them (vv. 15–17).

Judgment on Tyre: Tyre's Downfall (26:1–21)

Tyre was pleased by Judah's fall, because she saw it as being to her benefit (vv. 1–2). Because of its location on the Mediterranean coast, Tyre was a prosperous city that engaged in extensive maritime trade. It seems unlikely that Jerusalem's fall would enhance Tyre's already significant economic power, though it might open up caravan routes from the south.[75] Perhaps the imagery of verse 2 should be understood in political terms. With Judah gone,

---

73. On the purpose of the Egyptian oracles, in contrast to chapters 25–28, see Allen, *Ezekiel 1–19*, xxix–xxxi.

74. The phrase "people of the East" is literally "sons of the east," a phrase that appears in Gen. 29:1; Judg. 6:3, 33; 7:12; 8:10; 1 Kings 4:30; Job 1:3; Isa. 11:14; Jer. 49:28.

75. Daniel I. Block, *The Book of Ezekiel Chapters 25–48*, NICOT (Grand Rapids: Eerdmans, 1998), 36.

Tyre could play a more prominent role as a leader of the western Palestinian states.[76] The Lord had other ideas. Just as the waves of the sea crashed against the coast (an image that would be well understood in Tyre), so the Lord would send waves of nations against Tyre (v. 3). They would destroy her defenses, and the Lord would scrape away her rubble, leaving just a bare rock (v. 4). Fishermen would use the site to dry their nets (v. 5a). Tyre would be looted and her outlying settlements (literally, "daughters") ravaged by the sword (vv. 5b–6).

Verses 7–14 appear to give a more detailed account of how the prophecy of Tyre's fall would be realized. Nebuchadnezzar, king of Babylon, would attack it with his vast army from the north (v. 7). He is called "king of kings" because he ruled over a mighty empire, consisting of many nations.[77] This may explain why verse 3 refers to "many nations" coming in waves against Tyre. The Babylonian army enlisted troops from various provinces and consisted of soldiers from many different ethnic groups and nations.[78] Nebuchadnezzar would ravage the outlying settlements of Tyre and lay siege to the city (v. 8, cf. v. 6). His army would eventually breach Tyre's walls, sweep into the city, and cut down her people with the sword (vv. 9–11). The Babylonians would rob Tyre of her wealth, break down her walls, and throw the rubble into the sea (v. 12, cf. vv. 4, 5b). The Lord would put an end to Tyre's celebrations and make her a bare rock where fishermen dry their nets (vv. 13–14a, cf. v. 5a). She would never be rebuilt (v. 14b).

When and how was this prophecy of Tyre's destruction fulfilled? Nebuchadnezzar moved against Tyre in 585 B.C. and put the city under a siege that lasted thirteen years. The Babylonians did not reduce the city to rubble (see Ezek. 29:17–18, which is dated to 571 B.C.), though the evidence does suggest Tyre became subject to Babylonian authority.[79] Since the city was not devastated, how do we explain the apparent failure of the prophecy?

Some argue that the prophecy was fulfilled in 332 B.C., when Alexander the Great leveled the city, leaving it much the way Ezekiel describes. Proponents of this view make a distinction between the "many nations" that come in waves (v. 3) and Nebuchadnezzar's army (vv. 7–11). They also point to the switch from the singular "he" (i.e., Nebuchadnezzar) in verses 7–11 to the plural "they" (viewed as the "many nations") in verse 12. According to this view, an event in the immediate future, the Babylonian siege of Tyre, was blended with a more distant event (the ultimate destruction of the city). Such blending of the near and far is a feature of Hebrew prophecy (see

76. See Allen, *Ezekiel 20–48*, 75.
77. On the obvious literary connection between vv. 3 and 7, see Block, *Ezekiel Chapters 25–48*, 39.
78. Isa. 8:9 and 17:12–14 use similar language to describe the Assyrian army.
79. See Allen, *Ezekiel 20–48*, 109; Walthe; Zimmerli, *Ezekiel 2*, trans. J. D. Martin, Hermeneia (Philadelphia: Fortress, 1983), 23; and William A. Ward, "Phoenicians," in *Peoples of the Old Testament World*, ed. A. J. Hoerth, G. L. Mattingly, and E. M. Yamauchi (Grand Rapids: Baker, 1994), 191.

1 Kings 14:14–16). However, the proposed distinction between the "many nations" of verse 3 and Nebuchadnezzar's army seems overly subtle, in light of the reference to Nebuchadnezzar as "king of kings" (v. 7) and the multi-ethnic nature of his army. Nebuchadnezzar is the focal point of verses 7–11, but the actions described are those of an army. The subject of the plural forms in verse 12 is most naturally understood as the collective "army" (Heb. *'am*) of verse 7, which in turn can be seen as comprised of the "many nations" mentioned in verse 3 (see also the reference to "nations" in v. 5).

Block surveys various ways in which scholars have dealt with the problem raised by the apparent failure of the prophecy. He suggests quite plausibly that this prophecy, like so many others in the prophetic writings, was implicitly conditional and that Tyre's "submission to Babylon constituted a resignation to the will and plan of God," allowing the Lord to "suspend the threats he had pronounced upon the city, and indeed delay the actual fulfillment of the oracle for 250 years, until the time of Alexander the Great."[80]

Because so many nations around the Mediterranean world traded with Tyre, her fall would cause consternation in the coastal regions (vv. 15–16; see Isa. 23). Tyre's trading partners would lament her demise (vv. 17–18). Such mourning would be appropriate, for Tyre was as good as dead. Desolate and covered by the waters of the sea, she was ready to be ushered into the subterranean land of the dead from which no one can return (vv. 19–21).

Lamenting for Tyre (27:1–36)

Ezekiel's lament for Tyre sounds more like a taunting judgment speech. The lament recalls Tyre's prominence and wealth (27:1–4). All kinds of goods and riches flowed into Tyre from every direction of the compass, as the litany of Tyre's trading partners indicates (vv. 5–24). Tyre is compared to one of the impressive trading ships (literally "ships of Tarshish") that carried her goods throughout the Mediterranean world (v. 25). However, an east wind (perhaps symbolizing Babylon) wrecks the ship, and all her wealth sinks to the bottom of the sea (vv. 26–27). Tyre's trading partners along the coasts bitterly lament her demise, pointing out that the one who once enriched many nations is now taunted by merchants (vv. 28–36).

Taunting Tyre's King (28:1–19)

Ezekiel also taunted the ruler of Tyre, who at this time was Ethbaal. Ethbaal had delusions of grandeur and thought of himself as a "god" possessing su-

---

80. See Block, *Ezekiel Chapters 25–48*, 147–49. A possible parallel may be found in Mic. 3:12, which prophesies the ruin of Jerusalem. While the prophecy was circumvented in Micah's day by Hezekiah's repentance (see Jer. 26:17–19), the ruin of Jerusalem became a reality in 586 B.C., when the moral conditions prompting Micah's prophecy were duplicated in a later generation and no Hezekiah emerged to circumvent God's judgment.

pernatural wisdom (28:1–2a).[81] In his statement, "I am a god," the Hebrew word translated "a god" is El, the name of the Canaanite high god. It is possible that this deity is specifically in view here, for the ruler is depicted as enthroned "in the heart of the seas" and as possessing great wisdom. In the Ugaritic texts, El dwells "at the source of the rivers, amid the springs of the two oceans" and is portrayed as wise.[82] The ruler's wisdom (here he represents Tyre itself) was apparent in his ability to amass wealth through trade (vv. 4–5). He apparently thought he could even match or exceed the wisdom of Daniel (or perhaps the legendary Dan'el).[83] Despite his success he was a mere man, not a god (v. 2b). Because of his pride the Lord would kill him, using a ruthless invading army (the Babylonians) as his instrument of judgment (vv. 6–8). As the Tyrian ruler stood humiliated in the presence of his executioner, he would be very much aware of his mortality (vv. 9–10).

Another taunting lament against Ethbaal follows, in which Ezekiel depicts the king's humiliating fall from prominence. He is compared to a being who was once the model of perfection, wisdom, and beauty (vv. 11–13). Though he lived on God's mountain (v. 14), he used violence to expand his influence and was expelled from the divine presence (vv. 15–16; see Amos 1:9). His great pride led to his humiliating downfall (vv. 17–19).

This passage blends references to Tyre's commercial empire (vv. 13, 16a, 18–19) with allusions to an extrabiblical tradition that contains echoes of Genesis 2–3 and of ancient Near Eastern myths (vv. 12b–15, 16b–17). Verse 13 refers to the king's presence in "Eden, the garden of God," which certainly reminds one of Genesis 2–3. If one follows the traditional text of verse 14 ("you were an anointed, guardian cherub"), then it appears the king is compared to a cherub. Genesis 3:24 tells of guardian cherubim (plural) being placed at the entrance to the Garden of Eden, but it knows nothing of a proud cherub's fall from prominence such as we have in Ezekiel 28.[84] In this case, we must assume that Ezekiel draws on an extrabiblical Eden tradition about a guardian cherub, whom he utilizes as a metaphor for the king of Tyre.

However, the traditional interpretation of verse 14 is problematic. Verse 14 begins with the Hebrew form *'att,* which is the second-person *feminine*

81. Possessing supernatural wisdom was considered one of the primary characteristics of a divine being. See, for example, Gen. 3:5–6, 22, in which the "knowledge of good and evil" refers to divine wisdom, and Prov. 30:3, in which "wisdom" is defined as "knowledge of (i.e., belonging to) the holy ones" (the plural term, interpreted by NIV as an honorific plural, refers to members of the heavenly assembly; see Ps. 89:7).

82. For the pertinent Ugaritic texts, see Gibson, *Canaanite Myths and Legends,* 54, 59–60. See also Day, *Yahweh and the Gods,* 27.

83. On the debate over the identity of Daniel, see my comments on 14:14, 20.

84. Christian tradition identifies the serpent of Eden as Satan, but the serpent is portrayed as a member of the animal kingdom in Gen. 3, not as a cherub. For a critique of the view that sees Satan underlying the imagery of Ezek. 28, see Block, *Ezekiel Chapters 25–48,* 118–19.

singular form of the independent pronoun. Throughout these verses the king of Tyre is addressed with second-person *masculine* singular forms.[85] It is possible that *'att* is here a rare form of the masculine pronoun,[86] or that it should be repointed *'atta,* a defectively written (without the final vowel letter *he*) form of the masculine pronoun.[87] However, some prefer to follow the Septuagint and read the form as the preposition *'et,* "with."[88] In this case, one may translate, "With an anointed, guardian cherub I placed you."[89] In this case, the king of Tyre is compared to the first man, not a cherub. Verses 15–16 would then allude to the first man's creation, fall into sin, and expulsion from Eden. Furthermore, verse 12 accords well with the tradition, reflected in Job 15:7–8, that the first man was especially wise.[90]

Despite the similarities to Genesis 2–3, there are differences as well. Genesis 2–3 does not portray Adam as being covered with jewels nor does it know of a mountain of God from which the first man was thrown down (vv. 14, 16–17). To understand the significance of these elements, one must turn to ancient Near Eastern mythology. A neo-Babylonian myth contains a striking parallel to the imagery of the king's physical beauty.[91] As for the reference to a divine mountain, we should recall that the Canaanite high god El, perhaps already alluded to in the previous lament (see v. 2), lived on a mountain "at the source of the rivers." Though the biblical Eden is not specifically said to be on a mountain, it is the source of four rivers and seems to be located in the mountainous region of Armenia (see Gen. 2:10–14). Furthermore, there is evidence that El's mountain, like the biblical Eden, was located, at least in some traditions, at the source of the Euphrates.[92]

To summarize, it appears that Ezekiel 28:12–17 draws on an extrabibli-

85. Note especially the use of *'attah,* the second-person masculine singular form of the independent personal pronoun, in vv. 12 and 15.

86. There are two other apparent uses of *'att* as masculine. See Deut. 5:24 and Num. 11:15, as well as *GKC* 106, para. 32h.

87. See 1 Sam. 24:19; Neh. 9:6; Job 1:10; Ps. 6:3; Eccl. 7:22.

88. See, for example, Allen, *Ezekiel 20–48,* 91, Zimmerli, *Ezekiel 2,* 85, and Day, *Yahweh and the Gods,* 176. The preposition *'et* is collocated with the verb *natan* in Exod. 31:6.

89. This emendation requires one to remove the conjunction prefixed to the verb "I placed you" (again, as the Septuagint does). As the text stands, it reads, "You [were] an anointed, guardian cherub and I placed you, on the holy mountain of God you were, in the midst of the stones of fire you walked about." As Allen (*Ezekiel 20–48,* 91) points out, each of the verbs in v. 14b is placed at the end of its clause. If one removes the conjunction from "and I placed you," one achieves the same syntactical style (verb in final position) in v. 14a. In an effort to make sense of the resulting syntax, the conjunction was probably added sometime after the preposition was misunderstood as a pronoun. Furthermore, if one makes the proposed emendations in v. 14, one must follow the Septuagint and emend the difficult *wa'abbedka,* "and I expelled you," in v. 16 (on the form see *GKC* 186, para. 68k), to *wa'ibbadka,* "and [the guardian cherub] expelled you." See Allen, 91, and Zimmerli, *Ezekiel 2,* 86. As the Hebrew text stands, one must take "the guardian cherub," which appears right after the suffixed verb, as a vocative in apposition to the suffix, whereas the emended reading understands the guardian cherub as the subject of "expelled."

90. See Day, *Yahweh and the Gods,* 177–78, and Allen, *Ezekiel 20–48,* 94.

91. See Block, *Ezekiel Chapters 25–48,* 119.

92. See Day, *Yahweh and the Gods,* 28–32.

cal tradition, probably well-known in Tyre, in which the first man or a guardian cherub played a leading role. This tradition, while similar to Genesis 2–3, differs from the biblical account in certain details. It also appears to reflect Mesopotamian and Canaanite mythical elements. The man/cherub lived in the Garden of Eden, located on the mountain of God (perhaps the Canaanite El), and God adorned him with beauty and prestige. But then this man/cherub sinned and was cast down from the mountain. The use of such extrabiblical, mythological material has precedent in Isaiah 14:12–15, where Isaiah, in taunting the king of Babylon, utilizes imagery from the king's own religious context.

Judgment on Sidon (28:20–26)

Sidon was a Phoenician city-state located to the north of Tyre on the Mediterranean coast. Like the nations addressed in the preceding oracles, Sidon had apparently displayed hostility toward God's covenant people (v. 24). For this she must be punished (vv. 20–22). The Lord would use both a plague and the sword of an invader as his instruments of judgment (v. 23). The elimination of hostile enemies like Sidon would be accompanied by the return of the Lord's exiled people (vv. 25–26). As he resettled them securely in their land, he would punish their neighbors. At that time all observers would recognize the Lord's position as sovereign king (cf. "I will show myself holy," in v. 25), and his people would realize that he is Yahweh, their God, the one who delivers and protects them because he is faithful to his covenant promise to be with them.

Judgment on Egypt: The Lord Opposes Pharaoh (29:1–16)

In January 587 B.C., the Lord instructed Ezekiel to deliver a prophecy concerning the downfall of Egypt (29:1–2). The Lord opposed Pharaoh (Hophra by name), who is compared to the "great monster" that lurks in Egypt's streams (v. 3a). The Hebrew word translated "monster" (*tannin*)[93] often refers to a serpent (Exod. 7:9–10, 12; Deut. 32:33; Ps. 91:13) or to the large creatures that inhabit the sea (Gen. 1:21; Ps. 148:7). In several texts it takes on mythic proportions and is associated or identified with the chaotic sea or the multiheaded, serpentine sea creature Leviathan (Job 7:12; Ps. 74:13; Isa. 27:1; 51:9; Jer. 51:34 [?]).[94] Because of the Egyptian setting and the reference to the creature's scales (v. 4), most identify the reality behind the imagery of Ezekiel 29:3 as a crocodile.[95] Allen goes a step further and suggests that "this particular croc-

---

93. The Hebrew text actually reads *tannim,* normally meaning "jackals," which cannot be the referent here (see also 32:2). The form is either an alternate spelling or textual corruption of *tannin,* "serpent, sea monster." See Zimmerli, *Ezekiel 2,* 106.

94. In Ugaritic mythology, the term is used of the multiheaded sea creature associated or identified with Yam, the god of the sea. See Gibson, *Canaanite Myths and Legends,* 50.

95. Zimmerli, *Ezekiel 2,* 111. Note the reference to the creature's "feet" in 32:2b.

odile is larger than life and invested with mythological overtones."[96] Mettinger has shown that in Egypt the crocodile was a symbol of the forces of chaos.[97]

Pharaoh viewed himself as the owner of the Nile, the inundation of which was essential to Egyptian agriculture (v. 3b).[98] In Egyptian theology Pharaoh controlled the Nile.[99] However, the Lord would put a hook in the monster's jaws, pull him out of the water, and deposit him in a dry desert, where he would die and be eaten by scavengers (vv. 4–5). In the aftermath of Pharaoh's demise, the Egyptians would recognize the Lord's sovereignty (v. 6a).

Pharaoh had promised to help Judah against the Babylonian threat, but he had proven to be like a reed staff that easily breaks and injures the one leaning on it (vv. 6b–7; see Jer. 37:5–7). The Lord would cause Egypt to fall, proving to the people of Judah that he alone is the sovereign king (vv. 8–9a). To punish Pharaoh's pride, the Lord would turn Egypt into a desolate wasteland from north to south (vv. 9b–10). The Egyptians would go into exile, and Egypt's cities would lie in ruins for forty years (vv. 11–12). At the end of this period, the Lord would bring Egypt's exiles back to their land, but Egypt would be a minor kingdom and would never again occupy a prominent position among the nations (vv. 13–15). As the Lord's people witnessed all this, they would realize they had sinned by trusting in Egypt rather than the Lord (v. 16).

There is no historical evidence that Egypt suffered such a devastating defeat in the time of Ezekiel or that its people were taken into exile for forty years. In 525 B.C., the Persians conquered Egypt and reduced it to a province.[100] One might think that Ezekiel 29:1–16, using stylized, hyperbolic destruction language, anticipates this time. However, the next three oracles suggest otherwise. All three identify Nebuchadnezzar as God's instrument of judgment against Egypt (29:19; 30:10, 24–25), and the third associates the exile of the Egyptians with Nebuchadnezzar's invasion (30:26; cf. 29:12). Nebuchadnezzar invaded Egypt in 568–567 B.C., but few details of the campaign are available.[101] Perhaps this invasion constituted an essential fulfillment of the preceding prophecy, if one allows for the presence of stylized destruction language. However, one would have to label the language as exceedingly hyperbolic because Hophra's successor Amasis, who began ruling in 570 B.C., enjoyed a peaceful and prosperous reign.[102] A more likely op-

---

96. Allen, *Ezekiel 20–48*, 105. Day (*Yahweh and the Gods*, 103), who sees the creature as the mythical sea dragon, goes even further: "There are no grounds for supposing that a crocodile is thereby denoted, as some imagine."

97. See T. N. D. Mettinger, *In Search of God*, trans. F. Cryer (Philadelphia: Fortress, 1988), 195–98, where he discusses Behemoth and Leviathan as depicted in Job 40–41.

98. John D. Currid, *Ancient Egypt and the Old Testament* (Grand Rapids: Baker, 1997), 240–42.

99. Ibid., 243–44.

100. For the details of Cambyses's invasion of Egypt, see Edwin Yamauchi, *Persia and the Bible* (Grand Rapids: Baker, 1996), 95–124.

101. For a fragmentary report of this event, see James Pritchard, *Ancient Near Eastern Texts Relating to the Old Testament* (Princeton: Princeton University Press, 1969), 308.

102. Yamauchi, *Persia and the Bible*, 101.

tion is that the prophecy was implicitly conditional. Apparently historical developments and circumstances prompted God to modify his plan to some degree so that Egypt did not suffer to the extent envisioned by the prophet.

Nebuchadnezzar's Plunder (29:17–21)

Nebuchadnezzar's siege of Tyre had not yielded the loot his worn-out soldiers had anticipated (v. 18; see my comments on chapter 26). In this prophecy, given in 571 B.C., the Lord announced he would give Egypt to Nebuchadnezzar as a consolation prize because, after all, the Babylonian king had served as his instrument of judgment (vv. 19–20). Nebuchadnezzar would plunder Egypt and give its riches to his army. While Egypt was being looted, the Lord would revive the power of his own people (v. 21).[103]

Lamenting for Egypt (30:1–19)

The time had come to lament because the "day" of the Lord's judgment had arrived, bringing with it ominous clouds and a flashing sword (30:1–4a). The sword would cut down the people of Egypt and the neighboring nations and foreign peoples who allied with her (vv. 4b–6).[104] The "people of the covenant land" may refer to an unidentified nation that had allied with Egypt, though many see here an allusion to Jewish mercenaries living in Egypt.[105] These lands would be left in ruins, forcing the victims of divine judgment to recognize the sovereignty of the Lord (vv. 7–8). As the time of judgment drew near, the Lord himself would begin to spread terror in the region with the news of impending invasion (v. 9). Nebuchadnezzar would arrive with his mighty army and devastate the land (vv. 10–11). The Lord would "dry up the streams of the Nile," an act that would destroy Egypt's economy (v. 12). As city after city fell to the invader, the Egyptian gods, represented by their idols and images, would be exposed as weak and infinitely inferior to the sovereign Lord (vv. 13–20). The terms used to describe the "idols" and "images" in verse 13 are very derogatory. The first is used thirty-nine times by Ezekiel to describe pagan idols. The emphasis in many contexts is on the defiling effect that these idols have on their worshipers.[106] The second term literally means "weak, worthless things."[107]

---

103. On the apparent failure of the prophecy, see my comments on the preceding oracle in 29:1–16.

104. NIV's "Arabia" is probably a mistranslation of the Hebrew phrase *kol-ha'ereb* in v. 5. In Jer. 25:20 and 50:37, NIV translates the same expression "all the foreign people/foreigners." The phrase may refer to foreign mercenaries who served in the armies of the nations cited in these texts. See Zimmerli, *Ezekiel 2*, 129–30.

105. See ibid., 130, and Block, *Ezekiel Chapters 25–48*, 159–60.

106. See H. D. Preuss, "גִּלּוּלִים," *TDOT* 3:2–3. The derivation of the term is debated, but some theorize that the word, at least originally, meant "dung rolls."

107. Because this is the only use of the term in Ezekiel, some prefer to read *'elim*, "rulers," a term that does appear elsewhere in Ezekiel (see 17:13; 31:11; 32:21; 34:17). This reading appears to underlie the Septuagint. Note that the next line refers to a "prince."

Breaking Pharaoh's Arm (30:20–26)

In April 587 B.C., after Pharaoh Hophra's aborted attempt to relieve Jerusalem from the Babylonian threat, the Lord taunted the defeated Egyptian king (v. 20). He boasted that he had "broken the arm of Pharaoh" and that the king's injured arm had not yet healed. In fact the king's arm was so weak that he could not even hold a sword (v. 21). The language is, of course, metaphorical. Pharaoh's "arm" is a symbol of his military power. The Lord was not through with Pharaoh. He intended to break the king's other "arm," leaving him completely incapacitated (v. 22). The Lord would energize the king of Babylon, who would conquer Egypt and take the Egyptians into exile (vv. 23–26).[108]

A Cedar Falls (31:1–18)

Two months later, in June 587 B.C., the Lord again denounced the king of Egypt (31:1). Pharaoh was proud of his royal splendor (v. 2), but he needed to learn a lesson from history about what happens to arrogant rulers. Assyria was once like a majestic, well-watered cedar that towers above the other trees (vv. 3–5).[109] The imagery alludes to Assyria's great empire and the wealth she accumulated from the tribute she received from conquered nations. This cedar had great branches, and all the nations lived in its shade (v. 6). None of the other trees of the forest could begin to rival it in beauty (vv. 7–9). But the cedar became proud, so the Lord handed it over to "the ruler of the nations" (v. 11), probably a reference to the Babylonian king Nabopolassar, who conquered Nineveh in 612 B.C. He chopped the great cedar down, and none would ever rival its splendor again (vv. 12–14). The cedar's demise and descent into the land of the dead prompted lamentation in some quarters and fear in others (vv. 15–17). The great trees that had preceded this cedar into the underworld—probably a reference to mighty kingdoms that had preceded Assyria in history—were consoled when they realized that Assyria had met the same fate that they had (v. 16b). In the same way, proud Pharaoh would meet his demise (v. 18).

Lamenting for Pharaoh (32:1–16)

In March 585 B.C., the Lord revealed to Ezekiel a lament pertaining to Pharaoh and his land (32:1–2a, 16). Pharaoh was like a powerful lion or the great monster that inhabited the seas (v. 2b).[110] However, the Lord did not

---

108. On the apparent failure of the prophecy to be fulfilled, see my comments on chapter 29.

109. I translate v. 3a, "Look! Assyria [was] a cedar in Lebanon." In this case, vv. 3–17 describe Assyria. See Block, *Ezekiel Chapters 25–48,* 185. Some emend *'ashur* "Assyria," in v. 3a to *te'ashur,* "cypress," which makes a fitting parallel with "cedar" (see Isa. 41:19; 60:13), and read v. 3a, "Look! A cypress! A cedar of Lebanon!" In this case, vv. 3–18 in their entirety refer to Egypt. For this view see Zimmerli, *Ezekiel 2,* 141–53, and Allen, *Ezekiel 20–48,* 121–27.

110. On the latter image, see my comments on 29:3.

fear him. He would enlist "a great throng of people" (a reference to the Babylonian hordes; see vv. 11–12) and hunt Pharaoh down with his net (v. 3). The Lord would throw the sea monster onto the land, where it would be devoured by various scavengers (vv. 4–5). The creature's blood would flow through the countryside, and its flesh would be scattered in the valleys and ravines (v. 6). The darkness of judgment would overtake the cosmos, and kings would be terrified when they heard of Pharaoh's demise (vv. 7–10). Using the Babylonian army as his instrument of judgment, the Lord would devastate the land of Egypt (vv. 11–15).

The Demise of Egypt's Army (32:17–32)

In this seventh and final judgment speech against Egypt, given in 585 B.C., the prophet is told to wail in anticipation of the impending violent death of Egypt and her allies (vv. 17–21). As Pharaoh and his armies descended into the grave (see vv. 28, 31–32), other fallen warriors from defeated nations would be there to meet them. The Egyptians would join the Assyrians, Elamites, and the hordes of Meshech and Tubal, all of whom had terrorized the earth (vv. 22–28). The Edomites and Sidonians would be present as well (vv. 29–30). The Assyrian Empire had fallen between the years 612–609 B.C. Prior to that, during the reign of the Assyrian king Ashurbanipal (668–627 B.C.), the Assyrians had devastated the Elamites.[111] Meshech and Tubal (see 38:2 as well) were located in Anatolia (modern Turkey). The names appear as Mushku and Tabal in Assyrian texts.[112] The downfall of the Edomites and Sidonians, while seemingly assumed in verses 29–30, is viewed as future elsewhere in Ezekiel (see 25:12–14; 28:20–26). Apparently the prophet expected those nations to have already met their prophesied destiny by the time Egypt arrived in the land of the dead. Such a scenario makes sense, for the Babylonians would march through these regions on their way to Egypt.

The Restoration of Israel (Ezekiel 33–48)

This final major section of the Book of Ezekiel anticipates the fulfillment of God's ideal for his covenant community. Following a renewal of his commission (chapter 33), the prophet envisioned a time when the Lord would shepherd his sheep and raise up a new David to lead them (chapter 34). Archenemies would be defeated, and the Lord would restore prosperity to Israel as he cleansed and transformed his people (chapters 35–36). The Lord would bring the covenant community back from the dead and create a reunited people under the leadership of a new David (chapter 37). The Lord would put down one last threat by the hostile nations of the earth (chapters

---

111. See Georges Roux, *Ancient Iraq* (Middlesex, England: Penguin Books, 1966), 300–04.
112. See Edwin M. Yamauchi, *Foes from the Northern Frontier* (Grand Rapids: Baker, 1982), 24–27.

38–39). He would then reinstitute pure worship in Jerusalem and once again take up residence among his people (chapters 40–48).

Ezekiel's Renewed Commission (33:1–20)

The Lord reminded Ezekiel of his commission to be Israel's "watchman" (33:7, cf. 3:17–21). Using the analogy of a watchman who signals an enemy invasion, the Lord explained that those who disregard the signal are responsible for their own death (vv. 1–5). However, if the watchman fails to warn sinners of impending doom, the watchman is held accountable for the sinner's death, even though the sinner receives what he deserves (v. 6). In the same way, Ezekiel was to warn the wicked of approaching judgment (vv. 7–9).

The Lord also instructed Ezekiel to confront the people's faulty notions about God's character. The prophet's fellow exiles felt weighed down by their sin and were pessimistic about their future (v. 10). The Lord reminded them that he does not take pleasure in the death of the wicked, but instead desires sinners to repent and live (v. 11; see 18:23). The Lord holds a person individually accountable for his or her behavior. If a righteous person pursues sin, the Lord must judge that individual (vv. 12–13; see 18:24). On the other hand, anyone who responds to God's warning will escape judgment and live (vv. 14–16; see 18:21–22). The exiles accused God of being unjust, but they were the ones who were unjust (vv. 17–20; see 18:25–29). He was being more than fair with them. They held their destiny in their own hands. If they persisted in sin, they would die, but if they turned back to God, they would live.

The Vindication of a Prophet (33:21–33)

In January 585 B.C., a refugee arrived from Jerusalem and announced that the city had fallen (v. 21), an event that had occurred months before in the summer of 586. The evening before his arrival, the Lord freed the prophet from the restriction he had placed upon him several years before (v. 22; see 3:26–27). Prior to this Ezekiel could speak only with the Lord's permission.

Ezekiel also received a message from the Lord for the occasion. Those who remained among the ruins back in Israel were convinced the Promised Land now belonged to them (vv. 23–24). After all, Abraham gained divine title to the land before he even had a child (see Gen. 15). By comparison to Abraham, those remaining in the land were a multitude, so they reasoned that they would possess the land. However, the Lord corrected their faulty thinking. The remnant in the land broke God's ritual standards (eating meat with the blood still in it violated the Levitical code; see Lev. 19:26). They broke the Ten Commandments by worshiping idols and committing murder and adultery (vv. 25–26). The Lord could not allow such sinners to possess the land. On the contrary, the Lord would kill them and leave the land a desolate waste (vv. 27–29).

As for Ezekiel's fellow exiles, they seemed to care about what the prophet had to say, but their interest in his message was superficial (vv. 30–31). They found the prophet entertaining, but they had no desire to internalize his words and change their ethically bankrupt attitudes and actions (v. 32). However, when Ezekiel's prophecy came true, they would be forced to acknowledge that a genuine prophet of the Lord, not a mere singer, had been among them (v. 33).

A Shepherd Gathers His Sheep (34:1–31)

The Lord denounced the leaders of the covenant community for failing to carry out their responsibilities. Comparing them to shepherds and his people to a flock, he accused the leaders of looking out for their own interests, not the well-being of the sheep (vv. 1–2). They took milk and wool from the flock and even slaughtered and ate some of the sheep (v. 3). They did not care for the injured sheep or find the strays (v. 4). The sheep were scattered and devoured by wild animals (vv. 5–6). For these reasons the Lord would punish the shepherds, remove them from their position, and deliver his sheep from their oppressive ways (vv. 7–10). The Lord would find his sheep and regather them from the nations where they had been scattered (vv. 11–12). He would bring them back to the land of Israel and lead them to rich grazing areas (vv. 13–14).

The reality underlying the shepherd metaphor is the kingship of the Lord. Like any good king, the Lord would promote justice in his realm. He would show special consideration to the strays and the injured (symbolizing the oppressed and poor), but the "sleek and strong" (symbolizing the oppressors of the poor) he would destroy (vv. 15–16). As the extended metaphor in verses 17–21 makes clear, there were some sheep in the flock that ate what they needed (in the best area of the pasture) and then trampled down the rest of the pasture so the rest of the sheep had nothing to eat. They drank the water they needed and then muddied what remained so others could not get a drink. These well-fed and watered sheep grew big and strong and drove the undernourished sheep away. But the divine shepherd would rescue the weak (v. 22) and would assign them to the care of his special servant, David (vv. 23–24; see also 37:24–25). As elsewhere in the prophets, the ideal Davidic king of the future is here depicted as the second coming of David himself (see my comments on Isa. 11:1; Jer. 30:9; Hos. 3:5; and Mic. 5:2). The use of the term "prince" (v. 24) does not mean that this ruler is subordinate to the messianic king, nor should it be taken to mean that the reference is to the literal, resurrected David ruling as a vice-regent under the Messiah's authority. In 37:22–25, this "David" is called both "king" and "prince." The term "prince" is probably used here to facilitate a contrast with the "princes" (i.e., kings) of the Davidic dynasty who are denounced in earlier oracles (see 7:27; 12:10, 12; 19:1; 21:25; 22:6, 25).[113] Jesus the Messiah is the one toward whom these prophecies look and through whom they will be fulfilled.

The Lord would make a "covenant of peace" with his regathered flock that would assure their security (v. 25a; see also Num. 25:12; Isa. 54:10; Ezek. 37:26). The sheep would be safe because the Lord would eliminate the dangerous predators (v. 25b). The Lord would send the rain in its season, causing the fruit trees to flourish and the crops to grow (vv. 26–27a). His people would recognize him as Yahweh, their savior and protector (vv. 27b–31).

Paying Back Old Debts (35:1–36:15)

A judgment speech directed against Edom now appears, suggesting that the "wild animals" in the preceding prophecy (see vv. 5, 8, 25, 28) symbolize the hostile neighboring nations that took advantage of Judah's demise (35:1–2). Because the Edomites had shown such hostility toward God's people, the Lord would turn Edom over to the sword of an invading army and turn Edom's towns into ruins (vv. 3–9). The Edomites hoped to take over both Israel's and Judah's territory, even though the land belonged to the Lord (v. 10). The Lord would treat them the same way they had treated his people, pouring out his rage and hatred on them (v. 11). The Edomites had gloated over the demise of God's people and insulted the Lord himself, but the Lord would turn their joy into sorrow by turning their land into a desolate ruin (vv. 12–15).

Other nations had shared Edom's greedy desire to take possession of Israel's mountains (36:1–2). They plundered and taunted their helpless victims (vv. 3–5). The Lord would take vengeance on the surrounding nations for their merciless treatment of his covenant people (vv. 6–7). As for the mountains of Israel, they would once again flourish, for the Lord would bring his exiled people back to their land, where they would increase in numbers, rebuild their towns, experience material prosperity, and enjoy national security (vv. 8–15).

Moral Cleansing (36:16–38)

Sinful Israel was an embarrassment to God. They defiled the land with their idolatry and murderous deeds. To emphasize how repulsive their sin was to him, he compares it to a menstrual cloth (vv. 16–18). For this reason he scat-

113. Block suggests that Ezekiel uses this term in these earlier texts in order to "downplay the roles of Israel's monarchs." See Daniel I. Block, "Bringing Back David: Ezekiel's Messianic Hope," in *The Lord's Anointed,* ed. P. E. Satterthwaite, R. S. Hess, and G. J. Wenham (Grand Rapids: Baker, 1995), 175.

tered them among the nations (v. 19). Their removal from the land brought dishonor to God, for the nations reasoned that they lost their land because God was unable to defend them against their enemies (v. 20). Therefore, for the sake of his own reputation, the Lord decided that he must demonstrate his sovereign power and restore his honor among the nations (vv. 21–23). He would accomplish this by restoring his people to their land and by rebuilding what had been destroyed (vv. 24, 36).

However, simply bringing his sinful people back to the land would not suffice. They must be cleansed and transformed into a new community that would obey God. Using the imagery of ritual cleansing, the Lord promised to wash away their moral impurities and idolatry (v. 25). He would transform their hearts and spirits, enabling them to give him their undivided loyalty (v. 26; see 11:19; 18:31). The "heart" is viewed here as the seat of the will. At the present time they had a "heart of stone," that is, a dead heart (cf. 1 Sam. 25:37), an image suggesting they were stubborn and unresponsive. But the Lord would give them a "heart of flesh," that is, a living, beating heart, an image suggesting responsiveness and life. He would also place his Spirit within them, enabling them to obey his commandments (v. 27). The ancient covenantal ideal, expressed in the statement, "You will be my people, and I will be your God" (v. 28; cf. Exod. 6:7) would become a reality. The transformed and obedient community would then experience God's rich material blessings (vv. 29–30), express contrition over their past sins (vv. 31–32), and resettle the land, which would bloom like the Garden of Eden (vv. 33–35). The Lord's reputation would be exonerated as his people increased in numbers and filled the land (vv. 36–38).

Israel Is Resurrected and Reunited (37:1–28)

In perhaps his most famous vision, Ezekiel was taken to a valley filled with dried-out bones (37:1–3). At the Lord's command, Ezekiel urged the bones to hear the word of the Lord (v. 4). The Lord announced that he would breathe life into the bones, attach tendons to them, and cover them with flesh (vv. 5–6). As Ezekiel carried out the Lord's command, the bones began to reattach, as tendons and flesh appeared on them (v. 7a). However, the bodies still had no breath in them (v. 7b). The Lord commanded his life-giving breath to infuse them, and suddenly a vast army of people stood to their feet (vv. 8–10).

The Lord explains the meaning of the vision in verses 11–14. The bones symbolize the "whole house of Israel," which had given up any hope of being revived as a nation. They had been buried, as it were, in the foreign lands to which they had been exiled. But the Lord would open their graves and bring them back to the land. His Spirit would infuse the nation, and it would once again live.

The Lord next instructed Ezekiel to perform an object lesson. He was to write on one stick of wood the words "belonging to Judah and the Israelites associated with him" (vv. 15–16a). On another piece of wood, he was to write: "Belonging to Joseph, the stick of Ephraim and all the house of Israel associated with him" (v. 16b). Joseph (Ephraim was one of the sons of Joseph) symbolizes the northern kingdom. Ezekiel was then to join the two sticks together in his hand so that they appeared to be one (v. 17). This action symbolized what the Lord would do for his exiled people. He would bring both the Israelite and Judahite exiles back to the land and make them one nation again, ruled by one king, David (vv. 18–22, 24a, 25; see my comments on 34:23–24). They would reject their idols and obey the Lord, who would cleanse them from their past sins (vv. 23, 24b). The Lord would make a lasting "covenant of peace" with them and dwell among his people as their God (vv. 26–28; see 34:25). This prophecy of the reunification of Israel was not fulfilled in Ezekiel's time or in the postexilic period. Its essential fulfillment will occur when the Jewish people are reconciled to God (see Rom. 11:25–31, as well as my comments on Isa. 11:12–14 and Jer. 31:31–40).

The "covenant of peace" prophesied by Ezekiel is the same as the "new covenant" predicted by Jeremiah (see Jer. 31:31–37). This covenant is made in conjunction with the restoration of the exiles to their land (Jer. 31:23–30; Ezek 37:1–23) and is accompanied by the forgiveness of sins, spiritual cleansing, and the realization of the ancient covenantal ideal (Jer. 31:33–34; Ezek. 36:25; 37:23, 27). The former (Mosaic) covenant demanded obedience but provided no enablement to obey (Jer. 31:32). This new covenant of peace empowers God's people to obey his demands (Jer. 31:33–34), for it is accompanied by the gift of his indwelling Spirit (Ezek. 36:27), who transforms their will and gives them a new desire and capacity to obey (Jer. 31:33; Ezek. 36:26–27).

Just as the former (Mosaic) covenant was inaugurated with a blood sacrifice (Exod. 24:4–8), so the new covenant was established by the shed blood of Jesus, the ideal sacrifice (Luke 22:20; 1 Cor. 11:25). In the present era the church is God's new covenant community and experiences the reality of this covenant through the gift of the Spirit (see 2 Cor. 3:6; Gal. 4:24–31; Heb. 8:6–13; 9:15; 10:13–18, 29; 12:22–24; 13:20). Ethnic Israel, although presently alienated from God, will someday be reconciled to God and experience the reality of the new covenant as well (Rom. 11:25–27).

On the surface, New Testament references to the realization of the new covenant in the present era are problematic, for Jeremiah and Ezekiel spoke of this covenant being made with Israel, not the Gentiles. Some argue that the church is the new "Israel" through which the Old Testament promise is fulfilled. Others, insisting on a sharp distinction between Israel and the church, propose that the new covenant mentioned in the New Testament is distinct from the one promised in the Old Testament. A better solution is to propose an "already/not yet" model, which sees a present realization of the promises in the church and a future fulfillment for ethnic Israel. Only this mediating view does justice to the language of both the Hebrew prophets and the New Testament. Just because the Hebrew prophets mention only Israel as the recipient of the covenant does not mean that others could not be recipients as well; just because the New Testament focuses on a present realization through the church does not preclude a future fulfillment for Israel.

The prophets were like men looking through a tunnel. In the light at the end of the tunnel, they saw God reconciling Israel to himself. But as we walk to the end of the tunnel and look outside with Paul and the author of Hebrews, we gain the advantage of peripheral vision and discover that God's new covenant involves others that the prophets could not see with their "tunnel vision." At the same time, the existence of peripheral participants in the lighted world should not distract us from the fact that Israel continues to stand straight ahead of us, right where the prophets saw her, awaiting the time when her people too will become participants in this new covenant, just as the prophets envisioned.

The Last Battle (38:1–39:29)

The preceding oracles envision a time when reunified Israel would enjoy prosperity and security. Chapter 38 assumes this scenario; it depicts Israel as restored from exile (38:8; see 36:8–12, 34–35) and as living in safety under God's protective care (38:11, 14; see 34:27). However, a coalition of hostile nations, misinterpreting Israel's sense of security for vulnerability (see the reference to unwalled towns in v. 11), invade Israel's land and try to destroy God's people.

The leader of the hostile nations is called "Gog of the land of Magog, the chief prince of Meshech and Tubal" (38:2). Attempts to identify these proper names with modern Russian place names are anachronistic. Perhaps Gog is to be identified with the Gugu mentioned in Assyrian texts from the seventh century B.C. This Gugu is known to historians as Gyges, king of Lydia in western Anatolia (modern Turkey). Meshech is the ancient region of Mushku, located in central Anatolia, while Tubal is to be identified with ancient Tabal in eastern Anatolia. The inhabitants of these areas are mentioned in Assyrian inscriptions as resisting Assyria's imperialistic efforts.[114] The names Magog, Meshech, and Tubal (as well as Gomer and Togarmah; see v. 6) appear in Genesis 10:2–3 as descendants of Japheth. Some translations take the Hebrew word *rosh* in 38:2 as a proper name and translate, "the prince of Rosh, Meshech, and Tubal." However, it is far more likely that the word is appositional to "prince."[115] Gog heads up a coalition of nations that includes Persia from the distant east, Cush (Ethiopia) and Put (Libya) from

114. See Yamauchi, *Foes from the Northern Frontiers,* 19–27.
115. See Block, *Ezekiel Chapters 25–48,* 434–35, and Zimmerli, *Ezekiel 2,* 305.

the distant south, as well as Gomer and Beth Togarmah from the distant north (vv. 5–6).[116] As Block observes, the appearance of seven nations (Meshech, Tubal, Persia, Cush, Put, Gomer, Beth Togarmah) suggests "totality" and "completeness."[117]

This army marches against Israel, expecting to loot and plunder the land (vv. 7–15). Little do they realize that their attack is orchestrated by the Lord, who prophesied the event long ago and intends to demonstrate his sovereign power to the watching world and to his people by defeating this enemy horde (vv. 16–17, 23; 39:1–2, 7–8).[118] The Lord stops the invaders in their tracks (vv. 2–3) and supernaturally annihilates them (vv. 18–22; 39:3–6). In the aftermath of the battle, the people of Israel gather the weapons of the enemy and burn them as fuel (vv. 9–10). Many of the corpses are devoured by scavengers (vv. 5, 17–20); the rest are given a mass burial that takes seven months to complete (vv. 11–16). Following this display of divine power, the Lord's reputation will be fully exonerated (vv. 21–22). The nations will realize that Israel's exile was due to sin, not weakness on God's part (vv. 23–24; see 36:20–21).

In 38:1–39:24, the prophet describes a consummating battle that occurs after Israel has been restored to the land from exile. As this oracle concludes (vv. 25–29), the perspective shifts back to the exilic period (note "now" in v. 25).[119] The Lord promises to bring his people back from exile, show them his compassion, and pour out his Spirit upon them. They will repudiate their former sinful ways and recognize that he is their sovereign king.

How is this prophecy to be fulfilled? The only later biblical reference to this prophecy places this battle at the end of the millennial age (see Rev. 20:7–10). This is consistent with the portrait in Ezekiel 38, which indicates that this invasion comes while the land is populated and experiencing peace (38:8, 11, 14). The people have been forgiven by the Lord and reinstated to the land (cf. 38:8 with 36:33). Some object that Revelation 20:7 associates Gog and Magog with all the nations, rather than the specific areas mentioned in Ezekiel 38–39. But John's language, while abbreviated, is consistent with the description in Ezekiel 38:2–6, which pictures a coalition of distant nations from three of the four points of the compass. Furthermore, both passages (cf. Rev. 20:9b with Ezek. 39:6) describe the enemy being destroyed

---

116. Block (ibid., 439–40) prefers to see the Hebrew *paras,* traditionally translated "Persia," as a reference to a western ally of Egypt (see 27:10, where it is associated with Lydia and Put) or perhaps an alternative spelling for Pathros (see Isa. 11:11; Jer. 44:15; Ezek. 29:14; 30:14), a designation for southern (i.e., Upper) Egypt.

117. Ibid., 441.

118. There are no other prophecies in the Hebrew Bible that foretell an invasion of Israel by the forces named in chapter 38. Verse 17 must be referring to earlier, more general prophecies of how the Lord would defeat an end-time coalition of hostile nations. See, e.g., Isa. 13:1–16; 14:26; 24:1–23; 34:1–17; 63:1–6.

119. See Block, *Ezekiel Chapters 25–48,* 485, who notes that the preceding oracle referred to the "future years" (38:8) and "days to come" (38:16).

by fire from heaven.[120] Since the distinct nations mentioned in Ezekiel's prophecy have disappeared, it is best to take Gog and his hordes as archetypes of the hostile nations of the world whom God will defeat in a culminating cosmic battle.[121] In other words, Ezekiel's description of this battle was contextualized for his sixth-century B.C. audience. These distant, mysterious nations, located on the very perimeter of Israel's world, made apt archetypes because of their "foreignness."[122]

The Lord Restores Pure Worship (40:1–48:35)

In 573 B.C., Ezekiel was transported in his spirit to the land of Israel, where, from his vantage point on a high mountain, he saw a series of visions depicting the reconciliation of God and his people (40:1–2). As Ezekiel gazed at the temple mount, he saw an angelic surveyor who instructed him to record the content of his visions (vv. 3–4). Ezekiel describes in vivid and exact detail the structure and measurements of the rebuilt temple complex (40:4–42:20). He records the dimensions so the people may build it just as the Lord has specified (43:10–11). The description is so precise that modern readers are able to draw blueprints and sketches of the structure.[123] John Schmitt has even constructed an elaborate scale model of the temple complex and its inner rooms.[124]

Ezekiel's verbal blueprint of the rebuilt temple culminates with an exciting vision of the Lord's return to his house. Several years earlier Ezekiel had witnessed the departure of the Lord from the temple (see chapter 10). But now he witnesses the return of the Lord's glory from the east, the direction to which it had earlier departed (43:1–3; see 10:19; 11:23). The divine glory enters and fills the temple (vv. 4–5; see also 44:4). As it does, the Lord announces that he will now establish his throne in the temple and dwell there forever among his purified people (vv. 6–9). The entire top of the temple mount will be considered holy territory (v. 12).

Ezekiel next gives detailed instructions concerning temple regulations and service. He describes the design of the altar (vv. 13–17) and gives instructions for the dedicatory sacrifices that are to be offered upon it for seven

120. Scholars have constructed the chronology of events in Ezek. 38–39 in a variety of ways. Many place these events just before, during, or at the end of the seven-year "tribulation" period that precedes the millennial kingdom. See Harold W. Hoehner, "The Progression of Events in Ezekiel 38–39," in *Integrity of Heart, Skillfulness of Hands*, ed. C. H. Dyer and R. B. Zuck (Grand Rapids: Baker, 1994), 82–92. For a helpful survey and critique of various viewpoints, see Ralph H. Alexander, "Ezekiel," in *The Expositor's Bible Commentary*, ed. F. Gaebelein (Grand Rapids: Zondervan, 1986), 6:937–40.

121. For a brief discussion of archetypal language in prophetic literature, see Robert B. Chisholm Jr., *From Exegesis to Exposition* (Grand Rapids: Baker, 1998), 173–74.

122. See Block, *Ezekiel Chapters 25–48*, 436.

123. See, for example, ibid., 508–9, 520, 541, 550, 565, 572–73, and Alexander, "Ezekiel," 961, 965, 972.

124. See John W. Schmitt and J. Carl Laney, *Messiah's Coming Temple: Ezekiel's Prophetic Vision of the Future Temple* (Grand Rapids: Kregel, 1997), 77–103, 187.

days (vv. 18–27). After the altar's dedication, which involved burnt and sin offerings, the altar could be used for regular burnt and fellowship offerings. The east gate of the temple's outer court would be permanently shut to commemorate the Lord's arrival through it upon his return (44:1–2). Only the "prince" would be allowed to sit inside the gateway as he ate "in the presence of the Lord" (v. 3).

Who is the "prince" identified in verse 3 and in several other subsequent texts in these chapters?[125] The most likely explanation is that this "prince" is the new David prophesied in 34:23–24; 37:24–25. This ideal Davidic ruler, who is designated "king" and "prince" in both passages, stands in contrast to the Davidic "princes" of Ezekiel's day mentioned earlier in the book. However, some scholars prefer to distinguish the "prince" of chapters 44–48 from the Davidic prince mentioned earlier because the figure depicted in the later chapters seems to occupy the role of a worship leader, not a king (see especially 45:17, 22; 46:4, 10). However, this "prince" is also depicted as promoting justice, which was a royal function (45:7–12; 46:18).[126] It is also important to recall that both David and Solomon assumed the role of worship leader on important occasions, including the return of the ark to Jerusalem (2 Sam. 6) and the dedication of the temple (1 Kings 8). On both occasions, the king offered sacrifices before the Lord.

The Lord gives Ezekiel several regulations to govern temple worship (44:5). First of all, foreigners are prohibited from entering the temple (vv. 6–9). Isaiah anticipated a day when foreigners would become loyal followers of the Lord and worship in the new temple (Isa. 56:6–8). Ezekiel is not talking about such proselytes. His reference to foreigners who are "uncircumcised in heart and flesh" indicates that he has in mind people who have not committed themselves to the Lord and remain attached to their pagan practices.

A second series of regulations pertains to the Levites. Because of their past unfaithfulness, their new duties will be limited. They can serve at the temple gates and slaughter sacrifices, but they are not allowed to handle any of the holy objects or offerings (vv. 10–14). Only the descendants of Zadok, who remained faithful to the Lord, are permitted to enter his sanctuary (vv. 15–16). These Zadokite priests are given very specific regulations to follow in carrying out their duties (vv. 17–31).

A third series of regulations deals with prescribed offerings to be made on holy days and during feasts (45:13–46:24). As noted above, the prince plays a prominent role in leading the people in worship. He provides the var-

---

125. See 45:7–9, 16–17, 22; 46:2, 4, 8, 10, 12, 16–18; 48:21–22. For a detailed discussion of this issue, see Jon Douglas Levenson, *Theology of the Program of Restoration of Ezekiel 40–48* (Missoula, Mont.: Scholars Press, 1976), 57–73.

126. In this regard, see Moshe Weinfeld, *Social Justice in Ancient Israel and in the Ancient Near East* (Minneapolis: Fortress, 1995), 55–56.

ious offerings that "make atonement for the people" (45:17), offers a sin offering for himself and the people at the Passover (45:22), participates in the
Sabbath observance (46:2, 4), and worships among the people during appointed feasts (46:10, 12).

The Lord also specifies how the land around the temple complex is to
be allotted (45:1–7; 48:9–22). The Zadokite priests are given territory con-
tiguous to the temple, while the Levites and the "prince" receive adjoining
portions to the south and east/west, respectively.[127] The city allotted to the
"whole house of Israel" (45:6) borders Levite territory to the south. Included
within this area are houses and pastureland. The city proper is a square with
each of its four walls having three gates named for the tribes of Israel (48:30–
35). The name of the city is "The LORD is there."

Another special feature of Ezekiel's vision is a stream that originates in
the temple and flows eastward to the Dead Sea (47:1–12). Near its point of
origin the stream is only ankle deep, but eventually it becomes a deep river.
Fruit trees line the bank of the river, which flows into the Dead Sea and
transforms its salt water into fresh water. The sea teems with all kinds of fish
and attracts fishermen, who line its shores with their nets. The vision differs
slightly from that of Zechariah, who describes rivers flowing both eastward
and westward from the temple (see Zech. 14:8). Both visions depict God's
temple as the source of life and renewed blessing, symbolized by the water
that originates from it.

The prophecy also describes the land's boundaries and tribal allotments
(47:13–48:29).[128] Restored Israel's territory extends from Lebo Hamath in
the distant north to Kadesh in the far south. From north to south the tribal
arrangement is as follows: Dan, Asher, Naphtali, Manasseh, Ephraim, Reuben, Judah, Benjamin, Simeon, Issachar, Zebulun, Gad. The temple, city,
and territories reserved for the priests, Levites, and prince are located between Judah and Benjamin.

Ezekiel's vision of a new temple and a restored nation was not fulfilled
in the postexilic period. How then should we expect the vision to be fulfilled? Scholars have answered this question in a variety of ways. On one end
of the interpretive spectrum are those who see the vision as purely symbolic
and as fulfilled in the New Testament church. On the opposite end are the
hyper-literalists, who contend that the vision will be fulfilled exactly as described during the millennial age. In attempting to answer the question, one
must first recognize that Ezekiel's vision is contextualized for his sixth-century B.C. audience. He describes the reconciliation of God and his people in
terms that would be meaningful to this audience.[129] They would naturally

127. For a chart showing the arrangement, see Block, *Ezekiel Chapters 25–48,* 733.

128. For a map showing the boundaries and tribal allotments, see ibid., 711.

129. See Mark F. Rooker, "Evidence from Ezekiel," in *A Case for Premillennialism,* ed. D. K. Campbell and J. L. Townsend (Chicago: Moody, 1992), 133.

conceive of such reconciliation as involving the rebuilding of the temple, the reinstitution of the sacrificial system, the renewal of the Davidic dynasty, and the return and reunification of the twelve exiled tribes. Since the fulfillment of the vision transcends these culturally conditioned boundaries, we should probably view it as idealized to some extent and look for an essential, rather than an exact fulfillment of many of its features.

The vision anticipates the restoration of ethnic Israel, an event predicted by Paul (Rom. 11:25–32). However, the northern tribes never returned to the land and disappeared as they were assimilated into the surrounding culture. Ezekiel's vision of national restoration will be fulfilled through the Jewish people, who are descended from Judah, Benjamin, and Levi (see my comments on Isa. 11:13–14; Jer. 31:31–37; Ezek. 37:15–28).

The inclusion of so many minute details suggests that the temple described here will be a literal reality in the Jerusalem of the future (see Isa. 2:2–4; Hag. 2:9).[130] However, the final sacrifice of Jesus Christ has made the Levitical system obsolete (see Heb. 9:1–10:18). To return to this system, with its sin offerings and such, would be a serious retrogression.[131] Ezekiel's audience would have found it impossible to conceive of a restored covenant community apart from the sacrificial system.[132] Now that the fulfillment of the vision transcends that cultural context, we can expect it to be essentially fulfilled when the Israel of the future celebrates the redemptive work of their savior in their new temple.[133]

Ezekiel's portrait of the Davidic king, or "prince," is also contextualized to some degree. The king leads the community in worship and must even offer sacrifices for himself. Ezekiel also seems to anticipate the establishment of a dynastic succession (see 45:8; 46:16–18). Ezekiel's audience would have found this portrayal quite natural. However, Jesus, the one who fulfills the vision, will have no need to offer such sacrifices, nor will he institute a dynasty. On the contrary, he will reign over his kingdom forever.

Bibliography

Commentaries

Alexander, R. H. "Ezekiel." In *The Expositor's Bible Commentary*, edited by F. E. Gaebelein, 12 vols., 6:737–996. Grand Rapids: Zondervan, 1978–92.
Allen, L. C. *Ezekiel 1–19*. WBC. Dallas: Word, 1994.
———. *Ezekiel 20–48*. WBC. Dallas: Word, 1990.
Blenkinsopp, J. *Ezekiel*. Interpretation. Louisville: John Knox, 1990.

---

130. Ibid., 128–31.
131. Some scholars argue that the sacrificial system will be reinstituted in the millennial age with the sacrifices being commemorative of Christ's work. For a well-reasoned defense of this view, see Alexander, "Ezekiel," 946–52.
132. See H. A. Ironside, *Expository Notes on Ezekiel the Prophet* (New York: Loizeaux, 1949), 305.
133. See Rooker, "Evidence from Ezekiel," 131–34.

Block, D. I. *The Book of Ezekiel Chapters 1–24.* NICOT. Grand Rapids: Eerdmans, 1997.
———. *The Book of Ezekiel Chapters 25–48.* NICOT. Grand Rapids: Eerdmans, 1998.
Cooper, L. E., Sr. *Ezekiel.* NAC. Nashville: Broadman & Holman, 1994.
Eichrodt, W. *Ezekiel.* OTL. Translated by C. Quin. Philadelphia: Westminster, 1970.
Greenberg, M. *Ezekiel 1–20.* AB. Garden City, N.Y.: Doubleday, 1983.
———. *Ezekiel 21–37.* AB. New York: Doubleday, 1997.
Hals, R. M. *Ezekiel.* FOTL. Grand Rapids: Eerdmans, 1989.
Zimmerli, W. *Ezekiel 1.* Hermeneia. Translated by R. E. Clements. Philadelphia: Fortress, 1979.
———. *Ezekiel 2.* Hermeneia. Translated by J. D. Martin. Philadelphia: Fortress, 1983.

Recent Studies

General

Allen, L. C. "Some Types of Textual Adaptation in Ezekiel." *ETL* 71 (1995): 5–29.
Boadt, L. E. "Mythological Themes and the Unity of Ezekiel." In *Literary Structure and Rhetorical Strategies in the Hebrew Bible,* edited by L. J. de Regt et al., 211–31. Assen: Van Gorcum, 1996.
———. "A New Look at the Book of Ezekiel." *TBT* 37 (1999): 4–9.
Burke, D. L. "Style and Rhetoric in Ezekiel: A Syntactical Approach." Ph.D. diss., Annenberg Research Institute, 1992.
Clements, R. E. *Ezekiel.* Louisville: Westminster John Knox, 1996.
Cook, S. L. "Apocalypticism and Prophecy in Post-exilic Israel: The Social Setting of the Apocalyptic Sections of Joel, Ezekiel, and I-Zechariah." Ph.D. diss., Yale University, 1992.
Darr, K. P. "Ezekiel among the Critics." *Currents in Research: Biblical Studies* 2 (1994): 9–24.
———. "Ezekiel's Justifications of God: Teaching Troubling Texts." *JSOT* 55 (1992): 97–117.
Duguid, I. M. *Ezekiel and the Leaders of Israel.* VTSup 56. Leiden: Brill, 1994.
Galambush, J. *Jerusalem in the Book of Ezekiel: The City as Yahweh's Wife.* SBLDS 130. Atlanta: Scholars Press, 1992.
Greenberg, M. "Notes on the Influence of Tradition on Ezekiel." *JANES* 22 (1995): 29–37.
Halperin, D. J. *Seeking Ezekiel: Text and Psychology.* University Park, Pa.: Pennsylvania State University Press, 1993.
Hamilton, P. C. "Theological Implications of the Divine Title Adonai Yehovah in Ezekiel." Ph.D. diss., Southwestern Baptist Theological Seminary, 1990.
Joyce, P. M. "King and Messiah in Ezekiel." In *King and Messiah in Israel and the Ancient Near East,* edited by J. Day, JSOTSup 270, 323–37. Sheffield: Sheffield Academic Press, 1998.
———. "Synchronic and Diachronic Perspectives on Ezekiel." In *Synchronic or Diachronic? A Debate in Old Testament Exegesis,* edited by J. C. de Moor, 115–28. Leiden: Brill, 1995.
Kingsley, P. "Ezekiel by the Grand Canal: Between Jewish and Babylonian Traditions," *Journal of the Royal Asiatic Society,* 3d ser., no. 2 (1992): 339–46.
Kutsko, J. F. *Between Heaven and Earth: Divine Presence and Absence in the Book of Ezekiel.* Winona Lake, Ind.: Eisenbrauns, 2000.
Levitt Kohn, R. "A New Heart and a New Soul: Ezekiel, the Exile, and the Torah." Ph.D. diss., University of California, San Diego, 1997.
Lust, J. "Exile and Diaspora: Gathering from Dispersion in Ezekiel." In *Lectures et Relectures de la Bible: Festschrift P.-A. Bogaert,* edited by J.-M. Auwers and A. Wénin, 99–122. Louvain: Peeters, 1999.

McKeating, H. *Ezekiel.* Old Testament Guides. Sheffield: JSOT, 1993.
———. "Ezekiel the 'Prophet Like Moses'?" *JSOT* 61 (1994): 97–109.
Odendaal, M. "Exile in Ezekiel: Evaluating a Sociological Model." *NGTT* 40 (1999): 133–39.
Patton, C. L. "Pan-Deuteronomism and the Book of Ezekiel." In *Those Elusive Deuteronomists: The Phenomenon of Pan-Deuteronomism,* edited by L. S. Schearing and S. L. McKenzie, JSOTSup 268, 200–215. Sheffield: Sheffield Academic Press, 1999.
Renz, T. "The Use of the Zion Tradition in the Book of Ezekiel." In *Zion, City of Our God,* edited by R. S. Hess and G. J. Wenham, 77–103. Grand Rapids: Eerdmans, 1999.
Rooker, M. F. *Biblical Hebrew in Transition: The Language of the Book of Ezekiel.* JSOTSup 90. Sheffield: JSOT, 1990.
———. "The Use of the Old Testament in the Book of Ezekiel." *Faith and Mission* 15 (1998): 45–52.
Sloan, I. B. "Ezekiel and the Covenant of Friendship." *BTB* 22 (1992): 149–54.
Uffenheimer, B. "Theodicy and Ethics in the Prophecy of Ezekiel." In *Justice and Righteousness: Biblical Themes and Their Influence,* edited by H. G. Reventlow and Y. Hoffman, JSOTSup 137, 200–227. Sheffield: JSOT, 1992.
Vawter, B., and L. J. Hoppe. *A New Heart: A Commentary on the Book of Ezekiel.* Grand Rapids: Eerdmans, 1991.
Witherup, R. D. "Apocalyptic Imagery in the Book of Ezekiel." *TBT* 37 (1999): 10–17.

Ezekiel 1–24

Allen, L. C. "The Structure and Intention of Ezekiel i." *VT* 43 (1993): 145–61.
———. "The Structuring of Ezekiel's Revisionist History Lesson (Ezekiel 20:3–31)." *CBQ* 54 (1992): 448–62.
Beenjes, P. C. "What a Lioness Was Your Mother: Reflections on Ezekiel 19." In *On Reading Prophetic Texts,* edited by B. Becking and M. Dijkstra, 21–35. Leiden: Brill, 1996.
Block, D. I. "Ezekiel's Boiling Cauldron: A Form-Critical Solution to Ezekiel xxiv 1–14." *VT* 41 (1991): 12–37.
Braulik, G. "Ezekiel and Deuteronomy—'Clan Liability' in Ezekiel 18:20 and Deuteronomy 24:16 in Consideration of Jeremiah 31:29–30 and 2 Kings 14:6." *NGTT* 40 (1999): 270–92.
Brown, N. R. "The Daughters of Your People: Female Prophets in Ezekiel 13:17–23." *JBL* 118 (1999): 417–33.
Christman, A. G. R. "Ezekiel's Vision of the Chariot in Early Christian Exegesis." Ph.D. diss., University of Virginia, 1995.
Dempsey, C. J. "The Whore of Ezekiel 16: The Impact and Ramifications of Gender-Specific Metaphors in Light of Biblical Law and Divine Judgement." In *Gender and Law in the Hebrew Bible and the Ancient Near East,* JSOTSup 262, 57–78. Sheffield: Sheffield Academic Press, 1998.
Dijkstra, M. "Goddesses, Gods, Men, and Women in Ezekiel 8." In *On Reading Prophetic Texts,* edited by B. Becking and M. Dijkstra, 83–114. Leiden: Brill, 1996.
Eslinger, L. "Ezekiel 20 and the Metaphor of Historical Teleology: Concepts of Biblical History." *JSOT* 81 (1998): 93–125.
Franke, C. "Divine Pardon in Ezekiel." *TBT* 37 (1999): 24–28.
Fredericks, D. C. "Diglossia, Revelation, and Ezekiel's Inaugural Rite." *JETS* 41 (1998): 189–99.
Gravett, S. "That All Women May Take Warning: Reading the Sexual Ethnic Violence in Ezekiel 16 and 23." Ph.D. diss., Duke University, 1996.
Gross, C. D. "Ezekiel and Solomon's Temple." *BT* 50 (1999): 207–14.

Harland, P. J. "What Kind of 'Violence' in Ezekiel 22?" *ExpT* 108 (1996–97): 111–14.

Joyce, P. M. "Dislocation and Adaptation in the Exilic Age and After." In *After Exile: Essays in Honour of Rex Mason,* edited by J. Barton and D. J. Reimer, 45–58. Macon, Ga.: Mercer, 1996.

Korpel, M. C. A. "Avian Spirits in Ugarit and in Ezekiel 13." In *Ugarit, Religion, and Culture,* edited by N. Wyatt et al., 99–113. Münster, Germany: Ugarit-Verlag, 1996.

Lenchak, T. A. "Puzzling Passages: Ezekiel 4:4–5." *TBT* 37 (1999): 387.

Lust, J. "Ezekiel Salutes Isaiah: Ezekiel 20,32–44." In *Studies in the Book of Isaiah: Festschrift Willem A. M. Beuken,* edited by J. van Ruiten and M. Vervenne, 367–82. Louvain: Peeters, 1997.

Lutzky, H. C. "On 'the Image of Jealousy' (Ezekiel viii 3, 5)." *VT* 46 (1996): 121–25.

Matties, G. H. *Ezekiel 18 and the Rhetoric of Moral Discourse.* SBLDS 126. Atlanta: Scholars Press, 1990.

McBride, G. J. "The Nature of God's Judgment against Israel in Ezekiel 1–24." Ph.D. diss., New Orleans Baptist Theological Seminary, 1995.

Miller, J. E. "The Thirtieth Year of Ezekiel 1:1." *RB* 99 (1992): 499–503.

Odell M. S. "The Inversion of Shame and Forgiveness in Ezekiel 16.59–63." *JSOT* 56 (1992): 101–12.

———. "The Particle and the Prophet: Observations on Ezekiel ii 6." *VT* 48 (1998): 425–32.

———. "You Are What You Eat: Ezekiel and the Scroll." *JBL* 117 (1998): 229–48.

Patton, C. "'I Myself Gave Them Laws That Were Not Good': Ezekiel 20 and the Exodus Traditions." *JSOT* 69 (1996): 73–90.

Pope, M. H. "Mixed Marriage Metaphor in Ezekiel 16." In *Fortunate the Eyes That See: Essays in Honor of David Noel Freedman in Celebration of His Seventieth Birthday,* edited by A. B. Beck et al., 384–99. Grand Rapids: Eerdmans, 1995.

Swanepoel, M. G. "Ezekiel 16: Abandoned Child, Bride Adorned, or Unfaithful Wife?" In *Among the Prophets: Language, Image, and Structure in the Prophetic Writings,* edited by P. R. Davies and D. J. A. Clines, 84–104. Sheffield: JSOT, 1993.

van der Horst, P. W. "I Gave Them Laws That Were Not Good: Ezekiel 20:25 in Ancient Judaism and Early Christianity." In *Sacred History and Sacred Texts in Early Judaism: A Symposium in Honour of A. S. van der Woude,* edited by J. N. Bremmer and F. G. Martínez, 94–118. Kampen: Kok Pharos, 1992.

van Dijk-Hemmes, F. "The Metaphorization of Woman in Prophetic Speech: An Analysis of Ezekiel xxiii." *VT* 43 (1993): 162–70.

Ezekiel 25–32

Barr, J. "'Thou Art the Cherub': Ezekiel 28.14 and the Post-Ezekiel Understanding of Genesis 2." In *Priests, Prophets, and Scribes: Essays on the Formation and Heritage of Second Temple Judaism in Honour of Joseph Blenkinsopp,* edited by E. Ulrich et al., JSOTSup 149, 213–23. Sheffield: JSOT, 1992.

Geyer, J. B. "Ezekiel 27 and the Cosmic Ship." In *Among the Prophets: Language, Image, and Structure in the Prophetic Writings,* edited by P. R. Davies and D. J. A. Clines, 105–26. Sheffield: JSOT, 1993.

Jeppesen, K. "You Are a Cherub, but Not God!" *SJOT* 1 (1991): 83–94.

Lewis, T. J. "*CT* 13.33–34 and Ezekiel 32: Lion-Dragon Myths." *JAOS* 116 (1996): 28–47.

Miller, J. E. "The Maelaek of Tyre (Ezekiel 28,11–19)." *ZAW* 105 (1993): 497–501.

Noort, E. "Gan-Eden in the Context of the Mythology of the Hebrew Bible." In *Paradise Interpreted: Representations of Paradise in Judaism and Christianity,* edited by G. Luttikhuizen, 21–36. Leiden: Brill, 1999.

Porter, J. R. "Ezekiel xxx 16—A Suggestion." *VT* 47 (1997): 128.
Strong, J. T. "Ezekiel's Oracles against the Nations within the Context of His Message." Ph.D. diss., Union Theological Seminary, 1993.
———. "Ezekiel's Use of the Recognition Formula in His Oracles against the Nations." *Perspectives in Religious Studies* 22 (1995): 115–33.

Ezekiel 33–48

Allen, L. C. "Structure, Tradition, and Redaction in Ezekiel's Death Valley Vision." In *Among the Prophets: Language, Image, and Structure in the Prophetic Writings,* edited by P. R. Davies and D. J. A. Clines, 127–42. Sheffield: JSOT, 1993.
Block, D. I. "Bringing Back David: Ezekiel's Messianic Hope." In *The Lord's Anointed,* edited by P. E. Satterthwaite, R. S. Hess, and G. J. Wenham, 167–88. Grand Rapids: Baker, 1995.
———. "Gog in Prophetic Tradition: A New Look at Ezekiel xxxviii 17." *VT* 42 (1992): 154–72.
Cook, S. L. "Innerbiblical Interpretation in Ezekiel 44 and the History of Israel's Priesthood." *JBL* 114 (1995): 193–208.
Dijkstra, M. "The Altar of Ezekiel: Fact or Fiction?" *VT* 42 (1992): 22–36.
Engelhard, D. H. "Ezekiel 47:13–48:29 as Royal Grant." In *"Go to the Land I Will Show You": Studies in Honor of Dwight W. Young,* edited by J. E. Coleson and V. H. Matthews, 45–56. Winona Lake, Ind.: Eisenbrauns, 1996.
Fikes, B. A. "A Theological Analysis of the Shepherd-King Motif in Ezekiel 34." Ph.D. diss., Southwestern Baptist Theological Seminary, 1995.
Hullinger, J. M. "The Problem of Animal Sacrifices in Ezekiel 40–48." *BSac* 152 (1995): 279–89.
———. "A Proposed Solution to the Problem of Animal Sacrifices in Ezekiel 40–48." Ph.D. diss., Dallas Theological Seminary, 1993.
Irwin, B. P. "Molek Imagery and the Slaughter of Gog in Ezekiel 38 and 39." *JSOT* 65 (1995): 93–112.
Kasher, R. "Anthropomorphism, Holiness, and Cult: A New Look at Ezekiel 40–48." *ZAW* 110 (1998): 192–208.
Odell, M. S. "The City of Hamonah in Ezekiel 39:11–16: The Tumultuous City of Jerusalem." *CBQ* 56 (1994): 479–89.
Polan, G. J. "Ezekiel's Covenant of Peace." *TBT* 37 (1999): 18–23.
Seitz, C. R. "Ezekiel 37:1–14." *Int* 46 (1992): 53–56.
Sharon, D. M. "A Biblical Parallel to a Sumerian Temple Hymn? Ezekiel 40–48 and Gudea." *JANES* 24 (1997): 99–109.
Stevenson, K. R. *Vision of Transformation: The Territorial Rhetoric of Ezekiel 40–48.* SBLDS 154. Atlanta: Scholars Press, 1996.
Tanner, J. P. "Rethinking Ezekiel's Invasion by Gog." *JETS* 39 (1996): 29–46.
Tuell, S. S. "Ezekiel 40–42 as Verbal Icon." *CBQ* 58 (1996): 649–64.
———. *The Law of the Temple in Ezekiel 40–48.* HSM 49. Atlanta: Scholars Press, 1992.

Daniel

Introduction

Date, Author, and Literary Genre

The Book of Daniel appears in the English Bible between Ezekiel and Hosea and is classified with the Major Prophets. In the Hebrew Bible, which is divided into three sections (the Law, Prophets, and Writings), Daniel is in the Writings. Even so, the New Testament (Matt. 24:15) and the Jewish historian Josephus call Daniel a "prophet." The ancient Greek versions of Daniel include material that does not appear in the Hebrew text. The Prayer of Azariah and the Song of the Three Young Men are included in chapter 3, while the stories of Susanna and of Bel and the Dragon are appended to the book. The Roman Catholic Church accepts this additional material as canonical, but Protestants regard the additions as apocryphal.

On the basis of the book's internal evidence (see Dan. 8:1; 9:2, 22; 10:2) and statements in the New Testament (see, e.g., Matt. 24:15), authorship of the book is traditionally ascribed to Daniel, who lived in the seventh to sixth centuries B.C. Traditional scholarship also understands the narratives in chapters 1–6 as historically accurate biographical accounts and assumes that the book's prophecies are genuine. With the rise of higher criticism, many scholars have rejected the traditional position.[1] Most modern scholars date chapters 1–6 to the third century B.C. and discount the essential historicity of the narratives.[2] They date the prophetic material in chapters 7–12 to the second century B.C. Most critics understand the "fulfilled" prophecies as re-

---

1. Actually the philosopher Porphyry (A.D. 233–304) anticipated many of the arguments of modern higher criticism. See Edward J. Young, *The Prophecy of Daniel* (Grand Rapids: Eerdmans, 1949), 317–20. For a brief survey of higher critical opinion, see Raymond B. Dillard and Tremper Longman III, *An Introduction to the Old Testament* (Grand Rapids: Zondervan, 1994), 332.

2. For example, John J. Collins identifies the literary genre of chapters 1–6 as "court legend." See his *Daniel with an Introduction to Apocalyptic Literature*, FOTL (Grand Rapids: Eerdmans, 1984), 42.

ally made after the fact and the "unfulfilled" prophecies as genuine, albeit inaccurate, predictions. Collins calls the book a "historical apocalypse" and claims that it is "characterized by *ex eventu* [after the fact] prophecy of history and by eschatology that is cosmic in scope and has a political focus."[3] According to Collins, other examples of historical apocalypses include *Jubilees, 4 Ezra, 2 Baruch,* and the Book of Dreams and the Apocalypse of Weeks in *1 Enoch.*[4]

Daniel's prophecies do indeed share many of the characteristics of apocalyptic literature, including a long-range eschatological vision emerging out of a historical setting of oppression, revelation mediated through angels, unusual and highly symbolic imagery, and a deterministic view of history.[5] Many apocalyptic books are pseudonymous and utilize "prophecy" after the fact.[6] The latter technique uses the style of prediction (prophecy) to record events that had already taken place when the author wrote. While acknowledging that Daniel exhibits many of the features of the apocalyptic genre, most evangelicals argue that the book is not pseudonymous and that its prophecies are genuine. In this regard the debate focuses on chapter 11 (see the discussion of this chapter below).

Modern critics also argue on linguistic grounds for the later date of the book. For example, S. R. Driver stated: "The *Persian* words presuppose a period after the Persian Empire had been well established: the Greek words *demand,* the Hebrew *supports,* and the Aramaic *permits,* a date *after the conquest of Palestine by Alexander the Great* (B.C. 332)."[7] Evangelicals have challenged this conclusion. Archer, for example, argues that there are only three Greek loanwords in the book, all of which are technical terms for musical instruments. He shows that the Assyrians and Babylonians had contacts with Cyprus and Ionia and suggests that the instruments in question could have been known in Mesopotamia at a relatively early date.[8] The Persian loanwords number fifteen; all are governmental or administrative terms that could have been known to Daniel, who served under a Persian regime.[9] Archer also concludes on linguistic grounds that the Aramaic and Hebrew of the book differ significantly from that of texts originating in the third to second century B.C. and must therefore date to an earlier period.[10]

3. Ibid., 33.
4. Ibid., 6–14.
5. See Longman and Dillard, *Introduction,* 342–44.
6. Ibid., 344.
7. S. R. Driver, *An Introduction to the Literature of the Old Testament,* 8th ed. (Edinburgh: T. & T. Clark, 1909), 508.
8. See Gleason L. Archer Jr., "Daniel," in *The Expositor's Bible Commentary,* ed. F. E. Gaebelein, vol. 7 (Grand Rapids: Zondervan, 1985), 20–21.
9. Ibid., 21–22.
10. Ibid., 23–24. For a recent study of the linguistic features of the Aramaic of Daniel, see Zdravko Stefanovic, *The Aramaic of Daniel in the Light of Old Aramaic* (Sheffield: Sheffield Academic Press, 1992).

Historical Problems

The Book of Daniel poses several historical problems that have caused many to question or deny its historicity.

1. Daniel 1:1 speaks of a Babylonian invasion of Judah in 605 B.C., but there is no extrabiblical evidence for this. However, the Babylonian Chronicle states that Nebuchadnezzar attacked Egypt during the summer of that year, following his victory at Carchemish, and claims that he conquered "the whole area of Hatti." Bullock reasons: "Thus the foray into the Judean hill country, resulting in the captivity of Daniel and other members of the nobility, most likely occurred while the Babylonian army was en route to Egypt or very soon after the Egyptian operation in early August of 605 B.C."[11]

2. According to some critics, the account of Nebuchadnezzar's insanity (Dan. 4) is a legend. For example, Collins states: "The legendary character of the story is shown by the frequent intrusions of the marvelous: the dream, the voice from heaven, and the miraculous transformations of the king."[12] According to Collins, a variant form of this tradition appears in the "Prayer of Nabonidus," fragments of which have been discovered in Cave 4 at Qumran.[13] In this prayer, Nabonidus, king of Babylon, tells how he was afflicted with an ulcer for seven years in the city of Tema. An unnamed Jewish exorcist healed him and urged him to praise the true God and to repudiate idolatry. Collins points out that the account in Daniel 4 and the Prayer of Nabonidus "share some basic features," including, "the humiliation and restoration of a Babylonian king, the duration of seven years, the mediating role of a Jewish exile, and probably also the king's dream." Collins proposes that both texts "are ultimately based on the account of Nabonidus's withdrawal from Babylon for ten years to the desert oasis of Tema, such as is recorded in the Harran inscriptions."[14]

However, the many differences in details between the two texts make this proposal unlikely.[15] In fact, the only specific parallel is the reference in both texts to the illness lasting seven years, but the frequent symbolic use of the number seven in Semitic literature makes the significance of this parallel rather slight.[16]

3. Daniel 5 calls Belshazzar the son of Nebuchadnezzar, when in reality

---

11. C. Hassell Bullock, *An Introduction to the Old Testament Prophetic Books* (Chicago: Moody, 1986), 282.

12. Collins, *Daniel with an Introduction*, 62.

13. For translations of this text, see G. Vermes, *The Dead Sea Scrolls in English*, 3d ed. (London: Penguin, 1987), 274, and Michael A. Knibb, *The Qumran Community* (Cambridge: Cambridge University Press, 1987), 203–6.

14. Collins, *Daniel with an Introduction*, 62.

15. Archer, "Daniel," 15.

16. For a recent study of the similarities and differences between the two texts, see Matthias Henze, *The Madness of King Nebuchadnezzar* (Leiden: Brill, 1999), 63–73.

he was the son of Nabonidus, who was not a descendant of the royal Chaldean line but was made king by Babylonian noblemen.[17] However, Nabonidus may have married one of Nebuchadnezzar's daughters, making Belshazzar a grandson of the great king (the words "father" and "son" can be used of grandfathers and grandsons, respectively). Another possibility is that the words "father" and "son" are used figuratively, as in Shalmaneser III's Black Obelisk inscription, which refers to Jehu as the "son of Omri," even though Jehu wiped out the family of Omri and established his own dynasty.[18]

4. Critics regard the references to Darius the Mede, son of Xerxes, as inaccurate and confused (see 5:31; 9:1). Collins writes: "No such figure as Darius the Mede is known to history. Many attempts have been made to identify him with Gobryas (Ugbaru), Cyrus's general who occupied Babylon, but no satisfactory reason has been proposed why he should be called Darius the Mede. The name Darius can be attributed far more plausibly to confusion with Darius I of Persia (522–486). Darius had to put down two revolts by Babylonian pretenders and it is possible that these operations were later confused with the original conquest of Babylon. In Daniel 9:1, Darius is said to be the son of Ahasuerus (Xerxes). In fact, Xerxes I was son of Darius."[19]

However, the language used in 9:1 ("who was made ruler") suggests Darius the Mede was appointed as a vice-regent by someone else. Some identify him with Gubaru, the governor of Babylon under Cyrus (who should be distinguished from Ugbaru, a general involved in the conquest of Babylon who died three weeks after the takeover of the city), or with Cyrus himself.[20]

Literary Structure

The Book of Daniel displays two concurrent structures. When considering literary genres, one sees a distinct break between chapters 6 and 7. Chapters 1–6 contain narratives recounting the experiences of Daniel and his friends while in exile in Babylon. Chapters 7–12 contain the prophetic visions of Daniel. However, the material in 1:1–2:4a and chapters 8–12 is written in Hebrew, while 2:4b–7:28 is in Aramaic. There is no obvious reason for this variation, though some suggest that the Aramaic section pertains more to Gentile rulers and kingdoms. The Aramaic segment displays a symmetrical design that sets it off from its immediate context. Chapters 2 and 7 contain

---

17. See H. W. F. Saggs, *The Greatness That Was Babylon* (New York: New American Library, 1962), 150, and William W. Hallo and William K. Simpson, *The Ancient Near East: A History* (New York: Harcourt Brace Jovanovich, 1971), 147.

18. See Archer, "Daniel," 16, and Joyce G. Baldwin, *Daniel* (Leicester, England: InterVarsity, 1978), 22–23.

19. Collins, *Daniel with an Introduction*, 69.

20. For summaries of these proposals, see Archer, "Daniel," 16–19; Baldwin, *Daniel*, 23–28; and Bullock, *Old Testament Prophetic Books*, 284–85.

prophecies of four successive world empires, the last of which is supplanted by the kingdom of God. Chapters 3 and 6 tell stories of miraculous deliverance, and chapters 4 and 5 focus on God's sovereignty over the arrogant rulers of Babylon.

God Reveals His Power in Babylon (Daniel 1–6)

Daniel in Exile (1:1–21)

In 605 B.C., Nebuchadnezzar, having defeated the Egyptians at Carchemish, marched southward against Egypt. During this campaign he besieged Jerusalem, carried off some of the temple treasures, and took some of Judah's nobility to Babylon (1:1–2). The king of Babylon picked the best young men of Judah to serve on his palace staff (vv. 3–4a). He instructed Ashpenaz, the chief of his royal court, to train the young men and to give them a daily provision of fine food and wine from the king's own table (vv. 4b–5). Four members of this select group are singled out by name: Daniel, Hananiah, Mishael, and Azariah (v. 6). All four were given new Babylonian names: Daniel (whose Hebrew name means "my judge is God") was renamed Belteshazzar, Hananiah ("the Lord has been gracious") became Shadrach, Mishael ("Who is what God is?") received the name Meshach, and Azariah ("the Lord has helped") was renamed Abednego (v. 7). With the exception of Abednego (meaning "servant of Nego"), the meaning of the Babylonian names is uncertain. However, the renaming suggests that the young men were now viewed by their captors as Babylonian subjects.

Despite being renamed, the young men were determined to maintain their ritual purity in this foreign place. Daniel asked that they not be forced to eat the king's food and wine (v. 8). It is not entirely clear why Daniel viewed the king's food and wine as ritually defiling. Various reasons have been suggested.[21] It is unlikely that the king's food would have been prepared in accordance with the standards of the Mosaic law. It is also possible that it would have been previously offered to Babylonian gods in a pagan temple.

God made Ashpenaz kindly disposed to Daniel, but the official was fearful that the young men's health would suffer if they did not eat properly and that he would then be severely punished for neglecting their well-being (vv. 9–10). However, Daniel convinced the guard to whom the official had assigned the young men to consent to a ten-day testing period (vv. 11–14). During this period the young men would eat only vegetables and drink only water. At the end of the ten days, they looked healthier than the others, despite their meager diet, so the guard did not make them eat the king's provisions (vv. 15–16).

21. See John E. Goldingay, *Daniel*, WBC (Dallas: Word, 1989), 18–19.

God rewarded their devotion by giving them special wisdom, and he enabled Daniel to interpret visions and dreams (v. 17). When their training period was over, the king interviewed them and found them to be superior to all the others (vv. 18–19). They were assigned to the royal court and quickly surpassed all the king's divination experts in wisdom (v. 20). Daniel became a fixture in the palace and served the Babylonian kings for more than sixty years (v. 21).

Daniel Interprets the King's Dream (2:1–49)

The event recorded in chapter 2 occurred during the second year of Nebuchadnezzar's reign. The chronological reference poses a problem because the previous chapter indicates that a three-year testing period passed between Daniel's introduction to Nebuchadnezzar's royal court and his official acceptance into the king's service (see 1:5, 18). Perhaps the incident recorded in chapter 2 is a flashback into this three-year period, but this is unlikely since chapter 2 seems to presuppose the events of 1:18–20 and depicts Daniel and his friends as full-fledged members of the king's advisory staff. The problem can be solved if we understand the way the Babylonians reckoned a king's accession year. In the Babylonian system the year during which the king came to the throne (his accession year) was not counted as his first regnal year. Instead, his first full year on the throne was designated his first regnal year. So the king's second official regnal year was actually his third year on the throne.[22]

Nebuchadnezzar had a dream that greatly disturbed him (2:1). He summoned his wise men and asked them to interpret it for him (vv. 2–3). However, there was a catch. Apparently Nebuchadnezzar was skeptical about their abilities, so he demanded that they describe for him the dream and then interpret it (vv. 4–9). The wise men protested, pointing out that it was humanly impossible to do such a thing (v. 10). Only the gods could reveal the content of the king's dream (v. 11). Angered by their response, the king ordered the execution of all his wise men, including Daniel and his friends (vv. 12–13). When Daniel heard the news, he asked for a temporary stay of execution (vv. 14–16). He and his friends prayed for divine mercy, and during the night God revealed the king's dream to Daniel (vv. 18–19). Daniel praised God, acknowledging him as the source of all wisdom before whose penetrating gaze everything lies exposed (vv. 20–23). He then went to the king and told him that God had revealed the dream to him (vv. 24–30).

In his dream, the king saw a great statue with a head of gold, chest and arms of silver, belly and thighs of bronze, and legs of iron. Its feet were a mixture of iron and clay (vv. 31–33). He also saw a rock, apparently prepared by God, smash the statue's feet, causing the whole image to disintegrate (vv.

22. See Young, *Prophecy of Daniel*, 55–56.

34–35a). The debris was blown away by the wind and the rock grew into a great mountain that filled the earth (v. 35b).

Daniel interpreted the dream for the king (v. 36). The head of gold symbolized Nebuchadnezzar, to whom the Lord had given widespread dominion (vv. 37–38). The silver, bronze, and iron portions of the image represented subsequent kingdoms that would arise in succession (vv. 39–40). The fourth, though of inferior quality (iron), would be the strongest of all and supercede its predecessors. Yet this kingdom would be divided (v. 41). The mixture of iron and clay indicated that this divided kingdom, despite its strength, was vulnerable (vv. 42–43). The rock symbolized God's indestructible, eternal kingdom that would destroy the kingdoms of the world (vv. 44–45a).

Though the differing metals within the image represent four chronologically successive kingdoms, the single statue suggests that these kingdoms, though diverse in their identity, actually comprise one entity, a world empire opposed to God. This explains why the entire statue is depicted as destroyed by the rock with a single blow delivered to the feet (vv. 34–35, 44b) and why this event is said to occur "in the time of those kings," that is, the kings of the four kingdoms symbolized in the vision (v. 44a). The steadily declining value of the metal as one moves from head to foot (gold-silver-bronze-iron-iron mixed with clay) ironically points to the empire's downfall. While iron symbolizes strength (v. 40), the steady decline in value indicates that the essential substance of the world empire grows increasingly inferior. The mixture of iron and clay in the feet reveals its inherent vulnerability.

Impressed by Daniel's abilities, Nebuchadnezzar honored him and praised Daniel's God (vv. 45b–47). The king made Daniel a provincial governor over Babylon and lavished him with gifts (v. 48a). He placed him in charge of all the wise men and, at Daniel's request, assigned Daniel's three friends to important administrative posts (vv. 48b–49).

There is no scholarly consensus on the identity of the three kingdoms that succeed Nebuchadnezzar.[23] Since four individuals are specifically called kings in Daniel, it is possible that the four successive kingdoms are those of Nebuchadnezzar (3:1), Belshazzar (5:1), Darius the Mede (6:6), and Cyrus (10:1).[24] The second kingdom (symbolized by silver) is said to be "inferior" to Nebuchadnezzar (2:39). This might suggest that Nebuchadnezzar's Babylonian successors, particularly Nabonidus and Belshazzar, are in view. However, if one follows this scheme, it is difficult to see how Cyrus's kingdom was supplanted by the kingdom of God. Later visions, consistent with history, depict Alexander's Greek empire, not the kingdom of God, as the immediate successor to the Persian Empire (see chapters 7–8).

For this reason, many identify the chest and arms of silver as the Medes,

23. For a survey of the numerous proposals that have been made during the long history of the text's interpretation, see ibid., 73–75.

24. See Goldingay, *Daniel,* 51, 174.

the bronze belly and thighs as the Persians, and the legs of iron as the Greek empire under Alexander the Great. In this view the feet of iron and clay symbolize the division of Alexander's kingdom after his death. The mixture of the two substances alludes to the intermarriage that occurred between the Seleucids of Syria and the Ptolemies of Egypt. This view is attractive because later visions focus on Alexander's successors (especially the Seleucids and Antiochus IV Epiphanes) and their relationship with the Jewish people (see chapters 8 and 11).

However, the proposed distinction between Media and Persia is problematic since Cyrus ruled over both, a fact recognized by the text's references to "the Medes and Persians" as a unified entity (see 5:28; 6:8, 12, 15). Proponents of the view respond by pointing out that the reign (or perhaps "kingdom") of Darius the Mede seems to be distinguished from that of Cyrus the Persian (6:28). However, there is no reason why their reigns cannot be concurrent, with Darius being a subordinate of Cyrus. According to 5:28, Belshazzar's kingdom was given to the Medes and Persians, and 9:1 says that Darius was "made ruler over the Babylonian kingdom," suggesting he was appointed by a higher authority. Furthermore, in chapter 8 a two-horned ram symbolizes Media and Persia (see v. 20), reflecting the unity between these groups as well as their ethnic diversity.[25]

It seems more likely that the arms and chest of silver symbolize the Medo-Persian Empire which supplanted Babylon. In this case the bronze belly and thighs represent the Greek empire under Alexander the Great, while the iron legs symbolize a subsequent empire. The vision in chapter 7 supports this. If we assume there is a correlation between the four successive kingdoms depicted in chapters 2 and 7 (which form an *inclusio* for the Aramaic section of the book), then the bronze belly and thighs of chapter 2 correspond to the leopard of chapter 7 (see 7:6).[26] The latter has four heads, most likely symbolizing the four kingdoms that emerged from Alexander's Greek empire (see 8:21–22), which was divided among his four generals after his death. Since the Seleucid kingdom receives special attention in chapters 8 and 11, one might think it is the reality behind the fourth kingdom of chapters 2 and 7, but later visions, consistent with what history tells us, picture the Seleucids originating in Alexander (see 7:6; 8:21–25). For this reason, many see the fourth kingdom as a distinct successor to Alexander's empire, probably Rome and/or an end-time world empire.

If the second kingdom in Nebuchadnezzar's dream is the Medo-Persian Empire, in what sense can it be viewed as inferior to the Babylonian Empire (see 2:39)? After all, Cyrus conquered Babylon. Furthermore, the Persian Empire lasted much longer than Nebuchadnezzar's dynasty and extended

25. See Young, *Prophecy of Daniel*, 285–86.
26. Goldingay (*Daniel*, 174) is not willing to concede that chapters 2 and 7 need to be correlated in this way.

over a larger area. Perhaps the ethnic diversity within the Medo-Persian kingdom suggests an inherent weakness. A more likely option is that the statement simply reflects proper court etiquette and is added out of deference to Nebuchadnezzar. In this regard, it is noteworthy that Daniel identifies the golden head specifically as the king, not his kingdom, and that he calls Nebuchadnezzar "king of kings" (v. 37).

Daniel's Friends in a Fiery Furnace (3:1–30)

In chapter 1, God demonstrates his ability to bless his faithful followers, even when they are enslaved in a distant land. In chapter 2, he demonstrates his capacity to know all things, even the dream of a king. Ironically this dream anticipates the destruction of the Gentile world empire inaugurated by Nebuchadnezzar and the coming of God's kingdom. In chapter 3, God demonstrates his ability to protect his faithful followers, even when they are the objects of a mighty king's anger.

Nebuchadnezzar erected a huge gold-plated statue (3:1). The text does not give the specific identity of the image, but the association of the statue with the worship of Nebuchadnezzar's gods (vv. 12, 14) suggests it probably represented a deity, perhaps Nabu, the god after whom the king was named. Nebuchadnezzar summoned all his administrative officials and demanded that they bow down to the image (vv. 2–5). Anyone refusing to do so would be burned in a fiery furnace (v. 6). When Daniel's three friends refused to obey the king's edict, some of the king's officials reported them to Nebuchadnezzar (vv. 7–12). The news angered the king, who summoned the three men and gave them one more chance to comply with his order (vv. 13–15a). He warned them that continued disobedience would result in death and boasted that no god could rescue them (v. 15b).

The three men stood their ground. They told the king their God was capable of saving them from the fire (vv. 16–17). Even if he chose not to do so, they would not worship the king's gods or bow down before the golden statue (v. 18). Verse 17 reads literally, "If our God whom we serve exists, he is able to deliver us from the blazing, fiery furnace, and from your hand, O king, he will deliver." At first glance the statement seems to express doubt about God's existence, but their willingness to disobey the king and face the furnace suggests otherwise. The phraseology is purely rhetorical and reflects, perhaps sarcastically, the king's warped perspective. Earlier he had acknowledged Daniel's God as "the God of gods and the Lord of kings" (2:47), but now he speaks as if this sovereign God no longer exists (see 3:15).

Overcome by rage, Nebuchadnezzar ordered the furnace to be heated to its maximum temperature (the probable meaning of "seven times hotter") and commanded the guards to tie up the three men and throw them into the fire (vv. 19–21). The flames were so hot the executioners died from the heat as they threw the men into the furnace (vv. 22–23). But the men were not consumed by the fire. In fact, to the king's amazement, he saw them walking around untied, accompanied by a fourth figure (vv. 24–25). Concerning this fourth figure, the king said, "the fourth looks like a son of the gods." In verse 28, Nebuchadnezzar explains what he means as he identifies the figure as God's "angel" (literally, "messenger"). The identification of this angel as a "son of the gods" is consistent with the use of the comparable Hebrew expressions "sons of God/gods," which consistently refer in the Hebrew Bible to members of God's heavenly assembly (see Gen. 6:2, 4; Job 1:6; 2:1; 38:7; Ps. 29:1; 89:6, as well as Deut. 32:8 in the Dead Sea Scrolls).[27] Another reference to God's "angel" appears in Daniel 6:22, in which Daniel tells Darius that God sent "his angel" to shut up the mouths of the lions.

Nebuchadnezzar ordered Shadrach, Meshach, and Abednego out of the furnace (v. 26). They emerged completely unscathed, without even the smell of fire on their clothes (v. 27). The king praised their God as one who delivers his loyal and courageous followers (v. 28). He issued an edict that anyone who spoke against their God be executed, and he then promoted the three men (v. 29).

God Humbles Nebuchadnezzar (4:1–37)

In chapter 3, God demonstrates his superiority to Nebuchadnezzar by delivering his followers from the king's furnace. In chapter 4, he reveals his sovereignty over Nebuchadnezzar in an even more remarkable and direct manner by humbling the arrogant king. The chapter is framed by the king's autobiographical account of his life-changing experience (vv. 1–18, 34–37) into which is embedded a third-person report of the king's judgment and eventual restoration (vv. 19–33).

The chapter opens with Nebuchadnezzar addressing the peoples of the earth (4:1). He states his intention to tell them of the mighty acts of the Most High God, whose greatness and universal sovereignty he now recognizes (vv. 2–3). He recalls a time when he had a dream that frightened him (vv. 4–5). His wise men were unable to interpret the significance of the dream, so the king turned to Daniel (known in the Babylonian court by his Babylonian name, Belteshazzar) for an explanation, because he knew that he possessed "the spirit of the holy gods" (vv. 6–8, 18). In his dream, the king saw a great tree that provided shelter for the birds and wild animals (vv. 9–12). A heavenly messenger commanded that the tree be cut down and its stump and roots wrapped in iron and bronze (vv. 13–15a). The remainder of the messenger's command indicates that the stump symbolizes a person. The messenger announces that the one whom the stump represents is to live

---

27. The expression *bn 'lm,* "sons of gods" (or perhaps "sons of El"), appears in a concluding curse offered up by King Azitawadda in an inscription dating to around 800 B.C. See James Pritchard, *Ancient Near Eastern Texts Relating to the Old Testament* (Princeton: Princeton University Press, 1969), 499–500. The phrase refers to the pantheon of deities associated with Baalshamem, El, and the sun god.

outside with the wild animals and act like an animal for seven "times" (vv. 15b–16).[28] The episode would demonstrate the Most High God's sovereignty over mere human kingdoms and rulers (v. 17).

The dream disturbed Daniel, but Nebuchadnezzar encouraged him to reveal its significance (vv. 18–19a). Daniel wished he could tell the king that the dream pertained to his enemies, but this was not so (v. 19b). The tree symbolized the king in all his strength and splendor (vv. 20–22). But the king would be humbled. For seven "times" he would live away from human society and act like an animal (vv. 23–25a). However, the preservation of the stump and roots held out hope for the future. When his time of punishment ended, the king would be restored to his throne if he acknowledged the sovereignty of the Most High God (vv. 25b–26). Daniel hoped that the punishment envisioned in the dream might be averted through repentance. He urged Nebuchadnezzar to repent of his sins and promote justice in his realm in hopes that the king's success might continue uninterrupted (v. 27).

A year later, as the king was reflecting on his success and royal splendor, a voice from heaven announced that the dream was about to become reality (vv. 28–32). Suddenly he was struck with insanity, and for seven "times" he lived away from human society and took on the appearance of a wild animal (v. 33). At the end of this period, the Lord restored his sanity and his royal position (vv. 34a, 36). The king acknowledged the sovereignty of the Most High, who rules justly over the world and abases the proud (vv. 34b–35, 37).

Some are tempted to dismiss this account as sheer legend because of its bizarre account of how the king became like an animal. However, this condition is known in medical circles as boanthropy, a form of insanity in which a person takes on the mind-set of an animal and exhibits animal behavior. R. K. Harrison witnessed such a case in a British institution in 1946. The patient in question became antisocial and during the day roamed the grounds of the institution eating grass. Even during the cold, rainy winter months, he dressed lightly, but never contracted any illness. His hair lengthened, and his nails grew coarse and thick. Harrison observes: "Without institutional care the patient would have manifested precisely the same physical conditions as those mentioned in Daniel 4:33." He adds, "It seems evident that the author of the fourth chapter of Daniel was describing quite accurately an attestable, if rather rare, mental affliction."[29]

The End Comes for Babylon (5:1–31)

In chapter 5, God again demonstrates his sovereignty over kings and kingdoms as he announces in a startling, supernatural manner the demise of Babylon. The episode recorded here occurred in 539 B.C., the year of Cyrus's conquest of Babylon. By this time Nebuchadnezzar had died and Belshazzar

---

28. Many assume that the expression "seven times" refers to seven years, but this is not certain.
29. R. K. Harrison, *Introduction to the Old Testament* (Grand Rapids: Eerdmans, 1969), 1116–17.

was ruling Babylon. Nabonidus was the actual king of Babylon, but he had spent several years in Tema and left his son Belshazzar in charge of Babylon. Verse 29 hints at this state of affairs, informing us that Belshazzar elevated Daniel to "the third-highest ruler in the kingdom," the highest position that he, the second in command, could offer (see also vv. 7, 16).

Belshazzar held a great banquet for his nobles (5:1). He ordered the golden and silver goblets taken from the Jerusalem temple by Nebuchadnezzar to be brought to the banqueting hall so that he and his guests might drink from them (vv. 2–3). As they drank from these holy goblets, they praised their gods (v. 4). This sacrilege did not go unnoticed by God. Suddenly, human fingers appeared in the air and wrote a message on the wall of the palace (v. 5). The king's face turned white with terror, and he almost collapsed from fright (v. 6). He summoned his wise men and offered the position of "third-highest ruler in the kingdom" to the one who was able to interpret the message (v. 7). Much to the king's dismay, none of the wise men could do so (vv. 8–9). However, the queen mother remembered Daniel, who by now was probably in his eighties, and urged the king to send for him (vv. 10–12). The king offered Daniel presents and the position of third-highest ruler in the kingdom if he could interpret the message (vv. 13–16). Daniel refused the king's gifts, but he did agree to read the message (v. 17). But first he reminded the king of Nebuchadnezzar's humbling experience and how he had subsequently acknowledged the sovereignty of the Most High God (vv. 18–21). In contrast to Nebuchadnezzar, Belshazzar was proud. He offended God by desecrating the holy goblets and refused to pay homage to the one true God (vv. 22–23). For this reason, his kingdom would fall, as announced in the message written on the wall (v. 24).

The message itself was terse, being pronounced *mene' mene' teqel uparsin* (v. 25). At the surface level, the words meant literally "a mina, a mina, a shekel, and half-shekels." These units of measure suggested an image of monetary weights being placed on a scale. As such, each word carried a double meaning. The term *mene'* sounded like the verb *menah*, meaning "to number." God had numbered the days of Belshazzar's reign, and the king's time was up (v. 26). The word *teqel* sounds like the verb *teqal,* meaning "to weigh." Belshazzar had been weighed on God's scales and found wanting (v. 27). The term *uparsin* (combining the conjunction "and" and the plural of *peres,* "half-shekel") sounded like the verb *peras,* "to break in two." Belshazzar's kingdom had been broken and would be handed over to the Medes and Persians (v. 28). True to his word and against Daniel's earlier objection (see vv. 16–17), the king clothed Daniel in purple, put a golden chain around his neck, and officially promoted him to third in the kingdom (v. 29). But the king's gifts were meaningless. That very night Babylon fell, the king was killed, and Darius the Mede ascended his throne (vv. 30–31).[30]

30. On the historical problem of identifying Darius the Mede, see my earlier introductory remarks.

Daniel in the Lion's Den (6:1–28)

As in chapter 3, the Lord once more demonstrates his ability to protect his faithful followers. Darius knew talent when he saw it and assigned Daniel to an important administrative post under his regime (6:1–2). Daniel so distinguished himself that Darius planned to promote him to the position of prime minister (v. 3). The other administrators, filled with envy, plotted to destroy Daniel (vv. 4–9). Knowing that Daniel faithfully prayed to his God, they convinced the king to issue an edict prohibiting prayers to any god or man other than the king for a one-month period. Violators would be punished by being fed to the lions. The vain king made the edict a royal law, which could not be altered. As his enemies suspected, the law did not keep Daniel from praying to God three times a day (v. 10). The enemies barged in while Daniel was praying in his room and, after getting Darius to reiterate that the law was unalterable, reported Daniel's act of disobedience to the king (vv. 11–12). Despite his efforts to find a loophole in the law, Darius was forced to throw Daniel into the lions' den (vv. 13–16a). As he did so, he prayed that Daniel's God would rescue his faithful servant (v. 16b). The narrator of the story draws out the suspense by refusing to tell us immediately what happened. Instead, he informs us that the lions' den was sealed with the king's own signet ring (v. 17) and that the troubled king spent a sleepless night in his palace (v. 18).

In the morning the king rushed to the lions' den and called out to Daniel, asking him if his God had been able to rescue him from the beasts (vv. 19–20). Much to the king's and our delight, Daniel answered, informing the king that God's angel had kept the mouths of the lions shut and protected the innocent Daniel (vv. 21–22). Delighted that Daniel was alive, the king ordered his release. He also commanded that Daniel's enemies, along with their wives and children, be thrown to the lions, which devoured their victims alive before their bodies even reached the floor (vv. 23–24). The execution of the evildoers' wives and children may seem unfair and cruel, but it reflects the principle of corporate solidarity that was so common in the biblical world.[31] Their destiny contrasts sharply with that of Daniel, who prospered throughout the concurrent reigns of Darius and his superior, Cyrus (v. 28).

Once more the self-revelation of God elicited praise from a pagan king. Darius issued a decree that everyone in his kingdom worship Daniel's God because he is the sovereign, eternal king of the world who has the capacity to rescue his faithful followers from harm (vv. 25–27). The progression of praise in chapters 2–6 is noteworthy. In chapter 2, Daniel praises God as the source of all wisdom (2:20–23). His interpretive abilities prompt Neb-

---

31. See my comments on Hos. 4:5–6 and Amos 7:17, as well as Joel S. Kaminsky's important study, *Corporate Responsibility in the Hebrew Bible* (Sheffield: Sheffield Academic Press, 1995).

uchadnezzar to do homage to Daniel and to praise Daniel's God as the "God of gods and Lord of kings" (2:47). In chapter 3, Nebuchadnezzar, after witnessing the deliverance of Daniel's friends from the fiery furnace, praises their God and prohibits any blasphemy against him (3:28–29). Following his humiliation and restoration, Nebuchadnezzar issues a formal announcement of praise throughout his kingdom and calls Daniel's God "the Most High God" and "the King of heaven" (4:1–3, 34–37). Chapter 5 records no words of praise from the doomed Belshazzar, who seems more impressed with Daniel's abilities than with the God who empowers him. Darius the Mede, like Nebuchadnezzar, issues a formal announcement of praise throughout his kingdom (6:25–27). He praises "the living God" and goes one step further than Nebuchadnezzar by commanding his people to "fear and reverence" Daniel's God.

God Reveals His Plan for the Future (Daniel 7–12)

God Establishes His Kingdom (7:1–28)

The vision recorded in this chapter occurred during Belshazzar's first regnal year (7:1). Since Belshazzar ruled under Nabonidus, this must refer to the year when he was appointed to his post of vice-regent. A Babylonian text indicates that Nabonidus, who ruled from 556–539 B.C., made this appointment in his third year (approximately 553).

Daniel saw the four winds of heaven churning up the sea, from which emerged in succession four great beasts (vv. 2–3). The first resembled a lion, but it also had the wings of an eagle. When its wings were torn off, it stood upright like a man and was given a human heart (v. 4). The second beast resembled a bear (v. 5). It was "raised up on one of its sides." Perhaps this means it was crouching or rearing up, as if ready to attack. It also had "three ribs in its mouth between its teeth," as if it had just devoured the flesh of an animal.[32] However, the portrait is somewhat unclear and it is possible that the creature was hideously deformed.[33] At any rate, this bearlike beast was told to get up and devour flesh. The third beast resembled a leopard, though it also possessed four wings and four heads (v. 6). The fourth beast, which apparently resembled no animal known to Daniel, was the most terrifying and powerful of the four (v. 7). It had iron teeth and crushed underfoot

---

32. An alternative view is that the term usually translated "ribs" refers instead to fangs or tusks. In this case this aspect of the description would simply emphasize the beast's capacity to destroy and devour.

33. In this regard, Porter draws parallels between the beasts described in Dan. 7 and 8 and the deformed human and animal births referred to in Mesopotamian divination texts. One of these texts describes a deformity in which the right or left shoulder is raised. The bearlike creature in Dan. 7:5 is described as being "raised up on one of its sides." One of the divination texts speaks of a deformity in which the lungs are in the mouth, much like the ribs of the bearlike beast in Daniel's vision. See Paul A. Porter, *Metaphors and Monsters: A Literary-Critical Study of Daniel 7 and 8* (Lund: CWK Gleerup, 1983), 17.

whatever was left of its victims. It also had ten horns, but a little horn sprouted up and uprooted three of the other horns (v. 8a). This little horn had human eyes and spoke boastfully (v. 8b).

The scene suddenly shifted. Thrones were set up and the "Ancient of Days" took his place on one of them (v. 9a). His clothing and hair were pure white. His throne had wheels and consisted of flaming fire, which flowed like a river from before him (vv. 9b–10a). As innumerable attendants stood around him, the other members of the court were seated and scrolls were opened (v. 10b). As the little horn continued to spew out his arrogant words, the beast was killed and thrown into the fire (v. 11). The other beasts had already been stripped of their authority (v. 12). As Daniel continued to watch, "one like a son of man" arrived in the clouds of heaven and approached the Ancient of Days, who gave to him everlasting royal authority over the entire earth (vv. 13–14).

Disturbed by what he had seen, Daniel asked one of the bystanders what it all meant (vv. 15–16). The interpreter explained that the four beasts symbolized four kings who would arise on the earth, but God's eternal kingdom, delivered as a gift to the "saints [lit., "holy ones"] of the Most High," would supplant these earthly kingdoms (vv. 17–18).[34] Daniel wanted to know more about the fourth beast and its horns (v. 19a). At this point Daniel gives more details about what he saw. We are told that the beast had bronze claws (v. 19b) and that the little horn had successfully waged war against God's holy ones until the Ancient of Days decreed their victory (vv. 20–22). The interpreter explained that the fourth beast would be unique in its ability to conquer and destroy (v. 23). The ten horns symbolize ten kings who would emerge from this kingdom. Another king would arise and subdue three of these ten rulers (v. 24). He would wage war against God and oppress his holy ones for "a time, times and half a time," probably meaning three and a half years (v. 25).[35] But then the heavenly tribunal would decree his demise, and the earth's kingdoms would be handed over to "the people of the holy ones of the Most High," who would rule eternally (vv. 26–27). Daniel was visibly shaken by this experience, but he kept the matter to himself (v. 28).

While the interpreter's explanation of the vision clarifies its general meaning, many questions are left unanswered:

1. Why are the beasts depicted as arising out of the sea? This question

---

34. The verb translated "receive" is used in 2:6 of receiving a gift in exchange for services rendered, and in 5:31 of Darius the Mede receiving the kingdom of Babylon.

35. In 4:16, 23, 25, 32, the phrase "seven times" appears, though it is not certain if this refers to seven years. In Dan. 12:7, an equivalent Hebrew expression ("a time, times and half a time") is used of a period of either 1,290 or 1,335 days (vv. 11–12). Rev. 11:2–3 and 13:5, both of which seem to anticipate the oppressive reign of the little horn depicted in Dan. 7, appear to interpret the expression "a time, times, and half a time" as forty-two months/1,260 days (thirty-day, lunar months are in view), that is, three and a half years.

raises a more fundamental one: What is the background for the imagery of the vision? It appears that much of the imagery of the vision is rooted in ancient West Semitic mythology as well as archaic biblical symbolism. In mythology the god of the sea opposes Baal's rule, while in the Hebrew Bible the sea symbolizes the chaotic forces that seek to destroy God's creative order and covenant community. It is no surprise then that these destructive, monstrous kingdoms rise from the sea in Daniel's vision.[36] There are other links with mythological literature. As Day observes, the Ancient of Days "is reminiscent of the supreme Canaanite god El, who is called 'the Father of Years' and has grey hair."[37] In the myths the god Baal receives his authority to rule from El, just as the one like the son of man receives his right to rule from the Ancient of Days in Daniel's vision. Furthermore, as Day points out, "the one like a son of man comes with the clouds of heaven, just as Baal's stock epithet was 'rider on the clouds.'"[38] The scene depicted in verses 9–10 is also reminiscent of the divine assembly of the myths and of the heavenly assembly described in 1 Kings 22:19–22.

2. What is the precise identity of the four kingdoms? As in chapter 2, there is no consensus on the identity of the four kingdoms depicted here. If one assumes that they correspond to those in chapter 2, then the lion represents the Babylonian Empire, which was still in power at the time of the vision. The image of the lion conveys strength and ferocity, while the eagle's wings suggest speed. Perhaps the removal of the wings and the transformation of the lion into a man reflects Nebuchadnezzar's restoration from his animal-like condition (see chapter 4).

As in chapter 2, some identify the second kingdom as Media, the third as Persia, and the fourth as Greece. However, the proposed distinction between Media and Persia is problematic since the text views "the Medes and Persians" as a unified entity (see 5:28; 6:8, 12, 15), and a two-horned ram, reflecting diversity within unity, symbolizes Media and Persia in 8:20. If the bearlike creature symbolizes the Medo-Persian Empire, then the ribs in its mouth, presumably the leftovers of a meal, probably symbolize devoured nations. Perhaps Lydia, Babylon, and Egypt, all of which were conquered by Medo-Persia between 546–525 b.c., are in view. The third beast, a winged leopard, is an apt symbol for Alexander the Great, who is famous for his rapid conquests. The four heads probably represent the four kingdoms that emerged from Alexander's empire following his death (see 8:21).[39] If Greece

36. See John J. Collins, *Daniel, First Maccabees, Second Maccabees* (Wilmington, Del.: Michael Glazier, 1981), 72–76.

37. John Day, *Yahweh and the Gods and Goddesses of Canaan* (Sheffield: Sheffield Academic Press, 2000), 106.

38. Ibid.

39. Those who see a distinct Persian Empire as the third beast sometimes identify the four heads as the four Persian rulers referred to in 11:2. See Andre Lacocque, *The Book of Daniel*, trans. D. Pellauer (Atlanta: John Knox, 1979), 140.

is the third empire, then the fourth kingdom is most likely a successor, perhaps the Roman Empire and/or an end-time world power (but see the following discussion of the ten horns and little horn).

3. Who specifically are the ten horns and the little horn that sprouts up among them? Many, including some who take Alexander's Greek empire as the third beast, understand the ten horns as Alexander's successors in the region of Syria (known as the Seleucids). The Seleucids play an important role in Daniel's subsequent visions (see the references to the "king of the North" in chapter 11) and were especially hostile to the Jews. One particular member of this dynasty, Antiochus IV Epiphanes, who ruled from 175–163 B.C., is given special attention and depicted as an archenemy of God and his people (see 8:9–14, 23–25; 11:21–39). In 8:9–10, he is symbolized by a small horn that grows so powerful it can throw down some of the host of heaven. Some correlate this image with that of chapter 7, arguing that the little horn in both cases is Antiochus IV.

As for the ten horns of 7:8, 20, the first seven can be viewed as the predecessors of Antiochus IV:

> Seleucus I Nicator (312–280 B.C.)
> Antiochus I Soter (280–262)
> Antiochus II Theos (262–246)
> Seleucus II Callinicus (246–226)
> Seleucus III Ceraunus (226–223)
> Antiochus III the Great (223–187)
> Seleucus IV Philopator (187–175)

In this scheme the three displaced horns can be identified as Demetrius I (oldest son of Seleucus IV), Antiochus (youngest son of Seleucus IV), and Heliodorus. All three aspired to kingship, but were displaced by Antiochus IV.[40]

Some of the details of the vision fit well with the view that Antiochus IV is the little horn. Antiochus waged war with God's people and oppressed them (vv. 21–22, 25a). He changed the "set times" and "laws" of the Jews (v. 25b) by forcing them to give up many of their cherished traditions and religious practices (see 1 Macc. 1:44–49). In 167 B.C. he desecrated the temple in Jerusalem (1 Macc. 1:54–55; see Dan. 8:11–14). The temple remained in a ritually polluted condition for three years and ten days (cf. 1 Macc. 1:54 with 4:52) before the victorious Judas Maccabeus ordered it to be ritually cleansed and rededicated, an event celebrated to this day as Hanukkah (meaning "dedication").[41]

---

40. See Goldingay, *Daniel,* 179–80, for a discussion of this approach, as well as George Wesley Buchanan, *The Book of Daniel* (Lewiston, N.Y.: Mellen Biblical Press, 1999), 173. Some identify one of the displaced horns as Ptolemy VI of Egypt, whom Antiochus IV defeated in battle.

41. According to 7:25b, the little horn would oppress the holy ones for "a time, times and half a time," which suggests a period of three and a half years. If Antiochus is in view here, this figure would not

However, there are some problems with this line of interpretation:
(1) The vision appears to view the ten horns of the fourth beast as contemporary, not successive rulers. (2) There are significant differences between the little horn of chapter 7 and the little horn of chapter 8.[42] The little horn of chapter 7 is associated with the fourth beast, which, unlike the first three, is not compared to a specific animal. It grows up among ten horns and supplants three. The little horn of chapter 8 grows from a goat. It sprouts up from one of four horns.[43] (3) One is hard pressed to explain how the eternal kingdom of God was inaugurated by the Maccabees in conjunction with the fall of Antiochus IV.

For these reasons many prefer to identify the ten horns with a later kingdom, either the Roman Empire or an end-time world power, viewed by some as an extension or revival of its Roman predecessor.[44] Proponents of this approach typically identify the little horn of chapter 7 with the figure known as Antichrist (see 1 John 2:18). Paul refers to this individual as "the man of lawlessness" (2 Thess. 2:3–9), and Revelation 13 pictures him as a beast that exhibits the same hostility to God and his people as the little horn of Daniel 7.[45] Similarities between Antiochus IV and Antichrist are explained as typological in nature.[46]

4. Who is the Ancient of Days, and why is he depicted as wearing white clothes and having white hair (v. 9)? The Ancient of Days is the Most High God, portrayed here as the sovereign king of the world who grants authority to his vice-regent and pronounces judgment against the little horn (vv. 13–14, 21–22). His snow-white clothing probably points to the purity of his judgments. His title and his white hair depict him as aged, suggesting he is exceedingly wise.

5. Who is the "one like a son of a man"?[47] The humanlike appearance of this figure sharply contrasts with the animal-like beasts depicted earlier in the vision. His arrival in the clouds of heaven also contrasts with the earlier

---

be restricted to the period during which the temple was defiled, but would include the months leading up to this culminating act of sacrilege.

42. See Young, *Prophecy of Daniel*, 275–79.

43. Goldingay (*Daniel*, 174) is aware of these differences, but does not feel that "at any point the portraits of the small horn are incompatible." He states: "They *could* denote different kings, but—juxtaposed in the same book—this is not the natural understanding." Goldingay argues that Antiochus IV is the reality behind the small horn in both chapters. He contends that "the different images and details complement each other."

44. In Rev. 17:12–14, ten horns are identified as future kings who will oppose Christ. These horns grow on a seven-headed beast upon which a woman called "Babylon" (that is, Rome) rides.

45. The imagery of Dan. 7 has influenced John's description of the beast; it emerges from the sea and resembles a leopard, bear and lion.

46. See Archer, "Daniel," 99.

47. For a thorough study of the identity of this figure, see Maurice Casey, *Son of Man: The Interpretation and Influence of Daniel 7* (London: SPCK, 1979).

beasts, who emerged from the sea. Some identify this figure as the angel Michael, who is depicted in a later vision as the "great prince" (12:1; see also 10:13, 21).[48] Proponents of this view point out that the figure is "like" a son of man, indicating that he has a human appearance but is not human in essence. In other passages in Daniel, angelic beings are called men (9:21; 10:5; 12:6–7) and are described as looking like men (8:15; 10:16, 18).[49] However, while there is no doubt that the Book of Daniel assigns Michael a prominent role as the defender of God's people (12:1), it hardly pictures him as the eternal king of the world (cf. 7:14).

Others interpret the "one like a son of man" in a representative or corporate sense and understand the referent to be the "people of the holy ones of the Most High" mentioned in verse 27. The parallelism between verses 13–14 and 26–27 supports this, for both the "one like a son of man" and the "people of the saints of the Most High" receive an everlasting kingdom.[50] However, since the phrase "one like a son of man" more naturally suggests an individual is in view, it is more likely that it refers to the ruler of the people to whom the kingdom is delivered. The people receive the kingship (vv. 22, 27) through their royal representative (v. 14). Though the use of "like" (v. 13) might suggest the figure is only humanlike, not really human, one should note that a simile sometimes points to the reality underlying a metaphor.[51] In such cases the preposition ke-, normally translated "like, as," carries the force of "in every respect like," or "in every way like."[52]

If one understands the little horn of the vision as Antiochus Epiphanes (see above), then one might identify the "one like a son of man" as Judas Maccabeus, who led the Jewish revolt against Antiochus between 168–164 B.C. (see our earlier discussion of the identity of the little horn above).[53] However, Judas did not inaugurate an everlasting kingdom (7:14). Eventually, Jesus appropriates the title, announcing that he, "the Son of Man," will come, like the figure described in Daniel 7:13, "on the clouds of the sky,

48. Proponents of this view also see the "saints of the Most High" (see vv. 18, 21–22, 25, 27) as angelic beings.

49. Note, however, that the equivalent Hebrew phrase "son of man" is used of Daniel in 8:17.

50. In v. 27b the singular pronouns are best understood as referring back to the "people" mentioned in v. 27a, not to the Most High (a comparison to vv. 13–14 favors this). Since "people" is a collective noun, pronouns referring to it can be grammatically singular, though plural in sense. To avoid confusion one could translate v. 27b: "Their [i.e., the people just mentioned] kingdom will be an everlasting kingdom, and all rulers will worship and obey them [i.e., the people]." See Young, Prophecy of Daniel, 162.

51. See E. W. Bullinger, Figures of Speech Used in the Bible (reprint, Grand Rapids: Baker, 1968), 728–29.

52. See Bruce K. Waltke and M. O'Connor, An Introduction to Biblical Hebrew Syntax (Winona Lake, Ind.: Eisenbrauns, 1990), 203. For example, in Joel 1:15, the day of the Lord is said to "come like [i.e., in every respect like] destruction from the Almighty," meaning that it would indeed be such an instance of divine destruction. See also Isa. 1:7–8, where the expressions "as when overthrown by strangers" (literally, "[in every respect] like an overthrow by strangers") and "[in every respect] like a city under siege" point to the fact that Judah was indeed overrun by foreign invaders and that Jerusalem was indeed under siege.

53. See Buchanan, The Book of Daniel, 231.

with power and great glory" (Matt. 24:30; see also Matt. 26:64; Mark 13:26; 14:62; Luke 21:27).

6. Who are the holy ones of the Most High? Some identify this group as the angelic assembly, while others understand it to be God's covenant people (note the NIV translation, "saints"). In both the Aramaic and Hebrew portions of the book, angels are called "holy ones" (4:13, 17, 23; 8:13) and the expression is used of angelic beings elsewhere in the Hebrew Bible (see Deut. 33:3; Job 5:1; 15:15; Ps. 89:5, 7; Prov. 30:3; Zech. 14:5). However, the phrase can also refer to God's people (see Ps. 34:9).

The evidence in chapter 7 is ambiguous. The little horn, which symbolizes a human ruler, fights against the holy ones and oppresses them (7:21, 25). Since the little horn is human, it is natural to think that his victims are as well. However, in 8:9–10 the little horn (symbolizing Antiochus) is pictured as actually throwing some of the starry host (symbolizing angels) to the ground and trampling on them.

According to 7:18, the holy ones receive the kingdom, just as the "people of the holy ones" do in verse 27. This might suggest that the people and the holy ones are to be identified, but the phrase "people of the holy ones" in verse 27 (see also the Hebrew equivalent in 8:24) seems to indicate that the "people" are distinct from the holy ones. The holy ones (understood as angels) may be viewed as protectors of God's people and as co-heirs of the kingdom (see the depiction of Michael in 10:21 and 12:1). However, "people" and "holy ones" may very well be in apposition in verse 27, signifying "the people who are the holy ones."[54]

The Vision of the Horned Goat (8:1–27)

Two years later, during Belshazzar's third year (approximately 551 B.C., see 7:1), Daniel received another vision in which he saw himself in the Elamite citadel of Susa, an important Persian provincial city (see Neh. 1:1; Esth. 1:2) (8:1–2). This vision pertained to "the time of the end" (v. 17b), "the appointed time of the end" (v. 19b), and "the distant future" (v. 26b). The angel Gabriel interpreted the vision for Daniel, upon whom it had a disturbing impact (vv. 15–19, 26–27).

Daniel saw a ram standing beside the Ulai Canal, a waterway near Susa (v. 3a). The ram had two long horns; one was longer than the other, even though it had sprouted up later (v. 3b). The ram charged to the west, to the north, and to the south, defeating all who opposed it (v. 4). As we discover

---

54. Other examples of "people" in apposition to a following plural substantive include Exod. 1:9 (literally, "the people of the sons of Israel" = "the people, that is, the sons of Israel"); Ps. 95:10 (literally, "the people of the ones who err in heart" = "the people who err in heart"); Jer. 31:2 (literally, "the people of the survivors of the sword" = "the people who survived the sword"); Dan. 11:15 (literally, "the people of his chosen ones" = "the people who are his chosen ones"); Dan. 11:32 (literally, "the people of the knowers of his God" = "the people who know their God").

in verse 20, this ram symbolized the Medo-Persian Empire. The longer horn represented the Persians, who rose to prominence later than the Medes but eventually became the more dominant of the two.

As Daniel pondered the significance of the ram, he saw a goat with a large horn cross the earth from the west (v. 5). The goat attacked the ram, broke its two horns, and trampled it underfoot (vv. 6–7). The goat became very powerful, but at the height of its power, the large horn was broken off (v. 8a). Four horns grew up in its place (v. 8b). Verse 21 tells us that the goat symbolized Greece and the large horn its king, the great conqueror Alexander, who died prematurely. His kingdom was eventually divided up among his generals, symbolized by the four horns that grew up in place of the large horn (v. 22). Cassander ruled Macedonia, Lysimachus controlled Thrace and Asia Minor, Seleucus was in charge of Syria, and Ptolemy took Egypt.[55] This geographical diversity explains why the four horns are described as growing toward the four winds of heaven (v. 8b).

A little horn sprouted up from one of the goat's four horns. Though small at first, it grew toward the south and east and even threatened Palestine, called here "the beautiful (one)" (v. 9). This same term is used later of Palestine (11:16, 41) and of the temple mount in Jerusalem (11:45).[56] This powerful horn even pulled down some of the stars of heaven and trampled on them. He viewed himself as if he were the "Prince of the host" (perhaps referring to the angel Michael; see 12:1) (vv. 10–11a). He defiled the temple for a period of "2,300 evenings and mornings" (vv. 11b–14).[57] We discover in verses 23–25 that this horn symbolizes a particularly evil king who would declare war on God's people but would be supernaturally destroyed (v. 25b).

The little horn depicted in chapter 8 is Antiochus IV Epiphanes, ruler of the Seleucid kingdom from 175–163 b.c. The vision alludes to his conquest of the south (Egypt; see 1 Macc. 1:16–19), subjugation of Palestine (1 Macc. 1:20–28), desecration of the temple (1 Macc. 1:44–49, 54–59), and atrocities against the people (1 Macc. 1:60). His assault on God took the form of encouraging disobedience to God's law, sacrificing pigs on the sacred altars, burning copies of God's law, and executing any who kept copies in their possession. The language of verses 10–11a, while hyperbolic, does accurately reflect his arrogance. Second Maccabees 9:10 describes him as one who "thought that he could touch the stars of heaven," and his coins picture a star above his head.[58] As prophesied in Daniel 8:25b, Antiochus met his

55. For a brief historical survey of this period, see Harold W. Hoehner, "History and Chronology of the New Testament," in *Foundations for Biblical Interpretation*, ed. D. S. Dockery, K. A. Mathews, and R. B. Sloan (Nashville: Broadman & Holman, 1994), 458–59.
56. In Ezek. 20:6, 15, the Promised Land (Israel) is called the "most beautiful of all lands."
57. This could refer to 2,300 days (comprised of evenings and mornings) or to 1,150 days. For a discussion of the options, see Young, *Prophecy of Daniel*, 173–75.
58. See Goldingay, *Daniel*, 210.

demise by nonhuman agency. According to 1 Maccabees 6:1–16, he died of grief after hearing of the Maccabean victories over his forces. An alternate tradition in 2 Maccabees 9 gives a more detailed and embellished account of the king's demise. According to verses 5–6, the Lord "struck him an incurable and unseen blow" which caused him to have severe abdominal pains. He then fell out of his chariot and was severely wounded (vv. 7–8). The wound became infested with worms and his body began to rot. The stench was so putrid no one wanted to get near him (vv. 9–11). He confessed his sins, but was rejected by God and died a broken man (vv. 12–29).

Daniel's Prayer Is Answered (9:1–27)

Several years later, in the first year of Darius the Mede's rule (539–538 B.C.), Daniel was reading or at least reflecting upon Jeremiah's prophecy that Jerusalem would lie desolate for seventy years (9:1–2). Two passages in Jeremiah state this. In 25:11–12 (in a message dated in 605 B.C.), the Lord declared that the whole country would become desolate and would serve the king of Babylon for seventy years. In 29:10 (in a letter dated sometime after 597 B.C.), the Lord promised he would bring his people back to the land "when seventy years are completed for Babylon." If the beginning of this period was 605 B.C., when Daniel went into exile, then approximately sixty-six years had passed, and the prophesied period of time was approaching an end. If the beginning of the period is taken as 597 or 586 B.C., then the number "seventy" is more likely metaphorical, suggesting a lifetime.[59] Either way, from Daniel's perspective the period was drawing to a close.

Aware that the Lord had announced his intention to restore his people after the designated time of punishment, Daniel decided to pray for the Lord's promised intervention (v. 3). This suggests that he may not have seen the prophesied period of time as set in stone. God intended for the exile to end after this period, but Daniel's action suggests he may have understood repentance to be a prerequisite for fulfillment. Daniel addressed the Lord as the covenant God who is faithful to his obedient people (v. 4). Of course, God's people had not been obedient, so Daniel, speaking on behalf of the exiled nation, confessed their corporate guilt and acknowledged that they had rejected the Lord's prophetic servants (vv. 5–6). Before their righteous judge, the entire exiled community was covered with shame and guilt (vv. 7–11a). The well-deserved judgments threatened in the law of Moses had fallen upon them and left Jerusalem in ruins (vv. 11b–14). Reminding the Lord of his past deliverance of the nation from Egypt, Daniel prayed that he might show mercy to Jerusalem and forgive the sin that brought her to ruin (vv. 15–19a). After all, Jerusalem was the Lord's city, and the exiled people bore the Lord's own name (v. 19b).

---

59. For a discussion of the issue, see my comments on Jer. 25:11.

As soon as Daniel began to pray, the Lord issued an answer to his prayer because he was "highly esteemed" by God (v. 23). Gabriel arrived on the scene to give Daniel insight into God's plan for Jerusalem (vv. 20–22). Before discussing the details of this plan, we first offer an annotated translation of verses 24–27:

24 Seventy "weeks"[60] have been determined with respect to your people and your holy city, for the purpose of putting an end to[61] rebellion, bringing to completion[62] sin, atoning for iniquity, bringing about perpetual[63] righteousness, sealing up a prophetic vision,[64] and anointing what is most holy.[65] **25** Now know and understand this: From the going forth of a decree[66] to rebuild Jerusalem until an anointed one, a ruler [arrives], [there will be a period of] seven "weeks." And [during a period of] sixty-two "weeks"[67] a plaza and a trench will be rebuilt, but in distressing times. **26** And after [the period of] sixty-two "weeks" an anointed one will be cut off and have nothing.[68] The people of the ruler who is to come will destroy the

---

60. The Hebrew word *shabua'*, which appears in v. 24 in the plural, means literally "a period of seven." Elsewhere it is used of a week (a period of seven days) (see Gen. 29:27–28 [cf. Judg. 14:12]; Exod. 34:22; Lev. 12:5; Num. 28:26; Deut. 16:9–10, 16; 2 Chron. 8:13; Jer. 5:24; Dan. 10:2–3). Here in Dan. 9:24–27 it is usually understood to refer to seven "weeks" of years, that is to a seven-year period. The "seventy weeks" then constitute 490 years. However, see the discussion below.

61. The Hebrew consonantal text (Kethib) reads the verb *kala'*, meaning "to restrain, withhold." The translation follows the marginal reading of the scribes (Qere), which has the verb *kalah*, meaning (in the Piel stem), "to put an end to."

62. The Hebrew consonantal text (Kethib) reads the verb *katam*, meaning "to seal up." The translation follows the marginal reading of the scribes (Qere), which has the verb *tamam*, meaning (in the Hiphil stem) "to bring to completion." The Kethib reading has probably been influenced by the appearance of the verb "seal up" later in the verse.

63. The plural is probably used for emphasis.

64. The text literally reads, "a vision and a prophet," but the phrase is probably a hendiadys in which the second word qualifies the first.

65. The precise referent is not indicated, but the phrase is invariably used elsewhere of holy places, objects, or sacrifices, not people.

66. Literally, "a word." A formal decree announcing or permitting the rebuilding of the city is in view here.

67. The text reads literally, "seven weeks, and sixty-two weeks." Some combine the numbers and understand the text to mean, "until an anointed one, a ruler [arrives], [there will be a period of] sixty-nine weeks." However, this would be an odd way of expressing the number sixty-nine. Elsewhere, numbers in the sixty range are expressed by combining "sixty" with the other number. For example, sixty-two is literally "two and sixty" (Dan. 5:31) or "sixty and two" (Dan. 9:25–26), sixty-five is "sixty and five" (Isa. 7:8), sixty-six is "sixty and six" (Gen. 46:26; Lev. 12:5), and sixty-eight is "sixty and eight" (1 Chron. 16:38). The traditional scribal punctuation of Dan. 9:27 marks a clear break between "seven weeks" and "sixty-two weeks." The latter is best taken as a temporal adverbial phrase that begins the following clause. The reference to "sixty-two weeks" (not "seven weeks and sixty-two weeks") in v. 26 shows the sixty-two weeks are understood as distinct from the seven weeks. For a defense of the view expressed here, see Thomas E. McComiskey, "The Seventy 'Weeks' of Daniel against the Background of Ancient Near Eastern Literature," *WTJ* 47 (1985): 19–25. McComiskey marshals compelling grammatical evidence in support of the traditional punctuation in the Hebrew text.

68. The Hebrew text literally reads, "and there [will] not [be] to him," that is, "he will have nothing." Some emend the text, adding the noun, "wickedness." In this case the text would read, "though he had not wickedness."

city and the sanctuary. Its end will be with a flood. Until the end of war, desolation is decreed. 27 He will ratify a covenant with many [for a period of] one "week." In the middle of the "week" he will put an end to sacrifice and offerings. Upon the wing[69] there will be an abomination that makes desolate,[70] until the end that has been decreed engulfs that which makes desolate.

Understanding the syntax of verse 25 in the way outlined above means that the seventy "weeks" (or "sevens") are divided into three distinct periods of seven weeks, sixty-two weeks, and one week. The first period of seven weeks begins with a decree to rebuild Jerusalem and ends with the arrival of an anointed ruler, whose task appears to be to carry out the decree. A period of sixty-two weeks then follows, during which the city is rebuilt and after which an anointed one (not referred to as a ruler) is cut off. Jerusalem is destroyed by the people (or army) of a ruler who is to come. War persists to the end, when an unidentified individual (presumably the ruler who is to come) ratifies a covenant with many for one week, but then desecrates the temple before meeting his demise.

When was the decree to rebuild Jerusalem given?[71] Most attempt to identify the decree as a royal edict issued by a Persian ruler. The four options are the decrees of Cyrus (in 538 B.C.), Darius (519 or 518), Artaxerxes to Ezra (458 or 457), and Artaxerxes to Nehemiah (444). The decrees of Cyrus (2 Chron. 36:22–23; Ezra 1:1–4; 6:3–5) and Darius (Ezra 6:1–12) pertain to the rebuilding of the temple, not the city per se. Likewise, Artaxerxes' decree to Ezra (Ezra 7:11–26) makes no mention of rebuilding the city. Nehemiah 2:1–9 refers to letters given by Artaxerxes to Nehemiah authorizing the rebuilding of the city. Using this date (444) as a starting point, some calculate that there was a period of sixty-nine weeks (or 483 years) between the decree to rebuild the city and the triumphal entry of the "anointed" one, Jesus the Messiah, who is then "cut off."[72] However, if the syntactical analysis of Daniel 9:25 proposed above is correct, this view cannot be sustained, for the "anointed one" of verse 25 would have to appear around 396 (as-

69. The precise referent is unclear. As the text stands, the term appears to go with the following word, "the wing of abominations," but what this might mean is uncertain. Some see the referent as the "wing of the temple" (see Matt. 4:5), but how this would relate to a sacrifice is not clear. Others see the hornlike projections of an altar to be in view.

70. A comparison with 11:31 and 12:11 indicates that the word *shiqqutsim*, "abominations," goes with the term that follows, "that which makes desolate" (a singular participle). The plural form should probably be read as singular to agree with the following singular participle (the singular form *shiqquts* also appears in 11:31 and 12:11). The final *mem* is probably dittographic or enclitic.

71. The following discussion is not able to survey all of the interpretations of the seventy-"weeks" prophecy. For a helpful survey of the major views held currently, see Stephen R. Miller, *Daniel*, NAC (Nashville: Broadman & Holman, 1994), 252–57.

72. For a detailed presentation of this view, see Harold W. Hoehner, "Daniel's Seventy Weeks and New Testament Chronology," in *Vital Old Testament Issues*, ed. R. B. Zuck (Grand Rapids: Kregel, 1996), 171–86.

suming, as this system of reckoning does, that seven weeks is the equivalent of forty-nine years).

Since Daniel was aware of Jeremiah's prophecy concerning the desolation of Jerusalem, it is more likely that the decree to which Gabriel refers is also found in Jeremiah's prophecy. One finds such a prophetic decree in Jeremiah 30:18, a passage that can be dated sometime between 597–586 B.C. (see 29:1–2) and is thematically linked to the message recorded in chapter 29. If one takes the first period of seven weeks as equivalent to forty-nine years, as many do, then one would expect the arrival of an anointed ruler sometime between 548 and 539 B.C. It was during this period that the Persian ruler Cyrus, under whom Daniel served at the time he offered this prayer, began to gain momentum in his quest to build an empire. In Isaiah 45:1, Cyrus is actually called God's "anointed one," right after he is pictured decreeing the rebuilding of Jerusalem (44:28).[73] It should be noted that the "anointed" one referred to in Daniel 9:25 (also called a "ruler" here) and 9:26 (not called a "ruler") need not be the same individual. If the "ruler" mentioned in verse 26b can be different than the "ruler" of verse 25, as many argue, then the "anointed" one of verse 25 need not be the same as the "anointed" one of verse 26.

If one begins the entire period of seventy weeks sometime between 597–586 and terminates the first period of seven weeks sometime between 548–539, when does the second period of sixty-two weeks end? If one uses the method of literal calculation (that is, one week = seven years), the period would be equivalent to 434 years. Counting down from the time of Cyrus, one would then arrive at a date sometime between 114–105 B.C. Utilizing this system, Pierce concludes that the events prophesied in verses 26–27 were fulfilled during the reigns of the Hasmonean rulers Aristobulus I and Alexander Jannaeus.[74] However, since these historical figures play no role elsewhere in Daniel, this proposal seems unlikely.

Most prefer not to calculate the sixty-two weeks in such a literal manner. Instead, they correlate the events described in verses 26–27 with Antiochus IV Epiphanes' reign of terror. Some understand the "anointed" one of verse 26 as the high priest Onias III (probably referred to in Dan. 11:22), who was murdered in 171 B.C. (see 2 Macc. 4:33–36). The scenario outlined in verses 26–27 fits into the events of 171–164, especially the latter half of the period, when Antiochus (the "ruler" of v. 26) overran Jerusalem, made a covenant with the Hellenized Jews, burned the city, and desecrated the temple (1 Macc. 1:30–61). This view is attractive because of the way it correlates the text with other passages in the immediate context that pertain to

---

73. For a defense of the view proposed here (that the decree to rebuild the city is found in the context of Jeremiah 29 and that Cyrus is the anointed one of Dan. 9:25), see McComiskey, "The Seventy 'Weeks' of Daniel," 25–29.

74. See Ronald W. Pierce, "Spiritual Failure, Postponement, and Daniel 9," *TJ* 10 (1989): 211–22.

Antiochus IV (see especially 8:9–14 and 11:31–32). Antiochus erected "the abomination that causes desolation" (a pagan altar; see 1 Macc. 1:54, 59), in the temple (11:31). The phrase may even be a play on the name Baal Shamem (or Zeus), a deity worshiped by Antiochus.[75]

Since Jesus spoke of the abomination prophesied by Daniel as having a future fulfillment (Matt. 24:15), many prefer to see the hostile ruler depicted in Daniel 9:27 as Antichrist. In this view Jesus is usually understood as the "anointed" one who is "cut off" and the Romans are the "people" of the future ruler who destroy Jerusalem (v. 26). Proponents of this view are forced to see a gap between the events of the first century A.D. (v. 26) and the final, seventieth week (v. 27). McComiskey avoids this problem by seeing both verses 26 and 27 as prophesying the fall of Antichrist, who is both the "anointed" one that is "cut off" and the "ruler who is to come." He correlates this passage with 7:26 and 11:45, both of which in his view prophesy the fall of Antichrist.[76]

Perhaps pitting Antiochus IV against Antichrist is not the way to resolve this interpretive problem. If the little horn of chapter 8 (Antiochus) foreshadows Antichrist (the little horn of chapter 7), then it is possible that both figures are merged in 9:26–27 and that the passage has a double fulfillment.[77] In this scheme, verses 26–27 would depict the atrocities and downfall of Antiochus (also described in chapters 8 and 11), as well as the crimes and demise of the Antiochus-like Antichrist (also described in chapter 7). Jesus' reference to a future abomination as prophesied by Daniel demands that there be a future fulfillment of the prophecy, but it does not preclude an earlier, partial fulfillment as well. Indeed, most would agree that Daniel 11:31 describes an abomination of desolation (cf. v. 27) in the time of Antiochus IV. In this view, typological thinking underlies Jesus' use of the passage. Antiochus is a shadow of Antichrist and the period from 171–164, with its atrocities and sacrilege, is a shadow of the tribulation period, when such deeds will be repeated.

How do the prophesied events fit into the scheme of seventy weeks? Obviously, if we (a) understand the grammar of 9:25 as distinguishing between a period of seven weeks and another of sixty-two weeks, (b) take the decree of verse 24 as Jeremiah's prophecy that the city would be rebuilt, and (c) identify Cyrus the Persian as the "anointed" one who comes at the end of the seven weeks, then the period of seventy weeks cannot refer to a literal period of 490 years. Cyrus did arrive approximately forty-nine years after the decree, and there are textual indications that the seventieth week is seven

75. See Day, Yahweh and the Gods, 83–84.
76. McComiskey, "The Seventy 'Weeks' of Daniel," 29–35.
77. Some argue that Antiochus and Antichrist are closely associated in chapter 11 as well. See the discussion below.

years in duration,[78] but a period of 434 years (the intermediate period of sixty-two weeks) does not fit into a precise chronological scheme where one week equals seven years. The period from Cyrus to Antiochus (roughly 539 to 171 B.C.) is less than 434 years, while the period from Cyrus to Christ or the Antichrist (depending on the identity of the "anointed" one of v. 26) is longer than this.

For these reasons it is better to take the designation seventy weeks in a symbolic manner. As McComiskey points out, the term "week" simply connotes a unit of seven, not necessarily a "week" of seven years.[79] The image of seventy units of seven (or "weeks") is probably calendrical, with the symbolism of seven and seventy suggesting completeness. The symbolic use of the number seven and of multiples of seven in the ancient Near East is well-attested.[80] The use of seven weeks to designate the first period (from the decree to Cyrus) suggests a full period. But this was only the beginning of God's program, for the complete plan encompassed seventy weeks. McComiskey explains:

> [T]he seven weeks may be understood to represent a full measure of time, but not the fullest measure. The latter is denoted by the numerical concept seventy, which is ten times seven. That is, the numerical seven may have been applied to the first period of the structure because it represented a full period—which was the period of Israel's exile in Babylon. The numeral seven signifies the completion of that period. It indicates that the desolation of Jerusalem during the time of the exile would come to an end and the people would return. However, Daniel learned from the vision that the seven represented only a penultimate end to the desolations of Jerusalem. The desolation would cease ultimately only when seventy [weeks] had run their course and the supreme Desolator had been destroyed.[81]

It is quite natural that the ultimate consummation of God's program would be concentrated in a single seventieth week. The intermediate sixty-two weeks designate the long period between Cyrus and the beginning of this culminating week. Though this period of sixty-two weeks may be disproportionate to the first period of seven weeks, this is only problematic for those who demand mathematical precision. However, such precision may be foreign to the apocalyptic literary genre. In the intertestamental Apocalypse of Weeks found in *1 Enoch*, history is divided into successive weeks that are, when measured by the dating provided in the *Book of Jubilees*, disproportionate in duration.[82]

---

78. Dan. 9:27 says the abomination is set up in "the middle of the seven," while Dan. 12:7, 11 indicate that the desecration will continue for "a time, times and half a time," that is, 1,290 days, or approximately three and a half years.
79. Ibid., 40–41.
80. Ibid., 37–40.
81. Ibid., 41.
82. Ibid., 43–44.

Daniel's Final Vision (10:1–12:13)

This final vision is dated to "the third year of Cyrus king of Persia" (10:1). This probably refers to the third year of Cyrus's reign over the conquered city of Babylon (that is, 536 or 535 B.C.).

Daniel Meets an Angelic Visitor (10:1–11:1)

Daniel's vision pertained to a coming war and left him in mourning for three weeks (vv. 2–3). On the twenty-fourth day of the first month (Nisan, that is March–April), as he was standing on the bank of the Tigris River, he saw a "man," who radiated with brilliance and spoke with a loud voice (vv. 4–6). The vision of this angelic figure all but paralyzed Daniel, who fell into a trancelike sleep (vv. 7–9). The angel told Daniel he had been sent with a message for him and assured him that he need not fear (vv. 10–12). Though the angel had been dispatched as soon as Daniel had prayed, he had encountered opposition along the way, causing his arrival to be delayed for twenty-one days, the exact amount of time Daniel had been in mourning (v. 13; see v. 3). A powerful enemy, called here "the prince of the Persian kingdom," blocked his way. Michael, "one of the chief princes," intervened, enabling him to complete his mission. We are not told exactly why this "prince" opposed the angel sent to Daniel, but it seems likely that he wanted to prevent the delivery of a message announcing the downfall of the Persian Empire (see 11:2–3).[83] This "prince" was most likely a hostile angelic power. Though the term "prince" (Heb. *sar*) sometimes refers in Daniel to human rulers (see 9:6, 8; 11:5), it is also used of angelic powers (10:13, 21; 12:1). Since the angelic "prince" Michael here opposes the "prince" of Persia, it is likely that the latter is an angelic power as well.[84]

This mysterious but enlightening passage alludes to dissension and conflict among God's heavenly assembly. God has given jurisdiction over the nations to members of his heavenly assembly, but some of these delegated authorities have abused their position and rebelled against God. The original text of Deuteronomy 32:8 reads, "When the Most High gave the nations their inheritance, when he divided all mankind, he set up boundaries for the peoples according to the number of the sons of God."[85] But in Psalm 82,

---

83. See Goldingay, *Daniel*, 292.

84. See David E. Stevens, "Daniel 10 and the Notion of Territorial Spirits," *BSac* 157 (2000): 411–18. Verse 13b refers to the human rulers of Persia, but it uses a different term, translated "king," in this case. Actually the plural form is used in v. 13b (contrary to NIV), which one may translate, "I was left there near the kings of Persia." The reason for the plural is unclear. Perhaps Cyrus and his son Cambyses are the referents. See Stevens, 425.

85. The Hebrew text reads "sons of Israel," but this is a misinterpretation of the phrase "sons of God," a reading that is attested in a manuscript of the text from Qumran. The Septuagint has "angels of God," correctly interpreting the phrase as a reference to God's heavenly assembly. See Michael S. Heiser, "Deuteronomy 32:8 and the Sons of God," *BSac* 158 (2001): 52–74, as well as Robert B. Chisholm Jr., *From Exegesis to Exposition* (Grand Rapids: Baker, 1998), 26–27.

God denounces these "gods" for failing to promote justice on the earth. The New Testament makes it clear that these rebellious angels, under the authority of Satan, oppose God's work on earth (Eph. 6:12) and fight with the angels who have remained loyal to God (Rev. 12:7).

The angel had been sent to Daniel to explain to him the significance of the vision he had seen earlier (see v. 1), especially as it pertained to Israel (v. 14). Yet Daniel was still so overwhelmed by the presence of the angelic messenger that he fell on his face speechless (v. 15). The angel touched Daniel's lips and enabled him to speak, but Daniel could only describe how terrified he was (vv. 16–17). The angel imparted strength to Daniel, who was now ready to hear what the angel had to say (vv. 18–19). The angel reiterated that his task was to reveal the future to Daniel (v. 21). He also pointed out that he would soon have to return to spiritual combat against the angels who had been given jurisdiction over the kingdoms of Persia and Greece. This struggle had been going on for about three years (10:20; 11:1).

The Kings of the North and South Collide (11:2–45)

The angel outlined future events for Daniel. He explained that three more kings would appear in Persia, followed by a fourth, whose wealth would exceed that of his predecessors (v. 2). This fourth king would also launch a campaign against the Greeks. The identity of these four Persian rulers is not entirely certain. Twelve kings followed Cyrus on the Persian throne before Alexander the Great (see vv. 3–4) brought the dynasty to an end. So the reference to just four kings indicates a selective list is in view. Xerxes I (486–465 B.C.) would seem to be the fourth king. He was wealthy and campaigned against the Greeks. If Xerxes is the fourth king, then the first three would be his predecessors, Cambyses (530–522), Smerdis (522), and Darius I (522–486). Since Smerdis was such a minor figure, it is possible that Cambyses, Darius I, and Xerxes I are the first three kings, with Artaxerxes I (465–424) being the fourth. However, since either of these proposals would leave a significant chronological gap between the fourth Persian king and Alexander (336–323), who is mentioned in verse 3, some prefer to identify the fourth king as Darius III (336–330).

Verse 3 depicts the greatness of Alexander, while verse 4 focuses on the eventual disintegration of his kingdom. Alexander defeated the Persians but died suddenly and prematurely, leaving no legitimate heir to his throne. His empire was not passed on to descendants but was divided up among his generals (see 8:22). Cassander ruled Macedonia, Lysimachus controlled Thrace and Asia Minor, Seleucus was in charge of Syria, and Ptolemy took Egypt and southern Palestine.

Two of these kingdoms, Syria and Egypt, play a prominent role in the remainder of chapter 11, which describes how the kings of the north (the Seleucid rulers of Syria) collided with the kings of the south (the Ptolemaic rulers of Egypt).[86] The titles "king of the north" and "king of the south" refer in a generic way to the Seleucid or Ptolemaic rulers, respectively. The following chart shows the specific rulers referred to in these verses:

	King of the South	King of the North
v. 5	Ptolemy I (322–285 B.C.)	Seleucus I (312–280 B.C.)[87]
6	Ptolemy II (285–246)	Antiochus II (262–246)
7–9	Ptolemy III (246–221)	Seleucus II (246–226)
10		Seleucus III (226–223) Antiochus III (223–187)[88]
11–19		Antiochus III
(11–12)	Ptolemy IV (221–203)	
(14–17)	Ptolemy V (203–180)	
20		Seleucus IV (187–175)[89]
21–35		Antiochus IV (175–163)[90]
(25)	Ptolemy VI (180–145)	
36–45		???
(40)	???	

Ptolemy I was a powerful king, but eventually Seleucus I, who had fled to Egypt under pressure and served as one of Ptolemy's generals, reclaimed his lost territory and surpassed Ptolemy in power (v. 5). Several years later, around 250, Ptolemy II and Antiochus II made an alliance (v. 6). In an attempt to solidify the treaty, Ptolemy gave Antiochus his daughter Bernice as a wife. Antiochus divorced his wife Laodice in favor of Bernice and cut off his two sons by Laodice from their inheritance. Before too long Antiochus returned to Laodice, but she murdered him, Bernice, and the child Bernice had borne to Antiochus.

Bernice's brother, Ptolemy III, became the ruler of Egypt in 246 (v. 7a). He invaded Syria and carried away a great deal of loot (vv. 7b–8). Seleucus II tried to retaliate, but his campaign against Ptolemy was unsuccessful (v. 9).

86. For a helpful study of Daniel 11 as it relates to Near Eastern history, see Walter K. Price, *In the Final Days* (Chicago: Moody, 1977).
87. The king of the north is not specifically identified as such here, but v. 6 makes his identity clear.
88. Neither is called "king of the north" in v. 10, but it is clear that both are sons of the king of the north of v. 9.
89. He is not called "king of the north" here, but he is referred to as the successor of the king of the north described in the previous verses.
90. Antiochus IV is referred to as one of two kings in v. 27, but this section never actually calls him "king of the north." NIV's "king of the North" in v. 28 is interpretive; the Hebrew text does not have the phrase. The ruler described in v. 26a is Ptolemy, not Antiochus. Furthermore, the word "king" does not appear there in the Hebrew text (contrary to NIV).

His sons, Seleucus III and Antiochus III, renewed hostilities with Egypt (v. 10), but Ptolemy IV raised a large army and in 217 defeated Antiochus's forces at Raphia (vv. 11–12).

In 202, Antiochus III invaded Palestine at a time when Egypt, weakened by internal dissension, was not in a position to resist him effectively (vv. 13–14a). Some Jews attempted to resist Antiochus, but failed (v. 14b).[91] The forces of Antiochus defeated the Egyptians, who retreated to Sidon, where they surrendered (v. 15). Antiochus now controlled Palestine (v. 16). He made a treaty with Egypt and gave his daughter Cleopatra in marriage to Ptolemy V, hoping that this would allow him to control the Egyptian ruler (v. 17a). The plan backfired, for Cleopatra sided with her husband, rather than her father (v. 17b).

Wanting to expand his power even more, Antiochus III turned to the west and invaded Greece, but a Roman army defeated him and forced him to retreat (v. 18). He became a subject of Rome, which demanded tribute of him. He tried to rob a temple at Elymais and was assassinated by some irate residents of the town (v. 19). Seleucus IV succeeded Antiochus and attempted to raise funds to pay the tribute demanded by the Romans. He sent a tax collector named Heliodorus to rob the temple in Jerusalem. Eventually this same Heliodorus assassinated Seleucus (v. 20).

In 175, Antiochus IV, brother of Seleucus IV, seized the throne, even though Seleucus's son Demetrius, a political prisoner in Rome, was the rightful heir (v. 21). The text characterizes Antiochus as a "contemptible person," an assessment which is supported and illustrated by ancient historians.[92] He gave himself the title Theos Epiphanes, "God Revealed," though his enemies called him Epimanes, "Madman." He controlled Palestine and removed from power the high priest Onias III, probably the "prince of the covenant" mentioned here (v. 22). He made a deal with Jason, the brother of Onias. In exchange for the position of high priest, Jason agreed to promote Antiochus's interests, which involved forcing Hellenistic culture upon the Jewish people (vv. 23–24; see 2 Macc. 4:7–20).

Antiochus launched a campaign against Egypt and defeated the forces of Ptolemy VI (vv. 25–26; see 1 Macc. 1:17–19). The Egyptians placed Ptolemy's brother on the throne, prompting Antiochus to plot with Ptolemy VI to regain the throne (v. 27). The victorious Antiochus headed home, but on the way he stopped to rob the temple in Jerusalem and terrorize the population (v. 28; see 1 Macc. 1:20–28). Shortly thereafter he invaded Egypt again, but this time the Egyptians, aided by the Romans, turned him back (vv. 29–30a). Upset by his failure, he took his anger out on Jerusalem, desecrating the temple altar and committing atrocities against the people (vv. 30b–31;

91. Goldingay suggests that the pro-Egyptian Tobiads are in view here. See *Daniel*, 297.
92. See Price, *In the Final Days*, 56–72.

see 8:9–14, 23–25; 1 Macc. 1:54–60). Though some Jews supported Antiochus, others resisted him (v. 32). Certain godly leaders, called here the "wise," urged many to stand against Antiochus (v. 33a). This probably refers to the priest Mattathias and his sons (known as the Maccabeans), who organized a guerrilla army (1 Macc. 2:1–28). They suffered some setbacks (v. 33b), but eventually emerged victorious. They received "a little help" from an alliance with Rome (see 1 Macc. 8), though some impostors also infiltrated their ranks (v. 34).[93] Some of the leaders (the "wise") were even martyred (v. 35a; see 1 Macc. 9:14–27). However, their seemingly tragic demise is seen through the eyes of faith as purifying them "until the time of the end" when they would be vindicated and rewarded (v. 35b; see v. 40 and 12:2–3).[94]

Verses 32–35, which summarize the early years of the Maccabean revolt, take us a few years beyond the death of Antiochus IV. But verses 36–39 appear to pick up the description of his blasphemous deeds begun in verses 31–32. Like his father before him (see v. 16), he did as he pleased (v. 36a). He claimed to be divine, magnified himself above the pagan gods, and even blasphemed the one true God (vv. 36b–37). The reference to the "one desired by women" (v. 37) is cryptic. Apparently it refers to a deity who was particularly attractive to women, perhaps the god Tammuz (see Ezek. 8:14). Antiochus gave special honor to one particular god as he launched attacks against fortified cities (vv. 38–39; see v. 24). This "god of fortresses" was probably Zeus, whom Antiochus made the patron god of the Seleucids.[95]

Some argue that verses 36–39 describe Antichrist (identified as the little horn of chapter 7), not Antiochus IV. The description of his arrogant blasphemy in verse 36 has a parallel in the description of the little horn in 7:25. Some also argue that Antiochus did not magnify himself above all gods.[96] However, one must make some allowance for hyperbole here.[97] Second Maccabees 9:8 states that Antiochus thought "he could command the waves of the sea" and "weigh the high mountains in a balance," as if he were the sovereign creator and king of the world.

93. See Buchanan, The Book of Daniel, 354–59.
94. If one translates the preposition 'ad as "until," it gives the impression that the events of the Maccabean period, described in the preceding verses, are chronologically distinct from those during "the time of the end." In this case, the events prophesied in 11:36–12:4 would have to be later than the time of Antiochus and the Maccabees. However, 8:17 indicates that Antiochus's career is included in the period designated "the time of the end." Therefore, it is better to understand the phrase "until the time of the end" in 11:35 in the sense of "until the time of the end is completed" or "during the time of the end." The preposition 'ad has the nuance "to the end of, during" in biblical Aramaic (see BDB 1105; cf. Dan. 6:7, 12; 7:12, 25) and occasionally in biblical Hebrew (BDB 724, 2b). In this case, "the time of the end" in Daniel encompasses the career of Antiochus (8:17, 19; 11:40) as well as culminating eschatological events, including the resurrection of the Maccabean martyrs (11:35; 12:4, 9–10).
95. See Goldingay, Daniel, 304–5, and Lacocque, The Book of Daniel, 231–32. Zeus was probably identified with the Syrian god Baal Shamem. See Day, Yahweh and the Gods, 83–85.
96. See, for example, Archer, "Daniel," 144.
97. Similar hyperbole is utilized in Isa. 14:12–15, which depicts the proud king of Babylon as a petty deity who tries to ascend above the gods and usurp the high god's position.

Perhaps the best way to resolve this interpretive issue is not to pit Antiochus against Antichrist. Most likely Antiochus is a type of Antichrist, just as his abominable altar (11:31; see 1 Macc. 1:54, 59) foreshadowed a future desecration of the temple (Matt. 24:15).[98] His disrespect for God foreshadowed the attitude of the lawless one described by Paul (see 2 Thess. 2:3–9).

The story appears to continue in verses 40–45, which tell how the king of the north would beat back another assault by the king of the south, invade Palestine, conquer Egypt, and set up his tents between the Mediterranean and the Dead Sea before meeting his demise. However, these verses do not correspond to historical events during the final days of Antiochus IV. After desecrating the temple, he did not engage in another battle with the king of the south nor did he die in Palestine. How then is this apparent failure of prophecy explained?

Most modern scholars argue that Daniel 11 was written in 165 B.C. Verses 2–39 are viewed as "after the fact prophecy" (written in prophetic style, but actually postdating the events they allegedly predict), while verses 40–45 contain genuine, albeit unfulfilled prophecy. For example, Collins writes concerning chapter 11:

> The main focus of attention is Antiochus IV Epiphanes, to whose reign more than half the chapter is devoted. The preceding review of Hellenistic history bridges the gap between the supposed time of Daniel and the actual composition of the book. It is presented as a prediction and follows the cryptic style of prophecy. In this way it suggests that the course of history has been determined in advance. It also lends credibility to the real prophecy with which the passage concludes. If the "predictions" are known to have been accurate down to the present, then they are likely to be reliable for the future too. In fact, the concluding prophecy of the death of the king was not fulfilled, and so Daniel 11 provides a clear indication of the time when the book was composed.[99]

Most evangelicals reject this consensus and treat chapter 11 as genuine prophecy delivered in the time of Daniel. They typically argue that the referent changes from Antiochus IV to Antichrist, either at verse 36 (with the reference to "the king") or verse 40 (with the reference to "at the time of the end"). In this case the latter is depicted as an Antiochus-like figure who brings to culmination all the hostility expressed by his historical and typological predecessor. He is identified with the little horn of chapter 7, who is distinguished from the little horn of chapter 8. For support, proponents of this position appeal to statements by (a) Jesus, who anticipated a future abomination of desolation like that of Antiochus's time (cf. Matt. 24:15 with Dan. 11:31), (b) Paul, who foresaw the coming of a lawless one who opposes God (2 Thess. 2:3–9), and (c) the Apostle John, who spoke of a coming Antichrist (1 John 2:18) and envisioned an end-time world ruler rising up from

98. See my comments on Dan. 9:26–27.
99. John J. Collins, *The Apocalyptic Imagination* (New York: Crossroad, 1987), 88.

the sea (Rev. 13:1–10). Advocates of this view also point out that the events described in 11:40–45 occur at the "time of the end" and culminate in the resurrection (see 12:1–4).

Critics object to this reading of Daniel 11. For example, Collins states:

> The conservative argument that the concluding verses refer to the Antichrist of a distant eschaton is gratuitous: the text gives no indication of a change of referent. The author knows Antiochus's two campaigns to Egypt, the desecration of the temple in Jerusalem, and the fortification of the Akra, but not the reconsecration of the temple or the actual death of the king late in 164 B.C.[100]

In response to this objection, several observations are in order:

1. Changes in referent are not consistently indicated in this chapter. Changes in referent occur in the following verses:

Verses 5–6: The king of the south is Ptolemy I in verse 5 and Ptolemy II in verse 6, but no change is indicated. The powerful king of verse 5 is Seleucus I, and the king of the north in verse 6 is Antiochus II, but no change is indicated.

Verses 6 and 7–9: The king of the south is Ptolemy II in verse 6 and Ptolemy III in verses 7–9. A change in referent is implied in verse 7. The king of the north is Antiochus II in verse 6 and Seleucus II in verses 7–9, but no change is indicated.

Verses 7–9 and 10–19: The king of the south is Ptolemy III in verses 7–9, Ptolemy IV in verses 11–12, and Ptolemy V in verses 14–17, but the changes in referent are not indicated. The king of the north is Seleucus II in verses 7–9 and Antiochus III in verses 11–19, but, even though Seleucus II's sons are mentioned in verse 10, it is not entirely clear literarily if the king of the north in verses 11–19 is Seleucus II or one of his sons.

Verses 19–20: The text makes it clear that the ruler of verse 20 (Seleucus IV) is the successor of the king of the north (Antiochus III) of verses 11–19.

Verses 20–21: The text makes it clear that the ruler of verses 21–35 (Antiochus IV) is the successor of Seleucus IV (v. 20).

Verses 14–17 and 25: The king of the south is Ptolemy V in verse 17 and Ptolemy VI in verse 25, but there is no indication of a change of referent.

2. The reference to "the king" in verse 36 could signal a transition from Antiochus IV to another ruler or at least suggest that the description is now typological and transcends Antiochus. Though Antiochus seized the kingdom of the north (v. 21) and is one of the "two kings" mentioned in verse 27, he is never specifically called "the king" or even "the king of the north" in verses 21–35. As noted earlier, NIV's "king of the North" in verse 28 is interpretive;

100. Collins, *Daniel with an Introduction*, 101.

the Hebrew text does not have the phrase. The ruler described in verse 26a is Ptolemy, not Antiochus. Furthermore, the word "king" does not appear there in the Hebrew text (contrary to NIV). The close literary link between verse 36 (note "will do as he pleases") and earlier descriptions of the Medo-Persian Empire (8:4), Alexander the Great (11:3), and Antiochus III (11:16) may suggest that the king of verses 36–39 epitomizes the pride and power of these previous kings and transcends the historical Antiochus IV. If so, the title "the king" (which occurs only here in Daniel 11) is quite appropriate.

Some argue that verse 40 describes an attack by the kings of the north and the south upon "the king" of verses 36–39. If this is the case, then "the king" cannot be equated with Antiochus, for the latter is viewed as a usurper of the northern kingdom. However, it is more likely that verse 40 describes a conflict between the king of the south and the king of the north ("the king" of vv. 36–39). This would be consistent with the pattern of conflict already established earlier in the chapter and with the portrayal in verses 40b–43, which describe an invader sweeping down through Palestine into Egypt.

3. The reference to "the time of the end" in verse 40 (see also v. 35 and 12:4, 9) may mark a transition from the time of Antiochus IV to a culminating period. However, this argument is not as strong as it first appears, for the phrase "time of the end" is used in 8:17 with reference to Antiochus's career (see also v. 19). For this reason, the presence of this phrase actually favors the view that verses 40–45 refer to Antiochus (see further discussion below).

4. The purpose of this chapter is not to give a complete account of the various kings' careers. Rather, it traces the escalating strength of the northern kings and with it the increased oppression of God's people. In verses 5–12 the king of the south dominates the scene, but beginning in verse 13 the tables are turned and the king of the north prevails. Antiochus IV receives the most attention because he violated the temple. His disdain for God's people makes him a prime candidate for typological use. It would not be necessary to describe his demise here because (*a*) his death has already been announced (8:25) and (*b*) the ultimate failure of his oppressive program would be implied in the destruction of the one he typifies (11:45).

5. Typological patterning is attested elsewhere in the Bible. For example, several prophets speak of Israel's return from exile as a second exodus. Isaiah pictures the Servant of the Lord as a new Moses who leads this return from bondage. Some prophets call the coming messianic king "David," because he will rule in the spirit and power of his illustrious ancestor. Such typological patterning sometimes results in the blending of parallel yet distinct events in prophetic visions. For example, many prophets place God's judgment on specific nations of their time within the framework of a final, cosmic judgment prior to the inauguration of God's kingdom (see Isa. 13–27). Jesus

himself employs such a technique in the Olivet Discourse, where he blends into one vision scenes of the fall of Jerusalem in A.D. 70 and culminating end-time events (see Matt. 24 and Luke 21).

Both of the approaches outlined above understand verses 36–45 (or at least 40–45) to be in chronological sequence with what precedes. But is this necessarily the case? Could these verses be a recapitulation of earlier events, rather than in chronological sequence to what is outlined in the preceding verses? Buchanan argues that verses 40–45 actually pertain to Antiochus III, whose career is outlined in verses 11–19. He theorizes that the final editor of the book possessed two complementary versions of Antiochus III's exploits. Rather than merging the two into a composite account, he simply included one of them (vv. 40–45) as an appendix to the chapter. Later interpreters failed to recognize this, leading to the interpretive confusion we see today.[101]

However, there are problems with Buchanan's proposal. Verse 40 seems to link the king of the north with the ruler depicted in verses 36–39. The pronoun "him" in the statement "will engage him in battle" most naturally refers to the king described in verses 36–39 (whom Buchanan agrees is Antiochus IV). Furthermore, the reference to the "time of the end" in verse 40 militates against this proposal, for the phrase is applied to Antiochus IV's career in 8:17.

A more likely proposal is that verses 36–45 recapitulate the career of Antiochus IV, for the reference to the "time of the end" in verse 40, as noted earlier, is associated with Antiochus's reign of terror in 8:17.[102] In this view, verses 36–39 summarize his arrogant attitude and militarism (see vv. 24, 31–32). Like verse 24, they depict him as one who assaults "fortresses." Verses 40–43 review his successes against Egypt and domination of Palestine (vv. 21–26). The description of his army in verse 40 is almost identical to that given in 1 Maccabees 1:17: "So he invaded Egypt with a strong force, with chariots and elephants and cavalry and with a large fleet." Verse 44 probably refers to an episode that occurred in the aftermath of Antiochus's second Egyptian campaign (see v. 29). When a rumor of Antiochus's death reached Jerusalem, a rebellion broke out there as Jason, who had been supplanted by Menelaus as high priest, sought to regain his office. When reports of the rebellion reached Antiochus, he marched to Jerusalem. Second Maccabees 5:11 states: "When news of what had happened reached the king, he took it to mean that Judea was in revolt. So, raging inwardly, he left Egypt and took the city by storm." Atrocities followed as Antiochus ordered his troops to slaughter the people (2 Macc. 5:12–14). Verse 45a describes Antiochus's op-

101. Buchanan, *Book of Daniel,* 363–67, 420–23. To make this proposal work, he argues that v. 45 does not refer to the end of Antiochus III's life, but to a decline in his influence and power.
102. Albert Barnes argued that vv. 40–45 recapitulate the career of Antiochus IV. See his *Daniel,* ed. R. Frew, 2 vols. (reprint, Grand Rapids: Baker, 1979), 2:246–47.

pressive presence in Palestine, while verse 45b looks ahead to his eventual demise. But what of the fact that Antiochus did not die in Palestine? Actually this is not nearly the problem some have made it. These verses give a very streamlined profile of Antiochus's career. Verse 45 need not mean or imply that he would die in Palestine. It simply makes the point that, despite his designs on Jerusalem and Judea, he would ultimately fail.[103]

Culminating Events (12:1–13)

Just as the situation looked most desperate for God's people, Michael, the angelic protector of Israel, would intervene and deliver them (12:1). Those who see Antichrist as the referent in 11:36–45 understand this verse as referring to the tribulation period described in the Book of Revelation, during which Michael plays a significant role (see Rev. 12:7). However, if the preceding verses pertain to Antiochus, it is more likely that 12:1 refers to the distress experienced by Jerusalem in 167–164 B.C. The oppression of Antiochus, because of its desecration of the temple sacrifices and widespread slaughter, could well be viewed as the worst time of persecution ever experienced by God's people up to that point (see 1 Macc. 1:20–62; 2 Macc. 5).

The reference to Michael's intervention need not point to an end-time event. According to Jewish tradition, angelic intervention highlighted the Maccabean wars of independence. According to 2 Maccabees 10:29–30, "five resplendent men on horses" came down from heaven in one battle and supernaturally protected Judas Maccabeus from death. They "showered arrows and thunderbolts upon the enemy, so that, confused and blinded, they were thrown into disorder." Before his battle with Lysias, Judas asked the Lord to send "a good angel to save Israel" (2 Macc. 11:6). As his army prepared for battle, "a horseman appeared at their head, clothed in white and brandishing weapons of gold" (v. 8). The vision energized the men, who charged fearlessly into battle and defeated the enemy (vv. 9–12). Lysias "realized that the Hebrews were invincible because the mighty God fought on their side" (v. 13). Before his battle with Nicanor, Judas prayed again that the Lord would send "a good angel" to overwhelm the enemy, just as he had done to Sennacherib's army in the days of Hezekiah (2 Macc. 15:22–23). The men prayed as they fought and won a decisive victory, which left them "gladdened by God's manifestation" (vv. 26–27).

Michael's victory would culminate with the resurrection of the dead,

---

103. Even if the statement intends to say that Antiochus would die in Palestine, that he died elsewhere is not as problematic as some think. Sometimes prophecies are fulfilled in essence, but not with the precision one might expect. For example, in 1 Kings 21:19 Elijah prophesies to Ahab: "In the place where dogs licked up Naboth's blood, dogs will lick up your blood—yes, yours." The prophecy was fulfilled (1 Kings 22:38), though the dogs licked Ahab's blood in Samaria, not Jezreel, where Naboth was executed (see 1 Kings 21:1–14). Ironically, the prophecy, perhaps in a revised version, seems to have received a more literal fulfillment when Jehu assassinated Ahab's son Joram and threw his corpse on the field belonging to Naboth (2 Kings 9:24–26).

some to everlasting life and others to everlasting shame (v. 2). At that time the "wise," many of whom had been martyred (see 11:33–35), would be vindicated and honored (v. 3). Some see the resurrection here as metaphorical, referring to the revival of the nation's fortunes (see Isa. 26:19 and Ezek. 37:1–14). However, the reference to evildoers also being raised from the dead and the literary link with 11:33–35, where the literal death of martyrs is envisioned, indicates that a literal resurrection of the dead is in view here. The prophecy leaps ahead from the Maccabean era to the future resurrection of the dead in order to make it clear that those who gave their lives resisting the godless Antiochus did not die in vain. Their vindication will come.

Those who see 11:36–45 as referring to Antichrist may think this reference to resurrection favors their view, since no resurrection occurred in conjunction with the Maccabean victory. However, in response one need only point out that the blending of events that are separated in history is a characteristic of prophecy. Indeed, they themselves propose that such a blending occurs between 11:35 and 11:36.

The angel instructed Daniel to close up the scroll containing the vision (v. 4a), just as he had been told to do following his earlier vision of Antiochus's career (see 8:26). This withholding of divine revelation would cause many to wander about in search of a word from God (v. 4b).[104] However, the vision was not quite completed. Daniel saw two more angelic figures, one standing on one side of the river (the Tigris; see 10:4), the other on the opposite side (v. 5). One of them asked the angel clothed in linen (with whom Daniel had been speaking; see 10:5) how long it would take for the prophesied events to be fulfilled (v. 6). The question is similar to the one asked by an angel in 8:13. The answer (v. 7a, "a time, times and half a time") is reminiscent of 7:25, which states that the little horn would oppress God's holy ones for this same period of time, probably three and a half years. God's people would be shattered by oppression, but the promised deliverance would then come (v. 7b).

Daniel asked for clarification of the message (v. 8). The angel told Daniel to go on his way and assured him that he would someday inherit his reward for being a godly follower of the Lord (vv. 9, 13). The trial to come would purify the godly, who, in contrast to the wicked, would possess insight into how these events fit into the divine program (v. 10). Once the abominable altar was set up, a period of 1,290 days would ensue, followed by another period of forty-five days (vv. 11–12). Apparently the first of these numbers pertains to the period of persecution, while the additional forty-five days is the time it would take for complete restoration and purification to occur. The figure of 1,290 days is probably meant to correspond to the "time, times and half a time," or three and a half years. If one uses a lunar

---

104. See Goldingay, *Daniel*, 309.

calendar (thirty days per month for forty-two months), three and a half years would add up to 1,260 days (see Rev. 11:2–3 and 13:5), but the figure here may include an intercalated month, added to make the calendar correspond to the solar year.[105]

If the oppression of Antiochus is in view, then this period began when Antiochus outlawed sacrifices in the temple (see 1 Macc. 1:44–45) sometime before desecrating it in 167 B.C. According to 1 Maccabees, the temple remained in a ritually polluted condition for three years and ten days (cf. 1 Macc. 1:54 with 4:52) before the victorious Judas Maccabeus ordered it to be ritually cleansed and rededicated. This adds up to 1,090 days (1,120 days if one includes an intercalated month), not 1,290, but the period in question probably includes the time between the edict outlawing sacrifices and the setting up of the abominable altar, both of which are mentioned in verse 11. It is unclear how the figures given here relate to the 2,300 evenings and mornings (1,150 days?) mentioned in 8:14 as the time that would elapse before the temple would be reconsecrated.

Those who identify Antichrist as the oppressive king of 11:36–45 prefer to see this final vision as referring to the tribulation period. If the little horn of chapter 7 is Antichrist, then the reference to "a time, times and half a time" in both 7:25 and 12:7 lends some support to this proposal. However, in Revelation 11:2–3 and 13:5, the beast's control of Jerusalem lasts for forty-two months/1,260 days, not 1,290 days. No matter how one interprets Daniel 12, it is apparent that the oppression of Antiochus, which lasted roughly three and a half years in its most intensive stage, foreshadows a similar period of persecution by Antichrist during the tribulation period. If the little horn of chapter 7 is indeed Antichrist, then this typological relationship between the periods of oppression is already apparent in the Book of Daniel.

Bibliography

Commentaries

Archer, G. L. "Daniel." In *The Expositor's Bible Commentary*, edited by F. E. Gaebelein, 12 vols., 7:1–157. Grand Rapids: Zondervan, 1978–92.
Baldwin, J. G. *Daniel*. TOTC. Leicester, England: InterVarsity, 1978.
Buchanan, G. W. *The Book of Daniel*. Mellen Biblical Commentary. Lewiston, N.Y.: Mellen Biblical Press, 1999.
Collins, J. J. *Daniel*. Hermeneia. Minneapolis: Fortress, 1993.
Goldingay, J. E. *Daniel*. WBC. Dallas: Word, 1989.
Hartman, L. F., and A. A. Di Lella, *The Book of Daniel*. AB. New York: Doubleday, 1978.
Lacocque, A. *The Book of Daniel*. Translated by D. Pellauer. Atlanta: John Knox, 1979.
Miller, S. R. *Daniel*. NAC. Nashville: Broadman & Holman, 1994.

105. See ibid., 309–10.

Montgomery, J. A. *A Critical and Exegetical Commentary on the Book of Daniel.* ICC. Edinburgh: T. & T. Clark, 1927.

Porteous, N. W. *Daniel.* OTL. Rev. ed. Philadelphia: Westminster, 1979.

Walvoord, J. F. *Daniel: The Key to Prophetic Revelation.* Chicago: Moody, 1971.

Young, E. J. *The Prophecy of Daniel.* Grand Rapids: Eerdmans, 1949.

Recent Studies

General

Aaron, C. L., Jr. "Loosening a Knot: Theological Development in the Book of Daniel." Ph.D. diss., Union Theological Seminary (Va.), 1996.

Baldwin, D. D. "Free Will and Conditionality in Daniel." In *To Understand the Scriptures: Essays in Honor of William H. Shea,* edited by D. Merling, 163–72. Berrien Springs, Mich.: Institute of Archaeology/Siegfried H. Horn Archaeological Museum Andrews University, 1997.

Choi, J. J. "The Aramaic of Daniel: Its Date, Place of Composition, and Linguistic Comparison with Extra-biblical Texts." Ph.D. diss., Trinity Evangelical Divinity School, 1994.

Cryer, F. H. "The Problem of Dating Biblical Hebrew and the Hebrew of Daniel." In *In the Last Days: On Jewish and Christian Apocalyptic and Its Period,* edited by K. Jeppesen et al., 185–98. Århus, Denmark: Århus University Press, 1994.

David, P. S. "The Composition and Structure of the Book of Daniel: A Synchronic and Diachronic Reading." Ph.D. diss., Louvain, 1991.

Helberg, J. L. "The Determination of History according to the Book of Daniel: Against the Background of Deterministic Apocalyptic." *ZAW* 107 (1995): 273–87.

Lucas, E. C. "Daniel: Resolving the Enigma." *VT* 50 (2000): 66–80.

————. "The Source of Daniel's Animal Imagery." *TynB* 41 (1990): 161–85.

Mastin, B. A. "Wisdom and Daniel." In *Wisdom in Ancient Israel: Essays in Honour of J. A. Emerton,* edited by J. Day et al., 161–69. Cambridge: Cambridge University Press, 1995.

Meadowcroft, T. J. *Aramaic Daniel and Greek Daniel: A Literary Comparison.* JSOTSup 198. Sheffield: Sheffield Academic Press, 1995.

Miller, J. E. "The Redaction of Daniel." *JSOT* 52 (1991): 115–24.

Patterson, R. D. "Holding on to Daniel's Court Tales." *JETS* 36 (1993): 445–54.

Péter-Contesse, R., and J. Ellington. *A Handbook on the Book of Daniel.* New York: United Bible Societies, 1994.

Pfandl, G. "The Later Days and the Time of the End in the Book of Daniel." Ph.D. diss., Andrews University, 1990.

Stefanovic, Z. *The Aramaic of Daniel in the Light of Old Aramaic.* JSOTSup 129. Sheffield: JSOT, 1992.

Thompson, H. O. *The Book of Daniel: An Annotated Bibliography.* New York: Garland, 1993.

van der Woude, A. S., ed. *The Book of Daniel in the Light of New Findings.* Louvain: Peeters, 1993.

Vermes, G. "Josephus' Treatment of the Book of Daniel." *JJS* 42 (1991): 149–66.

Woodard, B. L., Jr. "Literary Strategies and Authorship in the Book of Daniel." *JETS* 37 (1994): 39–53.

Daniel 1–6

Armistead, D. B. "The Images of Daniel 2 and 7: A Literary Approach." *Stulos Theological Journal* 6 (1998): 63–66.

Arnold, B. T. "Wordplay and Narrative Techniques in Daniel 5 and 6." *JBL* 112 (1993): 479–85.

Avalos, H. I. "The Comedic Function of the Enumerations of Officials and Instruments in Daniel 3." *CBQ* 53 (1991): 580–88.

Brewer, D. I. *"Mene Mene Teqel Uparsin:* Daniel 5:25 in Cuneiform." *TynB* 42 (1991): 310–16.

Colless, B. E. "Cyrus the Persian as Darius the Mede in the Book of Daniel." *JSOT* 56 (1992): 113–26.

Coxon, P. W. "Another Look at Nebuchadnezzar's Madness." In *The Book of Daniel in the Light of New Findings,* edited by A. S. van der Woude, 211–22. Louvain: Peeters, 1993.

———. "Nebuchadnezzar's Hermeneutical Dilemma." *JSOT* 66 (1995): 87–97.

Dyer, C. H. "The Musical Instruments in Daniel 3." *BSac* 147 (1990): 426–36.

Ferguson, P. "Nebuchadnezzar, Gilgamesh, and the 'Babylonian Job.'" *JETS* 37 (1994): 321–31.

Fröhlich, I. "Daniel 2 and Deutero-Isaiah." In *The Book of Daniel in the Light of New Findings,* edited by A. S. van der Woude, 266–70. Louvain: Peeters, 1993.

Henze, M. *The Madness of King Nebuchadnezzar: The Ancient Near Eastern Origins and Early History of Interpretation of Daniel 4.* Leiden: Brill, 1999.

Hilton, M. "Babel Reversed—Daniel Chapter 5." *JSOT* 66 (1995): 99–112.

Holm, T. L. "A Biblical Story-Collection: Daniel 1–6." Ph.D. diss., Johns Hopkins University, 1997.

Kruschwitz, R. B., and P. L. Redditt, "Nebuchadnezzar as the Head of Gold: Politics and History in the Theology of the Book of Daniel." *Perspectives in Religious Studies* 24 (1997): 399–416.

Lawson, J. N. "'The God Who Reveals Secrets': The Mesopotamian Background to Daniel 2:47." *JSOT* 74 (1997): 61–76.

Lust, J. "The Septuagint Version of Daniel 4–5." In *The Book of Daniel in the Light of New Findings,* edited by A. S. van der Woude, 39–53. Louvain: Peeters, 1993.

Mitchell, T. C. "And the Band Played On . . . but with What Did They Play On?" *BRev* 15, no. 6 (1999): 32–39.

Paul, S. M. "Decoding a 'Joint' Expression in Daniel 5:6, 16." *JANES* 22 (1995): 121–27.

Pfandl, G. "Interpretation of the Kingdom of God in Daniel 2:44." *AUSS* 35 (1997): 249–68.

Prinsloo, G. T. M. "Two Poems in a Sea of Prose: The Content and Context of Daniel 2.20–23 and 6.27–28." *JSOT* 59 (1993): 93–108.

Soesilo, D. "Why Did Daniel Reject the King's Delicacies? (Daniel 1.8)." *BT* 45 (1994): 441–44.

van der Toorn, K. "In the Lions' Den: The Babylonian Background of a Biblical Motif." *CBQ* 60 (1998): 626–40.

van Deventer, H. J. M. "'We Did Not Hear the Bagpipe': A Note on Daniel 3." *OTE* 11 (1998): 340–49.

———. "Would the Actually 'Powerful' Please Stand? The Role of the Queen (Mother) in Daniel 5." *Scriptura* 70 (1999): 241–51.

Wenthe, D. O. "The Old Greek Translation of Daniel 1–6." Ph.D. diss., University of Notre Dame, 1991.

Wills, L. M. *The Jew in the Court of the Foreign King: Ancient Jewish Court Legends.* Minneapolis: Fortress, 1990.

Wolters, A. "The Riddle of the Scales in Daniel 5." *HUCA* 62 (1991): 155–77.

———. "Untying the King's Knots: Physiology and Wordplay in Daniel 5." *JBL* 110 (1991): 117–22.

Daniel 7–12

Adler, W. "The Apocalyptic Survey of History Adapted by Christians: Daniel's Prophecy of 70 Weeks." In *The Jewish Apocalyptic Heritage in Early Christianity,* edited by J. C. VanderKam and W. Adler, 201–38. Minneapolis: Fortress, 1996.

Anderson, L. O. "The Michael Figure in the Book of Daniel." Ph.D. diss., Andrews University, 1996.

Avalos, H. "Daniel 9:24–25 and Mesopotamian Temple Rededications." *JBL* 117 (1998): 507–11.

Collins, J. J. "Stirring up the Great Sea: The Religio-Historical Background of Daniel 7." In *The Book of Daniel in the Light of New Findings,* edited by A. S. van der Woude, 121–36. Louvain: Peeters, 1993.

David, P. "Daniel 11,1: A Late Gloss?" In *The Book of Daniel in the Light of New Findings,* edited by A. S. van der Woude, 505–14. Louvain: Peeters, 1993.

Dequeker, L. "King Darius and the Prophecy of Seventy Weeks: Daniel 9." In *The Book of Daniel in the Light of New Findings,* edited by A. S. van der Woude, 187–210. Louvain: Peeters, 1993.

Dimant, D. "The Seventy Weeks Chronology (Dan 9,24–27) in the Light of New Qumranic Texts." In *The Book of Daniel in the Light of New Findings,* edited by A. S. van der Woude, 57–76. Louvain: Peeters, 1993.

Farris, M. H. "The Formative Interpretations of the Seventy Weeks of Daniel." Ph.D. diss., University of Toronto, 1990.

Gardner, A. E. "The Great Sea of Dan. vii 2." *VT* 49 (1999): 412–15.

———. "The Way to Eternal Life in Dan 12:1e–2 or How to Reverse the Death Curse of Genesis 3." *Australian Biblical Review* 40 (1992): 1–19.

Grabbe, L. L. "The Seventy-Week Prophecy (Daniel 9:24–27) in Early Jewish Interpretation." In *The Quest for Context and Meaning: Studies in Biblical Intertextuality in Honor of James A. Sanders,* edited by C. A. Evans and S. Talmon, 594–611. Leiden: Brill, 1997.

Gulley, N. R. "Why the Danielic Little Horn is Not Antiochus IV Epiphanes." In *To Understand the Scriptures: Essays in Honor of William H. Shea,* edited by D. Merling, 191–97. Berrien Springs, Mich.: Institute of Archaeology/Siegfried H. Horn Archaeological Museum Andrews University, 1997.

Kalafian, M. *The Prophecy of the Seventy Weeks of Daniel: A Critical Review of the Prophecy as Viewed by Three Major Theological Interpretations and the Impact of the Book of Daniel on Christology.* Lanham, Md.: University Press of America, 1991.

Kaltner, J. "Is Daniel Also among the Prophets? The Rhetoric of Daniel 10–12." In *Vision and Persuasion: Rhetorical Dimensions of Apocalyptic Discourse,* edited by G. Carey and L. G. Bloomquist, 41–59. St Louis: Chalice, 1999.

Laato, A. "The Seventy Yearweeks in the Book of Daniel." *ZAW* 102 (1990): 212–25.

Lurie, D. H. "A New Interpretation of Daniel's 'Sevens' and the Chronology of the Seventy 'Sevens.'" *JETS* 33 (1990): 303–9.

Otzen, B. "Michael and Gabriel: Angelological Problems in the Book of Daniel." In *The Book of Daniel in the Light of New Findings,* edited by A. S. van der Woude, 114–24. Louvain: Peeters, 1993.

Owusu-Antwi, B. "An Investigation of the Chronology of Daniel 9:24–27." Ph.D. diss., Andrews University, 1993.

Patterson, R. D. "The Key Role of Daniel 7." *Grace Theological Journal* 12 (1991): 245–61.

Ray, P. J., Jr. "The *Abomination of Desolation* in Daniel 9:27 and Related Texts: Theology of Retributive Judgment." In *To Understand the Scriptures: Essays in Honor of William H. Shea,* edited by D. Merling, 205–13. Berrien Springs, Mich.: Institute of Archaeology/Siegfried H. Horn Archaeological Museum Andrews University, 1997.

Redditt, P. L. "Calculating the 'Times': Daniel 12:5–13." *Perspectives in Religious Studies* 25 (1998): 373–79.

———. "Daniel 11 and the Sociohistorical Setting of the Book of Daniel." *CBQ* 60 (1998): 463–74.

Stele, A. A. "Resurrection in Daniel 12 and Its Contribution to the Theology of the Book of Daniel." Ph.D. diss., Andrews University, 1996.

van der Woude, A. S. "Prophetic Prediction, Political Prognostication, and Firm Belief: Reflections on Daniel 11:40–12:3." In *The Quest for Context and Meaning: Studies in Biblical Intertextuality in Honor of James A. Sanders,* edited by C. A. Evans and S. Talmon, 63–73. Leiden: Brill, 1997.

van Henten, J. W. "Antiochus IV as a Typhonic Figure in Daniel 7." In *The Book of Daniel in the Light of New Findings,* edited by A. S. van der Woude, 223–43. Louvain: Peeters, 1993.

Waterhouse, S. D. "Why Was Darius the Mede Expunged from History?" In *To Understand the Scriptures: Essays in Honor of William H. Shea,* edited by D. Merling, 173–89. Berrien Springs, Mich.: Institute of Archaeology/Siegfried H. Horn Archaeological Museum, Andrews University, 1997.

Wilson, G. H. "The Prayer of Daniel 9: Reflection on Jeremiah 29." *JSOT* 48 (1990): 91–99.

Minor Prophets

Introduction

"Minor Prophets" is the title given to the last twelve books of the English Old Testament. In the Hebrew Bible, which is divided into three sections (the Law, Prophets, and Writings), these prophetic books appear in the Prophets, where they are known collectively as "the Twelve."

These books originated in different time periods over a span of roughly three hundred years. Hosea, Amos, and Micah prophesied in the eighth century B.C., while Nahum, Zephaniah, and Habakkuk delivered their messages in the seventh century B.C., probably toward the end of the century. Haggai, Zechariah, and Malachi are clearly postexilic books. Haggai's and Zechariah's ministries are specifically dated to the late sixth century B.C.; Malachi may originate as late as the mid–fifth century B.C.

The date of origin for the Books of Joel and Obadiah has been debated by scholars. Some regard these books as the earliest in the Twelve and date them to the ninth century B.C., but the internal evidence suggests that both originate much later. Joel probably originates in the early postexilic era, perhaps in the late sixth century B.C., while Obadiah was likely written during the exile (sixth century B.C.), though it may have originated as late as the mid–fifth century B.C. Since the arrangement of the Twelve seems to follow a roughly chronological sequence, some regard the placement of Joel and Obadiah in the first half of the corpus as proof of their early date. However, it is likely that the placement of these two books reflects thematic similarities to the Book of Amos, not chronological factors. Joel 4:16 is very similar to Amos 1:2, and Obadiah, with its denunciation of Edom, develops Amos 9:12 nicely.[1]

The Book of Jonah is unique among the Minor Prophets. It is primarily

---

1. See Hans W. Wolff, *Joel and Amos*, Hermeneia, trans. W. Janzen et al. (Philadelphia: Fortress, 1977), 3–4, and the same author's *Obadiah and Jonah*, trans. M. Kohl (Minneapolis: Augsburg, 1986), 17.

biographical, rather than hortatory. It tells a prophet's story, while the other books of the Twelve record, for the most part, messages delivered by the prophets to Israel and/or Judah. Though Jonah's ministry is best dated in the eighth century B.C., it is not certain when the Book of Jonah was actually written.

Restoring a Wayward Wife (Hosea)

Introduction

Hosea prophesied during the eighth century B.C. According to the book's heading, his career began while Jeroboam II was ruling Israel (he reigned from 793–753 B.C.) and Uzziah was king over Judah (792–740 B.C.). His prophetic ministry continued through the reigns of the Judahite kings Jotham (750–731 B.C.) and Ahaz (735–715 B.C.) and concluded sometime during the rule of Hezekiah (715–686 B.C.). Oddly enough, the heading does not mention the six Israelite kings who followed Jeroboam. The reason for this is unclear; the omission of their names may indicate that the book's final editor considered them to be insignificant.

The Book of Hosea does not display a sophisticated macrostructure; it appears to be a loose anthology of speeches rather than a tightly structured collection. Chapters 1 and 3 describe Hosea's dealings with Gomer, which serve as an object lesson of God's love for Israel (chapter 2). Chapters 4–14 are a collection of speeches that probably originate from different time periods in the prophet's long career. Though there is no overarching structure, some loose structural patterns can be observed. Chapters 4 and 5 both begin with a call to "hear," suggesting that they contain parallel speeches, the first addressed to Israel in general (see 4:1), the second to the priests, the "house of Israel" ("Israelites" NIV), and the royal establishment (see 5:1). The call to repentance in 6:1–3 (note "come, let us return to the LORD" in v. 1) seems to conclude this section on a positive note. The prophet's call to "return" to the Lord in 14:1 appears to correspond to this call to repentance and signals the book's upbeat conclusion. Both of these exhortations to "return" to the Lord echo the prophecy of 3:5 ("the Israelites will return and seek the LORD"), which concludes the introductory section of the book.

A Family Affair (1:1–2:1)

At the very beginning of Hosea's ministry, the Lord gave him some strange instructions. He commanded the prophet to acquire "an adulterous wife and children of unfaithfulness" (v. 2). They were to be part of an object lesson of Israel's unfaithfulness to the Lord. Hosea played the role of the Lord in this gut-wrenching real-life drama, while his wife played the role of adulterous Israel. The children born during this time received names symbolizing God's rejection of his people.

In obedience to the Lord's command, Hosea married a woman named Gomer (v. 3). Why did Hosea pick Gomer? Did she already have a reputation as a loose woman? Was she a prostitute? Some think so, but the text does not really answer these questions. The phrase "adulterous wife" in verse 2, rather than describing Gomer's status at the time of her marriage to Hosea, more likely anticipates what Gomer would become—an unfaithful wife. The symbolism seems to demand this understanding of the phrase. Gomer's subsequent unfaithfulness to her husband Hosea became an object lesson of Israel's lack of commitment to her "husband," the Lord. Just as Hosea's wife cheated on him and violated her marriage vows, so Israel broke her covenant with the Lord and committed spiritual adultery (see 2:2; 4:12; 5:4). Of course, while the phrase "adulterous wife" need not mean that Gomer was sexually active at the time Hosea married her, it is quite possible that he selected such a woman to assure that the Lord's stated purpose would be realized. Some argue that Gomer must have been pure at the time of the marriage for the symbolism to work properly. After all, Israel was "pure" at the time she entered into a covenant with the Lord (see 2:15 in this regard). However, it is not necessary for a symbolic metaphor to "walk on all fours." Gomer's subsequent unfaithfulness, no matter what her status at the time of the marriage, was enough to satisfy the intended symbolism.

Who were the "children of unfaithfulness" (v. 2), and in what sense can they be labeled as such? If Gomer was a prostitute at the time of the marriage, they could be illegitimate children whom she brought into the marriage with her. The wording of the text may even suggest this, for "children," like "wife," is an object of the verb "take," which seems to have the nuance "acquire" here. However, it seems more likely that the children in view are the three mentioned in the following context. If so, the language of verse 2 must be elliptical (the verb "have" is unexpressed but assumed)[2] and proleptic (it anticipates Hosea's acquiring children through Gomer).

In what sense are they "children of unfaithfulness"? The qualifying term "unfaithfulness" most likely refers to their mother, not the children themselves. The entire expression should be paraphrased "children (born to a mother) of unfaithfulness."[3] Does this mean they were not Hosea's? In the case of the first child, Jezreel, the text specifically indicates that Gomer "bore him [that is, Hosea] a son" (v. 3), but the text does not specifically identify

2. One would expect the text to say, "Take for yourself an adulterous wife and *have* children of unfaithfulness." See Jer. 29:6, which reads literally, "take wives and produce [literally, "cause to be born"] sons and daughters."
3. A similar construction occurs in Gen. 44:20, where the phrase "a child of old age" means "a child born to a father who is old at the time of the child's birth."

Hosea as the father of Lo-ruhamah (v. 6) or Lo-ammi (v. 8). For this reason, some argue that these two children were fathered by other men. Support for this view also comes from 2:4–5, which speaks of disowned children conceived "in disgrace," and 5:7, where Israel is accused of giving birth to illegitimate children.

Though one can make a case for this view, it is not entirely convincing. The omission of any reference to Hosea in 1:6, 8 does not preclude his being the father of the second and third children. In Genesis 29:32–35, Jacob's name is omitted from the birth announcements of Leah's sons because the context makes it clear that Jacob was the father. One could argue that verse 3 provides such contextual clarity in Hosea 1. The statement in 2:5 has been mistranslated in NIV. The Hebrew text actually reads, "The one who conceived them has acted disgracefully." This need not mean that she conceived them through a disgraceful (that is, adulterous) act. They could very well be legitimate children, but their mother's disgraceful behavior called the children's legitimacy into question.

It is probably best to respect the ambiguity of the text. Though the first child was Hosea's, Gomer's subsequent behavior cast a shadow over the second and third children. In the metaphorical application of the situation in 2:4–5, this uncertainty prompts the father (the Lord in this case) to threaten to disown the children.

As instructed by the Lord, Hosea gave the name Jezreel to the son born to him and Gomer (vv. 3–4). The name was an omen of the demise of the Israelite royal dynasty. It would end in violence, just as it had risen to power several decades before through a violent coup at Jezreel. In 841 B.C., Jehu, at the instigation of the Lord and his prophets, overthrew the Omride dynasty, which had ruled Israel since 885 B.C. Jehu assassinated King Ahab's successor Joram, killed the queen mother Jezebel, and wiped out Ahab's descendants (see 1 Kings 19:17–18; 2 Kings 9–10). Jehu assassinated Joram outside the walls of Jezreel by shooting an arrow through his heart. He rode into Jezreel and commanded the palace servants to throw Jezebel out the window to the street below, where her body smashed against the pavement, was trampled by horses, and eaten by dogs. He then sent a letter to the royal officials at Samaria, ordering them to execute Ahab's sons and send their heads to Jezreel. When the order was carried out, the heads, which arrived in baskets, were placed in two piles at Jezreel's city gate.

As one can readily see, Jehu's coup was a violent, bloody affair. But now, ironically, the violence and bloodshed that stained the streets of Jezreel would be repeated. This time Jehu's dynasty would be the victim. The prophecy was fulfilled in 752 B.C., when Shallum assassinated Zechariah, the fourth of Jehu's descendants to rule on his throne (2 Kings 15:10).

Hosea 1:4 is often interpreted to mean that Jehu's dynasty would be punished for the bloodshed and violence it dished out at Jezreel. This is, of course, problematic since the Lord himself commissioned Jehu to wipe out Ahab's house (2 Kings 9:6–10) and commended him when the job was done (2 Kings 10:30).

The original text of Hosea 1:4 demands a closer look. In the Hebrew text the statement in question reads literally, "I will visit the bloodshed of Jezreel upon the house of Jehu." What does this statement mean? Many times in the Hebrew Bible one finds the expression "to visit iniquity [or "sin"] upon [a person or place]."[4] When this expression is used, it means "to punish [the person or place named] for iniquity." Hosea 1:4 differs from this in that the object of the verb "visit" is not "iniquity," but "bloodshed." In four other passages a term other than "iniquity" (or "sin") appears as the object of the verb "visit" in a context where judgment (i.e., a hostile visitation) is in view.[5] Jeremiah 15:3 reads (literally), "I will visit upon them [the sinful people denounced in vv. 1–2] four destroyers." In this case the object of the verb identifies the instrument of divine judgment. In Jeremiah 51:27, one reads, "Visit upon [or perhaps "summon/appoint against"] her [Babylon] a commander." Again the object of the verb identifies the instrument of divine judgment. Hosea 2:13 (v. 15 in the Hebrew text) reads, "I will visit upon her [wayward Israel] the days of the Baals." In this case "the days of the Baals," an allusion to Israel's unfaithfulness, identifies the reason for the visitation. Because an underlying iniquity is in view, one may translate, "I will punish her for the days of the Baals." Finally, in Hosea 4:9 one reads, "I will visit upon him [the representative sinner mentioned in the previous line] his ways [i.e., sinful deeds]." As the next line makes clear (see also Hos. 12:2, where we read "according to his ways"), "his ways" identifies the reason for the visitation. Iniquity is in view, so one may translate, "I will punish him for his ways."

What is one to make of Hosea 1:4? Is "bloodshed" simply the instrument of punishment, as it were, or does the term hint at the underlying reason for the coming judgment? One could make a case for the former. It seems that the fundamental idea of the construction "visit upon" in the five relevant texts is "cause to [re]appear" (in the experience of the one being judged).[6] In two of the texts (Hos. 2:13; 4:9) it is a former transgression that reappears, as it were, as a reason for judgment. But in the two texts in Jeremiah, it is an instrument of judgment that appears. One could argue that the "bloodshed of Jezreel" will reappear in the royal dynasty's experience as an instrument of judgment. As McComiskey explains, "If we understand Hosea

4. When this expression is used in the Hebrew Bible any one of various terms for "iniquity" (or "sin") can appear as the direct object of the verb "visit"; the term 'awon, "iniquity," is used most often.

5. The construction in view contains the verb "visit," accompanied by a direct object and a prepositional phrase introduced by 'al, "upon." In four of the five examples to be discussed, the prepositional phrase appears before the direct object; Hos. 1:4 is the lone exception.

6. In this regard see Thomas McComiskey, "Hosea," in *The Minor Prophets: An Exegetical and Expositional Commentary*, ed. T. McComiskey, vol. 1 (Grand Rapids: Baker, 1992), 20–21.

1:4 in this way, it states that the bloodshed at Jezreel will reappear hauntingly in Jehu's dynasty, bringing it to end."[7] In this case there is great irony, for the dynasty ends in the same way it began, suggesting that it had become just as guilty and defiled as the dynasty it so violently replaced.

However, most prefer to see the "bloodshed" of Jezreel in the sense of "bloodguilt" and to understand this as an underlying reason for God's judgment on Jehu's dynasty. After all, the two other uses of the grammatical construction in Hosea work this way, and "bloodshed" is often viewed as sinful in the Hebrew Bible. If one chooses to interpret the passage in this way, the apparent conflict with the account in 1–2 Kings is unavoidable. As noted above, the Kings account clearly depicts Jehu's bloody revolt as authorized and commended by the Lord himself. For this reason, some argue that Hosea 1:4 reflects an alternative view of Jehu's revolt that interprets his coup in a negative sense.[8] Andersen and Freedman suggest that Hosea viewed Jehu's revolt in "a dual light," just as the prophets view Assyria and Babylon as the Lord's instruments of punishment but then turn right around and condemn these cruel nations for their excesses and haughty attitude.[9]

The name Jezreel would also serve as a portent of the demise of Israel's armies, which would suffer a crushing defeat in the Valley of Jezreel (v. 5). This prophecy was fulfilled in 733 B.C. when the Assyrian king Tiglath-pileser III defeated an Aramean-Israelite alliance. He executed King Rezin of Damascus and made Syria into an Assyrian province (see 2 Kings 16:9). In Israel, Hoshea assassinated King Pekah and became an Assyrian puppet king (see 2 Kings 15:29–30). Israel's territory was greatly reduced, as the northern regions of the nation became Assyrian provinces.[10] It is likely that military operations occurred in the Valley of Jezreel during this campaign.[11]

The Lord instructed Hosea to name Gomer's second child Lo-ruhamah, which means "Unloved" (v. 6). This name foreshadowed the Lord's rejection of Israel, which is portrayed in more vivid detail in the next chapter (see 2:2–13).

---

7. Ibid., 21. While the term "bloodshed" might suggest wrongdoing ("bloodguilt"), it need not have this connotation. Perhaps here it simply has the nuance "massacre." See Douglas Stuart, *Hosea-Jonah*, WBC (Waco, Tex.: Word, 1987), 29, as well as McComiskey, "Hosea," 21–22.

8. See, for example, James L. Mays, *Hosea*, OTL (Philadelphia: Westminster, 1969), 27–28, and William R. Harper, *A Critical and Exegetical Commentary on Amos and Hosea*, ICC (Edinburgh: T. & T. Clark, 1905), 211.

9. See Francis I. Andersen and David Noel Freedman, *Hosea*, AB (Garden City, N.Y.: Doubleday, 1980), 178–80. They also raise the possibility that Jehu's attack on the royal house of Judah may have been viewed as excessive. In this regard see Robert B. Chisholm Jr., *Interpreting the Minor Prophets* (Grand Rapids: Zondervan, 1990), 24.

10. For more detailed accounts of the Assyrian invasion of the west in 734–732 B.C., see W. T. Pitard, *Ancient Damascus* (Winona Lake, Ind.: Eisenbrauns, 1987), 186–89, and B. Otzen, "Israel under the Assyrians," in *Power and Propaganda*, ed. M. T. Larsen (Copenhagen: Akademisk Forlag, 1979), 251–61.

11. See Yohanan Aharoni, *The Land of the Bible: A Historical Geography*, translated and edited by A. F. Rainey, rev. ed. (Philadelphia: Westminster, 1979), 372–74.

Although the Lord would withhold his compassion from the northern kingdom, he would continue to extend his favor to Judah (v. 7). He would personally intervene and supernaturally deliver Judah from its enemies without the use of weapons or chariots. This promise of Judah's preservation anticipates the miraculous deliverance of Jerusalem in 701 B.C. Because this reference to Judah seems intrusive here, some regard it as a later editorial addition.[12] However, it is possible that this statement prepares the way rhetorically and thematically for the reversal in tone that occurs in verses 10–11 and sets the stage for the main theme of chapters 2–3. The future of the northern kingdom, whether they wanted to admit it or not, was intertwined with Judah's destiny. Someday the two nations would be reunited (1:11) under a Davidic king (3:5). For this reason, a reference to Judah's preservation makes sense here.

By divine command Gomer's third child was named Lo-ammi, meaning "Not My People" (vv. 8–9). Like Lo-ruhamah, this boy's name foreshadowed the Lord's rejection of Israel. In a tragic reversal of the covenantal ideal (see Exod. 6:7; Lev. 26:12), the Lord would sever his relationship with Israel and no longer be "their God."[13]

Though the Lord would reject Israel, the separation would not be final. Eventually the Lord would restore his favor, and Israel would become the great nation envisioned in God's promise to Abraham (v. 10a; see Gen. 22:17; 32:12). Those once called "not my people" would be renamed "sons of the living God" (v. 10b), a God who defeats his people's enemies and gives them a land (see Josh. 3:10). Israel and Judah would reunite under one leader (v. 11a), the Davidic king (see Hos. 3:5). Rather than being a negative portent associated with a geographical site, the name Jezreel, which means "God plants," would take on new significance (v. 11b). Reunited Israel and Judah would take root and sprout up from the ground, as it were, for the Lord would reinstate them to their land and renew his blessings (see 2:14–23, especially v. 23, in which "plant" translates the verb *zara'*, the same verb that appears in the name Jezreel).[14] Though God had once rejected Israel, the citizens of this new nation would be his people and would experience his love (2:1).

12. See, for example, G. I. Davies, *Hosea,* NCB (Grand Rapids: Eerdmans, 1992), 47, and Harper, *Amos and Hosea,* 213.

13. The Hebrew text of the last line of verse 9 reads, "and I, I will not be for you." It is likely that a scribal error has occurred and that the phrase "for God" has been accidentally omitted. The text should be reconstructed to read, "and I, I will not be to you for God," meaning "I will not be your God." See Jer. 11:4; 24:7; 30:22; 32:38; Ezek. 11:20; 14:11; 34:24; 36:28; 37:23; and Zech. 8:8 for the same or similar construction (though the verb is not negated as in Hos. 1:9). Some retain the Hebrew text and, seeing an allusion to Exod. 3:14, translate, "And I am not I AM for you." See Mays, *Hosea,* 22, 29.

14. NIV reads "will come up out of the land" in v. 11, as if the text is describing a return from exile. Note the reference in 2:15 to Israel's coming up "out of Egypt." Some see "the land" in 1:11 as a reference to Egypt, viewed symbolically as the place of Israel's exile (see 8:13; 9:3, 6; 11:5). However, it is more likely that "the land" refers to the land of Israel (as in 1:2; 2:18, 23; 4:1, 3) or to the surface of the ground (as in

For rhetorical effect, some of these children of the future are actually addressed in 2:1. They are urged to call their "brothers" and "sisters" (the rest of the restored covenant community of the future) "My people" (Heb. *ammi*) and "My loved one" (Heb. *ruhamah*), respectively. These names, which are an obvious reversal of those given to Hosea's children, symbolize God's renewed relationship with his people.

Radical Discipline Brings Radical Transformation (2:2–23)

The Lord continues to address these children in verse 2. In the preceding verse they were told to address their brothers and sisters; here they are instructed to rebuke their "mother." This "mother," who is also the Lord's "wife," personifies the land of Israel (see 1:2). She can be viewed as the mother of these children of the future because they would sprout up from her soil, as it were (see 1:11).

The Lord instructs his future children, in their dramatic role, to bring a formal charge against their mother on his behalf (v. 2a). The verb "rebuke" refers here to a formal, legal accusation against an offending party, not just a mere word of correction (see Hos. 4:1, where the related noun form is translated "charge"). The charge begins with a startling statement ("she is not my wife, and I am not her husband") that makes it sound as if the relationship is already terminated, but the following context makes it clear this is not really the case. An exhortation to adulterous Israel immediately follows (v. 2b), to which are attached a stern warning of the consequences of continued disobedience (vv. 3–4) and a description of the disciplinary measures the Lord plans to take in order to win back his wayward wife (vv. 5–13). Because the Lord clearly intends to reclaim his wife, the statement in verse 2a must be viewed as exaggerated for shock effect.

Israel must turn from her adulterous ways. Verse 2b, which reads literally, "Let her put away her unfaithfulness from her face, and her adultery from between her breasts," may allude to the makeup and jewelry she wore to attract her lovers.[15] If Israel did not change her ways, the Lord threatened to punish her severely (v. 3). He would humiliate her by stripping the clothes off her back and publicly exposing her nakedness. The penalty was appropriate for a sexual crime and was sometimes preliminary to the execution of an adulteress (see Ezek. 16:36–40). The Lord also threatened to remove her fertility, making her like an arid desert. The background for the imagery may be the removal of conjugal rights and with it, the possibility of having legitimate children. The image of a fertile land being turned into a desert is especially appropriate in this case, because the personified land is here cast in

2:21–22 and 6:3, where the phrase is translated "the earth" in NIV). The people of reunited Israel and Judah are viewed as plants growing up from the ground and repopulating the land.

15. See Stuart, *Hosea-Jonah*, 47, and Andersen and Freedman, *Hosea*, 224–25.

the role of the Lord's wife (see 1:2). Last but not least, the Lord would withdraw his love from her children, because her adulterous behavior cast a shadow of doubt over their legitimacy (vv. 4–5a). The "children" mentioned here are not the children of the future addressed in verses 1–2, but rather Hosea's contemporary generation (the same group addressed in 1:9).

Despite this threat of harsh treatment, the Lord was not ready to give up on his adulterous wife. In fact, he had a clear-cut strategy for winning her back. Because she was so obsessed with her lovers, whom she regarded as the source of her food and clothing (v. 5b), the Lord would be forced to do something drastic. He would "block her path" and "wall her in," making it impossible for her to reach her lovers (v. 6). Frustrated in her efforts to find them, she would come to her senses and return to her husband (v. 7).

At this point reality pushes aside metaphor, as the Lord accuses Israel of ingratitude and idolatry. Israel did not acknowledge the Lord as the source of her blessings, which included the staples of life, as well as great wealth (v. 8a). Instead, she insisted on worshiping Baal, the Canaanite storm and fertility god, for she thought he was the source of her prosperity (v. 8b).

For this reason, the Lord would take away Israel's crops and herds (v. 9a). With no wool or linen, Israel, now pictured again as a woman, would have no clothes to wear and would be forced to walk naked before her helpless lovers (vv. 9b–10). Religious celebrations, which had been corrupted by paganism (see v. 13), would come to an end (v. 11), and the vineyards and fig orchards, once thought to be blessings from Baal, would become thickets populated by wild animals (v. 12). The punishment would fit the crime. Israel had worshiped Baal in order to ensure abundant crops and herds. Appropriately, the Lord, the forgotten one, would remove that abundance (v. 13).

Depriving his adulterous wife of her lovers and her blessings was only the first stage in the Lord's strategy to reclaim her. Having brought her to the point of desperation (see v. 7b), he would lead her out to an isolated place and make romantic advances toward her (v. 14).

The reference to the Lord leading Israel out to the desert anticipates the nation's exile, but it also looks back to an earlier period in Israel's history, when the people wandered in the wilderness. Though Pentateuchal tradition presents this episode in a negative light (see also Ezek. 20:10–21), later tradition sometimes idealizes it as a pristine time in the nation's history, when Israel, like a new bride, expressed her love for the Lord and in turn experienced his protection (see Hos. 13:5; Jer. 2:2–3). The Lord here exploits this nostalgic viewpoint for rhetorical purposes. The "desert" clearly has a positive connotation, for it is the site of a renewed romance between the Lord and his wife.

The image is a bold one; the Lord speaks seductively and romantically to his wife in an effort to win back her favor. The verb translated "allure" is used elsewhere in romantic contexts, where it describes a man seducing a young woman (Exod. 22:16) and a young woman enticing her lover (Samson in both cases) into revealing a secret (Judg. 14:15; 16:5). The expression "speak tenderly" (literally, "speak to the heart") can also have a romantic connotation (see Gen. 34:3; Judg. 19:3).

Once the relationship was revived, the Lord would restore the nation's agricultural prosperity (symbolized by the "vineyards") and lead her back into the land (v. 15). As in the time of the Israelite conquest, the gateway to the land was the Valley of Achor (see Josh. 7). On that earlier occasion this valley was a place of "trouble" (the meaning of the name Achor), for it was there that Israel executed Achan, who had sinned against the Lord by stealing some of the riches of Jericho. Israel piled rocks over Achan's corpse and named the place the Valley of Achor, a name it permanently retained (see Josh. 7:26) as a reminder of how sin jeopardized Israel's future. However, all of this would change in the future. The valley of "trouble" would be transformed into a "door of hope," for restored Israel would respond favorably to the Lord's overtures of love.[16]

Israel would again acknowledge the Lord as her husband (v. 16). She would address him as "my husband" (Heb. *'ishi*), not "my master" (Heb. *ba'li*), for the latter form of address, though a common way to refer to one's husband in ancient Israelite patriarchal society,[17] had negative connotations. Since Israel's former lover was the Canaanite god Baal (Heb. *ba'al*, which means "master"), calling the Lord "my master" might bring back painful memories for both parties, and the Lord was determined to remove all traces of Israel's adulterous past (v. 17).

The Lord would also restore Israel's security (v. 18). He would negotiate a deal, as it were, between Israel and the wild animals so that the latter would no longer devour Israel's vineyards and trees (see v. 12). Invading armies would also be turned back. This promise literally reads, "Bow and sword and battle I will break from the land." It echoes the earlier prophecy of judgment, "I will break Israel's bow" (see 1:5), and in so doing draws attention to the reversal in Israel's situation. The Lord once shattered Israel's military power, but in the future he would destroy the might of the would-be invader.

In verses 19–20, the Lord speaks of his renewed relationship with Israel in terms of betrothal, as if the past did not exist. Having pursued the object of his love (v. 14), he was now ready to "tie the knot," as it were. In ancient

16. The Hebrew verb *'anah* usually means "to answer, respond." In v. 15, NIV translates it "sing," apparently understanding the verb here as a homonym (see *HALOT* 854, which, however, does not list Hos. 2:15 under this verbal root).

17. Second Samuel 11:26 shows that the terms *'ish*, "husband," and *ba'al*, "master," were interchangeable synonyms when referring to a woman's husband. The passage reads literally, "When the wife of Uriah heard that Uriah her husband (*'ish*) was dead, she mourned for her master (*ba'al*)." See also Deut. 24:3–4.

Israel betrothal was a legally binding commitment to marriage (see Deut. 22:23–24) in which the future husband would pay a price to secure his future wife (see 2 Sam. 3:14). As his betrothal payment the Lord here offers his protective care, compassionate love, and undying commitment.[18] In exchange for his loyalty, he anticipates Israel's devotion. The verb translated "acknowledge" (Heb. *yada*, "know") is used here in its covenantal sense of "acknowledge (or "recognize") as Lord." Such recognition of lordship required faithfulness demonstrated concretely through obedience to the Lord's commands. In Hosea 4:1–6, the absence of such recognition is associated with failure to keep the covenantal demands made in the law of Moses (see also 8:1–2).

The reconciliation of the Lord and his wife would be marked by the return of agricultural prosperity. The coming judgment would deprive Israel of the staples of life (see vv. 8–9), but the Lord would restore them (vv. 21–22). Using personification, the Lord vividly depicts this renewal of divine blessing. Jezreel (apparently being used here as a name for Israel; see v. 23, where the Lord says, "I will plant *her*") is pictured as speaking to the crops, perhaps asking them to appear. The crops in turn address the soil from which they must grow. The soil then speaks to the skies, the source of the life-giving rains, which in turn address the Lord. The Lord responds to the sky, the implication being that he commands the rain to fall so that the crops can grow again and provide Jezreel with the staples of life.

The agricultural imagery continues in verse 23, but with a slight alteration. Playing on the name Jezreel (meaning "God plants"), the Lord announces that he will "plant" Jezreel (apparently the antecedent of the pronoun "her") in the land, meaning that she will take root and produce a crop of children, as it were (see 1:11).[19] As in 1:11–2:1, the Lord reverses the negative symbolism attached to the names of Gomer's children. In the near future Jezreel would be the site of Israel's military demise (see 1:5), but the name also anticipated the day of restoration beyond judgment when God would replant Israel (see 1:11). Lo-ruhamah ("Unloved") and Lo-ammi ("Not My People") were reminders that the Lord would reject his people for a time (see 1:6, 9), but a day would come when God would restore his love and would again address Israel as his people (see 2:1). At this point a metamorphosis occurs as the sinful children of Hosea's generation (addressed in

18. The terms translated "righteousness" and "justice" refer here to the Lord's vindication of Israel's just cause through protection and deliverance from enemies.

19. Andersen and Freedman (*Hosea*, 288) argue that "plant her" means here "inseminate her" and that this verse refers to the consummation of the marriage anticipated in vv. 19–20. In Num. 5:28, planting imagery is used of insemination. That text reads literally, "and she may be sown with seed." The woman is viewed as a field in which seed (= semen) is sown. However, it is unlikely that such imagery is present in Hos. 2:23, where Israel (i.e., Jezreel) is not the field, but the seed sown in the field (note "in the land"). A similar construction occurs in Hos. 10:12, in which the Lord urges the people, "sow for yourselves [cf. "for myself" in 2:23] righteousness." In this case "righteousness," like Jezreel in 2:23, corresponds to the seed planted in the field.

1:9 and referred to in 2:4) become the blessed children of the future (referred to in 1:10 and addressed in 2:1–2).

Retrieving a Wife (3:1–5)

In this autobiographical account, Hosea tells how the Lord instructed him to retrieve his wayward wife Gomer. By renewing his relationship with Gomer and reaching out to her in love, Hosea would become a living object lesson of the Lord's love for idolatrous Israel (v. 1). Some scholars argue that Gomer is not the woman in view here, but the analogy demands that Hosea retrieve his wayward wife, not pick a new one.[20]

Hosea's and Gomer's relationship had been severed, probably by divorce.[21] Verse 2 makes it clear that she became the property of someone else, for Hosea had to pay a price to acquire her. This would not have been necessary if he were still married to her and owned her. The text does not give the identity of her new owner. Once divorced by Hosea, Gomer may have turned for sustenance to one of her illicit lovers. However, it is possible that she returned to her father's house (see Lev. 22:13; Judg. 19:2).

As translated by NIV, verse 1 appears to indicate that Gomer's owner was one of her lovers (see the phrase "loved by another"), but this interpretation is doubtful. The Hebrew text reads literally, "a woman loved by a friend." The Hebrew term "friend" could refer to someone other than Hosea, but it is more probable that Hosea is the referent. In Jeremiah 3:20 the word is used of an unfaithful woman's husband. NASB reflects this interpretation of Hosea 3:2, "Love a woman who is loved by her husband."

If Hosea had already divorced Gomer, then how can she legitimately be called an "adulteress" at this point (v. 1)? While the language might appear to be technically incorrect, it need not be pressed into such an overly technical mold. It characterizes Gomer from Hosea's perspective and reflects what she had done to him in the past. If Hosea had divorced Gomer, then a reference to him as Gomer's "friend [i.e., husband]" also seems to be problematic. But again, the language need not be taken so technically; the term could be equivalent here to "former husband."

Once Hosea paid the stipulated price to secure possession of Gomer (v. 2), he gave her clear instructions (v. 3).[22] She was to wait "many days" for Hosea to marry her.[23] During this betrothal period she must abstain from

---

20. See Harper, *Amos and Hosea*, 216–17. The Hebrew text of 3:1a is not as clear-cut on this issue as the NIV makes it sound. The Hebrew text says literally, "Again go, love a woman loved by a friend and an adulteress." Because the text refers simply to "a woman," some argue that this refers to a woman other than Gomer. But "woman" does not appear in isolation; it is modified by "loved by a friend" (a probable reference to Hosea; see my comments on v. 2) and collocated with "adulteress."

21. Though the threat in 2:2–4 is made by the Lord, it is likely that it reflects Hosea's experience.

22. If Hosea bought Gomer from her father, the silver and barley were the betrothal price.

23. Hosea's first statement to Gomer reads literally in the Hebrew text: "Many days you will remain [or "sit"] for me." The idiom (the verb *yashab*, "sit," collocated with the preposition *le-*, "for") here means

any further adulterous relationships and refrain from marrying anyone else.[24] While she patiently waited for this trial period to end, Hosea would commit himself to her care.[25]

Hosea's treatment of Gomer mirrored, of course, the Lord's announced strategy for reclaiming Israel (see 2:14–15) and anticipated Israel's experience in exile (v. 4). For "many days," exiled Israel would be deprived of its national independence (symbolized by "king" and "prince") and be denied the opportunity to offer sacrifices to God at an authorized worship center. But this experience would not be as bad as it might appear, for Israel would also be separated from the pagan influences of the land of Canaan, including the forbidden "sacred stones" utilized in the worship of Baal (see Hos. 10:1, as well as Lev. 26:1; Deut. 16:22; 2 Kings 3:2; 10:26–27; 17:10; Mic. 5:13) and unauthorized divination devices, such as the "ephod" and "idol." The term "ephod" sometimes refers to a garment or object worn by priests, but at other times it refers to an object used to receive direct revelation from the Lord (see 1 Sam. 23:9–10; 30:7–8). Such objects could be easily misused, as Judges 8:27, which refers to a golden ephod that eventually became an object of idolatrous worship, makes clear. Here in Hosea 3:4 the reference to an "ephod" has a negative connotation because of its association with an "idol." The term translated "idol" refers to household idols (see Gen. 31:19; 1 Sam. 19:13, 16) that were used for divination (Ezek. 21:21). Their use was forbidden by the Lord (see 1 Sam. 15:23; 2 Kings 23:24). Both an ephod and such an idol are mentioned together in Judges 17–18, where they are listed among the objects in Micah's homemade shrine (see 17:5; 18:14). The Danites eventually stole them and made them a part of their unauthorized worship center (Judg. 18:17–18, 20).

Delivered from the spell of paganism, the Israelites would come to their senses (see 2:7). They would seek the Lord's favor and recognize the Davidic king as their divinely chosen ruler (v. 5). Having experienced the Lord's discipline, they would exhibit a healthy fear of his power and enjoy his renewed blessings.

"to wait for," as in Exod. 24:14; Judg. 16:9; and Jer. 3:2. See Andersen and Freedman, *Hosea*, 301 (although four of the five examples of the idiom which they cite are invalid).

24. The Hebrew text reads literally, "you will not commit adultery and will not be for a man." The idiom "be for a man" (the verb *hayah*, "be," collocated with *le'ish*, "for a man") means "be married" (see Lev. 22:12; Num. 30:7; Deut. 21:15).

25. The last clause of v. 3 is especially problematic. It reads literally, "and also I toward you." The presence of the adverb *gam*, which often has the nuance "also," suggests some type of symmetry with what precedes. (See Andersen and Freedman, *Hosea*, 304–5.) Here the adverb is best taken as emphasizing what follows ("and moreover") or as introducing a rhetorical climax ("and certainly"). The verb *hayah*, "be," can be supplied from the preceding line (assuming an ellipsis). Normally the resulting collocation *hayah 'el*, "be toward," has the nuance "be against" or "come to" (when "word" is the subject), but neither idea makes sense here. In Ezek. 45:16 the collocation means "be liable for, obliged to," referring to the people's obligation to contribute to the temple offerings. See Leslie C. Allen, *Ezekiel 20–48*, WBC (Dallas: Word Books, 1990), 240, 247, as well as the sources cited there.

The reference to "David their king" should not be understood in an overly literalistic manner. The prophets view the ideal Davidic ruler of the future as the second coming of David (see Isa. 11:1–10; Mic. 5:2) and even call him "David" on occasion (see Jer. 30:9; Ezek. 34:23–24; 37:24–25). This "David" carries out royal functions that cannot be distinguished from those assigned to the messianic king. Other texts make it clear that this "David" is actually a descendant of David (see Jer. 23:5–6; 33:15–16) who comes in his ancestor's spirit and power, much like John the Baptist came in the spirit and power of Elijah and thus fulfilled the prophecy of Malachi 4:5 (see Matt. 11:10–14; 17:11–12; Mark 1:2–4; Luke 1:17, 76; 7:27).

A Broken Covenant (4:1–19)

The prophet summoned the Israelites to hear the Lord's formal charge against them (v. 1a). Israel was unfaithful; she was no longer committed to the Lord and no longer recognized his authority over her (v. 1b). The phrase "acknowledgment of God" refers here to recognizing the Lord's authority within the context of the covenantal relationship that he established with Israel. Such recognition was demonstrated through obedience (see Jer. 22:16).

But Israel demonstrated that she did not recognize the Lord's authority, for she blatantly violated his covenantal laws, including the Ten Commandments, which were the central core of the covenant. Verse 2 specifically mentions violations of five of the Ten Commandments (see Exod. 20:1–17; Deut. 5:6–21). "Cursing" does not refer here to obscene speech but rather to the misuse of oaths and imprecations. An imprecation was a formal curse, made in the name of a deity, in which one person would call calamity down upon another (see Job 31:29–30). Such imprecations were allowed when the one offering them had a just cause (see, for example, Num. 5:19–23; Judg. 9:20, 56–57), but unjustified curses made in the Lord's name were a violation of the third commandment (see Exod. 20:7).

Because the people had broken the covenant with their cursing and violent deeds, the Lord would punish the land severely (v. 3).[26] The picture of the land mourning and withering depicts a drought that would destroy the land's crops and cause the wildlife to die. Such a drought was one of the forms of judgment threatened in the "curse" lists of the Mosaic law (see Lev. 26:19; Deut. 28:23–24). Appropriately, those who killed their fellow Israelites (note the references to "murder" and "bloodshed" in v. 2) would watch their land die, as it were. Those who called curses down on others would experience the "curse" of God.

The judgment would be harsh, but the people had no right to accuse

---

26. The Hebrew imperfect verbal forms in v. 3 are best translated as future, for the verse describes the coming judgment on the land. See Hos. 2:9–12.

God of being unjust (v. 4a).[27] As far as God was concerned, these rebels were as brazen as those who have the audacity to formally charge a priest, one of God's designated civil authorities (v. 4b). Such defiance of priestly authority was a capital crime, according to the law (see Deut. 17:12).

The priests deserved respect, yet they were not immune from divine punishment if they abused their office and neglected their God-given responsibility. In fact, God addresses the priests in verses 4–6 (see especially v. 6) and accuses them of ignoring his law.[28] Their failure to provide adequate spiritual leadership was partially responsible for the people's failure to recognize the Lord's authority. The priests, as well as the majority of the prophets, were no better than the people. Because of their elevated position and great responsibility, the priests would be special targets of the Lord's anger. (To whom much is given, much is required.) Because the people under their guidance were destroyed by their failure to recognize God's authority, the Lord would destroy the priests' mothers (vv. 5b–6a). Because the priests themselves had rejected God's authority, the Lord would reject them (v. 6b). Because the priests had ignored God's law, the Lord would ignore their children (v. 6c), preventing the continuation of their priestly office.[29] To the modern Western mind, it might seem unfair that the priests' mothers and children should be punished for their sins. But the concept of corporate guilt and punishment was common in ancient Israel and is frequently reflected in the Hebrew Bible. Because of their close biological association with the priests, they shared in their guilt and would be punished as well.[30]

The Lord's judgment on the sinful people and priests would be severe, but just and appropriate (vv. 7–11a). Both would be repaid for their sinful deeds (v. 9). The priests were feeding on the sins of the people (v. 8), in the sense that they encouraged the people to multiply their hypocritical sacrifices (see Hos. 6:6; 8:11–13), a portion of which was taken by the priests. Appropriately, both the priests and the people would be deprived of food (v. 10a). Both verses 8 and 10 use the Hebrew verb 'akal, "feed, eat." The

---

27. The Hebrew text of v. 4a reads literally, "Let not a man bring a charge! Let not a man accuse!" NIV assumes that this refers to bringing charges against another human being. In this case, the point would be that the Israelites have no right to take one another to court, for all are guilty. However, it seems more likely that a counteraccusation against God is in view here. He had brought a charge against them (v. 1), but they had no legitimate defense and no right to claim that the announced punishment was unfair.

28. In the Hebrew text of vv. 4–6, the Lord uses second masculine singular pronominal and verbal forms in addressing the priests. The singular is used either collectively (the priesthood is addressed as an institution or group, see vv. 7–9) or in a representative manner (a typical priest is addressed as representative of the entire group).

29. The verbal repetition highlights the appropriate nature of the punishment. See Patrick D. Miller Jr., *Sin and Judgment in the Prophets* (Chico, Calif.: Scholars Press, 1982), 12–14.

30. Ancient curses were often transgenerational, as was divine judgment in the Hebrew Bible. See the comments on v. 5b by Andersen and Freedman, *Hosea*, 352. For a more general study of corporate responsibility for sin in the Hebrew Bible, see Joel S. Kaminsky, *Corporate Responsibility in the Hebrew Bible* (Sheffield: Sheffield Academic Press, 1995).

word repetition draws attention to the correlation between the crime and the punishment and suggests that the latter is appropriate.[31] With the apparent approval of the priests, the people overstepped the boundaries of God's law (see v. 2b). They even turned to pagan fertility rites involving "sacred" prostitution in an effort to ensure a good harvest and increase the population of the nation (v. 10). Appropriately, the land would not yield enough crops for them to eat, and the people would not increase in number. Once more, word repetition is used to suggest the idea of poetic justice. Verse 2 uses the Hebrew verb *parats*, "break out," to describe how the people "break all bounds" (the text reads literally, "they break out"). Verse 10 uses this same verb when describing their failure to multiply in number (see NIV "but not increase," which reads literally, "and they will not break out").

The pagan fertility rites in which Israel engaged are described in great detail in verses 11–14. To win the favor of the fertility god Baal and the goddess Asherah, the Canaanites engaged in "sacred" prostitution, which involved ritual sexual acts with "sacred" prostitutes. These rituals took place at special shrines located on hills under the shade of trees and were designed to promote fertility in the land. These rituals involved drinking intoxicating wine, consulting pagan gods through divination, and offering sacrifices. The Israelites encouraged their daughters to visit the shrines, hoping that their participation in ritual sex with the priests of Baal and Asherah would encourage these gods to give them numerous children. But their fathers were just as guilty, for they too visited the shrines and had sexual relations with the priestesses there in an effort to enhance their own virility.

With the northern kingdom so corrupt, it was always possible that Judah, her neighbor to the south, would be contaminated by Israel's sin. The prophet interrupted his indictment of Israel to warn Judah not to follow her example (v. 15a). The people of Judah must stay away from Israel's defiled worship centers (v. 15b).[32] Although Gilgal, the place where Israel renewed its covenant with the Lord after crossing the Jordan River (see Josh. 5:1–9), had an important place in the nation's history, it was now characterized by religious hypocrisy (see Hos. 9:15; 12:11; Amos 4:4; 5:5). Bethel, once "the house of God" (see Gen. 28:17), was so corrupted by sin and paganism that the prophet gave it a new name, Beth Aven, meaning "House of Wickedness." That this is a derogatory name for Bethel is apparent from 10:5, which mentions the calf-idol placed there by Jeroboam I (see 1 Kings 12:28–33).

---

31. See Miller, *Sin and Judgment,* 14–15.

32. Some regard this exhortation to Judah as not being a part of Hosea's original message. However, such an appeal to Israel's southern neighbor is very effective rhetorically. By warning Judah to stay clear of Israel, the prophet emphasized the degree of Israel's sin and the magnitude of the approaching judgment. Also, one must not assume that Hosea's message was restricted to Israel. Throughout his long career he ministered in Judah as well and may have later adapted his earlier messages to Israel so they would be relevant to a southern audience.

It was imperative that Judah avoid Israel because the latter was doomed. Their persistent paganism would activate the powerful wind of God's judgment, which would sweep them away into exile (vv. 16–19). Once again the prophet employs word repetition to highlight the appropriate nature of the punishment. The Hebrew noun translated "whirlwind" in verse 19, also appears in verse 12, where it describes the "spirit of prostitution" that was leading Israel astray (see also 5:4). Israel's own unfaithful "spirit" (Heb. *ruakh*) was leading her away from God; a "whirlwind" (*ruakh*) sent from God would finish the job Israel had started, sweeping her away to destruction.

A Lion Ready to Pounce (5:1–15)

The Lord addressed all Israel, though the priests and royal house were singled out. These religious and civil authorities had misled the people by encouraging them to engage in hypocritical and perhaps even idolatrous worship at Mizpah and Tabor (v. 1). The precise identification of Mizpah here is uncertain. Either Mizpah in Gilead or Mizpah in Benjamin may be in view. Tabor refers to the mountain of that name located in northern Israel southwest of the Sea of Galilee. The names were probably chosen as representative of various religious sites scattered throughout the land. If Mizpah in Gilead is in view, then the name pair refers to cult sites both east and west of the Jordan River. If Mizpah in Benjamin is in view, then the name pair refers to cult sites from the south to north.[33]

This deception of Israel occurred despite the Lord's efforts to correct his people (v. 2). NIV, like most commentators, interprets the second half of the verse as describing God's future response to Israel's sin. However, the Hebrew text reads literally, "and I [was? am? will be?] discipline to all of them." The statement is a verbless sentence, which can be translated with the past, present, or future tense depending on the demands of the context. As many interpreters note, the word translated "discipline" often has a positive connotation in the Hebrew Bible, referring to the instruction and discipline that a father imparts to his children. For that reason many observe that the term seems to be too mild to describe the severe judgment God was about to bring upon Israel (see vv. 8–14). Therefore it seems more likely that the statement refers to the Lord's past efforts to discipline Israel. The clause, which can be taken as concessive, is best translated, "even though I was [a source of] discipline to all of them." It refers to the Lord's attempts to correct Israel before

33. Verse 2 may add a third name to the list. NIV translates the first line, "The rebels are deep in slaughter," but some emend the text to read, "a pit at Shittim [which] they dug deep." Shittim was located east of the Jordan (Num. 25:1). The reference to a metaphorical "pit" would provide a nice parallel to the metaphors of a "snare" and "net" in v. 1. See Stuart, *Hosea-Jonah*, 88, and Hans W. Wolff, *Hosea*, trans. G. Stansell, Hermeneia (Philadelphia: Fortress, 1974), 94. However, Andersen and Freedman argue against this emendation. See *Hosea*, 386–88.

it was too late (see Amos 4:6–12). Unfortunately, his efforts had proven futile.

Israel could not hide its sin from God (v. 3a). Despite their hypocritical attempts to worship him (v. 6a), their guilt was as plain as day. They had committed spiritual adultery and become "corrupt" (v. 3b), a word used in Numbers 5:20, 27–28, to describe an adulterous woman. They even gave birth to "illegitimate children" (v. 7a). The language may be purely metaphorical, depicting what typically happened when a woman was unfaithful to her husband. However, there may be an allusion to Israel's participation in pagan fertility rites (see 4:13–15), which likely produced many such children. Israel did all of this with a brazen attitude. They could not disguise their arrogance, which "testified" against them and, as pride always does (see Prov. 16:18), had caused them to "stumble" and fall (v. 5). They were obsessed with their false gods, refused to acknowledge the Lord's authority, and were beyond the point of repentance (v. 4). For this reason, the Lord had withdrawn from them (v. 6b) and would soon destroy them (v. 7b). NIV translates the last line of verse 7, "Now their New Moon festivals will devour them and their fields," but the statement is better rendered, "Now he [the Lord] will devour them and their fields [at the time of] the New Moon festival."[34] The text is dripping with irony. The New Moon festivals were occasions for Israel to celebrate God's protective presence among them (see Num. 10:10), but they would soon be transformed into a day of judgment.

The irony continues in verse 8. Trumpets were blown to celebrate the arrival of the New Moon festivals (see Num 10:10), but God's impending judgment would soon cause a different trumpet signal to sound. Trumpets would be blown, but they would signal an impending battle, not a festival. These warning trumpets would be heard in Gibeah and Ramah, both of which were located in Benjaminite territory just a few miles north of Jerusalem, as well as in Beth Aven (that is, Bethel; see 4:15), located near the southern border of Israel.[35] Because Gibeah, the closest to Jerusalem of the three towns mentioned, is listed first, and Bethel, the farthest from Jerusalem of the three, is mentioned last, some see an allusion to an invasion of Israel from the south. However, it is not necessary to see an order of march alluded to here. It is more likely that Hosea pictures an enemy invader sweeping through Ephraim to the north (see v. 9) and then threatening the very borders of Judah. After all, Judah had rejected the Lord's warning (see

---

34. See Davies, *Hosea*, 145.

35. The last line of v. 8 (translated in NIV as "lead on, O Benjamin") reads literally, "After you, Benjamin." The meaning of this cryptic statement is uncertain. In Judg. 5:14, the same expression appears and apparently describes how Ephraim followed Benjamin to Tabor to fight for Barak against the Canaanite forces of Sisera. Perhaps in Hos. 5:8 it is to be construed with what follows. The prophet, writing from the perspective of one standing in Judah, views Ephraim as being to the rear of Benjamin. He warns Benjamin that an invader is approaching from the direction of Ephraim.

4:15) and followed Israel's example (see 5:5). The Lord's judgment would descend on both the northern and southern kingdoms.

In fulfillment of a divine decree, Ephraim would be devastated (v. 9) and Judah inundated by a flood of divine anger (v. 10b). In Judah social injustice was rampant (v. 10a). By comparing Judah's leaders to those who move boundary stones, the Lord accused them of theft and injustice. Boundary stones marked the legal boundary between property. By moving them, one could obscure the boundary and steal a portion of land from one's neighbor. The practice was denounced in the law (see Deut. 19:14; 27:17).

Actually, God had already begun to judge Ephraim and Judah, both of which are compared to one who has been overcome by a serious illness (vv. 11, 13a). Like a clothes-eating moth (Job 13:28; Isa. 50:9; 51:8), he was eating away Israel's very fabric. Like a progressive bone disease (see Prov. 12:4; 14:30; Hab. 3:16), he was silently robbing Judah of its strength.

Sensing her desperate situation, Israel had formed an alliance with Assyria, thinking this would restore their national stability (v. 13b). This could refer to the pro-Assyrian policies of Menahem, who ruled Israel from 752–742 B.C., or to those of Hoshea, who ruled from 732–722 B.C. as an Assyrian puppet king. However, Assyria could not cure Israel's disease. The Lord would pounce on both Israel and Judah like a powerful lion, ripping them to shreds and then carrying them off to be devoured (v. 14). He would retreat to his lair and not return until both repented of their sins (v. 15). This prophecy anticipates the downfall of Israel in 722 B.C. and the Assyrian invasion of Judah in 701 B.C.

A Call to Repentance (6:1–3)

An abrupt shift in mood occurs here as an unidentified speaker, perhaps the prophet speaking as the representative of the people, calls the covenant community to repentance. Because the Lord denounces Israel's and Judah's hypocrisy in the following speech (see v. 4), some argue that verses 1–3 are not to be taken at face value. Rather than being a sincere call to repentance, some understood the speech as a misguided attempt to attract God's favor. In this view the reference to the Lord restoring his people "after two days . . . on the third day" (v. 2) is taken as proof of the people's blindness. They take their sin so lightly that they think God will quickly restore them if they make just a token move in his direction.[36] God then rebukes their shallow efforts in verse 4 (see also 8:2).

This cynical understanding of verses 1–3 should be rejected. Hosea's sinful contemporaries are not speaking here. The perspective is that of a future generation that would experience God's severe judgment (compare v. 1 with 5:14). The prophet included this prayer as a model for that generation to fol-

---

36. See, for example, Harper, *Amos and Hosea*, 281–83.

low once judgment had fallen. Realizing that God will not restore his favor until the people seek him in repentance (see 5:15), the speaker urges them to return to the Lord and experience his healing. In the past they had refused to "acknowledge" the Lord and were incapable of returning to him (see 5:4), but the speaker is confident that renewed commitment to the Lord will bring a restoration of divine blessings. The speaker's confidence, rather than being presumptuous, is rooted in the mercy of God, who suddenly replaces the dark night of judgment with the light of deliverance (see Ps. 30:5), and in the Lord's ancient covenantal promise made through Moses (see Deut. 30:1–10). The rebuke in verse 4 need not be taken as the Lord's response to this speech. It is better interpreted as resuming the diatribe of chapters 4–5 after the brief interlude of verses 1–3. Similar shifts in focus, from judgment to salvation and back to judgment, occur in 1:9–2:2 and in 11:7–12.

Lack of Loyalty (6:4–11a)

With a tone of exasperation, the Lord asks rhetorically: "What can I do with you, Ephraim? What can I do with you, Judah?" (v. 4a). The Lord demanded his people's devotion, but any allegiance they might show quickly disappeared, like the morning mist or the dew on the grass (v. 4b). The Hebrew term translated "love" refers to commitment or devotion to the Lord that is based on a recognition of his sovereign authority and is demonstrated through obedience to his covenantal laws. God desired such allegiance above all else, even sacrifices (see v. 6, where "mercy" translates this same Hebrew word).[37]

But the people had broken the covenant (v. 7), prompting God to judge them severely (v. 5). Through his prophets he had first announced judgment and then made his threats a reality. He used the prophets like a sword to cut his people down. The punishment was appropriate, for the people, including even the priests, were guilty of shedding blood in violation of the sixth commandment of the Decalogue (vv. 8–9; see Exod. 20:13). Ironically, such crimes even took place in the cities of Ramoth Gilead[38] and Shechem, both of which had been designated by Joshua as cities of refuge, where one who had accidentally killed another could find asylum from a bloodthirsty avenger (see Josh. 20:1–2, 7–8).

As translated in NIV, verse 7 draws a comparison between rebellious Israel and Adam, who disobeyed God by eating the forbidden fruit in the Garden of Eden. However, it is highly unlikely that the text actually draws this

---

37. The first line in v. 6 might be interpreted to mean that God rejects sacrifice altogether in favor of loyalty. But overstatement is utilized here, as the second line makes clear. This line should be translated, "and acknowledgement of God more than burnt offerings." Sacrifices had their place in Israel's relationship to God, but only when offered by obedient people. God placed a higher priority upon obedience.

38. Gilead (see v. 8) was a region, not a city. Since v. 8 specifically calls Gilead a "city," in this case the town of Ramoth Gilead, located east of the Jordan River, is probably in view here.

comparison. Because the adverb "there" in the next line demands an antecedent, it is reasonable to assume that Adam is a geographical name here, referring to a town located near the Jordan River (see Josh. 3:16).[39] Place names also appear in the following verse.

If murder were not bad enough, Israel topped off its rebellion against God with an even worse sin, called a "horrible (or perhaps "disgusting") thing" (v. 10).[40] The reference is to idolatry, a violation of the second commandment of the Decalogue (v. 10; see Exod. 20:4). Though idolatry is not specifically mentioned in the verses that immediately precede, the metaphor of "prostitution" certainly points in that direction (see 4:10–18), as does the reference to Israel being "defiled" (the Hebrew term is the same one translated "corrupt" in 5:3, where it likely depicts Israel as an adulterous woman).

As noted earlier, Judah was following in Ephraim's moral footsteps (see 5:5, 10; 6:4). Consequently they would also experience God's judgment (v. 11a; see 5:14), which is compared here to a harvest because it was appointed for a specific time and would involve the people being cut down with a sickle, as it were, and carried off to be threshed (see Jer. 51:33; Joel 3:13).[41]

Turmoil Within and Without (6:11b–7:16)

God was willing to restore and heal his people, but Israel's sins prevented reconciliation (6:11b–7:2). Theft, another violation of the Decalogue (see Exod. 20:15), is highlighted here. Even the royal court encouraged sin and deceit (v. 3). From top to bottom the nation was filled with "adulterers" who had been unfaithful to God and his moral standards (v. 4a). The prophet compares their passion for sin to a fire in a baker's oven that has been left unattended and is blazing hot (v. 4b).

From 752–732 B.C., four of Israel's kings were assassinated (see 2 Kings 15). This political turmoil is the setting for verses 5–7, which describe how the conspirators and assassins typically carried out their plots against the king. On a festive occasion they would wait until the king was drunk and then strike quickly. Utilizing the imagery of verse 4, the prophet compares them to fire in an oven that smolders all night long and then, at just the right time, is stoked into a blazing flame. In the same way, the conspirators hatched their plots and waited patiently until an opportune time, when they carried out their murderous schemes.

---

39. The proposed reading "in Adam," as opposed to "like Adam," requires a slight emendation of the Hebrew preposition *ke-*, "like," to *be-*, "in." The letters *kaph* and *beth* are easily confused. See Ellis Brotzman, *Old Testament Textual Criticism* (Grand Rapids: Baker, 1994), 109, and P. Kyle McCarter, *Textual Criticism* (Philadelphia: Fortress, 1986), 44.

40. A related Hebrew term is used in Jer. 29:17 of rotten, inedible figs.

41. On harvesting and threshing practices in ancient Israel, see Oded Borowski, *Agriculture in Iron Age Israel* (Winona Lake, Ind.: Eisenbrauns, 1987), 57–65.

Israel's political instability made it vulnerable, but no one looked to the Lord for national security (vv. 7b, 10). Instead, Israel formed alliances with the superpowers of the day, Egypt and Assyria (v. 11b). Just as those baking cakes mix flour with oil, so Israel mixed with foreigners (v. 8a), but this strategy would backfire. Israel would come to ruin, like an unturned cake that gets charred on one side and must be thrown away (v. 8b). Israel's foreign masters demanded heavy tribute that sapped the nation's wealth (v. 9a). Israel was like a man who fails to recognize that he is getting older because the signs of aging, such as the graying of one's hair, occur so gradually (v. 9b). Israel's attempt to find security through these powerful nations was misguided and doomed to fail. Like a dove, she lacked sense (v. 11a) and would be easily ensnared in the Lord's net of judgment (v. 12).

The Lord was willing to deliver his people, but they "strayed" from him and "rebelled" against his authority (v. 13). Their rebellion was perhaps most clearly seen in their paganism. Rather than looking to the Lord for grain and wine, they engaged in the pagan rites of Baal worship. NIV translates verse 14, "They gather together for grain and new wine," but the traditional Hebrew text has suffered corruption here. A few medieval Hebrew manuscripts and the Septuagint preserve the original text of this verse, which reads, "They slash themselves for grain and new wine."[42] Self-mutilation was practiced by worshipers of the fertility god Baal during times of drought (see 1 Kings 18:28). According to Canaanite belief, drought resulted when Baal was temporarily subdued and imprisoned by his archenemy Mot, the god of death. To facilitate Baal's return to the land of the living, his worshipers would mourn his death and cut themselves.[43] In the Ugaritic myths, the god El mourns Baal's death by putting dust on his head, clothing himself in sackcloth, shaving his facial hair, and cutting his body.[44] Hosea 7:14 pictures the Israelites as engaging in such mourning rites. They wailed in sorrow and cut themselves in an effort to resurrect Baal so he could restore the crops the Lord had taken away in judgment (see 2:9).

In the past the Lord had "trained" and "strengthened" his people (v. 15a). The language may depict the Lord as giving Israel the strength to win battles (see 2 Kings 14:25–28). In Ezekiel 30:24–25 the expression "strengthen the arms" (the literal reading of the statement translated "strengthened" in NIV) describes how the Lord empowered the king of Babylon militarily, enabling him to defeat the king of Egypt. Israel repaid the Lord's efforts with hostility (v. 15b). Utilizing another military metaphor, the prophet compares unfaithful, morally unreliable Israel to a "faulty bow" that does not function properly in the heat of battle (v. 16a; see Ps. 78:57).

---

42. For a discussion of the text-critical issues involved here, see Chisholm, *From Exegesis to Exposition,* 21–22.

43. Cutting oneself is associated with mourning the dead in Deut. 14:1; Jer. 16:6; 47:5.

44. See J. C. L. Gibson, *Canaanite Myths and Legends,* 2d ed. (Edinburgh: T. & T. Clark, 1978), 73.

Israel's insolence would bring destruction and humiliation. Their leaders would fall by the sword, and Egypt, one of the nations to whom they looked for help (v. 11), would mock their demise (v. 16b).

Reaping What They Sow (8:1–14)

Addressing an unidentified watchman (perhaps Hosea), the Lord calls for the alarm to sound in Israel (v. 1a; see 5:8). A mighty eagle (symbolizing the Assyrian army) was circling over the nation, ready to swoop down and carry it away in its powerful claws (v. 1b; see Deut. 28:49, which may provide the literary background for the imagery). Though Israel claimed to be loyal to the Lord, they had broken his law, prompting the Lord to send an enemy against them (vv. 1b–3).

Israel had rejected the Lord's authority in a number of ways. They set up king after king without seeking the Lord's guidance in the matter (v. 4a). Worse yet, they worshiped idols, including the calf-idol of Samaria (vv. 4b–6). There is no other reference in the Hebrew Bible to a calf-idol in Samaria. For this reason, "Samaria" probably refers here to the northern kingdom as a whole (see 1 Kings 13:32), and the calf-idol in question is likely the one set up in Bethel by Jeroboam I (see Hos. 10:5). The Lord found this idol particularly repulsive, and he warned that he would destroy it. Israel had "rejected what is good" (the Lord and his law) (v. 3); now, appropriately, he would reject their beloved calf-idol (v. 5). NIV translates the first line of verse 5a, "Throw out your calf-idol, O Samaria!" However, the Hebrew text actually has a third-person verb form, "He has rejected (the verb is the same one translated "rejected" in v. 3) your calf-idol, O Samaria."[45]

Israel would get exactly what she deserved (v. 7a). By her idolatrous worship she had planted the "wind," which here symbolizes that which lacks substance and value. She would reap the "whirlwind," which symbolizes destructive divine judgment (see Ps. 83:15; Isa. 29:6). By utilizing the imagery of planting and harvesting, the Lord makes it clear that Israel planted the seeds of her own destruction when she turned to idols.

Agricultural imagery continues in the second half of verse 7. Israel's idolatrous attempts to attain prosperity were futile. They are compared to a stalk that has no grain in it and, therefore, yields no flour. Even if the nation's efforts did yield some "grain" (prosperity), foreign nations would swallow it up. This too would be appropriate and ironic, for Israel was seeking security through alliances with these nations (v. 8). She willingly submitted herself to Assyria and Egypt, but her efforts would backfire (vv. 9–10).

Despite Israel's idolatry and foreign alliances, she still had the audacity

---

45. Some emend the verb form to an imperative, because it is awkward to find a third-person reference to God in a divine speech. However, such inconsistency in person is attested elsewhere in speeches by God in Hosea (see 1:7; 4:10–12; 8:13). On the significance of the wordplay involving "reject," see Miller, *Sin and Judgment in the Prophets,* 17–18.

to offer sacrifices to the Lord (v. 11a). However, because Israel had rejected the law of the Lord (v. 12), he regarded their "worship" as sinful hypocrisy (v. 11b) and refused to accept their offerings (v. 13a). Because Israel had forgotten their "Maker," the one who made them a nation by delivering them from bondage in Egypt, the Lord would send them back into slavery (vv. 13b–14a). They would "return to Egypt," as it were. Of course, Assyria, not Egypt, was the destination of exiled Israel, but "Egypt" is used here as a symbol of slavery to indicate that the nation's salvation history would be reversed.

God's judgment upon Israel would spill over into Judah. Though Judah had "fortified many towns" to make themselves secure from invasion, the Lord would send the fire of judgment upon them (v. 14b). As in Hosea 5:14, the prophecy of verses 13b–14 anticipates the downfall and exile of Israel in 722 B.C., as well as the Assyrian invasion of Judah in 701 B.C., when Sennacherib conquered forty-six of Judah's "strong cities" and "walled forts."[46]

Weep for the Children (9:1–17)

Israel was not to rejoice in anticipation of an abundant harvest (v. 1a). Because Israel had looked to Baal for food, she would be deprived of grain and wine (vv. 1b–2). Israel's worship of Baal is compared to prostitution. She gave herself to Baal in exchange for the "wages of a prostitute," namely the agricultural prosperity she erroneously thought Baal could provide (see 2:5). But the threshing floors and winepresses would be empty, and Israel would be sent into exile (v. 3). Symbol and reality are mixed, as both Egypt (the place where Israel had once been enslaved) and Assyria (the destination of the future exiles) are mentioned. Imprisoned in a foreign land, Israel would have to eat ceremonially "unclean" food (see Ezek. 4:13) and would be unable to offer acceptable sacrifices to God or observe their religious festivals (vv. 4–5). The people would die in a foreign land, while the riches they left behind in Israel would lie among the ruins of their homes, which would be overgrown with briers and thorns (v. 6). With rhetorical flair, the prophet warned that the Egyptian city of Memphis, a famous Egyptian burial site, would be the exiles' cemetery.

Israel's many sins demanded repayment (vv. 7a, 9b). Israel's hostility toward God was perhaps most clearly seen in the way she rejected the Lord's prophets (vv. 7b–8). The prophets were Israel's "watchmen," sent by God to warn the people of impending doom. But the people considered them to be insane fools and threatened them with violence. The Lord considered such hostility comparable to the horrible sin committed at Gibeah by an earlier generation (v. 9a). The prophet here alludes to the incident recorded in Judges 19, which tells how the Benjaminites of Gibeah tried to rape a Levite

---

46. For Sennacherib's highly propagandized account of the invasion, see James Pritchard, *Ancient Near Eastern Texts Relating to the Old Testament* (Princeton: Princeton University Press, 1969), 287–88.

who sought shelter in their city for the evening. They settled for his helpless concubine, whom they gang-raped all night long.

The Lord had not always found Israel so repulsive. In fact, at the beginning of their relationship, he looked upon her with great delight, as one does when he finds grapes in the desert or sees the early fruit on a fig tree (v. 10a). The latter was considered a tasty and irresistible delicacy (see Isa. 28:4; Jer. 24:2; Mic. 7:1). However, the Lord's view of Israel quickly changed, for at Baal Peor they worshiped other gods and engaged in fertility rites with foreign women (Num. 25:1–5).

Hosea's generation had repeated these sins, hoping that Baal would grant them numerous children. The Lord would judge them harshly, but appropriately. He would prevent the Israelite women from conceiving and giving birth (v. 11). He would cause those women who did conceive to miscarry (v. 14) and would hand over to ruthless invaders any babies that did happen to be born (vv. 12–13, 16). Like a husband who has decided to divorce an unfaithful wife, he would drive his people from his house and make them wander among the nations (vv. 15, 17).

This denunciation of Israel effectively uses the literary devices of irony and literary allusion. The name "Ephraim," which predominates in verses 11–16, is chosen for a specific reason. The name, which was popularly thought to mean "doubly fruitful" (see Gen. 41:52), suggests the concepts of fertility and fruitfulness. Ironically, Ephraim, the "doubly fruitful" one, would end up like a withered root and yield no fruit (v. 16a). The reference to Gilgal in conjunction with the threat of exile is also ironic. Gilgal was Israel's first campsite once they crossed the Jordan River under Joshua (see Josh. 4). As such, it symbolized Israel's possession of the Promised Land. But now the sins committed there necessitated Israel's expulsion from the land. The same verb (Heb. *garash*, "drive out") used of God's expulsion of the Canaanites (see Deut. 33:27, for example) is now used to describe how the Lord would "drive out" his people from his house (v. 15). This verb is also used in Genesis 4:14 of Cain's expulsion from God's presence. An analogy may be intended, since the Israelites' hostility toward the prophets was comparable to Cain's hatred of his brother Abel. Like Cain, Israel would become a wanderer. The word translated "wanderers" (a form of the Hebrew verb *nadad*, "wander") in Hosea 9:17 is also used to describe Cain's destiny in Genesis 4:12, 14.

The Yoke of Sin and Judgment (10:1–15)

With a touch of nostalgia, the prophet recalls early Israel's prosperity as she spread out like a vine in the Promised Land (v. 1a; see Ps. 80:8–11; Ezek. 19:10–11). However, realism quickly sets in as the prophet also recalls how ungrateful and hypocritical Israel eventually turned to idolatry (v. 1b). The altars mentioned here symbolize the empty formalism that characterized Is-

rael's religion (see 8:11), while the sacred stones symbolize their pagan idolatry (see 3:4). Their hollow and insincere attempts to worship the Lord left
them guilty of hypocrisy (v. 2a). For this reason, the Lord would destroy
both the altars and sacred stones (v. 2b).

The coming judgment would deprive Israel of her independence, symbolized by her king. The people would acknowledge their failure to fear the
Lord as the cause of this calamity, which would be so devastating that even
a king could not reverse it (v. 3).

The deceit that characterized Israel's relationship with the Lord (see vv.
1–2) also pervaded the people's dealings with one another (v. 4). They broke
their promises and showed no regard for the oaths they had sworn. This inevitably led to a rash of lawsuits, which the prophet compares to weeds in a
plowed field.

The Lord's judgment would strike at the heart of pagan Israel. The people were especially devoted to the "calf-idol of Beth Aven" (that is, Bethel),
but the Assyrians would haul it away into exile, leaving the humiliated people and priests to mourn its departure (vv. 5–6). The rare term translated
"idolatrous priests" is used elsewhere of the priests of Baal (see 2 Kings 23:5;
Zeph. 1:4). Samaria's king would "float away" into exile, like a twig carried
along by the current of a stream (v. 7; see also v. 15). The pagan shrines
would be destroyed and overgrown with thorns and thistles (v. 8a). As their
whole world crumbled around them, the people would beg the mountains
and hills to fall on them and end their misery (v. 8b).

For centuries, going all the way back to the horrible crime committed
against the Levite's concubine in Gibeah (see 9:9, as well as Judg. 19), Israel
had persisted in sin (v. 9). The Lord announced that the time for punishment had arrived (v. 10). Borrowing imagery from the agricultural realm, the
Lord compares Israel to a calf that has been trained to thresh grain (v. 11).
This job was relatively easy because the animal was allowed to eat some of
the grain on the threshing floor (see Deut. 25:4). However, Israel's easy days
were over. The Lord would put a yoke on Ephraim and Judah and make
them do the hard work of plowing.

The prophet extends the image of plowing in verses 12–13a. He urged
the people to do some plowing and planting in the moral and ethical sphere.
He told them to plant justice. If they responded positively, the Lord would
send showers of deliverance,[47] which in turn would yield the harvest of his
"unfailing love." Of course, this vision of potential prosperity contrasted
with reality. The people had actually planted wickedness and reaped a crop
of evil and deception.

Rather than depending on the Lord for their security, Israel trusted in its

---

47. NIV translates the Hebrew term as "righteousness," but the word likely refers here to God's deliverance. See Hos. 2:19.

own military power (v. 13b). For this reason, the Lord would destroy their army and allow an invader to sweep through the land (vv. 14–15). Israel's fortified cities would be devastated, the people would be the victims of horrible atrocities, Bethel (where the calf-idol was located) would fall, and the king of Israel would be removed.

The prophet compared the upcoming disaster to Shalman's ruthless conquest of Beth Arbel, an event that apparently was familiar to Hosea's audience (v. 14). Unfortunately, modern scholarship has been unable to find any other references to this event in biblical or extrabiblical literature. Both the identity of Shalman and the precise location of Beth Arbel are uncertain.[48]

God's Great Compassion (11:1–11)

Once again the Lord wistfully recalls Israel's early history (v. 1; see 9:10 and 10:1). Israel was God's "son," the special object of his fatherly love. The Lord's supreme act of love was the exodus, when he summoned his "son" out of bondage in Egypt in order to establish a covenant relationship with him.[49] But Israel turned to idols, especially the Baals, despite the Lord's protective care (vv. 2–4).[50]

Israel's rebellion made judgment inevitable. They would be conquered by Assyria and taken into exile (symbolized again as a return to Egypt, v. 5; see 8:13; 9:3). Hosea uses wordplay here to emphasize that this punishment would be appropriate. Israel refused to "repent" (Heb. *shub,* "return"), so they would "return" (Heb. *shub*) to bondage. Enemy swords would flash through Israel's cities, bringing her proud plans to an abrupt end and leaving her helpless in the face of judgment (vv. 6–7).[51]

Suddenly the Lord has a change of heart, prompting him to temper his judgment with mercy (v. 8). Utilizing rhetorical questions, he makes it clear that he could never totally destroy his people as he did Admah and Zeboiim, which were wiped out along with Sodom and Gomorrah (Deut. 29:23; see also Gen. 10:19; 14:2, 8). Those wicked cities had been "overturned" by

48. For discussion of various options offered by scholars, see Wolff, *Hosea,* 188, and Davies, *Hosea,* 248–49.

49. On Matthew's typological application of this verse to Christ, see my comments on Isa. 7:14 under the heading "Immanuel as a Type."

50. The translation and interpretation of v. 2a are especially problematic. The Hebrew text reads literally, "they called to them, so they walked from before them." Many understand the plural subject of "called" to be the prophets, through whom the Lord called Israel to faithfulness. Andersen and Freedman (*Hosea,* 577–78) suggest an allusion to the Baal Peor incident (see Hos. 9:10), in which case the subject of "called" might be the pagan women who invited the Israelites to their fertility rites. (See Num. 25:2, where NIV uses "invited" to translate the same Hebrew verb translated "called" in Hos. 11:2.) They alter the second line of Hos. 12:2a to read, "they walked from before me," taking the *he-mem* combination at the end of the form as an independent third masculine plural pronoun that goes with the next line. The Septuagint supports this textual alteration. NIV follows the Septuagint in reading "I called" at the beginning of the line and "from me" at the end.

51. The translation and interpretation of v. 7b are problematic. As the Hebrew text stands, it defies meaning, reading literally, "and to upon they call him, together he does not exalt them." NIV assumes that

God's judgment (see Gen. 19:25, where NIV translates the verb "overthrew"), but in Israel's case the Lord's "heart," viewed as the seat of his emotions, would be "turned" (NIV "changed" translates the same verb rendered "overthrew" in Gen. 19:25), and his compassion would replace his anger. The Lord would not attack Ephraim with blind rage; he would stop short of annihilating them (v. 9). Human beings sometimes are so filled with anger that they are unable to demonstrate any restraint or mercy as they seek revenge. But the Lord, the "Holy One," is God, not a man.[52] He has the capacity to show mercy and is able to keep his emotions in perfect balance.

Some theologians argue that God does not possess emotions. Of course, to make such an assertion they must dismiss as anthropopathic the many biblical texts that attribute emotions to God. Hosea 11:9 demonstrates that this view of God's nature is erroneous and unbiblical. God, like human beings whom he made in his image, is capable of a wide range of emotions, but God, unlike human beings, expresses his emotions in perfect balance. The distinction between God and human beings does not lie in some supposed absence of divine emotion, but in God's ability to control his emotions and express them appropriately.

Having stated that he would preserve his people, the Lord anticipated a time when they would readily follow him (vv. 10–11). Earlier the Lord pictured himself as a powerful lion ready to tear his people to shreds (see 5:14). Here he uses the image of a lion in a completely different way. A day would come when the Lord would roar like a lion to summon his people. With genuine fear of the Lord (note the reference to "trembling"), they would answer his summons and return to the Promised Land, where the Lord would resettle them. Earlier the Lord depicted Israel as senseless and easily deceived, like a dove that is ensnared by a hunter (see 7:11). But here he uses the dove image differently, comparing Israel's future return to the land to the swift flight of the dove.

Lessons from the Past (11:12–12:14)

After this brief flight into the future, the Lord returns to the cold, hard present. Despite God's faithfulness, both Israel and Judah had rebelled against their king, called here "the Holy One," a title that emphasizes his sovereign position as their king and moral authority (11:12).[53] The people pursued a

---

Hebrew 'al, "upon," is an abbreviated form of the divine name "Most High." In this case Israel is pictured as calling in desperation to the Lord, only to have him reject their plea for help. Others prefer to emend 'al, "upon," to ba'al, "Baal." In this case they cry out to Baal, but he is unable to deliver them from God's judgment. See Wolff, Hosea, 192, and Mays, Hosea, 150, 156.

52. The title "Holy One" here depicts God as transcendent and absolutely unique.

53. In the Hebrew text the form translated "Holy One" appears here in the plural to emphasize the Lord's sovereignty. Hebrew sometimes uses the plural to indicate the degree or magnitude of a quality or characteristic inherent in the noun.

deceitful lifestyle that was empty and self-destructive. The prophet compares it to feeding on the wind, a practice that will eventually cause one to starve (12:1a). Social injustice (note the reference to "lies and violence") plagued the land, and its leaders, rather than looking to God for security, sought safety in foreign alliances (v. 1b). The Lord could not let such sin go unpunished; he was bringing formal charges against his people. Having demonstrated their guilt, he would then repay them for their sinful deeds (v. 2).

The proceedings begin with a history lesson (vv. 3–5). God's deceitful people (see 11:12–12:1) were just like Jacob, the father of the nation.[54] While he was still in the womb, Jacob's greedy and deceitful character was evident. At the time of his birth, he grabbed his brother Esau's heel, seemingly in an effort to keep Esau from being the firstborn (see Gen. 25:26). This action foreshadowed his conflict with Esau, in which Jacob used deceit in his effort to achieve security and prosperity. After several years of conflict with his uncle Laban, Jacob finally began to realize that God's supernatural blessing, not his own scheming, was the only way he could succeed (see Gen. 31:42). Facing the prospects of meeting an angry Esau, Jacob's inner struggle culminated in a wrestling match with God's angel (Gen. 32:22–32).[55] The conflict ended with Jacob demanding and receiving a divine blessing in accordance with God's earlier promise (see Gen. 28:13–15). At the beginning of his life, Jacob bargained with God (see Gen. 28:20–22), but he came to the point where he recognized his dependence on God's help (Gen. 32:26).

Jacob's deceitful descendants should have followed his example. The prophet urged them to repent, promote social justice, and trust in God for security and prosperity (v. 6). This demanded a radical turnabout, for the economic practices of the land were corrupt and royal bureaucrats were proud of their wealth (vv. 7–8).[56] If changes were not forthcoming, the Lord would remove the people from the land and make them live in a wilderness, just as he did after he brought them out of Egypt (v. 9). Israel commemorated this past experience by observing the Feast of Tabernacles, when the people would live in temporary shelters for a week (Lev. 23:33–43). Ironically, celebration would become harsh reality as the wilderness wanderings would be reactualized in exile. The Lord had sent his prophets to confront and warn the people (v. 10), but the people persisted in their sin and engaged

54. The same Hebrew word translated "deceit" in Hos. 11:12 is used of Jacob's deceitful treatment of his father in Gen. 27:35.

55. According to the Genesis account, Jacob wrestled with God himself; Hosea appears to reflect an alternate, less anthropomorphic tradition according to which Jacob wrestled with an angel sent from God. Perhaps Jacob's words in Gen 48:15–16, where he appears to refer to God as an "angel," influenced the tradition expressed in Hosea.

56. For a study of the socioeconomic background of the time, see John A. Dearman, *Property Rights in the Eighth-Century Prophets,* SBLDS 106 (Atlanta: Scholars Press, 1988).

in hypocritical worship at places like Gilgal (v. 11a). Appropriately, the coming judgment would reduce the altars at such shrines to "piles of stones" (v. 11b). The statement is more arresting in the Hebrew text, where the word translated "piles of stones" (Heb. *gallim*) sounds like the name Gilgal (note the "g" and "l" sounds in both terms).

More lessons from history were in order. The nation's destiny was in the Lord's hands. If Israel somehow thought they were immune to exile, they should have considered the experience of their father Jacob. Following his deception of Esau, he had to leave the Promised Land and travel to the home of his uncle, where he was forced to work hard and long to acquire a wife (v. 12). Later, after Jacob and his family were forced to go to Egypt because of a famine, the Lord delivered his people from bondage through a prophet (v. 13). Israel had ignored the prophets, but they should have realized that the prophets were often God's instruments in accomplishing his purposes for his people (see v. 10, as well as 9:8). Israel could not escape God's providential control. They had angered him with their violence and would now suffer the consequences of their sin (v. 14).

Death Receives an Invitation (13:1–16)

There was a time when Ephraim, the most prominent tribe in the northern kingdom, exercised leadership in Israel and was highly respected. Israel's first king, Jeroboam I, was from Ephraim (see 1 Kings 11:26; 12:25). But then Ephraim turned to Baal worship and "died," as it were (v. 1). This statement is highly ironic, for Baal worship was designed to promote life and fertility. In pagan mythology Baal's arch-rival was Mot, the god of death. Ephraim worshiped Baal in order to achieve life; instead, they got death.

The situation went from bad to worse, as the people sinned even more and continued to manufacture and worship idols (v. 2). Their devotion to their false gods was best illustrated by their practice of kissing the calf-idols as a sign of homage (see 1 Kings 19:18). Imagine the absurdity of human beings, made in the image of God, kissing the images of calves made by their own hands.

NIV's translation of verse 2b, which understands human sacrifice to be in view, is questionable. The Hebrew text reads literally, "Sacrificers of men kiss calves." Some interpret this to mean, "Those who sacrifice men kiss calves," taking "men" as the object of "sacrifice." According to this view, the Israelites were offering human sacrifices in conjunction with their Baal worship. The Israelites apparently did offer child sacrifices to the god Molech (see Lev. 18:21; 20:2–5; 2 Kings 23:10), a practice that was in some way associated with Baal worship (Jer. 32:35). However, it is unlikely that this abominable practice is in view in Hosea 13:2. The Hebrew term translated "men," more likely refers to adults, not children. The construction "sacrificers of men" is probably an idiom, with "men" identifying the broader category of which the "sacrificers" are a part. It is like the expression "poor of men," meaning "the poor among men" or "men who are poor" (see Isa. 29:19). By using this construction the prophet draws attention to the absurdity of men kissing calves.

Because of its idolatry, Israel would soon disappear from the scene (v. 3). Four metaphors are used to picture this: the morning mist being dispelled by the light of the sun, the early dew evaporating, chaff being blown away by the wind, and smoke escaping through a window. In addition to picturing how quickly Israel would vanish, the metaphors also suggest that idolatrous Israel lacked the spiritual substance that gives stability.

The Lord offered a defense of his actions. He delivered his people from bondage in Egypt, demonstrating that he is the only God worthy of their worship (v. 4). He cared for his people as they wandered in the wilderness and settled them in a land where they were well fed and satisfied (vv. 5–6a).[57] Despite the Lord's kindness, Israel became proud and "forgot" the Lord (v. 6b).

The Lord would not tolerate such ingratitude from his people. The Lord would attack them like a vicious wild animal and tear them to pieces (vv. 7–8; see 5:14). The only one who could help Israel had become their enemy, and no one, not even their king, could prevent divine judgment from falling (vv. 9–10a). After all, the Lord had reluctantly given Israel a king in the first place, and he certainly had the authority to take away what he had granted (vv. 10b–11).

It is not certain if verse 11 refers to a specific historical event or is a general statement about God's dealings with Israel. As translated in NIV, the verse refers to a particular king, perhaps Saul (1 Sam. 8–31) or Jeroboam I (see 1 Kings 12–14). However, the Hebrew verbal forms used here can just as easily be translated as generalizing presents, "So in my anger I give you a king, and in my wrath I take him away." In this case the verse summarizes the history of God's dealings with the northern kingdom. Disobedient king after disobedient king came and went.[58] This pattern would be repeated with the current king (see v. 10). The Lord's accusations against Israel were not vague, unfounded charges. Israel's sins were well documented, as it were, in God's record book, ready to be produced as evidence at the appropriate time (v. 12).

The initial stage of God's judgment was already evident, signaling more severe punishment to come. The Lord compared this to the labor pains that signal the birth of a child (v. 13a). Extending the metaphor, he then compared Israel to a baby that fails to come out of its mother's womb when the

57. Verse 6 does not specifically mention Israel's entry into the Promised Land, but it is likely that the reference to the Lord feeding his people alludes to the period after the conquest when the Lord settled Israel in the land. See Wolff, *Hosea*, 226; Mays, *Hosea*, 175; and Davies, *Hosea*, 290.
58. For this interpretation of v. 11, see Wolff, *Hosea*, 221, 227; and Davies, *Hosea*, 293.

time of birth arrives (v. 13b). Such a delay can, of course, be deadly. The metaphor illustrates Israel's lack of wisdom and spiritual sensitivity. Though God's judgment was already upon them, they failed to see the "handwriting on the wall," as it were.

Having demonstrated the nation's guilt and insensitivity, the Lord invited personified death to be his instrument of judgment against Israel (v. 14). As translated by NIV, the first half of verse 14 sounds like a promise of salvation. While the translation is possible, it is highly unlikely in this context, for the immediately following verses depict harsh and unrelenting judgment. It is true that Hosea sometimes makes abrupt shifts in mood (see 1:10–11; 2:2; 6:1, 4; 11:8, 12), but such a shift seems premature here. Not until the call to repentance at the beginning of chapter 14 does the prophecy take a turn for the better. For this reason, it is preferable to translate the two statements in verse 14a as rhetorical questions expecting a negative reply: "Will I ransom them from the power of the grave? Will I redeem them from death?"[59] The two questions that follow then become invitations to death to do its destructive work as the instrument of divine judgment.

Paul utilizes Hosea 13:14b in 1 Corinthians 15:55. Having stated that death will be "swallowed up in victory" at the time of the resurrection (v. 54), he then issues a defiant challenge to death. The questions might be paraphrased as follows: "Where, O death, is your victory *now?* Where, O death, is your sting *now?*" As employed by Paul, the questions point to the defeat of death, which he calls the "last enemy" (v. 26). Paul may be intentionally giving the questions an ironic twist, though it is possible that his use of the text simply reflects a later interpretive tradition. In the latter case, Paul's interpretation does not reflect the meaning of Hosea 13:14b in its original context, but utilizes the words of Scripture as traditionally understood.

God would not relent from sending judgment. NIV translates the last line of verse 14 as follows, "I will have no compassion." The text reads literally, "Compassion is hidden from my eyes," apparently meaning that God would not show compassion as he carried out judgment against his people. This statement appears to contradict Hosea 11:8, where the Lord indicates that his "compassion" would be aroused, preventing him from totally destroying his people. The terms translated "compassion" in these texts, though slightly different, are derived from the same Hebrew verb (*nakham*). In some contexts, this verb means "to be moved to pity, show compassion" (see Judg. 2:18; 21:6, 15; Ps. 90:13). This shade of meaning appears to be behind the noun used in Hosea 11:8. However, many other times the verb carries the idea, "to regret, relent, change one's mind." This shade of meaning may be behind the term employed in 13:14. In this case the Lord is stating that he

---

59. See Wolff, *Hosea*, 221, and Stuart, *Hosea-Jonah*, 207. For a statement of the opposite position (that v. 14a is a promise of salvation), see McComiskey, "Hosea," 223–24.

would not "relent" from sending the announced judgment. However, this decision to send judgment does not preclude his showing some compassion. God would not change his mind concerning his decision to punish his people, but, according to 11:8–9, he would temper this judgment with mercy and not allow it to exceed its proper limits.

Though tempered by God's compassion, the judgment would still be very severe (vv. 15–16). The prophet pictured this judgment as a hot east wind that blows in from the desert and dries up all the water sources, even those normally fed by underground streams.[60] Invaders would rob Israel's storehouses and, worse yet, slaughter even infants and pregnant women. This warning, though painful to read and envision, is a sober reminder that children sometimes suffer the consequences of their parents' sin. Normally we rightly consider the wholesale slaughter of babies to be outright murder, even in the context of warfare. However, as this passage illustrates, God sometimes kills babies as an act of judgment on rebellious sinners (note v. 16a). Such judicial killing, even when it involves infants, is justifiable from the standpoint of God, the moral authority of the universe.

A Final Call to Repentance (14:1–9)

The hideous image of infants being hurled to the ground and pregnant women being sliced open fades into the background, giving way to a final call to repentance (v. 1). The prophet urged sinful Israel to return to the Lord; he even gave them a model prayer to use as they confessed their sins (vv. 2–3). If the people asked for forgiveness, they would then be able to offer genuine, pure praise to God. They also needed to repudiate their foreign alliances and false gods, and acknowledge the Lord as their only source of help.

At this point, the Lord chimed in and promised to restore his wayward people if they repented. He promised to turn from his anger and extend his love to them (v. 4). Comparing himself to dew, the Lord promised to restore Israel's vitality (vv. 5–7). Israel would "blossom like a lily" (see Song of Sol. 2:2) and become deeply rooted, like one of the great cedars of Lebanon. The metaphors suggest attractiveness and stability. Several botanical metaphors follow. Israel would be as luxuriant as an olive tree, as aromatic as a cedar, and as fruitful as a grapevine. These images of vibrant plant life depict the restoration of God's blessings.

Reminding Israel that he was their source of vitality, the Lord promised to respond to their prayers and "care" (Heb. *shur*) for them (v. 8). This promise stands in stark contrast to the threat issued in 13:7, where the Lord warned that he would "lurk" (Heb. *shur*) by the path like a dangerous leopard, ready to pounce on his people. The use of the same Hebrew verb in both

---

60. On the characteristics and effects of these easterly winds, see Luis I. J. Stadelmann, *The Hebrew Conception of the World* (Rome: Pontifical Biblical Institute, 1970), 102–7.

texts (albeit with different shades of meaning) draws attention to the contrast. Sinful Israel would experience God as a "lurking" leopard; repentant Israel would experience him as a "caring" protector.

The prophet concluded his message with a proverbial statement (v. 9). He pointed out that those who are wise will recognize three principles: (1) The Lord's "ways" (referring to his commandments) are right, (2) the godly willingly "walk in" (i.e., obey) them, and (3) sinful rebels find them to be a stumbling block that leads to their destruction.

The Day of the Lord Is Near! (Joel)

Introduction

The heading to this book simply identifies the prophet without giving the historical setting of his ministry. Because of the book's canonical position between Hosea and Amos, both of whom prophesied in the eighth century B.C., some assume that Joel's ministry must have occurred during this same time period, perhaps even earlier. However, this argument is inconclusive, for Joel's position may be due to the literary parallels between Joel 3 and Amos 1, not chronological considerations.[61] The internal evidence of the book suggests it was written in the early postexilic period. In 3:2–3, the Lord announced that he would punish the nations for the way in which they had scattered his people, divided up his land, and sold children into slavery. The Hebrew verb forms are most naturally taken as narratival here, describing events that had already occurred.[62] Since several texts refer to the temple as standing (see 1:14, 16; 2:17), Joel must have delivered the prophecy after the second temple was built in 515 B.C. Several other internal features, such as the reference to slave trade with the Greeks (3:6) and the absence of any reference to a king over Judah, are consistent with a postexilic date.

The Book of Joel has two major sections, with the turning point coming at 2:18. In the first half of the book the prophet urged the people to mourn over the devastating effects of a recent locust invasion (1:2–20), warned that more "locusts" were coming (2:1–11), and called the community to repent (2:12–17). The second half of the book, having noted that the Lord did take pity on his people (2:18), then records the Lord's promise to call off the threatened invasion, restore the nation's crops, and vindicate his humiliated people (2:19–3:21).[63]

61. See Wolff, *Joel and Amos,* 3–4.

62. Proponents of an early date sometimes suggest that 2 Chron. 21:16–17 provides the background for the description of Joel 3:2–3, but the exile of the royal family described in the former passage hardly satisfies Joel's description. Proponents of an early date also explain the verb forms in Joel 3:2–3 as future perfects, but this explanation is tendentious.

63. NIV translates 2:18–19a with the future tense, as if they contain statements designed to motivate a positive response to the preceding call to repentance. But the verb forms in the Hebrew text are most nat-

Unprecedented Disaster (1:1–20)

The prophet called the people and their leaders (designated "elders") to attention, for the land had experienced an unprecedented disaster that would be a topic of conversation for generations to come (vv. 2–3). Waves of locusts had swept through the land, stripping it of its vegetation (v. 4).[64]

Four different Hebrew terms for locusts are used in verse four. The terms may be synonymous, though some have seen them as referring to different species or as reflecting different stages in a locust's physical development. In verse 4 the variation of terms within an overall repetitive structure (note the pattern "what . . . has left . . . have eaten") likely depicts wave after wave of destructive locusts, each of which left an ever smaller amount of vegetation for the next until everything was devoured.

With a sarcastic, but effective, rhetorical touch, the prophet told the drunkards to weep and wail because no wine was available (v. 5). With lion-like capacity to rip and tear, the innumerable swarms had devoured the vines and stripped even the bark from the fig trees, leaving the branches white (vv. 6–7).

Joel next urged the personified land[65] to lament as a young bride would mourn the death of her husband (v. 8).[66] In particular, the priests should weep because the destruction of the land's vegetation meant there could be no grain offerings, which included flour and oil, or drink offerings, which included wine (vv. 9–10, 13; see Num. 28:5, 7). The destruction of grains and fruits was especially devastating for the farmers, who were urged to join the priests in weeping over the disaster (vv. 11–12). The lengthy itemized list of destruction draws attention to the extent of the devastation. Eight items are specified, suggesting that the locusts were more than thorough. A sevenfold list would have indicated completeness, but by adding an eighth item to the list, the prophet stressed the utter and total destruction caused by the locusts.[67]

The extent of this disaster demanded more than sorrow. Joel instructed

---

urally taken as narratival and as reporting how the Lord took pity on his people in Joel's day, apparently as a result of a positive response to the prophet's exhortation.

64. For eyewitness accounts of locust invasions, see S. R. Driver, *Joel and Amos,* 2d ed. (Cambridge: Cambridge University Press, 1915), 40, 89–93; George A. Smith, *The Book of the Twelve Prophets,* rev. ed., 2 vols. (New York: Harper & Brothers, n.d.), 2:391–95; and John D. Whiting, "Jerusalem's Locust Plague," *National Geographic* 28, December 1915, 511–50. For a helpful survey of the characteristics of locusts, see Raymond B. Dillard, "Joel," in *The Minor Prophets: An Exegetical & Expositional Commentary,* ed. T. E. Mc-Comiskey, vol. 1 (Grand Rapids: Baker, 1992), 255–56.

65. The verb translated "mourn" is feminine singular in the Hebrew text, suggesting the personified land is in view here (see 2:18).

66. The term translated "virgin" may refer here to a woman who has been betrothed to a young man, only to have him die before the wedding. See Deut. 22:23–24, which refers to a betrothed woman as both a "virgin" and the "wife" of a man.

67. The eight items include wheat, barley, the vine, fig tree, pomegranate, palm, apple tree, and all the trees of the field. The phrase "harvest of the field" in v. 11b is not treated as a separate item because it refers to the wheat and barley mentioned in the previous clause.

the priests to call a "sacred assembly" in which the people would fast and cry
out to the Lord for mercy (v. 14). Fasting was often associated with repentance (see 1 Sam. 7:6; Neh. 9:1–2; Jon. 3:5). This response of brokenness
and repentance was necessary because the locusts were merely a foreshadow-
ing of imminent divine judgment (v. 15), just as the locust plague had been
in Egypt (see Exod. 10–11). The Deuteronomic "curses" also warned that a
locust invasion would accompany divine judgment (see Deut. 28:38–42).

The "day of the LORD" was near (v. 15a). This expression, which appears
frequently in the Hebrew Bible, refers to a day when the Lord intervenes in
the world to judge his enemies. The phrase is applied to various events; here
it refers to a day of judgment upon Joel's contemporaries.[68] This "day" would
bring destruction (Heb. *shod*) from the Almighty (Heb. *shaddai*) (v. 15b).
The similarity in sound between the key terms draws attention to the seri-
ousness of the situation and contributes to the portrayal of God as judge.
The name Shaddai depicts God as the sovereign king who is capable of protecting or judging.[69]

The prophet took up a lament in which he described the devastating effects of the locust invasion and cried out to the Lord for help (vv. 16–20).
He focused on the empty granaries and the starving cattle and used the imagery of fire to depict the drought and resulting famine that had followed the
invasion.

An Army on the March (2:1–11)

Assuming the role of a watchman, the Lord called for the trumpet to sound
an alarm in Zion, for a day of war was imminent (v. 1). The Lord's "day" (see
1:15) was approaching, bringing with it the dark clouds of impending doom
and destruction (v. 2a). Locusts had invaded the land; now an even more terrifying invader was approaching. The Lord himself was leading a mighty
army toward the land (vv. 2b, 11). Like an uncontrollable fire, it devoured
all the vegetation in its path, leaving a wasteland behind (v. 3). This army,
which resembled horses in appearance and sounded like chariots, moved
with great speed, causing the nations in its path to panic (vv. 4–6). Its divi-
sions marched ahead with precision, and no defenses could resist it (vv. 7–9).
This terrifying army even frightened the cosmos, causing the earth to shake
and the luminaries to grow dark (v. 10).

What kind of "army" is depicted here? Some argue that another locust
invasion is depicted, one even more devastating than the invasion that had
already occurred. Several features of the text appear to support this interpretation. The invaders cause the sky to darken and devour vegetation, just as
swarming locusts do. They are *compared* to a human army, suggesting that

---

68. For a more detailed discussion of the concept, see my comments on Isa. 13:6.
69. For a more detailed discussion of this divine name, see my comments on Isa. 13:6.

they are not human (see vv. 4–5, 7). They invade buildings, but are not described as killing anyone. According to verse 20, this army is eventually destroyed by being driven into the sea. Eyewitness accounts of locust invasions in Palestine sometimes describe the locusts being driven by the wind into the Mediterranean Sea.[70]

Others maintain that the invader, though depicted as "locustlike," is actually a human army. In other texts depicting the day of the Lord, literal armies are the instruments of divine judgment (see, for example, Isa. 13). The invader is said to come from the north (see v. 20), but locusts normally invade Palestine from the south or southeast. Though locust invasions from the north have occurred, it seems more likely that the depiction of the army as "northern" points to a literal army, for invaders often entered Palestine from that direction (see Isa. 14:31; Jer. 6:1, 22; Ezek. 26:7; 38:15). Other elements in the description (the darkening of the sky, the devouring of crops, the depiction of the army as locusts) can be understood as the stereotypical language of judgment.[71] The comparisons in verses 4–5, 7 would seem to preclude identifying the invader as a literal army, but in Hebrew a simile sometimes points to the reality underlying a metaphor.[72] In such cases the Hebrew preposition *ke-*, normally translated "like, as," carries the force of "in every respect like," or "in every way like."[73] For example, in Joel 1:15, the day of the Lord is said to "come *like* [i.e., in every respect like] destruction from the Almighty," meaning that it would indeed be such an instance of divine destruction.[74]

A third view understands the language of 2:1–11 as describing an army of "locustlike apocalyptic creatures," similar to the creatures described in Revelation 9:2–11.[75] In this case, the imagery is probably used for shock effect to emphasize the terrifying reality of impending judgment.

Urgent Warning! Repent! (2:12–17)

The looming presence of this terrifying army demanded an urgent response. The Lord urged his people to "return" to him and to demonstrate their humility by "fasting and weeping and mourning" (v. 12). The prophet seconded the Lord's exhortation, explaining that their repentance must be genuine and

70. See Driver, *Joel and Amos,* 62–63; Smith, *Twelve Prophets,* 2:411.

71. See, for example, Isa. 1:7; 5:30; 13:10; Jer. 51:27. For ancient Near Eastern texts comparing armies to locusts, see J. A. Thompson, "Joel's Locusts in the Light of Near Eastern Parallels," *JANES* 14 (1955): 52–55.

72. See E. W. Bullinger, *Figures of Speech Used in the Bible* (reprint, Grand Rapids: Baker, 1968), 728–29.

73. See Bruce K. Waltke and M. O'Connor, *An Introduction to Biblical Hebrew Syntax* (Winona Lake, Ind.: Eisenbrauns, 1990), 203.

74. See also Isa. 1:7–8, where the expressions "as when overthrown by strangers" (literally, "[in every respect] like an overthrow by strangers") and "[in every respect] like a city under siege" point to the fact that Judah was indeed overrun by foreign invaders and that Jerusalem was indeed under siege.

75. See Wolff, *Joel and Amos,* 42.

internal, not a mere outward show (v. 13a). He encouraged the people by reminding them of God's "gracious and compassionate" nature that prompts him to be patient with sinners, to extend his love to them, and to relent from sending judgment (v. 13b). This description of God's character is rooted in Exodus 34:6–7, where God is described in similar terms after relenting from judgment following Israel's sin with the golden calf (see Exod. 32:14).

Some dismiss biblical references to God "relenting" from judgment as anthropomorphic, arguing that an unchangeable God would never change his mind once he has announced his intentions. While it is true that God will not deviate from an announced course of action once he has issued a formal, unconditional decree (see Num. 23:19; 1 Sam. 15:29; Ps. 110:4), he is often depicted as "changing his mind" in contexts where he has given only a warning or made a conditional statement about what he will do.[76] Since Joel 2:13 lists God's capacity to "change his mind" as one of his fundamental attributes (see also Jon. 4:2), one cannot dismiss this characteristic as anthropomorphic. As Richard Rice states, "Formulations like these demonstrate that repentance is not an exceptional action on God's part, let alone something that is out of character for him. To the contrary, it is typical of God to relent from punishment. . . . In fact, it is his very nature to do so. Accordingly, God does not repent in spite of the fact that he is God; he repents precisely *because* he is God."[77]

However, Joel was not willing in this instance to presume upon God's grace and to guarantee that repentance would prompt God to relent. The Lord's call to repentance certainly made it seem as if this would be the case (see v. 12), but since the exhortation had no promise attached to it, one could not be entirely certain. For this reason, Joel asked, "Who knows?" before holding out the possibility of deliverance and renewed blessing (v. 14). God had given Joel a vision of impending doom, but it was not certain if this judgment had been decreed. Following the Lord's lead, Joel urged the people to repent with the hope that the threatened judgment would prove to be conditional and would be averted.[78]

Picking up on the second half of the Lord's exhortation (see v. 12b), Joel called for a formal assembly of the people in which they would fast and pray

76. See my discussion of Jer. 18:7–10, as well as Robert B. Chisholm Jr., "Does God Change His Mind?" *BSac* 152 (1995): 387–99. An abridged version of this article appears in *Kindred Spirit* 22, no. 2 (summer 1998): 4–5.

77. Richard Rice, "Biblical Support for a New Perspective," in *The Openness of God*, ed. C. Pinnock et al. (Downers Grove, Ill.: InterVarsity, 1994), 31.

78. King David responded in a similar fashion (2 Sam. 12:22) to Nathan's prophecy of judgment, which sounded unconditional but was not formally marked as such (2 Sam. 12:14). In this case David's lament was ineffective, for the prophecy proved to be a decree, making the prophesied judgment unconditional. The Ninevite king responded in a similar manner (Jon. 3:9) to Jonah's prophecy of Nineveh's judgment (Jon. 3:4). In this case the prophecy, though seemingly unconditional in tone, proved to be conditional, and God relented from judgment in response to the Ninevites' repentance (Jon. 3:10). This angered Jonah, who complained that such a response is typical of God (Jon. 4:2).

for God's deliverance (vv. 15–17). No one was exempt, not even nursing children or newlyweds. In their prayer for divine mercy, the people were to appeal to God's concern for his own reputation. If he punished his people and once again made them "an object of scorn," the nations might get the wrong impression about God, perhaps concluding that he was not interested in his people or was incapable of helping them. This type of prayer may seem like an attempt to manipulate God, but such arguments typically appear in the prayers of lamentation in the Hebrew Bible (Ps. 42:3; 79:10; see as well Exod. 32:12 and Ps. 74:11).

Mercy and a Promise (2:18–27)

Apparently the people responded positively to the prophet's warning, for verse 18 informs us that God's devotion (or "zeal") for his land was rekindled and that he took pity on his people.[79] The Lord would change from enemy to defender and drive the army he had been leading into the sea (v. 20). He also promised that he would restore the crops the locusts had devoured (vv. 19a, 21–22, 24–26a). In place of drought and famine, he would send the rains at the proper time (v. 23).[80] His people would acknowledge him as the only true God, and he would never again subject them to such humiliating judgment (vv. 19b, 26b–27).

God's people were subsequently humiliated on several occasions, making this promise sound rather hollow. However, just as God's warnings of judgment are often conditional and can be averted by repentance, so his promises of prosperity are often contingent on their recipients remaining loyal to God (see Jer. 18:7–10). The promise given here, while obviously implicitly conditional, was an honest statement of God's commitment to his people. If they had sustained their renewed devotion to him, he would sustain his blessings. As Allen remarks, "Here is expressed a divine desire, an implicit wish that the people for their part may be ever mindful of their obligations in return."[81]

An Outpouring of the Spirit (2:28–32)

The Lord moved beyond the immediate future and announced that sometime after the restoration of blessing depicted in verses 19–27 he would pour

79. As noted earlier, the verb forms in the Hebrew text are most naturally taken as narratival (contrary to NIV).

80. The significance of the Hebrew phrase translated "autumn rains in righteousness" by NIV is unclear. Since the word *moreh* can mean "teacher," some see a reference here to an eschatological figure, who is then labeled "the teacher of righteousness." This fanciful interpretation has no support from context or usage elsewhere in the Hebrew Bible. Others see a reference to "rain" (see the next line) as an "instructor in righteousness," in the sense that this restoration of divine blessing illustrates the important lesson that godly behavior pays off. However, it is more likely that *moreh* here refers to the "early rains," just as it does later in the verse and in Ps. 84:6. In this case the phrase "in righteousness" means "in accordance with what is proper," that is, in accordance with the covenantal principle that repentance brings restored blessing. See Leslie C. Allen, *Joel, Obadiah, Jonah, and Micah,* NICOT (Grand Rapids: Eerdmans, 1976), 93–94.

81. Ibid., 96. Allen finds an appropriate parallel in Deut. 5:29.

out his Spirit upon the covenant community (vv. 28–29). The reference to "all people" (literally, "all flesh") in verse 28 might suggest a worldwide outpouring of the divine Spirit, but the immediately following statement makes it clear that all classes of people within the covenant community are in view without regard to age, gender, or social status (see also Ezek. 39:29; Zech. 12:10). In the past the Spirit was given to a select few, primarily prophets. But this future outpouring of the Spirit would mark the dawning of a new era and fulfill the wish of Moses, who on one occasion told Joshua, "I wish that all the Lord's people were prophets and that the Lord would put his Spirit on them!" (Num. 11:29)

In conjunction with this outpouring of the Spirit, ominous signs in the heavens (the darkening of the luminaries) and on the earth (blood, fire, and smoke are all earmarks of warfare) would signal the approaching day of the Lord's judgment (vv. 30–31). However, the destruction of divine judgment would not be indiscriminate; all in Jerusalem who looked to the Lord in genuine faith would be delivered (v. 32). These loyal followers of the Lord are presumably the recipients of the Spirit described in verses 28–29.

According to the Apostle Peter, the prophecy of the outpouring of the Spirit was fulfilled, at least in part, on the day of Pentecost, when the Spirit of the Lord came upon a large crowd of Jews and supernaturally enabled them to speak in other languages (Acts 2:1–21).[82] Of course, many are quick to point out that the events described in Joel 2:30–32 did not occur at Pentecost. Was Peter wrong? Did he simply get carried away in his exuberance? Peter correctly saw the outpouring of the Spirit as initiating the fulfillment of the prophecy. He urged the people to repent so that the promise might be fully realized (see Acts 2:33, 38–39) and the "times of refreshing," culminating in the return of Jesus, might arrive (see 3:19–21). But the Jewish leadership rejected God's offer (Acts 4). Eventually, Peter came to realize that Jewish unbelief would delay Jesus' return and that Gentiles would also receive the gift of the Spirit (see Acts 10:44–48). In light of these later developments, we could say that the fulfillment of Joel's prophecy was suspended (the prophetic videotape is on "pause," as it were). However, since Jesus gives his Spirit to each new believer during the present era, it is probably better to view Joel 2:28–29 as being gradually fulfilled during this age, with verses 30–32 awaiting realization at the very end of the age (in this case the prophetic videotape is still moving forward, but in "slow motion"). Joel envisioned the outpouring of the Spirit as being confined to Jews, but in the progress of revelation and history, we discover that Gentiles are included as well, for they too are incorporated into the new covenant community.[83]

82. Note that Peter does not say this event is merely "like" the one prophesied by Joel. Instead he says, "This [the outpouring of the Spirit on Pentecost] is what was spoken by the prophet Joel" (Acts 2:16).

83. For a fuller discussion of how the new covenant promises find fulfillment in both the present age and in the age to come, see my comments on Jer. 31:31–34.

Payback Time (3:1–21)

While the day of the Lord would bring a restoration of Judah's and Jerusalem's fortunes, it would be a time of judgment for those who had taken God's people into exile and scattered them among the nations (vv. 1–3). This judgment would take place in "the Valley of Jehoshaphat" (see also v. 12), an otherwise unknown site.[84] The name is probably symbolic and chosen because its meaning, "The LORD judges," encapsulates what would transpire there. If, as the temporal references in verse 1 might suggest, this judgment occurs in conjunction with the culminating events depicted in 2:28–32, then the judgment cannot be literal, for the nations responsible for Judah's exile have disappeared from the scene. Rather than describing a literal day of judgment, it is more likely that the prophecy was fulfilled gradually throughout history as these nations and peoples passed from the scene.[85] In this case, one must understand the language of verse 1 ("in those days and at that time") as referring in a very general way to the entire time period following Joel's day. The use of "afterward" in 2:28 suggests as much. This means that Joel's vision of the future in chapter 3, like the prophecy in 2:28–32, encompasses events that actually occur over several centuries. Some of the vision has already been fulfilled, while other aspects of it await complete realization.[86]

In the aftermath of Jerusalem's fall to the Babylonians in 586 B.C., some of the surrounding peoples, including the Phoenicians and Philistines, had exploited the situation by looting Judah's wealth and selling refugees into slavery (vv. 4–6).[87] But the Lord would turn the tables on these greedy foreigners. The people of Judah would someday sell the descendants of the Phoenicians and Philistines as slaves (vv. 7–8). If, as suggested above, one can understand the judgment prophesied in verses 2–3 as being gradually realized in history, then this prophecy may have been fulfilled in the fourth century B.C. in conjunction with the conquests of Alexander the Great.[88]

Joel now dramatizes the coming judgment of the nations. He summons both the nations and the Lord to meet for battle (vv. 9–11). The Lord then speaks, challenging the nations to congregate in the Valley of Jehoshaphat for judgment (v. 12). Comparing the nations to a ripe harvest and grapes in a winepress, the Lord commands his warriors to "swing the sickle" and "trample the grapes" (v. 13). The prophet describes the scene as the nations

---

84. For a survey of attempts to locate this valley, see Dillard, "Joel," 300–301.

85. This is not to imply that Joel's generation would have understood the prophecy in this way. Based on the description given in chapter 3, they probably would have anticipated a single event when God judged all the nations for their atrocities against Judah.

86. See as a paradigm the prophecy in 1 Kings 14:10–16, which was fulfilled in stages spanning approximately two hundred years (see 1 Kings 14:17–18; 15:25–30; 2 Kings 17:7–23).

87. The "Greeks" mentioned in v. 6 were actually Ionians who lived along the coast of Asia Minor and traded with Phoenician cities during the sixth century B.C. See Arvid S. Kapelrud, *Joel Studies* (Uppsala: A. B. Lundequistska Bokhandeln, 1948), 154, as well as Ezek. 27:13, 19.

88. See Allen, *Joel, Obadiah, Jonah, and Micah,* 114.

crowd into the "valley of decision" (v. 14). The luminaries grow dark (v. 15; see 2:31), and the Lord emerges like a roaring lion from Jerusalem, causing the entire cosmos to shake before him (v. 16a). But his people need not fear, for he comes to protect them from their enemies (v. 16b; see 2:32). Though the nations are clearly identified earlier in the chapter with those responsible for Judah's exile and humiliation (see vv. 2–3), the cosmic dimension of the judgment and the thematic links with 2:30–32 suggest that Joel's vision may go beyond God's historical judgments upon the Phoenicians, Philistines, and other ancient peoples and depict the culminating judgment of the nations.[89]

God's intervention would vividly demonstrate to his people that he has set Jerusalem apart and made it his special dwelling place (v. 17a). Foreigners would never again invade the city (v. 17b), and Judah would be agriculturally prosperous once more (v. 18). This stylized, hyperbolic vision of the future pictures wine and milk flowing down the hillsides, seasonal streams flowing with water, and a fountain, symbolizing life and fertility, rising up from the temple and flowing through the "valley of acacias," the precise location of which is uncertain. (For similar visions, see Ezek. 47:1–12 and Zech. 14:8.) Since acacias typically grow in dry regions, the vision depicts a transformation of arid terrain.

By way of contrast, Egypt and Edom, the traditional enemies of God's people, would remain desolate, for both had oppressed and exploited Israel (v. 19). The text alludes here to Edomite atrocities in the aftermath of the Babylonian invasion of Judah in 586 B.C. (see Obad.) and perhaps also to Pharaoh Necho's invasion of Judah not long before that (see 2 Kings 23:29–35). Jerusalem and Judah would be inhabited (v. 20) and enjoy the safety afforded by the Lord's presence (v. 21b), but Egypt and Edom would pay for their crimes (v. 21a). The NIV translation of verse 21a makes it sound as if the Lord was announcing that he would forgive Judah and Jerusalem. However, it is more likely that "their bloodguilt" refers to the crimes committed by Egypt and Edom against Judah (see v. 19). It makes better sense to translate verse 21a: "And shall I let their shed blood [i.e., the shed blood of God's people] go unpunished? I will not let it go unpunished!"[90] This aspect of the prophecy may refer to Edom's eventual downfall and Egypt's decline in power and influence. If one insists that the situation described in verse 19 be coterminous with the ultimate restoration of Judah depicted in the immediate context, then the fulfillment must be viewed as essential, not exact, with Egypt and Edom being archetypal.[91] In this case, rather than de-

89. For this same technique, see Isa. 13–14, 24–27, and 34.

90. For a defense of this proposal and a slightly different translation of the statement, see Allen, *Joel, Obadiah, Jonah, and Micah*, 117.

91. Note that other prophets describe Egypt's eschatological situation differently. Isa. 19:19–25 depicts the Egyptians as full-fledged worshipers of the Lord, while Zech. 14:18–19 makes divine blessing accessible to Egypt, but contingent upon their worshiping the Lord.

scribing literal geopolitical realities of this future age, the text makes the point that the restored Israel of the future will be dominant on the world scene and safe from the threats of potentially hostile nations.[92]

A Lion Roars (Amos)

Introduction

The heading to the book states that Amos prophesied at a time when Uzziah ruled over Judah and Jeroboam II reigned over Israel. Uzziah, after a long co-regency with his father Amaziah, ruled Judah from 767–740 B.C., while Jeroboam II, who also served as a co-regent for a time, was independent ruler of Israel from 782–753 B.C. Thus it would appear that Amos's ministry took place between 767–753 B.C. The heading also informs us that Amos prophesied two years before a particularly well-known earthquake. There appears to be archaeological evidence at Hazor for an earthquake during this general time period, though it is impossible to pinpoint its date.[93]

The Book of Amos exhibits a macrostructure of sorts. Following the heading and introductory portrayal of the Lord as judge (1:1–2), a series of judgment oracles appears (1:3–2:16), each of which begins with the words, "For three sins of [name of city or state], even for four, I will not turn back my wrath." The list culminates with the northern kingdom, Israel. The prophet then delivers three judgment speeches to Israel, each of which begins with the summons, "Hear this word" (3:1–15; 4:1–13; 5:1–17). Two woe oracles lend strength to these speeches (5:18–27; 6:1–14). A series of visions follows (7:1–9; 8:1–3), with a biographical account of the prophet's encounter with Amaziah, the priest of Bethel, inserted between the third and fourth visions (7:10–17). The first, second, and fourth visions begin with the words, "this is what the Sovereign LORD showed me," while the third begins simply, "this is what he showed me." The final section of the book contains a judgment speech (8:4–14), another vision (simply introduced with "I saw") to which a judgment speech is attached (9:1–10), and a portrait of a time beyond the coming judgment when God would restore the prestige and prosperity of his covenant people (9:11–15).

A Bad Omen (1:1–2)

The book's heading not only tells us when Amos prophesied, but it also provides validation for his ministry. Amos was not a prophet by profession; he was a herdsman and vinedresser (see 7:14) who lived in Tekoa, located in Judah about five miles south of Bethlehem. Yet the Lord commissioned him

---

92. See my comments on Isa. 11:13–14 and Amos 9:12.

93. See Philip J. King, *Amos, Hosea, Micah—An Archaeological Commentary* (Philadelphia: Westminster, 1988), 21.

to travel to the northern kingdom and to warn Israel of impending judgment (see 7:15). By giving Amos's occupation and hometown, the heading authenticates his ministry. After all, why would anyone leave his job, travel to hostile territory, and incite the authorities there with an unpopular message (see 7:10–17), if he were not called by God?

The reference to the earthquake also authenticates Amos's message. In this culture an earthquake would not have been viewed as a mere natural occurrence, but as an omen of judgment. Amos had warned that the Lord would shake the earth (see 8:8; 9:1, 5, as well as 4:12–13). When the earthquake occurred just two years after he delivered his message, it signaled that the Lord was ready to make the words of Amos a reality.

The introductory verse (v. 2) reinforces this by depicting the Lord as a roaring lion (see 3:8). The Lord's powerful roar, which emanates from his temple in Jerusalem, not only makes the earth shake, but also shrivels up the vegetation growing in the pasturelands and well-wooded regions (like Carmel). This image of drought suggests an accursed condition, brought about by divine judgment (see Deut. 28:23–24).

Placing the Noose around Israel's Neck (1:3–2:16)

The people of the northern kingdom anticipated the arrival of the day of the Lord (see Amos 5:18). They expected it to be a glorious day when the Lord would defeat the surrounding nations, ushering in a new era of prosperity for Israel. Indeed, Jeroboam II, the king of Israel during this time, set out to revive Israel's fortunes and, with the Lord's approval, achieved great success in this regard (see 2 Kings 14:25–28). At first, Amos's oracles of judgment seem to reflect Israel's optimism. He announced that the Lord was coming to judge the surrounding nations. The litany of judgment starts with outright foreigners (the Arameans, Philistines, Phoenicians), moves to distant relatives (the Edomites, Ammonites, and Moabites),[94] and appears to culminate with Judah, Israel's brother to the immediate south. Judah, the seventh nation mentioned, seems to cap off the list, making it complete. Israel must have delighted in the news that Judah was to be judged, for the two kingdoms had engaged in military hostilities shortly before this (see 2 Kings 13:12; 14:8–14), and Judah was now flexing its muscles under King Uzziah (see 2 Chron. 26).

But all was not as it appeared. Jeroboam was an evil king who persisted in the sins of his ancestors (2 Kings 14:23–24). Though the Lord used him to bring his suffering people some relief, Israel's renewed strength would be temporary. Suddenly Amos expands his list from seven to eight by adding Israel. Despite what the people thought, the approaching day of the Lord

---

94. The Edomites were descendants of Esau (see Gen. 36), while the Ammonites and Moabites were the offspring of Lot (Gen. 19:30–38).

would be a time of darkness, not light, for Israel. Rather than being the beneficiary of the Lord's judgment on the surrounding nations, Israel would be the focal point of the Lord's anger.

A close reading of the oracles shows that the prophet was hinting at this all along. Each of the oracles begins with the formula "For three sins of [name of city or state], even for four, I will not turn back my wrath."[95] Based on structural parallels with proverbial statements that use the "three, even four" numerical pattern (see Prov. 30:15–16, 18–19, 21–23, 29–31), one expects to find a list of four specific sins in each oracle. But this never happens in the first seven oracles. After specifying one or two sins, the prophet breaks off the list, announces judgment, and then moves on to the next nation as if the real target of God's anger lies somewhere else. This stylistic device does not become a bad omen for Israel until the list of Judah's sins is left truncated, suggesting that another nation, which proves to be Israel, will follow.

The oracles may be outlined as follows:

1. Oracle against Damascus (the Arameans) (1:3–5)
   a. Introductory formula (1:3a)
   b. Sin list (1:3b; *one sin* listed)
      "Because *she threshed* Gilead with sledges having iron teeth"
   c. Announcement of judgment (1:4–5)

2. Oracle against Gaza (the Philistines)(1:6–8)
   a. Introductory formula (1:6a)
   b. Sin list (1:6b; *one sin* listed)
      "Because *she took captive* whole communities in order to sell them to Edom"[96]
   c. Announcement of judgment (1:7–8)

3. Oracle against Tyre (the Phoenicians)(1:9–10)
   a. Introductory formula (1:9a)
   b. Sin list (1:9b; *two sins* listed)
      (1) "Because *she sold* whole communities of captives to Edom,
      (2) *disregarding* a treaty of brotherhood."
   c. Announcement of judgment (1:10)

95. The introductory formula reads literally, "For three sins of [name of city or state], even for four, I will not bring it [or "him"] back." The referent of the pronominal object on the verb "bring back" is uncertain. The NIV assumes that it refers to God's anger (see Isa. 5:25; 9:12, 17, 21; 10:4). The expression "turn back anger" does appear elsewhere (see Ezra 10:14; Job 9:13; Ps. 78:38; 85:3; Prov. 24:18; 29:8), though "anger" is not specifically mentioned here. The pronoun may refer to the following decree of judgment or to the punishment announced therein. (See Shalom M. Paul, *Amos,* Hermeneia [Minneapolis: Fortress, 1991], 46–47.) In this case the formula apparently marks the announced judgment as an irreversible, unconditional decree. Another option is to understand the pronoun as referring to the city or state mentioned, "I will not take him back." (See Michael L. Barré, "The Meaning of *l' sybnw* in Amos 1:3–2:6," *JBL* 105 [1986]: 622.) In this case, the Lord announces that he will not resume treaty relations with the city/state that is mentioned.

96. NIV reads "and sold them to Edom," but this line is introduced with an infinitive construct indicating a purpose clause that is subordinate to the preceding main clause. Since two actions (kidnapping and slave trade) are described, one could see two sins here, but the grammatical structure suggests that one crime, comprised of two related actions, is in view.

4. Oracle against Edom (1:11–12)
    a. Introductory formula (1:11a)
    b. Sin list (1:11b; *two sins* listed with emphasis)[97]
        (1) "Because *he pursued* his brother with a sword,
            and *wiped out* his allies;[98]
        (2) because his anger *raged* continually
            and his fury *flamed* unchecked."
    c. Announcement of judgment (1:12)

5. Oracle against Ammon (1:13–15)
    a. Introductory formula (1:13a)
    b. Sin list (1:13b; *one sin* listed)
    "Because *he ripped open* the pregnant women of Gilead in order to extend his borders."[99]
    c. Announcement of judgment (1:14–15)

6. Oracle against Moab (2:1–3)
    a. Introductory formula (2:1a)
    b. Sin list (2:1b; *one sin* listed)
    "Because *he burned,* as if to lime, the bones of Edom's king."
    c. Announcement of judgment (2:2–3)

7. Oracle against Judah (2:4–5)
    a. Introductory formula (2:4a)
    b. Sin list (2:4b; *two sins* listed with emphasis)[100]
        (1) "Because *they have rejected* the law of the LORD and have not kept his decrees,
        (2) because *they have been led astray* by false gods, the gods their ancestors followed."
    c. Announcement of judgment (2:5)

8. Oracle against Israel (2:6–16)
    a. Introductory formula (2:6a)
    b. Sin list with intervening reminder of God's kind deeds (2:6b–12; *four sins* listed with emphasis)[101]
        (1) "*They sell* the righteous for silver,
            and the needy for a pair of sandals—
            those who[102] trample on the heads
                of the poor as upon
            the dust of the ground and deny justice to the oppressed.

97. Only two sins are listed, but the repetition through synonymous parallelism emphasizes Edom's crimes.

98. NIV reads, "stifling all compassion," but the text is better interpreted as a second reference to Edom's hostility toward its former allies. See the discussion on these verses in the commentary that follows.

99. Since two actions (wartime atrocities and imperialism) are described, one could see two sins here, but the grammatical structure suggests that one crime, comprised of two related actions, is in view.

100. Only two sins are listed, but the repetition through synonymous parallelism emphasizes Judah's crimes.

101. The synonymous parallelism used throughout vv. 6b–8, 12 emphasizes Israel's crimes.

102. NIV reads, "they trample," but the Hebrew form is actually a substantival participle that identifies the subject of the verb "they sell."

> (2) Father and son *use* the same girl
> and so profane my holy name.[103]
> (3) *They lie down* beside every altar on garments taken in
> pledge.
> In the house of their god *they drink* wine taken as
> fines. . . .[104]
> (4) But *you made* the Nazirites *drink* wine
> and *commanded* the prophets not to prophesy."[105]
> c. Announcement of judgment (2:13–16)

The oracles view the nations as subjects of the Lord who have violated a covenant with him. The noun translated "sins" in the introductory formula refers to "acts of rebellion" against one in authority (see its use in 1 Kings 12:19; 2 Kings 1:1; 3:5, 7; 8:22). The use of this noun suggests that the cities/states addressed are viewed as rebellious subjects who violated the covenant stipulations of their divine king. This is readily apparent in the case of Judah and Israel, who had broken the law of Moses, but what covenantal arrangement with the God of Israel had the surrounding nations violated? Some suggest that the nations had offended the Lord by attacking Israel, but atrocities committed against Israel are specifically mentioned only in the oracles against Damascus and Ammon (1:3, 13). The Moabite king is denounced for committing crimes against Edom, not Israel (see 2:1). It is more likely that the Noahic mandate, recorded in Genesis 9:5–7, provides the background for the Lord's indictment. In the mandate to Noah (which applies, by extension, to the entire human race), the Lord prohibited murder because it represents a blatant attack upon the image of God in man. Each of the nations indicted in Amos 1–2 had violated this mandate, at least in principle, by committing atrocities in conjunction with their imperialistic wars against their neighbors.[106]

An Oracle against Damascus (1:3–5)

The first oracle indicts Damascus, the capital city of the Arameans, who lived to the northeast of Israel. The Lord would judge the Arameans because of the atrocities they had committed against Gilead, located on the eastern side of the Jordan River. Perhaps he alludes to the Aramean invasion of Gilead during the second half of the ninth century b.c. (see 2 Kings 10:32–33). The Lord compared the Arameans' deeds to threshing "with sledges hav-

---

103. Since two actions (using the same girl and profaning the Lord's name) are described, one could see two sins here, but the grammatical structure suggests that one crime, comprised of two related actions, is in view.

104. Again two actions (lying down and drinking) are described, but one crime, abusing the system of pledges and fines, is in view.

105. Once more, two actions (making the Nazirites drink wine and forbidding the prophets to speak) are described, but one crime, disrespect for religious leaders, is in view.

106. See as well my comments on Isa. 24:5, another passage that appears to hold nations responsible for infractions of the mandate to Noah.

ing iron teeth."[107] The imagery comes from the threshing floor, where a wooden board with sharp nails embedded on the underside was pulled over the grain in order to separate the grain from the husk.[108]

Several proper names mentioned in verses 4–5 require comment. Hazael was the king of Damascus for most of the second half of the ninth century B.C., while the Ben-hadad mentioned here may have been his son and successor (2 Kings 13:3, 22–25).[109] The "Valley of Aven," which means "Valley of Evil," is probably a derogatory name for the Biq'ah Valley in Lebanon, while "Beth Eden" probably refers to Bit Adini, an Aramean state located on the Euphrates River two hundred miles to the north-northeast of Damascus.[110] The references thus provide the southern and northern limits of the Aramean kingdom. Finally, Kir, the precise location of which is unknown, was the original home of the Arameans (see Amos 9:7).[111] In the aftermath of the Arameans' defeat, they would be deported back to Kir. This prophecy was fulfilled in 732 B.C. when the Assyrian king Tiglath-pileser III conquered Damascus (2 Kings 16:9).

An Oracle against Philistia (1:6–8)

The Lord would also judge the Philistines, who lived to the southwest of Israel along the Mediterranean coast. Four of the five major Philistine towns are mentioned here (Gath being conspicuous by its absence, but see 6:2). The Philistines had conducted raids on neighboring communities (probably in Judah; see 2 Chron. 21:16–17; 28:18), kidnapped the people, and sold them to the Edomites as slaves. For this reason, God's judgment of fire would sweep through Philistine territory, bringing thorough destruction in its wake. This prophecy was fulfilled later in the eighth century when the Judahite kings Uzziah and Hezekiah invaded Philistia (see 2 Chron. 26:6–7; 2 Kings 18:8) and when a succession of Assyrian conquerors captured these towns.[112] Tiglath-pileser III (who ruled from 745–727 B.C.) listed Ashkelon and Gaza among his subjects, while Sargon II conquered Ashdod in 712 B.C. and made it an Assyrian province. In 701 B.C., Sennacherib deported the disloyal king of Ashkelon and conducted a successful campaign against Ekron.

107. Other passages compare military conquest to threshing. See 2 Kings 13:7; Isa. 41:15; Mic. 4:13; Hab. 3:12.

108. See Borowski, *Agriculture in Iron Age Israel,* 64–65.

109. For a detailed study of these two kings, see Pitard, *Ancient Damascus,* 145–75.

110. See Paul, *Amos,* 52–54, as well as Francis I. Andersen and David N. Freedman, *Amos,* AB (New York: Doubleday, 1989), 255–56. Some prefer to understand Beth Eden, which could be taken to mean "House of Pleasure," as a sarcastic title for the Aramean king's palace.

111. Kir was apparently located in Mesopotamia. Isa. 22:6 mentions Kir along with Elam, which was located east of Babylon. See Paul, *Amos,* 55, and Andersen and Freedman, *Amos,* 257.

112. For accounts of the Assyrian victories in the west, see Pritchard, *Ancient Near Eastern Texts,* 282–88, as well as King, *Amos, Hosea, Micah—An Archaeological Commentary,* 52–54.

An Oracle against Tyre (1:9–10)

Divine judgment would also fall on the city-state of Tyre, located north of Israel on the Mediterranean coast. Like the Philistines, Tyre had kidnapped entire communities and sold the people to Edom as slaves. Tyre's crime was even more reprehensible because it involved breaking a treaty. The phrase "treaty of brotherhood" refers to a parity treaty between Tyre and an unidentified neighboring state. In the ancient Near East, neighboring kings would sometimes establish such treaties in the interests of trade and national security. Biblical examples include the agreement between Hiram of Tyre and Solomon (1 Kings 9:13) and the treaty between Ben-hadad of Damascus and Ahab (2 Kings 20:32–33). Such treaties were to be characterized by peaceful relations.[113] When and how this prophecy was fulfilled is not clear. Though many kings attacked and besieged Tyre, the city was not actually destroyed until 332 B.C., when Alexander the Great conquered it.

An Oracle against Edom (1:11–12)

The Lord next turns his attention to Edom, already implicated in the slave trade denounced in the two preceding oracles. Like Tyre, Edom violated a treaty of brotherhood as it ruthlessly turned on its former partner with unbridled rage. Because Esau, the progenitor of the Edomites, was Jacob's brother, some see Israel or Judah as the referent of "his brother." However, it seems more likely that the term "brother" is used in its idiomatic sense of "treaty partner" (as in v. 9). The parallel line (translated by NIV, "stifling all compassion") supports this interpretation as well. The Hebrew term translated "compassion" by NIV is better understood here as a reference to Edom's "allies."[114] As in the case of Tyre, the precise details of when and how this prophecy was fulfilled remain unclear, but Edom had apparently been devastated by the time of Malachi (see Mal. 1:3), perhaps by the Babylonians.[115]

An Oracle against Ammon (1:13–15)

Ammon too had violated the Lord's moral standard and would experience his fierce judgment. In an effort to extend their border into Gilead (located just north of Ammon), the Ammonites had committed genocidal acts

---

113. See, for example, the parity treaty made between Rameses II of Egypt and the Hittite king Hattusilis. See Pritchard, *Ancient Near Eastern Texts*, 199.

114. See Michael Fishbane, "The Treaty Background of Amos 1, 11 and Related Matters," *JBL* 89 (1970): 313–18, and the same author's "Additional Remarks on *rḥmyw* (Amos 1:11)," *JBL* 91 (1972): 391–93. See as well Michael L. Barré, "Amos 1:11 Reconsidered," *CBQ* 47(1985): 420–27. Andersen and Freedman (*Amos*, 266–67) translate "allies," but see this as a double entendre referring to Israel/Judah and reflecting "both kinship and covenantal associations." Still another option is offered by Paul (*Amos*, 43, 64–65), who understands the term as referring to young women (he relates the form to the term found in Judg. 5:30) and translates "womenfolk."

115. See Kenneth G. Hoglund, "Edomites," in *Peoples of the Old Testament World*, ed. A. J. Hoerth, G. L. Mattingly, and E. M. Yamauchi (Grand Rapids: Baker, 1994), 342.

against the residents of Gilead (probably Israelites). They even resorted to ripping open pregnant women. This form of military atrocity is mentioned elsewhere in the Hebrew Bible (see 2 Kings 8:11–12; 15:16; Hos. 13:16) and in ancient Near Eastern literature.[116] Ammon's capital, Rabbah, would be burned with fire as the storm of divine judgment swept through her fortresses. The Ammonite king and his royal court would be taken into exile. Once again the precise details of the prophecy's fulfillment escape us, but the Babylonians apparently conquered Ammon in the sixth century B.C.[117]

An Oracle against Moab (2:1–3)

Moab is next in the series of judgment oracles. The Moabites were guilty of desecrating an Edomite royal tomb. They took the bones of one of Edom's deceased kings and burned them into ashes. Modern readers may not fully appreciate the implications of such an action, which would have been viewed in ancient Palestine as an extreme measure expressing intense hostility (see 2 Kings 23:15–16). Receiving a proper burial was considered very important in this culture, and tombs were protected by curses inscribed on them.[118] This atrocity epitomized the Moabites' hatred and cruelty. The Lord would devastate Moab and destroy her leaders. As with the prophecies against Edom and Ammon, precise details of the oracle's fulfillment are unavailable, but Moab did fall to the Babylonians in the sixth century B.C.[119]

An Oracle against Judah (2:4–5)

The prophet moved closer to home as he turned to Israel's neighbor to the south and announced Judah's impending judgment. Just as the pagan nations had violated their covenantal relationship with God, so Judah had broken the Mosaic covenant, which God made with his people at Mount Sinai. It is not clear what specific violation(s) Amos had in mind. The Hebrew text of verse 4b reads literally, "their lies, after which their fathers walked, have led them astray." Most identify these "lies" as false gods or idols. Though the Hebrew term does not refer to idols or gods elsewhere in the Hebrew Bible, the expression "walk after" is used of idolatry in several texts (see, for example, Deut. 6:14; 8:19; 13:3; 28:14; Judg. 2:12). Because "lies" more commonly refer to false prophecies, others prefer to identify the "lies" as the misleading words of false prophets.[120]

116. See Mordechai Cogan, " 'Ripping Open Pregnant Women' in Light of an Assyrian Analogue," *JAOS* 103 (1983): 755–57.
117. See Randall W. Younker, "Ammonites," in Hoerth, Mattingly, and Yamauchi, *Peoples of the Old Testament World*, 314.
118. For examples of such tomb inscriptions containing curses upon violators, see Pritchard, *Ancient Near Eastern Texts*, 661–62.
119. See Gerald L. Mattingly, "Moabites," in Hoerth, Mattingly, and Yamauchi, *Peoples of the Old Testament World*, 328.
120. See Andersen and Freedman, *Amos*, 301–6.

An Oracle against Israel (2:6–16)

The litany of judgment culminates with Israel. A royal military bureaucracy ruled Israel at this time. As this bureaucracy expanded, it acquired more and more land and gradually commandeered the economy and legal system. At various administrative levels, it invited bribery and other dishonest practices. The common people outside the administrative centers, through confiscatory taxation, conscription, excessive interest rates, and other oppressive measures, were gradually disenfranchised and lost their landed property and, with it, their means of survival and their rights as citizens.

Amos denounced such oppressive practices, which included selling debtors as slaves and denying the poor any kind of legal recourse (vv. 6b–7a). The oppressors seized the very clothes of the poor as collateral for debts and exacted taxes from the people in the form of wine (v. 8).[121] Having virtually extorted these items from the poor, they had the audacity to take them along when they went to offer sacrifices. It is not clear if verse 8 refers to "their God" (that is, the Lord), in which case hypocrisy is the crime in view, or to "their gods" (that is, pagan gods), in which case they compounded the sin of social injustice with idolatry.

It is unclear how verse 7b fits into the prophet's indictment. The Hebrew text reads literally, "a man and his father go to the young woman, thereby profaning my holy name." Most understand this statement as referring to a father and son having sexual relations with the same girl, usually understood to be a slave, a member of the oppressed poor class, or a cult prostitute. However, the Hebrew expression translated "go to" (Heb. *halak 'el*, in contrast to the idiom *bo' 'el*, "come to") is never used elsewhere in the Hebrew Bible of sexual intercourse. It seems more likely that this verse alludes to the pagan *marzeah*-banquet, an institution alluded to in Amos 6:4–7 (see also Jer. 16:5–9) and referred to elsewhere in ancient literature.[122] The *marzeah*-banquet was apparently a sort of religious social club where wealthy patrons would eat and drink to excess, perhaps in conjunction with mourning ceremonies for the deceased. According to Barstad, the "young woman" mentioned here was the hostess of such a banquet.[123] In this view, verse 7b, rather than denouncing sexual promiscuity, pictures a father and son attending such a banquet. Their presence there epitomizes the kind of lifestyle they enjoy at the expense of the poor and illustrates their willingness to assimilate pagan customs.

---

121. On the socioeconomic background of these verses, see Dearman, *Property Rights*, 19–25. Such practices are also alluded to in 2 Kings 4:1–7. For an extrabiblical text referring to illegal seizure of a garment, see Pritchard, *Ancient Near Eastern Texts*, 568, and Simon B. Parker, *Stories in Scripture and Inscriptions* (New York: Oxford University Press, 1997), 15–18.

122. See King, *Amos, Hosea, Micah*, 137–61, where he discusses the background of Amos 6:4–7. King does not interpret Amos 2:7b against this background, however.

123. Hans M. Barstad, *The Religious Polemics of Amos* (Leiden: Brill, 1984), 33–36.

Before concluding his indictment, the Lord rehearsed Israel's past, recalling how he had delivered them from Egypt, preserved them through the wilderness, and defeated the powerful Amorites so that Israel might occupy the Promised Land (vv. 9–10). He also raised up prophets, through whom he revealed his will to the nation, and Nazirites, whose religious vows (see Num. 6:2–21) provided a model of dedication to the Lord (v. 11). But the nation was ungrateful; the people tried to silence the prophets and encouraged the Nazirites to violate their vow of abstinence by drinking wine (v. 12). The sinful nation had become a heavy burden to the Lord, who is depicted as groaning under the weight of their sin, just as a cart creaks and groans when weighted down with a load of grain (v. 13).[124]

For all of these reasons, divine judgment would fall on Israel. The Lord skipped over the formal announcement of divine intervention and moved right to a description of the effects of judgment. Verses 14–16 contain seven descriptive statements, suggesting that the judgment would be thorough and complete. Israel's army, including swift infantry, archers, and horsemen, would be entirely destroyed.

Mangled Sheep and Broken Altars (3:1–15)

God's people, whom he had delivered from bondage in Egypt, occupied a privileged position among the nations of the world. The Lord had chosen them as his special covenant people (vv 1–2a).[125] He expected them to be a model society characterized by social justice. By obeying God's commandments, they would magnify both the Lord and his law among the nations (see Deut. 4:5–8). But God's people failed, and so the Lord would punish them for their sins (v. 2b). To whom much is given, much is required.

Before describing the coming judgment, Amos first validated his message and his role as God's prophetic spokesman. He asked a series of rhetorical questions that establish the principle of cause and effect. The questions in verses 3–5 expect the answer, "No, of course not!" The question in verse 6a expects the answer, "Yes, of course!" The question in verse 6b (which is the seventh in the list) makes the point that a cause-effect pattern is also at work when calamity overtakes a city. When disaster falls on a city, the Lord is the cause behind it. This probably refers to the impending disaster prophesied by Amos, though it may also allude to judgments that had already

---

124. The meaning of verse 13 is notoriously difficult. I am assuming that the Hiphil verb form is intransitive and that the root is related to an Arabic cognate meaning "groan." In this case one may translate, "I groan beneath you, just as a cart filled with grain groans." Many commentators prefer to see this statement as an announcement of judgment, rather than a comment on the nation's sin (see Paul, *Amos,* 94, for a survey of opinion). The NIV ("I will crush you as a cart crushes") reflects such an understanding of the verse.

125. The Hebrew text reads literally, "Only you have I known." This obviously does not mean that God was aware of only Israel. The verb "know" is here used in the sense of "recognize in a special way," which by metonymy can mean "choose" (see NIV).

fallen. (See 4:6–11, especially the reference to famine in every city in v. 6.) Apparently the people, because of their fundamental misunderstanding of the upcoming day of the Lord (see 5:18–20), thought they were immune to judgment (see 9:10). But within the theocratic context of ancient Israel, disaster could indeed come as the result of sin, and one could be certain that if it did, the Lord was the source.[126]

The images in verses 3–6 are carefully chosen. The unit begins with a picture of two people walking along together, but this peaceful image is suddenly replaced by visions of lions roaring, birds being ensnared, and disaster overtaking a city. But the God who decrees disastrous judgment is also merciful and typically reveals his intentions before sending destruction. He does so through his prophetic servants, like Amos (v. 7). When God, depicted here as a roaring lion (v. 8; see 1:2), announces impending judgment, the proper response is fear, which implies repentance in this context. As for the prophet, he has no alternative but to proclaim what the Lord has spoken (v. 8).

Having made it clear that he spoke by divine compulsion, Amos was ready to proclaim the Lord's word. With a touch of sarcasm, the Lord invited the Philistines (see the reference to Ashdod, one of the Philistines' major cities) and Egyptians to assemble on the mountains of Samaria to witness the social injustice among God's people (v. 9). Issuing such an invitation to these two groups was appropriate, for both were traditional oppressors of God's people. They would certainly enjoy viewing the cruelty that characterized Israelite society. This invitation is biting, for it suggests that the Israelites shared the same immoral character with these hated pagans. (It would be like an opponent of abortion inviting Hitler and his Nazi cohorts to come and view the butchery taking place in America's abortion "clinics." Such a rhetorical technique would strongly imply that the "clinics" are similar to the ovens of Auschwitz.)

The Lord denounced the greed of the rich oppressors, who hoarded wealth taken from their victims (v. 10). Appropriately, an enemy would overrun the land and take away these riches (v. 11). The oppressors would discover firsthand what it feels like to be robbed. The judgment would be devastating, comparable to when a lion rips a sheep to bits. When that happened, a shepherd tried to salvage a bone or piece of an ear to prove to his employer that the missing sheep was indeed killed, not stolen (see Exod. 22:13). In the aftermath of God's judgment, Israel would resemble such an animal.[127]

126. Verse 6 should not be understood as teaching divine pancausality. Fredrik Lindström observes: "The intention of the passage in *Amos 3,6b* is to force its audience to recognize the connexion between YHWH's actions and the catastrophes which affected Northern Israel. . . . there is nothing in the text to suggest that the prophet attempts to assign all disasters in general to the agency of YHWH." See his *God and the Origin of Evil* (Lund: CWK Gleerup, 1983), 237.

127. The irony is especially apparent in the Hebrew text. The verb translated "saves" and "saved" often carries a positive connotation "to rescue," but here it simply means "to salvage." Israel would not be "rescued" from the coming judgment; only a ripped and shredded remnant would be "salvaged."

Addressing the Philistines and Egyptians again, the Lord invited them to be witnesses against his people (v. 13). As experts in brutality, they would certainly know injustice when they saw it. By placing them in the position of witnesses, the Lord implied that they were morally superior to Israel.

The Lord's judgment would target the "altars of Bethel," the "horns" of which would be "cut off" (v. 14). The Israelites thought that their religious tradition, in which Bethel played such an important role, and their religious rituals would insulate them from judgment. But this startling announcement indicates otherwise. Despite its glorious past (see Gen. 28), Bethel was the scene of hypocritical religious formalism (see 4:4) and would be devastated in the coming judgment (see 5:5–6). The "horns" of an altar were the projections on its four corners.[128] Fugitives seeking asylum could grab hold of the horns of an altar and be granted justice and safety (see Exod. 21:14; 1 Kings 1:50–51; 2:28). By depicting the altar's horns being cut off, the Lord made it clear that Israel would find no place of asylum from the coming judgment.

The Lord would also demolish the fine homes of Israel's wealthy class, which they had built and decorated at the expense of their victims (v. 15). These homes had ivory paneling and were decorated with furniture containing ivory inlays.[129] Some of the rich had both winter and summer houses, a luxury usually limited to kings in the ancient Near East.[130] Even some kings did not have two palaces. In a West Semitic inscription dating to the eighth century b.c., King Barrakab of Samal refers to his predecessors having only a single palace, which had to serve as both their summer house and winter house.[131]

Persistence in Sin (4:1–13)

Continuing his verbal attack against the rich, the prophet turned to the wives of the wealthy bureaucrats who lived in Samaria. He sarcastically addressed them as "cows of Bashan." Like the livestock raised in the trans-Jordanian region of Bashan (see Deut. 32:14; Ps. 22:12; Ezek. 39:18), these women were well-fed by their husbands, who satisfied their greedy wives' cravings by exploiting the poor of the land (v. 1). Of course, the metaphor is dripping with irony, for the implication is that these "cows of Bashan" were being fattened for slaughter. Utilizing a different metaphor, the prophet pictured a time when these women would be hauled away into exile like fish packed in containers and sent off to the market place (vv. 2–3). Though the precise meaning of verse 2b is not entirely clear, S. Paul makes a good case

128. For a picture of such an altar, see King, *Amos, Hosea, Micah,* 103.
129. See ibid., 139.
130. See ibid., 64–65.
131. See Pritchard, *Ancient Near Eastern Texts,* 501.

for the following translation, "you shall be transported in baskets, And the very last one of you, in fishermen's pots."[132]

The sarcastic tone of the speech intensifies as the Lord instructs sinful Israel to go to Bethel and Gilgal and sin (v. 4a). The Lord, of course, did not really want his people to sin, but he uses biting sarcasm here to make a point. The people were fond of visiting traditional worship centers like Bethel and Gilgal and making offerings to God (vv. 4b–5). They thought this kind of religious ritual would win God's favor and ensure his blessing. By calling such practices "sin," the Lord made it clear that their religion was nothing but empty and hypocritical. Until they rejected their unjust socioeconomic practices, he would reject their attempts to worship him (see 5:21–24).

The Lord next recalled his failed attempts to get Israel's attention (vv. 6–11). The Mosaic law warned that persistent disobedience would bring judgment in the form of famine, drought, crop failure, locusts, contagious diseases, and military setbacks (see Lev. 26 and Deut. 28). The Lord had brought all these judgments upon the land, but the people had refused to repent.

The time had come for a direct confrontation between Israel's God and his sinful people (v. 12). After announcing that he would intervene in judgment, he instructed Israel: "Prepare to meet your God." The prophet then described this God with whom Israel had an appointment (v. 13). He is the creator of the mountains and the wind. Perhaps the mountains represent what is tangible or stable, while the wind represents what is intangible and transitory. Together they represent the totality of reality.[133] This sovereign creator intervenes as judge in the world. Before he comes in judgment, he reveals his intentions through his prophets.[134] Then he descends in the storm, turning the bright dawn into ominous darkness[135] as he "treads" on the "high places of the earth." The imagery is that of the storm clouds, which veil God's presence (see Ps. 18:9, 11), moving along the mountaintops. The prophet capped off his description of the divine judge by identifying him by name—he is the "Lord God Almighty" (literally "the Lord God of Hosts"). The title "God of Hosts" (or "Armies") is especially appropriate here, for it depicts the Lord as a mighty warrior-king who leads his armies into battle.

Some scholars are puzzled by the fact that God, though stating "this is what I will do to you" (v. 12), did not give a specific description of what he would do at this point. The statement could look back to the judgment pre-

132. See Paul, *Amos*, 128–35.
133. Ibid., 154.
134. The statement "he reveals his thoughts to man" probably refers to God's revelation of his plans, a theme articulated in an earlier speech (see 3:7). However, some understand the pronoun "his" as referring to "man," in which case the statement alludes to God's ability to read the thoughts of human beings.
135. The meaning of the Hebrew text is not entirely clear; it reads literally, "he makes dawn, darkness." Another option is to read, "he makes dawn and darkness," in which case the statement is a reminder that the Lord is the source of both life/blessing (symbolized by dawn) and death/judgment (symbolized by darkness).

dicted in 3:11–15 and/or anticipate the devastation described in the follow-ing speech. However, it is possible that the Lord left the statement unfin-ished for rhetorical effect, allowing the audience to imagine with dread what the judgment would entail.[136]

Death Is around the Corner (5:1–17)

Anticipating the destructive effects of divine judgment, the prophet took up a lament for Israel, comparing her to a helpless young woman who has been struck down, never to rise again (vv. 1–2). The tragic image depicts one who is ready to enter into full womanhood, only to have her life suddenly taken from her. The reality behind the image is Israel's devastating military defeat in which the nation would experience a casualty rate of 90 percent (v. 3).

Even in the face of impending doom, God's mercy was evident. Before coming in judgment, the Lord invited Israel to repent (vv. 4–6). He urged the people to seek him so they might live. Failure to do so would inevitably bring God's fiery judgment down upon the land.

When the people heard God say "seek me," they were inclined to head for one of the well-known sanctuaries in the land, such as Bethel, Gilgal, or Beersheba. Bethel, a name meaning "the house of God," was a logical place to expect to find God. It was here that God revealed himself to Jacob, the fa-ther of the nation (see Gen. 28) and officially changed the patriarch's name to Israel (see Gen. 35). Gilgal, Israel's first campsite after they crossed the Jor-dan River in the days of Joshua (see Josh. 4:19–24), was the place where a new generation of Israelites submitted to the rite of circumcision and com-mitted themselves to God (see Josh. 5). Beersheba, located in the far south of the land in Judah's territory, was an important religious site as well, for it was here that Abraham worshiped God (Gen. 21:33) and that God revealed himself to Isaac (Gen. 26:23–25) and to Jacob (Gen. 46:1–4) and reiterated his promise to them.

But God was not interested in Israel's religious rituals (see 4:4–5). In fact, if the people did not repent, these famous sites would experience judg-ment just like the rest of the land. Ironically, even the residents of Gilgal, which symbolized Israel's possession of the land, would go into exile. To highlight this irony, the prophet employed sound-play. The Hebrew text reads *haggilgal galoh yigleh,* "Gilgal will surely go into exile." The statement "will surely go into exile" *(galoh yigleh)* sounds like the name Gilgal. The rep-etition of "g" and "l" sounds draws attention to the statement. Even Bethel was not immune from divine judgment. Ironically, the "house of God" would be "reduced to nothing."

---

136. In this regard, see ibid., 149–50. Andersen and Freedman (*Amos,* 450–52) understand the first-person verb form as a preterite (past tense) and paraphrase: "Therefore thus have I done to you, O Israel! Because [or inasmuch as] I have done this to you: [and because you have not returned to me] prepare to confront your God, O Israel!" In this case the verb refers to the judgments described in 4:6–11.

Rather than religious ritual, the Lord desired genuine repentance, which entailed seeking and loving what was "good" and rejecting what was "evil" (vv. 14–15). By correlating verses 4–5 with verses 14–15, one discovers that seeking the Lord meant first and foremost pursuing his moral will. More specifically, this meant reestablishing and promoting socioeconomic and legal justice in the land. The rich royal bureaucrats placed an oppressive tax burden on the farmers (v. 11a). Judges took bribes in exchange for favorable decisions (v. 12) and perverted justice, turning it into something distasteful and bitter to its victims (v. 7). Anyone who dared stand up for fairness was treated with contempt (v. 10). The situation had gotten so bad that anyone with any sense turned the other way and kept quiet (v. 13)—except the Lord and his prophet Amos, of course.

Using a hymnic descriptive style, Amos once more reminded sinful Israel that they had an appointment with their sovereign king, who rules over the cycles of nature (v. 8). The constellations Pleiades and Orion were associated with the changing of the seasons.[137] Verse 8 thus pictures God as the one who established the seasons, regulates the day-night cycle, and sends the rain at the appropriate time. Surely this sovereign king possesses both the authority and the power to destroy proud sinners and overturn the unjust society they had created (v. 9). This sovereign judge threatened to deprive the rich of their "stone mansions" and "lush vineyards," acquired at the expense of the poor (v. 11b). He would pass through the land, bringing death and sorrow in his wake (vv. 16–17).

The nation's only hope was to heed the Lord's call to repent. If the people repented, they just might experience God's mercy (v. 15b). However, despite the Lord's appeal in verses 4–5, God's grace is held out only as a possibility in verse 15, not a guarantee (note "perhaps" in v. 15b). Israel had fallen so deeply into sin, any continued delay might close the door that God had left just slightly open.

Some scholars, arguing that verses 8–9 fit awkwardly in the speech and seemingly interrupt the accusation of verses 7 and 10, propose that verses 8–9 are not original to this speech. However, this proposal begs the real question, for it is apparent that someone (a later editor in their view) felt this hymnic description of God was appropriate here. Actually the very awkwardness of these verses draws attention to them and highlights their content. Furthermore, as several scholars have observed, this speech is arranged in a chiastic fashion with verses 8–9 occupying the central and pivotal position.

One may outline the structure of the speech as follows:

A Israel's demise deserves a *lament* (vv. 1–3).
  B The people must *repent* for judgment is imminent (vv. 4–6)
    C and they are *guilty of injustice* (v. 7).

137. See Paul, *Amos,* 168.

> D They will encounter the *divine Judge*
>   (vv. 8–9).
> C′ The people are *guilty of injustice* and judgment
>   is imminent (vv. 10–13),
>   B′ so the people must *repent* (vv. 14–15).
> A′ Divine judgment will bring widespread *lamentation* (vv. 16–17).

The chiastic structure makes the second half of the speech somewhat repetitious, but the B′ and A′ elements clarify and elaborate upon the B and A elements, respectively. The C′ section outlines in far more detail (see vv. 10–13) the injustice mentioned in C (see v. 7), while the B′ section (vv. 14–15) clarifies what it means to seek the Lord (the B section in vv. 4–6 indicates only what it does *not* mean). The A′ element extends the lamentation from the prophet (see v. 1 in the A section) to all of society (see vv. 16–17). The internal logic of the speech may be outlined as follows:

> A Death is around the corner (vv. 1–3)!
>   B You need to repent (vv. 4–6),
>   C because you stand guilty and doomed before God (v. 7),
>   D the all-powerful, sovereign Judge (vv. 8–9)!
>   C′ You stand guilty and doomed before him (vv. 10–13),
>   B′ so you need to repent (vv. 14–15)!
> A′ Otherwise death is around the corner (vv. 16–17)!

Israel's Funeral (5:18–27)

Verses 16–17 picture widespread sorrow and lamentation. It is quite appropriate then that the next two speeches (see 5:18; 6:1) begin with the word "woe." This term was used in ancient Israel as a mourning cry at funerals (see 1 Kings 13:30; Jer. 22:18–19). In fact, an alternate form of the word appears in verse 16, where NIV translates "cries of anguish." When Amos's audience heard this word, images of death must have appeared in their minds. By prefacing his remarks with this word, the prophet suggested that the rebellious nation's funeral was imminent.

As noted earlier, the Israel of Amos's time anticipated the arrival of the day of the Lord. They expected it to be a glorious day when the Lord would defeat the surrounding nations, ushering in a new era of prosperity for Israel. Indeed, Jeroboam II, the king of Israel during this time, set out to revive Israel's fortunes and, with the Lord's approval, achieved great success in this regard (see 2 Kings 14:25–28). But, as Amos made clear, this era of renewed divine blessing would be short-lived. The "day of the LORD" was coming, but for Israel it would be a dark day of inescapable destruction, not a sunny day of salvation (vv. 18, 20). To illustrate the point, the prophet compared Israel to a man who runs away from a dangerous lion, only to encounter an equally dangerous bear. He then darts inside a house, and leans against a wall to rest, only to have a snake bite him (v. 19). In the same way, Israel would not be able to avoid the day of judgment.

Developing themes introduced in earlier speeches, the Lord denounced in strong terms (note "I hate, I despise") hypocritical Israel's religious formalism and meaningless rituals (vv. 21–23; see 4:4–5; 5:5). In the previous speech Amos accused the people of hating those who stand up for justice and urged them to "hate" instead their evil ways (see 5:10, 15). Now the Lord declares his hatred of their religious formalism (5:21). The repetition of the verb "to hate" draws attention to the correspondence between their sin and God's response to it. They hated social justice, so God in turn hated their hypocritical religion, which was a false substitute for ethical living. God did not desire Israel's offerings but rather demanded that they establish and promote justice throughout the land (v. 24; see 5:15). No mere token effort would do. Justice must become a permanent feature of the landscape, like a river that flows continually, in contrast to seasonal streams that dry up during hot weather.

The Lord used a history lesson to illustrate how ineffective their sacrifices were (v. 25). Recalling the period of the wilderness wandering, he asked, "Did you bring me sacrifices and offerings forty years in the desert, O house of Israel?" The question appears to anticipate a negative answer. This raises a problem since the Pentateuch clearly depicts Israel sacrificing to God during this period. The question may be exaggerated for effect. Though Moses gave Israel numerous laws about sacrifices and offerings, the sacrificial system per se could not be fully implemented until the people settled in the land. Though important, sacrifices were never the essence of God's relationship with his people. Loyalty, expressed through obedience, was always the highest priority. Sacrifices had significance only when offered by one who was committed to God and obedient to his moral will.[138] One could rephrase the question, "Did you bring me only sacrifices and offerings?" The implied answer would be: "No, I required and still do demand something much more basic from you—obedience."

Another option is to subordinate the question of verse 25 to the statement in the next verse and translate, "When you brought me sacrifices and offerings forty years in the desert, O house of Israel, did you lift up Sikkuth, your king and Kiyyun, your images . . . ?"[139] In this case, the point may be paraphrased as follows: "You think sacrifices are so important because they

138. See Jer. 7:21–23, which makes the same point as this text. See as well the comments of Paul, *Amos*, 193–94; Jeffrey Niehaus, "Amos," in *The Minor Prophets: An Exegetical and Expositional Commentary*, ed. T. E. McComiskey, vol. 1 (Grand Rapids: Baker, 1992), 433; Yehezkel Kaufmann, *The Religion of Israel*, trans. M. Greenberg (Chicago: University of Chicago Press, 1960), 365; and Roland de Vaux, *Ancient Israel*, 2 vols. (New York: McGraw-Hill, 1965), 2:428.
139. See Thomas J. Finley, *Joel, Amos, Obadiah* (Chicago: Moody, 1990), 253–54.

were inaugurated from the very beginning of your history. But when you offered sacrifices to me back then, did you also worship idols, like you do today? No! Though they are a fundamental part of your relationship with me, your sacrifices will do you no good because of your idolatry."

Of course, not all scholars understand verse 26 to be looking backward. Many combine it with verse 27 and take it as predictive. In this case one may translate: "You will lift up Sikkuth, your king and Kiyyun, your images . . . and I will send you into exile. . . ." Israel's idols would be unable to rescue them from God's judgment, but even as the people marched into exile, their commitment to these false gods would remain unshaken.

Whether one takes verse 26 as looking backward or forward, it is clear that Israelite worship, in addition to being characterized by hypocritical formalism, was also idolatrous. Two gods are mentioned here—Sikkuth and Kiyyun. Sikkuth was a Mesopotamian deity who is identified with Ninurta in a list of gods found at Ugarit. Kiyyun was another Mesopotamian god, associated with the planet Saturn.[140] The proper vocalization of the names is Sakkuth and Kayyamanu, respectively. Both names have been given an "i-u" vowel pattern in the Hebrew text, probably to mimic the vowel pattern of shiqquts, "detestable thing," and gillul, "idol."[141]

Exile and Defeat (6:1–14)

Another "woe" oracle follows, addressed to the wealthy royal bureaucrats of both Judah and Israel (v. 1). Since Amos's ministry and message focused on the northern kingdom (see vv. 6, 14), it is possible that the reference to "Zion" (Jerusalem) in verse 1 represents a later adaptation of the prophet's message to a southern audience. However, the coming judgment would include Judah (see 2:4–5), so the reference may well be original.[142]

These complacent leaders felt secure and were oblivious to the approaching disaster (vv. 2–3). Verse 2 may contain a quotation of what these rulers said to their people (see v. 1b).[143] In this case, the rhetorical questions can be understood as follows: "Are they [i.e., Calneh, Hamath, and Gath] better than these kingdoms [i.e., Judah and Israel]? No! Is their territory greater than your territory? No!" As far as the leaders of Judah and Israel were concerned, these other kingdoms were inferior.[144] However, since there is no introductory statement indicating that the leaders are speaking here, many prefer to understand verse 2 as the prophet's sarcastic words to the leaders.

---

140. See Paul, *Amos,* 194–97.
141. See ibid., 196, and Andersen and Freedman, *Amos,* 533.
142. See ibid., 199–200, and Andersen and Freedman, *Amos,* 553–59.
143. For a defense of this view, see David A. Hubbard, *Joel and Amos,* TOTC (Downers Grove, Ill.: InterVarsity, 1989), 190–91.
144. Calneh and Hamath were located in Syria, a significant distance to the north-northeast of Israel, while Gath was located in Philistine territory.

After all, the prophet speaks in both verses 1 and 3. In this case the rhetorical questions can be understood as follows: "Are you [i.e., Judah and Israel] any better than these kingdoms [i.e., Calneh, Hamath, and Gath]? No! You will be conquered just as they were! Is their territory greater than your territory? No! And in the same way your territory will be reduced!"[145] However, this interpretation seems to presuppose that these other kingdoms had already been conquered. Perhaps the prophet refers to Assyrian campaigns under Shalmaneser III in the ninth century B.C.[146] These kingdoms were also defeated by Tiglath-pileser III later in the eighth century B.C., well after the prophetic ministry of Amos. For this reason, many consider this verse to be a later addition to the text.

Israel's wealthy government officials ignored the approaching calamity and preferred to "live it up" (vv. 4–6).[147] They lounged around on ivory couches, eating meat, listening to music, and drinking wine from huge bowls normally used for sacrifices. The feasts described here were probably pagan religious banquets.[148]

The partying would soon come to an abrupt end (v. 7). An enemy army (the Assyrians) would invade the land and carry these prominent citizens away into exile. Amos uses sound-play to highlight the appropriate nature of God's judgment. The rich officials considered themselves to be rulers of the foremost (Heb. re'shit, v. 1) nation and enjoyed the finest (Heb. re'shit again, v. 6) lotions. Their attitude seemed to be "only the best for the best." How appropriate then that the Lord had reserved a special place for them right at the very front of the line of exiles. After all, it was only fitting that they should be the first (Heb. ro'sh, v. 7a, which is derived from the same root as the term re'shit, "foremost, finest") to be carried away, since it was their failure to obey God that had led to Israel's demise in the first place. With poetic flair the prophet also announced that their "lounging" (Heb. serukhim, v. 7b) would "end" (Heb. sar, v. 7b). The sound-play (both words have the sound sequence "s-r") draws attention to the statement and contributes to the theme of poetic justice.[149]

Using a solemn oath formula, the Lord denounced Israel's pride and announced that he would deliver Samaria over to an enemy (v. 8). The devastating judgment decreed by God would bring widespread death and destruction (vv. 9–11). As the few survivors went about the task of burying the

145. See Finley, Joel, Amos, Obadiah, 263.

146. See Paul, Amos, 203.

147. The phrase "ruin of Joseph" in v. 6 refers to either the approaching judgment upon Israel or the social disintegration of Israel caused by the officials' unjust practices.

148. The use of the Hebrew term mirzakh, "feasting," in v. 7 suggests that these banquets may have been associated with the marzeah institution (see my earlier comments on Amos 2:7). For more detailed discussion, see Barstad, Religious Polemics of Amos, 127–42, and King, Amos, Hosea, Micah, 137–61.

149. See Miller, Sin and Judgment, 23.

dead, they would be careful not to mention the Lord's name, for fear that it might prompt another outburst of divine anger.

Again the Lord gets to the root of the problem as he exposes Israel's perversion of justice (v. 12). The first part of the verse should probably be translated: "Do horses run on a cliff? Does one plow the sea with an ox?"[150] Both questions present ludicrous, bizarre images and expect the answer, "Of course not!" Such actions would be irrational. However, Israel had done something equally absurd in the legal realm by perverting justice. The courts had become a place where the powerful exploited the powerless.

Though Israelite society was disintegrating, Israel boasted of their recent military victories under the leadership of Jeroboam II (see 2 Kings 14:25, 28). They bragged that they had conquered Karnaim, a name that means "double horned" or "two horns." Since the horn of a wild ox was often used as a symbol of strength (see Deut. 33:17), the Israelites apparently felt this victory was an especially significant demonstration of their military power. But the Lord can pun on the meaning of names as well. He pointed out that they also rejoiced over their victory at Lo Debar, a name that means "nothing." As far as the Lord was concerned, all this bragging was just empty boasting, for Israel had accomplished nothing of lasting significance. An enemy invader would soon sweep through the land from north (Lebo Hamath) to south (the Valley of the Arabah), swiftly erasing Israel's military exploits (in this regard, see 2 Kings 14:25).

God's Patience Runs Out (7:1–8:3)

Amos next records a series of four visions that he received from the Lord. An account of Amos's hostile encounter with Amaziah the priest is inserted between the third and fourth visions. The structure of the first and second visions is similar:

Vision described (7:1, 4)
Amos's response (7:2, 5)
Lord's counterresponse (7:3, 6)

Both visions are like motion pictures as they depict in horrifying detail the destruction of the land. In the first vision swarms of locusts strip the land of its crops, leaving the people without food and destined to die from starvation. In the second vision fire devours everything in the land. Both visions, because they focus on the awful effects of judgment, elicited an emotional

150. The Hebrew text reads literally, "Do horses run on a cliff? Or does one plow with oxen?" While the first question expects the answer, "Of course not," the second seems to expect a positive response—"Yes, one normally plows with oxen." It is obvious that the poetic parallelism as well as the second half of the verse require an equally absurd second question. For this reason, many redivide the Hebrew text, changing *babbeqarim*, "[Does one plow] with oxen," to *babbaqar yam*, "[Does one plow] the sea with an ox." Another option is to understand the word for "cliff" as implied in the second line: "Do horses run on a cliff? Does one plow [a cliff] with oxen?" This interpretation underlies the NIV translation.

response from the prophet, who naturally sympathized with the people. He cried out to the Lord and begged him not to send the judgment. After the first vision, he asked God to "forgive," suggesting that he was aware that the punishment was deserved. However, after the second vision he simply cried out, "Stop." In both cases God relented (or "changed his mind") and announced that he would withhold judgment. God's patience and mercy are evident.

The third vision differs from the first two in several ways (vv. 7–9). Rather than giving Amos another video clip of judgment, God presented him with a symbolic scene that resembled a still life or snapshot. This time God initiated the dialogue and made it clear that he could no longer withhold judgment. Apparently convinced of the necessity of judgment, Amos offered no objections.

The traditional understanding of this vision sees the Lord standing beside a wall (symbolizing Israel) that was built true to plumb. He holds in his hand a plumb line (perhaps symbolizing God's moral standards), which reveals that the wall is now slanted and ready to fall (symbolizing Israel's failure to measure up to God's standard). By focusing Amos's attention on the reason for judgment, rather than its effects, God convinces Amos of the necessity for judgment.

However, many modern scholars reject this interpretation. The meaning of the word translated "plumb" or "plumb line" is uncertain. Traditionally it was taken to mean "lead," suggesting that a plumb line, to which a lead weight was attached, was in view. But recent research seems to indicate that the word refers to "tin," not lead.[151] In this case, the text would read: (7) "This is what he showed me: The Lord stood upon [or "beside"] a wall of tin, with tin in his hand. (8) The LORD said to me, 'What do you see Amos?' I replied, 'Tin.' Then the Lord said, 'Look, I am placing tin in the midst of my people Israel. I will no longer spare them.'"

But what is the symbolic value of tin in the vision? Unfortunately, scholars have not been able to offer a convincing explanation, though various proposals have been made. Since metal walls (made of iron or bronze) sometimes symbolize strength in ancient Near Eastern literature and in the Hebrew Bible (see Jer. 1:18; Ezek. 4:3), a tin wall might symbolize weakness and vulnerability to attack.[152] However, what would be the significance of the tin in the Lord's hand and the implication of placing tin in the midst of the people? Some suggest that tin, because it was used to form bronze, symbolizes weapons here, but surely the Lord could have described bronze weapons in a more direct way. Another possibility is that wordplay is involved, as in the fourth vision (see 8:1–3 below). In postbiblical Hebrew

151. The term in question, which occurs only here in the Hebrew Bible, is usually understood as an Akkadian loanword, *annaku*, "tin."
152. See Paul, *Amos*, 235.

there is a homonym meaning "grief." Perhaps verse 8b utilizes this homonym. In this case the tin (the Hebrew word is pronounced *'anak*) wall and the tin (*'anak*) in the Lord's hand ominously foreshadowed the day when the Lord would place "grief" (also pronounced *'anak*) among the people.[153]

Despite the uncertainty surrounding the symbolism of the vision, it is apparent that its details point to impending judgment. The Lord would destroy the corrupt religious centers of the land and launch a direct attack on King Jeroboam's dynasty (or "house"). The prophecy was fulfilled in 752 B.C. when, shortly after Jeroboam's death, his son Zechariah was assassinated (see 2 Kings 15:8–12).

Though Amos had sympathy for Israel and initially objected to God's plan to judge the nation, he eventually came to the point where he agreed with God's decision. Perhaps his personal experience helped convince him that judgment was inevitable. The biographical account that follows the third vision tells how Amos came face to face with the northern kingdom's royal power structure (vv. 10–17). In his encounter with Amaziah, the priest of the royal sanctuary at Bethel, Amos saw firsthand how corrupt Israel's leadership had become.[154]

Obviously upset by Amos's message, Amaziah sent a letter to Jeroboam accusing Amos of agitating the people to revolt against the king (v. 10). He gave a capsulized report of Amos's message, claiming that Amos had prophesied that Jeroboam would die by the sword and that Israel would be taken into exile (v. 11). The second part of the accusation is certainly accurate (see 5:5, 27; 6:7), but the first part of the statement misrepresents the prophet's message. According to 7:9, the Lord himself would attack the dynasty of Jeroboam, but Amaziah omitted any reference to Amos's divine authority and claimed that Amos said that the king himself would die by the sword. By tampering with Amos's message in this subtle manner, Amaziah made Amos appear to be the opponent of the king.

Amaziah then turned his attention to Amos and demanded that he return to Judah and make his living there (v. 12), implying that Amos's motives were primarily mercenary. He reminded Amos that Bethel was a royal sanctuary (v. 13), implying that Amos must respect the king's authority and recognize the official state religion as legitimate. Amos's reply was quick and hard-hitting. He pointed out that he was not a prophet by birth or training, but rather a sheep herder and agricultural laborer (v. 14).[155] He left his job

---

153. See Andersen and Freedman, *Amos*, 759. They actually see three homonyms in vv. 7–8. Appealing to another postbiblical root, they understand the wall to be a "plastered" wall.

154. Since Amos is spoken of in the third person in vv. 10–17 (in contrast to 5:1; 7:1–8; 8:1–3; 9:1), it is possible that the book's final editor, perhaps one of the prophet's disciples, inserted this biographical account.

155. Amos's statement in v. 14 may be translated, "I was neither a prophet nor a prophet's son," in which case he emphasized that he was not a prophet by birth or training, but became one through a special calling. Another option, however, is to translate with the present tense, "I am not a prophet nor a prophet's

as a herdsman when God called him to carry out a prophetic mission to Israel (v. 15).

In response to Amaziah's demand that he cease prophesying against Israel, Amos delivered a prophecy against Amaziah (vv. 16–17). He utilized Amaziah's version of his message (see v. 11b), keeping the second half of the message intact (compare v. 17b with v. 11b), but removing the first half (pertaining to Jeroboam) and replacing it with an announcement of judgment against Amaziah. God's judgment would strike at Amaziah and his immediate family circle. In the aftermath of the wider judgment upon Israel, Amaziah's wife would become a prostitute just to stay alive. His sons and daughters would, like Jeroboam's dynasty (see v. 9), die by the sword, bringing the priest's own dynasty to an end. Amaziah would lose his wealth and die in exile in a "pagan" (lit., "unclean") land. The punishment is especially ironic since priests were supposed to carefully distinguish the clean from the unclean and keep themselves from being ritually defiled (Lev. 10:10).

Modern readers might wonder why Amaziah's family should have to suffer for his sins, but the principle of corporate solidarity was integral to Israelite thinking. Though modern Westerners tend to emphasize individualism, ancient Israelites were very much aware that the actions of individuals profoundly affect others in their social context and that one's social context impacts the individual adversely or positively.[156]

The biographical account provides tangible evidence of the necessity of judgment. It explains why God could no longer relent from judgment (the point of the first three visions) and lays a solid foundation for the fourth vision in the series. As in the third vision (see 7:7–9), the Lord showed Amos a still life (8:1). Once again God initiated the dialogue, explained the symbolism of the vision, and made it clear that he could no longer withhold judgment (v. 2). This time Amos saw a basket of ripe fruit. Such fruit (including figs and pomegranates) was harvested at the very end of the agricultural season, during August and September.[157] The term translated "ripe fruit" (Heb. *qayits*), because it sounds like the Hebrew *qets*, "end," can be used here to foreshadow Israel's fate. When Amos, in response to the Lord's question, said that he saw a basket of ripe fruit *(qayits)*, the Lord responded, "The end [Heb. *qets*] has come for my people Israel" (v. 2). As in the third vision, the Lord announced he could spare Israel no longer. He then de-

---

son." In this case he denied being a prophet in the professional sense, even though he was carrying out an ad hoc prophetic mission by divine command.

156. The principle is illustrated nicely in Josh. 7, where God accuses Israel of having sinned (v. 11), even though an individual (Achan) was the actual culprit. Achan's animals and children were then executed along with him. For a discussion of the theological principle of corporate solidarity, see Kaminsky, *Corporate Responsibility in the Hebrew Bible*.

157. See Borowski, *Agriculture in Iron Age Israel*, 31, 38, 115. The month for gathering in summer fruit is listed last in the Gezer calendar. See Pritchard, *Ancient Near Eastern Texts*, 320.

scribed the aftermath of judgment, when singers would lament over the many corpses that would litter the ground (v. 3).

The Silence of God (8:4–14)

The prophet next addressed the oppressors of the poor (v. 4). He depicted them as greedy merchants who impatiently longed for religious holy days to end so they could resume their dishonest business practices (vv. 5–6). Two of their favorite tricks were "skimping the measure" and "boosting the price" (literally, "making the ephah small and making the shekel large"). When measuring out grain, they used a less than standard ephah (a unit of dry measure) so that the customer received less than he thought he was buying. At the same time they used a heavier than standard shekel-weight to measure the purchase price so that the customer actually paid more than he should. To top it off, these merchants used rigged scales and mixed some chaff in with the grain they sold. Their consciences were so seared that they even sold and traded people.

The Lord did not intend to let such behavior go unchecked (v. 7). He solemnly vowed that he would not overlook their oppressive and dishonest deeds. He made the vow by the "pride of Jacob." Though some (see, for example, NIV, which capitalizes "Pride") understand this phrase as a divine title, it is more likely that the Lord refers to Israel's arrogant attitude, expressed in its defiance of his law. In Amos 6:8, the phrase "pride of Jacob" refers to Israel's self-confidence, while Hosea 5:5 and 7:10 denounce the "pride of Israel." Since one typically swears by someone or something that is unchanging and constant, the statement sarcastically expresses the Lord's evaluation of Israel's moral character. As far as he was concerned, their pride was permanently ingrained.

The Lord would send judgment upon the land. The earth would quake at the divine Judge's approach (v. 8; see 1:1), and the sky would grow dark, ominously signaling the death and destruction to come (v. 9). Religious celebrations would be replaced by bitter lamentation, as when one loses an only son (v. 10). To make matters worse, the Lord's prophetic word, which Israel had rejected (see 2:12; 7:10–17), would cease (vv. 11–14). Comparing God's silence to a famine, the prophet pictured the idolatrous people desperately searching for a word from God, as one would food or water. But their search would prove futile, and even the most robust of the nation would fall dead from starvation and thirst.[158]

Inescapable Judgment (9:1–10)

Once more Amos saw a vision of the Lord (v. 1; see 7:7). This time he was standing beside "the altar," probably a reference to the royal sanctuary at

---

158. Though Israel's idolatry is alluded to in v. 14, the precise identity of the gods involved is not certain. See Barstad, *Religious Polemics*, 143–201.

Bethel (see 7:13), which epitomized Israel's empty ritualism (3:14). The Lord issued a command that the entire sanctuary be demolished, killing those worshiping inside. If any tried to escape, the Lord would cut them down with the sword. God's sinful people would not be able to escape the coming judgment, for God's dominion is worldwide (vv. 2–3). If they were to dig into the depths of Sheol, the subterranean land of the dead in ancient Israelite thought, God's hand would retrieve them. If they were to climb to the sky or hide on a mountaintop, God would still find them. Even if they were to swim to the bottom of the sea, God would command a poisonous sea serpent to bite them with its deadly fangs.[159] Israel would go into exile, but even there they would continue to experience divine punishment (v. 4).

At this point, Amos, utilizing a hymnic descriptive style, portrayed the Judge with whom Israel must reckon (vv. 5–6; see 4:13; 5:8–9). The prophet used the title "Lord Almighty" (literally, "Lord of Armies"), which pictures God as a mighty warrior-king. When he comes in judgment, the Lord is able to cause cosmic disturbances that rock the earth's very surface (v. 5; see 8:8). His royal palace encompasses the earth, and he controls the cycles of nature (v. 6).

Speaking directly to Israel, the Lord affirmed once more his intention to judge his people (vv. 7–10). Because of Israel's privileged position before God (see 3:2), they thought of themselves as immune to judgment and destined for glory (v. 10b; see 5:18). The Lord dismissed such arrogance with a startling rhetorical question that implies the Israelites were no different in his sight than the distant Cushites of Africa (v. 7a). The Lord controls the history of all nations, including Israel (v. 7b). He made Israel his covenant people, but their privileged status was the result of his sovereign choice, not any inherent superiority they might think they possessed. In fact, their special advantages made them more responsible and culpable in God's sight. For this reason, he would punish the nation for its sins (vv. 8–10). Yet the Lord's judgment is always discerning. While sinners would be destroyed, the Lord would preserve a remnant. God's discerning judgment is compared to a sieve used to separate grain from chaff and pebbles.[160]

Brighter Days Ahead (9:11–15)

Amos's message ends on a positive note as the prophet depicts a glorious era beyond the coming judgment. Because it so radically departs from the consistently negative tone of the prophecy up to this point, many scholars reject

159. Since this creature is called "the serpent" some identify it with Leviathan, a serpentine sea monster that symbolizes chaos in Ugaritic mythology and in biblical poetry (see Job 26:13; Isa. 27:1). However, the Hebrew article may be used to indicate a generic serpent (see 5:19 and note the NIV translation there, "a snake").

160. On the type of sieve used here, see Borowski, *Agriculture in Iron Age Israel*, 66–67, and Paul, *Amos*, 286.

the originality of these verses and attribute them to a later editor who wanted to give the book a happy ending. However, if a later editor could consider such an addition appropriate, why would a message of salvation be so antithetical to Amos's thinking? After all, Moses anticipated Israel's return from exile (Deut. 30:1–10), and God's promises to David and Abraham (alluded to in vv. 11 and 15) necessitated Israel's restoration.[161] Other eighth-century prophets (Isaiah, Hosea, Micah) combined messages of judgment with visions of a glorious future for Israel, so why not Amos?[162]

This vision of the golden era to come has two scenes. Verses 11–12 depict a time when the Davidic dynasty would be revived and would reconquer the surrounding nations. Verses 13–15 portray a time when exiled Israel would be restored to its land and enjoy prosperity and security.

By the time of Amos, the Davidic dynasty, compared here to a dilapidated shelter, had fallen on hard times and no longer enjoyed the glory and respect of the Davidic-Solomonic era. Approximately 170 years before, the northern tribes had broken away from the house of David. Since that time both the northern (Israel) and southern (Judah) kingdoms had struggled to maintain their independence against neighboring peoples and more distant powers. Whether either wanted to admit it or not, a unified nation would be more powerful and secure in a hostile world. That unity and security would come when the Lord revived the Davidic dynasty, which entailed the reunification of the nation (see also Isa. 9:1–7; 11:10–14; Hos. 1:11; 3:5). The Lord had made Edom and the other nations subject to David's rule (see 2 Sam. 8:1–14; 10:1–19; 1 Kings 11:15), but when the kingdom divided, they were eventually able to regain their independence (see, for example, 2 Kings 8:20–22). However, the revived house of David would conquer all these nations and reestablish the Davidic empire.[163] As in Isaiah 11:12–14, which also depicts a revived Davidic empire conquering its traditional enemies, we should expect an essential, not exact, fulfillment of this prophecy.[164]

161. Of course, critics typically deny Mosaic authorship of Deuteronomy and regard Deut. 30 as postdating the time of Amos.

162. For a defense of the authenticity of Amos 9:11–15, see Paul, *Amos*, 288–90; John H. Hayes, *Amos* (Nashville: Abingdon, 1988), 223–28; and Gerhard F. Hasel, *Understanding the Book of Amos* (Grand Rapids: Baker, 1991), 116–20.

163. In Acts 15:16–17, James uses an alternative form of this text to support his argument that God always intended to save the Gentiles. The Hebrew text of Amos 9:12a reads, "so that they may possess the remnant of Edom and all the nations that bear my name." The Old Greek translation of the passage misreads "possess" (Heb. *yarash*) as "seek" (Heb. *darash*), mistakes "Edom" for "mankind" (Heb. *'adam*), and makes "the remnant of men and all the nations" the subject of the verb, rather than its object. The resulting reading, "that the remnant of men and all the nations, over whom my name is called, may seek," is in need of an object. Later Greek witnesses supplied an object (either "me" or "the Lord"). James's citation follows the latter of these secondary readings and transforms a militaristic passage into a prophecy about the Gentiles seeking God. In its original context, the passage anticipates a new era of Davidic imperialism. Of course, from the Israelite perspective, the nations should have viewed subjugation to the Davidic king in a positive light (see Ps. 2).

164. See my earlier comments on Isa.11:12–14.

The second scene in the prophet's concluding vision depicts Israel enjoying the Lord's blessings. Having returned and rebuilt their once desolated cities, the people would plant their crops and enjoy an abundant harvest. With a burst of hyperbole, the Lord pictured a time when the crops would be so abundant that the reapers (who worked in April–May) would still be harvesting when the plowmen (who normally worked in October–November) arrived. The grape harvest (normally occurring in August–September) would still be underway when planting season (November–December) arrived. The wine would be so plentiful that it would overflow the vats and cascade down the hillsides. Playing on the planting imagery of these verses, the Lord capped off this scene by declaring that he would do some planting of his own. He would "plant" Israel in their land, never to be "uprooted" again (see Hos. 2:23).

Vengeance Is Mine (Obadiah)

Introduction

The book's heading identifies its author without giving any information about its historical setting. Because of its placement after Amos (who prophesied in the eighth century B.C.) and before Jonah (who lived during this same time period), some date the prophecy in the preexilic period, suggesting that it may have originated in the aftermath of the Edomite rebellion against Judah in the ninth century B.C. during the reign of Joram (see 2 Kings 8:20–22 and 2 Chron. 21:8–10). However, the events of this period hardly fit the picture of Judah's demise painted in Obadiah 10–14. Though Philistines and Arabian tribes invaded Judah and looted the royal palace during the reign of Joram, the account in 2 Chronicles 21:16–17 makes no mention of Edomite involvement, nor does it give any indication that Judah was devastated to the degree described by Obadiah.

It is far more likely that Obadiah prophesied in the aftermath of the Babylonian destruction of Jerusalem in 586 B.C., which culminated in the exile of large segments of the population. Like Obadiah, other texts dating from this time denounce Edom's involvement in Judah's demise (see Ps. 137:7; Lam. 4:21–22; Ezek. 25:12–14; 35:1–15). In fact, Obadiah may have borrowed from the prophet Jeremiah, who also prophesied the downfall of Edom (cf. Obad. 1–4 with Jer. 49:14–16; Obad. 5–6 with Jer. 49:9–10; Obad. 8 with Jer. 49:7; and Obad. 16 with Jer. 49:12).[165]

This short prophecy is a diatribe against Edom's pride and mistreatment

165. Proponents of the priority of Obadiah argue that Jeremiah borrowed from Obadiah, not vice versa. For a helpful discussion of the similarities and differences between Obadiah and Jeremiah 49, see Stuart, *Hosea-Jonah*, 414–16.

of Judah. In verses 1–9, the Lord denounces Edom's pride and announces Edom's impending doom. In verses 10–14, he gives the formal accusation against Edom. In Judah's day of distress, the Edomites allied themselves with Judah's enemies and exploited Judah's weakness to their own advantage. In verses 15–21, the Lord sets the judgment of Edom against the background of the "day of the LORD." In the aftermath of God's judgment on the nations, Jerusalem would be rejuvenated, while Edom would be devastated. God's people would reoccupy their land and take possession of Edomite territory as well.

Pride Goes before a Fall (1–14)

After the heading, which suggests that the prophecy came to Obadiah through a vision, the introductory formula makes it clear that God has something to say to Edom (v. 1a). This divine word begins in verse 2, where the Lord directly addresses Edom. However, prior to this, an unidentified group (probably the prophet and the exiles whom he represents) declares that they too have received a "message" from the Lord (v. 1b). Following this statement, there is a report about an envoy being sent to the nations to summon them to war against Edom. The "message" heard by the group may be the one delivered by the envoy to the nations, in which case verse 1b is parenthetical (see the punctuation in NIV). Another option is that the "message" heard by the group is the same as the one that begins in verse 2. In this case one may translate verse 1b: "We have heard a message from the LORD, *while* an envoy was sent to the nations to say, 'Rise, and let us go against her for battle.'" In either case the delivery of the message to Edom is concurrent with the mission of the envoy. As the Lord announced Edom's impending doom, he was already summoning his instruments of judgment to carry out their assigned task.

Edom felt secure and invulnerable in its impregnable rocky highlands, which the prophet compared to an inaccessible eagle's nest located on a high cliff.[166] But Edom's confidence would prove to be self-deception, for the Lord would bring the Edomites down from their lofty "nest" and humiliate them among the nations (vv. 2–4). Invaders would ransack Edom and rob it of all its wealth, including its hidden treasures (vv. 5–6). Thieves typically take what they desire, leaving unwanted items behind. Even grape pickers normally miss or drop a few grapes. But Edom's invaders would miss nothing and leave nothing behind. Edom would be thoroughly looted. To add insult to injury, Edom's own allies would betray her, but her wise men would not detect this treachery until it was too late (vv. 7–8). By then her warriors would be overcome with terror and would fall before the Lord's judgment (v. 9).

---

166. For a description of the topography of Edom, see Aharoni, *Land of the Bible,* 40.

Judgment would fall on Edom because of the way they had treated the people of Judah (vv. 10–14). When the Babylonians invaded and ransacked Jerusalem, the Edomites gloated over Judah's defeat and participated in the looting. To make matters worse, they even hunted down refugees from Judah and handed them over to the Babylonians. For dramatic effect the prophet uses a series of negative commands in verses 12–14, as if he were actually seeing firsthand Jerusalem's downfall and its aftermath. As he witnesses Edom's actions, he cries out in protest, urging them to refrain from such hostility. Edom's actions were especially contemptible because the Edomites were descendants of Jacob's brother Esau and therefore distant cousins of the people of Judah. But God's judgment would be appropriate; Edom would get what it deserved (see v. 15b). Just as the Edomites had "cut down" Judah's fugitives (v. 14), so they would be "cut down" (v. 9) and "destroyed" (v. 10).[167]

Revenge and Reversal (15–21)

God's judgment would not be confined to Edom. Edom would certainly be punished in just measure for its wrongdoing, but the Lord's "day" of judgment would also encompass the nations (v. 15). This judgment is compared to intoxicating wine, which the nations are forced to keep drinking (v. 16). Just as an intoxicating beverage eventually causes the one drinking it to become disoriented and to stagger, so God's judgment would cause the panic-stricken nations to stumble around in confusion.

The identification of the addressee in verse 16a is uncertain. On the surface, it would appear to be Edom, which is addressed in verse 15b and throughout the prophecy. However, when Edom is addressed, second-person *singular* forms are used in the Hebrew text. In verse 16a, the verb "you drank" is a *plural* form in Hebrew, suggesting that Edom is no longer addressed, at least solely. Perhaps Edom and the nations, mentioned in verse 15a, are addressed in verse 16a. However, since the nations are referred to in the third person in verse 16b, it seems unlikely that they are addressed here. Another option is to take the final *mem* on the Hebrew verb form (*shetitem*) as an enclitic particle and to revocalize the form as a singular verb (*shatita*) addressed to Edom. In this case verse 16a would allude to the time when Edom celebrated Jerusalem's defeat on Mount Zion, God's "holy hill." Verse 16b would then make the ironic point that just as Edom once drank in victory, so the nations (Edom included) would someday drink the cup of judgment. However, this interpretation is problematic for it necessitates taking the drinking metaphor in different ways (as signifying celebration and then judgment) within the same verse. Another option is that the exiled people of Judah are addressed. Just as God's people were forced to drink the intoxicating wine of divine judgment, so the nations, including those who humiliated

---

167. niv "destroyed" in v. 10 translates the same Hebrew word rendered "cut down" in vv. 9 and 14.

Judah, would be forced to drink this same wine. What goes around comes around. However, God's people are never addressed elsewhere in the prophecy, making this proposal problematic.[168]

While the nations would fall in judgment, God's people would be rejuvenated. The Lord would restore Mount Zion as his holy hill, and reunited Israel (called here "the house of Jacob") would again possess its land (v. 17). The Israelites (northerners included, as the phrase "house of Joseph" indicates) would annihilate the Edomites, leaving no survivors (v. 18). The judgment is appropriate, for the Edomites had mistreated the survivors of Judah following the fall of Jerusalem (see v. 14). The returning exiles would repopulate Israel and Judah, as well as the surrounding regions, including Philistine and Edomite territory (vv. 19–20).[169] Judah's rulers, called here "deliverers," would exercise dominion over this kingdom from Mount Zion (v. 21).

Was Obadiah's prophecy fulfilled? By Malachi's time (approximately 450 B.C.), Edom had suffered a devastating defeat (see Mal. 1:1–4), though not of the magnitude envisioned by Obadiah.[170] Obadiah's description of Edom's judgment is probably to some degree stylized and exaggerated. However, the cosmic dimension of the prophecy transcends historical developments and points to an end-time judgment of worldwide proportions. When viewed in this larger eschatological context, Edom serves as an archetype for all God's enemies, who will be crushed by his angry judgment (see also Isa. 34 and 63:1–6).

A Wayward Prophet Learns a Lesson (Jonah)

Introduction

Unlike the other prophetic books, the Book of Jonah is a prophetic biography. It tells the story of Jonah, an Israelite prophet from Gath-hepher, located in the northern kingdom on the border of Zebulun's tribal territory (see Josh. 19:13). Jonah is mentioned in one other passage in the Hebrew Bible. According to 2 Kings 14:25, he prophesied the military successes of King Jeroboam II, who ruled from 793–753 B.C.

Traditionally, the Book of Jonah has been understood as a historical account of an episode in the life of the prophet. Most modern scholars reject this notion and understand the book as legendary, allegorical, or parabolic.

---

168. The only other second-person masculine plural form occurs in v. 1, where the nations are told to "rise" and prepare to attack Edom. As noted above, an address to the nations in v. 16 is problematic.

169. Some of the other place names in vv. 19–20 require comment. Gilead was located east of the Jordan River, while Zarephath was situated on the Mediterranean coast south of Sidon. The identification of Sepharad is uncertain. Options include Spain, Sardis (located in Asia Minor), and Saparda, a region in Media where some of the Israelite exiles may have been taken (see 2 Kings 17:6).

170. See Hoglund, "Edomites," in *Peoples of the Old Testament World*, 342–43.

They argue that various elements in the book are too fantastic to be anything but fiction. For example, Jonah is preserved alive inside a large marine creature for three days and three nights and even prays (in beautiful Hebrew poetic verse) from within the insides of the fish.[171] When he preaches in Nineveh, which seems to be portrayed as much larger than it really was (see Jon. 3:3), the Ninevites repent en masse. Furthermore, secular history provides no evidence of such a spiritual revival among the Assyrians. Within just a few decades of their alleged conversion, they were once again building their empire with unprecedented cruelty.[172]

Despite the modern scholarly consensus that the book is fictional, many evangelicals continue to defend its historicity on presuppositional and philosophical grounds, arguing that a commitment to historicity, biblical inspiration, and supernaturalism demands such a view.[173] Defenders of the book's historicity argue that its alleged fanciful elements can be attributed to divine intervention. Indeed, other stories about prophets (for example, Moses, Elijah, Elisha, and Balaam) also record some unusual incidents.[174] They also point out that Jesus assumed its authenticity when he spoke of Jonah's ordeal in the belly of the fish and contrasted the repentant Ninevites with the unbelieving generation of his own day (see Matt. 12:39–42; Luke 11:29–32).[175]

171. Some defenders of the book's historicity have attempted to find other instances of men being preserved alive after being swallowed by marine animals, but at least some of these alleged parallels have been exposed as "fish stories." See Uriel Simon, *Jonah*, trans. L. J. Schramm, JPSBC (Philadelphia: Jewish Publication Society, 1999), xvi, and R. K. Harrison, *Introduction to the Old Testament* (Grand Rapids: Eerdmans, 1969), 907–8. While Harrison states that "not all of these ought to be dismissed as ridiculous," he points out that Jonah "was fully conscious and coherent, both mentally and emotionally, being able to compose a penitential psalm and worship his god before being regurgitated by the great fish." He adds: "This is a vastly different experience from that of any modern counterpart of Jonah, and in itself raises a major obstacle to the acceptance of a literal interpretation of the prophecy" (908).

172. For more thorough presentations of the case against the book's historicity, see Terence E. Fretheim, *The Message of Jonah* (Minneapolis: Augsburg, 1977), 61–72, and Allen, *Joel, Obadiah, Jonah, and Micah,* 175–81.

173. See, among others, Stuart, *Hosea–Jonah,* 440–42; Chisholm, *Interpreting the Minor Prophets,* 119–21; and C. Hassell Bullock, *An Introduction to the Old Testament Prophetic Books* (Chicago: Moody, 1986), 44–48. T. D. Alexander ("Jonah and Genre," *TynB* 36 [1985]: 35–59) attempts to demonstrate that the book fits the pattern of historical narrative, though he acknowledges that it also displays obvious literary and didactic elements. For a more noncommittal approach from an evangelical perspective, see Raymond B. Dillard and Tremper Longman III, *An Introduction to the Old Testament* (Grand Rapids: Zondervan, 1994), 392–93.

174. In response to this line of argumentation, Fretheim states that one must distinguish between "what God could have done" and "what he actually did do." He points out that the book's fantastic elements (for example, the Ninevites' repentance) are not consistently attributed to divine intervention (Fretheim, *Jonah,* 63). Allen observes that "the miracles do not fall into the landmark pattern, whereby biblical miracles tend to cluster around crucial points of history, the Exodus, the ministry of prophets engaged in repelling Baalism or secular involvement in power politics, and the inauguration of Christianity" (*Joel, Obadiah, Jonah, and Micah,* 176 n. 5).

175. In response, Allen states that Jesus' use of the story may reflect "popular Jewish understanding." He compares Jesus' reference to Jonah to a modern preacher challenging "his congregation with a reference to Lady Macbeth or Oliver Twist" (*Joel, Obadiah, Jonah, and Micah,* 180; see also Fretheim, *Jonah,* 62–63). Since Jonah actually did live, a more apt analogy might be a school teacher using a legendary incident from

The debate over the book's historicity will undoubtedly continue, because for some it is a litmus test of orthodoxy that proves whether or not one is committed to historical Christianity. Surely such an attitude makes a philosophical "mountain" out of a literary "molehill." Unlike the exodus and the resurrection of Jesus, the historicity of the Book of Jonah is not foundational to redemptive history and biblical faith.[176] Unfortunately, the debate over the book's historicity has often distracted interpreters from focusing on its theological message, which is not affected by how one understands the book's literary genre. Whether the book is labeled historical narrative, legend, parable, or something akin to a historical novella, its themes seem apparent. It assumes that the God of Israel is sovereign over the nations. It also affirms that he is merciful and compassionate, not willing that anyone should perish without being given an opportunity to repent. More profoundly, the book makes the point that God's justice must be tempered and balanced by his mercy if God's world is to continue.[177] It is also possible that the book is a polemic against sinful Israel, represented by the disobedient prophet. Despite all he knows about God, Jonah, because of his obsession with justice, is unwilling to carry out God's commands and get in line with God's program, in contrast to the pagans, who respond immediately and appropriately to God's revealed will and exhibit genuine fear before him.[178]

The book exhibits a symmetrical design in which chapters 1–2 stand parallel to chapters 3–4.[179] Several elements in part one have corresponding elements in part two, as the following outline of the story's structure indicates:

Part One (chapters 1–2)

A   The Lord commissions Jonah (1:1–2)
B   Jonah rejects his commission (1:3)
C   The sovereign Lord reveals his power (1:4)
D   The sailors submit to the Lord and avert disaster (1:5–16)
E   The Lord uses a fish to retrieve Jonah (1:17)
F   Jonah prays, thanking the Lord for saving his life (2:1–9)
G   The fish disgorges Jonah (2:10)

---

the story of George Washington to motivate his/her students to follow the example of America's revered founding father.

176. For a helpful study of the relationship of biblical historicity to faith, see V. Philips Long, *The Art of Biblical History* (Grand Rapids: Zondervan, 1994), especially 88–119.

177. For a superb discussion of this theme, see Simon, *Jonah*, xii–xiii.

178. For a similar type of contrast utilizing a foreigner, see 2 Kings 5, where the foreign general Naaman responds in faith to the God of Israel, while Gehazi (epitomizing sinful Israel?) is punished for his disobedience. Similarly, Ruth the Moabitess stands out like a bright light against the dark moral backdrop of the Judges period. Though not born an Israelite, she becomes, more by actions than words, a true follower of Israel's God, in contrast to rebellious and paganized Israel.

179. See Phyllis Trible, *Rhetorical Criticism: Context, Method, and the Book of Jonah* (Philadelphia: Fortress, 1994), 109–17, as well as Fretheim, *Jonah*, 55, and Simon, *Jonah*, xxiv–xxv.

Part Two (chapters 3–4)

A′ The Lord commissions Jonah (3:1–2)
B′ Jonah accepts his commission (3:3)
C′ The sovereign Lord reveals his plan (3:4)
D′ The Ninevites submit to the Lord and avert disaster (3:5–10)
E′ Jonah prays, complaining that the Lord has saved Nineveh (4:1–3)
F′ The Lord uses a plant and worm to teach Jonah a lesson (4:4–11)

The symmetry between chapters 1 and 3 is readily apparent. Both chapters begin with Jonah's response to his commission and then focus on the reaction of foreigners to God's self-revelation. Though the structural parallelism between chapters 2 and 4 is not as tight, both chapters present a prayer of Jonah and focus on the prophet's reaction to the Lord's intervention. There is a sharp contrast between chapter 2, where Jonah thanks the Lord for delivering him, and chapter 4, where he objects to God's saving the pagan Ninevites. Because of its poetic style and apparent incongruity with the author's presentation of Jonah's character, many scholars regard the thanksgiving song in 2:2–9 as a later addition to the book. However, as the outline above indicates, it is integral to the book's structure and provides a foil, as it were, for Jonah's prayer of complaint in 4:2–3.[180]

Prophet on the Run (1:1–16)

The Lord commissioned Jonah to warn Nineveh that judgment would soon fall because of the city's evil deeds (v. 2). Jonah refused to accept this commission and headed in the opposite direction, boarding a ship bound for the distant port of Tarshish (v. 3). To emphasize disobedient Jonah's audacity, the author informs us twice that Jonah fled "from the LORD" and tells us three times that he was heading "to Tarshish" (cf. the Hebrew text; NIV translates only two of these). The author does not reveal at this point Jonah's reason for running from the Lord; he saves this information until later (see 4:2), when he allows Jonah himself to explain his motives.

Though the precise identity of Tarshish is uncertain, it was apparently located somewhere on the coast of the Mediterranean Sea. Tarshish was named after one of Javan's sons, who were the ancestors of "the maritime peoples" referred to in Genesis 10:5. It was a distant coastal land (Ps. 72:10; Isa. 23:6, 10; 66:19) known for producing and trading silver, iron, tin, and lead (see Jer. 10:9 and Ezek. 27:12; 38:13). The "ships of Tarshish" (see Isa. 2:16; 23:1; Ezek. 27:25) were large trading ships capable of traveling to ports throughout the Mediterranean region. Scholars have suggested Tarsus in Asia Minor as a possible site, but it is more likely, based on a reference in an Assyrian inscription, that Tarshish is distinct from Tarsus and was located somewhere west of both Cyprus and the land of the Ionians. Perhaps it

---

180. For a fuller discussion of how the song contributes to the book's thematic development and to the characterization of Jonah, see the commentary below.

should be identified with a Phoenician colony located in ancient Tartessus in southwest Spain.[181]

The Lord was not about to let Jonah shirk his duty so easily. He "sent" (lit., "hurled") a powerful wind into the sea, causing a storm that threatened to break the ship in pieces (v. 4). To emphasize the severity of the storm, the author utilizes the device of personification and pictures the ship as actually thinking it would be destroyed. NIV translates the last clause in verse 4 as "the ship threatened to break up," but the Hebrew text literally says, "the ship thought [it] would be broken." The panic-stricken sailors began praying to their gods and throwing cargo overboard (v. 5a). However, while the sailors frantically tried to save themselves and the ship, Jonah was down in the hold of the ship sleeping (v. 5b).[182] Just as Jonah's trip to Tarshish was halted by the storm, so his sleep was interrupted by the captain (v. 6), who urged him to "get up and call" (lit., "get up and cry out") to his God. The captain's words should have sounded strangely familiar to Jonah, for they mimic the Lord's commission, which literally reads, "*Get up!* Go to Nineveh . . . and *cry out*" (see v. 2).

The sailors decided to "cast lots" in order to isolate the individual who was responsible for the calamity that had come upon them (v. 7). They assumed, rightly in this case, that such a mighty storm was an expression of divine anger at a sinner. Once again the text drips with irony. Jonah had been sent to Nineveh to confront pagans with their "wickedness" (Heb. *ra'ah*, used here in its moral sense). Having shirked his duty, he had brought "calamity" (Heb. *ra'ah* again, used in its nonmoral sense of the punishment that results from sin) down upon himself and the pagan sailors. The one chosen to help eliminate human evil from the pagan world was now the catalyst for an outpouring of divine punishment upon that same world.

The precise form of lot casting used here is not clear. Perhaps the sailors did something akin to drawing straws or rolling dice. Such a practice may seem to the modern mind as an odd and imprecise way of determining the facts of a case, but in this culture it was viewed as a means whereby a god could reveal vital information (see Prov. 16:33, as well as 1 Sam. 14:41–42).

Sure enough, "the lot fell on Jonah," who, in response to the sailors' questions concerning his identity and calling, explained that he was running away from the Lord (vv. 8–10). The irony of the account should not be missed. In a wonderful-sounding theological confession, Jonah claims that he "fears" (NIV translates the Hebrew term "worship") "the LORD, the God

181. For a discussion of the location of Tarshish, including an analysis of the Assyrian evidence, see Hans W. Wolff, *Obadiah and Jonah*, trans. M. Kohl (Minneapolis: Augsburg, 1986), 100–101.

182. The Hebrew text emphasizes the contrast between the frantic sailors and inactive Jonah by using a disjunctive clause, in which Jonah's name appears before the verb (see NIV, "but Jonah had gone below"). The use of the perfect verbal form makes it uncertain if Jonah went down into the hold prior to the actions of the sailors or at the same time that their activity commenced. For a discussion of the point see Simon, *Jonah*, 7.

of heaven, who made the sea and the land" (v. 9). If this is the case, however, why would he try to run away from this God? After all, if the Lord sees everything from his heavenly vantage point and is sovereign over the sea he created, how could the prophet possibly think he could escape? His actions make his words ring hollow.

At a loss to know what to do, the sailors asked Jonah for his advice (v. 11). He told them to throw him into the sea (v. 12). At first this seems like a noble response, but a closer examination reveals otherwise. The proper response would have been for Jonah to repent on the spot and to agree to go to Nineveh. But despite the captain's exhortation (see v. 6), Jonah never does pray in this scene, at least as far as we can tell. His instructions to the sailors betray his obstinate refusal to obey the Lord.[183] It is as if Jonah is saying: "Okay, if he won't let me go to Tarshish, then I'll just die in the sea! But I'm not going to Nineveh!"[184]

The sailors were not willing to resort to such a desperate measure. Instead, they tried to row to shore, but the storm became even more severe (v. 13). Finally, they gave up and prayed to Jonah's God, acknowledging his sovereign power and begging him not to hold them accountable for what they were about to do (v. 14). When Jonah hit the water, the storm stopped (v. 15) and the sailors, overcome with fear, offered sacrifices and made vows to God (v. 16).

In this episode the sailors are a foil for Jonah. In contrast to Jonah, who preaches but does not pray, the sailors offer prayers to God. In contrast to Jonah, who says he fears God but acts in a way that is inconsistent with his claim, the sailors, who barely know Jonah's God, respond to him in genuine fear.

Praying inside a Fish (1:17–2:10)

Jonah may have thought he could escape his commission through death, but once again the Lord frustrated his strategy. He prepared a great fish, which swallowed Jonah and carried him in its belly for three days and three nights (1:17) before disgorging him on to dry land (2:10). In ancient Near Eastern literature, the trip to the underworld land of the dead was viewed as a three-day journey.[185] It is possible that the text depicts the fish giving Jonah a return trip from the underworld, to which he had, by his own admission, descended (see 2:2, 6). Another option is that the time reference simply

---

183. In this regard, see the insightful comments by Trible, *Rhetorical Criticism,* 147, as well as those of Wolff, *Obadiah and Jonah,* 118.

184. One might ask why Jonah did not simply throw himself overboard. But, as Simon (*Jonah,* 13) points out, there are other examples of "passive suicide" in the Hebrew Bible (see Judg. 9:54 and 1 Sam. 31:4–5). Saul's actions suggest that it may have been considered less reprehensible to die by "assisted suicide" than by one's own hand.

185. George M. Landes, "The 'Three Days and Three Nights' Motif in Jonah 2:1," *JBL* 86 (1967): 246–50.

indicates how far the ship had traveled out to sea; it took the fish three days and three nights to return Jonah to his departure point.[186] Of course, it is possible that the fish deposited Jonah at a point on the Mediterranean coast north of Canaan in order to facilitate his trip to Nineveh. In this case the time reference indicates how long it took the fish to travel from the point where it swallowed Jonah to the spot where it vomited the prophet out.

From inside the belly of the fish, Jonah prayed to the Lord (2:1). The prayer takes the form of a thanksgiving song and utilizes stock terminology and idioms. Jonah recalled his time of desperate need, his prayer for deliverance, and the Lord's saving intervention (vv. 2–7). Contrasting himself with pagan idolaters (v. 8), he then promised to thank the Lord publicly and to fulfill the vows he had made when he sought the Lord's help (v. 9). He concluded the song with the declaration, "Salvation comes from the LORD." Jonah's prayer is surprising. We expect a penitential psalm in which the prophet confesses his sins, but, much to our surprise, he did not acknowledge his disobedience. He simply celebrated his deliverance, boasted of his superiority to pagans, and made promises.

Because the psalm seems incongruous in its context, many reject its authenticity. However, the prayer actually contributes to the story's irony and the author's characterization of Jonah. One might have viewed the experience of being swallowed by a fish as a cruel form of torture and as a prelude to death. But Jonah presumed, probably because of his privileged position as a prophet and an Israelite, that he had been saved. Furthermore, despite his earlier decision to choose assisted suicide over repentance, he was quite happy to be alive. Having come face-to-face with the horror of death, he greatly appreciated God's merciful deliverance. One would hope that his bout with death might give him some sympathy for the Ninevites' plight and a greater appreciation for the task God gave him. However, the disdain he showed for the pagans foreshadowed the attitude he would display in the story's final scene.

The Ninevites Repent (3:1–10)

Through Jonah's ordeal in the fish's belly, the Lord had gotten his prophet's attention. This time when the Lord commanded Jonah to go to Nineveh, the prophet obeyed (vv. 1–3a). Before telling us what happened there, the author stops and reminds us what a "great city" Nineveh was. He describes it literally as a "great city, to God, a journey of three days." The adjective "great" refers to the city's size, while the expression "to God" probably means "even by God's standards."[187] The phrase "a journey of three days"

186. Verse 13 seems to militate against this, for it indicates that the sailors thought it was possible to row to dry land, suggesting that the ship was close to land. However, though they may have been near an island or coastline, it need not have been their departure point in Canaan.

187. Other references in the Hebrew Bible to a "great city" or to "great cities" pertain to physical size (see Gen. 10:12; Num. 13:28; Deut. 1:28; 6:10; 9:1; Josh. 10:2; 14:12; 1 Kings 4:13; Jer. 22:8). On the

has often been understood as referring to the city's diameter, that is, to how long it took to travel through the city. This would mean that the city's diameter was about fifty miles.[188] Though Nineveh was large by ancient standards, it was nowhere near this size.[189] For this reason, some scholars point to this exaggerated description of the city's size as evidence of the fictional character of the Book of Jonah. However, others propose that the dimensions do not refer to the city proper, but to the entire administrative district of which Nineveh was a part. In this case "Greater Nineveh" is in view.[190] Stuart translates the expression "a three-day visit city," understanding it as referring to the city's importance as an administrative center or as alluding to the fact that a city as large as Nineveh would require a three-day preaching tour by the prophet to assure that the entire population heard the message.[191] Marcus suggests that the expression does not refer to Nineveh's size, but to the distance Jonah had to travel to get there. It is not to be understood literally, but as an idiom for a long journey, for Jonah would have needed more than three days to travel from the Mediterranean coast to Nineveh.[192]

Jonah's message was simple—in forty more days Nineveh would be destroyed by divine judgment (v. 4).[193] The message sounds unconditional, but the reference to "forty days" suggests there may be a window of opportunity for Nineveh to repent and be spared.[194] The Ninevites took the warning to heart and expressed their sorrow by donning sackcloth and declaring a city-wide fast (v. 5). When the news reached the king, he exchanged his royal robes for sackcloth and issued a proclamation that all people and animals should fast, wear sackcloth, cry out to God, and, most importantly, abandon their evil behavior (vv. 6–8). Though he was not sure if the announcement of judgment was unconditional or not, he reasoned that God might show the city mercy and relent from sending the judgment

---

significance of the expression "to God," see Allen, *Joel, Obadiah, Jonah, and Micah,* 221, and Wolff, *Obadiah and Jonah,* 148. Some prefer to see the expression "great city to God" as referring to the importance of the city in God's eyes. See Stuart, *Hosea-Jonah,* 487, and T. Desmond Alexander, "Jonah," in *Obadiah, Jonah, Micah,* by David W. Baker, T. Desmond Alexander, and Bruce K. Waltke (Downers Grove, Ill.: InterVarsity, 1988), 119.

188. See Allen, *Joel, Obadiah, Jonah, and Micah,* 221.

189. Ibid. Prior to the reign of Sennacherib (705–681 B.C.), the circumference of the city was less than three miles, but Sennacherib expanded the city's circumference to seven and a half miles.

190. Alexander, "Jonah," 57–58.

191. Stuart, *Hosea-Jonah,* 487–88.

192. David Marcus, "Nineveh's 'Three Days' Walk' (Jonah 3:3): Another Interpretation," in *On the Way to Nineveh: Studies in Honor of George M. Landes,* ed. S. L. Cook and S. C. Winter (Atlanta: Scholars Press, 1999), 42–53. In this view, v. 4 makes the point that Jonah arrived at Nineveh after a journey of only one day, an idiom for a short time. According to Marcus, the point is that he got there "lickety split" (47).

193. Verse 4a states literally, ". . . and Jonah began to go into the city a journey of one day." If the city's/district's diameter is in view, then the text describes him going one-third of the way through it.

194. On the implied conditionality of many announcements of judgment, see my remarks on Jer. 26:18 and Mic. 3:12, as well as Chisholm, "Does God Change His Mind?" 389–91.

(v. 9).[195] When God saw Nineveh's sincere response, he did indeed respond with compassion and relented from sending the announced judgment (v. 10).

A Pouting Prophet (4:1–11)

God's decision to spare Nineveh sickened and angered Jonah (v. 1). He apparently hated the Ninevites and believed that they deserved the swift justice of God, not his mercy. Jonah was sent on a mission to warn the Ninevites that God was about to judge their moral evil (Heb. *ra'ah*). His mission was successful; the Ninevites changed, prompting God to relent from sending calamity (Heb. *ra'ah* again). However, rather than celebrating God's mercy (the same mercy he had experienced when delivered from death), Jonah was displeased and overcome with anger. The statement "Jonah was greatly displeased" literally reads "Jonah was displeased [with] great displeasure." Ironically, the Hebrew term *ra'ah*, translated "displeasure" here, is used to describe Jonah's emotional state. At the beginning of the story the term characterized the evil Ninevites; by the end of the story it applies to Jonah— in more ways than one, as we shall see (see v. 6 below).

At this point we discover why Jonah rejected the commission initially and fled for Tarshish (v. 2). He knew that God, because of his loving and compassionate nature, would extend his mercy to the Ninevites if they repented. Jonah wanted no part in the moral reclamation of such a wicked city, so he refused to go and preach there.

Jonah's characterization of God's compassion is not unique; the same description occurs in Joel 2:13. It is rooted in Exodus 34:6–7, where God is described in similar terms after relenting from judgment following Israel's sin with the golden calf (see Exod. 32:14). Some dismiss biblical references to God "relenting" from judgment as anthropomorphic, arguing that an unchangeable God would never change his mind once he has announced his intentions. But both Jonah 4:2 and Joel 2:13 list God's capacity to "change his mind" as one of his fundamental attributes, one that derives from his compassion and demonstrates his love.[196]

Jonah's double standard is appalling. He knew God was merciful because he had extended his compassion to sinful Israel and to the disobedient prophet himself. But, in Nineveh's case, Jonah was unwilling to let God be God. He felt the pagan Ninevites did not deserve mercy, even though they repented of their sin. It is fine for God to forgive sinful Israel but not the sinful pagans.

195. Note that the king asks rhetorically, "Who knows?" For other examples of someone responding in this manner to an announcement of judgment, see 2 Sam. 12:22, where the announcement proved to be an unalterable decree, and Joel 2:14, where the announcement proved to be conditional and the threatened judgment was averted.
196. For a more detailed discussion, see Joel 2:13 as well as Chisholm, "Does God Change His Mind?" 387–99. An abridged version of this article appears in *Kindred Spirit* 22 (summer 1998): 4–5.

Jonah decided he would rather die than live with the knowledge that Nineveh had been spared, so he asked God to take his life (v. 3). The Lord responded with a rhetorical question, asking Jonah if it was proper for him to be so angry (v. 4).[197] Without responding to the Lord's question, the prophet went out to a spot east of the city, made a shelter, and waited to see what would happen (v. 5). Perhaps he hoped that God would decide to judge Nineveh after all or that the Ninevites would return to their sin, prompting an outbreak of divine anger. Or just maybe Jonah thought that his anger would bring God to his senses and prompt him to do what was just.

Little did Jonah realize that the Lord's agenda had a new focus. Having persuaded Nineveh to turn from its evil ways, the Lord now turned his attention to the angry, pouting prophet with the death wish on his lips. He decided to give Jonah an object lesson in order to deliver the prophet from his faulty way of thinking. The Lord caused a large plant to grow up suddenly over Jonah's shelter so that he might have additional shade "to ease his discomfort" (v. 6; lit., "to deliver him from his discomfort"). But there is more here than meets the eye. The word translated "discomfort" is the Hebrew *ra'ah,* the same term used earlier to describe the Ninevites' "evil" (see 1:2; 3:8) as well as Jonah's displeasure with God's decision to spare the city (see 4:1). On the surface, the term seems to refer in verse 6 to Jonah's physical "discomfort." But if God were concerned only with Jonah's physical comfort, he would not have destroyed the plant so quickly (see v. 7). God provided and then took away the plant for a more important reason. He used it as an object lesson to deliver Jonah from something more important than physical distress, namely Jonah's morally wrong attitude. The word *ra'ah* has a double meaning here. On the surface level it refers to Jonah's physical discomfort, but on a deeper level it refers to his "evil" way of thinking, expressed by his displeasure (see 4:1) over God's mercy.

Oddly enough, Jonah, who shortly before had asked to die, was elated over the extra shade provided by the plant (v. 6b). The intense heat, like his earlier experience in the sea, had brought him close to death. Having stared death in the face, the prophet was happy when relief came through the plant. One would hope that this might give him some insight into why God was willing to spare the Ninevites.

When God caused a worm to kill the plant, leaving Jonah without extra shelter from the elements, the prophet once more asked to die (v. 8). We then discover that his anger over the loss of the plant had brought him to this point (v. 9). God asked him if it was proper for him to be so angry over

197. In the Hebrew text, the Lord's question reads literally, "Doing well is there anger to you?" The expression "doing well" is usually taken in the sense "Is it right [for you to be angry]?" In this case the Lord questions the moral propriety of Jonah's anger. However, it is possible that the expression indicates degree or intensity. In this case one may translate, "Are you that deeply angry?" See Simon, *Jonah,* 38. In this case, the Lord's question seems to express surprise, or perhaps outrage, at the degree of Jonah's anger.

a plant. Jonah responded to God's question this time; he affirmed that he had every right to be angry—even to the point of wishing he were dead. Jonah's answer played right into God's hands. Using an argument from the lesser to the greater, God explained that Jonah felt remorse over the loss of a plant that he did not produce or cultivate (v. 10). If Jonah, out of self-interest, could develop such an attachment to a mere plant, how much more should God be allowed to feel remorse over the prospect of losing a great city filled with people and animals (v. 11).

In formulating his argument, God points out that there were 120,000 people in Nineveh who could not "tell their right hand from their left." Some understand this as referring to children who had not yet reached the age of moral discernment.[198] However, the Hebrew term used here (*'adam*) more naturally refers to the entire population of the city, especially when it is coordinated with the term "beast(s)" (translated "cattle" in NIV).[199] Their inability to discern "their right hand from their left" must refer to their moral ignorance. Though responsible for their evil deeds and subject to divine judgment (see 1:2), the Ninevites did not have the advantage of special divine revelation concerning the moral will of God. Morally and ethically speaking, they were like children.[200] Their relative ignorance, though not excusing their behavior, did make God predisposed to give them a window of opportunity and to be merciful to them when they repented.

The book ends abruptly without telling us how Jonah responded to the Lord's final argument. This is appropriate, for what could Jonah say? His obsession with justice had been exposed as wrongheaded, and the Lord had made an airtight case for showing mercy.

Sin Punished and Promises Fulfilled (Micah)

Introduction

Micah, a contemporary of Isaiah, prophesied in the late eighth century B.C. during the reigns of the Judahite kings Jotham (750–731 B.C.), Ahaz (735–715), and Hezekiah (715–686). He was from the town of Moresheth (probably the same as Moresheth-gath, mentioned in 1:14), located southwest of Jerusalem. Apart from this we know nothing about the prophet's background.

The Book of Micah has no overarching macrostructure; it appears to be a loosely arranged anthology of speeches. The book divides into three main

---

198. See, for example, ibid., 47.
199. See Lev. 27:28; Ps. 36:6; Jer. 32:43; 36:29; Ezek. 14:13, 17, 19; 25:13; 29:8; 36:11; Zeph. 1:3; and Zech. 2:4.
200. See Allen, *Joel, Obadiah, Jonah, and Micah*, 234–35.

sections: chapters 1–3, 4–5, and 6–7. The first three chapters focus on Judah's sin and impending doom. The initial speech (1:2–16) looks to the immediate future and anticipates the fall of Samaria, as well as the invasion of Judah. The next speech (2:1–11) focuses on the present and denounces the sins of Judah's leaders, including the false prophets. At the end of chapter 2 (vv. 12–13), the tone changes abruptly as the prophet looks beyond the coming judgment to the more distant future and depicts Israel's eventual deliverance from exile. In chapter 3, Micah picks up where he left off before the brief interlude. He returns to the present and again exposes the sin of Judah's leaders and false prophets (vv. 1–11). The chapter ends (v. 12) with the announcement that Jerusalem will be devastated, bringing to a climax the invasion depicted in chapter 1.

At the beginning of chapter 4 there is another abrupt thematic shift as the prophet looks beyond the coming judgment to a time when the Lord will rule from Jerusalem and establish his worldwide kingdom of peace (4:1–5). The remainder of chapter 4 and chapter 5 describe how this vision would come to be realized. Jerusalem and the Davidic dynasty would undergo humiliation in the immediate future, and the Lord would take away the people's sources of false security. But the Lord would eventually raise up a new David to lead his people into a glorious new era.

The book's final section contains a judgment speech (6:1–16) and a prophetic lament over Judah's sad moral condition (7:1–7). However, sadness turns to joy as the prophet portrays a time when Zion would be restored, God's exiled people would return home, and the Lord would show mercy to his people in fulfillment of his promise to the patriarchs (7:8–20).

The Lord Is on the Warpath (1:2–16)

The prophet called the nations to attention and announced that the Lord was ready to testify against them (v. 2). However, oddly enough, the message that follows does not denounce the nations or describe their punishment. Rather it focuses on Israel and Judah. Why then did Micah open his speech in this fashion? Most likely this is a rhetorical device to capture his audience's attention. He made it sound as if a judgment speech against Israel's and Judah's enemies would follow. Such a message would have certainly been welcomed by Israel and Judah. But having gained their attention, he then turned on them. Yes, God was coming to judge the nations, but the covenant community was not exempt. In fact, it was the focal point of God's judgment.

The prophet described the sovereign Judge's arrival on the scene (vv. 3–4). The Lord descends from his heavenly dwelling place and walks along the tops of the mountains, which disintegrate beneath him. The mountains melt like wax before fire, and the rocks slide down the mountain slopes as swiftly as water. At this point the prophet sprang his trap. It was Israel's rebellion against their covenant Lord that had prompted his judgment (v. 5). This rebellion was epitomized by idolatrous Samaria, the capital of the northern kingdom, and by Jerusalem, the capital of Judah.

The prophet first described God's judgment on Samaria (vv. 6–7). The Lord would reduce the city to a heap of rubble and a place where vineyards would be planted. Her stones would tumble into the valley below, the very foundations of the city would be exposed, and her idols would be shattered to bits and burned.[201] The idols are compared to a prostitute's wages, for they were made from metal donated to the Samarian temple by the idolaters who came to worship there. However, these idols would be melted down and used "as the wages of prostitutes." The precise meaning of this statement is not clear. Perhaps it means that the enemy soldiers would use the metal to hire prostitutes or that they would donate the metal to their own gods.

Having described Samaria's fall, the prophet was ready to move on to Jerusalem. He lamented what was about to happen, for he realized that Samaria's moral corruption had infected Judah as well and had even reached Jerusalem (vv. 8–9). However, before announcing Jerusalem's coming devastation (see 3:12), he depicted the enemy invasion of the Judahite countryside (vv. 10–15). The prophet began his description of the invasion with the words, "Tell it not in Gath" (v. 10a). David used these same words when he lamented the tragic deaths of Jonathan and Saul at the hands of the Philistines (see 2 Sam. 1:20). At that time Gath was one of the Philistines' major cities; David did not want the news of Israel's tragedy to be publicized in enemy territory. By Micah's time Gath may have been in Judah's hands (see 2 Chron. 26:6), but that is immaterial. Micah was using a traditional saying to make the point that Judah's demise should not be publicized. Her humiliation would be bad enough without the surrounding nations adding insult to injury.

The invaders would capture the towns of Judah one by one, until they stood at the very gate of the capital city. For rhetorical impact the prophet utilized sound-play and irony in his description. He urged the people of Beth Ophrah (which could be taken to mean "house of dust") to roll in the dust as an expression of their sorrow (v. 10b; see Jer. 25:34). The women of Shapir (meaning "beautiful") would be publicly exposed and humiliated, while the women of Zaanan (which sounds like the Hebrew verb "come out") would be trapped in their town and unable to "come out" (v. 11a).[202] All Beth Ezel, meaning the "house next door," could do was watch and weep (v. 11b). The expectations of Maroth (a name that sounds like the Hebrew

---

201. Samaria was situated on a hill, approximately three hundred feet above the valley below. See King, *Amos, Hosea, Micah—An Archaeological Commentary,* 36.

202. In the Hebrew text, the feminine singular is used to address the "inhabitant of Shapir" and the "inhabitant of Zaanan." Apparently the singular is collective, or a typical woman is addressed as a representative of the city.

marah, meaning "bitter") would go unrealized (v. 12), while those in Lachish needed to harness "the team" (the Hebrew noun translated "team" resembles the name Lachish) to their chariots in preparation for battle (v. 13).[203] Lachish would say good-bye to Moresheth Gath's citizens, much like a father who gives his daughter "parting gifts" at marriage (v. 14a). The name Moresheth sounds like the Hebrew word for "betrothed, engaged," facilitating the portrayal of the city as a daughter ready to leave home. The town of Aczib would prove "deceptive" (the word "deceptive" sounds like the name Aczib) to the kings of Judah (v. 14b). Mareshah would be invaded by a conqueror (the Hebrew word sounds like the name Mareshah), forcing the "glory of Israel," probably a reference to Judah's men of rank, to flee to Adullam for safety, just like David of old (v. 15).[204] In light of this coming tragedy, the prophet urged the inhabitants of Mareshah to lament over the exile of their children (v. 16).[205]

Judah's Leaders Denounced (2:1–3:12)

Using the language of death and lamentation, the prophet acted out in advance the funeral of Judah's sinful leaders. The interjection "woe" was a cry of mourning heard at funerals (see 1 Kings 13:30; Jer. 22:18–19; Amos 5:16). By using this word, the prophet suggested that they would soon die. They are characterized as "those who plot evil on their beds" and then carry out their schemes when morning comes (2:1). He accused them of stealing land and houses from people. As noted earlier (see my comments on Isa. 1:16–17), a huge, oppressive royal military bureaucracy had developed in Judah. As it grew in size and in power, it began to exploit the common people and, through a combination of oppressive measures, take their land from them.[206]

The Lord was not about to let them get away with their unjust practices. While the evildoers planned their sinful schemes (see v. 1), the Lord was doing some planning of his own and would send disaster on them (v. 3). They would lose the land they had stolen (v. 4), and they would be excluded from any future distribution of the land (v. 5).

203. Once again, the feminine singular is used, apparently in a collective or representative sense, in referring to the "inhabitant of Maroth" and in addressing the "inhabitant of Lachish."

204. NIV interprets "glory of Israel" as referring to an individual, perhaps the king, but the phrase more likely refers to the leaders in general, including the king. See Isa. 5:13, where NIV "men of rank" reads literally "his glory."

205. The second-person verbs and pronouns in v. 16 are feminine singular. It is possible that Zion, personified as a young woman, is addressed (see v. 13), but it is more likely that the addressees are the residents of Mareshah. The Hebrew text of v. 15 reads literally, "the conqueror I will bring against you [feminine singular], O inhabitant [feminine singular again] of Mareshah." A typical female resident, representing the city as a whole, is addressed. It is natural to assume that this address continues in v. 16. This same style is utilized in vv. 11–13 (see comments above).

206. For a study of the socioeconomic background of the time, see Dearman, *Property Rights in the Eighth-Century Prophets.*

Wordplay highlights the prophet's speech. The repetition of the word "plan" emphasizes that the Lord's response is an appropriate one. The word used to describe their evil deeds (v. 1, Heb. *ra'*) is almost identical to the term *ra'ah*, used in verse 3 of the "disaster" planned by the Lord and of the "calamity" that would overtake the sinners. Those who "take" away (Heb. *nasa'*, literally "lift up") the houses of the victims (v. 2) would be the objects of taunts as men "ridicule" (Heb. *nasa' mashal*, literally "lift up a taunt") them (v. 4). The tables would be turned as the oppressors became the victims of oppression. These oppressors-turned-victims would lament, "We are utterly ruined" (v. 4; Heb. *shadod neshaddunu*). Even these words testify to their guilt, for they sound like the word "fields" (v. 2, Heb. *sadot*) and remind us that the land for which they mourn was acquired unjustly.[207]

These evildoers rejected the prophets who confronted them with their sinful actions. They wanted to hear promises of prosperity (symbolized by "wine and beer," see v. 11). They told the Lord's prophets to stop their impassioned rhetoric of judgment, for they were confident that the Lord would not humiliate his people (vv. 6–7a). In response to their faulty reasoning, the Lord reminded them that he rewards only those who obey him (v. 7b), not those who treat their countrymen like enemies and steal their property (vv. 8–9). Their sin would bring disaster on the land (v. 10).

Before finishing his judgment speech against Judah's leaders, Micah stopped briefly to encourage the upright (vv. 12–13; see v. 7). Though exile was imminent (see 1:16; 2:10), the Lord would someday gather the exiled remnant like sheep and lead them out of exile (see 4:6 and 7:14–15 as well).

Because this oracle, if understood in a positive sense, does not fit smoothly into its immediate context, some understand it as containing the words of the false prophets (just mentioned in v. 11). Others argue that it depicts the Assyrian siege of Jerusalem in 701 B.C. In this case it pictures the remnant of Judah being herded into Jerusalem, only to be released by the Lord as he attacks the enemy outside the city's walls.[208] Since Micah appears to envision this event in 4:11–13, this interpretation of 2:12–13 is certainly possible. However, in this case a reference to the Lord "going up" from Jerusalem would be odd.[209] Furthermore, the oracle in 2:12–13 is part of a larger speech that anticipates the destruction of Jerusalem (see 3:12). As we shall see in our discussion of 3:12, this judgment was averted when Hezekiah repented. At that point, Micah's vision of the future, like that of Isaiah, changed, and he prophesied Jerusalem's fall to the Babylonians, rather than the Assyrians (see 4:10, as well as Isa. 39:6–7). To argue that 2:12–13 prophesies the events of 701 overlooks this progression in Micah's message.

207. For a helpful study of this passage, see Miller, *Sin and Judgment in the Prophets*, 29–31.
208. See, for example, Allen, *Joel, Obadiah, Jonah, and Micah*, 301–3.
209. See Delbert R. Hillers, *Micah*, Hermeneia (Philadelphia: Fortress, 1984), 39.

In chapter 3 the prophet continued his diatribe against Judah's leaders. He compared their cruel oppressive deeds to cannibalism (3:1–3) and warned that a day would come when the tables would be turned (v. 4; see 2:3–5). When that time arrived, the oppressors would cry out to the Lord for help, but their prayers would fall on deaf ears.

Many of the prophets had also compromised their position as God's spokesmen and misled the people (v. 5). If they received food in exchange for a prophetic message, these greedy prophets promised their clients peace, but, if not paid adequately, they prophesied calamity. Appropriately, a time would come when the Lord would shut off the channels of genuine prophetic revelation. All of the methods used by the prophets, including visions (which were legitimate) and the reading of omens (which was not an authorized means of receiving revelation from the Lord), would cease to yield information, leaving the prophets silent and disgraced (vv. 6–7).

Micah stopped at this point to defend the authenticity of his own ministry (v. 8). He possessed the Lord's Spirit, the source of genuine prophecy. He championed the cause of justice and boldly confronted Israel's sins. By way of contrast, Judah's leaders perverted justice (vv. 9–10), while the priests and prophets were concerned only with material gain (v. 11a) and naively denied that judgment would come upon the nation (v. 11b).

For this reason, Jerusalem would fall (v. 12). After devastating the countryside of Judah, the invaders would reduce Zion, like Samaria, to a heap of rubble. Even the temple would be destroyed. This prophecy of Jerusalem's demise was not fulfilled, at least in Micah's day. We find out why in Jeremiah 26. Like Micah before him, Jeremiah prophesied that Jerusalem and the temple would be destroyed (see Jer. 26:6). When certain leaders demanded that Jeremiah be executed, some of the elders of the land gave them a history lesson. They recalled Micah's prophecy of Jerusalem's fall and then pointed out that the judgment had been averted when King Hezekiah repented (Jer. 26:17–19). This demonstrates that Micah's prophecy, though seemingly unconditional in tone, was implicitly conditional.[210] Because of Hezekiah's repentance, the prophesied judgment was postponed.[211]

Better Days Ahead (4:1–5:15)

Once more, Micah's tone shifted abruptly, as he looked beyond the immediate judgment to a new era characterized by justice and worldwide peace. In a text that is almost identical to Isaiah 2:2–4, Micah envisioned a time when the temple mount in Jerusalem would become the focal point of the world (4:1–3).[212]

---

210. See Chisholm, "Does God 'Change His Mind'?" 391, 397, as well as my comments on Jer. 26:19.

211. Micah's vision of Jerusalem's ruin did become a reality in 586 B.C.

212. It is not certain if Micah borrowed from Isaiah, or vice versa. Perhaps they both drew on an otherwise unknown common source.

The nations would stream to Jerusalem to learn the Lord's laws and submit their disputes to his wise and fair judgment. Wars would cease as the nations devoted their energies to more peaceful and worthwhile endeavors. At that time everyone would grow his crops without having to worry about enemy invaders (v. 4).[213] This exciting vision of the future prompted the prophet, speaking on behalf of God's people, to declare his allegiance to the Lord (v. 5).

Having described Jerusalem's ultimate destiny, Micah next explained how this new era would come about (vv. 6–8). The Lord would gather the exiles and form them into a strong nation. Kingship would be restored to Zion, as the Lord established his rule over his people. Jerusalem is called the "watchtower of the flock," because the Lord would keep a protective eye on his people from his throne.

In verses 9–10, the prophet drew closer to his own time (note "now" in v. 9, in contrast to "in the last days" in v. 1 and "in that day" in v. 6). Addressing personified Zion, he depicted her as a woman writhing in labor. Zion's pain was caused by the prospect of losing her king and being taken into exile. But this dual disaster would not happen immediately. Micah specifically mentioned Babylon as the place of exile. Like Isaiah, he foresaw the Lord's deliverance of Jerusalem from the Assyrian threat (vv. 11–13), but he also realized that exile would eventually come (see Isa. 39:6–7). This revision of Micah's message came in the wake of Hezekiah's repentance (see my comments on 3:12).

In chapter 5 the prophet repeated and expanded the major themes of 4:6–10, only in reverse order. This creates a chiastic structure for the central portion of the speech, which can be outlined as follows:

> A The Lord strengthens a remnant (4:6–7a)
> > B Dominion restored (4:7b–8)
> > > C Zion and her king are humiliated (4:9–10)
> > > > D Zion saved from the present crisis (4:11–13)
> > > C′Zion and her king are humiliated (5:1)
> > B′Dominion restored (5:2–6)
> A′The Lord strengthens a remnant (5:7–9)

Picking up on the theme of 4:9–10, the prophet pictured Zion under siege (5:1). This siege is not the one alluded to in 4:11, from which Zion would be delivered. Rather, it is accompanied by the humiliation of Zion's king, a theme present in 4:9, where the loss of kingship is associated with Zion's exile (see 4:10). The enemy is depicted as striking Zion's king with a scepter, normally a symbol of rulership (see Ps. 2:9), but here an instrument of humiliation.

But all is not lost, for dominion would return to Zion. In the first part of the speech, the prophet spoke of the Lord ruling from Zion (see 4:7b),

213. Verse 4 is unique to Micah.

but here it becomes clear that the Lord would exercise his dominion through a human king, who is depicted as another David, or perhaps even as the second coming of David himself (vv. 2–6). This king is introduced in riddle-like fashion as coming from Bethlehem Ephrathah, the home of David.[214] The final statement of verse 2 describes the coming king as one "whose origins are from of old, from ancient times." The time references indicate antiquity. The expression "from of old," refers elsewhere to antiquity in general (Isa. 45:21; 46:10; Hab. 1:12) and more specifically to Israel's early history (Ps. 74:12; 77:11), including the Davidic era (Neh. 12:46). The phrase "ancient times" (literally, "days of antiquity") likewise refers elsewhere to Israel's early history (Isa. 63:9, 11; Mic. 7:14; Mal. 3:4), including the time of David (Amos 9:11). The Hebrew term translated "origins" by NIV, literally means "goings out." The term may refer here to the coming king's genealogical roots. In this case the term pictures him as part of a long royal line extending back to David (see as well Jer. 23:5; 33:15). Another option is to understand the word as referring to the coming king's appearance.[215] In this case the king is depicted as an actual figure from the past who would reappear—the second coming of David, as it were. Since other prophets speak of the ideal king of the future as "David," this interpretation is certainly possible here (see Jer. 30:9; Ezek. 34:23–24; 37:24–25; Hos. 3:5). However, even if taken this way, the language is archetypal and should not be understood in a hyperliteralistic manner. This "David" carries out royal functions that cannot be distinguished from those assigned to the messianic king. He is actually a descendant of David who comes in his ancestor's spirit and power, much like John the Baptist came in the spirit and power of Elijah and thus fulfilled the prophecy of Malachi 4:5 (see Matt. 11:10–14; 17:11–12; Mark 1:2–4; Luke 1:17, 76; 7:27).

In 4:10, the prophet described Zion as a woman in labor, straining to give birth. He picked up that image again in 5:3 as he anticipated a time when she would finally give birth. The reality behind the image is the restoration of God's covenant people to their previously abandoned land. On that occasion the coming king's "brothers," apparently referring to his fellow Judahites, would join with the Israelites to form a revived united kingdom.

Energized by the Lord's power, the king would care for the people like a shepherd and establish a secure and peaceful environment for them (vv. 4–5a).[216] Supported by other competent leaders, he would beat back and conquer aggressive, imperialistic powers like the Assyrians (vv. 5b–6). The reference to "seven shepherds, even eight leaders of men," utilizes the numbers seven/eight to symbolize completeness. The king would have the help

---

214. Ephrathah is apparently an alternative name for Bethlehem. See Gen. 35:19; 48:7; Ruth 4:11.
215. A related term has the nuance "appearance" in Ps. 65:8 and Hos. 6:3.
216. Note how the shepherding motif of 5:4 corresponds to the imagery of 4:8.

of an ideal complement of associates who, with authority delegated by the king, would defeat and rule over Israel's defeated enemies.

Micah's vision of an Israelite empire was not realized in his time. In the meantime, the Assyrians have long since disappeared from the international scene. Only the most hyperliteral interpreter would suggest that a revived Assyrian Empire will reappear during the messianic era. Assyria is an archetype here. In terms that would have been very inspiring and meaningful to an eighth-century B.C. Israelite audience, Micah assured God's people that a time was coming, unlike their own day, when they would no longer be threatened by powerful, hostile nations. In other words, Micah's vision of Israel's future is contextualized so that his contemporaries might fully appreciate it. The essential point is that the new era will be one of peace and security for God's people where God's ideal king prevents the lionlike "Assyrians" of the world from terrorizing helpless sheep.

In 5:7–9, the prophet returned to the remnant theme of 4:6–7. He used two seemingly contradictory images to depict the remnant. In the first he compared the remnant to dew and rain on the grass, while in the second he likened the remnant to a powerful lion that "mauls and mangles" its victims. The second image is militaristic, as verse 9 makes clear. But what is the point of the comparison to dew and rain? The final statement in verse 7 is the key to interpreting the metaphor. The point is made that both the dew and rain are beyond human control. In the same way the animals of the forest cannot resist the powerful lion (v. 8b). The point of both metaphors seems to be that the remnant would become a mighty nation whose enemies would be unable to resist its power (v. 9).[217]

In the messianic era the Lord would remove all the false sources of security in which his misguided people had trusted, including chariots, fortified cities, divination, and idols (vv. 10–14). In the ancient Near East, armies utilized horse-drawn chariots in battle, but the Lord expected his people to trust in his supernatural protective power, not a modernized army (Deut. 20:1–4). The pagans used divination as a way of discerning the intentions of the gods, but the Lord prohibited it (Deut. 18:10–12) and revealed his will and intentions through his prophets. Israel would finally realize that true security is found in the Lord, for he is sovereign over the nations (v. 15).

What the Lord Requires (6:1–16)

Using the language of the courtroom, the Lord formally confronted his people and challenged them to defend themselves against the charges he was about to bring against them (v. 1). He summoned the personified mountains, which have been around since the beginning of time, to serve as witnesses, for they could testify accurately concerning God's relationship with

---

217. Dew is also used as a military metaphor in 2 Sam. 17:12.

his people (v. 2). Countering their charge that he had mistreated them, the Lord reminded his people that he had delivered them from Egyptian bondage, given them leaders, protected them from the hostility of Balak of Moab (see Num. 22–24), and led them into the Promised Land (vv. 3–5).[218] In verse 3, the Lord asks, "How have I burdened you?" He had, of course, done no such thing. On the contrary, he had delivered them from burdensome slavery. In verse 4, the Lord declares, "I brought you up out of Egypt." The similarity in sound between the Hebrew verbs translated "burdened" and "brought up" draws attention to the contrast between their false accusation and reality, or, as Allen states, between "wild theory" and "sober fact."[219]

Micah now chimed in. Playing the role of a worshiper, he asked the question, "With what shall I come before the LORD and bow down before the exalted God?" (v. 6a). Many of his fellow Israelites would have thought immediately in terms of sacrifices. Surely the Lord would expect burnt offerings from those worshiping him (v. 6b). Imagine how pleased he would be if one brought thousands of rams or one's firstborn child (v. 7). But Micah rejected this approach and reminded the people that God had already revealed where his priorities lie (v. 8). Before all else God wants his people to actively promote justice, to passionately devote themselves to the good of others, and to humbly (or perhaps "carefully") submit to the Lord's standards in all areas of one's life. This is what is "good" and what the Lord fundamentally requires from his people. The Hebrew word translated "mercy" in NIV refers more broadly to "loyalty, faithfulness, commitment, devotion." It is the pivotal term in this passage, for such devotion to others is proof of one's submission to God's authority, as well as the foundation for establishing a just society. To "love" devotion suggests a passion for it; those who "love devotion" actively seek the good of others.[220] In the New Testament, Jesus himself becomes the epitome and standard of such sacrificial love.

How does Micah's speech relate to the words of the Lord that precede it and to the judgment speech that follows? Apparently the people felt the Lord was being unfair to them. They brought plenty of sacrifices, but yet the Lord seemed displeased with them. Perhaps some thought the Lord wanted to burden them with more sacrifices. Micah refuted this kind of thinking by demonstrating that God's priorities are justice, loyalty, and obedience, not sacrifice. Reminding Israel of this fundamental truth sets up the judgment speech that follows (vv. 9–16), in which the Lord accuses his people of being unjust and announces that judgment would fall on those who had disregarded his priorities.

218. Shittim was the Israelites' campsite prior to crossing the Jordan River, while Gilgal was their first campsite after crossing. See Josh. 2:1; 3:1; 4:19–5:10.

219. Allen, *Joel, Obadiah, Jonah, and Micah,* 366.

220. For a helpful discussion of the importance of the concept of "loyalty" in Micah's argument, see Katharine D. Sakenfeld, *Faithfulness in Action: Loyalty in Biblical Perspective* (Fortress: Philadelphia, 1985), 101–4.

The judgment speech characterizes Judah as a "wicked house" where "ill-gotten treasures" have been hidden away (v. 10a). In violation of God's law (see Lev. 19:35–36; Deut. 25:13–16), merchants used dishonest means to increase their profits (vv. 10b–11), and the rich oppressors resorted to violence and deceit to get ahead (v. 12). Like the Israelite kings Omri and Ahab of the previous century, they abused their power (v. 16a).[221] God's judgment would be appropriate. An enemy invader would sweep through the land, depriving these greedy sinners of their crops (vv. 14–15) and leaving them an object of scorn among the surrounding nations (v. 16b).

The Prophet Laments (7:1–7)

As he surveyed the moral landscape of Judah, Micah lamented. He compared himself to one who walks through a vineyard or orchard in hopes that he will find a cluster of grapes or a delicious fig. But the harvesters have already passed through, and there is no fruit to be found (v. 1). In a similar way, the godly had disappeared from the land, which was now overrun by violent and dishonest men (vv. 2–3). No "fruit" could be found; there were only briers and thorns (v. 4a). God's judgment was inevitable; soon the panic-stricken watchmen on the city walls would announce its arrival (v. 4b). The situation had deteriorated to the point where one could not trust neighbors, friends, or even one's own family (vv. 5–6). However, the prophet had not lost hope. He continued to pray to and wait for his God, who would eventually vindicate the few godly people who remained (v. 7).

Looking Confidently to the Future (7:8–20)

The book ends on a positive note as both personified Zion and the nation confidently look to the future, and oracles of salvation affirm that their expectations will be realized. The structure of this section may be outlined as follows:

> *Confidence:* Zion anticipates vindication from the Lord (vv. 8–10).
> *Salvation oracle:* Vindication will indeed come (vv. 11–13).
> *Prayer:* May the Lord again shepherd his people (v. 14).
> *Salvation oracle:* The Lord will again reveal his power (v. 15).
> *Confidence:* The nation anticipates vindication from the Lord (vv. 16–17).
> *Hymn:* The nation praises God for his mercy and faithfulness (vv. 18–20).

Zion is not specifically identified as the speaker in verses 8–10, but several contextual clues suggest that she is. In verses 10b–11, where the speaker of verses 8–10a is addressed, feminine singular pronouns are used in the Hebrew text (see "your God" and "your walls"). Zion, of course, is typically portrayed as a woman in prophetic literature (see Mic. 1:13 and 4:10). The ref-

221. Omri ruled over the northern kingdom from 885–874 B.C., while Ahab reigned from 874–853 B.C. Ahab's treatment of Naboth (see 1 Kings 21) epitomized his attitude.

erence to "walls" in verse 11 suggests a city is in view, and the humiliation referred to in verse 8 corresponds thematically to Zion's plight as depicted in 4:9–10. Speaking to her enemies, Zion acknowledges she has suffered because of her sin, but she is confident that the Lord will take up her cause and vindicate her. The oracle (vv. 11–13) assures her that her walls will be rebuilt, her exiled people will return to her from the south and north, and the nations will be punished for their deeds.

A prayer is then offered on behalf of the nation (v. 14). The speaker is not identified, but the following context suggests the nation is here praying to the Lord. (Note the first-person plural pronouns "our" and "us" in vv. 17, 19–20, where the nation is clearly speaking.) The nation asks that the Lord might "shepherd" his people as he did in former times. Israel is depicted as isolated and vulnerable, but they long to feed, as it were, in rich pasture-lands, symbolized by the trans-Jordanian sites Bashan and Gilead. Both regions were well known as fertile grazing areas (see Num. 32:1–4; Deut. 32:14; Jer. 50:19). The oracle (v. 15) assures the nation that the Lord will indeed intervene for his people in a mighty, miraculous way, just as he did in the days of Moses.

With this word of assurance the nation anticipates a time when the once arrogant nations will be silenced and forced to grovel before the Lord's people (vv. 16–17). The nation marvels at the Lord's incomparable mercy. He is willing to forgive their sins so that they are no longer a barrier to his relationship with his people (v. 18). Two metaphors are used to picture the Lord's forgiveness (v. 19). In the first the Lord is depicted as crushing their sins underfoot as one would an enemy. In the second he hurls their sins into the depths of the sea, where they can never be recovered. What prompts the Lord to show his people such mercy? The answer comes in verse 20. The Lord forgives the nation for the sake of Abraham and Jacob. He promised the patriarchs on oath that he would multiply their descendants, give them the Promised Land, and make them a paradigm of divine blessing (see Gen. 12:2–3; 22:15–18; 28:13–15; 35:11–12). For these promises to be fulfilled, God must continue to extend mercy to Abraham's descendants until they finally come to the place where they obey the Lord (see Gen. 18:18–19a). Only then will the promises be fully realized (Gen. 18:19b).

The Downfall of Nineveh (Nahum)

Introduction

Nahum prophesied sometime between the fall of the Egyptian city Thebes in 663 B.C. and the fall of Nineveh in 612 B.C. He spoke of the former as a historical fact (see 3:8–10) and of the latter as still future.[222] Why was the fall of Nineveh so important to Nahum and to the people of Judah? Since the middle of the eighth century B.C., the Assyrians had been "public-enemy number one." When the Assyrians began to expand their empire into Palestine, Judah under foolish King Ahaz initially allied with them against Israel and the Arameans (see Isa. 7). When King Hezekiah rebelled against Assyria, Sennacherib invaded Judah and devastated the countryside, before being turned back by the Lord outside the walls of Jerusalem (see Isa. 36–37 and 1 Kings 18–19). Though defeated, he carried many of the people of Judah into exile. Eventually the Assyrians returned and made Judah one of their subjects. They even carried wicked King Manasseh away into exile (2 Chron. 33:11). One of the inscriptions of King Esarhaddon of Assyria, who ruled from 681–669 B.C., lists "Manasseh, king of Judah" as one of the Assyrian subjects.[223] In short, for Judah, the fall of Nineveh, one of the major cities of the Assyrian Empire, meant freedom from the oppressive hand of Assyria. No more would Judah have to go through the humiliating and economically draining experience of paying tribute to a demanding and ruthless foreign tyrant.

The book's introduction takes the form of a hymnic-style theophany (vv. 2–6), to which a judgment speech is attached (vv. 7–11). The main body of the prophecy, which is introduced with the words "This is what the LORD says," exhibits a chiastic structure:[224]

A Assyrian king taunted/Judah urged to celebrate (1:12–15)
  B Dramatic call to alarm (2:1–10)
    C Taunt (2:11–12)
      D Announcement of judgment (2:13)
        E Woe oracle (3:1–4)
      D´ Announcement of judgment (3:5–7)
    C´ Taunt (3:8–13)
  B´ Dramatic call to alarm (3:14–17)
A´ Assyrian king taunted as others celebrate (3:18–19)

In the calls to alarm (B/B´), the prophet plays the role of a watchman on Nineveh's walls. He urges the city to prepare for an attack and then describes its demise. The taunts (C/C´) begin with rhetorical questions and expose Nineveh's pride. The announcements of judgment (D/D´) begin with the words, "'I am against you,' declares the LORD Almighty."

---

222. For a variety of reasons, J. J. M. Roberts prefers a date between 640 and 630 B.C. See his *Nahum, Habakkuk, and Zephaniah*, OTL (Louisville: Westminster John Knox, 1991), 38–39. Richard D. Patterson opts for a date between 660 and 654 B.C. See his *Nahum, Habakkuk, Zephaniah* (Chicago: Moody, 1991), 5–7.

223. See Pritchard, *Ancient Near Eastern Texts*, 291.

224. For a thorough analysis of the book's structure, including the chiastic arrangement of formal units outlined here, see G. H. Johnston, "A Rhetorical Analysis of the Book of Nahum," Ph.D. diss., Dallas Theological Seminary, 1992, 46–214.

The Divine Warrior Appears (1:2–11)

The central theme of the prophecy is clear from its very beginning. Nahum affirms that the Lord is a God of vengeance who unleashes his raging anger against his enemies (v. 2). NIV translates the first statement, "The LORD is a jealous and avenging God." Though the Hebrew term translated "jealous" can sometimes refer to jealousy, in this context, where God appears as an angry warrior bent on revenge, the word more likely depicts him as one who is "zealous" or "filled with rage."[225]

Nahum adapts a traditional creedal statement in verse 3a. He describes the Lord as "slow to anger and great in power" and then observes that the Lord "will not leave the guilty unpunished." Elsewhere, when the phrase "slow to anger" is used of God, it is followed by the expression "abounding in love" (see Exod. 34:6; Num. 14:18; Neh. 9:17; Ps. 86:15; 103:8; 145:8; Joel 2:13; Jon. 4:2). The statement "he does not leave the guilty unpunished" also appears in Exodus 34:7 and Numbers 14:18, in both cases after a reference to God's willingness to forgive. Nahum alters the traditional formulation by changing "abounding in love" to "great in power" and by omitting any reference to God's forgiving nature. God had been patient with Nineveh, but his love and willingness to forgive were exhausted. Nineveh would experience his unbridled power and justice as he descended in the clouds of judgment (v. 3b).[226]

As the Lord arrives on the scene, he gives a mighty shout, or battle cry, which dries up the sea and rivers and causes even lush regions like Bashan and Carmel to wither (v. 4). The Hebrew verb translated "rebukes" in NIV does sometimes refer to scolding or rebuking (see Gen. 37:10; Ruth 2:16; Zech. 3:2), but in militaristic contexts like this one it more likely refers to a battle cry that terrifies and paralyzes the enemy.[227] The mountains, normally viewed as the epitome of stability, and all of the earth's inhabitants quake before the Lord, for they realize nothing can withstand his angry attack (vv. 5–6).

The theophanic vision of verses 2–6 is certainly terrifying, but it reflects only one side of God's character. The angry warrior-judge is also the protector of his people (v. 7). Nahum's message focuses on God's judgment of Nineveh, but there is another side to the coin. The judgment of Nineveh would mean deliverance and freedom for Judah (see vv. 12–13, 15). The Lord is

225. See also Isa. 42:13; 59:17; Ezek. 36:5–6; 38:19; Zeph. 1:18; 3:8, where a closely related term (derived from the same root) refers to the divine warrior's "zeal."

226. For helpful comments on Nahum's rhetorical technique here, see Roberts, *Nahum, Habakkuk, and Zephaniah,* 50.

227. See A. Caquot, "גָּעַר," *TDOT* 3:53, and note the use of the verb in Ps. 68:30; 106:9; as well as the related noun in Job 26:11; Ps. 9:5; 76:6; 104:7; Isa. 50:2; 51:20; 66:15. The motif of the warrior's powerful battle cry is a fairly common one in ancient Near Eastern literature. For examples, see Chisholm, *Interpreting the Minor Prophets,* 169–70.

good and proves to be "a refuge in times of trouble" who "cares for those who trust in him."[228] The verb translated "cares for" is literally "knows." The Lord "knows" his loyal followers in the sense that he recognizes their allegiance and rewards them for it.

Having balanced his portrait of God, the prophet returns to the theme of God's judgment. When the Lord comes as judge, he annihilates his foes and chases them into darkness, which here symbolizes death (v. 8b; see Job 18:18).[229] The Hebrew verb form translated "pursue" emphasizes the Lord's determination; it indicates an intensification of activity and suggests a persistent pursuit. Speaking directly to the Lord's enemies, the prophet assured them that the Lord would frustrate their efforts and quickly destroy them (vv. 9–10).[230]

In verse 11, the addressee becomes more specific as the prophet speaks to personified Nineveh. Though Nineveh is not actually mentioned (NIV's "O Nineveh" is interpretive), the prophet now uses a second-person feminine singular form, which is most likely understood as being addressed to the city (see 2:1–10). The Lord speaks here of the king of Assyria as one who has "come forth" from the city and "plots evil against the LORD."

Relief for Judah (1:12–15)

The main body of the prophecy begins with the Lord delivering a series of addresses to Judah (1:12–13), the king of Assyria (1:14), and then Judah again (1:15). He uses second-person feminine singular Hebrew pronominal forms in verses 12–13 in speaking to personified Judah. Though Judah is not specifically mentioned here (NIV's "O Judah" in v. 12 is interpretive), verse 15 makes it clear that Judah is the addressee. Judah is addressed by name in verse 15, and five second-person feminine singular Hebrew verbal and pronominal forms are used in the address. Verse 14 is clearly addressed to an enemy, not the Lord's people. Although NIV understands the addressee as Nineveh, it is more likely that the king of Assyria is addressed here. When Nineveh is addressed elsewhere in the book, second feminine singular verbal and pronominal forms are used in the Hebrew text (see 1:11; 2:13; 3:5–8, 11–17), but verse 14 uses second masculine singu-

---

228. The traditional verse division understands the first line of verse 8 as going with what follows, but it seems likely that it belongs with what precedes and corresponds to the phrase "in times of trouble" in the poetic structure. In this case, one may translate vv. 7–8a as follows: "The LORD is good, a refuge in times of trouble; he cares for those who trust in him when the overwhelming flood passes by." The point of both lines is the same: trouble may come, but the Lord protects his people from danger.

229. NIV translates the second line of v. 8, "he will make an end of Nineveh." However, "Nineveh" is not specifically mentioned here. The Hebrew text reads "he will make an end of her place." Since there is no antecedent for the pronoun "her," it is better to follow the ancient Greek translation in reading "those who rise against him." This reading requires only a slight emendation of the traditional Hebrew text and has the advantage of providing a better parallel with "his foes" in the following line. Though the *waw* at the beginning of v. 8 would seem to militate against this proposal, it can be easily explained as dittographic. Note the *waw* on the final form in v. 7.

230. The verb form translated "they plot" in v. 9a is actually second-person plural in the Hebrew text. The enemies referred to in v. 8b are the most likely addressee.

lar Hebrew verbal and pronominal forms. In 3:18–19, the Assyrian king is specifically addressed, and masculine singular forms are employed. This suggests that the king is also the addressee in 1:14. The content of the judgment speech in 1:14 also favors this interpretation (see the comments below).

Though the Lord has punished Judah in the past, he now assures her that her time of affliction is over and that he will deliver her from the oppressive Assyrians (vv. 12–13). Turning to the king of Assyria, the Lord announces that he will eradicate the royal dynasty, destroy the idols in the royal temple, and desecrate the royal tomb (v. 14).[231] Desecrating a tomb expressed intense hostility (see 2 Kings 23:15–16, as well as my comments on Amos 2:1–3). Receiving a proper burial was considered very important in this culture, and tombs were protected by curses inscribed on them.[232] By violating the Assyrian king's tomb, the Lord would show his utter disdain for both the king and the gods responsible for protecting it.

Turning back to Judah, the Lord tells her to look toward the mountains, for a messenger is approaching. He brings with him the good news of Assyria's fall (v. 15). Never again would the Assyrians invade the land of Judah. The people were free to celebrate their festivals and to repay the vows they had made to the Lord in their prayers for deliverance.

The Invasion of Nineveh (2:1–3:19)

Playing the role of a watchman on the city wall, the prophet announces that an enemy is approaching and urges the city to stand on guard and prepare for battle (2:1). Before describing the city's downfall (vv. 3–10), he stops to reiterate the theme of 1:12–15. Nineveh's fall signals a new era for Israel, whose splendor will be restored (v. 2).

Nahum's account of Nineveh's fall is written as if he were an eyewitness of the event (vv. 3–10). One sees the soldiers' shields and spears, as well as the war chariots darting about in the streets and squares. The Assyrian soldiers rush to defend the city wall, but the enemy invades and loots Nineveh's treasures as the people melt with fear. Nahum's vision of Nineveh's demise was fulfilled in 612 b.c. when the combined forces of the Babylonians and Medes conquered Nineveh after a siege of two months.[233] A Babylonian source describes the city's fall as follows: "[T]he city was seized and a great defeat he [the Babylonian king Nabopolassar] inflicted upon the entire population. . . . many prisoners of the city, beyond counting, they carried away. The city they turned into ruin-hills and heaps of debris."[234]

---

231. In the last line of v. 14, the Hebrew text reads, "I will place [i.e., prepare] your grave." But a slight emendation of the text yields the reading, "I will make desolate your grave."

232. For examples of such tomb inscriptions containing curses upon violators, see Pritchard, *Ancient Near Eastern Texts,* 661–62.

233. Georges Roux, *Ancient Iraq* (Middlesex, England: Penguin Books), 341–42.

234. Pritchard, *Ancient Near Eastern Texts,* 304–5.

Having previewed the fall of Nineveh, Nahum asked rhetorically, "Where now is the lions' den?" (v. 11). The mighty Assyrians had for many years been like a lion among sheep, stalking and eating whomever they desired (v. 12). But now the "den" would be empty; the LORD Almighty (v. 13; Hebrew "LORD of Armies") would destroy Nineveh's "young lions."

Nahum pronounces a woe oracle over the "city of blood, full of lies, full of plunder, never without victims" (3:1). The cry of "woe" suggests Nineveh's funeral is imminent, while the description of Nineveh that follows alludes to her crimes against humanity. Once more the prophet depicts the invasion of the city (vv. 2–3). Whips crack, chariots dart about, horsemen charge, swords flash, spears glitter, and Nineveh's corpses are piled so high, the panic-stricken survivors stumble over them as they attempt to flee to safety. Though the scene tends to arouse sympathy for the victims, the prophet reminds us that Nineveh's fate is well-deserved, for she enslaved others (v. 4).

The Lord once more speaks, again declaring to Nineveh, "I am against you" (v. 5; see 2:13). Picturing Nineveh as a prostitute (see v. 4), he announces that he will publicly humiliate her by exposing her nakedness and pelting her with filth (vv. 5–6). Observers will flee from her in terror, leaving her abandoned and in ruins with no one to mourn her fate (v. 7).

Nineveh thought she was invincible, but the prophet draws a lesson from Assyria's own history to illustrate that she was self-deceived. The city of Thebes seemed invincible as well, but in 663 B.C. the Assyrian army conquered this Egyptian fortress and carried its people into exile (vv. 8–10).[235] If it could happen to Thebes, it could and would happen to Nineveh. Terrified and confused, Nineveh would stagger like a drunkard and flee for shelter (v. 11). Her fortresses would be easy pickings for the enemy (v. 12), for Nineveh's defenders would be like helpless women before the invaders (v. 13).

Nahum again plays the role of watchman as he urges the city to prepare for a siege and strengthen her defenses (v. 14). However, Nineveh's efforts will prove futile, for the city will be destroyed by fire and sword as the enemy soldiers sweep through like locusts (v. 15a). The prophet sarcastically urges the people of Nineveh to multiply like locusts (v. 15b). He compares the city's many merchants to a locust swarm that strips the land bare and then flies away (v. 16). In the same way, the merchants, having made a profit in Nineveh during its golden era, will flee the city before its downfall. Nahum also compares the city's numerous guards and officials to locusts that hide in a wall on a cold day and then fly away when the sun comes out (v. 17). In the same way, Nineveh's leaders, who once felt secure inside the city, will disappear.

235. For an account of the Assyrian conquest of Thebes, see Daniel D. Luckenbill, *Ancient Records of Assyria and Babylonia*, 2 vols. (Chicago: University of Chicago Press, 1926–27), 2:351, par. 906.

Nahum concludes his prophecy by addressing the king of Assyria once more (vv. 18–19; cf. 1:14). Anticipating Nineveh's fall, he compares the city's leaders to shepherds who sleep on the job, allowing their sheep, who stand for the people of the city, to be scattered on the mountains, where they are vulnerable to predators. The prophet depicts the king as one who has been fatally wounded. Everyone who hears of the king's death will celebrate because all have been victims of his cruelty.

A Panorama of the Future (Habakkuk)

Introduction

Habakkuk prophesied in the late seventh century B.C., though it is impossible to pinpoint a precise date for his message. On the one hand, Habakkuk announced the Babylonians' rise to prominence as if it would be a surprise (1:5–6). This seems to presuppose a date prior to 605 B.C., when the Babylonians defeated the Egyptians at the battle of Carchemish and then invaded Judah (see Dan. 1:1–2). On the other hand, the prophecy seems to assume the Babylonians had already built a reputation as an imperialistic power (see 1:6–11, 15–17; 2:5–17). This seems to presuppose events following the battle of Carchemish, for it was only after this date that the Babylonians became a dominant power. It is possible that the description of the Babylonians is purely proleptic, anticipating what they would become. But the most natural way of reading the text is to assume that the Babylonians had already established their reputation. Perhaps the best way to resolve the problem is to understand the book as a collection of messages from different periods in the prophet's career.[236] For example, the speech in 1:5–11 combines the Lord's original announcement of the Babylonians' rise to prominence, made sometime prior to 605, with a later description of Babylonian imperialism postdating 605. Since Habakkuk expected an imminent Babylonian invasion that would devastate the land (see 3:16–19), the book in its final form must have been composed just before either Nebuchadnezzar's second invasion of Judah in 597 B.C. (2 Kings 24:10–17) or his third and most devastating invasion in 588–586, when Jerusalem was destroyed and looted (2 Kings 25).

The book exhibits the pattern of a dialogue, which may be outlined as follows:

> *Heading* (1:1)
> *Habakkuk's lament* (1:2–4): How long must the unjust triumph?
> *The Lord's response* (1:5–11): Justice is on the way!
> *Habakkuk's response* (1:12—2:1): You call this justice?

236. See Roberts, *Nahum, Habakkuk, and Zephaniah,* 82–84. Roberts argues that "some of the oracles date from before 605 B.C. and others from after 597 B.C." He suggests that the final form of the book reflects the prophet's "post–597 B.C. perspective."

> *The Lord's response* (2:2–20): Justice will indeed prevail in due time.
> *Habakkuk's response* (3:1–19): "I have heard . . . I will rejoice!"

The prayer in chapter 3 consists of three parts: (1) a petition asking the Lord to renew his mighty historical acts and to temper his anger with mercy (vv. 1–2); (2) a report of a theophany in which the Lord comes as a mighty warrior and annihilates his enemies (vv. 3–15); and (3) a song of confidence in which the prophet declares his faith in God's ability to protect him through the difficult times to come (vv. 16–19). The theophany is a detailed account of what the prophet had heard about the Lord.[237] It does not describe one particular event but is a poetic montage of various events in which the Lord intervened in Israel's early history. Some argue that verses 3–15 are strictly a vision of the future, but the Hebrew verb forms used in these verses indicate, for the most part, completed action, favoring the idea that this is a historical report.[238] Of course, since the prophet asks the Lord to "renew" his deeds (v. 2b), one can also view the report as a preview of coming judgment and as prophetic. History would repeat itself.

Because chapter 3 is set off by musical directions and displays an archaic poetic style, some argue that it is not part of the original prophecy. The absence of chapter 3 from the commentary on Habakkuk found at Qumran would seem to support this conclusion. However, the chapter completes the dialogue pattern of chapters 1–2 and resolves the problem posed at the beginning of the book. Complaint is transformed into confidence as the prophet, certain of God's protective care, anticipates the outpouring of divine justice. The musical directions may indeed have been added later, but the poetic style may simply indicate that the prophet utilized earlier poetic traditions. The absence of the chapter from the Qumran commentary may reflect sectarian concerns. Furthermore, chapter 3 does appear in a text from Murabb'at, dating to the second century A.D., and in the Greek Minor Prophets scroll found at Nahal Hever, dating to the first century A.D.[239]

Justice Is Perverted (1:2–4)

Habakkuk lamented that the society in which he lived had been torn apart by injustice. He used six different terms to describe the situation: "violence," "injustice," "wrong," "destruction," "strife," and "conflict." He pictured the law as "paralyzed." The term translated "paralyzed" is used elsewhere of a heart or hand growing numb (see Gen. 45:26; Ps. 77:2). When this happens, the affected body part cannot function normally. In the same way, the laws God had established to govern the socioeconomic life of the covenant com-

---

237. In v. 2, he declares "I have heard." In vv. 3–15, he reports what he had heard, and then in v. 16, having shared the report, he again states, "I heard."

238. Note how the NIV consistently uses the English past tense in translating vv. 3–15.

239. See Robert D. Haak, *Habakkuk* (Leiden: Brill, 1992), 3, 5.

munity were being ignored, causing the law to be incapacitated, as it were. The prophet also pictured justice as being "perverted." This term pictures God's just standards being "bent" or "twisted" by the wicked.

Some identify the "wicked" described here as a foreign power, either the Assyrians or the Babylonians. But the Assyrians are mentioned nowhere else in the book, and the Babylonians are presented as God's solution to the problem in verses 5–11. The reference to the "law" being paralyzed makes it more likely that the prophet had in view the unjust within Judah who were exploiting and oppressing their countrymen. Jeremiah, a contemporary of Habakkuk, also exposed and lamented the injustice that characterized Judah at this time (see Jer. 7:3–6; 9:1–6; 12:1–4; 15:10; 20:7–8; 22:3, 13–17).

With great boldness, Habakkuk challenged God to intervene and complained that the Lord seemed oblivious to his prayers and to Judah's disintegrating social fabric. Though the Lord is at times silent while evildoers overrun society, this silence must never be interpreted to mean that he is unaware of what is happening or that he does not care about justice. Eventually he will respond and intervene, as Habakkuk discovered.

God's Solution (1:5–11)

Habakkuk complained that the Lord made him "look" at injustice (v. 3), but suddenly the Lord told him to "look" out toward the nations, for he was about to do something amazing and unexpected (v. 5). He would raise up the Babylonians, who would be his instrument of justice (v. 6a). As noted above, this initial announcement of Babylon's rise to power was later filled out with a description of the Babylonian war machine (vv. 6b–11). The Babylonians were bent on world conquest. They struck fear into the hearts of other nations, for they were subject to no law but their own. They moved swiftly and swept down on their victims like a vulture. They scoffed at those who attempted to resist them. Such a lawless and violent army would be an appropriate instrument of divine judgment against those in Judah who violently oppressed their countrymen and ignored God's law.

Habakkuk's Response (1:12–2:1)

Habakkuk could no longer accuse God of being inactive, but God's solution was apparently not what the prophet had in mind. He was not entirely satisfied with the Lord's plan. Before registering his objection, however, he addressed the Lord as one who had been active in Israel's history from ancient times (v. 12). The Hebrew phrase rendered "from everlasting" by NIV is better translated "from antiquity." It refers elsewhere to antiquity in general (Isa. 45:21; 46:10) and more specifically to Israel's early history (Ps. 74:12; 77:11), including the Davidic era (Mic. 5:2; Neh. 12:46). Habakkuk was more concerned about the Lord's involvement in the life of the nation since earliest times (see 3:2–16) than he was in God's eternality in some philosophical sense.[240] The prophet also addressed God as "Holy One," recognizing the Lord's sovereign position as the world's moral authority, and as a "Rock," indicating that he is the protector of his people (see Isa. 17:10; 26:4; 30:29; 44:8).

Habakkuk clearly knew his theological creed: the Lord is the just ruler and protector of his people, and cannot tolerate evil and injustice (v. 13a). But it is this same creed that continued to cause such a problem for the prophet. If God really was the just king, then how could he elevate the Babylonians to such prominence? Yes, the Babylonians would dish out violence on the wicked oppressors within the nation of Judah, but what about the innocent people who would get swallowed up in the process (v. 13b). Practically speaking, how would a Babylonian invasion be any better for the innocent than the oppression they had been experiencing from their own countrymen? Indeed, by allowing the Babylonians to build an empire, God seemed to be showing little regard for the value of human life. The Babylonians were like fishermen who use nets to pull fish out of the water at will (vv. 14–15). In other words, in God's plan it seemed as if the nations had no value at all. They existed simply to satisfy the Babylonians' appetite. To make matters worse, the pagan Babylonians did not even recognize themselves as instruments of God. Instead, they worshiped their own power, symbolized by the nets (vv. 16–17). Having lodged his latest protest, the prophet waited eagerly for God's reply, ready to offer his own counterresponse (2:1).

An Assuring Word (2:2–20)

The Lord responded to Habakkuk's objection by assuring him that divine justice would prevail in the end. The Lord considered this message so important that he instructed Habakkuk to write it down on tablets (vv. 2–3). Prior to the fulfillment of the prophecy, this formal record of God's promise would serve as an assuring reminder to the godly remnant that they would eventually be vindicated. After its fulfillment it would serve as legal proof of God's faithfulness, as well as an incriminating witness against those who had rejected it.[241]

240. The next line may also affirm God's transcendence of history. The traditional Hebrew text has "we will not die" (see NIV), but an ancient scribal tradition suggests that the original text may have read, "you [referring to God] will not die." Some theorize the latter was altered so that the idea of death would not be associated with God in any way. See Roberts, *Nahum, Habakkuk, and Zephaniah*, 100–101. For a defense of the traditional reading ("we will not die"), see Haak, *Habakkuk*, 48–49.

241. Verse 3a is best translated: "For the vision is a witness at the appointed time, indeed a witness at the end that does not lie." The text has traditionally been translated something like this: "For the vision is still for the appointed time, and it hastens [lit. "pants"] toward the end, and does not lie." This reading assumes that *yapeakh* is a Hiphil prefixed verbal form from the root *puakh*, "breathe, blow," but this interpretation of the form is incorrect. It is actually a noun, meaning "witness." It appears in Ugaritic, where the most clearly attested readings use the word to introduce the names of witnesses to legal contracts. It occurs in several passages in Proverbs, where it stands parallel to the noun *'ed*, "witness" (6:19; 12:17; 14:5,

The message proper begins with a proverbial-style statement that contrasts the destinies of the wicked and the godly (v. 4). The verse presents special interpretive challenges and has been translated in various ways. NIV
translates the first line, "See, he is puffed up; his desires are not upright."[242]
In this case the statement is a comment on the pride and misplaced motives
of an unidentified subject. However, a better translation might be, "See, the
one whose desires are not upright faints." This translation assumes an emendation of the verb 'upelah to 'ullepah (in this case the traditional Hebrew text
is the product of an accidental transposition of the letters *pe* and *lamed*),
meaning "faints,"[243] and understands "his desires are not upright" as the substantival subject of the verb "faints" (possibly a euphemism for death). This
produces tighter contrastive parallelism with the second line:

> See, the one whose desires are not upright *faints,*
> but the godly one *lives* by his integrity.

Verse 4b reads literally, "and [the] godly [one] by his integrity will live."
The antecedent of the pronoun "his" has been debated. The pronoun could
refer to the prophecy (see vv. 2–3), in which case one might translate the
phrase "its reliability."[244] Another option is that the pronoun refers to God.
In this case the phrase might be translated "his faithfulness."[245] However, the
nearest and most likely antecedent is the "godly [one]" mentioned just before this. In this case the point is that the godly would be sustained through
the coming trial by their upright character.

Each of the terms in verse 4b requires discussion. The term translated
"godly [one]" (Heb. *tsaddiq*), used collectively here, probably refers in this
context to the innocent, godly people who were being oppressed. The same
Hebrew term is used in 1:4 of the innocent victims of oppression in Judah
and in 1:13 of the innocent who would be swallowed up by the Babylonians.[246] The verb "lives" (Heb. *yikhyeh,* from *khayah*) is used here in its most
basic sense of "live physically." In this context it refers to being preserved or
sustained through the coming invasion, which would strip the land of its

---

25; 19:5, 9). (In these passages the Masoretic tradition apparently understands the form as a verb, for it is
pointed with a *hireq-yod* theme vowel.) The proposed noun fits very well in Hab. 2:3a, where it would refer
to the vision functioning as a witness. If this interpretation of *yapeakh* is correct, then it is possible that *'od,*
"still," in the parallel line is a later misinterpretation of an original consonantal *'ed,* "witness," which forms
a word pair with *yapeakh* in the Proverbs passages cited above. For fuller discussion of the textual problem,
see Haak, *Habakkuk,* 55–57, and Roberts, *Nahum, Habakkuk, and Zephaniah,* 105–6.

242. In this view, the Hebrew verbal form *'upelah,* translated "is puffed up," is derived from a root,
attested in later Hebrew and in Arabic, meaning "be impudent, foolish."

243. The verbal root *'alap* is attested in the Pual stem (the form proposed here) in Isa. 51:20 and in
the Hithpael stem in Amos 8:13 and Jon. 4:8.

244. See Haak, *Habakkuk,* 59, and Roberts, *Nahum, Habakkuk, and Zephaniah,* 111–12.

245. In this regard, note that the LXX reads *pisteos mou,* which could be translated, "my [referring to
God] faithfulness."

246. See as well the use of the term in Isa. 3:10; 57:1; Hos. 14:9; Mal. 3:18.

food sources (see 3:17). The term translated "integrity" is the Hebrew noun *'emunah*. Though traditionally translated "faith" here on the basis of the New Testament use of the passage, the term is better rendered "integrity," "faithfulness," or "allegiance." The primary meaning of the term is "firmness, steadiness" (see Exod. 17:12). When used of human character and conduct, it refers to reliability (see Prov. 12:17, 22; Isa. 59:4; Jer. 5:3; 9:3) and integrity (see 2 Kings 12:15; 22:7; Jer. 5:1). Nowhere is it used of "faith" or "belief" per se. In the context of Habakkuk 2:4, the term probably refers to the law-abiding character of the oppressed, who refused to violate God's law by following the example of the deceitful and violent. The Lord's statement assured Habakkuk that such innocent folk would not be the target of his judgment.

Habakkuk 2:4b is one of the most well-known passages in the prophets, undoubtedly because it is quoted three times in the New Testament. In Romans 1:17, Paul quotes the passage as a proof-text for his thesis that "righteousness from God" comes "by faith." In Galatians 3:11 he cites Habakkuk 2:4b to prove that one is justified before God by faith, not by the Mosaic law. In both cases Paul does not include the pronoun "his" with "faith." Perhaps more significant, he seems to assign a meaning to the Hebrew term *'emunah* that is not attested in its use elsewhere in the Hebrew Bible. As noted above, in the Hebrew Bible the term refers to one's character and lifestyle, not "belief" in the sense referred to by Paul. However, one could argue that a righteous lifestyle was based, even in Old Testament times, upon an unwavering commitment to God coupled with trust in God's promise to reward and protect his loyal followers. In other words, faith and faithfulness were two sides of the same coin. Perhaps this close connection between the two concepts underlies Paul's thinking, though it is possible that his use of the passage simply reflects an interpretive tradition of Habakkuk 2:4 current in his time.[247] Habakkuk 2:4 is also cited in Hebrews 10:38, albeit in a different text form that puts the pronoun "my" before "righteous one" and omits the pronoun "his" before "faith."[248] The author of Hebrews uses Habakkuk 2:4 in a way that closely reflects its original meaning. He urged his readers to remain faithful despite their trials, for God would eventually reward their perseverance. In a similar way, the Lord reminded Habakkuk that persistent godliness would sustain the innocent through the difficult times ahead.

The statement about the ungodly in verse 4a is very general; it describes what typically happens to the wicked. It is general enough to encompass both the wicked within Judah and the cruel Babylonians. However, by verse

247. For a helpful discussion of Paul's use of Hab. 2:4b in Rom. 1:17, see Douglas Moo, *Romans 1–8* (Chicago: Moody, 1991), 71–73.
248. Heb. 10:37–38 actually cites Hab. 2:3b–4, essentially in its LXX text form, but with a reversal of the lines in v. 4.

5b it is clear that the primary referent is the Babylonians, as the references to worldwide conquest indicate (cf. 1:6). The Lord characterized the Babylonians as intoxicated with pride and greed. Like a drunkard who wants more and more wine, so the Babylonians' military successes made them want to expand their empire to include more and more nations. Like the grave, which always wants more and more bodies, so the Babylonians desired more and more victims.[249] In short, the Lord agreed with Habakkuk's assessment of the Babylonians' greed and pride (see 1:14–17) and he would not condone or ignore their actions. In fact, once he had used the Babylonians to accomplish his purposes, he would judge them severely.

The Babylonians would meet their demise, and in the aftermath of their judgment all of their victims would taunt their oppressor with a scathing funeral song containing five stanzas (v. 6a). The song may be outlined as follows: 6b–8, 9–11, 12–14, 15–17, 18–20. Each of the first four stanzas begins with "woe" (see vv. 6b, 9, 12, 15). As noted earlier, this word was a cry of mourning heard at funerals (see 1 Kings 13:30; Jer. 22:18–19; Isa. 1:4; Amos 5:16). Its appearance here indicates that Babylon was on the verge of death. The term also appears within the final stanza (see v. 19), which begins with a rhetorical question denouncing idols and idolaters (v. 18). The structural variation is probably a way of signaling closure for the song.

The Babylonians built an empire by robbing and killing (vv. 6, 9a, 10). They left behind them a trail of blood and ruined cities (vv. 8, 12, 17b). In their arrogance they even invaded the great forest of Lebanon and assaulted its trees and animals (v. 17a; see Isa. 14:8).[250] Like an eagle that builds a nest in a high place, they thought they were secure (v. 9b), but a day of reckoning would come. Babylon's empire seemed like a sturdy house, but the very stones and woodwork of this house (symbolizing the wealth taken from others) testified to its crimes (v. 11). Babylon's victims would rise up like merciless creditors and demand retribution, treating the Babylonians the way they had treated others (v. 7).[251] The Lord Almighty (literally, "Lord of Armies"), not Babylon, rules the earth and frustrates the imperialistic efforts of nations like Babylon (vv. 13–14). He would dish out to Babylon what she had dished out to others. Babylon is pictured as one who forces others to drink an intoxicating beverage until they are so drunk and silly that they expose themselves, much to taunting Babylon's amusement (v. 15). The underlying reality may be the practice of publicly humiliating prisoners by exposing their nakedness.[252] But now it was Babylon's turn to be humiliated

---

249. On the personification of death as having a voracious appetite, see my comments on Isa. 25:8.

250. Nebuchadnezzar transported timber from Lebanon for his building projects. See Roux, *Ancient Iraq*, 345–46, 359–60.

251. The Hebrew form translated "debtors" by NIV (v. 7) is better understood as referring to "creditors."

252. Roberts, *Nahum, Habakkuk, and Zephaniah*, 124.

(v. 16). The Lord's right hand, symbolizing his strength, was passing the cup of intoxicating beverage to Babylon. Babylon would be forced to drink to the point where, drunken and silly, it exposed its nakedness. The language of verse 16 is much more graphic than most translations indicate. The second line reads literally, "Drink, yes you, and expose your foreskin!"[253] While the Lord's glory extends throughout the earth (v. 14), Babylon's glory would turn to shame and disgrace. The Babylonians trusted in their idol-gods, which would be unable to protect them from divine judgment (vv. 18–19). In contrast to these man-made, lifeless "gods," the Lord rules the earth from his heavenly palace (v. 20a). In his presence the whole earth must stand in awestruck silence (v. 20b). This silence may very well be the prelude to his arrival in judgment (see chapter 3, as well as Zeph. 1:7).

Praying for History to Repeat Itself (3:1–15)

Habakkuk responded to the prophecy of Babylon's demise with a prayer (v. 1). He had heard of the Lord's mighty acts in Israel's past. In fact, the report was so impressive that it gripped the prophet with fear (v. 2a).[254] He asked the Lord to renew these deeds in his own day but also requested that he temper his angry judgment with mercy (v. 2b).

What exactly did this report entail? Why did it instill the prophet with such fear? In verses 3–15, Habakkuk gives a detailed description of the report he had heard. This report has two parts. Verses 3–7 speak of the Lord in the third person and picture his march from the south. In verses 8–15, the prophet directly addresses the Lord as he recalls what the report said about him. References to the Lord trampling the sea with his horses bracket the unit.

The Lord approaches from the direction of Teman and Mount Paran (v. 3). Teman was an Edomite city (see Amos 1:12; Obad. 9) located to the southeast of Judah. Mount Paran was a mountain range located to the south of Judah, near the Gulf of Aqaba. The tent-dwellers of Midian and Cushan, located in the southern Trans-Jordan, react with fear, realizing that they lie in the pathway of this mighty warrior's march (v. 7). The picture of the Lord coming from the south recalls earlier poetic descriptions of his march from this same area. Deuteronomy 33:2 describes him as coming from Sinai, Seir (that is, Edom), and Mount Paran to bless the Israelite tribes and lead them into the Promised Land. In Judges 5:4, he comes from Seir/Edom to fight against the Canaanite army of Sisera.

As the Lord arrives on the scene, the radiance of his royal splendor is

---

253. The text pictures personified Babylon as being uncircumcised. An alternative reading, found in the Dead Sea Scrolls and in the LXX, is "and stagger." For a defense of the traditional Hebrew text, see Miller, *Sin and Judgment in the Prophets*, 63–64, as well as Roberts, *Nahum, Habakkuk, and Zephaniah*, 116.

254. Verse 2a reads literally, "O LORD, I heard the report about you, I fear, O LORD, your work."

blinding and elicits praise from those who view it (v. 3b). According to NIV, verse 4 compares his glory to the rays of the sun at dawn. However, it is possible that the image is that of lightning.[255] The text reads literally, "and [his] radiance is like light, two horns from his hand to him." The Hebrew term translated "light" can refer to sunlight but does on occasion refer to lightning (see Job 36:32; 37:3, 11, 15). The reference to "two horns" may depict forked lightning. Mesopotamian gods are sometimes described as using "double lightning" as a weapon, and an Ugaritic text appears to call the storm god Baal's lightning a "horn."[256] Verse 9 pictures the Lord shooting arrows, which are often used as a metaphor for lightning in theophanic texts (see Ps. 18:14; 77:17–18; 144:6; Zech. 9:14).

The Lord is accompanied by personified "plague" and "pestilence," viewed here as part of his royal entourage (v. 5). Before this fearsome trio the earth shakes, the nations tremble, and the age-old mountains, long known for their stability, disintegrate (v. 6). The Hebrew term *reshep* is normally translated "pestilence" here because it is paired with the term *deber*, "plague," in the parallel structure of the verse. The word also refers to pestilence in Deuteronomy 32:24 and probably Psalm 78:48 as well.[257] In some biblical texts the term *reshep* simply means "arrows" (see Ps. 76:3; Song of Sol. 8:6). This secondary meaning can be explained by the fact that, in the ancient Near East, Resheph was a warlike deity whose arrows brought pestilence.[258]

Verse 8, through a series of questions, forces one to reflect on the object of God's anger. The Lord has climbed into his chariot to do battle, but against whom? Is he angry at the rivers and the sea? At first the question may seem strange, but verse 15 does indeed depict the hooves of the Lord's chariot horses stomping on the surging water of the sea. It becomes apparent as the vision unfolds that the sea is the object of the Lord's anger (see v. 10b as well). The imagery recalls the exodus, when the Lord dried up the sea. But the sea is a mere poetic symbol of the hostile nations (v. 12).

The report pictures the Lord as a warrior armed with several weapons (vv. 9–14). As he prepares to shoot his arrows, he formally commissions

255. Roberts, *Nahum, Habakkuk, and Zephaniah*, 152–53.

256. See E. D. van Buren, *Symbols of the Gods in Mesopotamian Art* (Rome: Pontifical Biblical Institute, 1945), 70–73, and Gibson, *Canaanite Myths and Legends*, 51.

257. One can make a good case for emending Hebrew *barad*, "lightning," in v. 48a to *deber*, "plague," in which case *reshapim* (the plural form of *reshep*) in v. 48b refers not to lightning bolts but to the sons of Resheph (see Job 5:7) who bring pestilence. These sons of Resheph may be the "destroying angels" mentioned in v. 49. See John Day, *Yahweh and the Gods and Goddesses of Canaan* (Sheffield: Sheffield Academic Press, 2000), 200–201.

258. See ibid., 197–99, 202–4. The iconographic evidence depicts Resheph as a warrior. See Izak Cornelius, *The Iconography of the Canaanite Gods Reshef and Ba'al* (Fribourg, Germany: Fribourg University Press, 1994). At Ugarit he was equated with Nergal, the Mesopotamian god of the underworld and plague. One Ugaritic text describes him as taking the life of a king's wife. See Day, *Yahweh and the Gods*, 198, and Gibson, *Canaanite Myths and Legends*, 82 (text 14 i 18–19). Resheph also aids the god Baal in his war with Yam, the god of the sea. See John Day, "New Light on the Mythological Background of the Allusion to Resheph in Habakkuk III 5," *VT* 29 (1979): 353–55.

them to do their deadly work (v. 9a). NIV translates the second line of verse 9 "you called for many arrows," but the Hebrew text (which reads literally, "adjured [are the] shafts [with a] word") is better rendered "you commission your arrows" (see NET).[259] In the ancient Near East, warriors would sometimes empower their weapons with a magical formula.[260] The Lord is depicted here as doing the same (see also Jer. 47:6–7).

As noted above, arrows are sometimes used in theophanies as a metaphor for lightning bolts. This is probably the case here, for storm imagery dominates verses 9b–10. A torrential downpour causes streams to flood their banks and run over the surface of the land, so that the earth appears to be split with rivers. The onslaught is so terrifying that the mountains shake and the great deep raises its hands (probably a reference to the surging waves produced by the strong wind accompanying the storm) and begs loudly for mercy.[261] The language is similar to Psalm 77:16–18, a poetic account of Israel's deliverance at the Red Sea that depicts the Lord coming in a storm and subduing the sea so that he might lead his people safely through it. The bright flash of the Lord's arrows and spear (both metaphors for lightning) paralyzes the sun and moon (v. 11).[262] Here the language is reminiscent of Joshua 10:12–14, which depicts the sun and moon standing still so that the Israelite forces could slaughter their Canaanite enemies before nightfall.

The Lord's primary purpose is to deliver his people and the Davidic king, referred to here as the Lord's "anointed one" (vv. 13–14a). The language seems to recall the military victories of David, who defeated many nations as he enjoyed supernatural deliverance and protection on the battlefield (see 2 Sam. 22).

The Lord focuses his attack on "the land (literally, "house") of wickedness." At this point the prophetic dimension of the report crowds out history, for the phrase "house of wickedness" alludes back to 2:9–11, where the Babylonian Empire is compared to a house built through unjust gain, and to 1:13, where the Babylonians are characterized as "wicked." The Lord's attack on this wicked "house" is violent and decisive. Verses 13b–14a are best trans-

---

259. The Hebrew term *mattot* is the plural form of *matteh*, which normally refers to a scepter or club. However, in this context, where a bow is mentioned in the parallel line, the term refers to the shafts of the warrior's arrows. The Ugaritic cognate of *matteh* is used in a mythological text of the "shafts" (that is, arrows) which the warrior goddess Anat shoots from her bow. See Gibson, *Canaanite Myths and Legends*, 47.

260. See Haak, *Habakkuk*, 95. In the Ugaritic myths, Baal's weapons are given a formal commission to destroy Yam, the god of the sea and Baal's mortal enemy. See Gibson, *Canaanite Myths and Legends*, 43–44.

261. Raising one's hands sometimes accompanied pleas for mercy. See Ps. 28:2 and Lam. 2:19.

262. An Ugaritic mythological text describes Baal as follows: "Seven lightning bolts he casts, eight magazines of thunder, he brandishes a spear of lightning." On this text see Marvin H. Pope and Jeffrey H. Tigay, "A Description of Baal," *UF* 3 (1971): 118; and Frank M. Cross Jr., *Canaanite Myth and Hebrew Epic* (Cambridge: Harvard University Press, 1973), 147–48.

lated as follows: "You crush the head of the house of wickedness, laying him open from the lower body to the neck. With his arrows you pierce the heads of his soldiers."[263] The "house of wickedness" is personified here as the Lord's rival in battle. With his battle club the Lord crushes the enemy's head and then, with his sword, slices his body open. Taking his foe's arrows, the Lord shoots them into the heads of the enemy's soldiers.[264]

Habakkuk Looks Confidently to the Future (3:16–19)

Having shared the report of the Lord's mighty historical deeds, the prophet again described the fear that it produced within him (v. 16a; see v. 2a). Such a display of divine anger and power cannot help but be terrifying to observers, even if they are not the objects of divine anger.

By the end of the book, Habakkuk knew that the God of Israel's past was still alive and ready to renew his mighty deeds among the nations. Nevertheless, the situation in Judah would get worse before final vindication arrived. While it was encouraging to reflect on the past and to realize that God would eventually renew his mighty deeds, the invasion of Judah (see 1:2–4) was on the immediate horizon (v. 16b). Yet Habakkuk could face the future with confidence, for he knew God would sustain his loyal followers (see 2:4b). Though food might disappear, Habakkuk would rejoice in the God who delivers his people from such crises (vv. 17–18). Somehow the Lord would enable him to negotiate the dangerous obstacles ahead, just as an agile deer is able to run on rugged terrain (v. 19).

The Judgment That Purifies (Zephaniah)

Introduction

According to the book's heading, Zephaniah prophesied during the reign of Josiah (640–609 B.C.). He anticipated the fall of Nineveh in 612 B.C. (see 2:13–15), and his description of Judah's religious corruption (see 1:4–18) appears to predate Josiah's reforms, which occurred in 622–621 B.C. (see 2 Kings 22–23).

Zephaniah may have been of royal descent. The heading traces his ancestry back four generations to a man named Hezekiah. Since the headings of prophetic books usually give only the name of the prophet's father (see Isa. 1:1; Jer. 1:1; Ezek. 1:3; Hos. 1:1; Joel 1:1) or, at most, two generations (Zech. 1:1), there must be some reason for the more extensive genealogy that

---

263. This translation understands Hebrew *ro'sh*, "head(s)," as collocated with the following phrase, "his warriors." Some (for example, NIV) take "his warriors" with what follows.

264. NIV "his own spear" translates a Hebrew form that literally means "his shafts." In v. 9, however, the term appears to refer to arrows.

appears in Zephaniah's case. The best explanation for this is that Zephaniah was a descendant of the famous king Hezekiah.

The book is comprised of three major sections (1:2–18; 2:4–3:7; 3:8b–20) connected by two transitional exhortations (2:1–3; 3:8a). The book's structure may be outlined as follows:

Part One

Announcement of worldwide judgment (1:2–3)
Announcement of judgment upon Judah/Jerusalem (1:4–6)
Proclamation of the approaching day of the Lord (1:7)
Announcement of judgment upon Jerusalem (1:8–13)
Proclamation of the approaching day of the Lord (1:14a)
Announcement of worldwide judgment (1:14b–18)
Transition: Exhortation (2:1–3)

Part Two

Announcement of judgment upon Philistia (2:4–7)
Announcement of judgment upon Moab and Ammon (2:8–11)
Announcement of judgment upon Cush (2:12)
Announcement of judgment upon Assyria (2:13–15)
Woe oracle against Jerusalem (3:1–7)
Transition: Exhortation (3:8a)

Part Three

Announcement of worldwide judgment (3:8b)
Announcement of worldwide salvation (3:9–10)
Announcement of salvation for Jerusalem (3:11–20)

In part one, references to the approaching "day of the Lord" appear in verses 7 and 14, dividing the section into three subunits (vv. 2–6, 7–13, 14–18). In verses 2–6, the Lord announces he will judge the world and, more specifically, Judah and Jerusalem. Verses 7–13 develop the latter theme (judgment of Jerusalem), while verses 14–18 expand the theme of worldwide judgment. The portraits of worldwide judgment (see vv. 2–3, 17–18) form a bracket around the section.

The first exhortation (2:1–3) provides a fitting conclusion to the announcement of the impending day of the Lord (cf. v. 3 with 1:7, 14, 18). Yet it is clearly transitional, for the Hebrew particle *kiy*, "for, because," appears at the beginning of verse 4 (NIV fails to translate the term), indicating a logical connection between the exhortation and the judgment oracle that follows it.

The judgment speeches in part two support the theme of worldwide judgment presented in part one. Representative nations from the four points of the compass are chosen: Philistia (to Judah's west), Moab and Ammon (to the east), Cush (to the south), and Assyria (to the north; see 2:13a).[265] The

---

265. Assyria was actually located northeast of Judah, but Assyrian armies invaded Palestine from the north. See Isa. 14:31.

list culminates with Jerusalem. As in chapter 1, the Lord's judgment is worldwide in scope but focuses on God's own covenant community as its primary target. However, the message is not entirely negative, as notices of salvation for both Judah (2:7, 9b) and the nations (2:11) appear, anticipating the dominant theme of part three.

The second exhortation (3:8a) is transitional, being logically connected to what precedes (note "therefore" at the beginning of the verse) and to what follows (note "for" in v. 8b). Part three begins with another announcement of worldwide judgment, continuing the primary theme of parts one and two. But the mood changes as the salvation theme, introduced briefly in part two, dominates.

The Destroyer Is Coming (1:2–6)

The Lord's judgment would devastate the entire surface of the earth, including mankind and animals. Even the birds in the sky and the fish in the sea would be destroyed. The extent of the devastation rivals that of the Noahic flood, to which allusion is made here (cf. the language of vv. 2–3 with that of Gen. 6:7; 7:4, 23). This judgment constitutes an undoing of creation in reverse order. Verse 3a speaks of mankind and animals (created on the sixth day) being eliminated, followed by the birds and fish (created on the fifth day).

The precise meaning of verse 3b is unclear. The Hebrew text reads literally, "and the stumbling blocks along with the wicked," or "and the things which cause the wicked to stumble." One option is that the noun translated "stumbling blocks" refers to idols made in the images of animals. This would explain why the judgment is so far-reaching in its scope. If humankind insists upon worshiping images of animals, then God will eliminate the inspiration for such images. The point is not that the animals were to blame for humankind's sin, but that idolatrous humankind had corrupted the animal kingdom by using it in a way that was never intended by the Creator. Another option is that the Hebrew term refers not to stumbling blocks of some sort but to the "ruins" (the causative form of the verb *kashal*, "to stumble," can mean "to overthrow, reduce to ruins") of humankind's cities. In Isaiah 3:6, the only other text where the noun occurs in the Hebrew Bible, it refers to a city that had been reduced to ruins. In this case, the text warns that the Lord would devastate the earth's cities as he unleashed his judgment upon wicked humankind.

This portrait of divine judgment on a cosmic scale provides the framework for the more focused judgment announced in verses 4–6. The primary target of God's judgment would be his very own people, who had rejected him and embraced pagan practices and gods. The second half of verse 5 reads literally "those who bow down, who swear allegiance to the LORD, and those who swear oaths by their king." Apparently this does not refer to two different groups (loyal followers of the Lord and idolaters), but to one group that engaged in the syncretistic worship of both the Lord and a pagan god referred to here as "their king." The identity of this god is not clear, though Baal (see v. 4), the Ammonite god Milkom (Heb. *malkam*, "their king," could be a deliberate play on this god's name), or Molech (see NIV) are prime candidates. These gods were popular during the reign of Josiah, who attempted to eliminate the worship of all three through his reforms (see 2 Kings 23:4–5, 10, 13).[266]

The Day of the Lord Is Near (1:7–18)

The appropriate response to this announcement of judgment was awestruck silence (v. 7a; see Hab. 2:20), for this revelation of the Lord's power in judgment was imminent. Zephaniah referred to this outbreak of divine judgment as "the day of the LORD." The expression appears frequently in the Hebrew Bible.[267] Though it is applied to various events, in the most basic sense it is a day when the Lord intervenes in the world to judge his enemies. Here it encompasses both the Babylonian conquest of Judah in 586 B.C. and a more far-reaching judgment on a worldwide scale. Zephaniah compared this "day" to a sacrifice, for the Lord would slaughter his victims, much as a priest slaughters sacrificial animals (v. 7b). These victims would include members of the royal family, whose clothing betrayed their paganism (v. 8), as well as those responsible for the social injustice in Judah (v. 9).

The latter group is described literally as "those who leap over the threshold, who fill up the house of their masters [by] violence and deceit." The reference to leaping over the threshold may allude to a pagan practice. According to 1 Samuel 5:5, after the incident involving the ark of the Lord, the Philistine priests at the god Dagon's temple in Ashdod avoided stepping on the threshold. Others suggest that this avoidance of the threshold reflects a common pagan belief that demons live near the threshold of a house. Still another option is that the statement describes the suddenness with which these oppressors entered their victims' homes or the eagerness they displayed as they returned home with the riches they had taken by violence and deceit. In the second half of the description, the identity of "their masters" is uncertain. Pagan gods may be in view (see NIV), but the phrase more likely refers to those who sent these individuals out on their mission of violence and deceit. If the plural is understood as indicating majesty, then a king or high-ranking official may be in view.

266. Contrary to NIV, 2 Kings 23:13 reads "Milkom" in the Hebrew text, not Molech (who is mentioned in v. 10).
267. See my earlier comments on Isa. 13. For studies of the origin and usage of the phrase, see Gerhard von Rad, "The Origin of the Concept of the Day of the Lord," *JSS* 4 (1959): 97–108; A. J. Everson, "The Days of the Yahweh," *JBL* 93 (1974): 329–37; and Douglas Stuart, "The Sovereign's Day of Conquest," *BASOR* 220/221 (December 1975–February 1976): 159–64.

The Lord's judgment would deprive the wealthy of their ill-gotten gain, which in turn would cause widespread weeping and wailing, especially from the merchants who were exploiting the oppressive socioeconomic policies of the royal bureaucracy (vv. 10–13). Many of the people had grown self-assured, thinking the Lord would remain aloof and indifferent to what was happening. The Lord compares them to wine that sits on its sediment too long and becomes thick and syrupy. In the same way, these people had become set in their ways and unwilling to reform their society in accordance with God's standards. But the Lord would teach these practical atheists a lesson, hunting them down wherever they tried to hide. In this regard he compares himself to men with lamps who look in every dark corner and alley to find the object of their search.

Again the prophet emphasized how near this day of judgment was (v. 14a). On this day the victims' cries of terror would be intermingled with the warriors' battle cries (v. 14b). It is portrayed as a day of divine anger, characterized by panic, ruin, darkness, and the sounds of warfare (vv. 15–16). Terror-stricken sinners would stumble about blindly and be struck down by the sword, leaving the earth soaked with their blood and littered with their intestines (v. 17). They would not be able to buy off the Lord with their riches, for his anger would consume the world like fire (v. 18).

Prepare for Judgment! (2:1–3)

The prophet interrupted his description of the day of the Lord at this point and delivered an exhortation to God's people. The first portion of the exhortation is addressed to the sinful nation in general (vv. 1–2). He urged them to bunch themselves together like kindling before the day of judgment arrived.[268] The image suggests their flammability; the Lord's fiery judgment would consume them (see 1:18).[269]

The second part of the exhortation is addressed to the Lord's faithful followers within the nation (v. 3). The prophet urged them to humbly obey the Lord, for if they did, they just might find shelter in the coming day of judgment. The inclusion of the little word "perhaps" is a bit disturbing. We might expect, based on the Lord's assuring words to Habakkuk (Hab. 2:4b) and the prophet's confession of trust (Hab. 3:16–19), that the Lord would certainly preserve the faithful through judgment. However, Zephaniah's "perhaps" reminds us that the godly, even if spared from the full wrath of God, do experience the effects of judgment to some extent because they live in a community of sinners. Despite his confidence, even Habakkuk anticipated going hungry (Hab. 3:17). It is also possible that Zephaniah included "perhaps" for rhetorical effect. If even the godly had no absolute guarantees

268. The Hebrew verb used here is derived from a noun meaning "straw," and expresses the idea "gather stubble, kindling." See Roberts, *Nahum, Habakkuk, and Zephaniah*, 186.

269. See Adele Berlin, *Zephaniah*, AB (New York: Doubleday, 1994), 96.

that they would be spared, what did that mean for the ungodly? They truly were like kindling waiting to be burned (cf. vv. 1–2).

Widespread Destruction (2:4–15)

The prophet next depicted God's judgment falling on various nations representing the four points of the compass. To the west, the four major Philistine cities would be reduced to uninhabited ruins and used as pasture by those in Judah who survived the judgment (vv. 5–7). To the east, the Moabites and Ammonites, both of whom were the offspring of Lot's incestuous relations with his daughters (see Gen. 19:30–38), would be annihilated (vv. 8–11). Because they had threatened and insulted Judah, the Lord would make them like Sodom and Gomorrah and hand their territory over to the remnant of his people. The reference to Sodom and Gomorrah is highly ironic, for Moab and Ammon were reminders that Lot had escaped the destruction of these ancient cities. But now that judgment would catch up with Lot, as it were. To the south the Cushites, the inhabitants of Ethiopia, would be cut down by the sword (v. 12), while to the north proud Nineveh, one of Assyria's major cities, would be reduced to a pile of rubble inhabited by grazing flocks and wild animals (vv. 13–15).

Despite the dominance of the judgment theme in this section, there is a silver lining in its dark clouds. The language of verse 7b is far more hopeful than that of verse 3b, for it pictures the Lord caring for the remnant of Judah and restoring their fortunes. He assigns his people the territory formerly held by the Philistines (v. 7a) and the Moabites/Ammonites (v. 9b; see Isa. 11:14). Verse 11b anticipates the distant nations worshiping the Lord in the aftermath of his judgment. This glimmer of hope bursts into a bright ray of salvation in the next chapter.

Jerusalem's Funeral (3:1–7)

Initially one might think that the woe oracle at the beginning of chapter 3 continues the announcement of judgment against Nineveh (see 2:13–15). Perhaps the city addressed in verse 1 is the same as the "carefree city" (Nineveh) of 2:15. But one quickly discovers this is not the case. The oppressive, rebellious city is none other than Jerusalem, whose residents had rejected the Lord (v. 2). Jerusalem's leadership was thoroughly corrupt. Her officials, compared to ravenous lions and wolves, exploited the weak and poor (v. 3), her prophets were proud and deceptive (v. 4a), and her priests polluted God's temple and broke his law (v. 4b). The Lord, who lived in the temple, demanded justice, but the city's leaders shamelessly perverted the Lord's just standards (v. 5). The Lord's judgment upon other nations should have made an impact on Jerusalem, convincing her that he repays wickedness appropriately. But it had no effect; the people continued to eagerly pursue their unjust ways (vv. 6–7).

Following such a lengthy accusation, one expects this woe oracle to conclude with a formal announcement of judgment. The word "therefore" at the beginning of verse 8 seems to signal such a transition, but once again (see my comments on 3:1 above) we are surprised. Instead of an announcement of judgment, the Lord exhorts an unidentified group to "wait" for him, because the worldwide judgment announced and described earlier (see especially chapters 1–2) is about to arrive. It is likely that the Lord speaks here to his obedient followers, whom he addressed in an earlier exhortation (see 2:3) and refers to in the third person shortly after this (see 3:12).[270] The exhortation to "wait" has a positive connotation here, where it carries the nuance "wait in faith" (see as well Ps. 33:20; Isa. 8:17; 30:18; 64:4; Hab. 2:3). Such hopeful expectation will sustain God's people through the difficult time to come, when God's anger will be poured out on the nations.

Better Days Ahead (3:9–20)

The faith of the godly would be rewarded, for the Lord's judgment would have a purifying effect and be followed by a time of salvation for both the nations and Jerusalem. Developing a theme already introduced in 2:11b, the Lord anticipated a time when he would "purify the lips of the peoples," enabling them to praise the Lord in unison as they serve him (vv. 9–10). The prophecy portrays a time when the people of the earth would again speak one language. It depicts a reversal of the Babel event, when God confused the speech of the people and caused them to scatter over the earth. At that time "the whole world had one language [literally, "one lip"] and a common speech" (Gen. 11:1, cf. v. 6). But the Lord "confused the language [literally, "lip"] of the whole world" (Gen. 11:9). However, in the day of salvation depicted in Zephaniah 3:9 the Lord would give the peoples a "purified lip." The appearance of the word "lip" to refer to language recalls the Babel episode and the term *berurah*, "purified," plays on the sound of the verb *balal*, "confused," employed in Genesis 11. The reference to the people being "scattered" (v. 10) also alludes to the Babel event, for the term used here appears three times in Genesis 11 to describe how the Lord "scattered" the people (see vv. 4, 8–9). At Babel the rebellious people joined forces to build a tower to heaven. They were punished by having their language confused and by being scattered over the globe. In the future age they would return from these distant lands where they were scattered, join forces (note "shoulder to

270. The exhortation to "wait" in 3:8 is a second-person masculine plural form in the Hebrew text, just like the verb forms used in 2:3. This form is distinct from the second-person feminine singular forms used in 3:11–19 to address personified Jerusalem.

shoulder" in Zeph. 3:9), and with a unified language worship the Lord they once defied.

The Lord next turned to personified Jerusalem and assured her that she would be restored.[271] The themes of verses 11–19 are arranged in a chiastic fashion:

> A Jerusalem's shame will be removed (v. 11a)
>> B The Lord will preserve and protect a remnant (vv. 11b–13)
>>> C Jerusalem is urged to rejoice over the Lord's saving presence (vv. 14–15)
>>> C′ Jerusalem is urged to take comfort in the Lord's saving presence (vv. 16–17)
>> B′ The Lord will restore a remnant (vv. 18–19a)
> A′ Jerusalem's shame is removed (v. 19b)

Within verses 14–17, certain key terms and phrases reoccur in a chiastic pattern:

> A *Sing* (v. 14a)
>> B *Be glad* (v. 14b)
>>> C he has turned back your enemy (v. 15a)
>>>> D The LORD . . . *is with you* (v. 15b)
>>>>> E never again will you *fear* (v. 15c)
>>>>> E′ Do not *fear* (v. 16a)
>>>> D′ The LORD . . . *is with you* (v. 17a)
>>> C′ he is mighty to save (v. 17b)[272]
>> B′ He will rejoice over you with *gladness* (v. 17c)[273]
> A′ he will rejoice over you with *singing* (v. 17d)

Jerusalem's sinful people, referred to as "those who rejoice in their pride" would be removed, leaving the godly to populate the city. The Lord would protect this remnant and, in contrast to the proud sinners of an earlier era, Jerusalem would "rejoice" (v. 14) in the Lord's deliverance (cf. v. 15). The returning exiles, compared to lame and scattered sheep, would return to the city and join the ranks of the godly. The book concludes with an assuring word to these exiles, who are promised honor and praise (v. 20).[274]

---

271. The second-person pronominal and verbal forms in vv. 11–19 are second feminine singular in the Hebrew text.

272. While the C′ element does not repeat a word or phrase from the C section, the themes closely correspond. The God who turns back the enemy proves he is mighty to save.

273. NIV reads here, "He will take great delight in you," but the Hebrew reads literally, "He will rejoice over you with gladness."

274. The second-person pronouns in v. 20 are masculine plural in the Hebrew text, indicating that the address has shifted from personified Jerusalem (see vv. 11–19) to the exiles.

The Dawning of a New Era (Haggai)

Introduction

Haggai prophesied in 520 B.C., the second year of the reign of King Darius of Persia (see Hag. 1:1). The book contains five messages, four of which are specifically dated:[275]

First message (1:1–11)	Sixth month, first day = August 29
Second message (1:13)	Sixth month, sometime between first and 24th day = August 29–September 21
Third message (2:1–9)	Seventh month, 21st day = October 17
Fourth message (2:10–19)	Ninth month, 24th day = December 18
Fifth message (2:20–23)	Ninth month, 24th day = December 18

By 520 B.C., a group of exiles had returned to Judah, which had become a Persian province. The rebuilding of the temple, begun in 536 B.C. (see Ezra 3:8–13; 5:16), had been suspended for sixteen years. In the meantime the people had not experienced prosperity. Haggai confronted them with their neglect and misplaced priorities. In response to his message, they resumed the project (1:12, 14–15). Haggai assured them that a new era was dawning in which God's glory would fill the temple and the Davidic dynasty would be elevated to unprecedented heights.

Misplaced Priorities (1:1–12)

In 536 B.C., under pressure from hostile neighboring peoples (see Ezra 4:1–5, 24), the returning exiles had ceased work on the temple, rationalizing that the time was just not right for the project to be completed (v. 2). Yet they had built nice homes for themselves. The Lord challenged their priorities (vv. 3–4). He also pointed out that their neglect of the temple had resulted in hard economic times (vv. 5–11). Though they had worked hard planting their crops, the harvest was small because the Lord had sent a drought upon the land. Ironically, the Hebrew word translated "drought" (v. 11, *khorab*) sounds like the word used to describe the ruined condition of the temple (NIV "a ruin" in vv. 4 and 9 translates the Hebrew *khareb*). The condition of their fields mirrored that of the temple. But all this could change if the people would resume building the temple. Once more wordplay is employed for rhetorical effect. The people had "harvested" (v. 6; literally, "brought in," Heb. *bo'*) little and had lost what they had "brought" (v. 9, Heb. *bo'* again) home. This situation would be reversed if they would

275. For the dates, see Carol L. Meyers and Eric M. Meyers, *Haggai, Zechariah 1–8*, AB (Garden City, N.Y.: Doubleday, 1987), xlvi.

go to the mountains and "bring down" (v. 8, Heb. *bo'* once more) timber to build the temple. The people responded positively to Haggai's message (v. 12). Led by their governor Zerubbabel and Joshua the high priest, they obeyed and secured the timber.[276]

An Encouraging Word (1:13–15)

Pleased by the people's positive response, the Lord assured them of his protective presence (v. 13). He also "stirred" Zerubbabel, Joshua, and the people to begin rebuilding the temple structure (v. 14). The project was resumed on September 21 (v. 15). The expression "stir the spirit" (v. 14) is the same one used in 2 Chronicles 36:22–23 to describe how the Lord moved Cyrus several years before to decree that the temple be rebuilt. These references to the Lord's moving human hearts to accomplish his will certainly attest to his sovereignty. However, it is noteworthy that the supernatural divine action described in Haggai 1:14 comes in response to and is set in motion by the people's obedient response to the challenge delivered to them. The sequence of divine challenge—human response (obedience)—divine response (assurance and enablement) is instructive. God is not portrayed here as a divine puppeteer who manipulates people, but as a sovereign king who rewards obedience by giving it a boost.

The Glory to Come (2:1–9)

On October 17, about a month after the people resumed the temple project, the Lord spoke to them again (vv. 1–2). Those who were old enough to remember the grandeur of Solomon's temple, which had been destroyed sixty-six years before, were surely discouraged when they looked at the rebuilt temple. Compared to the splendor of the Solomonic structure, the rebuilt temple must have seemed like nothing (v. 3). But the Lord did not want the people or their leaders to be discouraged by such comparisons. Assuring them of his presence, he reminded them of their legacy as his covenant people. Just as he lived among Moses' generation, so his Spirit was with the postexilic community (vv. 4–5). They were the link between the past and future. Before too long, the Lord would disrupt the world order and make this temple the focal point of his worldwide kingdom of peace (vv. 6–9). The nations would bring their tribute to the Lord and the glory of this temple would exceed that of the Solomonic temple.

Some understand the statement "and the desired of all nations will come" (v. 7) as a messianic prophecy. However, this interpretation seems unlikely. The verb "will come" is plural in the Hebrew text, suggesting that the subject should be grammatically plural. For this reason, the feminine singu-

---

276. Since v. 15 indicates that construction actually resumed twenty-four days after Haggai delivered this first message, v. 12 must refer to securing the timber necessary for the project.

lar form *khemdat*, "the desirable [thing]," should be taken as collective or changed to *khamudot*, "the desirable [things]," in agreement with the Septuagint, which has a plural noun here. These "desirable things" are identified in verse 8 as the silver and gold of the nations (see as well Isa. 60:5–9; Zech. 14:14).[277]

Though some see this prophecy being fulfilled in Herod's expansion of the second temple or in Jesus' appearance there, it is more likely that the fulfillment awaits a future age when God overturns the nations and establishes his rule on earth (see vv. 6–7a). Of course, this raises a problem because the second temple was destroyed in A.D. 70. However, it is important to note that verse 3 (note "this house in its former glory") appears to view the Solomonic temple and the second temple as one, not as distinct structures. In the same way, a future temple could be regarded as a later phase of this historical temple.

However, there is a more difficult problem that must be discussed. All of these proposals assume a fulfillment long after the time of Haggai, despite the fact that the words "in a little while" suggest a more immediate fulfillment of the prophecy (v. 6).[278] However, the events prophesied here did not materialize at any time in the postexilic period or in subsequent Jewish history, let alone in Haggai's day. Has prophecy failed? Should the prophet's words be dismissed as wishful thinking? Some think so, but there are better explanations that preserve the integrity of the prophecy. The language may be archetypal and contextualized. Perhaps the prophet used objects visible to the postexilic community (the rebuilt temple and the governor Zerubbabel; see vv. 20–23) to help them visualize ultimate realities. Another, perhaps more attractive, option is that the prophecy should be taken at face value, with the understanding that its fulfillment was implicitly contingent from the outset. The Lord desired to bring the prophecy to pass in the immediate future, but subsequent developments within the postexilic community pushed the fulfillment into the more distant future and transformed literal realities into archetypes.[279]

277. For more detailed discussion of this issue, see Pieter A. Verhoef, *Haggai and Malachi*, NICOT (Grand Rapids: Eerdmans, 1987), 103–4; and David L. Petersen, *Haggai and Zechariah 1–8*, OTL (Philadelphia: Westminster, 1984), 67–68.

278. The precise meaning of the words is uncertain. The Hebrew text reads literally, "Still one, a little it is." The construction occurs nowhere else in the Hebrew Bible. It is likely that the reading is a conflation of two variants: (*a*) "Still a little it is" (Heb. *'od me'at hi'*, omitting *'akhat*) and (*b*) "Yet once for all" (Heb. *'od 'akhat*, omitting *me'at hi'*). The first would mean that the shaking of the earth and so on would soon take place. The idiom "still a little" (Heb. *'od me'at*) means "shortly, soon, almost," in Exod. 17:4; Ps. 37:10; Isa. 10:25; 29:17; Jer. 51:33; and Hos. 1:4. The second statement, when combined with what follows, would read: "Yet once for all I will shake . . ." The word *'akhat* carries this sense in Ps. 89:36. If one were to follow this reading, then the prediction would not have the immediacy suggested by the traditional translation.

279. In this regard, note how Isa. 55 offers the exiled community the opportunity to renew their covenant with the Lord and to experience his blessings. Several passages in Isa. 40–55 seem to picture the return from exile as ushering in a new era of divine blessing and peace. But the vision did not materialize in

Blessing Is on the Way (2:10–19)

On December 18, about three months after the people began rebuilding the temple, the Lord encouraged them with a promise of renewed blessing (v. 10). He began with an illustration from ritual law. According to the ritual laws of the Mosaic system, consecrated meat made a garment in which it was carried holy (Lev. 6:27). However, holiness could not be transferred from the garment to another object it happened to touch (vv. 11–12). Ritual impurity worked differently. If a man touched a ritually unclean object, such as a corpse, he became defiled and in turn transferred his impure condition to any object he touched (v. 13, cf. Num. 19:22). In the same way, the postexilic community, because of their misplaced priorities (see chapter 1), had become spiritually defiled in the Lord's sight. For this reason, their deeds and offerings were defiled as well, making them unacceptable before the Lord (v. 14). As proof of this, they only had to consider what had happened before they resumed work on the temple. Their fields had yielded only a meager amount because the Lord had struck their crops with disease and hail (vv. 15–17). But all this would change. Though past crop failures meant they had no seed or fruit at the present, the Lord would bless them now that they had resumed building the temple (vv. 18–19).

The literary structure of verses 15–19 seems a bit confusing at first glance. The argument is best outlined as follows:[280]

> Verse 15a: " 'Now give careful thought from this day on—
>
> Verses 15b–17: Consider how things were before one stone was laid on another in the LORD's temple. When anyone came to a heap of twenty measures, there were only ten. When anyone went to a wine vat to draw fifty measures, there were only twenty. I struck all the work of your hands with blight, mildew, and hail, yet you did not turn to me,' declares the LORD—
>
> Verse 18a: 'From this day on, from this twenty-fourth day of the ninth month, give careful thought—
>
> Verses 18b–19a: From the day when the foundation of the LORD's temple was laid, give careful thought. Is there yet any seed left in the barn? Until now, the vine and the fig tree, the pomegranate and the olive tree have not borne fruit—
>
> Verse 19b: From this day on I will bless you.' "

Verses 15b–17 are parenthetical. Before completing the thought begun in verse 15a, the Lord urges the people to recall the crop failure that charac-

---

this way, for the exilic community as a whole failed to grab hold of God's promise, and the postexilic community, as anticipated in Isa. 56–66, failed to measure up to God's standards. See as well my comments on Peter's offer of the kingdom to the Jews (see Acts 2–4) in conjunction with our discussion of the fulfillment of Joel 2:28–32.

280. The following translation is based on the NIV, but changes have been made to reflect my interpretation of the logic of the Lord's argument.

terized the period prior to the resumption of the temple project. In verse 18a, the Lord briefly resumes the thought begun in verse 15a, but once more diverts the people's attention to the past. In verses 18b–19a, he urges them to recall how things have gone over the past sixteen years (that is, "from the day when the foundation of the LORD's temple was laid"). The absence of seed and fruit epitomizes the period. Finally, in verse 19b the Lord completes the sentence started in verse 15a and resumed in verse 18a. Having set the stage for a contrast between the past and the future, he announces he will bless his people from "this day" (that is, December 18) forward.[281]

The Lord's Signet Ring (2:20–23)

Haggai delivered a second message on December 18, this time for Zerubbabel, the governor of Judah and a descendant of King David (see 1 Chron. 3:18–19; Matt. 1:12). Once again he announced his intention to disrupt the world order (v. 21; see v. 6). The Lord would bring down the high and mighty kingdoms of the earth and shatter their military power (v. 22). At that time he would elevate Zerubbabel, his chosen ruler, to a position of prominence (v. 23). The governor would become the Lord's signet ring, as it were. In the ancient Near East, a king's signet ring contained the royal seal and was used to authorize royal documents and decrees (see 1 Kings 21:8; Esther 8:8, 10). In a similar way, Zerubbabel would be authorized as the Lord's representative on earth. This promise reversed the judgment pronounced against Zerubbabel's grandfather Jehoiachin (see Jer. 22:24–30) and restored hope for the Davidic dynasty.

But the prophecy was never fulfilled. God did not overthrow the kingdoms of the world in Zerubbabel's day, nor did the governor become a great king ruling on God's behalf. Did the prophecy fail? As with the rebuilt temple (see 2:1–9), it is possible that Zerubbabel is an archetype of the ideal Davidic king, who would be his descendant. In this case the prophet used the governor, as well as the rebuilt temple, to help the people visualize ultimate realities. Perhaps the prophecy should be taken at face value, but with an implicit element of contingency attached. The Lord may have desired to restore the glory of the Davidic throne in Zerubbabel's day, only to have subsequent developments within the postexilic community cause him to postpone that event, thereby relegating Zerubbabel to an archetype of the great king to come.

---

281. In the interpretation just presented, "the day when the foundation of the LORD's temple was laid" (v. 18) is understood as referring to the laying of the temple foundation in 536 B.C. Ezra 3:8–13 favors this. However, others prefer to understand v. 18 as referring to a refounding ceremony on December 18, 520 B.C. See Meyers and Meyers, *Haggai, Zechariah 1–8*, 63–64; and Petersen, *Haggai and Zechariah 1–8*, 93. Zech. 8:9 may refer to such a ceremony.

Restoring Zion and Her Leaders (Zechariah)

Introduction

Zechariah, like his contemporary Haggai, ministered to the early postexilic community. The first eight chapters contain three messages that are dated between 520–518 B.C.[282] The precise dates are:

First message (1:1–6)	Second year, eighth month = October–November 520 B.C.
Second message (1:7–6:15)	Second year, 24th day of the eleventh month = February 15, 519 B.C.
Third message (7:1–8:23)	Fourth year, fourth day of the ninth month = December 7, 518 B.C.[283]

The two "oracles" in the book's final chapters (see 9–11, 12–14) are not dated. The modern scholarly consensus is that Zechariah did not write these chapters, which are usually attributed to an anonymous "Second Zechariah."[284] On the one hand, some of the material in chapters 9–14 appears to reflect a preexilic setting. For example, Egypt and Assyria are presented as the enemies of God's people and Assyria's fall (which occurred in 612–609 B.C., almost one hundred years before Zechariah's ministry) is predicted (see 10:10–12). On the other hand, certain references, for example to a war between God's people and the Greeks (see 9:13), seem to point to a date well after the time of Zechariah. How is one to explain the evidence? While any theory must be labeled speculative, it is possible that Zechariah utilized earlier material in composing these prophecies and/or that a later editor-author supplemented his work.[285]

A Call for Repentance (1:1–6)

The book begins with a brief, but powerful call to repentance. Speaking in October–November, 520 B.C. (v. 1), shortly after the resumption of the temple project (on September 21; see Hag. 1:14–15), the Lord challenged his people to renew their commitment to him and to his covenantal standards. Their ancestors had experienced the Lord's anger (v. 2), but the Lord wel-

---

282. The first two messages originate in 520–519 B.C., the second year of the Persian ruler Darius's reign, while the third message is dated to this king's fourth year (518 B.C.).

283. For the dates, see Meyers and Meyers, *Haggai, Zechariah 1–8*, xlvi.

284. For a survey of the history of interpretation, see Paul D. Hanson, *The Dawn of Apocalyptic*, rev. ed. (Philadelphia: Fortress, 1979), 287–90, and Ralph L. Smith, *Micah–Malachi*, WBC (Waco, Tex.: Word Books, 1984), 169–73, 242–49. For a helpful summary and evaluation of the evidence from an evangelical perspective, see Dillard and Longman, *Introduction to the Old Testament*, 429–32.

285. See the commentary to follow for a discussion of the problems raised by specific passages.

comed a renewed relationship with this new generation. He urged them, "Return to me," promising that, if they did, he would return to them (v. 3). The Lord did not specify what returning to him entailed, but a later message suggests the Lord was especially concerned that the community establish social justice within its ranks (see 7:8–10; 8:16–19).

To support his message, the Lord gave the community a brief history lesson (vv. 4–6). The preexilic generation had ignored the prophets, through whom the Lord urged the people to repent of their evil lifestyle. While this generation and the prophets who preached to them had passed off the scene, their experience continued to teach a lesson. God's warnings of judgment had overtaken their unrepentant ancestors; the exile had come, just as God had predicted. But fortunately, many of the exiles had repented, acknowledging that their sins had been justly punished. The Lord had restored a remnant of his people to the land. The postexilic community held the key to the nation's future. If they heeded the Lord's word, the future would be bright.

Visions of a Bright Future (1:7–6:15)

In this lengthy message, delivered on February 15, 519 B.C. (v. 7), the Lord gave the prophet a series of eight night visions, culminating with instructions concerning a symbolic object lesson Zechariah was to perform (see 6:9–15). Throughout the visions, Zechariah interacted with an angel who interpreted the symbolism for him. The visions depict, among other things, the rebuilding of Jerusalem, the growth of the postexilic community, the restoration of royal and priestly leaders, and the spiritual cleansing of the land.

Vision One: A Man among the Myrtle Trees (1:8–17)

Zechariah saw a man mounted on a red horse among some myrtle trees in a ravine (v. 8a). As the vision unfolds, it becomes apparent that this "man" is the angel of the Lord (see v. 11). Behind him were riders mounted on red, brown, and white horses (v. 8b). These riders were scouts who had returned from a reconnaissance mission that had taken them throughout the earth (vv. 9–10). They reported that the "whole world" was "at rest and in peace" (v. 11). The angel of the Lord then asked the Lord how long he would withhold his mercy from Jerusalem and the towns of Judah (v. 12). Since the destruction of Jerusalem in 586 until the time of the vision in 519, a period of roughly seventy years, they had been in ruins.[286] In response to the angel's question, the Lord announced that he was committed to Jerusalem's well-being and had transferred his anger to the nations responsible for making her

---

286. The number "seventy" is a rounded figure here; the actual time elapsed between the destruction of Jerusalem and the time of the vision was sixty-seven years. The "seventy years" referred to here is distinct from the "seventy years" of exile spoken of by Jeremiah (see 25:11–12; 29:10), a period that concluded in 539–538 B.C. See 2 Chron. 36:20–23; Ezra 1:1; Dan. 9:2.

suffering worse than God intended it to be (vv. 13–15). He proclaimed the good news that he would return to Jerusalem and live in the rebuilt temple. Jerusalem would be rebuilt, and the towns of Judah would once more experience the Lord's blessings (vv. 16–17).

Some writers have tried to find symbolism in the many details of the vision, including the various colors of the horses, the myrtle trees, and the ravine. However, since the text itself provides no explanations or even clues in this regard, such interpretations are purely speculative and should be disregarded. Apparently these particular details were included simply for the sake of lending vividness and realism to the vision.

Vision Two: Four Horns and Four Craftsmen (1:18–21)

In his second vision, Zechariah saw four horns, which represented the nations that had taken Judah into exile (vv. 18–19, 21). This included Babylon, as well as the Ammonites, Moabites, Edomites, and Philistines, all of whom took advantage of Judah's defeat (see 2 Kings 24:2; Ezek. 25:1–17; Obadiah). The number four probably refers to the four points of the compass, suggesting that the enemies of God's people attacked from all directions. Support for this comes from 2:6, which speaks of the exiles being "scattered . . . to the four winds of heaven." Perhaps the horns of the vision are animal horns, which often symbolize strength and/or military power in the Hebrew Bible (see Deut. 33:17; 1 Sam. 2:10; Ps. 75:10; 89:17, 24; 92:10; 112:9; Jer. 48:25; Lam. 2:17; Ezek. 29:21).

The prophet next saw four craftsmen, whose task was to "terrify" and "throw down" the horns (vv. 20–21). Why "craftsmen" appear as God's instruments of judgment is not entirely clear. There may be an allusion here to Ezekiel's "craftsmen of destruction" (21:31; NIV, "men skilled in destruction"), or possibly the craftsmen are mentioned because they would forge weapons to be used against the horns (see Isa. 54:16–17). Perhaps the metaphor changes at this point, with the animal horns becoming the horns of an altar (see Exod. 27:2). The craftsmen who made the horned altar now come to destroy its horns (see Amos 3:14).[287] The vision is at least partially retrospective, because the Persians had already conquered Babylon twenty years before this.

Vision Three: A Man with a Measuring Line (2:1–13)

In Zechariah's third vision, he saw a man with a measuring line, who announced that he was ready to survey Jerusalem in preparation for rebuilding the city's walls (vv. 1–2). However, an angel ran after the man and told him not to bother taking measurements, for Jerusalem would be an unwalled city. Its population would be too great to fit within a walled city (vv. 3–4). Fur-

287. See Petersen, *Haggai and Zechariah 1–8*, 165–66.

thermore, the Lord announced that he would be a wall of fire around the city limits, protecting it from any would-be invaders (v. 5). The language is obviously exaggerated. Isaiah depicted the Jerusalem of the new era as having walls built by the once-hostile nations (see 60:10–11), but Zechariah goes beyond this by depicting the city as unwalled. Both prophets, in their own way, emphasized the same basic truth—Jerusalem of the future would be secure from invasion.

The Lord spoke to the exiles and urged them to return from Babylon and the other places where they had been scattered (v. 6). He even addressed Zion as if she were in exile and told her to escape from Babylon (v. 7). Zion had every reason to rejoice, for the Lord was on his way back and would again take up residence within the city (v. 10). Other nations would be incorporated into the covenant community, as Judah and Jerusalem were elevated to special prominence (vv. 11–12). As the Lord roused himself for action, the appropriate response from mankind was silent awe and reverence (v. 13).

The interpretation of verses 8–9 is difficult. The introductory formula (v. 8a) gives the impression that everything that follows is spoken by the Lord (see NIV), but the final sentence of verse 9, where the speaker says he has been sent by the Lord, makes this problematic. It is better to see two speakers—Zechariah and the Lord—in these verses. Note that the prophet speaks in the first person earlier in the vision (see vv. 1–3). If one follows this proposal, there are a couple of ways verses 8–9 may be outlined and translated/paraphrased:

Option A

Zechariah: "For this is what the LORD Almighty says (for his own glory he has sent me)[288] concerning[289] the nations who plundered you (for whoever touches you touches the pupil of his eye):
The Lord: 'I will surely raise my hand against them so that their slaves will plunder them.'
Zechariah: (When this happens), then you will know that the LORD Almighty has sent me."

Option B

Zechariah: "For this is what the LORD Almighty says:
(For his own glory he has sent me to[290] the nations who plundered you, for whoever touches you touches the pupil of his eye.)"

288. The Hebrew text reads literally, "after glory he sent me." The meaning of the statement is unclear. The translation offered here assumes that God's glory is in view and that it is the goal of the prophet's mission.
289. The Hebrew preposition used here, though often meaning "to," can have the sense "regarding, concerning." See H. G. Mitchell, "A Critical and Exegetical Commentary on Haggai and Zechariah," in *A Critical and Exegetical Commentary on Haggai, Zechariah, Malachi, and Jonah,* ICC (New York: Charles Scribner's Sons, 1912), 146.
290. In this case, the Hebrew preposition translated "to" is construed with "sent me."

The Lord: 'I will surely raise my hand against them so that their slaves will plunder them.'

Zechariah: (When this happens), then you will know that the LORD Almighty has sent me."[291]

In either case, the Lord announced that he would punish the nations appropriately, for they had attacked his people, who are compared to the "pupil" (traditionally translated "apple") of the eye to emphasize their great value in his sight. Those who plundered his people would in turn be plundered. When this came to pass, Zechariah would be vindicated as the Lord's spokesman.

Vision Four: The Cleansing of Joshua's Robes (3:1–10)

Zechariah next saw the high priest Joshua standing before the angel of the Lord (v. 1). At Joshua's right hand stood an accuser (see Ps. 109:6), called here literally "the adversary" (Heb. *hassatan*). The term *satan,* when used without the definite article, usually refers to a human adversary.[292] When the term appears with the article, as it does here and in Job 1–2, it is a title for a being who seems to serve as a prosecuting attorney in the heavenly court. In Job 1–2, he is impertinent toward God and exhibits an unduly hostile attitude toward Job. He calls into question both Job's motives and God's justice. Here in Zechariah 3:1–2, he does not speak, but the Lord's passionate response to his very presence suggests that the adversary has hostile intentions. In the progress of biblical revelation, as the character of this "adversary" comes into sharper focus, his title in the Hebrew Bible becomes a proper name, Satan. Though his evil nature is not fully revealed in the Hebrew Bible, he seems malevolent. While his role as a prosecutor in the divine court seems to be legitimate, he reminds one of Inspector Javert, the antagonist in Victor Hugo's novel *Les Miserables* who relentlessly hunts down the repentant reformed convict Jean Valjean. Javert's obsession with "justice" and "right" transforms him into an evil monster who has no place in his heart for mercy.

The angel of the Lord, speaking as the Lord's representative,[293] rebuked the adversary, making it clear that this was a time for salvation, not judgment

---

291. Extending this proposal to what follows, we see that v. 11 contains both the words of the Lord and the prophet. First the Lord, continuing the speech begun in v. 10, says, "Many nations will be joined with the LORD in that day and will become my people. I will live among you." Then the prophet adds, "And you will know that the LORD Almighty has sent me."

292. The one exception is in Num. 22:22, 32, where the angel of the Lord assumes the role of Balaam's adversary. In 1 Chron. 21:1, the term probably refers to a nearby nation, though some prefer to take the word in this context as a proper name, "Satan." For arguments against taking the term as a proper name, see Sarah Japhet, *I & II Chronicles: A Commentary,* OTL (Philadelphia: Westminster, 1993), 374–75.

293. Verse 2 gives the impression that the Lord himself spoke to the adversary (note "the LORD said to Satan"). However, the speaker then refers to "the LORD" in the third person two times, suggesting he is distinct from the Lord. It is likely that the Lord spoke through the angel referred to in v. 1. Since the angel represents the Lord, the introductory formula can attribute his words directly to the Lord himself.

(v. 2). The Lord was devoted to Jerusalem, and he had delivered the high priest, who represented the city and the postexilic community, from destruction, just as one snatches a stick from the fire before it is consumed. The angel ordered Joshua's filthy garments to be removed and replaced with ornate robes and a turban (vv. 3–5). The Lord was not blind to the community's past sins. The term translated "filthy" pictures the priest's garments as stained with excrement.[294] But the past is no barrier to the future where God's mercy is concerned. The door to a new era was open. If Joshua obeyed the Lord's commandments and governed the temple properly, he would enjoy prominence among the community (vv. 6–7).

Joshua's cleansing and new opportunity foreshadowed the transformation of the entire community. He and his associates (either his fellow priests or the civil leaders) were symbols of better days ahead (vv. 8–10). The Lord would raise up a servant, called here "the Branch," to purify the land of its sinful condition, and to restore prosperity to the community. Though "the Branch" is not specifically identified here, those familiar with Jeremiah's prophecies would recognize him as the ideal Davidic ruler to come (see 23:5; 33:15). In Zechariah's day this promise was attached to the person of Zerubbabel, a Davidic descendant and the governor of the community who would be instrumental in the rebuilding of the temple (see 4:6–12 and 6:9–15, as well as Hag. 2:20–23). However, Zerubbabel's accomplishments would hardly satisfy the portrait given by Jeremiah. In the progress of revelation, Jesus Christ emerges as the ideal ruler foreseen by Jeremiah, relegating Zerubbabel to a mere archetype.

The Lord pointed to a stone that he had set in front of Joshua (v. 9). The stone had seven "eyes" on it and would soon be engraved with an inscription. The identity and significance of the stone are unclear. Though scholars have proposed various interpretations, it seems most likely that the stone is the capstone of the rebuilt temple (see 4:7). In this case the "seven eyes" probably symbolize the Lord's watchful care (see 4:12), while the inscription would identify the structure as the Lord's. Another attractive proposal understands the "stone" as the golden plate attached to the high priest's turban and inscribed with the words "Holy to the Lord" (see Exod. 28:36–37).[295] Like the stone in Zechariah's vision, this golden plate was associated with the removal of sin (see Exod. 28:38). In this case, the "seven eyes" would be the facets of the stone.[296]

---

294. The Hebrew term used in v. 4 appears only here, but related words, derived from the same root, refer elsewhere to excrement (see Deut. 23:13; 2 Kings 18:27 = Isa. 36:12; Ezek. 4:12).

295. Petersen, *Haggai and Zechariah 1–8*, 211–12.

296. The Hebrew word translated "eye" does refer on occasion to the gleam of metal or jewels. See Ezek. 1:4, 7, 16, 22; 8:2; 10:9; Dan. 10:6. Note also the phrase *yn 'n*, "sparkling wine" (literally, "wine of an eye") in Ugaritic. For the pertinent text (*CTA* 6 iv 42), see Gibson, *Canaanite Myths and Legends*, 78.

Vision Five: A Lampstand and Two Olive Trees (4:1–14)

In Zechariah's next vision, he saw a golden lampstand with a bowl and seven lamps (vv. 1–2). The last part of verse 2 reads literally, "seven and seven [were] channels [or perhaps "spouts"] for the lamps which were on its top." What this means is uncertain. It may describe seven channels, or pipes, connecting the bowl with the lamps (NIV), but in this case the repetition of "seven" is problematic. It is more likely that the seven lamps were arranged around the edge of the bowl and that each of these lamps contained seven spouts or indentations, in each of which a wick was placed.[297] On each side of the lampstand was an olive tree that supplied the bowl with oil (v. 3; see vv. 11–12).

What do the various elements of the vision symbolize? The angel never explained the significance of the lampstand, but since the vision pertains to the rebuilding of the temple (vv. 7–10), it is possible that it stands for the temple. The Hebrew word translated "lampstand" (*menorah*) is used elsewhere (with one exception, 2 Kings 4:10) of the lampstand in the tabernacle or the lampstands in Solomon's temple. The seven lamps represent the "eyes of the LORD, which range throughout the earth" (v. 10b). In other words, the lamps are a reminder of the Lord's awareness of and sovereignty over what happens in the world. The fact that the lamps were positioned on the lampstand suggests the Lord was present in the temple. The olive trees are never identified. Zechariah asked what they symbolize (v. 11), but before the angel could answer, the prophet noticed two streams of oil flowing from the trees into two golden pipes which carried the oil into the bowl (v. 12).[298] When he asked about them, the angel specifically identified them as, literally, "the two sons of oil who stand before the Lord of the whole earth" (v. 14). The phrase "sons of oil" is typically interpreted to mean that the two individuals mentioned were anointed with oil as the Lord's special servants (see NIV). However, the word for "oil" used here (Heb. *yitshar*) does not refer to anointing oil elsewhere (the Hebrew term for such oil is *shemen*) but to fresh oil that symbolizes a land's agricultural abundance.[299] It is more likely, then, that the individuals are called "sons of oil" because under their leadership the Lord would restore agricultural prosperity to the land (see 3:10, as well as Hag. 2:19). These "sons of oil" were, of course, the high priest Joshua and the governor Zerubbabel (see 3:1–10; 4:7–10; 6:9–15). Through the supernatural power of his Spirit (4:6), the Lord would enable Zerubbabel to

297. On the structure of the lampstand, bowl, and lamps, see Joyce G. Baldwin, *Haggai, Zechariah, Malachi,* TOTC (London: InterVarsity, 1972), 119–20; Petersen, *Haggai and Zechariah 1–8,* 220–23; and Meyers and Meyers, *Haggai, Zechariah 1–8,* 234–38.
298. The Hebrew word translated "branches" in NIV elsewhere actually refers to "ears of grain," not tree branches. The term is better interpreted here as a homonym meaning "flowing stream." The term refers to streams of oil flowing from the tree into the pipes. See Petersen, *Haggai and Zechariah 1–8,* 235–36.
299. Ibid., 230–31.

overcome all obstacles and complete the temple project (vv. 7–10). Through Joshua's ministry, the religious activities of the temple would be resumed (3:7). Because both of these leaders would be instrumental in the restoration of worship in the temple, they could be portrayed as supplying the oil that lit the lamps on the temple lampstand.[300]

Vision Six: A Flying Scroll (5:1–4)

Zechariah next saw a huge unrolled scroll (thirty feet by fifteen feet) flying through the sky (vv. 1–2). The scroll is specifically identified as the "curse that is going out over the whole land" (v. 3). It is called a "curse" because it announced judgment upon evildoers. Written on one side of the scroll were the words "every thief will be banished," while the opposite side contained the warning "everyone who swears falsely will be banished." The Lord would send the scroll into the homes of thieves and those who took false oaths, where it would rot away the timber and stones, leaving the house in ruins (v. 4). The words on the scroll allude to two of the Ten Commandments. The third commandment prohibited taking false oaths, while the eighth condemned theft. The underlying concern of both commandments was that God's people not cheat and rob one another. The vision was a reminder to the postexilic community that they, like their forefathers, were still subject to God's standards for social conduct as expressed in the Decalogue. Failure to abide by these standards would bring slow, but certain destruction.

Vision Seven: A Woman in a Basket (5:5–11)

Zechariah's next vision was especially bizarre. He saw a woman in a basket who personified the wickedness and sin of the land (vv. 5–8). The heavy lid of the basket was secured. Then two other women, both of whom had wings like storks, grabbed the basket, flew into the sky, and set out for Babylon (literally, Shinar), where they would deposit the basket (vv. 9–11). The women are perhaps compared to storks because these birds were unclean, according to the law (Lev. 11:19; Deut. 14:18). Storklike women would make appropriate bearers of a contaminated basket. Likewise, Shinar, the distant unclean land where the exiles lived, was an appropriate destination for personified sin.[301] The point of the vision is clear. The Lord would not tolerate sin in the postexilic community. Those who violated his standards would be sent back into exile.

Vision Eight: Four Chariots (6:1–8)

In this final vision, Zechariah saw four chariots emerging from between two bronze mountains. The team of horses pulling each chariot differed in color from the other teams (vv. 1–4). The angel identified the chariots as "the four

300. Ibid., 233–34.
301. For the concept of a foreign land being unclean, see Amos 7:17.

winds of heaven," representing the four points of the compass (v. 5; see NIV margin, as well as 2:6).[302] The different colors of the horses, rather than having some symbolic value, simply help to distinguish the respective chariots and are included in the description for the sake of vividness. The symbolism of the bronze mountains is not explained. Bronze suggests strength (see Isa. 45:2; Jer. 1:18), and it is possible that the twin mountains mirror Solomon's temple, which had two bronze pillars situated at its entrance (1 Kings 7:15–22).

As the chariots emerged from God's presence, the one with black horses headed northward, followed by the one with white horses.[303] The chariot with dappled horses headed toward the south, while the one with red horses is not mentioned. Apparently it was held back in reserve. The mission of the chariots appears to be militaristic. Indeed, Jeremiah 49:36 indicates that the four winds (which the chariots symbolize; see v. 5) serve as instruments of divine judgment. Those going to the north appeased God's anger by bringing judgment upon the regions of the north.[304] Since this undoubtedly included Babylon (see 2:6–7), the vision is to some degree retrospective (see 1:18–21 as well). The Persians had conquered Babylon twenty years before.

A Symbolic Coronation (6:9–15)

This lengthy message (which began in 1:7) concludes with instructions for Zechariah to perform a symbolic coronation of the high priest Joshua. Using silver and gold collected from three of the returning exiles, Zechariah was to make a crown and place it on Joshua's head (vv. 9–11). After delivering a message pertaining to the rebuilding of the temple and the unification of the royalty and priesthood (vv. 12–13), Zechariah was to place the crown in the temple as a memorial to the exiles who had donated the silver and gold from which it was made (v. 14).[305] Their contribution foreshadowed the participation of other returning exiles in the rebuilding of the temple (v. 15).

---

302. Some translations understand the Hebrew word *rukhot* here as "spirits," but the appearance of the same phrase in 2:6 suggests that the winds are in view here. See Meyers and Meyers, *Haggai, Zechariah 1–8*, 322–23.

303. NIV gives the impression that the chariot with white horses went to the west. The Hebrew text reads literally, "and the white ones went out to after them." The expression *'el 'akhare*, "to after," elsewhere means "to/at a place behind" (see 2 Sam. 5:23; 2 Kings 9:18–19). This suggests that the white horses followed the black ones toward the north. However, many, assuming that the four winds need to move in the direction of all four points of the compass, prefer to emend the text to read, "and the white ones went out toward the sea," which would mean they headed westward. Proponents of this view usually also argue that a reference to the fourth chariot heading east must have been accidentally omitted from the text. See Baldwin, *Haggai, Zechariah, Malachi*, 131–32; and Petersen, *Haggai and Zechariah 1–8*, 263–64.

304. NIV translates v. 8, "Look, those going toward the north country have given my Spirit rest in the land of the north." However, it is more probable that the Hebrew word *ruakh*, which does frequently refer to the divine Spirit (see Zech. 4:6), refers here to God's angry disposition, which is appeased by judgment poured out on the objects of his anger (see 1:15). For examples where the Hebrew term refers to anger, see Job 15:13; Prov. 29:11; Eccles. 10:4.

305. Two of the names given in v. 10 are different in v. 14. In the Hebrew text of v. 14, Heldai is called Helem, while Zephaniah's son Josiah is called Hen. It is likely that Helem is a textual corruption of or an

The message accompanying the symbolic coronation requires special attention. As Zechariah placed the crown on Joshua's head, he was to announce that one designated "the Branch" would rebuild the temple and occupy a throne (vv. 12–13a). At first it appears that Joshua is identified as "the Branch," but this seems unlikely since the fourth and fifth visions, when correlated, identify Zerubbabel as the Branch who would rebuild the temple (see 3:8 and 4:7–10). Zechariah's message actually pertained to both Joshua and Zerubbabel and anticipated their cooperative relationship as leaders of the covenant community. Verses 11–13 display a chiastic structure:[306]

> A Joshua is crowned as the priestly ruler of the community (11).
> B Zerubbabel (the Branch) will rebuild the temple (12–13a).
> B'Zerubbabel will be the civil ruler of the community (13b).
> A'Joshua will be the priestly ruler of the community (13c).[307]
> *Conclusion:* There will be harmony between the two rulers (13d).

Justice, Not Ritual (7:1–8:23)

The people of Bethel sent a delegation to Jerusalem to ask if they should continue the practice of mourning during the fifth month to commemorate the destruction of Jerusalem in 586 B.C., an event that had occurred during the fifth month of the year (vv. 1–3; see 2 Kings 25:8; Jer. 52:12). In response to this inquiry, the Lord gave Zechariah a message for the people in which he emphasized that social justice must take priority over ritual. The structure of chapters 7–8 displays a chiastic arrangement of main themes, though the central elements (see D/D'–F/F' below) display some variation:

> A Messengers from Bethel come *to entreat* (Heb. *lekhallot*) the Lord (7:1–3)
>   B The Lord denounces meaningless fasts (7:4–7)
>   C The Lord's priority is social justice (7:8–12)
>   D The Lord sent his people into exile (7:13–14)
>   E The Lord will restore Jerusalem (8:1–3)
>   F The Lord will bless a remnant (8:4–6)
>   D'The Lord will bring back the exiles (8:7–8)
>   F'The Lord will bless a remnant (8:9–13)
>   E'The Lord will restore Jerusalem (8:14–15)
>   C'The Lord's priority is social justice (8:16–17)
>   B'The Lord will restore meaningful fasts (8:18–19)
> A'Many nations will come *to entreat* (Heb. *lekhallot*) the Lord (8:20–23)

---

alternate name for Heldai. See Meyers and Meyers, *Haggai, Zechariah 1–8*, 340. "Hen" may not be a proper name at all, but a title given to Josiah. (The actual title is *lekhen*, meaning "steward." See Petersen, *Haggai and Zechariah 1–8*, 278 n. 8.)

306. The outline included in the text is based on that of Eugene H. Merrill, *Haggai, Zechariah, Malachi* (Chicago: Moody, 1994), 199.

307. NIV ("And he will be a priest on his throne") makes it sound as if the Branch of vv. 12–13a is the referent here, but the Hebrew text is better translated at this point, "and there will be a priest on his throne."

The question posed by the Bethel delegation (v. 3) was a natural one. After all, a group of exiles had reoccupied the land, and the temple was being rebuilt. Could the people assume that the exile was officially over and that it was no longer necessary to commemorate the fall of Jerusalem nearly seventy years before? Could they assume that God would restore his blessing and that it was no longer necessary to mourn over the past? The Lord's response (vv. 4–6) reveals the people's shallow thinking and their failure to recognize God's priority. The Lord questioned the motives of those who had observed fasts in the fifth and seventh months for the past seventy years.[308] Whether fasting or eating, the people acted out of self-interest. They should have known that God did not place priority on fasting and other rituals, for the preexilic prophets, with whose teachings the exiles should have been familiar, had made this clear (v. 7; see especially Jer. 14:12).[309] The Lord was not concerned about fasting and rituals as much as he was ethical standards and justice. He urged the postexilic community to promote justice and to show compassion, especially toward the vulnerable in society (vv. 8–10). They must be different than their forefathers, who stubbornly rejected the commandments of God's law and the warnings of the prophets, prompting God's angry judgment to fall upon them (vv. 11–12). Because they did not heed God when he called them to repentance, God did not listen to their call for help (v. 13). Instead, he scattered them among the nations, leaving the land in ruins (v. 14).

However, God's judgment was not final. He was committed to Jerusalem and would once again take up residence in the city, making her "the City of Truth" and "the Holy Mountain" (8:1–3). The signs of a vibrant society would be present as the elderly sat in the streets, watching the boys and girls

308. The fast in the seventh month probably commemorated the death of the governor Gedaliah, who was assassinated by a Judahite fanatic in the seventh month of the year 586 b.c. (see 2 Kings 25:25–26). His death had negative repercussions for the people of Judah (see Jer. 40:7–41:18).

309. As it stands, the Hebrew text of v. 7 appears to be elliptical and unintelligible. It reads literally: "Is there not, the words which the Lord proclaimed by the former prophets when Jerusalem was inhabited and at rest, and its surrounding towns and the Negev and the Shephelah were inhabited?" The Hebrew text places the accusative sign before "the words," indicating that it is the object of a verb, but the verb does not appear. Something appears to have been accidentally omitted in the transmission of the text. I propose the following emended reading at the beginning of v. 7: *halo' 'attem hashome'im 'et-haddebarim*, "Are you not the ones who heard the words . . . ?" In this case, the existing Hebrew text can be easily explained as the result of an accidental scribal error. Having written the first two letters (*aleph* and *taw*) of the second masculine plural pronoun *'attem*, the scribe's eye accidentally jumped forward to the *aleph-taw* of the accusative sign, leaving out the intervening letters. In addition to making sense out of the text, the proposed emendation also has the advantage of creating a syntactical structure that reflects, at least partially, the construction in v. 6b, where *halo'* is followed by the second masculine plural pronoun *'attem* and a plural participle with the article ("Are you not the ones who ate?"). The verb *shama'*, "to hear, listen," is proposed in the emendation because it is so often collocated with the Lord's word(s). In this case the point would be that the exilic generation (see v. 5) had heard the words of the preexilic prophets, not directly, but through the prophetic tradition and their parents. However, one could propose a different verb in the ellipsis, such as *ma'as*, "reject," or *shakakh*, "forget." In this case the Lord chides their behavior as running counter to the time-honored principles laid down by the preexilic prophets.

playing (vv. 4–5). Though the restoration of the city might stagger the imagination of the people, the Lord would not share their amazement, for nothing is beyond his capability (v. 6).

The language of verses 5–6 alludes to the account in Genesis 18, where Sarah "laughed" (v. 12, Heb. *tsakhaq*) when told she would have a child. The Lord reprimanded her, asking, "Is anything too hard [Heb. *pala'*] for the Lord?" (v. 14). When the child was born, Sarah named him Isaac (Heb. *yitskhaq*, "he laughs"), explaining, "God has brought me laughter, and everyone who hears about this will laugh with me" (Gen. 21:6). In Zechariah 8:5–6 the key words from the Genesis account appear. In verse 5 the children are described as playing (literally, "laughing," from Heb. *sakhaq*, an alternate spelling of *tsakhaq*), while in verse 6 the point is made that even these remarkable developments will not seem marvelous (Heb. *pala'*) to the Lord. Like Sarah's joyful laughter over her newborn son, the laughter of Jerusalem's children would give proof that nothing is too amazing for the Lord to accomplish. Just as he gave barren Sarah a child, so he can revive the desolate land (see 7:14).

The Lord would bring the exiles back to the land and form them into a loyal community of worshipers (vv. 7–8). Times had been hard, but the Lord would prosper his people and give them abundant crops (vv. 9–11).[310] God's people had become a curse word among the nations, but they would become a prime example of a nation blessed by God (v. 13). Verse 13 reads literally, "And it will so happen [that] as you were a curse among the nations, O house of Judah and house of Israel, so I will save you and you will be a blessing." For Judah and Israel to "be a curse" meant that their names appeared in curse formulas.[311] Because Judah and Israel were prime examples of an accursed people, one pronouncing a curse would call a similar fate down upon his enemies. For Judah and Israel to "be a blessing" would mean that their names would be used in blessing formulas.[312] They would be recognized as a classic example of a people blessed by God. One pronouncing a blessing would ask that the object of the blessing prosper like Judah and Israel.

The Lord promised to reverse the effects of past judgment and to restore his favor to Judah and Jerusalem (vv. 14–15), but he also expected the people to commit themselves to his ethical standards. They must promote justice in the community and avoid evil and dishonest practices (vv. 16–17). Once the people got their priorities straight and experienced God's renewed

310. Verse 9 mentions the time when the temple foundation was laid. This would seem to refer to the time when the rebuilding of the temple was initiated in 536 B.C. (see Ezra 3:13). However, v. 10 refers to a time, prior to the laying of the foundation, when wages were low. This situation seems to correspond to what is described in Hag. 1:6 as taking place prior to 520 B.C., when work on the temple was resumed. Perhaps Zech. 8:9 refers then to a second foundation laying ceremony in 520. If so, Haggai and Zechariah are probably the prophets referred to in v. 9.

311. For an example of a curse formula, see Jer. 29:22.

312. For examples of blessing formulas, see Gen. 48:20 and Ruth 4:11.

blessings, their fasts would be transformed into joyful festivals (vv. 18–19).[313] People from throughout the land would willingly seek the Lord, joined by foreigners from distant lands (vv. 20–23).

The Lord Establishes His Kingdom (9:1–14:21)

As noted earlier, the final chapters of Zechariah contain two oracles. The first of these (chapters 9–11) depicts a glorious future for God's people, highlighted by the defeat of the nation's traditional enemies (9:1–8), the arrival of God's chosen king (9:9–10), the return of the exiles (9:11–12; 10:8–12), the supernatural rejuvenation of Israel's military power (9:13–15; 10:3–7; 11:1–3), and the restoration of divine blessing (9:16–17; 10:1–2). However, this portrait of the future is balanced by a highly symbolic account depicting the rejection of God's rulership by his people and a time of judgment (11:4–17). The second oracle (chapters 12–14) continues the story. Jerusalem is besieged by hostile nations, but the Lord supernaturally protects the city (12:1–9). The people grieve over their rejection of God, and he forgives their sin, purifies them, and renews his covenant with them (12:10–13:9). However, Jerusalem suffers greatly before the Lord intervenes just in the nick of time (14:1–7, 12–15; cf. 13:7b–8). Following his great victory, the Lord establishes his universal kingdom, and the nations worship him (14:8–11, 16–21).

The Rejuvenation of God's People (9:1–11:3)

The first oracle begins with an announcement of judgment upon the Arameans to the northeast (9:1), the Phoenicians to the north (vv. 2–4), and the Philistines to the west (vv. 5–7). Some find the fulfillment of this prophecy in Alexander the Great's conquests in the fourth century B.C., but it is more likely that these particular nations are mentioned because they were traditional enemies of God's people. Furthermore, their defeat would secure the borders of Israel and Judah (v. 8) and pave the way for the expansion of the nation to its idealized limits (see Deut. 1:7; Josh. 1:3–4).[314]

Though Jerusalem had been deprived of its independence since its fall in 586 B.C., kingship would be restored to the city. The Lord urges the personified city to rejoice and then directs her attention to the arrival of her king (v. 9a). Since the Lord is speaking in this context (see vv. 6–8, 10–13), the king of whom he speaks must be a human ruler, undoubtedly a Davidic

313. Four fasts are mentioned in v. 19. As noted earlier, the fast in the fifth month commemorated the destruction of Jerusalem in 586, while the one in the seventh month recalled Gedaliah's death (see 7:3, 5). The fast in the fourth month probably commemorated the Babylonian invasion of Jerusalem in 586 (see 2 Kings 25:3–4; Jer. 39:2; 52:6–7), while the one in the tenth month likely recalled the beginning of the siege of Jerusalem in 588 (see 2 Kings 25:1–2; Jer. 39:1; 52:4; Ezek. 24:1–2).

314. See Hanson, *Dawn of Apocalyptic*, 317, as well the comments of Merrill, *Haggai, Zechariah, Malachi*, 247–48.

descendant (see 12:8). The king is described as "just and victorious" (NIV "righteous and having salvation") and as riding on a donkey (v. 9b).[315] Kings often rode donkeys in the ancient Near East, so this mode of transportation was not inherently demeaning for royalty.[316] However, riding a donkey, rather than a chariot or warhorse, reflects his "humble" (NIV "gentle") character and the peaceful nature of his rule (see v. 10).[317] The prophecy finds its partial fulfillment in Jesus' triumphal entry into Jerusalem just prior to his crucifixion (see Matt. 21:1–11; Mark 11:1–11; Luke 19:28–38; John 12:12–15). However, because the Jewish nation rejected Jesus at that time, the complete fulfillment of the prophecy (especially the promises made in v. 10) awaits the second advent.

Having announced the arrival of the king, the Lord next promises Zion that he will free her captive people in fulfillment of his covenant promise to her (vv. 11–12).[318] It is possible that the phrase "blood of my covenant" alludes to Exodus 24:8, where it is used of the sacrifice that ratified God's covenant with Israel at Sinai. However, it is difficult to see how that covenant, at least on the surface, can be viewed as made with Zion or how it anticipates a return from exile.[319] It is more likely that Zechariah alludes here to Ezekiel 16:8, where the Lord recalls that he made a covenant with Zion when she was a young woman (see v. 60 as well). It is possible that the Mosaic covenant underlies Ezekiel's metaphor because Zion appears to represent the nation. In this case, Zechariah 9:11, if indeed alluding to Ezekiel 16:8, would probably refer to the promise (appended to the Deuteronomic version of the covenant) of an eventual return of God's people from exile (see Deut. 30:1–10). However, it seems more likely that God's choice of Zion as his dwelling place (a decision made during David's reign) underlies Ezekiel's metaphor. In this case, Zechariah 9:11, if drawing on Ezekiel 16, may allude to the promises of Psalm 132:13–17, which are closely associated with God's covenant with David (see vv. 11–12).

Zechariah also depicts the reunification of Judah and Israel, represented here by its most prominent tribe, Ephraim (v. 13a). Zion's sons would attack Javan's (NIV "Greece") sons (v. 13b). Shielded by his protective power, the Lord's people would defeat their enemies (vv. 14–15) and enjoy his renewed blessings (vv. 16–17).

Some see the reference to Greece (literally, "Javan") as an indication of a later date of authorship for this oracle or as evidence that this statement is a

315. Another option is to understand the Hebrew term *tsaddiq*, "just," in the sense of "vindicated" or "legitimate" here. See Merrill, *Haggai, Zechariah, Malachi*, 254.
316. See Baldwin, *Haggai, Zechariah, Malachi*, 165–66.
317. In this regard, contrast Absalom, who rode in a chariot (2 Sam. 15:1), with Solomon, who rode a mule to his coronation (1 Kings 1:33).
318. The second-person pronouns and verb forms in v. 11 are feminine singular, indicating that personified Zion is still being addressed (see v. 9).
319. Exod. 23 anticipates the conquest of the land, not a return from exile.

later addition to the prophecy. But the mere naming of Greece (= Javan) does not necessitate such a conclusion, for references to Javan also appear in Genesis 10:2, 4; Isaiah 66:19; and Ezekiel 27:13. More pertinent is that a war between God's people and the sons of Javan is depicted. For some this anticipates or reflects the struggles between the Maccabees and the Seleucids in the second century B.C. (see Dan. 8:21–25), but perhaps Javan is used here as representative of the distant nations that would be incorporated into the Lord's kingdom.[320]

Zechariah interrupted his description of the future and urged his contemporary audience to look to the Lord for renewed blessings (10:1). The postexilic community had not experienced agricultural prosperity (see Hag. 1:5–11; 2:16–17), but a renewed commitment to God and his ethical standards would bring the rains and cause the fields to yield an abundant harvest (see 8:12).

At this point the major themes of 9:11–16 are repeated in reverse order, creating a chiastic structure:

> A The Lord delivers the exiles (9:11–12)
>   B The Lord energizes Judah and Ephraim for battle (9:13–15)
>   C The Lord shepherds and blesses his people (9:16–17)
>   D Blessing is offered in the present (10:1)
>   C´ The Lord shepherds his people (10:2–3b)
>   B´ The Lord energizes Judah and Ephraim for battle (10:3c–7)
> A´ The Lord delivers the exiles (10:8–11:3)

The people were to look to the Lord as their source of blessing, not to divination experts and their devices (v. 2a).[321] In fact, because of such pagan practices God's covenant community was like lost sheep with no shepherd to guide and protect them (v. 2b). Those responsible for shepherding God's people had neglected their duties and would be severely disciplined by God (v. 3a).[322] The identity of these "shepherds/male goats" is not clear. They may represent oppressive foreign rulers (see 9:8; 10:5b, 11), but it is more likely, in light of the way the shepherd motif is employed in 11:4–17 and 13:7, that leaders within the covenant community are in view.

Dissatisfied with the incompetent leaders he appointed over his people, the Lord himself would assume the position of Judah's shepherd (10:3b). He

---

320. See Baldwin, *Haggai, Zechariah, Malachi,* 169.

321. The "idols" mentioned in v. 2 were used in divination. The term translated "idols" (Heb. *terapim*) refers to household idols (see Gen. 31:19; 1 Sam. 19:13, 16) that were used for divination (Ezek. 21:21; Hos. 3:4). Their use was forbidden by the Lord (see 1 Sam. 15:23; 2 Kings 23:24). Such idols are mentioned in Judg. 17–18, where they are listed among the objects in Micah's homemade shrine (see 17:5; 18:14). The Danites eventually stole them and made them part of their unauthorized worship center (Judg. 18:17–18, 20).

322. The Hebrew term translated "leaders" in NIV, refers literally to "male goats" that sometimes set the pace for the flock (see Jer. 50:8). Here it is a metaphor for rulers.

would transform Judah into a mighty military force, compared here to a warhorse (v. 3c). The Lord's power would give Judah stability and enable them to defeat their enemies (vv. 4–5).[323] The northern kingdom (represented by the "Ephraimites" of the "house of Joseph") would return from exile and be reunited with Judah (vv. 6–8). The Israelite exiles had been scattered among the nations, but they would return from Assyria and from Egypt (a symbol of slavery and exile; see Hos. 8:13; 9:6), populate Gilead and Lebanon, and become loyal followers of the Lord (vv. 9–10, 12). Using imagery from the past, the Lord pictured his people passing safely through the dangerous sea, as they did in the days of Moses (v. 11a). He would bring down the pride of Assyria and the royal power of Egypt (v. 11b). The Assyrians, of course, had long since disappeared from the international scene by Zechariah's time. It is possible that Zechariah used a preexilic source at this point, but such a proposal is not necessary to account for the anachronistic reference. Since Assyria and Egypt were the traditional enemies of Israel, the prophet was probably using them here as code words for the powerful nations of his own time or as archetypes for the hostile nations in general.

The downfall of Assyria and Egypt is depicted in highly poetic terms in 11:1–3. Fire sweeps through the forests of Lebanon and the region of Bashan (located east of the Jordan), destroying the trees and pasturelands. As the shepherds wail over the loss of their grazing areas, the fire sweeps on toward the Jordan River, burning up the thicket and driving the lions from their homes. The underlying reality behind the imagery is not specifically identified, but since these verses immediately follow the announcement of Assyria's and Egypt's defeat, it is reasonable to associate the fire with God's judgment upon the nations they symbolize. Isaiah used the cedars of Lebanon and oaks of Bashan to symbolize the proud objects of divine judgment (2:13). Isaiah compared Assyria to the trees of Lebanon (10:33–34), and Ezekiel pictured both Assyria and Egypt as great trees in the Lebanon forest (31:1–18).

The Flock Rejects Its Shepherd (11:4–17)

The reference to shepherds wailing (v. 3) provides the transition to the concluding section of this oracle, which contains an allegory about shepherds and sheep. The focus of the oracle to this point has been the glorious future

323. The precise meaning of v. 4 is unclear. The Hebrew text reads literally, "from him a cornerstone, from him a tent peg, from him a bow of war, from him goes out every ruler [or "oppressor"?] together." It is uncertain who or what is the antecedent of the third masculine singular pronoun. Options include (see v. 3) "the Lord of Hosts," "his [the Lord's] flock," and "the house of Judah" (see NIV). In my view, the Lord's flock or the house of Judah is the antecedent. The first three lines make the point that the Lord's flock/house of Judah would experience renewed stability (symbolized by the cornerstone and tent peg) and power (symbolized by the bow). Perhaps a royal figure is envisioned as emerging from Judah. (The metaphor of a cornerstone is used elsewhere of leaders. See Judg. 20:2 [NIV "leaders"]; 1 Sam. 14:38 [NIV "leaders"]; Isa. 19:13.) The meaning of the fourth line is debated. Because the cornerstone, tent peg, and bow seem to be

of Judah and Israel, but in verses 4–5 the mood changes, as we read about worthless shepherds who care nothing for their flock. The theme has already appeared briefly in the oracle. In 10:2b–3a, the Lord pictured his people as wandering sheep and denounced the shepherds who had abandoned them. In 11:4–17, he develops this theme in much more detail.

The Lord asked the prophet to play the role of a shepherd and instructed him to "pasture the flock marked for slaughter" (v. 4).[324] The Lord denounced three groups—those who sell the flock in order to get rich, those who buy the sheep in order to slaughter them for food, and the shepherds who do nothing to protect the flock (v. 5). The Lord then announced that he would show no more pity for the people (symbolized by the sheep) and that he would allow each one to be oppressed by "his neighbor" (referring to nearby nations?) and "his king" (referring to a leader of the community?) (v. 6). The prophet shepherded the flock, using two staffs, one named Favor and the other Union (v. 7). In the span of one month, he got rid of three shepherds (probably the negligent shepherds mentioned in v. 5), but the flock turned on him (v. 8), prompting him to renounce his commission and let the sheep die (v. 9). He broke the staff called Favor, which symbolized peaceful relations with the nations (vv. 10–11), threw away the meager amount of silver he was paid for his trouble (vv. 12–13), and then broke the staff called Union, which symbolized the unification of Judah and Israel (v. 14). At this point the Lord instructed the prophet to play a different role—that of a foolish shepherd who cares nothing for his sheep (v. 15). This foreshadowed a leader who would be raised up, ironically by the Lord himself. He would not only neglect the sheep, but also slaughter and eat them (v. 16). However, a judgment oracle is pronounced against this worthless shepherd (v. 17).

These verses, which are among the most cryptic in the Bible, have defied the efforts of interpreters to pin down their meaning. For this reason, the interpretations offered here must be considered provisional and to some degree speculative. Some understand the allegory, at least verses 4–14, as describing Israel's history prior to and including the exile.[325] Israel (the flock) was plagued by irresponsible leaders (shepherds). When the Lord attempted to help the sheep by removing these shepherds, his people rejected him. So he allowed the nations to oppress his people and divided his covenant com-

---

positive images of Judah's renewed stability and power, some want to understand the rulers of the fourth line as leaders of God's people. However, the term used here (Heb. *noges*) refers to oppressive tyrants elsewhere (see especially Zech. 9:8). For this reason, the fourth line probably refers to oppressive rulers being removed from God's flock/the house of Judah.

324. It is not certain how, if at all, the prophet carried out this commission. Perhaps he actually shepherded a flock for symbolic purposes, but it is possible that what is described in vv. 4–17 took place in a vision or dream.

325. See, for example, Merrill's treatment of vv. 4–14 (*Haggai, Zechariah, Malachi*, 287–301).

munity into two kingdoms. The Lord's judgment culminated with his people being handed over to a foolish shepherd, who possibly symbolizes the foreign powers responsible for the exile of God's people, though this shepherd may be a leader who would come after Zechariah's time.[326]

Others understand verses 4–17 against the backdrop of the early postexilic period, about which we know very little. If Zechariah is the author of these verses, then perhaps they reflect a time later in his career when the sociopolitical fabric of the community began to disintegrate and the leadership of the postexilic community became irresponsible (a scenario already anticipated in Isa. 56–66). When the Lord intervened, the community rejected him, prompting the Lord to walk away from them and give them over to oppressive neighbors. The reunification of the nation envisioned by earlier prophets became a shattered ideal. Worse yet, the Lord would give the flock over to a foolish leader of his own choosing, who would oppress his people but eventually be struck down by divine judgment. The demise of this ruler is depicted in 13:7, where the Lord commands that he be struck down.[327] His death would cause the sheep to be scattered. The Lord himself would attack the sheep and devastate the land, leaving only a remnant. Since God calls this ruler "my shepherd" and "the man who is close to me," he may be a Davidic descendant who governed the postexilic community at some point.[328]

The Lord Delivers Jerusalem (12:1–9)

The second oracle begins on a more positive note, as we see the Lord intervening for his people and delivering them from the hostile nations. The Lord is depicted as the creator of the world, including humankind. As such, he has both the authority and the ability to intervene in the affairs of nations (v. 1). The nations attack and besiege Judah and Jerusalem, but they are repelled and defeated (vv. 2–3, 9). Jerusalem is compared to a cup filled with an intoxicating beverage that causes those who drink it to stagger and to an immovable rock that resists the efforts of those who try to displace it. The Lord intervenes in the battle and strikes the horses of the attackers with blindness, prompting the leaders of Judah to recognize his protective presence and devotion to Jerusalem (vv. 4–5). These same leaders devour their enemies, like fire does a woodpile (v. 6). All of Judah, not just Jerusalem and the house of David, is saved (v. 7). The inhabitants of Jerusalem are energized by God's power, so that even the weakest of them possesses the military power of the

---

326. Merrill, though understanding vv. 4–14 as looking backward to preexilic times, understands vv. 15–17 as forward-looking. In his view they describe "the whole collective leadership of Israel from Zechariah's time forward, culminating at last in that epitome of godless despotism, the individual identified in the NT as the Antichrist" (see ibid., 303).

327. Hanson, *Dawn of Apocalyptic,* 350.

328. Ibid., 349–50.

great warrior David. As for the house of David, it displays superhuman prowess in battle, like that of God himself or the Lord's angel (v. 8).

The People Return to the Lord (12:10–13:9)

The day of deliverance would also be a day of purification and reconciliation. The Lord would, by an act of sovereign grace, prompt his people to turn to him (12:10a). They had rejected his shepherd-like protection (see 11:8), but now they would mourn over what they had done, just as one mourns the death of an only child or a firstborn son (vv. 10b–11).[329] The formal ceremony of lamentation would be led by the royal house and the priests (vv. 12–14).

Because of the Apostle John's citation of verse 10b (see John 19:37), some regard it as a messianic prediction. In the Hebrew text the second half of the verse reads: "and they will look toward me, the one whom they pierced and they will lament over him, as one laments an only child, and grieve over him, as one grieves over a firstborn son." In the Hebrew text the relative clause "the one whom they pierced" is preceded by the accusative sign, which specifies that the speaker (note "me") and "the one whom they pierced" are one and the same.[330] The use of the third-person singular pronoun later in the verse (note "him") makes it appear that the one who is pierced and lamented is distinct from the speaker, but it is more likely that the switch to the third person is purely grammatical. The third-person pronoun refers back to "the one whom they pierced," which in turn is equated with the speaker ("me").[331] In this context, in which the speaker is most naturally understood as God himself (see vv. 2–4, 6, 9–10), the piercing is purely metaphorical, referring to the people's rejection of their divine shepherd (see 11:8).

When the Roman soldier pierced Jesus' side, John saw in this a fulfillment of the statement in Zechariah (John 19:37). But if the statement in its original context is purely metaphorical and God himself is the one pierced, how is John's use of the text justified? In what way is the statement in Zechariah "fulfilled"? John's citation does not necessarily imply that he viewed the passage as a direct prediction of the Messiah's experience. His understanding of the prophecy and its relationship to Jesus is more subtle than this. The crucifixion of Jesus, capped off by the spear wound he received, was a spe-

---

329. Verse 11 compares the lamentation to that of Hadad Rimmon in the plain of Megiddo. Hadad Rimmon may be the name of a place, perhaps the site where Josiah's death in battle, which occurred on the plain of Megiddo, was mourned (see 2 Chron. 35:24–25). Another option is that v. 11 refers to mourning rites for Hadad Rimmon, a name for the Canaanite storm god. For a helpful discussion of the options, see Merrill, *Haggai, Zechariah, Malachi*, 323–24.

330. For other examples of this specifying use of the accusative sign, see Jer. 38:9 ("to Jeremiah the prophet, the one whom they threw into the cistern"); Ezek. 14:22; 37:19.

331. See ibid., 320.

cific example of Israel's rejection of God. More than that, it was the ultimate expression of this rejection—the culminating act in a long history of such rejection. By rejecting and executing Jesus, the nation put to death God in the flesh. As such, the event puts flesh on Zechariah's language as metaphor becomes literal reality. The general truth expressed in Zechariah is realized tangibly in the crucifixion of Jesus, giving the language a literal quality it does not possess in its original literary context.[332]

In response to the repentance of the people and the royal house, the Lord would "cleanse them from sin and impurity" (13:1). This would entail eliminating their idols and the false prophets (v. 2; see 10:2). Devotion to the Lord would be so intense that a false prophet's parents would willingly execute him, in obedience to the law of Moses (v. 3; see Deut. 13:6–11). False prophets would become so unpopular that those who formerly engaged in such activity would disguise the fact (vv. 4–6). The Lord would also purify the house of David by eliminating the foolish, worthless shepherd he had raised up (v. 7; see my earlier comments on 11:15–17). The elimination of this shepherd would be the first phase in his judgment of the whole land. He would unleash his judgment on the people, two-thirds of whom would die (v. 8a). But the Lord would preserve the remaining third and make them his covenant community (vv. 8b–9).

Verse 7 is a well-known passage, primarily because Jesus cited it on the night of his arrest as he predicted the disciples would abandon him (see Matt. 26:31; Mark 14:27). Jesus was not, of course, the foolish, worthless shepherd envisioned in Zechariah, so why did he cite this verse as if it seemingly predicted what would happen in Gethsemane? As with John's citation of Zechariah 12:10, Jesus' use of this passage does not necessarily imply that he understood it as a direct prediction of what would happen to him. It is more likely that he utilized it in a proverbial manner. In other words, when a shepherd is struck down, his sheep are typically scattered. In the same way, Jesus' arrest would cause his confused and fearful "sheep" to scatter in all directions.[333]

The Lord Is Victorious (14:1–21)

This final chapter of the book pulls together several thematic strands from the preceding chapters. The Lord's judgment of the land (see 13:8) would include Jerusalem. The nations would capture the city, loot its houses, rape its women, and carry half its residents off into exile (14:1–2). The scene de-

---

332. John 19:37 also uses Ps. 34:20 in a similar way, giving the metaphorical language of the psalmist a more literal twist. On John's use of Ps. 34:20 see Robert B. Chisholm, "A Theology of the Psalms," in R. B. Zuck, ed. *A Biblical Theology of the Old Testament* (Chicago: Moody, 1991), 291.

333. For a concise and helpful statement of this view of Jesus' use of the text, see Merrill, *Haggai, Zechariah, Malachi*, 339. Merrill, however, seems to want to move beyond this explanation and see the passage as messianic prophecy (339–40). It is, of course, possible that Jesus' use of the text reflects a messianic interpretation that may have been current in his day.

picted here differs greatly from the one described in 12:1–9, where Jerusalem appears to be impenetrable. Two different events may be envisioned, but it seems more likely that 14:1–2 supplements the earlier prophecy and makes it clear that Jerusalem would initially suffer before experiencing deliverance.

When all hope seemed gone, the Lord would suddenly intervene with his angelic army (called "holy ones"). His arrival on the Mount of Olives would cause an earthquake that would split the mountain in two, making a way of escape for the city's residents (vv. 3–5). The entire cosmos would be disrupted, and the normal cycle of day and night would be severely altered (vv. 6–7).

Before continuing his account of the Lord's victory over the nations (see vv. 12–15), the prophet described the conditions that would exist once the Lord established his worldwide rule (v. 9).[334] Jerusalem would become the source of life-giving water, with one stream flowing eastward to the Dead Sea, and another westward to the Mediterranean (v. 8). The area south of Jerusalem would become level like the Arabah (the area south of the Dead Sea), while the city, now inhabited again and forever secure, would be elevated for all to see (vv. 10–11).

The prophet now returns to the battle scene. The Lord would strike the foreign armies outside Jerusalem with a plague that would rot out their eyes and tongues (v. 12) and kill their animals (v. 15). Panic would sweep through the invading armies, causing them to attack one another (v. 13). The people of Judah would join the residents of Jerusalem in collecting the gold, silver, and clothing discarded by their defeated enemies (v. 14).

Having subdued the nations, the Lord would rule over them. The survivors among the nations would be required to make an annual pilgrimage to Jerusalem for the Feast of Tabernacles, which celebrated the fruit harvest (v. 16; see Deut. 16:13–15). Those who refused to comply would be punished with drought and deprived of a harvest (vv. 17–19). Jerusalem would become a holy city. Even ordinary items, such as the bells on the horses and the cooking pots, would be treated as holy, as if they were sacred bowls in the temple (vv. 20–21a). The rebuilt temple would no longer be polluted by the presence of foreigners (v. 21b).[335]

---

334. The Hebrew text of v. 9b reads literally, "In that day the Lord will be one, and his name [will be] one." The term "one" is used here in the sense of "unique, unparalleled." On this use of predicative "one" see also Song of Sol. 6:8.

335. The Hebrew text of v. 21b says literally, "There will no longer be a Canaanite in the house of the Lord of Hosts in that day." Some see "Canaanite" as an ethnic term here, but it seems more likely that the word here carries its secondary meaning of "merchant, trader," probably referring to foreign merchants in general (see the use of the term in Job 41:6; Prov. 31:24; Isa. 23:8; and Hos. 12:7). Babylonians may even be in view, for Ezek. 16:29 and 17:4 refer to Babylon as a "land of merchants."

Cleansing a Community (Malachi)

Introduction

Apart from his name (which means "my messenger"), we know virtually nothing about the prophet Malachi. Some regard "Malachi" as a title, not a proper name, but analogy with other prophetic books, all of which include their author's name in the heading, suggests otherwise. The absence of background information is not unique and does not necessitate taking the name as a title (see Obad. 1; Hab. 1:1; Hag. 1:1).

The prophecy is not specifically dated, but internal evidence suggests that it originated in the postexilic period, probably in the fifth century B.C. The term "governor" (1:8; Heb. *pekhah*) is used in the Book of Nehemiah for Persian governors and in Haggai of Zerubbabel (see 1:1, 14; 2:2, 21). Other parallels between Malachi and Ezra-Nehemiah include references to marriage with foreign wives (see Mal. 2:11; Ezra 9–10; Neh. 13:23–27), failure to pay tithes (Mal. 3:8–10; Neh. 13:10–14), and social injustice (Mal. 3:5; Neh. 5:1–13). Though the prophecy probably dates to the same general time period in which Nehemiah lived, Nehemiah was not the governor referred to in 1:8, for he refused to receive offerings from the people (Neh. 5:14, 18).

The structure of the book exhibits a recurring disputational pattern arranged in six units. Each of the six disputations includes an affirmation by the Lord or prophet, the people's response, and a conclusion:

Disputation	Introduction	Response	Conclusion
(1) 1:2–5	1:2a	1:2b	1:2c–5
(2) 1:6–2:9	1:6a, 7a	1:6b, 7b	1:7c–2:9
(3) 2:10–16	2:10–13	2:14a	2:14b–16
(4) 2:17–3:5	2:17a	2:17b	2:17c–3:5
(5) 3:6–12	3:6–7b, 8a	3:7c, 8b	3:8c–12
(6) 3:13–4:3	3:13a	3:13b	3:14–4:3

A brief appendix (4:4–6) contains an exhortation (v. 4) and an announcement of Elijah's reappearance (vv. 5–6).

The Lord Loves Jacob (1:2–5)

The book begins on a positive note as the Lord affirms his love for "Jacob," which refers here to Jacob's descendants, the postexilic community (v. 2a). However, the people respond with skepticism, demanding that the Lord provide evidence of this professed love (v. 2b). The trials and humiliation of the exile had apparently caused God's people to become cynical about his concern for them. As evidence of his abiding love, his people need only contrast their situation with that of Edom (vv. 2c–5). While the Lord had preserved his people through the ordeal of exile and restored them to their ancient land, he had judged severely Esau's descendants, the Edomites. This judgment is viewed as evidence of God's hatred for (i.e., opposition to) the Edomites, which is contrasted with his love for (i.e., continuing commitment to) Jacob's descendants. The Edomites planned to rebuild their devastated cities, but the Lord would oppose their efforts and demolish whatever they rebuilt. At that time the Lord's people would be forced to acknowledge his sovereignty, which extends beyond Israel's borders and encompasses all the nations.

Denouncing Corrupt Sacrifices (1:6–2:9)

In this second disputation (the longest in the book), the Lord denounces a corrupt priesthood. One would expect a son to honor his father or a servant to honor his master, but the priests had shown only contempt for their divine Master by offering him defiled sacrifices (1:6–7). Though the Mosaic law specifically prohibited offering blind, crippled, and diseased animals to the Lord (see Lev. 22:17–25; Deut. 15:21), these priests brought blemished sacrifices to the Lord (vv. 8, 12–13). If the community's governor would not regard such offerings as legitimate tribute, how could the priests expect the Lord, the sovereign ruler of the world, to accept them (vv. 8–9, 14b)? The Lord would someday be worshiped by all the nations, who would recognize his greatness and offer incense and pure sacrifices to him (v. 11). To offer blemished sacrifices to the great king of the universe was insulting and demeaning. The priests would be better off shutting the temple doors, for defiled sacrifices were an offense to the Lord, gave proof of the priests' deceitful nature, and brought a curse down upon those who offered them (vv. 10, 12, 14a).

Because there are no temporal indicators in verse 11, some translate the verse in the present tense ("My name *is* great . . . pure offerings *are* brought . . . my name *is* great among the nations"), rather than using the future tense. Some see a reference here to Jewish worship among the exiles, but the phrase "among the nations" suggests a broader referent. Others argue that this verse legitimizes sincere pagan worship as really being directed to the one true God. However, such a notion is antithetical to the militant monotheism that permeates Israel's Yahwistic theology. The prophets envisioned universal worship of the Lord as characterizing a future age, not the present era (see Isa. 2:2–4; 19:19–21; 24:14–16; 42:6; 45:22–24; 66:18–21; Mic. 4:1–3; Zeph. 3:8–9; Zech. 8:20–23; 14:16). For this reason, verse 11 is best translated in the future tense and interpreted as a prophecy of what will transpire when God establishes his kingdom on earth.[336]

The Lord issued the priests an ultimatum (2:1–3). If they did not change their ways, the Lord's "curse," which had already been pronounced against them, would fall upon them with full force. The priestly blessings they pronounced on others (see Lev. 9:22–23; Num. 6:23–26; 2 Chron. 30:27) would be ineffective (i.e., cursed), the priests' descendants would be rejected, and the priests themselves would be humiliated.[337] Using vivid and repulsive imagery, the Lord warned that he would smear the refuse of the sacrificial animals on the priests' faces and then carry them to a place outside the sanctuary where such refuse was burned (see Exod. 29:14; Lev. 4:11–12; 8:17; 16:27).

By confronting and, if need be, punishing the priests, the Lord hoped to motivate them to repent and thereby preserve his ancient covenant with Levi's descendants (v. 4). Though no such covenant is recorded in the Pentateuch, this must refer to the Lord's choice of the Levites, especially Aaron, to serve him in a priestly role (see Num. 3:12). A formal covenant with the Levites, also referred to in Jeremiah 33:21 and Nehemiah 13:29, was apparently made on this occasion.[338] The Lord promised Levi "life and peace" in exchange for reverent obedience (v. 5). In contrast to the disobedient priests of Malachi's time, who had violated the Levitical covenant (vv. 8–9), the early Levites had taken their priestly responsibilities seriously and given the Lord's people moral guidance (vv. 6–7). Some suggest that the prophet alludes here to the incidents recorded in Exodus 32:26–29 and Numbers 25:11–13. However, in those instances priests wielded the sword of divine discipline, while Malachi 2:6 seems to refer to verbal instruction offered by the priests, not punitive measures against fellow Israelites.

Denouncing Divorce (2:10–16)

In this third disputation, the prophet denounced the men of the community for their unfaithfulness to both God and their wives. God's covenant community was a family, brought into existence by their divine Father and Cre-

---

336. For more detailed analyses of this problem, see Verhoef, *Haggai and Malachi,* 227–28; Merrill, *Haggai, Zechariah, Malachi,* 399–401; and Beth Glazier-McDonald, *Malachi* (Atlanta: Scholars Press, 1987), 60–61.

337. The verb translated "rebuke" in v. 3 here is a synonym of "curse" and means here "to suppress an object's vitality or effectiveness." See Glazier-McDonald, *Malachi,* 66–67. The verb carries this same force in Ps. 106:9; Nah. 1:4; Zech. 3:2; and Mal. 3:11.

338. Num. 18:19 mentions a "covenant of salt" between the Lord and the Levites, but this pertains to the priests' assigned portion of a sacrifice, not priestly service in general. The covenant in Num. 25:12–13 was made with Phinehas and his descendants, not the entire tribe of Levi. It was an unconditional promise rewarding Phinehas's loyalty, whereas the covenant in view in Mal. 2:4 was a bilateral agreement in which blessing was contingent upon loyalty (see v. 5).

ator (v. 10a).[339] As such, they were to demonstrate loyalty to God and faithfulness in their dealings with one another (v. 10b). But the community had violated this principle of covenantal life (v. 11). Many of the men had married "the daughter of a foreign god." Some understand this expression as referring figuratively to a pagan goddess, but it seems more likely that intermarriage with foreign women is in view. Ezra 9–10 makes it clear that such unauthorized marriages occurred during the postexilic period. These marriages, by their very nature, threatened to destroy the ethnic purity and identity of the covenantal community and led the people into idolatry (see Exod. 34:15–16; Deut. 7:3–4; Judg. 3:6–7; 1 Kings 11:1–6). For this reason, the Lord would reject those who married foreign women, even if they brought him offerings and tearfully lamented God's anger (vv. 12–13). They were reprehensible in God's sight, especially those who had divorced their wives in order to marry these foreigners (v. 14). The Lord considered marriage to be a binding contract that was to be honored by the parties involved (v. 15). The Lord vehemently opposed divorce and considered it tantamount to an act of violence (v. 16).

The precise meaning of verse 16 is uncertain. The translation that appears in most English versions ("I hate divorce") does not reflect the traditional Hebrew text, which reads (literally): " 'For he hates divorce,' says the LORD God of Israel, 'and he covers over his garment [with] violence,' says the LORD Almighty." As it stands, the text is nonsensical, for it seems to indicate that one who hates divorce is guilty of violence. The Septuagint understands a second-person verb form addressed to the one guilty of divorcing his wife, " 'If you hate [her] and put [her] away,' says the LORD God of Israel, 'ungodliness will cover your thoughts,' says the LORD Almighty." In this case, it is the one who divorces his wife who is guilty of hatred. It is difficult to envision the present Hebrew text, if corrupt, deriving from such a reading. It is likely that this is the Greek translator's attempt to make sense out of a corrupt text. Perhaps the Hebrew text originally read, "For one who hates [his wife] divorces [his wife] . . . and covers his garment with violence."[340] In this case, as in the Greek translation, the one who divorces his wife is guilty of hatred. Another option is to reconstruct the Hebrew text so that it yields the traditional translation, "For I hate divorce . . . and the one who covers his garment with violence."[341]

339. Baldwin (*Haggai, Zechariah, Malachi*, 237) identifies the "father" as Abraham (see Isa. 51:2), but the synonymous parallel structure suggests that the nation's divine Father is in view. See Merrill, *Haggai, Zechariah, Malachi*, 414 n. 1.

340. In this case, one must (*a*) revocalize Hebrew *sane*, a third masculine singular perfect, as *sone*, a masculine singular active participle, functioning substantively, and (*b*) revocalize *shallakh*, an infinitive construct, as *shilleakh*, a third masculine singular Piel perfect.

341. In this case, one must reconstruct the first clause as *ki 'anoki sone' shallakh*. The construction *ki 'anoki* + participle is attested in Deut. 4:22. If it were original here, then the pronoun *'anoki* could have

Affirming Divine Justice (2:17–3:5)

The Lord next accuses his people of wearying the Lord by denying his just character (v. 17). This came in two forms. Some actually argued that God approved of evildoers, while others merely suggested he was disinterested in the affairs of humans. In response to this charge, the Lord announced that he would intervene in the world and demonstrate his justice to all (3:1–5). Divine judgment, compared here to "a refiner's fire" and "a launderer's soap" (v. 2), would purify the Levites (v. 3a) and destroy all evildoers, including those who oppressed the weak and deprived the needy of justice (v. 5). In the aftermath of this purifying judgment, the godly would offer acceptable sacrifices to the Lord (vv. 3b–4), in contrast to the hypocrites of Malachi's time (see 2:12–13).

In verse 1a, the Lord mentions a messenger who would be sent to pave the way for the Lord's arrival. In 4:5–6, this messenger is identified as the prophet Elijah. Verse 1 goes on to describe how "the Lord" would come to "his temple" and how one called "the messenger of the covenant" would arrive. In the Hebrew text, the parallelism, which is both chiastic and synonymous, strongly suggests that "the Lord" and "the messenger of the covenant" are one and the same. The text reads literally:

> And suddenly he will come to his temple
> the Lord whom you seek;
> and the messenger of the covenant whom you desire,
> behold, he is coming.

At first one might think that "my messenger" and "the messenger of the covenant" refer to the same individual, but the parallel structure suggests otherwise. Rather, the titles "the Lord" (Heb. *ha'adon*) and "the messenger of the covenant" appear to refer to the same individual, who is distinct from the forerunner.[342] Both of the titles used here are unique to this passage.[343] Though some see the owner of the titles as the messianic king, it seems more likely that the Lord himself is the referent, for the text pictures him coming to "his temple" (see Ps. 27:4, as well as Ezek. 43:1–9). But in what sense is the Lord a "messenger of the covenant"? What exactly does the title connote? The title may depict the Lord as the one who enforces the covenant by blessing the godly and punishing the wicked (see vv. 3–5). The use of "messen-

---

been dropped accidentally from the text by homoioteleuton with a subsequent alteration of the following *sone'* to *sane'*. In the second clause, one must understand a virtual relative clause. On the grammatical point, see *GKC* 488, para. 155n.

342. See Verhoef, *Haggai and Malachi,* 288–89. For a defense of the view that "my messenger" and "the messenger of the covenant" refer to the same individual, who is distinct from "the Lord," see Merrill, *Haggai, Zechariah, Malachi,* 431–32.

343. The title *ha'adon,* "the Lord," appears in seven other texts, but always with the name Yahweh after it. Only here does it appear in isolation.

ger" may allude to an ancient tradition depicting the Lord as a protective angel (see Gen. 48:15–16; Hos. 12:4) or at least closely associating him with such an angel (see Exod. 23:20–23; Isa. 63:9).[344]

Robbing God (3:6–12)

The Lord begins the next disputation with an affirmation of his faithfulness, "I the LORD do not change" (v. 6a). This declaration should not be taken in an overly philosophical manner, as if it were referring to God's being or essential nature. God is immutable (i.e., unchangeable) in his being and essential nature, but that is not the point of this passage. The context indicates that God's faithfulness is in view here, more specifically his fidelity to the covenantal relationship he established with his people (vv. 6b–7a).[345] Despite his people's rebellion, the Lord remained faithful to his promises and did not completely destroy them. He continued to reach out to the disobedient nation. He offered them the opportunity to repent and promised that he would in turn restore his relationship with them.

In their case, repentance must start with a renewed commitment to God's covenantal requirements. They had neglected to pay the tithes and offerings demanded by the law (see Num. 18:8, 11, 19, 21–24). The Lord, who regarded this failure as being tantamount to robbery, placed the nation under a "curse" (vv. 8–9). He challenged the people to bring the "whole tithe" to him. If they obeyed, he promised to pour his blessings upon them (vv. 10–12). He would send the rain down from heaven and protect their crops. As the surrounding nations witnessed their agricultural prosperity, they would recognize God's people as the objects of divine blessing.

Vindicating the Godly (3:13–4:3)

The sixth and final disputation further develops a theme raised earlier (see 2:17–3:5). The people had spoken harshly of the Lord. They claimed that it did not pay off to serve the Lord, and complained that the ungodly actually prospered (vv. 13–15). The implication was clear. In their way of thinking, God was disinterested in the affairs of humans or, even worse, unjust.

However, this verdict was not unanimous. Those who feared the Lord rallied together and attracted the attention of the Lord, who officially recorded their names (v. 16). The Lord promised that this group of God-fearers would become his "treasured possession" (v. 17a; see Exod. 19:5) and would experience his compassion and salvation (v. 17b). The Lord would make a sharp distinction between the ungodly and godly (v. 18). His de-

---

344. For further discussion of the significance of the phrase "the messenger of the covenant," see Verhoef, *Haggai and Malachi*, 289, and Glazier-McDonald, *Malachi*, 130–32.

345. See Ps. 89:34, where God declares "I will not violate my covenant or alter [Heb. *shanah*, the same verb translated "change" in Mal. 3:6] what my lips have uttered." The context (see especially v. 33) makes it clear that faithfulness to his covenantal promise to David is in view.

structive judgment would totally annihilate the ungodly (4:1), but the godly would emerge victorious and crush their enemies (vv. 2–3).

Elijah Is Coming (4:4–6)

The Lord concludes his message to the people with an exhortation to obey the law (v. 4). They had violated the laws pertaining to sacrifices (1:7–14), idolatry (2:10–11), and tithes (3:8–9), so the command is quite appropriate. The members of the postexilic generation were the heirs of God's ancient covenant with Israel, and they must take their responsibility seriously.

Elaborating on an earlier prophecy (see 3:1a), the Lord also revealed the identity of the messenger who would come prior to "the day of the LORD" (v. 5). The ancient prophet Elijah would return with the task of turning the community back to God so that the severe judgment of the wicked announced earlier in the prophecy might be averted (v. 6).[346] According to Jesus, this prophecy was essentially fulfilled in the person and ministry of John the Baptist, who resembled Elijah (cf. Matt. 3:4 with 2 Kings 1:8) and, like the ancient prophet, demanded radical repentance from God's people (see Matt. 11:10–14; 17:12–13; Luke 1:17, 76; 7:27).

According to NIV, verse 6 envisions Elijah restoring domestic peace in the community by reconciling fathers and children, who were presumably, in this view, warring with one another. However, the Hebrew text could be translated, "He will turn the hearts of the fathers along with those of the children, and the hearts of the children along with those of the fathers."[347] In this case the chiastic, complementary parallelism emphasizes that the entire community, including both the older and younger generations, would repent and return to the Lord (cf. 3:7).[348]

Bibliography

Recent Studies on the Minor Prophets

Barton, J. "The Canonical Meaning of the Book of the Twelve." In *After Exile: Essays in Honour of Rex Mason,* edited by J. Barton and D. J. Reimer, 59–73. Macon, Ga.: Mercer University Press, 1996.

Baumann, G. "Connected by Marriage, Adultery, and Violence: The Prophetic Marriage Metaphor in the Book of the Twelve and in the Major Prophets." *SBLSP* (1999): 552–69.

Ben Zvi, E. "A Deuteronomistic Redaction in/among 'The Twelve'? A Contribution from the Standpoint of the Books of Micah, Zephaniah, and Obadiah." *SBLSP* (1997): 433–59.

———. "Twelve Prophetic Books or 'The Twelve'? A Few Preliminary Considerations." In

---

346. The warning of v. 6 is directed primarily to the wicked, for the Lord had already promised to spare the godly (see 3:3–4; 4:1–3). See Glazier-McDonald, *Malachi,* 259–61.

347. For numerous examples of the preposition *'al* having the nuance "together with," see *BDB* 755.

348. See Glazier-McDonald, *Malachi,* 256.

Forming Prophetic Literature: Essays on Isaiah and the Twelve in Honor of John D. W. Watts, edited by J. W. Watts and P. R. House, JSOTSup 235, 125–56. Sheffield: Sheffield Academic Press, 1996.

Chisholm, R. B., Jr. *Interpreting the Minor Prophets.* Grand Rapids: Zondervan, 1990.

———. "A Theology of the Minor Prophets." In *A Biblical Theology of the Old Testament,* edited by R. B. Zuck, 397–433. Chicago: Moody, 1991.

Coggins, R. J. "The Minor Prophets: One Book of Twelve?" In *Crossing the Boundaries: Essays in Biblical Interpretation in Honour of Michael D. Goulder,* edited by S. E. Porter et al., 57–68. Leiden: Brill, 1994.

Conrad, E.W. "The End of Prophecy and the Appearance of Angels/Messengers in the Book of the Twelve." *JSOT* 73 (1997): 65–79.

Floyd, M. H. *Minor Prophets, Part 2.* FOTL 22. Grand Rapids: Eerdmans, 2000.

Fuller, R. "The Form and Formation of the Book of the Twelve: The Evidence from the Judean Desert." In *Forming Prophetic Literature: Essays on Isaiah and the Twelve in Honor of John D. W. Watts,* edited by J. W. Watts and P. R. House, JSOTSup 235, 86–101. Sheffield: Sheffield Academic Press, 1996.

House, P. R. "The Character of God in the Book of the Twelve." *SBLSP* (1998): 831–49.

———. *The Unity of the Twelve.* JSOTSup 97. Sheffield: Almond, 1990.

Jones, B. A. *The Formation of the Book of the Twelve: A Study in Text and Canon.* SBLDS 149. Atlanta: Scholars Press, 1995.

Nogalski, J. D. "The Day(s) of YHWH in the Book of the Twelve." *SBLSP* (1999): 617–42.

———. *Literary Precursors to the Book of the Twelve.* Berlin: de Gruyter, 1993.

———. *Redactional Processes in the Book of the Twelve.* Berlin: de Gruyter, 1993.

Redditt, P. L. "The Production and Reading of the Book of the Twelve." *SBLSP* (1997): 394–419.

Rendtorff, R. "Alas for the Day! The 'Day of the Lord' in the Book of the Twelve." In *God in the Fray: A Tribute to Walter Brueggemann,* edited by T. Linafelt and T. K. Beal, 186–97. Minneapolis: Fortress, 1998.

———. "How to Read the Book of the Twelve as a Theological Unity," *SBLSP* (1997): 420–32.

Hosea

Commentaries

Andersen, F. I., and D. N. Freedman. *Hosea.* AB. Garden City, N.Y.: Doubleday, 1980.

Davies, G. I. *Hosea.* NCB. Grand Rapids: Eerdmans, 1992.

Harper, W. R. *A Critical and Exegetical Commentary on Amos and Hosea.* ICC. Edinburgh: T. & T. Clark, 1905.

King, P. J. *Amos, Hosea, Micah—An Archaeological Commentary.* Philadelphia: Westminster, 1988.

Macintosh, A. A. *A Critical and Exegetical Commentary on Hosea.* ICC. Edinburgh: T. & T. Clark, 1997.

Mays, J. L. *Hosea.* OTL. Philadelphia: Westminster, 1969.

McComiskey, T. E. "Hosea." In *The Minor Prophets: An Exegetical and Expositional Commentary,* edited by T. E. McComiskey, 3 vols., 1:1–237. Grand Rapids: Baker, 1992–98.

Stuart, D. *Hosea-Jonah.* WBC. Waco, Tex.: Word, 1987.

Wolff, H. W. *Hosea.* Translated by G. Stansell. Hermeneia. Philadelphia: Fortress, 1974.

Recent Studies

Bosma, C. J. "Creation in Jeopardy: A Warning to Priests (Hosea 4:1–3)." *Calvin Theological Journal* 34 (1999): 64–116.

Botha, P. J. "The Communicative Function of Comparison in Hosea." *OTE* 6 (1993): 57–71.

Boudreau, G. R. "Hosea and the Pentateuchal Traditions: The Case of Baal of Peor." In *History and Interpretation: Essays in Honour of John H. Hayes,* edited by M. P. Graham et al., JSOTSup 173, 121–32. Sheffield: JSOT, 1993.

Brenneman, J. E. "Prophets in Conflict: Negotiating Truth in Scripture" [on Hos. 1:4–5]. In *Peace and Justice Shall Embrace—Power and Theopolitics in the Bible: Essays in Honor of Millard Lind,* edited by T. Grimsrud and L. L. Johns, 49–63. Telford, Pa.: Pandora, 1999.

Daniels, D. R. *Hosea and Salvation History: The Early Traditions of Israel in the Prophecy of Hosea.* Berlin: de Gruyter, 1990.

Dearman, A. "YHWH's House: Gender Roles and Metaphors for Israel in Hosea." *JNSL* 25 (1999): 97–108.

Eidevall, G. *Grapes in the Desert: Metaphors, Models, and Themes in Hosea 4–14.* Stockholm: Almqvist & Wiksell, 1996.

Fuller, R. A. "A Critical Note on Hosea 12:10 and 13:4." *RB* 98 (1991): 343–57.

Goldingay, J. "Hosea 1–3, Genesis 1–4, and Masculist Interpretation." *Horizons in Biblical Theology* 17 (1995): 37–44.

Hynniewta, M. J. "The Integrity of Hosea's Future Hope: A Study of the Oracles of Hope in the Book of Hosea." Ph.D. diss., Union Theological Seminary (Va.), 1996.

Holt, E. K. *Prophesying the Past: The Use of Israel's History in the Book of Hosea.* JSOTSup 194. Sheffield: Sheffield Academic Press, 1995.

Hornsby, T. J. "'Israel has become a worthless thing': Re-reading Gomer in Hosea 1–3." *JSOT* 82 (1999): 115–28.

Irvine, S. A. "Enmity in the House of God: (Hosea 9:7–9)." *JBL* 117 (1998): 645–53.

———. "Politics and Prophetic Community in Hosea 8:8–10." *JBL* 114 (1995): 292–94.

———. "The Threat of Jezreel (Hosea 1:4–5)." *CBQ* 57 (1995): 494–509.

Kruger, P. A. "The Divine Net in Hosea 7,12." *ETL* 68 (1992): 132–36.

———. "The Marriage Metaphor in Hosea 2:4–17 against Its Ancient Near Eastern Background." *OTE* 5 (1992): 7–25.

Kuan, J. K. "Hosea 9.13 and Josephus, *Antiquities* IX,277–287." *Palestine Exploration Quarterly* 123 (1991): 103–8.

Landy, F. *Hosea.* Sheffield: Sheffield Academic Press, 1995.

———. "In the Wilderness of Speech: Problems of Metaphor in Hosea." *Biblical Interpretation* 3 (1995): 35–59.

Lemche, N. P. "The God of Hosea." In *Prophets and Scribes: Essays on the Formation and Heritage of Second Temple Judaism in Honour of Joseph Blenkinsopp,* edited by E. Ulrich et al., JSOTSup 149, 241–57. Sheffield: JSOT, 1992.

Light, G. W. "Theory-Constitutive Metaphor and Its Development in the Book of Hosea." Ph.D. diss., Southern Baptist Theological Seminary, 1991.

Macintosh, A. A. "Hosea and the Wisdom Tradition: Dependence and Independence." In *Wisdom in Ancient Israel: Essays in Honour of J. A. Emerton,* edited by J. Day, 124–32. Cambridge: Cambridge University Press, 1995.

McComiskey, T. E. "Hos 9:13 and the Integrity of the Masoretic Tradition in the Prophecy of Hosea." *JETS* 33 (1990): 155–60.

———. "Prophetic Irony in Hosea 1,4: A Study of the Collocation עַל פָּקַד and Its Implications for the Fall of Jehu's Dynasty." *JSOT* 58 (1993): 93–101.

McKinlay, J. "Bringing the Unspeakable to Speech in Hosea." *Pacifica* 9 (1996): 121–33.

Moenikes, A. "The Rejection of Cult and Politics by Hosea." *Henoch* 19 (1997): 3–15.

Morris, G. P. *Prophecy, Poetry, and Hosea.* JSOTSup 219. Sheffield: Sheffield Academic Press, 1996.

Odell, M. S. "The Prophets and the End of Hosea." In *Forming Prophetic Literature: Essays on Isaiah and the Twelve in Honor of John D. W. Watts,* edited by J. W. Watts and P. R. House, JSOTSup 235, 158–70. Sheffield: Sheffield Academic Press, 1996.

———. "Who Were the Prophets in Hosea?" *Horizons in Biblical Theology* 18 (1996): 78–95.

Oestreich, B. "Metaphors and Similes for Yahweh in Hosea 14:2–9 (1–8): A Study of Hoseanic Pictorial Language." Ph.D. diss., Andrews University, 1997.

Olyan, S. M. "'In the Sight of Her Lovers': On the Interpretation of *nablūt* in Hos 2,12." *Biblische Zeitschrift* 36 (1992): 255–61.

Schmitt, J. J. "Yahweh's Divorce in Hosea 2—Who Is That Woman?" *SJOT* 9 (1995): 119–32.

Sherwood, Y. *The Prostitute and the Prophet: Hosea's Marriage in Literary-Theoretical Perspective.* JSOTSup 212. Sheffield: Sheffield Academic Press, 1996.

Smith, D. A. "Kinship and Covenant: An Examination of Kinship Metaphors for Covenant in the Book of the Prophet Hosea." Ph.D. diss., Harvard University, 1994.

———. "Kinship and Covenant in Hosea 11:1–4." *Horizons in Biblical Theology* 16 (1994): 41–53.

Snyman, G. "Social Reality and Religious Language in the Marriage Metaphor in Hosea 1–3." *OTE* 6 (1993): 90–112.

Swanepoel, M. G. "Solutions to the *Crux Interpretum* of Hosea." *OTE* 7 (1994): 39–59.

van Rooy, H. F. "The Names Israel, Ephraim, and Jacob in the Book of Hosea." *OTE* 6 (1993): 135–49.

Walker, T. W. "The Metaphor of Healing and the Theology of the Book of Hosea." Ph.D. diss., Princeton Theological Seminary, 1997.

West, G. "The Effect and Power of Discourse: A Case Study of a Metaphor in Hosea." *Scriptura* (1996): 201–12.

Weyde, K. W. "The References to Jacob in Hos 12:4–5: Traditio-Historical Remarks." In *Text and Theology: Studies in Honour of Professor dr. theol. Magne Saebø Presented on the Occasion of His Sixty-fifth Birthday,* edited by A. Tångberg et al., 336–58. Oslo: Verbum, 1994.

Whitt, W. D. "The Divorce of Yahweh and Asherah in Hos 2,4–7.12ff.." *SJOT* 6 (1992): 31–67.

———. "The Jacob Traditions in Hosea and Their Relation to Genesis." *ZAW* 103 (1991): 18–43.

Zulick, M. D. "Rhetorical Polyphony in the Book of the Prophet Hosea." Ph.D. diss., Northwestern University, 1994.

Joel

Commentaries

Allen, L. C. *Joel, Obadiah, Jonah, and Micah.* NICOT. Grand Rapids: Eerdmans, 1976.

Coggins, R. J. *Joel and Amos.* NCB. Sheffield: Sheffield Academic Press, 2000.

Crenshaw, J. L. *Joel.* AB. New York: Doubleday, 1995.

Dillard, R. "Joel." In *The Minor Prophets: An Exegetical and Expositional Commentary,* edited by T. E. McComiskey, 3 vols., 1:239–313 Grand Rapids: Baker, 1992–98.

Finley, T. J. *Joel, Amos, Obadiah.* Chicago: Moody, 1990.

Hubbard, D. A. *Joel and Amos.* TOTC. Downers Grove, Ill.: InterVarsity, 1989.

Stuart, D. *Hosea-Jonah.* WBC. Waco, Tex.: Word, 1987.

Wolff, H. W. *Joel and Amos.* Translated by W. Janzen et al. Hermeneia. Philadelphia: Fortress, 1977.

Recent Studies

Andiñach, P. R. "The Locusts in the Message of Joel." *VT* 42 (1992): 433–41.

Coggins, R. J. "Interbiblical Quotations in Joel." In *After Exile: Essays in Honour of Rex Mason,* edited by J. Barton and D. J. Reimer, 75–84. Macon, Ga.: Mercer University Press, 1996.

Crenshaw, J. L. "Freeing the Imagination: The Conclusion of the Book of Joel." In *Prophecy and Prophets: The Diversity of Contemporary Issues in Scholarship*, edited by Y. Gitay, 129–47. Atlanta: Scholars Press, 1997.

———. "Who Knows What YHWH Will Do? The Character of God in the Book of Joel." In *Fortunate the Eyes That See: Essays in Honor of David Noel Freedman in Celebration of His Seventieth Birthday*, edited by A. B. Beck et al., 185–96. Grand Rapids: Eerdmans, 1995.

Hurowitz, V. A. "Joel's Locust Plague in Light of Sargon II's Hymn to Nanaya." *JBL* 112 (1993): 597–603.

Leung, K. K. "An Intertextual Study of the Motif-Complex יום יהוה in the Book of Joel." Ph.D. diss., Fuller Theological Seminary, 1997.

Marcus, D. "Nonrecurring Doublets in the Book of Joel." *CBQ* 56 (1994): 56–67.

Noguchi, T. "A Study of the Verbs in Joel 2:4–9: The Author's Style or Aramaic Influence?" *Orient* 33 (1998): 103–14.

Pettus, D. D. "A Canonical-Critical Study of Selected Traditions in the Book of Joel." Ph.D. diss., Baylor University, 1992.

Prinsloo, W. S. "The Unity of the Book of Joel." *ZAW* 104 (1992): 66–81.

Simkins, R. A. "God, History, and the Natural World in the Book of Joel." *CBQ* 55 (1999): 435–52.

———. " 'Return to Yahweh': Honor and Shame in Joel." *Semeia* 68 (1994): 41–54.

———. *Yahweh's Activity in History and Nature in the Book of Joel*. Lewiston, N.Y.: Mellen, 1991.

Sweeney, M. A. "The Place and Function of Joel in the Book of the Twelve." *SBLSP* (1999): 570–95.

Treier, D. J. "The Fulfillment of Joel 2:28–32: A Multiple-Lens Approach." *JETS* 40 (1997): 13–26.

van Leeuwen, C. "The 'Northern One' in the Composition of Joel 2,19–27." In *Sacred History and Sacred Texts in Early Judaism: A Symposium in Honour of A. S. van der Woude*, edited by J. N. Bremmer and F. G. Martínez, 85–99. Kampen: Kok Pharos, 1992.

Wheeler, R. D. "The Development of Repentance in Joel: A Reader-Response Approach." Ph.D. diss., Southern Baptist Theological Seminary, 1992.

Amos

Commentaries

Andersen, F. I., and D. N. Freedman. *Amos*. AB. New York: Doubleday, 1989.

Coggins, R. J. *Joel and Amos*. NCB. Sheffield: Sheffield Academic Press, 2000.

Finley, T. J. *Joel, Amos, Obadiah*. Chicago: Moody, 1990.

Harper, W. R. *A Critical and Exegetical Commentary on Amos and Hosea*. ICC. Edinburgh: T. & T. Clark, 1905.

Hayes, J. H. *Amos*. Nashville: Abingdon, 1988.

King, P. J. *Amos, Hosea, Micah—An Archaeological Commentary*. Philadelphia: Westminster, 1988.

Mays, J. L. *Amos*. OTL. Philadelphia: Westminster, 1969.

Niehaus, J. "Amos." In *The Minor Prophets: An Exegetical and Expositional Commentary*, edited by T. E. McComiskey, 3 vols., 1:315–494. Grand Rapids: Baker, 1992–98.

Paul, S. M. *Amos*. Hermeneia. Minneapolis: Fortress, 1991.

Smith, B. K., and F. S. Page. *Amos, Obadiah, Jonah*. NAC. Nashville: Broadman & Holman, 1995.

Smith, G. V. *Amos: A Commentary*. Grand Rapids: Zondervan, 1989.

Stuart, D. *Hosea-Jonah*. WBC. Waco, Tex.: Word, 1987.

Wolff, H. W. *Joel and Amos*. Translated by W. Janzen et al. Hermeneia. Philadelphia: Fortress, 1977.

Recent Studies

Asen, B. A. "No, Yes, and Perhaps in Amos and the Yahwist." *VT* 43 (1993): 433–41.
Auld, A. G. "Amos and Apocalyptic: Vision, Prophecy, Revelation." In *Storia e tradizioni di Israele*, edited by D. Garrone and F. Israel, 3–13. Brescia, Italy: Queriniana, 1991.
Berquist, J. L. "Dangerous Waters of Justice and Righteousness." *BTB* 23 (1993): 54–63.
Bramer, S. J. "The Analysis of the Structure of Amos." *BSac* 156 (1999): 160–74.
———. "The Literary Genre of the Book of Amos." *BSac* 156 (1999): 42–60.
———. "The Structure of Amos 9:7–15." *BSac* 156 (1999): 278–81.
Bulkeley, T. "Cohesion, Rhetorical Purpose, and the Poetics of Coherence in Amos 3." *Australian Biblical Review* 47 (1999): 16–28.
Carroll R.. *Contexts for Amos: Prophetic Poetics in Latin American Perspective*. JSOTSup 132. Sheffield: JSOT, 1992.
———. "God and His People in the Nations' History: A Contexualised Reading of Amos 1–2." *TynB* 47 (1996): 39–70.
Ceresko, A. R. "Janus Parallelism in Amos's 'Oracles against the Nations' (Amos 1:3–2:16)." *JBL* 113 (1994): 485–90.
Chisholm, R. B., Jr. " 'For Three Sins . . . Even for Four': The Numerical Sayings in Amos." *BSac* 147 (1990): 188–97.
Clements, R. E. "Amos and the Politics of Israel." In *Storia e tradizioni di Israele*, edited by D. Garrone and F. Israel, 49–64. Brescia, Italy: Queriniana, 1991.
Clines, D. J. A. "Metacommentating Amos." In *Of Prophets' Visions and the Wisdom of the Sages: Essays in Honour of R. Norman Whybray on His Seventieth Birthday*, edited by H. A. McKay and D. J. A. Clines, JSOTSup 162, 142–60. Sheffield: JSOT, 1993.
Cooper, A. "The Meaning of Amos's Third Vision (Amos 7:7–9)." In *Tehillah le-Moshe: Biblical and Judaic Studies in Honor of Moshe Greenberg*, edited by M. Cogan et al., 13–21. Winona Lake, Ind.: Eisenbrauns, 1997.
Cotterell, P. "A Question of Peak." *BT* 49 (1998): 139–48.
Davies, P. R. "*Bytdwd* and *Skwt Dwyd*: A Comparison." *JSOT* 64 (1994): 23–24.
Dell, K. J. "The Misuse of Forms in Amos." *VT* 45 (1995): 45–61.
Dempster, S. "The Lord Is His Name: A Study of the Distribution of the Names and Titles of God in the Book of Amos." *RB* 98 (1991): 170–89.
Diop, A. G. "The Name 'Israel' and Related Expressions in the Books of Amos and Hosea." Ph.D. diss., Andrews University, 1995.
Dorsey, D. A. "Literary Architecture and Aural Structuring Techniques in Amos." *Bib* 73 (1992): 305–30.
Firth, D. G. "Promise as Polemic: Levels of Meaning in Amos 9:11–15." *OTE* 9 (1996): 372–82.
Freedman, D. N. "Confrontations in the Book of Amos." *Princeton Seminary Bulletin* 11 (1990): 240–52.
García-Treto, F. O. "A Reader-Response Approach to Prophetic Conflict: The Case of Amos 7.10–17." In *The New Literary Criticism and the Hebrew Bible*, edited by J. C. Exum and D. J. A. Clines, JSOTSup 143, 114–24. Sheffield: JSOT, 1993.
Gilbert, P. "A New Look at Amos' Prophetic Status (Amos 7:10–17)." *Eglise et Theologie* 28 (1997): 291–300.
Giles, T. "A Note on the Vocation of Amos in 7:14." *JBL* 111 (1992): 690–92.
Gillingham, S. " 'Who Makes the Morning Darkness': God and Creation in the Book of Amos." *SJT* 45 (1992): 165–84.
Grimsrud, T. "Healing Justice: The Prophet Amos and a 'New' Theology of Justice." In *Peace*

and Justice Shall Embrace—Power and Theopolitics in the Bible: Essays in Honor of Millard Lind, edited by T. Grimsrud and L. L. Johns, 64–85. Telford, Pa.: Pandora, 1999.

Hasel, G. F. *Understanding the Book of Amos.* Grand Rapids: Baker, 1991.

Hermanson, E. "Biblical Hebrew: Conceptual Metaphor Categories in the Book of Amos." *OTE* 11 (1998): 438–51.

Heyns, D. "In the Face of Chaos: Border-Existence as Context for Understanding Amos." *OTE* 6 (1993): 72–89.

———. "Space and Time in Amos 7: Reconsidering the Third Vision." *OTE* 10 (1997): 27–38.

———. "Space and Time in Amos 8: An Ecological Reading." *OTE* 10 (1997): 236–51.

———. "Theology in Pictures: The Visions of Amos." In *"Feet on Level Ground": A South African Tribute of Old Testament Essays in Honor of Gerhard Hasel,* edited by K. Van Wyk, 131–71. Berrien Center, Mich.: Hester, 1996.

Hoffmeier, J. K. "Once Again the 'Plumb Line' Vision of Amos 7.7–9: An Interpretative Clue from Egypt?" In *Boundaries of the Ancient Near Eastern World: A Tribute to Cyrus H. Gordon,* edited by M. Lubetski et al., JSOTSup 273, 304–19. Sheffield: Sheffield Academic Press, 1998.

Hope, E. R. "Problems of Interpretation in Amos 3.4." *BT* 42 (1991): 201–5.

Jeremias, J. "The Interrelationship between Amos and Hosea." In *Forming Prophetic Literature: Essays on Isaiah and the Twelve in Honor of John D. W. Watts,* edited by J. W. Watts and P. R. House, 171–86. Sheffield: JSOT, 1996.

Kleven, T. "The Cows of Bashan: A Single Metaphor at Amos 4:1–3." *CBQ* 58 (1996): 215–27.

Linville, J. R. "Visions and Voices: Amos 7–9." *Bib* 80 (1999): 22–42.

Mahaffey, E. L. "An Investigation of Social Justice as It Relates to the Message of Amos." Ph.D. diss., New Orleans Baptist Theological Seminary, 1993.

Marrs, R. R. "Amos and the Power of Proclamation." *Restoration Quarterly* 40 (1998): 13–24.

Melugin, R. F. "Amos in Recent Research." *Currents in Research: Biblical Studies* 6 (1998): 65–101.

Moltz, H. "A Literary Interpretation of the Book of Amos." *Horizons* 25 (1998): 58–71.

Moore, D. C. "Amos' Apologia: A Defense of His Prophetic Ministry." Ph.D. diss., Southwestern Baptist Theological Seminary, 1994.

Noble, P. R. "Amos' Absolute 'No'." *VT* 47 (1997): 329–40.

———. "Amos and Amaziah in Context: Synchronic and Diachronic Approaches to Amos 7–8." *CBQ* 60 (1998): 423–39.

———. "The Function of N'm Yhwh In Amos." *ZAW* 108 (1996): 623–26.

———. " 'I Will Not Bring "It" Back' (Amos 1,3): A Deliberately Ambiguous Oracle?" *ExpT* 106 (1994–95): 105–9.

———. "Israel among the Nations." *Horizons in Biblical Theology* 15 (1993): 56–82.

———. "The Literary Structure of Amos: A Thematic Analysis." *JBL* 114 (1995): 209–26.

———. "The Remnant in Amos 3–6: A Prophetic Paradox." *Horizons in Biblical Theology* 20 (1998): 122–47.

Nogalski, J. D. "The Problematic Suffixes of Amos ix 11." *VT* 43 (1993): 411–18.

O'Connell, R. H. "Telescoping N + 1 Patterns in the Book of Amos." *VT* 46 (1996): 56–73.

Ogden, D. K. "The Earthquake Motif in the Book of Amos." In *Goldene Äpfel in silbernen Schalen,* edited by K.-D. Schunck and M. Augustin, 69–80. Frankfurt am Main: Lang 1992.

O'Kennedy, D. F. " 'It Shall Not Be': Divine Forgiveness in the Intercessory Prayers of Amos (Am 7:1–6)." *OTE* 10 (1997): 92–108.

Olyan, S. M. "The Oaths of Amos 8.14." In *Priesthood and Cult in Ancient Israel,* edited by G. A. Anderson and S. M. Olyan, JSOTSup 125, 121–49. Sheffield: JSOT, 1991.

Paas, S. "'He Who Builds His Stairs into Heaven . . .' (Amos 9:6a)." *UF* 25 (1993): 319–25.

Park, S. H. "Eschatology in the Book of Amos: A Text-Linguistic Analysis." Ph.D. diss., Trinity Evangelical Divinity School, 1996.

Ramírez, G. "The Social Location of the Prophet Amos in Light of a Cultural Anthropological Model." Ph.D. diss., Emory University, 1993.

Rilett, W. J. L. "Amos: Prophecy as Performing Art and Its Transformation in Book Culture." Ph.D. diss., University of St. Michael's College, 1993.

Rosenbaum, S. N. *Amos of Israel: A New Interpretation.* Macon, Ga.: Mercer University Press, 1990.

Schmitt, J. J. "The Virgin of Israel: Referent and Use of the Phrase in Amos and Jeremiah." *CBQ* 53 (1991): 365–87.

Shelly, P. J. "Amos and Irony: The Use of Irony in Amos' Prophetic Discourse." Ph.D. diss., Iliff School of Theology and University of Denver, 1992.

Siqueira, R. W. "The Presence of the Covenant Motif in Amos 1:2–2:16." Ph.D. diss., Andrews University, 1996.

Smith, G. V. "Continuity and Discontinuity in Amos' Use of Tradition." *JETS* 34 (1991): 33–42.

Snyman, S. D. "A Note on Ashdod and Egypt in Amos iii 9." *VT* 44 (1994): 559–62.

———. "'Violence' in Amos 3,10 and 6,3." *ETL* 71 (1995): 30–47.

Soggin, J. A. "Amos and Wisdom." In *Wisdom in Ancient Israel: Essays in Honour of J. A. Emerton,* edited by J. Day, 119–23. Cambridge: Cambridge University Press, 1995.

Steinmann, A. E. "The Order of Amos's Oracles against the Nations: 1:3–2:16." *JBL* 111 (1992): 683–89.

Strijdom, P. D. F. "What Tekoa Did to Amos." *OTE* 9 (1996): 273–93.

Thompson, H. O. *The Book of Amos: An Annotated Bibliography.* London: Scarecrow, 1997.

Thompson, M. E. W. "Amos—A Prophet of Hope?" *ExpT* 104 (1992–93): 71–76.

Viberg, Å. "Amos 7:14: A Case of Subtle Irony." *TynB* 47 (1996): 91–114.

Watts, J. D. W. *Vision and Prophecy in Amos.* Expanded ed. Macon, Ga.: Mercer University Press, 1997.

Weiss, M. "Concerning Amos' Repudiation of the Cult." In *Pomegranates and Golden Bells: Studies in Biblical, Jewish, and Near Eastern Ritual, Law, and Literature in Honor of Jacob Milgrom,* edited by D. P. Wright et al., 199–214. Winona Lake, Ind.: Eisenbrauns, 1995.

Widbin, R. B. "Center Structure in the Center Oracles of Amos." In *"Go to the Land I Will Show You": Studies in Honor of Dwight W. Young,* edited by J. E. Coleson and V. H. Matthews, 177–92. Winona Lake, Ind.: Eisenbrauns, 1996.

Williamson, H. G. M. "The Prophet and the Plumb-Line: A Redaction-Critical Study of Amos vii." In *In Quest of the Past: Studies on Israelite Religion, Literature, and Prophetism,* edited by A. S. van der Woude, 101–21. Leiden: Brill, 1990.

Wood, J. R. "Tragic and Comic Forms in Amos." *Biblical Interpretation* 6 (1998): 20–48.

Obadiah

Commentaries

Allen, L. C. *Joel, Obadiah, Jonah, and Micah.* NICOT. Grand Rapids: Eerdmans, 1976.

Finley, T. J. *Joel, Amos, Obadiah.* Chicago: Moody, 1990.

Niehaus, J. "Obadiah." In *The Minor Prophets: An Exegetical and Expositional Commentary,* edited by T. E. McComiskey, 3 vols., 2:495–541. Grand Rapids: Baker, 1992–98.

Raabe, P. R. *Obadiah.* AB. New York: Doubleday, 1996.

Smith, B. K., and F. S. Page. *Amos, Obadiah, Jonah.* NAC. Nashville: Broadman & Holman, 1995.

Stuart, D. *Hosea-Jonah.* WBC. Waco, Tex.: Word, 1987.

Watts, J. D. W. *Obadiah: A Critical Exegetical Commentary.* Grand Rapids: Eerdmans, 1969.

Wolff, H. W. *Obadiah and Jonah.* Translated by M. Kohl. Minneapolis: Augsburg, 1986.

Recent Studies

Ben Zvi, E. *A Historical-Critical Study of the Book of Obadiah.* New York: de Gruyter, 1996.

Bliese, L. F. "Chiastic and Homogeneous Metrical Structures Enhanced by Word Patterns in Obadiah." *Journal of Translation and Textlinguistics* 6 (1993): 210–27.

Clark, D. J. "Obadiah Reconsidered." *BT* 42 (1991): 326–36.

Halpern, H. "Obadiah: The Smallest Book in the Bible." *The Jewish Biblical Quarterly* 26 (1998): 231–36.

Nogalski, J. D. "Obadiah 7: Textual Corruption or Politically Charged Metaphor?" *ZAW* 110 (1998): 67–71.

Snyman, S. D. "Yom (YHWH) in the Book of Obadiah." In *Goldene Äpfel in silbernen Schalen,* edited by K.-D. Schunck and M. Augustin, 81–91. Frankfurt am Main: Lang, 1992.

Wendland, E. R. "Obadiah's 'Day': On the Rhetorical Implications of Textual Form and Intertextual Influence." *Journal of Translation and Textlinguistics* 8 (1996): 23–49.

———. "Obadiah's Vision of 'The Day of the Lord': On the Importance of Rhetoric in the Biblical Text and in Bible Translation." *Journal of Translation and Textlinguistics* 7 (1995–96): 54–86.

Jonah

Commentaries

Allen, L. C. *Joel, Obadiah, Jonah, and Micah.* NICOT. Grand Rapids: Eerdmans, 1976.

Baldwin, J. "Jonah." In *The Minor Prophets: An Exegetical and Expositional Commentary,* edited by T. E. McComiskey, 3 vols., 2:543–90. Grand Rapids: Baker, 1992–98.

Limburg, J. *Jonah.* OTL. Louisville: Westminster John Knox, 1993.

Sasson, J. M. *Jonah.* AB. New York: Doubleday, 1990.

Simon, U. *Jonah.* JPSBC. Translated by L. J. Schramm. Philadelphia: Jewish Publication Society, 1999.

Smith, B. K., and F. S. Page. *Amos, Obadiah, Jonah.* NAC. Nashville: Broadman & Holman, 1995.

Stuart, D. *Hosea-Jonah.* WBC. Waco, Tex.: Word, 1987.

Wolff, H. W. *Obadiah and Jonah.* Translated by M. Kohl. Minneapolis: Augsburg, 1986.

Recent Studies

Barré, M. L. "Jonah 2,9 and the Structure of Jonah's Prayer." *Bib* 72 (1990): 237–48.

Bolin, T. M. *Freedom beyond Forgiveness: The Book of Jonah Re-examined.* JSOTSup 236. Sheffield: Sheffield Academic Press, 1997.

———. "'Should I Not Also Pity Nineveh': Divine Freedom in the Book of Jonah." *JSOT* 67 (1995): 109–20.

Brenner, A. "Jonah's Poem out of and within Its Context." In *Among the Prophets: Language, Image, and Structure in the Prophetic Writings,* edited by P. R. Davies and D. J. A. Clines, 183–92. Sheffield: JSOT, 1993.

Christensen, D. L. "Jonah and the Sabbath Rest in the Pentateuch." In *Biblische Theologie und gesellschaftlicher Wandeln: Für Norbert Lohfink SJ,* edited by G. Braulik et al., 48–60. Freiburg: Herder, 1993.

Cooper, A. "In Praise of Divine Caprice: The Significance of the Book of Jonah." In *Among the Prophets: Language, Image, and Structure in the Prophetic Writings,* edited by P. R. Davies and D. J. A. Clines, 144–63. Sheffield: JSOT, 1993.

Craig, K. M., Jr. *A Poetics of Jonah: Art in the Service of Ideology.* Columbia: University of South Carolina Press, 1993.

———. "Jonah and the Reading Process." *JSNT* 47 (1990): 103–14.

———. "Jonah in Recent Research." *Currents in Research: Biblical Studies* 7 (1999): 97–118.

Crouch, W. B. "To Question an End, to End a Question: Opening the Closure of the Book of Jonah." *JSOT* 62 (1994): 101–12.

Day, J. "Problems in the Interpretation of the Book of Jonah." In *In Quest of the Past: Studies on Israelite Religion, Literature, and Prophetism,* edited by A. S. van der Woude, 32–47. Leiden: Brill, 1990.

Dell, K. J. "Reinventing the Wheel: The Shaping of the Book of Jonah." In *After Exile: Essays in Honour of Rex Mason,* edited by J. Barton and D. J. Reimer, 85–101. Macon, Ga.: Mercer University Press, 1996.

Dyck, E. "Jonah among the Prophets: A Study in Canonical Context." *JETS* 33 (1990): 63–73.

Farmer, D. A. "Jonah 3–4." *Int* 54 (2000): 63–65.

Ferguson, P. "Who Was the 'King of Nineveh' in Jonah 3:6?" *TynB* 47 (1996): 301–14.

Frolov, S. "Returning the Ticket: God and His Prophet in the Book of Jonah." *JSOT* 86 (1999): 85–105.

Gitay, Y. "Jonah: The Prophecy of Antirhetoric." In *Fortunate the Eyes That See: Essays in Honor of David Noel Freedman in Celebration of His Seventieth Birthday,* edited by A. B. Beck et al., 197–206. Grand Rapids: Eerdmans, 1995.

Holmgren, F. C. "Israel, the Prophets, and the Book of Jonah: The Rest of the Story (the Formation of the Canon)." *Currents in Theology and Mission* 21 (1994): 127–32.

Houk, C. B. "Linguistic Patterns in Jonah." *JSOT* 77 (1998): 81–102.

Jonker, L. "Reading Jonah Multidimensionally: A Multidimensional Reading Strategy for Biblical Interpretation." *Scriptura* 64 (1998): 1–15.

Judisch, D. McC. L. "The Historicity of Jonah." *Concordia Theological Journal* 63 (1999): 144–57.

Krašovec, J. "Salvation of the Rebellious Prophet Jonah and of the Penitent Heathen Sinners." *Svensk Exegetisk Årsbok* 61 (1996): 53–75.

Lacocque, A., and P.-E. Lacocque. *Jonah: A Psycho-Religious Approach to the Prophet.* Columbia: University of South Carolina Press, 1990.

Levine, B. A. "The Place of Jonah in the History of Biblical Ideas." In *On the Way to Nineveh: Studies in Honor of George M. Landes,* edited by S. L. Cook and S. C. Winter, 201–17. Atlanta: Scholars Press, 1999.

Longacre, R. E., and S. J. J. Hwang. "A Textlinguistic Approach to the Biblical Hebrew Narrative of Jonah." In *Biblical Hebrew and Discourse Linguistics,* edited by R. D. Bergen, 336–58. Winona Lake, Ind.: Eisenbrauns, 1994.

Marcus, D. "Nineveh's 'Three Days' Walk' (Jonah 3:3): Another Interpretation." In *On the Way to Nineveh: Studies in Honor of George M. Landes,* edited by S. L. Cook and S. C. Winter, 42–48. Atlanta: Scholars Press, 1999.

Nel, P. J. "The Symbolism and Function of Epic Space in Jonah." *JNSL* 25 (1999): 215–24.

Niccacci, A. "Syntactic Analysis of Jonah." *Liber Annuus Studii Biblic Franciscani* 46 (1996): 9–32.

Person, R. F., Jr. *In Conversation with Jonah: Conversation Analysis, Literary Criticism, and the Book of Jonah.* JSOTSup 220. Sheffield: Sheffield Academic Press, 1996.

Ratner, R. J. "Jonah, the Runaway Servant." *Maarav* 5–6 (1990): 281–305.

Salters, R. B. *Jonah and Lamentations.* Old Testament Guides. Sheffield: JSOT, 1994.

Sherwood, Y. "Cross-Currents in the Book of Jonah: Some Jewish and Cultural Midrashim on a Traditional Text." *Biblical Interpretation* 6 (1998): 49–79.

———. "Rocking the Boat: Jonah and the New Historicism." *Biblical Interpretation* 5 (1997): 364–402.

Smelik, K. A. D. "The Literary Function of Poetical Passages in Biblical Narrative: The Case of Jonah 2:3–10." In *Give Ear to My Words: Psalms and Other Poetry in and around the Hebrew Bible. Essays in Honour of N. A. Uchelen,* edited by J. W. Dyk, 147–51. Amsterdam: Societas Hebraica Amstelodamensis, 1996.

Spangenberg, I. J. J. "Jonah and Qohelet: Satire versus Irony." *OTE* 9 (1996): 494–511.

Thompson, M. E. W. "The Mission of Jonah." *ExpT* 105 (1993–94): 233–36.

Trible, P. A. "Divine Incongruities in the Book of Jonah." In *God in the Fray: A Tribute to Walter Brueggemann,* edited by T. Linafelt and T. K. Beal, 198–208. Minneapolis: Fortress, 1998.

———. *Rhetorical Criticism: Context, Method, and the Book of Jonah.* Minneapolis: Fortress, 1994.

———. "A Tempest in a Text: Ecological Soundings in the Book of Jonah." In *On the Way to Nineveh: Studies in Honor of George M. Landes,* edited by S. L. Cook and S. C. Winter, 187–99. Atlanta: Scholars Press, 1999.

van Heerden, W. "Humour and the Interpretation of the Book of Jonah." *OTE* 5 (1992): 389–401.

van Wyk-Bos, J. W. H. "No Small Thing: The 'Overturning' of Nineveh in the Third Chapter of Jonah." In *On the Way to Nineveh: Studies in Honor of George M. Landes,* edited by S. L. Cook and S. C. Winter, 218–37. Atlanta: Scholars Press, 1999.

Wendland, E. R. "Recursion and Variation in the 'Prophecy' of Jonah: On the Rhetorical Impact of Stylistic Technique in Hebrew Narrative Discourse, with Special Reference to Irony and Enigma." *AUSS* 35 (1997): 67–98.

———. "Text Analysis and the Genre of Jonah." *JETS* 39 (1996): 191–206, 373–95.

Wilt, T. L. "Jonah: A Battle of Shifting Alliances." In *Among the Prophets: Language, Image, and Structure in the Prophetic Writings,* edited by P. R. Davies and D. J. A. Clines, 164–82. Sheffield: JSOT, 1993.

———. "Lexical Repetition in Jonah." *Journal of Translation and Textlinguistics* 5 (1992): 252–64.

Woodard, B. L. "Death in Life: The Book of Jonah and Biblical Tragedy." *Grace Theological Journal* 12 (1990): 3–16.

Micah

Commentaries

Allen, L. C. *Joel, Obadiah, Jonah, and Micah.* NICOT. Grand Rapids: Eerdmans, 1976.

Andersen, F. I., and D. N. Freedman. *Micah.* AB. New York: Doubleday, 2000.

Hillers, D. R. *Micah.* Hermeneia. Philadelphia: Fortress, 1984.

King, P. J. *Amos, Hosea, Micah—An Archaeological Commentary.* Philadelphia: Westminster, 1988.

Mays, J. L. *Micah.* OTL. Philadelphia: Westminster, 1976.

McKane, W. *The Book of Micah: Introduction and Commentary.* Edinburgh: T. & T. Clark, 1998.

Smith, R. L. *Micah-Malachi.* WBC. Waco, Tex.: Word, 1984.

Waltke, B. K.. "Micah." In *The Minor Prophets: An Exegetical and Expositional Commentary,* edited by T. E. McComiskey, 3 vols., 2:591–764. Grand Rapids: Baker, 1992–98.

Wolff, H. W. *Micah.* Translated by G. Stansell. Minneapolis: Augsburg, 1990.

Recent Studies

Andersen, F. I. "The Poetic Properties of Prophetic Discourse in the Book of Micah." In *Biblical Hebrew and Discourse Linguistics,* edited by R. D. Bergen, 520–28. Winona Lake, Ind.: Eisenbrauns, 1994.

Barker, K. L. "A Literary Analysis of the Book of Micah." *BSac* 155 (1998): 437–48.

Ben Zvi, E. "Micah 1.2–16: Observations and Possible Implications." *JSOT* 77 (1998): 103–20.

———. "Wrongdoers, Wrongdoing, and Righting Wrongs in Micah 2." *Biblical Interpretation* 7 (1999): 88–100.

Biddle, M. E. "'Israel' and 'Jacob' in the Book of Micah: Micah in the Context of the Twelve." *SBLSP,* vol. 2 (1998): 850–71.

Carroll, R. P. "Night without Vision: Micah and the Prophets." In *Sacred History and Sacred Texts in Early Judaism: A Symposium in Honour of A. S. van der Woude,* edited by J. N. Bremmer and F. G. Martínez, 74–84. Kampen: Kok Pharos, 1992.

Cook, S. L. "Micah's Deuteronomistic Redaction and the Deuteronomists' Identity." In *Those Elusive Deuteronomists: The Phenomenon of Pan-Deuteronomism,* edited by L. S. Schearing and S. L. McKenzie, JSOTSup 268, 216–31. Sheffield: Sheffield Academic Press, 1999.

Dempsey, C. J. "The Interplay between Literary Form and Technique and Ethics in Micah 1–3." Ph.D. diss., Catholic University of America, 1994.

———. "Micah 2–3: Literary Artistry, Ethical Message, and Some Considerations about the Image of YHWH and Micah." *JSOT* 85 (1999): 117–28.

Hutton, R. P. "What Happened from Shittim to Gilgal? Law and Gospel in Micah 6:5." *Currents in Theology and Mission* 26 (1999): 94–103.

Jenson, P. P. "Models of Prophetic Prediction and Matthew's Quotation of Micah 5:2." In *The Lord's Anointed,* edited by P. E. Satterthwaite, R. S. Hess, and G. J. Wenham, 189–211. Grand Rapids: Baker, 1995.

McKane, W. "Micah 1,2–7." *ZAW* 107 (1995): 420–34.

———. "Micah 2:1–5: Text and Commentary." *JSS* 42 (1997): 7–22.

———. "Micah 2:12–13." *JNSL* 21 (1995): 83–91.

Miller, D. E. "Micah and Its Literary Environment: Rhetorical Critical Studies." Ph.D. diss., University of Arizona, 1991.

Na'aman, N. "'The House-of-No-Shade Shall Take Away Its Tax from You' (Micah i 11)." *VT* 45 (1995): 516–27.

Petrotta, A. J. *Lexis Ludens: Wordplay and the Book of Micah.* New York: Lang, 1991.

Shaw, C. S. *The Speeches of Micah: A Rhetorical-Historical Analysis.* JSOTSup 145. Sheffield: JSOT, 1993.

Shoemaker, K. W. "Speaker and Audience Participants in Micah: Aspects of Prophetic Discourse." Ph.D. diss., Graduate Theological Union and University of California, Berkeley, 1992.

Strydom, J. G. "Micah of Samaria: Amos's and Hosea's Forgotten Partner." *OTE* 6 (1993): 19–32.

van der Wal, A. *Micah: A Classified Bibliography.* Amsterdam: Free University, 1990.

Wagenaar, J. A. "The Hillside of Samaria: Interpretation and Meaning of Micah 1:6." *Biblische Notizen* 85 (1996): 26–30.

Wessels, W. J. "Conflicting Powers: Reflections from the Book of Micah." *OTE* 10 (1997): 528–44.

———. "Wisdom in the Gate: Micah Takes the Rostrum." *OTE* 10 (1997): 125–35.

Williamson, H. G. M. "Marginalia in Micah." *VT* 47 (1997): 360–72.

Zapff, B. M. "The Perspective of the Nations in the Book of Micah as a 'Systematization' of the Nations' Role in Joel, Jonah, and Nahum? Reflections on a Context-Oriented Exegesis in the Book of the Twelve." *SBLSP* (1999): 596–616.

Nahum

Commentaries

Longman, T. "Nahum." In *The Minor Prophets: An Exegetical and Expositional Commentary,* edited by T. E. McComiskey, 3 vols., 2:765–829. Grand Rapids: Baker, 1992–98.

Patterson, R. D. *Nahum, Habakkuk, Zephaniah*. Chicago: Moody, 1991.
Roberts, J. J. M. *Nahum, Habakkuk, and Zephaniah*. OTL. Louisville: Westminster John Knox, 1991.
Robertson, O. P. *Nahum, Habakkuk, and Zephaniah*. NICOT. Grand Rapids: Eerdmans, 1990.
Smith, R. L. *Micah-Malachi*. WBC. Waco, Tex.: Word, 1984.

Recent Studies

Ball, E. "Interpreting the Septuagint: Nahum 2.2 as a Case Study." *JSOT* 75 (1997): 59–75.
Becking, B. "Divine Wrath and the Conceptual Coherence of the Book of Nahum." *SJOT* 9 (1995): 277–96.
———. "Passion, Power, and Protection: Interpreting the God of Nahum." In *On Reading Prophetic Texts*, edited by B. Becking and M. Dijkstra, 1–20. Leiden: Brill, 1996.
Bliese, L. F. "A Cryptic Chiastic Acrostic: Finding Meaning from Structure in the Poetry of Nahum." *Journal of Translation and Textlinguistics* 7 (1995): 48–81.
Charles, J. D. "Plundering the Lions' Den—A Portrait of Divine Fury (Nahum 2:3–11)." *Grace Theological Journal* 10 (1989): 183–201.
Christensen, D. L. "The Book of Nahum: A History of Interpretation." In *Forming Prophetic Literature: Essays on Isaiah and the Twelve in Honor of John D. W. Watts*, edited by J. W. Watts and P. R. House, JSOTSup 235, 187–94. Sheffield: Sheffield Academic Press, 1996.
Floyd, M. H. "The Chimerical Acrostic of Nahum 1:2–10." *JBL* 113 (1994): 421–37.
House, P. R. "Dramatic Coherence in Nahum, Habakkuk, and Zephaniah." In *Forming Prophetic Literature: Essays on Isaiah and the Twelve in Honor of John D. W. Watts*, JSOTSup 235, edited by J. W. Watts and P. R. House, 195–208. Sheffield: Sheffield Academic Press, 1996.
Johnston, G. H. "Nahum's Historical Allusions to the Neo-Assyrian Lion Motif." *BSac* 158 (2001): 287–307.
———. "Nahum's Rhetorical Allusions to Neo-Assyrian Conquest Metaphors." *BSac* 159 (2002): 21–45.
———. "A Rhetorical Analysis of the Book of Nahum." Ph.D. diss., Dallas Theological Seminary, 1992.
Nogalski, J. "The Radical Shaping of Nahum 1 for the Book of the Twelve." In *Among the Prophets: Language, Image, and Structure in the Prophetic Writings*, edited by P. R. Davies and D. J. A. Clines, 193–202. Sheffield: JSOT, 1993.
Patterson, R. D., and M. E. Travers, "Nahum: Poet Laureate of the Minor Prophets." *JETS* 33 (1990): 437–44.
Spronk, K. "Acrostics in the Book of Nahum." *ZAW* 110 (1998): 209–22.
———. *Nahum*. Kampen: Kok Pharos, 1997.
———. "Synchronic and Diachronic Approaches to the Book of Nahum." In *Synchronic or Diachronic? A Debate in Old Testament Exegesis*, edited by J. C. de Moor, 159–86. Leiden: Brill, 1995.
Sweeney, M. A. "Concerning the Structure and Generic Character of the Book of Nahum." *ZAW* 104 (1992): 364–77.
Wendland, E. R. "What's the 'Good News'—Check Out 'the Feet'! Prophetic Rhetoric and the Salvific Center of Nahum's 'Vision.' " *OTE* 11 (1998): 154–81.
Wessels, W. J. "Nahum, an Uneasy Expression of Yahweh's Power." *OTE* 11 (1998): 615–28.

Habakkuk

Commentaries

Bruce, F. F. "Habakkuk." In *The Minor Prophets: An Exegetical and Expositional Commentary*, edited by T. E. McComiskey, 3 vols., 2:831–96. Grand Rapids: Baker, 1992–98.

Patterson, R. D. *Nahum, Habakkuk, Zephaniah*. Chicago: Moody, 1991.

Roberts, J. J. M. *Nahum, Habakkuk, and Zephaniah*. OTL. Louisville: Westminster John Knox, 1991.

Robertson, O. P. *Nahum, Habakkuk, and Zephaniah*. NICOT. Grand Rapids: Eerdmans, 1990.

Smith, R. L. *Micah-Malachi*. WBC. Waco, Tex.: Word, 1984.

Recent Studies

Bliese, L. F. "The Poetics of Habakkuk." *Journal of Translation and Textlinguistics* 12 (1999): 47–75.

Copeland, P. E. "The Midst of Years." In *Text as Pretext: Essays in Honour of Robert Davidson*, edited by R. P. Carroll et al., JSOTSup 138, 91–105. Sheffield: JSOT, 1992.

Floyd, M. H. "Prophecy and Writing in Habakkuk 2,1–5." *ZAW* 105 (1993): 462–81.

———. "Prophetic Complaints about the Fulfillment of Oracles in Habakkuk 1:2–17 and Jeremiah 15:10–18." *JBL* 110 (1991): 397–418.

Haak, R. D. *Habakkuk*. VTSup 44. Leiden: Brill, 1992.

Hahlen, M. A. "The Literary Design of Habakkuk." Ph.D. diss., Southern Baptist Theological Seminary, 1992.

Heard, C. "Hearing the Children's Cries: Commentary, Deconstruction, Ethics, and the Book of Habakkuk." *Semeia* 77 (1997): 75–89.

Leigh, B. Y. "A Rhetorical and Structural Study of the Book of Habakkuk." Ph.D. diss., Golden Gate Baptist Theological Seminary, 1992.

O'Neal, G. M. "Interpreting Habakkuk as Scripture: An Application of the Canonical Approach of Brevard S. Childs." Ph.D. diss., Southern Baptist Theological Seminary, 1996.

Sweeney, M. A. "Structure, Genre, and Intent in the Book of Habakkuk." *VT* 41 (1991): 63–83.

Thompson, M. E. W. "Prayer, Oracle, and Theophany: The Book of Habakkuk." *TynB* 44 (1993): 33–53.

Trudinger, P. "Two Ambiguities in Habakkuk's 'Unambiguous' Oracle." *Downside Review* 113 (1995): 282–83.

Tsumura, D. T. "The 'Word Pair' *qšt* and *mt* in Habakkuk 3:9 in the Light of Ugaritic and Akkadian." In *"Go to the Land I Will Show You": Studies in Honor of Dwight W. Young*, edited by J. E. Coleson and V. H. Matthews, 353–61. Winona Lake, Ind.: Eisenbrauns,1996.

van Ruiten, J. T. A. G. M. "'His Master' s Voice'? The Supposed Influence of the Book of Isaiah in the Book of Habakkuk." In *Studies in the Book of Isaiah: Festschrift Willem A. M. Beuken*, edited by J. van Ruiten and M. Vervenne, 397–411. Louvain: Peeters, 1997.

Watts, J. W. "Psalmody in Prophecy: Habakkuk 3 in Context." In *Forming Prophetic Literature: Essays on Isaiah and the Twelve in Honor of John D. W. Watts*, edited by J. W. Watts and P. R. House, JSOTSup 235, 209–23. Sheffield: Sheffield Academic Press, 1996.

Wendland, E. "The 'Righteous Live by Their Faith' in a Holy God: Complementary Compositional Forces and Habakkuk's Dialogue with the Lord." *JETS* 42 (1999): 591–628.

Zephaniah

Commentaries

Berlin, A. *Zephaniah*. AB. New York: Doubleday, 1994.

Motyer, J. A. "Zephaniah." In *The Minor Prophets: An Exegetical and Expositional Commentary*, edited by T. E. McComiskey, 3 vols., 3:897–962. Grand Rapids: Baker, 1992–98.

Patterson, R. D. *Nahum, Habakkuk, Zephaniah.* Chicago: Moody, 1991.

Roberts, J. J. M. *Nahum, Habakkuk, and Zephaniah.* OTL. Louisville: Westminster John Knox, 1991.

Robertson, O. P. *Nahum, Habakkuk, and Zephaniah.* NICOT. Grand Rapids: Eerdmans, 1990.

Smith, R. L. *Micah-Malachi.* WBC. Waco, Tex.: Word, 1984.

Recent Studies

Ben Zvi, E. *A Historical-Critical Study of the Book of Zephaniah.* Berlin: de Gruyter, 1991.

Berlin, A. "Zephaniah's Oracles against the Nations and an Israelite Cultural Myth." In *Fortunate the Eyes That See: Essays in Honor of David Noel Freedman in Celebration of His Seventieth Birthday,* edited by A. B. Beck et al., 175–84. Grand Rapids: Eerdmans, 1995.

Haak, R. D. "'Cush' in Zephaniah." In *The Pitcher Is Broken: Memorial Essays for Gösta A. Ahlström,* edited by S. W. Holloway and L. K. Handy, JSOTSup 190, 238–51. Sheffield: Sheffield Academic Press, 1995.

King, G. A. "The Day of the Lord in Zephaniah." *BSac* 152 (1995): 16–32.

———. "The Message of Zephaniah: An Urgent Echo." *AUSS* 35 (1997): 211–22.

———. "The Remnant in Zephaniah." *BSac* 151 (1994): 414–27.

———. "The Theological Coherence of the Book of Zephaniah." Ph.D. diss., Union Theological Seminary (VA), 1996.

Nysse, R. W. "A Theological Reading of Zephaniah's Audience." In *All Things New: Essays in Honor of Roy A. Harrisville,* edited by A. J. Hultgren et al., 65–73. St. Paul, Minn.: Word & World, 1993.

Rudman, D. "A Note on Zephaniah." *Bib* 80 (1999): 109–12.

Ryou, D. H. *Zephaniah's Oracles against the Nations: A Synchronic and Diachronic Study of Zephaniah 2:1–3:8.* Leiden: Brill, 1995.

Sweeney, M. A. "A Form-Critical Reassessment of the Book of Zephaniah." *CBQ* 53 (1991): 387–408.

———. "Zephaniah: A Paradigm for the Study of the Prophetic Books." *Currents in Research: Biblical Studies* 7 (1999): 119–45.

Haggai

Commentaries

Baldwin, J. G. *Haggai, Zechariah, Malachi.* TOTC. London: InterVarsity, 1972.

Merrill, E. H. *Haggai, Zechariah, Malachi.* Chicago: Moody, 1994.

Meyers, C. L., and E. M. Meyers. *Haggai, Zechariah 1–8.* AB. Garden City, NY.: Doubleday, 1987.

Motyer, J. A. "Haggai." In *The Minor Prophets: An Exegetical and Expositional Commentary,* edited by T. E. McComiskey, 3 vols. Grand Rapids: Baker, 1992–98. 3:963–1002.

Petersen, D. L. *Haggai and Zechariah 1–8.* OTL. Philadelphia: Westminster, 1984.

Redditt, P. L. *Haggai, Zechariah, Malachi.* NCB. Grand Rapids: Eerdmans, 1995.

Smith, R. L. *Micah-Malachi.* WBC. Waco, TX.: Word, 1984.

Verhoef, P. A. *Haggai and Malachi.* NICOT. Grand Rapids: Eerdmans, 1987.

Wolff, H. W. *Haggai.* Translated by M. Kohl. Minneapolis: Augsburg, 1988.

Recent Studies

Bedford, P. R. "Discerning the Time: Haggai, Zechariah, and the 'Delay' in the Rebuilding of the Jerusalem Temple." In *The Pitcher Is Broken: Memorial Essays for Gösta A. Ahlström,* JSOTSup 190, edited by S. W. Holloway and L. K. Handy, 71–94. Sheffield: Sheffield Academic Press, 1995.

Christensen, D. L. "Impulse and Design in the Book of Haggai." *JETS* 35 (1992): 445–56.

Clark, D. J. "Discourse Structure in Haggai." *Journal of Translation and Textlinguistics* 5 (1992): 13–24.

Clines, D. J. A. "Haggai's Temple, Constructed, Deconstructed, and Reconstructed." *SJOT* 7 (1993): 51–77.

Craig, K. M., Jr. "Interrogatives in Haggai-Zechariah: A Literary Thread?" In *Forming Prophetic Literature: Essays on Isaiah and the Twelve in Honor of John D. W. Watts,* JSOTSup 235, edited by J. W. Watts and P. R. House, 224–44. Sheffield: Sheffield Academic Press, 1996.

Floyd, M. H. "The Nature of the Narrative and the Evidence of Redaction in Haggai." *VT* 45 (1995): 470–90.

Holbrook, D. J. "Narrowing Down Haggai: Examining Style in Light of the Discourse and Content of Haggai." *Journal of Translation and Textlinguistics* 7 (1995): 1–12.

Sim, R. J. "Notes on Haggai 2:10–21." *Journal of Translation and Textlinguistics* 5 (1992): 25–36.

Sykes, S. "Time and Place in Haggai-Zechariah 1–8: A Bakhtinian Analysis of a Prophetic Chronicle." *JSOT* 76 (1997): 97–124.

Tollington, J. E. *Tradition and Innovation in Haggai and Zechariah 1–8.* JSOTSup 150. Sheffield: JSOT, 1993.

Wendland, E. R. "Temple Site or Cemetery?—A Question of Perspective: The Influence of World View on the Interpretation of Haggai 2:10–19 and Its Implications for the Handling of Implicit Information in Bible Translation." *Journal of Translation and Textlinguistics* 5 (1992): 37–85.

Zechariah

Commentaries

Baldwin, J. G. *Haggai, Zechariah, Malachi.* TOTC. London: InterVarsity, 1972.

McComiskey, T. E. "Zechariah." In *The Minor Prophets: An Exegetical and Expositional Commentary,* edited by T. E. McComiskey, 3 vols., 3:1003–1244. Grand Rapids: Baker, 1992–98.

Merrill, E. H. *Haggai, Zechariah, Malachi.* Chicago: Moody, 1994.

Meyers, C. L. and E. M. Meyers. *Haggai, Zechariah 1–8.* AB. Garden City, N.Y.: Doubleday, 1987.

———. *Zechariah 9–14.* AB. New York: Doubleday, 1993.

Petersen, D. L. *Haggai and Zechariah 1–8.* OTL. Philadelphia: Westminster, 1984.

———. *Zechariah 9–14 and Malachi.* OTL. London: SCM, 1995.

Redditt, P. L. *Haggai, Zechariah, Malachi.* NCB. Grand Rapids: Eerdmans, 1995.

Smith, R. L. *Micah-Malachi.* WBC. Waco, Tex.: Word, 1984.

Recent Studies

Butterworth, M. *Structure of the Book of Zechariah.* JSOTSup 130. Sheffield: JSOT, 1992.

Clark, D. J. "Vision and Oracle in Zechariah 1–6." In *Biblical Hebrew and Discourse Linguistics,* edited by R. D. Bergen, 529–60. Winona Lake, Ind.: Eisenbrauns, 1994.

Cook, S. L. "The Metamorphosis of a Shepherd: The Tradition History of Zechariah 11:17 + 13:7–9." *CBQ* 55 (1993): 453–66.

Craig, K. M., Jr. "Interrogatives in Haggai-Zechariah: A Literary Thread?" In *Forming Prophetic Literature: Essays on Isaiah and the Twelve in Honor of John D. W. Watts,* edited by J. W. Watts and P. R. House, JSOTSup 235, 224–44. Sheffield: Sheffield Academic Press, 1996.

Floyd, M. H. "Cosmos and History in Zechariah's View of the Restoration (Zechariah 1:7—

6:15)." In *Problems in Biblical Theology: Essays in Honor of Rolf Knierim*, edited by H. T. C. Sun, 125–44. Grand Rapids: Eerdmans, 1997.

———. "The Evil in Ephah: Reading Zechariah 5:5–11 in Its Literary Context." *CBQ* 58 (1996): 51–68.

Fox, H. "The Forelife of Ideas and the Afterlife of Texts." *RB* 105 (1998): 520–25.

Good, R. "Zechariah 14:13 and Related Texts: Brother against Brother in War." *Maarav* 8 (1992): 39–47.

Gordon, R. P. "Inscribed Pots and Zechariah xiv 20–1." *VT* 42 (1992): 120–23.

Hartle, J. A. "The Literary Unity of Zechariah." *JETS* 35 (1992): 145- 57.

Hobbs, T. R. "The Language of Warfare in Zechariah 9–14." In *After Exile: Essays in Honour of Rex Mason*, edited by J. Barton and D. J. Reimer, 103–28. Macon, Ga.: Mercer University Press, 1996.

Hoppe, L. J. "Zechariah 3: A Vision of Forgiveness." *TBT* 38 (2000): 10–16.

Kline, M. G. "The Structure of the Book of Zechariah." *JETS* 34 (1991): 179–93.

Kruger, P. A. "Grasping the Hem in Zech 8:23: The Contextual Analysis of a Gesture." In *"Feet on Level Ground": A South African Tribute of Old Testament Essays in Honor of Gerhard Hasel*, edited by K. Van Wyk, 172–92. Berrien Center, Mich.: Hester, 1996.

Laffey, A. L. "Zechariah 1: A Vision of Compassion." *TBT* 38 (2000): 4–9.

Larkin, K. *The Eschatology of Second Zechariah: A Study of the Formation of a Mantological Wisdom Anthology*. Kampen: Kok Pharos, 1994.

LaRocca-Pitts, B. "Zechariah 6: A Vision of Peace." *TBT* 38 (2000): 23–28.

Laubscher, F. du T. "Epiphany and Sun Mythology in Zechariah 14." *JNSL* 20 (1994): 125–38.

Marinkovic, P. "What Does Zechariah 1–8 Tell Us about the Second Temple? In *Second Temple Studies*, vol. 2: *Temple Community in the Persian Period*, edited by T. C. Eskenazi and K. H. Richards, JSOTSup 175, 88–103. Sheffield: JSOT, 1994.

Meyers, C. L., and E. M. Meyers. "The Future Fortunes of the House of David: The Evidence of Second Zechariah." In *Fortunate the Eyes That See: Essays in Honor of David Noel Freedman in Celebration of His Seventieth Birthday*, edited by A. B. Beck et al., 207–22. Grand Rapids: Eerdmans, 1995.

———. "Jerusalem and Zion after the Exile: The Evidence of First Zechariah." In *"Sha'arei Talmon": Studies in the Bible, Qumran, and the Ancient Near East Presented to Shemaryahu Talmon*, edited by M. Fishbane et al., 121–35. Winona Lake, Ind.: Eisenbrauns, 1992.

Meyers, E. M. "The Crisis of the Mid–Fifth Century B.C.E. Zechariah and the 'End' of Prophecy." In *Pomegranates and Golden Bells: Studies in Biblical, Jewish, and Near Eastern Ritual, Law, and Literature in Honor of Jacob Milgrom*, edited by D. P. Wright et al., 713–23. Winona Lake, Ind.: Eisenbrauns, 1995.

———. "Messianism in First and Second Zechariah and the 'End' of Biblical Prophecy." In *"Go to the Land I Will Show You": Studies in Honor of Dwight W. Young*, edited by J. E. Coleson and V. H. Matthews, 127–42. Winona Lake, Ind.: Eisenbrauns,1996.

Nash, K. S. "Zechariah 4: A Vision of Small Beginnings." *TBT* 38 (2000): 17–22.

Nielsen, E. "A Note on Zechariah 14, 4–5." In *In the Last Days: On Jewish and Christian Apocalyptic and Its Period*, edited by K. Jeppesen et al., 33–37. Århus, Denmark: Århus University Press, 1994.

Nurmela, R. *Prophets in Dialogue: Inner-Biblical Allusions in Zechariah 1–8 and 9–14*. Turku, Finland: Åbo Akademis Förlag, 1996.

Peachey, B. F. "A Horse of a Different Colour: The Horses in Zechariah and Revelation." *ExpT* 110 (1999): 214–16.

Person, R. F. *Second Zechariah and the Deuteronomistic School*. JSOTSup 167. Sheffield: JSOT, 1993.

Redditt, P. L. "Nehemiah's First Mission and the Date of Zechariah 9–14." *CBQ* 56 (1994): 664–78.

———. "The Two Shepherds in Zechariah 11:4–17." *CBQ* 55 (1993): 676–86.

———. "Zechariah 9–14, Malachi, and the Redaction of the Book of the Twelve." In *Forming Prophetic Literature: Essays on Isaiah and the Twelve in Honor of John D. W. Watts,* edited by J. W. Watts and P. R. House, JSOTSup 235, 245–68. Sheffield: Sheffield Academic Press, 1996.

———. "Zerubbabel, Joshua, and the Night Visions of Zechariah." *CBQ* 54 (1992): 249–59.

Rhea, R. "Attack on Prophecy: Zechariah 13,1–6." *ZAW* 107 (1995): 288–93.

Rose, W. H. *Zemah and Zerubbabel: Messianic Expectations in the Early Postexilic Period.* JSOTSup 304. Sheffield: Sheffield Academic Press, 2000.

Rubenstein, J. L. "Sukkto, Eschatology, and Zechariah 14." *RB* 103 (1996): 161–95.

Schaefer, K. R. "The Ending of the Book of Zechariah: A Commentary." *RB* 100 (1993): 165–238.

———. "Zechariah 14: A Study in Allusion." *CBQ* 57 (1995): 66–91.

———. "Zechariah 14 and the Composition of the Book of Zechariah." *RB* 100 (1993): 368–98.

Sykes, S. "Time and Place in Haggai–Zechariah 1–8: A Bakhtinian Analysis of a Prophetic Chronicle." *JSOT* 76 (1997): 97–124.

Tigchelaar, E. J. C. *Prophets of Old and the Day of the End: Zechariah, the Book of Watchers, and Apocalyptic.* Leiden: Brill, 1996.

Tollington, J. E. *Tradition and Innovation in Haggai and Zechariah 1–8.* JSOTSup 150. Sheffield: JSOT, 1993.

VanderKam, J. C. "Joshua the High Priest and the Interpretation of Zechariah 3." *CBQ* 53 (1991): 553–70.

Wilbur, K. C. "Analysis of Poetic and Prose Expression in Zechariah 9–11." Ph.D. diss., Boston University, 1994.

Witt, D. A. "Zechariah 12–14: Its Origins, Growth, and Theological Significance." Ph.D. diss., Vanderbilt University, 1991.

Wolters, A. "Semantic Borrowing and Inner-Greek Corruption in LXX Zechariah 11:8." *JBL* 118 (1999): 685–707.

Malachi

Commentaries

Baldwin, J. G. *Haggai, Zechariah, Malachi.* TOTC. London: InterVarsity, 1972.

Hill, A. E. *Malachi.* AB. New York: Doubleday, 1998.

Merrill, E. H. *Haggai, Zechariah, Malachi.* Chicago: Moody, 1994.

Petersen, D. L. *Zechariah 9–14 and Malachi.* OTL. London: SCM, 1995.

Redditt, P. L. *Haggai, Zechariah, Malachi.* NCB. Grand Rapids: Eerdmans, 1995.

Smith, R. L. *Micah-Malachi.* WBC. Waco, Tex.: Word, 1984.

Stuart, D. "Malachi." In *The Minor Prophets: An Exegetical and Expositional Commentary,* edited by T. E. McComiskey, 3 vols., 3:1245–1396. Grand Rapids: Baker, 1992–98.

Verhoef, P. A. *Haggai and Malachi.* NICOT. Grand Rapids: Eerdmans, 1987.

Recent Studies

Berry, D. K. "Malachi's Dual Design: The Close of the Canon and What Comes Afterward." In *Forming Prophetic Literature: Essays on Isaiah and the Twelve in Honor of John D. W. Watts,* edited by J. W. Watts and P. R. House, JSOTSup 235, 269–302. Sheffield: Sheffield Academic Press, 1996.

Clark, D. J. "A Discourse Approach to Problems in Malachi 2.10–16." *BT* 49 (1998): 415–25.

Clendenen, E. R. "Old Testament Prophecy as Hortatory Text: Examples from Malachi." *Journal of Translation and Textlinguistics* 6 (1993): 336–53.

Curtis, B. G. "The Daughter of Zion Oracles and the Appendices to Malachi: Evidence on the Latter Redactors and Redactions of the Book of the Twelve." *SBLSP,* vol. 2 (1998): 872–92.

Fuller, R. "Text-Critical Problems in Malachi 2:10–16." *JBL* 110 (1991): 47–57.

Heath, E. A. "Divorce and Violence: Synonymous Parallelism in Malachi 2:16." *Ashland Theological Journal* 28 (1996): 1–8.

Hugenberger, G. P. *Marriage as a Covenant: A Study of Biblical Law and Ethics Governing Marriage Developed from the Perspective of Malachi.* Leiden: Brill, 1994.

Kugler, R. A. "A Note on the Hebrew and Greek Texts of Mal 2,3aα." *ZAW* 108 (1996): 426–29.

———. "The Levi-Priestly Tradition: From Malachi to 'Testament of Levi.'" Ph.D. diss., University of Notre Dame, 1994.

Lewis, J. P. " 'Sun of Righteousness' (Malachi 4:2): A History of Interpretation." *Stone-Campbell Journal* 2 (1999): 90–110.

Mariottini, C. F. "Malachi: A Prophet for His Time." *The Jewish Biblical Quarterly* 26 (1998): 149–57.

O'Brien, J. M. "Judah as Wife and Husband: Deconstructing Gender in Malachi." *JBL* 115 (1996): 241–50.

———. "Malachi in Recent Research." *Currents in Research: Biblical Studies* 3 (1995): 81–94.

———. "On Saying 'No' to a Prophet." *Semeia* 72 (1995): 111–24.

———. *Priest and Levite in Malachi.* SBLDS 121. Atlanta: Scholars Press, 1990.

Redditt, P. L. "The Book of Malachi in Its Social Setting." *CBQ* 56 (1994): 240–55.

Reynolds, C. B. "Malachi and the Priesthood." Ph.D. diss., Yale University, 1993.

Snyman, S. D. "A Structural Approach to Malachi 3:13–21." *OTE* 9 (1996): 486–94.

Viberg, Å. "Wakening a Sleeping Metaphor: A New Interpretation of Malachi 1:11." *TynB* 45 (1994): 297–319.

Williams, D. T. "The Windows of Heaven." *OTE* 5 (1992): 402–13.

Subject Index